FIELDS OF
WRITING

A71TETS1395

FIELDS OF

WRITING

READINGS ACROSS
THE DISCIPLINES

Nancy R. Comley
QUEENS COLLEGE, CUNY

David Hamilton
UNIVERSITY OF IOWA

Carl H. Klaus
UNIVERSITY OF IOWA

Robert Scholes
BROWN UNIVERSITY

Nancy Sommers
RUTGERS UNIVERSITY

St. Martin's Press
NEW YORK

ACKNOWLEDGMENTS

James Agee, "Buster Keaton," from *Agee on Film*, vol. I, by James Agee. © 1958 by the James
Agee Trust. Permission granted by Grosset & Dunlap, Inc.

Frederick Lewis Allen, "Crash!," from Chapter XIII, "Crash!" (pp. 266–281), in *Only Yesterday:
An Informal History of the 1920's* by Frederick Lewis Allen. Copyright © 1931 by Frederick
Lewis Allen. By permission of Harper and Row, Publishers, Inc.

Othmar H. Ammann, "Tentative Report on the Hudson River Bridge," reprinted by permission of
the Port Authority of New York.

Maya Angelou, "Graduation," from *I Know Why the Caged Bird Sings*, by Maya Angelou. Copyright © 1969 by Maya Angelou. Reprinted by permission of Random House, Inc.

Isaac Asimov, "My Built-In Doubter," from *Fact and Fancy* by Isaac Asimov. Copyright © 1961
by the Mercury Press. Reprinted by permission of Doubleday & Company, Inc.

W. H. Auden, "The Water of Life." Copyright 1952 by W. H. Auden. Reprinted from *Forewards
and Afterwards*, by W. H. Auden, by permission of Random House, Inc.

James Baldwin, "Autobiographical Notes," from *Notes of a Native Son* by James Baldwin. Copyright
© 1955 by James Baldwin. Reprinted by permission of Beacon Press.

Roland Barthes, "The Eiffel Tower," from *The Eiffel Tower and Other Mythologies* by Roland
Barthes, translated by Richard Howard. Copyright © 1979 by Farrar, Straus and Giroux, Inc.
Reprinted by permission of Hill and Wang, a division of Farrar, Straus and Giroux, Inc.

Eric Bentley, "To Impersonate, to Watch, and to be Watched," from *The Life of the Drama*.
Copyright © 1964 by Eric Bentley. Reprinted with the permission of Atheneum Publishers.

John Berger, "The Question of Zoos," from *About Looking*, by John Berger. Copyright © 1980 by
John Berger. Reprinted by permission of Pantheon Books, a division of Random House, Inc.

Bruno Bettelheim, "Joey: A 'Mechanical Boy,' " reprinted with permission. Copyright © 1959 by
Scientific American, Inc. All rights reserved.

Michael Brown, "Love Canal and the Poisoning of America." Copyright 1979 by Michael Brown.
Reprinted from *Having Waste: Love Canal and the Poisoning of America*, by Michael Brown,
by permission of Pantheon Books, a division of Random House, Inc.

Ronald Bryden, "Olivier's Moor—Othello: National Theatre." Reprinted by permission of the
author.

Carol Caldwell, "You Haven't Come a Long Way, Baby: Women in Television Commercials,"
from *The Commercial Connection*, edited by John W. Wright.

Acknowledgments and copyrights continue at the back of the book on pages 763–766,
which constitute an extension of the copyright page.

For Instructors

From start to finish, our goal in *Fields of Writing* has been to produce a composition reader that is truly cross-curricular. A quick glance at the table of contents, for example, will reveal the breadth of its subject matter, which covers topics ranging from the Egyptian pyramids to *Star Wars*, from the bubonic plague of the fourteenth century to contemporary causes of environmental stress, from the evolution of language to the theory of relativity. But we have not been content to go after curricular variety in a casual or haphazard way. We have confined ourselves only to material that is genuinely disciplined—that is well informed, well developed, and well written. And we have drawn this material equally from the arts and humanities, from the social sciences and public affairs, and from the sciences and technologies. Thus, you will find in this collection a balanced spread of writing that reflects the major areas of the curriculum in both their academic and applied forms.

Our commitment to well-informed writing has led us to feature the work of persons who are major scholars and thinkers in their fields—Goodall and Mead in anthropology, Thurow and Smith in economics, Carr and Tuchman in history, Freud and Piaget in psychology, Darwin and Eiseley in the biological sciences, Einstein and Oppenheimer in the physical sciences. Our commitment to provide models of writing has also led us to include pieces that represent major forms of composition across the curriculum, such as reviews, case studies, policy statements, position papers, and research reports. Overall, then, our selections are as various in subject, form, and purpose as are the many different kinds of reading that students actually encounter—and the many different kinds of writing they are actually expected to produce—in the many different areas of undergraduate education. As various, too, as the different kinds of reading and writing they are likely to carry on in the world outside the classroom.

We have organized our collection according to four broad rhetorical categories—"Reporting," "Explaining," "Arguing," and "Reflecting"—which constitute aims of writing that are integral to the work of virtually every academic or professional area. In every field, persons need to convey information (reporting), to make sense of information (explaining), to debate controversial ideas and issues (arguing), and to contemplate past experience and knowledge (reflecting). Within each of these four categories, we have grouped the selections

v

For Instructors

according to three broad curriculum areas—"Arts and Humanities," "Social Sciences and Public Affairs," and "Sciences and Technologies." This combined system of organization will enable you to identify and consider selections both in terms of their rhetorical purpose and in terms of their curricular affiliation.

To explain these important frameworks for reading and writing, we have discussed them in our general introduction, "For Students," as well as in the more detailed introductions to each of the four main sections, "Reporting," "Explaining," "Arguing," and "Reflecting." These sectional introductions, which are illustrated with passages from the anthologized readings, define each type of writing, discuss its relevance within a broad range of fields, compare and contrast its use in differing fields and situations, as well as identify and explain methods of achieving its aims. Thus, the introductions show, for example, how description and narration are basic in reporting or how analogy, comparison and contrast, definition, and illustration are basic in explaining.

The concepts and terms that figure in the sectional introductions are, in turn, applied throughout the remainder of our editorial apparatus. So, you will find that our headnote for each piece identifies, and where necessary explains, the professional field of its author and the rhetorical context or source of its original publication. Likewise, our questions following each selection call for reading and writing that relate form and style to purpose, subject, and academic field. Beyond these highly focussed questions following each piece, you will find a more broadly based set of "Writing Suggestions" at the end of each main section. These assignments bring together two or more pieces from a particular section, relating them in terms of an academic, professional, personal, or rhetorical topic. And at the end of the collection, you will find our most spacious and challenging set of ideas for composition, "Suggestions for Writing Across the Disciplines." These assignments offer opportunities to pull together several readings and encourage the exploration of broad issues, questions, and problems that are of concern in every academic and professional field.

Because the material in this collection is intended to help students develop their reading and writing abilities, we have prepared two appendices that offer special guidance in these areas. "Reading and Rereading" explains the important relationship between reading and writing and illustrates several approaches to reading, focusing on an essay by E. B. White. "Writing and Rewriting," in turn, explains and illustrates the composing process through a detailed discussion of the same essay by White, including the previously unpublished notes and drafts that White prepared in the process of writing the piece. These appendices, then, are meant to present reading and writing not in abstract terms, but through examples that demonstrate what is actually involved in each activity.

As you look through our table of contents, you will probably notice that pieces that are related in subject or theme have been placed side by side. These relationships, of course, cut across individual sections as well, so we have highlighted them all in a "Topical Guide to the Contents," making it possible to approach the readings in terms of particular subjects of study or themes of interest. We have also put together a "Rhetorical Index" that takes into account all of the rhetorical aims and modes that are discussed in our critical apparatus. Thus, our collection has been designed to serve a full range of approaches to reading and writing across the disciplines.

ACKNOWLEDGMENTS

A reader of this size and complexity is invariably a collaborative undertaking—and not just among the persons whose names appear on the cover. So we have a number of people to thank for helping us make our way across the disciplines.

For their expert reviews of the organization, table of contents, and critical apparatus, we are grateful to Professors Toby Fulwiler (University of Vermont), Frank Hubbard (University of Wisconsin, Milwaukee), Malcolm Kiniry (University of California, Los Angeles), Linda Robertson (Wichita State University), Christopher Thaiss (George Mason University), and Stephen Witte (University of Texas). For their knowledgeable suggestions of readings to consider, we are grateful to Deborah Asher (Union County College), James Farber (Bell Labs), Miriam Gilbert (University of Iowa), Antonia Hamilton (Hansen, Lind, Meyer Architects), James Hanlon (Shippensburg State College), Patrick Hays (Bell Labs), Marshall H. Klaus (Michigan State University Medical School), Susan Long (Bell Labs), Donald McQuade (Queens College, CUNY), JoAnn Putnam-Scholes (Barrington, Rhode Island), Elizabeth Robertson (University of Iowa), and Steven Weiland (National Federation of State Humanities Boards). For their expert consultation on technical matters in their particular fields, we are grateful to Professors Keith Marshall (University of Iowa—Anthropology), Eugene Spaziani (University of Iowa—Zoology), and James Van Allen (University of Iowa—Astronomy). For their special insights as students, we are grateful to Hilary Broadbent (Barnard College) and Geoffrey Soriano (Brown University). For their discerning reactions to draft versions of the introductory sections, we are grateful to Kate Franks (Iowa City) and Professor Nancy Jones (University of Iowa). For her assistance in preparing material for a segment of the Instructor's Manual, we are grateful to Nancy Moore (University of Iowa), and for her assistance in procuring material for one of the appendices, we are grateful to Carol Singley (Brown University). For their generous assistance in reading proof, we are grateful to Cynthia Putnam (Barrington, Rhode Island) and Richard Putnam (Barrington, Rhode Island). For her thoughtful editing of the manuscript, we are grateful to Marcia Muth. For their excellent work in bringing this book into print, we are grateful to the staff of St. Martin's Press, especially Mark

Gallaher, Assistant Editor, and Ronald Aldridge, Project Editor. Above all, we are indebted to the two English Editors whose contributions to this book have been inestimable, Thomas Broadbent and Nancy Perry.

N.R.C.
D.H.
C.H.K.
R.S.
N.S.

Contents

Contents

CONTENTS

Contents

CONTENTS

Sciences and Technologies

Arts and Humanities

Contents

xiv

CONTENTS

Contents

CONTENTS

Topical Guide to the Contents

WRITING

HISTORY

MYTH AND FANTASY

Topical Guide to the Contents

SYMBOLS AND SYMBOLISM

ART

MEDIA

Topical Guide to the Contents

Topical Guide to the Contents

HUMAN BEHAVIOR

PUBLIC AFFAIRS

TOPICAL GUIDE TO THE CONTENTS

Topical Guide to the Contents

TIME, SPACE, NUMBER

KNOWLEDGE AND BELIEF

For Students

Fields of Writing: Readings Across the Disciplines has been designed to reflect the broad areas of study and writing you are likely to discover as you begin to acquaint yourself with academic life at your school. Our collection of material, like your introductory college English course itself, is intended to help you develop the abilities in reading and writing that you will need as you move from one course to another, one field of study to another, throughout your college career. In some senses, of course, all areas of study will expect the same things of you—namely, close and careful reading as well as clear and exact writing, with an attentiveness above all to information and ideas. But as you will discover, the particular kinds of information, ideas, and concerns that distinguish each field of study also call for somewhat different reading and writing abilities. As you might imagine, for example, a book report for a literature course requires a different form and style from a lab report in physics. So, in putting together this collection, we have tried to give you a sampling of the varied fields of writing you are likely to encounter in the academic world.

Most undergraduate schools are organized around some version of the traditional division of studies into "the humanities," "the social sciences," and "the sciences." The humanities generally include fields of learning that are thought of as having a cultural orientation, such as language, literature, history, philosophy, and religion. The social sciences, including such fields as anthropology, economics, education, political science, psychology, and sociology, deal with social institutions and their members, analyzing the functions of larger and smaller groups in relation to each other. The sciences generally include fields of knowledge that are concerned with the natural and physical world, such as astronomy, botany, chemistry, physics, and zoology.

These traditional divisions of study are not entirely stable. History and psychology, just to name two, are often regarded as a social science and a science respectively, rather than as a humanity and a social science. Workers in many fields will migrate from one broad area of learning to another, according to the orientation of their own studies on particular occasions. Moreover, these traditional divisions of study are closely affiliated with applied areas of work and study that exist not only in colleges and universities but also in the professional world outside higher education. The humanities, for example, are closely affiliated with the arts; the social sciences, with public affairs such as business and government; and the sciences, with technology. So, if you look through the table of contents, you will find that we have used these basic divisions and clusterings of fields as a major organizing principle of our book. So, too, for this reason have we called it *Fields of Writing*.

An introductory college writing course attentive to these "fields of writing" would probably attempt to work through a variety of academic writing systematically. Such a course would be concerned, no doubt, with examining both boundaries and continuities among these fields. One element of writing that continues from history to business to physics, for example, is the purpose of the writer who is responsible for a given piece of work. Few people write without purpose. Purposes, naturally, are always complex, too complex to unravel completely and to restrict to a single idea. Nevertheless, we can imagine a great deal about the intentions and motivations that guide a particular writer at work on a particular essay, and we can say something about the purpose that writer shows. By focusing on those purposes, no matter how fuzzy they may be around the edges, we begin to see important ways by which writings from all areas of learning relate to each other.

Thus, in organizing the readings in this anthology, we have subordinated areas of academic specialization—Arts and Humanities, Social Sciences and Public Affairs, Sciences and Technologies—to the *purposes* of writing that we wish to define and come to understand better.

Reporting, Explaining, Arguing, and Reflecting—the titles of the primary sections of this reader—are the names that seem to indicate best the purposes we wish to isolate for your consideration. Of course these purposes overlap and are impossible to keep wholly apart from each other. Even so they form an idealized sequence of mental events by which we can consider the varying relations of writer to subject to audience.

Think of all writing, for a moment, as following from a certain amount of investigation, from some process by which the writer becomes familiar with the material at hand. And, to make matters as concrete as possible, think further of that investigation as being analogous to the physical exploration of a new territory or a new world. "Reporting," then, would correspond to our early contact with the unfamiliar territory. In those reports we describe our arrival, our getting acquainted with the place, our discovering terms by which to know it, and our establishing a working relation to the territory we have decided to explore.

That stage of initial investigation can continue indefinitely, but at some point we will discover that we have become familiar with an area, that in some sense we have settled in. "Explaining" is the writing we are most likely to produce when we have reached the stage of settler rather than explorer. By the time we are able to explain the place, we will have answered a certain number of early questions. We will have established boundaries, defined landmarks, and accommodated ourselves to any earlier inhabitants. Now we are able to record our more detailed understanding of place and circumstance. We are in possession of information unknown to others. We are the ones, after all, who have done the work of settling in, and we seek to make our expertise, our familiarity with things, clear.

To carry this metaphor a step further, we must imagine confronting a rival settler, someone who presumes to know our territory as well as we do, someone who challenges our claim to possession of the place. That rival has come up with an alternative explanation, no doubt. "Arguing," then, is the process of contesting rival understandings. When we argue, we dig in deeper; we entrench ourselves against counterattack; we consider carefully the rival explanation while striving to defend our own. Of course, we hope to demonstrate the superiority of our own understanding, but a degree of compromise may be necessary. When that is the case, the territory will need to be redefined.

Assuming some success in that idealized sequence of mental events—the steps of exploring, settling into, and defending territory we have chosen to make our own—it is likely that we would want to step back, eventually, and consider the meaning of our achievement. Hence the stage of "Reflecting" placed at the end of this sequence. Reflection comes after struggle and conflict; it follows from extended experience and a certain amount of adjusting to what we have encountered. If one were to *begin* a writing course with "Reflecting," it would have to be with reflection upon work and experience that had occurred outside the course. "Reflecting" is the mirror image of "Reporting," and through it we are likely to come to different terms with our experience than we had known.

Clearly, these stages of learning and writing don't exist as absolute divisions among purposes for writing anywhere except in a textbook. In this text, you will undoubtedly find evidence of "explaining" in essays labelled "argument," or "reflecting," or even "reporting." In some cases, you may even feel certain that an essay would have been better placed in a different section of the reader. We hope that won't happen often, for we feel confident of the reasons that led us to place most pieces where they are. More important, we are confident that you will find these stages useful to consider separately. They seem to us the natural stages of learning, and insofar as writing depends on learning, insofar, in fact, as the two are intertwined, they seem to us the natural stages of writing as well. Furthermore, these purposes establish continuities within the variety of this reader. Understanding them will give you access to a wider range of written work.

One thing a systematic study of academic writing surely challenges is your inclination for one topic and hesitation toward another. This reader includes writing on many different subjects. Of course, you won't instantly like it all or be ready for all of it either. The range of difficulty varies, and your preparedness for different topics will vary at least as much. One reason, then, for our organizing this reader as we have and for our stressing these stages of learning and purposes for writing throughout is that those ideas should make the more difficult essays on less familiar topics more accessible to you. They can give you a purpose for reading that does not depend on your mastery of the subject being discussed.

Each section of this reader begins with an essay on "Reporting," "Explaining," "Arguing," or "Reflecting" that explains in far more detail than would be useful here that stage of learning and purpose for writing as we understand it. Each essay within each section is accompanied by a brief headnote, explanatory footnotes when necessary, and a set of questions for study and writing. There are also brief sections "On Reading" and "On Writing" and separate sets of writing suggestions that are addressed to more than one essay, sometimes to more than a single writing purpose. All this apparatus is meant to help you further. The rest is up to you, to your classmates, and to your instructor. We hope you will find *Fields of Writing* and the course it suggests useful to the purpose we suppose you have of becoming a more effective college writer.

REPORTING

REPORTING

Here in "Reporting" you will find writing that reflects a wide array of academic and professional situations—an anthropologist describing the rhythm of daily life in a primitive South Seas culture, a brain surgeon detailing the progress of a delicate operation, a historian telling about the plague that swept through Europe in the mid-fourteenth century, a journalist recounting a memorable day on the New York Stock Exchange during the crash of 1929. Informative writing is basic in every field of endeavor, and the writers in this section seek to fulfill that basic need by reporting material drawn from various sources— a ticker tape, a data bank, a microscope, a telescope, articles, books, public records, or firsthand experience and observation. Working from such various sources, these writers aim to provide detailed and reliable accounts of things— to give the background of a case, to convey the look and smell and feel of a place, to describe the appearance and behavior of people, to tell the story of recent or ancient events.

Though reporting depends heavily on the gathering of reliable information, it is by no means a mechanical and routine activity that consists simply of getting some facts and writing them up. Newspaper editors and criminal investigators, to be sure, often speak longingly of wanting "just the facts," but they know at last that in one way or another the facts are substantially shaped by the point of view of the person who is reporting them. By point of view, we mean both the physical and the mental standpoint from which a person observes or investigates something. Each of us, after all, stands at a particular point in space and time, as well as in thought and feeling, whenever we look at any subject. And wherever we stand in relation to the subject—whether we observe it close up or at a distance, in sunlight or in shadows—will determine the particular aspects of it that we perceive and bring out in an account.

This essential element of reporting can be seen in the following passage from an article about events at the New York Stock Exchange on October 24, 1929:

> The weird roar compounded of the voices of thousands of shouting men held to its steady volume. It never rose, it never fell, but rumbled to the high ceiling in mighty monotone. It was the voice of the Street, now hopeful, now tragic, making audible the history of a momentous day in the market. It could be heard on the Broad Street sidewalk.
>
> The hand of the clock crawled on. William R. Crawford, superintendent of

3

the Exchange's reporting department, stood up in his balcony. He looked oddly like a judge about to charge a jury or deliver an oral decision. The brokers below were rushing about even more intensively as they realized that only seconds were left in which to execute orders.

Suddenly Mr. Crawford seized a gavel and as the minute hand touched three he sounded the gong, ending trading for the day. In long, quivering notes the cease-business warning clanged through the medley of noise. Thrice Mr. Crawford sounded the gong. There was a second of silence, during which the telegraph wires sped the news of the close of trading to all points.

Then the roar from the floor was resumed, swelling to a new height and then gradually receding.

This report, which appeared in the *New York Times* on October 25, 1929, was evidently written by someone close enough to the immediate flow of events to provide a vividly detailed account of the various impressions and sensations—the sights and sounds—we might have experienced had we been there ourselves, watching the brokers rush about, listening to the roar of their voices, silenced only "a second" by the sound of Mr. Crawford's gong. And this is just one of several scenes in and around the Exchange that you will find depicted in the article, which the *Times* ran under a long but catchy title, "Weird Roar Surges From Exchange Floor During Trading in a Record Smashing Day." As you make your way through this piece, however, you will discover that it reports very little about the financial events that accounted for that "Record Smashing Day." The anonymous author of "Weird Roar" evidently chose to focus attention almost entirely on the striking images and "wild scenes" of that day at the Exchange, from the brokers roaring on the market floor to their office boys "shouting and whooping through the streets." Indeed, the report covers not only the spectacle itself but also a notable array of spectators observing it, from Winston Churchill standing in the balcony of the Exchange to movie makers filming scenes in the surrounding financial district.

To see how decisively point of view can influence what comes through in a report, you need only look at a different account of that same day on the Exchange—in Frederick Lewis Allen's "Crash!" In Allen's piece you will not find any mention of Mr. Crawford and his gong, nor of Winston Churchill looking on, nor of office boys running through the streets, nor of movie makers shooting the scene. And the "roar from the floor," which was featured in the title and opening paragraphs of the *Times* piece, receives only a single sentence in Allen's account. Conversely, some matters that are barely touched on in the *Times* report are amply covered in Allen's account. In particular, Allen centers on the financial drama of the day, from the "torrent of selling" that took place during the early hours of trading, to the falling prices that followed, to the panic and confusion brought on by the steep decline, to the "desperate remedy" devised by five powerful bankers who met at noon in the office of J. P. Morgan & Company and "agreed in behalf of their respective institutions to put up forty millions apiece to shore up the stock market."

4

Given such striking differences in the emphasis of these two pieces, you might wonder which one offers a more accurate report of the day. Actually, both are true to the day within the limits of their points of view on it. The *Times* reporter, for example, concentrates on a close, firsthand observation of the Exchange and the immediately surrounding area, and this standpoint brings into focus the vivid array of spectacles to be seen on that "Record Smashing Day." Allen, by contrast, covers the day in the process of chronicling the "crash" that took place in the stock market between early September and mid-November of 1929. Thus Allen views the day in a broader context and from a greater distance—from the distance, in fact, of more than a year and a half later, through the medium of previously written and published reports. And this perspective enables him to see the events of the day as revealing "that the economic structure had cracked wide open." Thus each point of view affords a special angle on the day, obscuring some aspects of it, revealing others. And these are only two of many standpoints from which the day might have been seen and reported. Imagine, for example, how Mr. Crawford might have viewed the events from his position as "superintendent of the Exchange's reporting department," or how Winston Churchill might have reported on events as "former Chancellor of the Exchequer of Great Britain," or how one of those five bankers might have covered events from his special perspective within the secret meeting at J. P. Morgan & Company, or how a broker on the Exchange, or an office boy, or a small stockholder might have seen events and reported on them. Or imagine what might be discovered and reported about that day by an economist, historian, journalist, or market researcher of our own time.

Once you try to imagine the various perspectives from which anything can be observed or investigated, then you will see that no one person can possibly uncover everything there is to be known about something. For this reason, above all, point of view is an important aspect of reporting to be kept in mind by both readers and writers. As a reader of reportorial writing, you should always attempt to identify the point of view from which the information was gathered so as to help yourself assess the special strengths and weaknesses in the reporting that arise from that point of view as distinct from others. By the same token, in your own reporting you should carefully decide upon the point of view that you already have or plan to use in observing or gathering information about something. Once you begin to pay deliberate attention to point of view, you will come to see that it is closely related to the various purposes for which people gather and report information in writing.

THE RANGE OF REPORTORIAL WRITING

The purpose of reporting is in one sense straightforward and self-evident, particularly when it is defined in terms of its commonly accepted value to readers. Whether it involves a firsthand account of some recent happening or the documented record of a long past sequence of events, reportorial writing informs readers about the various subjects that may interest them but that they cannot possibly observe or investigate on their own. You may never get to see chimpanzees in their native African habitats, but you can get a glimpse of their behavior through the firsthand account of Jane Goodall. So, too, you will probably never have occasion to make your way through the many public records and personal reports of the bubonic plague that beset Europe in the mid-fourteenth century, but you can get a synoptic view of the plague from Barbara Tuchman's account, which is based on an investigation of those sources. Reporting thus expands the range of its readers' perceptions and knowledge beyond the limits of their own immediate experience. From the outlook of readers, then, the function of reporting does seem to be very clear-cut.

But if we shift our focus and look at it in terms of the purposes to which it is evidently put by writers, reporting often turns out to serve a more complex function than might at first be supposed. An example of this complexity can be seen in the following passage from Goodall's account:

> Suddenly I stopped, for I saw a slight movement in the long grass about sixty yards away. Quickly focusing my binoculars I saw that it was a single chimpanzee, and just then he turned in my direction. I recognized David Graybeard.
>
> Cautiously I moved around so that I could see what he was doing. He was squatting beside the red earth mound of a termite nest, and as I watched I saw him carefully push a long grass stem down into a hole in the mound. After a moment he withdrew it and picked something from the end with his mouth.

This passage seems on the whole to be a very neutral bit of scientific reporting that details Goodall's observation of a particular chimpanzee probing for food in a termite nest. The only unusual aspect of the report is her naming of the creature, which has the unscientific effect of personifying the animal. Otherwise, she is careful in the opening part of the description to establish the physical point of view from which she observed the chimpanzee—sixty yards away, looking at it through binoculars. And at the end of the passage she is equally careful not to identify or even conjecture about "something" beyond her range of detailed vision. As it turns out, however, this passage is not only a record of her observations but also a pivotal moment in the story of how she came to make an important discovery about chimpanzees—that they are tool users—and thus how she came to regard their behavior as being much closer to that of human beings than had previously been supposed. So she climaxes her previous description of the chimpanzee with this sentence:

> I was too far away to make out what he was eating, but it was obvious that he was actually using a grass stem as a tool.

Here as elsewhere, then, her reporting is ingeniously structured and worded to make a strong case for her ideas about chimpanzee and human behavior. Thus, she evidently intends her report to be both informative and persuasive.

6

A different set of purposes can be seen in yet another firsthand account of animal behavior—this time of salmon swimming upriver to spawn, as observed by Edward Hoagland:

> Like mountain climbers, the most active fish would wiggle twenty yards further on and gain a new cranny. It might require a number of tries, but they were the freshest fish, unscarred, and occasionally one would get into some partially sheltered corner of the chute itself, in one of the zigs or zags. These dozen desperate niches were so packed that they were like boxfuls of crated fish set into the bullet-gray water. The salmon who were able to battle upcurrent did so by shimmying and thrusting more than by leaping, although they did leap now and again. This was the cruelest sight of all, because they were like paper airplanes thrown into the hydrant blast. The water shattered and obliterated the leap and then banged the limp, tender body down the same stretch of rapids that it had been fighting its way up for perhaps the past day and a half.

In this passage, Hoagland conveys the extreme difficulties that the salmon faced in trying to swim up this particular river—the opposing current, the overcrowding, and the exhaustion brought on by fighting to overcome these physical obstacles. The salmon's difficulties are clearly depicted through Hoagland's extensive use of figurative language—through metaphors and similes that put these aspects of the scene in vividly familiar terms. He conveys the force of the opposing current, for example, by speaking of it as a "hydrant blast." And he depicts the obstacles as well as the overcrowding by reporting that the "niches were so packed that they were like boxfuls of crated fish set into the bullet-gray water." But it is also clear from some of the other similes in this passage that Hoagland aims to convey what he felt to be at once the heroic and pathetic efforts of the salmon to overcome these difficulties. Thus in the opening of the passage he compares them to "mountain climbers" but later on to "paper airplanes thrown into the hydrant blast." Here as elsewhere Hoagland's report is calculatedly structured and worded to express his sympathies and arouse our feelings for the salmon. Clearly he intends his report to be moving as well as informative.

For yet another combination of purposes, you might look at Farley Mowat's entertaining, self-mocking, but informative account of his firsthand encounter with the territorial behavior of wolves. Or you might turn to the *Times* report we discussed earlier and find that it is evidently intended not only to convey the sights and sounds of that day on the Exchange floor, but also to suggest through an accumulation of loaded phrases, such as "weird roar," "wild scenes," and "mad market," that the world of the Exchange had lost control of itself. Or you might look at Ronald Bryden's account of Laurence Olivier performing the role of Othello, and you will see a reporter who clearly regards himself not simply as providing information to help persons decide whether to attend the production but also as establishing an authoritative written record of a performance so remarkable as to deserve preservation for "posterity."

As is apparent from just this handful of selections, writers invariably seem to use reporting for a combination of purposes—not only to provide information but also to convey their attitudes, beliefs, or ideas about it as well as to influence the views of their readers. This joining of purposes is hardly surprising, given the factors involved in any decision to report on something. After all, whenever we make a report, we do so presumably because we believe that the subject of our report is important enough for others to be told about it. And presumably we believe the subject to be important because of what we have come to know and think about it. So, when we are faced with deciding what information to report and how to report it, we inevitably base our decisions on these ideas. At every point in the process of planning and executing a report, we act on the basis of our particular motives and priorities for conveying information about the subject. And how could we do otherwise? How else could Ronald Bryden have decided exactly what to focus on amid all the details that he witnessed in a full-scale production of *Othello?* How else could Jane Goodall have decided what information to report out of all she must have observed during her first few months in Africa? Without controlling and shaping purposes for reporting, our records of events would be as long as the events themselves.

Reporting, as you can see, necessarily serves a widely varied range of purposes—as varied as are the writers and their subjects. Thus whenever you read a piece of reportorial writing, you should always try to discover for yourself what appear to be its guiding purposes by examining its structure, its phrasing, and its wording, much as we have earlier in this discussion. And once you have identified the purpose, you should then consider how it has influenced the selection, arrangement, and weighting of information in the report. When you turn to doing your own writing, you should be equally careful in determining your purposes for reporting and in planning the overall method of your report so as to put the information in a form that is true to what you know and think about the subject.

METHODS OF REPORTING

In planning a piece of reportorial writing, you should begin by deciding upon the basic form of presentation best suited to both the nature of your information and your purposes for reporting it. For example, if the information concerns a single detailed event or covers a set of events spread over time, then the most natural way to present it is in the form known as narration—the form of story telling—in a more or less chronological order. This is the basic form that Goodall uses in recounting her first few months of observation in Africa, and it proves to be a very clear and persuasive form for gradually unfolding her discoveries about the behavior of chimpanzees. If the information concerns a single place or spectacle, then the most natural way to present it is in the form known as description, using a spatial or some other visually controlled way of taking your reader through the scene. This is the basic form that Hoagland uses in "River-Gray, River-Green," first giving us a distant, overhead view of the river from a helicopter, then forcing us to see it up close—a filmlike shifting of perspective that enables him to emphasize the horrific spectacle of the dying fish, struggling to make their way upriver.

Although narration, description, and other related forms are often treated separately for purposes of convenience in identifying each of them, it is good to keep in mind that they usually end up working in some sort of combination with one another. Narratives, after all, involve not only events but also persons and places, sights and sounds, so it is natural that they include descriptive passages, as in the earlier excerpt from Goodall's "First Observations." By the same token, descriptions of place frequently entail stories about the events taking place in them, as in the earlier excerpt from Hoagland's "River-Gray, River-Green." In writing, as in other activities, it is best to think of form as following function rather than being forced to fit arbitrary rules.

Once you have settled upon a basic form, you should then devise a way of managing your information within that form—of selecting, arranging, and pro-portioning it—so as to achieve your purposes most effectively. To carry out this task, you will need to review all of the material you have gathered with an eye to determining what you consider to be the most important information to report. Some bits or kinds of information, after all, will strike you as more significant than others, and these are the ones that you should want to feature in your report. Conversely, you will probably find that some information is simply not important enough even to be mentioned in your report. Only by deliberately sorting through your material and focusing on the most significant details will you be able to produce a report that makes a clear and decisive impression on your readers. Ronald Bryden, for example, in reporting on the National Theatre production of *Othello*, produces a striking account precisely because he focuses immediately on Laurence Olivier in the role of Othello— "All posterity will want to know is how he played." And Bryden maintains this focus so relentlessly that he only mentions other actors, or other aspects of the production, as they serve to highlight Olivier's performance. Similarly, Jane Goodall's account is so memorable because she focuses primarily on her obser-vation of chimpanzees, subordinating all of the other material she reports to her discoveries about the behavior of chimpanzees. Thus only on a couple of oc-casions does she include observations about the behavior of animals other than chimpanzees—in particular about the timidities of a bushbuck and a leopard. And she only includes these observations to point up by contrast the distinctively sociable behavior of chimpanzees. For much the same reasons, she proportions her coverage of the several chimpanzee episodes she reports so as to give the greatest amount of detail to the one that provides the most compelling indication of their advanced intelligence—namely, the final episode, which shows the chimpanzees to be tool users, a behavior previously attributed only to human beings.

To help achieve your purposes, you should also give special thought to deciding on the perspective through which you present your information to the reader. Do you want to present the material in first or third person? Do you want to be present in the piece, as are Goodall and Hoagland? Or do you want to be invisible, as are Allen and Bryden? To some extent, of course, your answer to this question will depend upon whether you gathered the information through firsthand observation and then want to convey your firsthand reactions to your observation of the subject, as Goodall and Hoagland do in their pieces. But just to show that there are no hard-and-fast rules on this score, you might look at "A Delicate Operation" by Roy C. Selby, Jr. You will notice at once that, although Dr. Selby must have written this piece on the basis of firsthand experience, he tells the story in third person, removing himself almost completely from it except for such distant-sounding references to himself as "the surgeon." Clearly, Dr. Selby is an important part of the information of this report, yet he evidently decided to de-emphasize himself in making the report. In order to see just how important it is to consider these alternatives in planning any report, you might look at another doctor's account based on firsthand experience, namely Richard Selzer's "The Discus Thrower." Dr. Selzer, as you will see, reports his observations of a particular patient through a first-person perspective, despite the fact that you might suppose him to be a relatively unimportant aspect of the information. If you tried your hand at revising the perspectives of these two medical reports, you would see at once that both the nature of the information and the effect of the report are a function not only of *what* a writer gathers from various sources but also of *how* a writer presents the information.

In the pieces that follow in this section, you will have an opportunity to see how more than twenty different writers report things in language. In later sections, you will see how reporting combines with three other kinds of writing—explaining, arguing, and reflecting.

Arts and Humanities

THE RING OF TIME
E. B. White

*Elwyn Brooks White (b. 1899) began writing in various
capacities for* The New Yorker *in 1926, soon after the magazine's inception. Since 1957 he has lived at his farm in
Maine and has continued to write. White has been called
with some justice "the finest essayist in the United States"
because of the grace and clarity of his writing and the range
of his interests. As White himself says, the essayist thoroughly enjoys his work because "he can pull on any sort of
shirt, be any sort of person, according to his mood or his
subject matter." Here, in "The Ring of Time," we see him
as "recording secretary" for circus lovers, taking a small event
and endowing it with significance.*

FIDDLER BAYOU, March 22, 1956—After the lions had returned to their   1
cages, creeping angrily through the chutes, a little bunch of us drifted away and
into an open doorway nearby, where we stood for a while in semidarkness,
watching a big brown circus horse go harumphing around the practice ring. His
trainer was a woman of about forty, and the two of them, horse and woman,
seemed caught up in one of those desultory treadmills of afternoon from which
there is no apparent escape. The day was hot, and we kibitzers were grateful to
be briefly out of the sun's glare.[1] The long rein, or tape, by which the woman
guided her charge counterclockwise in his dull career formed the radius of their
private circle, of which she was the revolving center; and she, too, stepped a
tiny circumference of her own, in order to accommodate the horse and allow
him his maximum scope. She had on a short-skirted costume and a conical

---

[1]kibitzers: a Yiddish word for people who interfere and who give advice gratuitously; meddlesome
onlookers. [Eds.]

straw hat. Her legs were bare and she wore high heels, which probed deep into the loose tanbark and kept her ankles in a state of constant turmoil. The great size and meekness of the horse, the repetitious exercise, the heat of the afternoon, all exerted a hypnotic charm that invited boredom; we spectators were experiencing a languor—we neither expected relief nor felt entitled to any. We had paid a dollar to get into the grounds, to be sure, but we had got our dollar's worth a few minutes before, when the lion trainer's whiplash had got caught around a toe of one of the lions. What more did we want for a dollar?

Behind me I heard someone say, "Excuse me, please," in a low voice. She was halfway into the building when I turned and saw her—a girl of sixteen or seventeen, politely threading her way through us onlookers who blocked the entrance. As she emerged in front of us, I saw that she was barefoot, her dirty little feet fighting the uneven ground. In most respects she was like any of two or three dozen showgirls you encounter if you wander about the winter quarters of Mr. John Ringling North's circus, in Sarasota—cleverly proportioned, deeply browned by the sun, dusty, eager, and almost naked. But her grave face and the naturalness of her manner gave her a sort of quick distinction and brought a new note into the gloomy octagonal building where we had all cast our lot for a few moments. As soon as she had squeezed through the crowd, she spoke a word or two to the older woman, whom I took to be her mother, stepped to the ring, and waited while the horse coasted to a stop in front of her. She gave the animal a couple of affectionate swipes on his enormous neck and then swung herself aboard. The horse immediately resumed his rocking canter, the woman goading him on, chanting something that sounded like "Hop! Hop!" 2

In attempting to recapture this mild spectacle, I am merely acting as recording secretary for one of the oldest of societies—the society of those who, at one time or another, have surrendered, without even a show of resistance, to the bedazzlement of a circus rider. As a writing man, or secretary, I have always felt charged with the safekeeping of all unexpected items of worldly or unworldly enchantment, as though I might be held personally responsible if even a small one were to be lost. But it is not easy to communicate anything of this nature. The circus comes as close to being the world in microcosm as anything I know; in a way, it puts all the rest of show business in the shade. Its magic is universal and complex. Out of its wild disorder comes order; from its rank smell rises the good aroma of courage and daring; out of its preliminary shabbiness comes the final splendor. And buried in the familiar boasts of its advance agents lies the modesty of most of its people. For me the circus is at its best before it has been put together. It is at its best at certain moments when it comes to a point, as through a burning glass, in the activity and destiny of a single performer out of so many. One ring is always bigger than three. One rider, one aerialist, is always greater than six. In short, a man has to catch the circus unawares to experience its full impact and share its gaudy dream. 3

The ten-minute ride the girl took achieved—as far as I was concerned, who wasn't looking for it, and quite unbeknownst to her, who wasn't even striving 4 for it—the thing that is sought by performers everywhere, on whatever stage, whether struggling in the tidal currents of Shakespeare or bucking the difficult motion of a horse. I somehow got the idea she was just cadging a ride, improving a shining ten minutes in the diligent way all serious artists seize free moments to hone the blade of their talent and keep themselves in trim. Her brief tour included only elementary postures and tricks, perhaps because they were all she was capable of, perhaps because her warmup at this hour was unscheduled and the ring was not rigged for a real practice session. She swung herself off and on the horse several times, gripping his mane. She did a few knee-stands—or whatever they are called—dropping to her knees and quickly bouncing back up on her feet again. Most of the time she simply rode in a standing position, well aft on the beast, her hands hanging easily at her sides, her head erect, her straw-colored ponytail lightly brushing her shoulders, the blood of exertion showing faintly through the tan of her skin. Twice she managed a one-foot stance—a sort of ballet pose, with arms outstretched. At one point the neck strap of her bathing suit broke and she went twice around the ring in the classic attitude of a woman making minor repairs to a garment. The fact that she was standing on the back of a moving horse while doing this invested the matter with a clownish significance that perfectly fitted the spirit of the circus—jocund, yet charming. She just rolled the strap into a neat ball and stowed it inside her bodice while the horse rocked and rolled beneath her in dutiful innocence. The bathing suit proved as self-reliant as its owner and stood up well enough without benefit of strap.

The richness of the scene was in its plainness, its natural condition—of horse, of ring, of girl, even to the girl's bare feet that gripped the bare back of her proud and ridiculous mount. The enchantment grew not out of anything that happened or was performed but out of something that seemed to go round and around and around with the girl, attending her, a steady gleam in the shape of a circle—a ring of ambition, of happiness, of youth. (And the positive pleasures of equilibrium under difficulties.) In a week or two, all would be changed, all (or almost all) lost: the girl would wear makeup, the horse would wear gold, the ring would be painted, the bark would be clean for the feet of the horse, the girl's feet would be clean for the slippers that she'd wear. All, all would be lost. 5

As I watched with the others, our jaws adroop, our eyes alight, I became painfully conscious of the element of time. Everything in the hideous old building seemed to take the shape of a circle, conforming to the course of the horse. The rider's gaze, as she peered straight ahead, seemed to be circular, as though bent by force of circumstance; then time itself began running in circles, and so the beginning was where the end was, and the two were the same, and one thing ran into the next and time went round and around and got nowhere. The girl wasn't so young that she did not know the delicious satisfaction of having a perfectly behaved body and the fun of using it to do a trick most people can't do, but she was too young to know that time does not really move in a circle at all. I thought: "She will never be as beautiful as this again"—a thought that 6

13

made me acutely unhappy—and in a flash my mind (which is too much of a busybody to suit me) had projected her twenty-five years ahead, and she was now in the center of the ring, on foot, wearing a conical hat and high-heeled shoes, the image of the older woman, holding the long rein, caught in the treadmill of an afternoon long in the future. "She is at that enviable moment in life [I thought] when she believes she can go once around the ring, make one complete circuit, and at the end be exactly the same age as at the start." Everything in her movements, her expression, told you that for her the ring of time was perfectly formed, changeless, predictable, without beginning or end, like the ring in which she was traveling at this moment with the horse that wallowed under her. And then I slipped back into my trance, and time was circular again—time, pausing quietly with the rest of us, so as not to disturb the balance of a performer.

Her ride ended as casually as it had begun. The older woman stopped the horse, and the girl slid to the ground. As she walked toward us to leave, there was a quick, small burst of applause. She smiled broadly, in surprise and pleasure; then her face suddenly regained its gravity and she disappeared through the door. 7

It has been ambitious and plucky of me to attempt to describe what is indescribable, and I have failed, as I knew I would. But I have discharged my duty to my society; and besides, a writer, like an acrobat, must occasionally try a stunt that is too much for him. At any rate, it is worth reporting that long before the circus comes to town, its most notable performances have already been given. Under the bright lights of the finished show, a performer need only reflect the electric candle power that is directed upon him; but in the dark and dirty old training rings and in the makeshift cages, whatever light is generated, whatever excitement, whatever beauty, must come from original sources—from internal fires of professional hunger and delight, from the exuberance and gravity of youth. It is the difference between planetary light and the combustion of stars. 8

QUESTIONS

1. In paragraph 3, White describes his role as "recording secretary" for those who love circus riders. In the first two paragraphs, he does record or report what he observed. But how is paragraph 3 different from the first two? How much of the essay is actually devoted to reporting events?

2. The events in the essay are presented chronologically, but in what different ways is time felt and described within that structure? Why is this essay entitled "The Ring of Time"?

3. Why does White say the circus is "as close to being the world in microcosm as anything I know" (paragraph 3)? How would you describe the circus? What circus performers do you prefer watching? Why?

4. Why does White say at the end that he has failed in attempting "to describe what is indescribable" (paragraph 8)? Do you agree with him? In what sections of the essay do you find him most successful at describing?

5. Write a paragraph or two in which you report the same events from the girl's point of view. You will have to decide whether she would be aware of how she looked, or of the audience watching her.

6. For an essay of your own, observe a practice session of an orchestra, an athletic team, a drama group, or a studio art or ballet class. Concentrate on one person in the group you are observing, and report that person's actions. Then consider that person as representative of the entire group and what they are practicing for.

TUTANKHAMEN'S TOMB IS OPENED
New York Times

*The Egyptian king Tutankhamen died at the age of eighteen
after enjoying but a brief reign during the late fourteenth
century B.C. However, he is well known to us because his
was the first royal tomb discovered virtually intact and almost untouched by grave robbers. On the front page of the
New York Times on February 17, 1923, the editor gave the
story a three-column headline on the right side of the page,
accompanied by a picture of King Tut and the following
unsigned dispatch from Luxor, Egypt. The writer apparently
had his problems, both because of the close control over the
material exercised by Lord Carnarvon, the sponsor of the
expedition, and because of the difficulty of finding language
that would not be too technical yet would be adequate to
the items being described.*

Tut-Ankh-Amen's Tomb Is Opened, Revealing Undreamed of Splendors, Still Untouched After 3,400 Years

KING IN NEST OF SHRINES

SERIES OF ORNATE COVERS ENCLOSE PHARAOH'S SARCOPHAGUS

Whole Fills Large Room

MORTUARY CHAMBER OPENS INTO ANOTHER ROOM, CROWDED WITH GREAT TREASURE

Explorers Are Dazzled

Tutankhamen's Tomb Is Opened

WEALTH OF OBJECTS OF HISTORIC AND ARTISTIC INTEREST EXCEEDS ALL THEIR WILDEST VISIONS

The Times (London) World Copyright, by Arrangement with the Earl of Carnarvon. Copyright, 1923, by the New York Times Company. Special Cable to THE NEW YORK TIMES

LUXOR, Egypt, Feb. 16.—This has been, perhaps, the most extraordinary day in the whole history of Egyptian excavation. Whatever anyone may have guessed or imagined of the secret of Tut-Ankh-Amen's tomb, they surely would not have dreamed the truth as now revealed. 1

The entrance today was made into the sealed chamber of the tomb of Tut-Ankh-Amen, and yet another door opened beyond that. No eyes have yet seen the King, but to practical certainty we know that he lies there close at hand in all his original state, undisturbed. 2

Moreover, in addition to the great store of treasures which the tomb has already yielded, today has brought to light a new wealth of objects of artistic, historical, and even intrinsic value which is bewildering. 3

It is such a hoard as the most sanguine excavator can hardly have pictured, even in visions in his sleep, and puts Lord Carnarvon's and Mr. Carter's discovery in a class by itself and above all previous finds.[1] 4

OFFICIAL OPENING SUNDAY.

Though the official opening of the sealed mortuary chamber of the tomb has been fixed for Sunday, it was obviously impossible to postpone until then the actual work of breaking in the entrance. This was a job involving some hours of work, because it had to be done with the greatest care, so as to keep intact as many of the seals as possible, and also to avoid injury to any of the objects on the other side which might be caused by the falling of material dislodged. 5

All this could not be done on Sunday while the official guests were kept waiting in the singularly unpleasant atmosphere of the tomb, so an agreement was made with the Egyptian authorities by which the actual breaking through of the wall should be done in their presence today. 6

Consequently, Howard Carter was very busy inside the tomb all morning with Professor Breasted and Dr. Alan Gardiner, whose assistance has been in- 7

---

[1]Lord Carnarvon and Mr. Carter: Howard Carter (1873–1939) was an English Egyptologist and the discoverer of the tomb of Tutankhamen. George Edward Stanhope Molyneux Herbert, 5th Earl of Carnarvon (1866–1923), was an amateur archaeologist and the patron of Carter's dig. He died of the effects of a mosquito bite several weeks after the official opening of the tomb. [Eds.]

valuable from the beginning of the work of examining seals and deciphering and copying inscriptions of all kinds. They had finished by noon, and the tomb was closed till after luncheon, at which Lord Carnarvon, Mr. Carter and Lady Evelyn Herbert entertained all those invited to be present today.

OFFICIAL STORY OF INNER TOMB.

It was after 1 o'clock when the official party entered the tomb, and the operation was begun which was to result in such astounding discoveries, of which I am able to give the following authoritative description: 8

Today between the hours of 1 and 3 in the afternoon the culminating moment in the discovery of Tut-Ankh-Amen's tomb took place when Lord Carnarvon and Howard Carter opened the inner sealed doorway in the presence of Lady Evelyn Herbert; Abdel Hamid Suliman Pasha, Under Secretary of Public Works; Pierre Lacau, Director General of the Antiquities Department; Sir William Garstin; Sir Charles Cuph; Mr. Lythgoe, the curator of the Metropolitan Museum of Art of New York; Mr. Winlock, Director of the Egyptian expedition of the Metropolitan Museum, together with other representatives of the Government. 9

The process of opening this doorway, bearing the royal insignia and guarded by the protective statues of the King, had taken several hours of careful manipulation under the intense heat. It finally ended in a wonderful revelation, for before the spectators was the resplendent mausoleum of the King, a spacious and beautifully decorated chamber, completely occupied by an immense shrine covered with gold inlaid with brilliant blue faience. This beautiful wooden construction towers nearly to the ceiling and fills the great sepulchral hall within a short span of its four walls. Its sides are adorned with magnificent religious texts and fearful symbols of the dead and it is capped with a superb cornice and a tyrus molding like the propylaeum of a temple,[2] in fact, indeed, the sacred monument. 10

ANOTHER SHRINE WITHIN.

On the eastern end of this shrine are two immense folding doors, closed and bolted. Within it, is yet another shrine, closed and sealed, bearing the cipher of the Royal Necropolis.[3] On this inner shrine hangs the funerary pall, studded with gold, and by the evidence of the papyrus of Rameses IV,[4] there must be 11

---

[2]propylaeum: an elaborate vestibule or entrance to a temple area. [Eds.]

[3]cipher of the Royal Necropolis: the seal of the royal City of the Dead, depicting the jackal Anubis and nine slaves, which was affixed to the outer doorway of a royal tomb. [Eds.]

[4]Rameses IV: a pharaoh of the Twentieth Dynasty, which ruled Egypt from 1200 to 1085 B.C. [Eds.]

a series of these shrines within, covering the remains of the King lying in the sarcophagus.

Around the outer canopy, or shrine, stand great protective emblems of a mystic type finely carved and covered with gilt, and upon the floor lie seven oars for the King's use in the waters of the other world. 12

In the further end of the eastern wall of this sepulchral hall is yet another doorway, open and never closed. It leads to another chamber, the store chamber of the sepulchre. There at the end stands an elaborately and magnificently carved and gilded shrine of indescribable beauty. It is surmounted by tiers of uraei and its sides are protected by open-armed goddesses of the finest workmanship,[5] their pitiful faces turned over their shoulders toward the invader. This is no less than the receptacle for the four canopic jars which should contain the viscera (brain, heart &c.) of the King. 13

Immediately at the entrance to this chamber stands the jackal god Anubis,[6] in black and gold, upon his shrine, which again rests upon a portable sled, strange and resplendent. Behind this again is the head of the bull, emblem of the underworld. 14

Stacked on the south side of the chamber in great numbers are black boxes and shrines of all shapes, all closed and sealed, save one with open doors in which are golden effigies of the King standing upon black leopards. Similarly at the end of the chamber are more of these cases, including miniature coffins, sealed, but no doubt containing funerary statuettes of the monarch, servants for the dead in the coming world. On the south side of the deity Anubis is a tier of wonderful ivory and wooden boxes of every shape and design, studded with gold and inlaid with faience, and beside them yet another chariot. 15

This sight is stupendous and its magnificence indescribable, and as the time was fast creeping on, and dusk was falling, the tomb was closed for further action and contemplation. 16

The foregoing narrative is necessarily hasty and may be subject to correction in details as a result of future investigation. The truth is that all those who were privileged to share in today's unparalleled experiences were and still are so bewildered that it is not easy for any of them to give a consecutive narrative. All, however agree in describing as overwhelming the impression produced by the discovery of the great shrine or canopy, splendid in its blue and gold and almost filling the entire space of the new chamber. 17

QUESTIONS

1. One of the headlines reads "Explorers Are Dazzled." How would you describe the condition of the reporter of this article?

---

[5]uraei: representations of the sacred serpents that symbolized sovereignty on the headdresses of Egyptian monarchs and gods. [Eds.]
[6]Anubis: god of the dead. [Eds.]

2. What does the introduction (paragraphs 1 to 4) lead the reader to expect from the article? Does the writer fulfill those expectations? Does he, for example, make clear why this day might be considered "the most extraordinary day in the whole history of Egyptian excavation"?

3. In paragraph 16, the writer states that "this sight is stupendous and its magnificence indescribable." How often in this article does the writer actually describe objectively what happened and what he saw?

4. How would you edit the introductory paragraphs to produce an objective report?

5. Visit a place where you have never been before, such as a museum, a large public building, or a new shopping mall. Write two reports of your visit to this place. In the first, take care to describe objectively its most important features for an audience that has never seen this place. In the second report, describe the place from a subjective point of view, so that your audience will know how you felt about what you saw.

LEARNING TO READ AND WRITE
Frederick Douglass

Frederick Augustus Washington Bailey (1817–1895) was born into slavery on the Eastern Shore of Maryland. His mother was a black slave; his father, a white man. After his escape from the South in 1838, he adopted the name of Douglass and worked to free other slaves and later (after the Civil War) to protect the rights of freed slaves. He was a newspaper editor, a lecturer, United States minister to Haiti, and the author of several books about his life and times. The Narrative of the Life of Frederick Douglass: An American Slave *(1841), from which the following chapter has been taken, is his best-known work.*

I lived in Master Hugh's family about seven years. During this time, I suc- 1
ceeded in learning to read and write. In accomplishing this, I was compelled to resort to various stratagems. I had no regular teacher. My mistress, who had kindly commenced to instruct me, had, in compliance with the advice and direction of her husband, not only ceased to instruct, but had set her face against my being instructed by any one else. It is due, however, to my mistress to say of her, that she did not adopt this course of treatment immediately. She at first lacked the depravity indispensable to shutting me up in mental darkness. It was at least necessary for her to have some training in the exercise of irresponsible power, to make her equal to the task of treating me as though I were a brute.

My mistress was, as I have said, a kind and tender-hearted woman; and in 2
the simplicity of her soul she commenced, when I first went to live with her, to treat me as she supposed one human being ought to treat another. In entering upon the duties of a slaveholder, she did not seem to perceive that I sustained to her the relation of a mere chattel, and that for her to treat me as a human being was not only wrong, but dangerously so. Slavery proved as injurious to her as it did to me. When I went there, she was a pious, warm, and tender-hearted woman. There was no sorrow or suffering for which she had not a tear. She had bread for the hungry, clothes for the naked, and comfort for every mourner that came within her reach. Slavery soon proved its ability to divest her of these heavenly qualities. Under its influence, the tender heart became stone, and the lamblike disposition gave way to one of tiger-like fierceness. The first step in her downward course was in her ceasing to instruct me. She now commenced to practise her husband's precepts. She finally became even more

21

violent in her opposition than her husband himself. She was not satisfied with simply doing as well as he had commanded; she seemed anxious to do better. Nothing seemed to make her more angry than to see me with a newspaper. She seemed to think that here lay the danger. I have had her rush at me with a face made all up of fury, and snatch from me a newspaper, in a manner that fully revealed her apprehension. She was an apt woman; and a little experience soon demonstrated, to her satisfaction, that education and slavery were incompatible with each other.

From this time I was most narrowly watched. If I was in a separate room   3
any considerable length of time, I was sure to be suspected of having a book, and was at once called to give an account of myself. All this, however, was too late. The first step had been taken. Mistress, in teaching me the alphabet, had given me the *inch*, and no precaution could prevent me from taking the *ell*.

The plan which I adopted, and the one by which I was most successful, was   4
that of making friends of all the little white boys whom I met in the street. As many of these as I could, I converted into teachers. With their kindly aid, obtained at different times and in different places, I finally succeeded in learning to read. When I was sent on errands, I always took my book with me, and by going one part of my errand quickly, I found time to get a lesson before my return. I used also to carry bread with me, enough of which was always in the house, and to which I was always welcome; for I was much better off in this regard than many of the poor white children in our neighborhood. This bread I used to bestow upon the hungry little urchins, who, in return, would give me that more valuable bread of knowledge. I am strongly tempted to give the names of two or three of those little boys, as a testimonial of the gratitude and affection I bear them; but prudence forbids;—not that it would injure me, but it might embarrass them; for it is almost an unpardonable offence to teach slaves to read in this Christian country. It is enough to say of the dear little fellows, that they lived on Philpot Street, very near Durgin and Bailey's ship-yard. I used to talk this matter of slavery over with them. I would sometimes say to them, I wished I could be as free as they would be when they got to be men. "You will be free as soon as you are twenty-one, *but I am a slave for life!* Have not I as good a right to be free as you have?" These words used to trouble them; they would express for me the liveliest sympathy, and console me with the hope that something would occur by which I might be free.

I was now about twelve years old, and the thought of being *a slave for life*   5
began to bear heavily upon my heart. Just about this time, I got hold of a book entitled "The Columbian Orator."[1] Every opportunity I got, I used to read this book. Among much of other interesting matter, I found in it a dialogue between a master and his slave. The slave was represented as having run away from his

---

[1]*The Columbian Orator:* a popular schoolbook designed to introduce students to argument and rhetoric. [Eds.]

master three times. The dialogue represented the conversation which took place between them, when the slave was retaken the third time. In this dialogue, the whole argument in behalf of slavery was brought forward by the master, all of which was disposed of by the slave. The slave was made to say some very smart as well as impressive things in reply to his master—things which had the desired though unexpected effect; for the conversation resulted in the voluntary emancipation of the slave on the part of the master.

In the same book, I met with one of Sheridan's mighty speeches on and in behalf of Catholic emancipation.[2] These were choice documents to me. I read them over and over again with unabated interest. They gave tongue to interesting thoughts of my own soul, which had frequently flashed through my mind, and died away for want of utterance. The moral which I gained from the dialogue was the power of truth over the conscience of even a slaveholder. What I got from Sheridan was a bold denunciation of slavery, and a powerful vindication of human rights. The reading of these documents enabled me to utter my thoughts, and to meet the arguments brought forward to sustain slavery; but while they relieved me of one difficulty, they brought on another even more painful than the one of which I was relieved. The more I read, the more I was led to abhor and detest my enslavers. I could regard them in no other light than a band of successful robbers, who had left their homes, and gone to Africa, and stolen us from our homes, and in a strange land reduced us to slavery. I loathed them as being the meanest as well as the most wicked of men. As I read and contemplated the subject, behold! that very discontentment which Master Hugh had predicted would follow my learning to read had already come, to torment and sting my soul to unutterable anguish. As I writhed under it, I would at times feel that learning to read had been a curse rather than a blessing. It had given me a view of my wretched condition, without the remedy. It opened my eyes to the horrible pit, but to no ladder upon which to get out. In moments of agony, I envied my fellow-slaves for their stupidity. I have often wished myself a beast. I preferred the condition of the meanest reptile to my own. Any thing, no matter what, to get rid of thinking! It was this everlasting thinking of my condition that tormented me. There was no getting rid of it. It was pressed upon me by every object within sight or hearing, animate or inanimate. The silver trump of freedom had roused my soul to eternal wakefulness. Freedom now appeared, to disappear no more forever. It was heard in every sound, and seen in every thing. It was ever present to torment me with a sense of my wretched condition. I saw nothing without seeing it, I heard nothing without hearing it, and felt nothing without feeling it. It looked from every star, it smiled in every calm, breathed in every wind, and moved in every storm.

I often found myself regretting my own existence, and wishing myself dead;

6

7

---

[2]Richard Brinsley Sheridan (1751–1816): British dramatist, orator, and politician. Catholics were not allowed to vote in England until 1829. [Eds.]

and but for the hope of being free, I have no doubt but that I should have killed myself, or done something for which I should have been killed. While in this state of mind, I was eager to hear any one speak of slavery. I was a ready listener. Every little while, I could hear something about the abolitionists. It was some time before I found what the word meant. It was always used in such connections as to make it an interesting word to me. If a slave ran away and succeeded in getting clear, or if a slave killed his master, set fire to a barn, or did any thing very wrong in the mind of a slaveholder, it was spoken of as the fruit of *abolition*. Hearing the word in this connection very often, I set about learning what it meant. The dictionary afforded me little or no help. I found it was "the act of abolishing"; but then I did not know what was to be abolished. Here I was perplexed. I did not dare to ask any one about its meaning, for I was satisfied that it was something they wanted me to know very little about. After a patient waiting, I got one of our city papers, containing an account of the number of petitions from the north, praying for the abolition of slavery in the District of Columbia, and of the slave trade between the States. From this time I understood the words *abolition* and *abolitionist*, and always drew near when that word was spoken, expecting to hear something of importance to myself and fellow-slaves. The light broke in upon me by degrees. I went one day down on the wharf of Mr. Waters; and seeing two Irishmen unloading a scow of stone, I went, unasked, and helped them. When we had finished, one of them came to me and asked me if I were a slave. I told him I was. He asked, "Are ye a slave for life?" I told him that I was. The good Irishman seemed to be deeply affected by the statement. He said to the other that it was a pity so fine a little fellow as myself should be a slave for life. He said it was a shame to hold me. They both advised me to run away to the north; that I should find friends there, and that I should be free. I pretended not to be interested in what they said, and treated them as if I did not understand them; for I feared they might be treacherous. White men have been known to encourage slaves to escape, and then, to get the reward, catch them and return them to their masters. I was afraid that these seemingly good men might use me so; but I nevertheless remembered their advice, and from that time I resolved to run away. I looked forward to a time at which it would be safe for me to escape. I was too young to think of doing so immediately; besides, I wished to learn how to write, as I might have occasion to write my own pass. I consoled myself with the hope that I should one day find a good chance. Meanwhile, I would learn to write.

The idea as to how I might learn to write was suggested to me by being in Durgin and Bailey's ship-yard, and frequently seeing the ship carpenters, after hewing, and getting a piece of timber ready for use, write on the timber the name of that part of the ship for which it was intended. When a piece of timber was intended for the larboard side, it would be marked thus—"L." When a piece was for the starboard side, it would be marked thus—"S." A piece for the

8

larboard side forward, would be marked thus—"L. F." When a piece was for starboard side forward, it would be marked thus—"S. F." For larboard aft, it would be marked thus—"L.A." For starboard aft, it would be marked thus—"S. A." I soon learned the names of these letters, and for what they were intended when placed upon a piece of timber in the ship-yard. I immediately commenced copying them, and in a short time was able to make the four letters named. After that, when I met with any boy who I knew could write, I would tell him I could write as well as he. The next word would be, "I don't believe you. Let me see you try it." I would then make the letters which I had been so fortunate as to learn, and ask him to beat that. In this way I got a good many lessons in writing, which it is quite possible I should never have gotten in any other way. During this time, my copy-book was the board fence, brick wall, and pavement; my pen and ink was a lump of chalk. With these, I learned mainly how to write. I then commenced and continued copying the Italics in Webster's Spelling Book, until I could make them all without looking on the book. By this time, my little Master Thomas had gone to school, and learned how to write, and had written over a number of copy-books. These had been brought home, and shown to some of our near neighbors, and then laid aside. My mistress used to go to class meeting at the Wilk Street meetinghouse every Monday afternoon, and leave me to take care of the house. When left thus, I used to spend the time in writing in the spaces left in Master Thomas's copy-book, copying what he had written. I continued to do this until I could write a hand very similar to that of Master Thomas. Thus, after a long, tedious effort for years, I finally succeeded in learning how to write.

QUESTIONS

1. As its title proclaims, Douglass's book is a narrative, the story of his life. So, too, is this chapter a narrative, the story of his learning to read and write. Separate out the main events of this story, and list them in chronological order.

2. Douglass is reporting some of the events in his life in this selection, but certain events are not simply reported. Instead, they are described so that we may see, hear, and feel what was experienced by those people who were present on the original occasions. Which events are described most fully in this narrative? How does Douglass seek to engage our interest and direct our feelings through such scenes?

3. In this episode from his life, as in his whole book, Douglass is engaged in evaluating an institution—slavery—and arguing a case against it. Can you locate the points in the text where reporting gives way to argumentation? How does Douglass support his argument against slavery? What are the sources of his persuasiveness?

4. The situation of Irish Catholics is a subtheme in this essay. You can trace it by

locating every mention of the Irish or of Catholicism in the text. How does this theme relate to Afro-American slavery? Try to locate *The Columbian Orator* in your library, or find out more about who "Sheridan" was and why he had to argue on behalf of "Catholic emancipation" (paragraph 6).

5. There is a subnarrative in this text that tells the story of Master Hugh's wife, the "mistress" of the household in which Douglass learned to read and write. Retell *her* story in your own words. Consider how her story relates to Douglass's own story and how it relates to Douglass's larger argument about slavery.

6. Put yourself in the place of Master Hugh's wife, and retell all events in her words and from her point of view. To do so, you will have to decide both what she might have come to know about all these events and how she would feel about them. You will also have to decide when she is writing. Is she keeping a diary during this very time (the early 1830s), or is she looking back from the perspective of later years? Has she been moved to write by reading Douglass's own book, which appeared in 1841? If so, how old would she be then, and what would she think about these past events? Would she be angry, bitter, repentant, embarrassed, indulgent, scornful, or what?

GRADUATION
Maya Angelou

*In her four volumes of autobiography, Maya Angelou (b.
1928) has written vividly of her struggles to achieve success
as an actress, a dancer, a songwriter, a teacher, and a
writer. An active worker in the civil rights movement in the
1960s, Angelou continues to focus much of her writing on
racial issues. The following selection is from* I Know Why
the Caged Bird Sings *(1969), in which she writes, "I speak
to the Black experience, but I am always talking about the
human condition."*

The children in Stamps trembled visibly with anticipation.[1] Some adults 1
were excited too, but to be certain the whole young population had come down
with graduation epidemic. Large classes were graduating from both the grammar
school and the high school. Even those who were years removed from their
own day of glorious release were anxious to help with preparations as a kind of
dry run. The junior students who were moving into the vacating classes' chairs
were tradition-bound to show their talents for leadership and management. They
strutted through the school and around the campus exerting pressure on the
lower grades. Their authority was so new that occasionally if they pressed a little
too hard it had to be overlooked. After all, next term was coming, and it never
hurt a sixth grader to have a play sister in the eighth grade, or a tenth-year
student to be able to call a twelfth grader Bubba. So all was endured in a spirit
of shared understanding. But the graduating classes themselves were the nobility.
Like travelers with exotic destinations on their minds, the graduates were remarkably forgetful. They came to school without their books, or tablets or even
pencils. Volunteers fell over themselves to secure replacements for the missing
equipment. When accepted, the willing workers might or might not be thanked,
and it was of no importance to the pregraduation rites. Even teachers were
respectful of the now quiet and aging seniors, and tended to speak to them, if
not as equals, as beings only slightly lower than themselves. After tests were
returned and grades given, the student body, which acted like an extended
family, knew who did well, who excelled, and what piteous ones had failed.

Unlike the white high school, Lafayette County Training School distin- 2
guished itself by having neither lawn, nor hedges, nor tennis court, nor climbing
ivy. Its two buildings (main classrooms, the grade school and home economics)
were set on a dirt hill with no fence to limit either its boundaries or those of

---

[1]Stamps: a town in Arkansas. [Eds.]

bordering farms. There was a large expanse to the left of the school which was used alternately as a baseball diamond or basketball court. Rusty hoops on swaying poles represented the permanent recreational equipment, although bats and balls could be borrowed from the P.E. teacher if the borrower was qualified and if the diamond wasn't occupied.

Over this rocky area relieved by a few shady tall persimmon trees the graduating 3 class walked. The girls often held hands and no longer bothered to speak to the lower students. There was a sadness about them, as if this old world was not their home and they were bound for higher ground. The boys, on the other hand, had become more friendly, more outgoing. A decided change from the closed attitude they projected while studying for finals. Now they seemed not ready to give up the old school, the familiar paths and classrooms. Only a small percentage would be continuing on to college—one of the South's A & M (agricultural and mechanical) schools, which trained Negro youths to be carpenters, farmers, handymen, masons, maids, cooks and baby nurses. Their future rode heavily on their shoulders, and blinded them to the collective joy that had pervaded the lives of the boys and girls in the grammar school graduating class.

Parents who could afford it had ordered new shoes and ready-made clothes 4 for themselves from Sears and Roebuck or Montgomery Ward. They also engaged the best seamstresses to make the floating graduating dresses and to cut down secondhand pants which would be pressed to a military slickness for the important event.

Oh, it was important, all right. Whitefolks would attend the ceremony, and 5 two or three would speak of God and home, and the Southern way of life, and Mrs. Parsons, the principal's wife, would play the graduation march while the lower-grade graduates paraded down the aisles and took their seats below the platform. The high school seniors would wait in empty classrooms to make their dramatic entrance.

In the Store I was the person of the moment. The birthday girl. The center. 6 Bailey had graduated the year before,[2] although to do so he had had to forfeit all pleasures to make up for his time lost in Baton Rouge.

My class was wearing butter-yellow piqué dresses, and Momma launched 7 out on mine. She smocked the yoke into tiny crisscrossing puckers, then shirred the rest of the bodice. Her dark fingers ducked in and out of the lemony cloth as she embroidered raised daisies around the hem. Before she considered herself finished she had added a crocheted cuff on the puff sleeves, and a pointy crocheted collar.

I was going to be lovely. A walking model of all the various styles of fine 8 hand sewing and it didn't worry me that I was only twelve years old and merely graduating from the eighth grade. Besides, many teachers in Arkansas Negro schools had only that diploma and were licensed to impart wisdom.

The days had become longer and more noticeable. The faded beige of former 9

---

[2]Bailey: the brother of the author. [Eds.]

times had been replaced with strong and sure colors. I began to see my classmates' clothes, their skin tones, and the dust that waved off pussy willows.
Clouds that lazed across the sky were objects of great concern to me. Their
shiftier shapes might have held a message that in my new happiness and with
a little bit of time I'd soon decipher. During that period I looked at the arch of
heaven so religiously my neck kept a steady ache. I had taken to smiling more
often, and my jaws hurt from the unaccustomed activity. Between the two
physical sore spots, I suppose I could have been uncomfortable, but that was
not the case. As a member of the winning team (the graduating class of 1940)
I had outdistanced unpleasant sensations by miles. I was headed for the freedom
of open fields.

Youth and social approval allied themselves with me and we trammeled   10
memories of slights and insults. The wind of our swift passage remodeled my
features. Lost tears were pounded to mud and then to dust. Years of withdrawal
were brushed aside and left behind, as hanging ropes of parasitic moss.

My work alone had awarded me a top place and I was going to be one of   11
the first called in the graduating ceremonies. On the classroom blackboard, as
well as on the bulletin board in the auditorium, there were blue stars and white
stars and red stars. No absences, no tardinesses, and my academic work was
among the best of the year. I could say the preamble to the Constitution even
faster than Bailey. We timed ourselves often: "WethepeopleoftheUnited
Statesinordertoformamoreperfectunion . . ." I had memorized the Presidents of
the United States from Washington to Roosevelt in chronological as well as
alphabetical order.

My hair pleased me too. Gradually the black mass had lengthened and   12
thickened, so that it kept at last to its braided pattern, and I didn't have to yank
my scalp off when I tried to comb it.

Louise and I had rehearsed the exercises until we tired out ourselves. Henry   13
Reed was class valedictorian. He was a small, very black boy with hooded eyes,
a long, broad nose and an oddly shaped head. I had admired him for years
because each term he and I vied for the best grades in our class. Most often he
bested me, but instead of being disappointed I was pleased that we shared top
places between us. Like many Southern Black children, he lived with his grandmother, who was as strict as Momma and as kind as she knew how to be. He
was courteous, respectful and soft-spoken to elders, but on the playground he
chose to play the roughest games. I admired him. Anyone, I reckoned, sufficiently afraid or sufficiently dull could be polite. But to be able to operate at a
top level with both adults and children was admirable.

His valedictory speech was entitled "To Be or Not to Be." The rigid tenth-   14
grade teacher had helped him write it. He'd been working on the dramatic
stresses for months.

The weeks until graduation were filled with heady activities. A group of small   15
children were to be presented in a play about buttercups and daisies and bunny
rabbits. They could be heard throughout the building practicing their hops and

their little songs that sounded like silver bells. The older girls (nongraduates, of course) were assigned the task of making refreshments for the night's festivities. A tangy scent of ginger, cinnamon, nutmeg and chocolate wafted around the home economics building as the budding cooks made samples for themselves and their teachers.

In every corner of the workshop, axes and saws split fresh timber as the woodshop boys made sets and stage scenery. Only the graduates were left out of the general bustle. We were free to sit in the library at the back of the building or look in quite detachedly, naturally, on the measures being taken for our event.

Even the minister preached on graduation the Sunday before. His subject was, "Let your light so shine that men will see your good works and praise your Father, Who is in Heaven." Although the sermon was purported to be addressed to us, he used the occasion to speak to backsliders, gamblers and general ne'er-do-wells. But since he had called our names at the beginning of the service we were mollified.

Among Negroes the tradition was to give presents to children going only from one grade to another. How much more important this was when the person was graduating at the top of the class. Uncle Willie and Momma had sent away for a Mickey Mouse watch like Bailey's. Louise gave me four embroidered handkerchiefs. (I gave her crocheted doilies.) Mrs. Sneed, the minister's wife, made me an undershirt to wear for graduation, and nearly every customer gave me a nickel or maybe even a dime with the instruction "Keep on moving to higher ground," or some such encouragement.

Amazingly the great day finally dawned and I was out of bed before I knew it. I threw open the back door to see it more clearly, but Momma said, "Sister, come away from that door and put your robe on."

I hoped the memory of that morning would never leave me. Sunlight was itself young, and the day had none of the insistence maturity would bring it in a few hours. In my robe and barefoot in the backyard, under cover of going to see about my new beans, I gave myself up to the gentle warmth and thanked God that no matter what evil I had done in my life He had allowed me to live to see this day. Somewhere in my fatalism I had expected to die, accidentally, and never have the chance to walk up the stairs in the auditorium and gracefully receive my hard-earned diploma. Out of God's merciful bosom I had won reprieve.

Bailey came out in his robe and gave me a box wrapped in Christmas paper. He said he had saved his money for months to pay for it. It felt like a box of chocolates, but I knew Bailey wouldn't save money to buy candy when we had all we could want under our noses.

He was as proud of the gift as I. It was a soft-leather-bound copy of a collection of poems by Edgar Allan Poe, or, as Bailey and I called him, "Eap." I turned to "Annabel Lee" and we walked up and down the garden rows, the cool dirt between our toes, reciting the beautifully sad lines.

GRADUATION

Momma made a Sunday breakfast although it was only Friday. After we 23 finished the blessing, I opened my eyes to find the watch on my plate. It was a dream of a day. Everything went smoothly and to my credit. I didn't have to be reminded or scolded for anything. Near evening I was too jittery to attend to chores, so Bailey volunteered to do all before his bath.

Days before, we had made a sign for the Store, and as we turned out the 24 lights Momma hung the cardboard over the doorknob. It read clearly: CLOSED. GRADUATION.

My dress fitted perfectly and everyone said that I looked like a sunbeam in 25 it. On the hill, going toward the school, Bailey walked behind with Uncle Willie, who muttered, "Go on, Ju." He wanted him to walk ahead with us because it embarrassed him to have to walk so slowly. Bailey said he'd let the ladies walk together, and the men would bring up the rear. We all laughed, nicely.

Little children dashed by out of the dark like fireflies. Their crepe-paper 26 dresses and butterfly wings were not made for running and we heard more than one rip, dryly, and the regretful "uh uh" that followed.

The school blazed without gaiety. The windows seemed cold and unfriendly 27 from the lower hill. A sense of ill-fated timing crept over me, and if Momma hadn't reached for my hand I would have drifted back to Bailey and Uncle Willie, and possibly beyond. She made a few slow jokes about my feet getting cold, and tugged me along to the now-strange building.

Around the front steps, assurance came back. There were my fellow "greats," 28 the graduating class. Hair brushed back, legs oiled, new dresses and pressed pleats, fresh pocket handkerchiefs and little handbags, all homesewn. Oh, we were up to snuff, all right. I joined my comrades and didn't even see my family go in to find seats in the crowded auditorium.

The school band struck up a march and all classes filed in as had been 29 rehearsed. We stood in front of our seats, as assigned, and on a signal from the choir director, we sat. No sooner had this been accomplished than the band started to play the national anthem. We rose again and sang the song, after which we recited the pledge of allegiance. We remained standing for a brief minute before the choir director and the principal signaled to us, rather desperately I thought, to take our seats. The command was so unusual that our carefully rehearsed and smooth-running machine was thrown off. For a full minute we fumbled for our chairs and bumped into each other awkwardly. Habits change or solidify under pressure, so in our state of nervous tension we had been ready to follow our usual assembly pattern: the American national anthem, then the pledge of allegiance, then the song every Black person I knew called the Negro National Anthem. All done in the same key, with the same passion and most often standing on the same foot.

Finding my seat at last, I was overcome with a presentiment of worse things 30 to come. Something unrehearsed, unplanned, was going to happen, and we were going to be made to look bad. I distinctly remember being explicit in the

31

choice of pronoun. It was "we," the graduating class, the unit, that concerned me then.

The principal welcomed "parents and friends" and asked the Baptist minister to lead us in prayer. His invocation was brief and punchy, and for a second I thought we were getting on the high road to right action. When the principal came back to the dais, however, his voice had changed. Sounds always affected me profoundly and the principal's voice was one of my favorites. During assembly it melted and lowed weakly into the audience. It had not been in my plan to listen to him, but my curiosity was piqued and I straightened up to give him my attention.

He was talking about Booker T. Washington, our "late great leader," who said we can be as close as the fingers on the hand, etc. . . . Then he said a few vague things about friendship and the friendship of kindly people to those less fortunate than themselves. With that his voice nearly faded, thin, away. Like a river diminishing to a stream and then to a trickle. But he cleared his throat and said, "Our speaker tonight, who is also our friend, came from Texarkana to deliver the commencement address, but due to the irregularity of the train schedule, he's going to, as they say, 'speak and run.' " He said that we understood and wanted the man to know that we were most grateful for the time he was able to give us and then something about how we were willing always to adjust to another's program, and without more ado—"I give you Mr. Edward Donleavy."

Not one but two white men came through the door off-stage. The shorter one walked to the speaker's platform, and the tall one moved to the center seat and sat down. But that was our principal's seat, and already occupied. The dislodged gentleman bounced around for a long breath or two before the Baptist minister gave him his chair, then with more dignity than the situation deserved, the minister walked off the stage.

Donleavy looked at the audience once (on reflection, I'm sure that he wanted only to reassure himself that we were really there), adjusted his glasses and began to read from a sheaf of papers.

He was glad "to be here and to see the work going on just as it was in the other schools."

At the first "Amen" from the audience I willed the offender to immediate death by choking on the word. But Amens and Yes, sir's began to fall around the room like rain through a ragged umbrella.

He told us of the wonderful changes we children in Stamps had in store. The Central School (naturally, the white school was Central) had already been granted improvements that would be in use in the fall. A well-known artist was coming from Little Rock to teach art to them. They were going to have the newest microscopes and chemistry equipment for their laboratory. Mr. Donleavy didn't leave us long in the dark over who made these improvements available to Central High. Nor were we to be ignored in the general betterment scheme he had in mind.

He said that he had pointed out to people at a very high level that one of   38
the first-line football tacklers at Arkansas Agricultural and Mechanical College
had graduated from good old Lafayette County Training School. Here fewer
Amen's were heard. Those few that did break through lay dully in the air with
the heaviness of habit.

He went on to praise us. He went on to say how he had bragged that "one   39
of the best basketball players at Fisk sank his first ball right here at Lafayette
County Training School."

The white kids were going to have a chance to become Galileos and Madame   40
Curies and Edisons and Gauguins, and our boys (the girls weren't even in on
it) would try to be Jesse Owenses and Joe Louises.

Owens and the Brown Bomber were great heroes in our world, but what   41
school official in the white-goddom of Little Rock had the right to decide that
those two men must be our only heroes? Who decided that for Henry Reed to
become a scientist he had to work like George Washington Carver, as a boot-
black, to buy a lousy microscope? Bailey was obviously always going to be too
small to be an athlete, so which concrete angel glued to what country seat had
decided that if my brother wanted to become a lawyer he had to first pay penance
for his skin by picking cotton and hoeing corn and studying correspondence
books at night for twenty years?

The man's dead words fell like bricks around the auditorium and too many   42
settled in my belly. Constrained by hard-learned manners I couldn't look behind
me, but to my left and right the proud graduating class of 1940 had dropped
their heads. Every girl in my row had found something new to do with her
handkerchief. Some folded the tiny squares into love knots, some into triangles,
but most were wadding them, then pressing them flat on their yellow laps.

On the dais, the ancient tragedy was being replayed. Professor Parsons sat,   43
a sculptor's reject, rigid. His large, heavy body seemed devoid of will or willingness, and his eyes said he was no longer with us. The other teachers examined
the flag (which was draped stage right) or their notes, or the windows which
opened on our now-famous playing diamond.

Graduation, the hush-hush magic time of frills and gifts and congratulations   44
and diplomas, was finished for me before my name was called. The accomplishment was nothing. The meticulous maps, drawn in three colors of ink,
learning and spelling decasyllabic words, memorizing the whole of *The Rape of
Lucrece*[3]—it was for nothing. Donleavy had exposed us.

We were maids and farmers, handymen and washerwomen, and anything   45
higher that we aspired to was farcical and presumptuous.

Then I wished that Gabriel Prosser and Nat Turner had killed all whitefolks   46
in their beds and that Abraham Lincoln had been assassinated before the signing
of the Emancipation Proclamation,[4] and that Harriet Tubman had been killed

---

[3]*The Rape of Lucrece*: an 1,855-line narrative poem by William Shakespeare. [Eds.]
[4]Gabriel Prosser and Nat Turner: leaders of slave rebellions during the early 1800s in Virginia.
[Eds.]

by that blow on her head and Christopher Columbus had drowned in the *Santa Maria*.[5]

It was awful to be a Negro and have no control over my life. It was brutal   47
to be young and already trained to sit quietly and listen to charges brought against my color with no chance of defense. We should all be dead. I thought I should like to see us all dead, one on top of the other. A pyramid of flesh with the whitefolks on the bottom, as the broad base, then the Indians with their silly tomahawks and teepees and wigwams and treaties, the Negroes with their mops and recipes and cotton sacks and spirituals sticking out of their mouths. The Dutch children should all stumble in their wooden shoes and break their necks. The French should choke to death on the Louisiana Purchase (1803) while silkworms ate all the Chinese with their stupid pigtails. As a species, we were an abomination. All of us.

Donleavy was running for election, and assured our parents that if he won   48
we could count on having the only colored paved playing field in that part of Arkansas. Also—he never looked up to acknowledge the grunts of acceptance—also, we were bound to get some new equipment for the home economics building and the workshop.

He finished, and since there was no need to give any more than the most   49
perfunctory thank-you's, he nodded to the men on the stage, and the tall white man who was never introduced joined him at the door. They left with the attitude that now they were off to something really important. (The graduation ceremonies at Lafayette County Training School had been a mere preliminary.)

The ugliness they left was palpable. An uninvited guest who wouldn't leave.   50
The choir was summoned and sang a modern arrangement of "Onward, Christian Soldiers," with new words pertaining to graduates seeking their place in the world. But it didn't work. Elouise, the daughter of the Baptist minister, recited "Invictus,"[6] and I could have cried at the impertinence of "I am the master of my fate, I am the captain of my soul."

My name had lost its ring of familiarity and I had to be nudged to go and   51
receive my diploma. All my preparations had fled. I neither marched up to the stage like a conquering Amazon, nor did I look in the audience for Bailey's nod of approval. Marguerite Johnson, I heard the name again, my honors were read, there were noises in the audience of appreciation, and I took my place on the stage as rehearsed.

I thought about colors I hated: ecru, puce, lavender, beige and black.   52

There was shuffling and rustling around me, then Henry Reed was giving   53
his valedictory address, "To Be or Not to Be." Hadn't he heard the whitefolks? We couldn't *be*, so the question was a waste of time. Henry's voice came out

---

[5]Harriet Tubman: an escaped slave who conducted others to freedom on the Underground Railroad and worked as an abolitionist. [Eds.]

[6]"Invictus": a poem by the nineteenth-century English poet, William Ernest Henley. Its inspirational conclusion is quoted here. [Eds.]

clear and strong. I feared to look at him. Hadn't he got the message? There was no "nobler in the mind" for Negroes because the world didn't think we had minds, and they let us know it. "Outrageous fortune"? Now, that was a joke. When the ceremony was over I had to tell Henry Reed some things. That is, if I still cared. Not "rub," Henry, "erase." "Ah, there's the erase." Us.

Henry had been a good student in elocution. His voice rose on tides of promise and fell on waves of warnings. The English teacher had helped him to create a sermon winging through Hamlet's soliloquy. To be a man, a doer, a builder, a leader, or to be a tool, an unfunny joke, a crusher of funky toadstools. I marveled that Henry could go through with the speech as if we had a choice. 54

I had been listening and silently rebutting each sentence with my eyes closed; then there was a hush, which in an audience warns that something unplanned is happening. I looked up and saw Henry Reed, the conservative, the proper, the A student, turn his back to the audience and turn to us (the proud graduating class of 1940) and sing, nearly speaking, 55

> "Lift ev'ry voice and sing
> Till earth and heaven ring
> Ring with the harmonies of Liberty . . ."

It was the poem written by James Weldon Johnson. It was the music composed by J. Rosamond Johnson. It was the Negro national anthem. Out of habit we were singing it.

Our mothers and fathers stood in the dark hall and joined the hymn of encouragement. A kindergarten teacher led the small children onto the stage and the buttercups and daisies and bunny rabbits marked time and tried to follow: 56

> "Stony the road we trod
> Bitter the chastening rod
> Felt in the days when hope, unborn, had died.
> Yet with a steady beat
> Have not our weary feet
> Come to the place for which our fathers sighed?"

Each child I knew had learned that song with his ABC's and along with "Jesus Loves Me This I Know." But I personally had never heard it before. Never heard the words, despite the thousands of times I had sung them. Never thought they had anything to do with me. 57

On the other hand, the words of Patrick Henry had made such an impression on me that I had been able to stretch myself tall and trembling and say, "I know not what course others may take, but as for me, give me liberty or give me death." 58

And now I heard, really for the first time: 59

35

"We have come over a way that with tears
has been watered,
We have come, treading our path through
the blood of the slaughtered."

While echoes of the song shivered in the air, Henry Reed bowed his head,   60
said "Thank you," and returned to his place in the line. The tears that slipped
down many faces were not wiped away in shame.

We were on top again. As always, again. We survived. The depths had been   61
icy and dark, but now a bright sun spoke to our souls. I was no longer simply
a member of the proud graduating class of 1940; I was a proud member of the
wonderful, beautiful Negro race.

Oh, Black known and unknown poets, how often have your auctioned pains   62
sustained us? Who will compute the lonely nights made less lonely by your
songs, or the empty pots made less tragic by your tales?

If we were a people much given to revealing secrets, we might raise monu-   63
ments and sacrifice to the memories of our poets, but slavery cured us of that
weakness. It may be enough, however, to have it said that we survive in exact
relationship to the dedication of our poets (include preachers, musicians and
blues singers).

QUESTIONS

1. Why was graduation such an important event in Stamps, Arkansas? Note the rituals
and preparations associated with this event. How do they compare with those accompanying your own high school graduation?

2. At the beginning of the graduation ceremony, the writer was "overcome with a
presentiment of worse things to come. Something unrehearsed, unplanned, was going
to happen" (paragraph 30). What "unrehearsed, unplanned" event does occur? How does
the writer convey to the reader the meaning of this event?

3. Toward the end of the essay we are told, "I was no longer simply a member of
the proud graduating class of 1940; I was a proud member of the wonderful, beautiful
Negro race" (paragraph 62). How did the experience of the graduation change the writer's
way of thinking about herself and her people?

4. Understanding the structure of this essay is important for understanding the meaning of the essay. How does the writer organize her material, and how does this organization reflect the writer's purpose? Why do you think the writer changes her point of
view from third person in the first five paragraphs to first person in the rest of the essay?

5. Think of an event in your life that didn't turn out as you expected. What were
your expectations of this event? What was the reality? Write an essay in which you show
the significance of this event by contrasting how you planned for the event with how it
actually turned out.

6. We have all had experiences that have changed the directions of our lives. These
experiences may be momentous, such as moving from one country to another or losing

a parent, or they may be experiences that did not loom so large at the time but that changed the way you thought about things, such as finding that your parents disapproved of your best friend because of her race. Recall such a turning point in your life, and present it so as to give the reader a sense of what your life was like before the event and how it changed after the event.

BUSTER KEATON
James Agee

Born in Knoxville, Tennessee, in 1909, James Agee graduated from Harvard in 1932 and began work as a writer for Fortune *magazine, moving to* Time *in 1936. For some years he reviewed books and films for both* Time *and the* Nation, *sometimes giving the same film more extended critical discussion in the* Nation *after a brief notice in* Time. *He is best known for his film reviews; his documentary book on the Depression,* Let Us Now Praise Famous Men, *with Walker Evans's photographs; and the unfinished memoir of his family, which was made into a play,* A Death in the Family, *after his early death in 1955. The following paragraphs on Buster Keaton first appeared in* Life *magazine in 1949 in an article called "Comedy's Greatest Era," which received one of the greatest responses in the magazine's history. The whole article may be found in the first volume of* Agee on Film.

Buster Keaton started work at the age of three and one-half with his parents   1
in one of the roughest acts in vaudeville ("The Three Keatons"); Harry Houdini
gave the child the name Buster in admiration for a fall he took down a flight
of stairs.[1] In his first movies Keaton teamed with Fatty Arbuckle under Sennett.
He went on to become one of Metro's biggest stars and earners; a Keaton feature
cost about $200,000 to make and reliably grossed $2,000,000. Very early in his
movie career friends asked him why he never smiled on the screen. He didn't
realize he didn't. He had got the dead-pan habit in variety; on the screen he
had merely been so hard at work it had never occurred to him there was anything
to smile about. Now he tried it just once and never again. He was by his whole
style and nature so much the most deeply "silent" of the silent comedians that
even a smile was as deafeningly out of key as a yell. In a way his pictures are
like a transcendent juggling act in which it seems that the whole universe is in
exquisite flying motion and the one point of repose is the juggler's effortless,
uninterested face.

Keaton's face ranked almost with Lincoln's as an early American archetype;   2
it was haunting, handsome, almost beautiful, yet it was irreducibly funny; he
improved matters by topping it off with a deadly horizontal hat, as flat and thin
as a phonograph record. One can never forget Keaton wearing it, standing erect

---

[1]Harry Houdini (1874–1926): American magician and author. [Eds.]

at the prow as his little boat is being launched. The boat goes grandly down the skids and, just as grandly, straight on to the bottom. Keaton never budges. The last you see of him, the water lifts the hat off the stoic head and it floats away.

No other comedian could do as much with the dead pan. He used this great, sad, motionless face to suggest various related things: a one-track mind near the track's end of pure insanity; mulish imperturbability under the wildest of circumstances; how dead a human being can get and still be alive; an awe-inspiring sort of patience and power to endure, proper to granite but uncanny in flesh and blood. Everything that he was and did bore out this rigid face and played laughs against it. When he moved his eyes, it was like seeing them move in a statue. His short-legged body was all sudden, machinelike angles, governed by a daft aplomb. When he swept a semaphorelike arm to point, you could almost hear the electrical impulse in the signal block. When he ran from a cop his transitions from accelerating walk to easy jogtrot to brisk canter to headlong gallop to flogged-piston sprint—always floating, above this frenzy, the untroubled, untouchable face—were as distinct and as soberly in order as an automatic gearshift.   3

Keaton was a wonderfully resourceful inventor of mechanistic gags (he still spends much of his time fooling with Erector sets); as he ran afoul of locomotives, steamships, prefabricated and over-electrified houses, he put himself through some of the hardest and cleverest punishment ever designed for laughs. In *Sherlock Jr.*, boiling along on the handlebars of a motorcycle quite unaware that he has lost his driver, Keaton whips through city traffic, breaks up a tug-of-war, gets a shovelful of dirt in the face from each of a long line of Rockette-timed ditch-diggers, approaches a log at high speed which is hinged open by dynamite precisely soon enough to let him through and, hitting an obstruction, leaves the handlebars like an arrow leaving a bow, whams through the window of a shack in which the heroine is about to be violated, and hits the heavy feet-first, knocking him through the opposite wall. The whole sequence is as clean in motion as the trajectory of a bullet.   4

Much of the charm and edge of Keaton's comedy, however, lay in the subtle leverages of expression he could work against his nominal dead pan. Trapped in the side-wheel of a ferryboat, saving himself from drowning only by walking, then desperately running, inside the accelerating wheel like a squirrel in a cage, his only real concern was, obviously, to keep his hat on. Confronted by Love, he was not as dead-pan as he was cracked up to be, either; there was an odd, abrupt motion of his head which suggested a horse nipping after a sugar lump.   5

Keaton worked strictly for laughs, but his work came from so far inside a curious and original spirit that he achieved a great deal besides, especially in his feature-length comedies. (For plain hard laughter his nineteen short comedies—the negatives of which have been lost—were even better.) He was the only major comedian who kept sentiment almost entirely out of his work, and he brought pure physical comedy to its greatest heights. Beneath his lack of   6

39

James Agee

emotion he was also uninsistently sardonic; deep below that, giving a disturbing tension and grandeur to the foolishness, for those who sensed it, there was in his comedy a freezing whisper not of pathos but of melancholia. With the humor, the craftsmanship and the action there was often, besides, a fine, still and sometimes dreamlike beauty. Much of his Civil War picture *The General* is within hailing distance of Mathew Brady.[2] And there is a ghostly, unforgettable moment in *The Navigator*, when, on a deserted, softly rolling ship, all the pale doors along a deck swing open as one behind Keaton and, as one, slam shut, in a hair-raising illusion of noise.

Perhaps because "dry" comedy is so much more rare and odd than "dry" wit, there are people who never much cared for Keaton. Those who do cannot care mildly. 7

QUESTIONS

1. What research did the writer do? How much information comes from watching Keaton's films? How much might have come from interviews with or articles and books about Keaton?

2. Which parts of this essay report what Keaton did? Which parts tell us how he did it?

3. Find some examples of figurative language using similes to compare Keaton's actions to something else. Why does the writer use such language? How does it affect the reader?

4. How close to his subject is the writer? What passages suggest that he admires Keaton?

5. Using the sentence in paragraph 4 that starts "In *Sherlock Jr.* . . . ." as a model, construct an equally complex sentence in which you record a series of actions or events that you have observed. Some suggestions are a hockey player moving the puck, a barroom brawl in a western film, or a short-order cook in a busy diner.

6. Consider why you find your favorite comedian funny. Describe a scene from a film, a television program, or a stage show, giving your audience an idea of the performer's body movements, facial expressions, speech patterns, or clothing or of whatever makes this performer distinctive.

7. After completing the writing assignment for question 6, find reviews of and articles about your comedian, and write an article in which you summarize this person's career. Then, as Agee does, concentrate on those characteristics that you and others find most distinctive about this performer.

---

[2]Mathew Brady (1823–1896): New York portrait photographer best known for his haunting and graphic photographs of Civil War battlefields. [Eds.]

ISADORA DUNCAN
Winthrop Palmer

Winthrop Palmer was born in 1899 across the street from Carnegie Hall in New York City and has been actively interested in music for many years. A poet and writer of children's books, she was also an associate editor of Dance News *for fifteen years and the author of* Theatrical Dancing in America *(1945, revised 1978). The following piece on Isadora Duncan (1878–1927) is an excerpt from an article on the development of modern dance in America. Duncan, who early in her career rejected the prescribed forms of classic ballet, felt that dance should exhibit personal feelings. The "Greek" style of dance that she introduced became one of the major influences on the development of modern dance as we know it today.*

Isadora Duncan, born in San Francisco of Irish-American parents in 1878, was prepared for life by a mother who gave music lessons all day to support her family, and who played Beethoven, Mozart, and Chopin or read Shakespeare, Keats, and Burns to them in the evening. A handsome father was seldom home. 1

At the age of eleven Isadora was teaching a new system of dancing to the little girls of the neighborhood. She recited a poem and taught the children to follow its meaning in gesture and movement. One of the first dances was to Longfellow's poem "I Shot an Arrow into the Air." Her classes grew in size and the youthful teacher, who put up her hair and let down the hem of her dress in order to look older, was invited to give lessons "in the richest houses in San Francisco." And all this after pronouncing that lessons with the most famous ballet teacher in San Francisco (she quit after the third lesson) did not please her. The stiff and commonplace gymnastics he called dancing only disturbed her dream of a dance that would express the feelings and the emotions of humanity. 2

Influenced by books she had read, she decided her true place was in the theatre. She called on the manager of a traveling company and danced Mendelssohn's *Songs Without Words* in a little white tunic. The manager watched her move about the big, bare stage. After some time he addressed Mrs. Duncan, who had played her daughter's accompaniment. "I advise you to take your little girl home," he said, "this sort of thing is no good for a theatre. It's more for a church." 3

Isadora thought otherwise. She and her mother left for Chicago. But the Chicago managers repeated the San Francisco manager's opinion with a slight 4

41

variation. They called the dance "very lovely," but they did not book the young lady. Of course, if she decided to pep the dance up a little. . . .? Nothing came of this proposition until Isadora had pawned the last of her grandmother's jewels and lived on a box of tomatoes for a week. She consented then to do a "peppery" dance under an assumed name in the Masonic Temple Roof Garden. She was an immediate success. The delighted roof garden manager offered her a prolonged engagement, or even a tour. The offer was declined. The dancer made it plain she had had enough of trying to amuse the public with something that was against her ideals. . . .

Isadora struggled along in Chicago for a while. Artists and literary people   5
paid her to give her "religious" dance at the club meetings. Then, one day, she happened to read in a newspaper that Augustin Daly was in town. She was told three times that the great producer could not give her an interview. The fourth try succeeded. She walked into his office and made a speech. Mr. Daly could not afford to turn her away, she said. Nonplused, Mr. Daly stalled. He was putting on a pantomime in New York next October with Jane May from Paris as the star. If Isadora could get herself to New York, and if she suited, there might be a part for her.

The Duncans got to New York on borrowed money. Isadora suited. She was   6
given a Directoire costume of blue silk, a blond wig and a big straw hat. She made love to Jane May who played the role of a fickle Pierrot. But she hated the whole performance. The last thing she had bargained for was to be imprisoned in what seemed to her a false and vapid form of theatre, "neither the art of the actor nor that of the dancer, something that falls between the two in hopeless sterility."

The pantomime closed after three weeks, but Daly kept the new youngster   7
on. She danced grudgingly in his productions of *The Tempest* and *A Midsummer Night's Dream.* But when he assigned her a "singing" role in *The Geisha* she quit. "What's the good of having me here with my genius when you make no use of me?" she said reprovingly, and shrugged off his explanation that *The Geisha* was a financial necessity.

In 1899 she embarked for Europe on a cattle boat, and in London and Paris   8
she found her only true masters, Greek sculpture and Greek vases. Inspired by the classic figures on friezes and bas-reliefs in the British Museum and in the Louvre, she composed dances that became the talk of Paris. The French press urged that no one miss the opportunity to see Isadora Duncan. "With her the dance is no longer *divertissement.* It is a work of art."

From then on Isadora danced in every European capital. She spent one year   9
in Greece, she established a school in Berlin and, finally, she went to Russia. She danced in St. Petersburg, in Moscow and, according to Russian commentators, had great influence on Michel Fokine himself. At that time (1905), Fokine was the center of a battle between the supporters of the old and the new styles in Russian Ballet. He created a Greek ballet after Isadora's visit, with his

corps de ballet in tunics and sandals. Isadora had come a long way from her "little religious dance" in San Francisco. . . .

She returned to New York in August, 1908, to dance *Iphigenia* and Bee- 10
thoven's *Seventh Symphony* at the Criterion Theater, under the management of Charles Frohman. As in Europe, she instantly commanded a passionate following of painters, sculptors, poets, and dancers. The young revolutionaries of Greenwich Village—George Bellows, Percy MacKaye, Max Eastman, Edwin Arlington Robinson—were Isadora's worshipers, but their loyalty did not make her New York season a success. Audiences were small and cold, and Frohman, regretfully realizing that Duncan was not Broadway, sent her out on a six months' tour. Her performances were reviewed by music critics who were friendly and eloquent in their praise: "This is something different. . . . a Greek frieze come to life. . . . exquisite tableaux. . . ." But no matter how favorable the reviewers, the public stayed home in town after town. "Your art is considerably over the heads of Americans," remarked Frohman, and he advised the disappointed young artist to return to Europe.

She revisited Russia, opened a school in France, and kept coming back to 11
the United States, from time to time, to dance for the few who remained faithful to her personification of ideal beauty. But she never won the heart of a bewildered public who were either shocked or bored by her natural expression of feeling. They learned better and, strangely enough, the instruction came through the very channels Isadora had despised.

QUESTIONS

1. What does Isadora Duncan's experience in America tell us about the kinds of dance preferred by Americans at that time?

2. What was Duncan doing that was new or different from traditional forms of dance?

3. What is the writer's opinion of Duncan? How objective is she? In organizing her research material, what choices did she make? For example, in gathering information about Duncan's childhood, what might she have been looking for? Why is Duncan's father mentioned only once and then briefly?

4. In paragraph 10, we are told about Duncan's return to New York in 1908. Choose one of the other names in that paragraph and find in a biography or in a newspaper or magazine of that period more information about that person. Or, if you are interested in what dance forms the public preferred, look for an article on the dance season in New York City in 1908. Then write a report in which you tell how you went about gathering your information and give a summary of what you found.

OLIVIER'S MOOR—OTHELLO: NATIONAL THEATRE
Ronald Bryden

*Born in the West Indies in the late 1920s, Ronald Bryden
went to school there and in Canada before emigrating to
England to finish his education at Cambridge. Since then
he has worked mostly as a reviewer, first of books and finally
of plays, of which he says, "If I found myself giving more
and more space to acting, that . . . was from my own growing fascination with the challenge of describing an art ten
times more difficult to write about than writing, which [act-
ing] would perish but for the theatre critic." The review
reprinted here, of Laurence Olivier playing Shakespeare's*
Othello *in 1964, won him his job as theater reviewer for the*
New Statesman, *and he reprinted it as the leading piece in
his collection of reviews* The Unfinished Hero *(1969).*

All posterity will want to know is how he played. John Dexter's National   1
Theatre *Othello* is efficient and clear, if slow, and contains some intelligent
minor novelties. But in the long run all that matters is that it left the stage as
bare as possible for its athlete. What requires record is how he, tackling Burbage's
role for the first time at 57, created the Moor.[1]

He came on smelling a rose, laughing softly with a private delight; barefooted,   2
ankleted, black. He had chosen to play a Negro. The story fits a true Moor
better: one of those striding hawks, fierce in a narrow range of medieval passions,
whose women still veil themselves like Henry Moore sleepers against the blowing
sand of Nouakchott's surrealistically modern streets.[2] But Shakespeare muddled,
giving him the excuse to turn himself into a coastal African from below the
Senegal: dark, thick-lipped, open, laughing.

He sauntered downstage, with a loose, bare-heeled roll of the buttocks; came   3
to rest feet splayed apart, hip lounging outward. For him, the great Richard III
of his day, the part was too simple. He had made it difficult and interesting for
himself by studying, as scrupulously as he studied the flat vowels, dead grin and

---

[1]Burbage . . . Moor: Richard Burbage, in 1604, was the first actor to play Othello, the Moor;
Moors are Muslims of the mixed Arab and Berber people who controlled much of Spain in the
Middle Ages. [Eds.]

[2]Henry Moore . . . Nouakchott: Moore (b. 1898) is an English sculptor whose subjects have
included many reclining figures. Nouakchott is the capital of the West African nation of Mauritania.
[Eds.]

hunched time-steps of Archie Rice, how an African looks, moves, sounds.[3] The make-up, exact in pigment, covered his body almost wholly: an hour's job at least. The hands hung big and graceful. The whole voice was characterized, the o's and a's deepened, the consonants thickened with faint, guttural deliberation. Keep up your bright swords, or de dew will rus' dem': not quite so crude, but in that direction.

It could have been caricature, an embarrassment. Instead, after the second performance, a well-known Negro actor rose in the stalls bravoing. For obviously it was done with love; with the main purpose of substituting for the dead grandeur of the Moorish empire one modern audiences could respond to: the grandeur of Africa. He was the continent, like a figure of Rubens allegory.[4] In Cyprus, he strode ashore in a cloak and spiked helmet which brought to mind the medieval emirates of Ethiopia and Niger. Facing Doge and senators, he hooded his eyes in a pouting ebony mask: an old chief listening watchfully in tribal conclave. When he named them "my masters" it was proudly edged: he had been a slave, their inquisition recalled his slavery, he reminded them in turn of his service and generalship.

He described Desdemona's encouragement smiling down at them, easy with sexual confidence.[5] This was the other key to the choice of a Negro: Finlay's Iago,[6] bony, crop-haired, staring with the fanatic mule-grin of a Mississippi redneck, was to be goaded by a small white man's sexual jealousy of the black, a jealousy sliding into ambiguous fascination. Like Yeats's crowd staring, sweating, at Don Juan's mighty thigh,[7] this Iago gazed, licking dry lips, on a black one. All he need do is teach his own disease.

Mannerisms established, they were lifted into the older, broader imagery of the part. Leading Desdemona to bed, he pretended to snap at her with playful teeth. At Iago's first hints, he made a chuckling mock of twisting truth out of him by the ear. Then, during the temptation, he began to pace, turning his head sharply like a lion listening. The climax was his farewell to his occupation: bellowing the words as pure, wounded outcry, he hurled back his head until the ululating tongue showed pink against the roof of his mouth like a trumpeting elephant's. As he grew into a great beast, Finlay shrunk beside him, clinging to his shoulder like an ape, hugging his heels like a jackal.

---

[3]Richard III: Shakespeare's play of the same name portrayed the English king as villainous and humpbacked. Olivier's brilliant film version of the play was produced in 1956. Olivier also delivered a flawless performance as Archie Rice, a music-hall comedian who is the lead character in John Osborne's *The Entertainer*.

[4]Rubens allegory: the Flemish painter Peter Paul Rubens (1577–1640) is noted for his large-scale paintings, many of them religious and political allegories. [Eds.]

[5]Desdemona: the wife of Othello. [Eds.]

[6]Finlay's Iago: Frank Finlay played Iago, Othello's ensign and the villain of the play. [Eds.]

[7]The reference is to lines from W.B. Yeats's "On Those That Hated 'The Playboy of the Western World,' 1907": "Once when midnight smote the air,/Eunuchs ran through Hell and met/On every crowded street to stare/Upon great Juan riding by:/Even like these to rail and sweat/Staring upon his sinewy thigh." [Eds.]

He used every clue in the part, its most strenuous difficulties. Reassured by   7
Desdemona's innocence, he bent to kiss her—and paused looking, sickened, at
her lips. Long before his raging return, you knew he had found Cassio's kisses
there.[8] Faced with the lung-torturing hurdle of "Like to the Pontic sea," he
found a brilliant device for breaking the period: at "Shall ne'er look back," he
let the memories he was forswearing rush in and stop him, gasping with pain,
until he caught breath. Then, at "By yon marble heaven," he tore the crucifix
from his neck (Iago, you recall, says casually Othello'd renounce his baptism
for Desdemona) and, crouching forehead to ground, made his "sacred vow" in
the religion which caked Benin's altars with blood.[9]

Possibly it was too early a climax, built to make a curtain of Iago's "I am   8
your own for ever." In Act Four he could only repeat himself with increased
volume, adding a humming animal moan as he fell into his fit, a strangler's
look to the dangling hands, a sharper danger to the turns of his head as he
questioned Emilia. But it gave him time to wind down to a superb returned
dignity and tenderness for the murder. This became an act of love—at "I would
not have thee linger in thy pain," he threw aside the pillow and, stopping her
lips with a kiss, strangled her. The last speech was spoken kneeling on the bed,
her body clutched upright to him as a shield for the dagger he turns on himself.

As he slumped beside her in the sheets, the current stopped. A couple of   9
wigged actors stood awkwardly about. You could only pity them: we had seen
history, and it was over. Perhaps it's as well to have seen the performance while
still unripe, constructed in fragments, still knitting itself. Now you can see how
it's done; later, it will be a torrent. But before it exhausts him, a film should be
made. It couldn't save the whole truth, but it might save something the unborn
should know.

QUESTIONS

1. Often theater or movie reviews are written to help us decide, on the basis of the
reviewer's opinion, whether or not to see a particular play or film. What is different
about this review?

2. In order to report how Olivier created his role, Bryden must transform a multi-
dimensional experience into words. What strategies does he use to do this?

3. In paragraph 2, Bryden describes Olivier's entrance on stage, telling us what he
looked like and how his choice of playing Othello as a Negro was a departure from
Shakespeare's intention. Where else in the review are we told that Olivier is creating
something different from previous interpretations of the role?

4. What does it mean to *create* a role? Aside from makeup, what else does Bryden
describe to help us see Olivier creating Othello?

---

[8]Cassio: Othello's lieutenant. [Eds.]
[9]Benin: a former African kingdom, now part of Nigeria. [Eds.]

5. Part of the effectiveness of Bryden's review derives from his knowledge of *Othello* and his experience of seeing a number of previous performances of the play and of seeing Olivier create other roles. Consider your own experience as a viewer of television, films, plays, or other performances. Observe a performance, and analyze how a performer creates a particular role. (If, for example, you are a regular viewer of *Dallas*, describe Larry Hagman's interpretation of J. R. Ewing in a particular show. If you have seen Hagman in other roles or in interviews, you will be even more aware of what he does to create J. R.) Concentrate on physical movements, facial expressions, speech patterns, clothing, or whatever you consider most important and effective in the creation of the role. Write a review of the performance. Remember that your audience may be counting on your review to know whether or not they should watch the performer you describe.

6. If you are a student who holds a job or who rushes from college to home to be a spouse or parent, what changes do you make in dress, behavior, or speech as you shift from one role to another? Write a review of yourself as the creator or actor of roles.

"THIS IS THE END OF THE WORLD": THE BLACK DEATH

Barbara Tuchman

For over twenty-five years Barbara Wertheim Tuchman (b. 1912) has been writing books on historical subjects, ranging over the centuries from the Middle Ages to World War II. Her combination of careful research and lively writing has enabled her to produce books like The Guns of August *(1962) and* A Distant Mirror *(1978), which please not only the general public but many professional historians as well. She has twice won the Pulitzer Prize.* A Distant Mirror, *from which the following selection has been taken, was on the* New York Times *best-seller list for over nine months.*

In October 1347, two months after the fall of Calais, Genoese trading ships put into the harbor of Messina in Sicily with dead and dying men at the oars. The ships had come from the Black Sea port of Caffa (now Feodosiya) in the Crimea, where the Genoese maintained a trading post. The diseased sailors showed strange black swellings about the size of an egg or an apple in the armpits and groin. The swellings oozed blood and pus and were followed by spreading boils and black blotches on the skin from internal bleeding. The sick suffered severe pain and died quickly within five days of the first symptoms. As the disease spread, other symptoms of continuous fever and spitting of blood appeared instead of the swellings or buboes. These victims coughed and sweated heavily and died even more quickly, within three days or less, sometimes in 24 hours. In both types everything that issued from the body—breath, sweat, blood from the buboes and lungs, bloody urine, and blood-blackened excrement—smelled foul. Depression and despair accompanied the physical symptoms, and before the end "death is seen seated on the face."

The disease was bubonic plague, present in two forms: one that infected the bloodstream, causing the buboes and internal bleeding, and was spread by contact; and a second, more virulent pneumonic type that infected the lungs and was spread by respiratory infection. The presence of both at once caused the high mortality and speed of contagion. So lethal was the disease that cases were known of persons going to bed well and dying before they woke, of doctors catching the illness at a bedside and dying before the patient. So rapidly did it spread from one to another that to a French physician, Simon de Covino, it

48

seemed as if one sick person "could infect the whole world." The malignity of the pestilence appeared more terrible because its victims knew no prevention and no remedy.

The physical suffering of the disease and its aspect of evil mystery were expressed in a strange Welsh lament which saw "death coming into our midst like black smoke, a plague which cuts off the young, a rootless phantom which has no mercy for fair countenance. Woe is me of the shilling in the armpit! It is seething, terrible . . . a head that gives pain and causes a loud cry . . . a painful angry knob . . . Great is its seething like a burning cinder . . . a grievous thing of ashy color." Its eruption is ugly like the "seeds of black peas, broken fragments of brittle sea-coal . . . the early ornaments of black death, cinders of the peelings of the cockle weed, a mixed multitude, a black plague like half-pence, like berries. . . ."

Rumors of a terrible plague supposedly arising in China and spreading through Tartary (Central Asia) to India and Persia, Mesopotamia, Syria, Egypt, and all of Asia Minor had reached Europe in 1346. They told of a death toll so dev-astating that all of India was said to be depopulated, whole territories covered by dead bodies, other areas with no one left alive. As added up by Pope Clement VI at Avignon, the total of reported dead reached 23,840,000. In the absence of a concept of contagion, no serious alarm was felt in Europe until the trading ships brought their black burden of pestilence into Messina while other infected ships from the Levant carried it to Genoa and Venice.

By January 1348 it penetrated France via Marseille, and North Africa via Tunis. Shipborne along coasts and navigable rivers, it spread westward from Marseille through the ports of Languedoc to Spain and northward up the Rhône to Avignon, where it arrived in March. It reached Narbonne, Montpellier, Carcassonne, and Toulouse between February and May, and at the same time in Italy spread to Rome and Florence and their hinterlands. Between June and August it reached Bordeaux, Lyon, and Paris, spread to Burgundy and Nor-mandy, and crossed the Channel from Normandy into southern England. From Italy during the same summer it crossed the Alps into Switzerland and reached eastward to Hungary.

In a given area the plague accomplished its kill within four to six months and then faded, except in the larger cities, where, rooting into the close-quartered population, it abated during the winter, only to reappear in spring and rage for another six months.

In 1349 it resumed in Paris, spread to Picardy, Flanders, and the Low Coun-tries, and from England to Scotland and Ireland as well as to Norway, where a ghost ship with a cargo of wool and a dead crew drifted offshore until it ran aground near Bergen. From there the plague passed into Sweden, Denmark, Prussia, Iceland, and as far as Greenland. Leaving a strange pocket of immunity in Bohemia, and Russia unattacked until 1351, it had passed from most of Europe by mid-1350. Although the mortality rate was erratic, ranging from one fifth in some places to nine tenths or almost total elimination in others, the overall estimate of modern demographers has settled—for the area extending from India to Iceland—around the same figure expressed in Froissart's casual words: "a third of the world died." His estimate, the common one at the time, was not an inspired guess but a borrowing of St. John's figure for mortality from plague in Revelation, the favorite guide to human affairs of the Middle Ages.

A third of Europe would have meant about 20 million deaths. No one knows in truth how many died. Contemporary reports were an awed impression, not an accurate count. In crowded Avignon, it was said, 400 died daily; 7,000 houses emptied by death were shut up; a single graveyard received 11,000 corpses in six weeks; half the city's inhabitants reportedly died, including 9 cardinals or one third of the total, and 70 lesser prelates. Watching the endlessly passing death carts, chroniclers let normal exaggeration take wings and put the Avignon death toll at 62,000 and even at 120,000, although the city's total population was probably less than 50,000.

When graveyards filled up, bodies at Avignon were thrown into the Rhône until mass burial pits were dug for dumping the corpses. In London in such pits corpses piled up in layers until they overflowed. Everywhere reports speak of the sick dying too fast for the living to bury. Corpses were dragged out of homes and left in front of doorways. Morning light revealed new piles of bodies. In Florence the dead were gathered up by the Compagnia della Misericordia— founded in 1244 to care for the sick—whose members wore red robes and hoods masking the face except for the eyes. When their efforts failed, the dead lay putrid in the streets for days at a time. When no coffins were to be had, the bodies were laid on boards, two or three at once, to be carried to graveyards or common pits. Families dumped their own relatives into the pits, or buried them so hastily and thinly "that dogs dragged them forth and devoured their bodies."

Amid accumulating death and fear of contagion, people died without last rites and were buried without prayers, a prospect that terrified the last hours of the stricken. A bishop in England gave permission to laymen to make confession to each other as was done by the Apostles, "or if no man is present then even to a woman," and if no priest could be found to administer extreme unction, "then faith must suffice." Clement VI found it necessary to grant remissions of sin to all who died of the plague because so many were unattended by priests. "And no bells tolled," wrote a chronicler of Siena, "and nobody wept no matter what his loss because almost everyone expected death. . . . And people said and believed, 'This is the end of the world.' "

In Paris, where the plague lasted through 1349, the reported death rate was 800 a day, in Pisa 500, in Vienna 500 to 600. The total dead in Paris numbered 50,000 or half the population. Florence, weakened by the famine of 1347, lost three to four fifths of its citizens, Venice two thirds, Hamburg and Bremen, though smaller in size, about the same proportion. Cities, as centers of transportation, were more likely to be affected than villages, although once a village was infected, its death rate was equally high. At Givry, a prosperous village in Burgundy of 1,200 to 1,500 people, the parish register records 615 deaths in the space of fourteen weeks, compared to an average of thirty deaths a year in the previous decade. In three villages of Cambridgeshire, manorial records show a death rate of 47 percent, 57 percent, and in one case 70 percent. When the last survivors, too few to carry on, moved away, a deserted village sank back into the wilderness and disappeared from the map altogether, leaving only a grass-covered ghostly outline to show where mortals once had lived.

In enclosed places such as monasteries and prisons, the infection of one 12 person usually meant that of all, as happened in the Franciscan convents of Carcassonne and Marseille, where every inmate without exception died. Of the 140 Dominicans at Montpellier only seven survived. Petrarch's brother Gherardo, member of a Carthusian monastery, buried the prior and 34 fellow monks one by one, sometimes three a day, until he was left alone with his dog and fled to look for a place that would take him in. Watching every comrade die, men in such places could not but wonder whether the strange peril that filled the air had not been sent to exterminate the human race. In Kilkenny, Ireland, Brother John Clyn of the Friars Minor, another monk left alone among dead men, kept a record of what had happened lest "things which should be remembered perish with time and vanish from the memory of those who come after us." Sensing "the whole world, as it were, placed within the grasp of the Evil One," and waiting for death to visit him too, he wrote, "I leave parchment to continue this work, if perchance any man survive and any of the race of Adam escape this pestilence and carry on the work which I have begun." Brother John, as noted by another hand, died of the pestilence, but he foiled oblivion.

The largest cities of Europe, with populations of about 100,000, were Paris 13 and Florence, Venice and Genoa. At the next level, with more than 50,000, were Ghent and Bruges in Flanders, Milan, Bologna, Rome, Naples, and Palermo, and Cologne. London hovered below 50,000, the only city in England except York with more than 10,000. At the level of 20,000 to 50,000 were Bordeaux, Toulouse, Montpellier, Marseille, and Lyon in France, Barcelona, Seville, and Toledo in Spain, Siena, Pisa, and other secondary cities in Italy, and the Hanseatic trading cities of the Empire. The plague raged through them all, killing anywhere from one third to two thirds of their inhabitants. Italy, with a total population of 10 to 11 million, probably suffered the heaviest toll. Following the Florentine bankruptcies, the crop failures and workers' riots of 1346–47, the revolt of Cola di Rienzi that plunged Rome into anarchy, the plague came as the peak of successive calamities. As if the world were indeed in the grasp of the Evil One, its first appearance on the European mainland in January 1348 coincided with a fearsome earthquake that carved a path of wreckage from Naples up to Venice. Houses collapsed, church towers toppled, villages were crushed, and the destruction reached as far as Germany and Greece. Emotional response, dulled by horrors, underwent a kind of atrophy epitomized

51

by the chronicler who wrote, "And in these days was burying without sorrowe and wedding without friendschippe."

In Siena, where more than half the inhabitants died of the plague, work was 14 abandoned on the great cathedral, planned to be the largest in the world, and never resumed, owing to loss of workers and master masons and "the melancholy and grief" of the survivors. The cathedral's truncated transept still stands in permanent witness to the sweep of death's scythe. Agnolo di Tura, a chronicler of Siena, recorded the fear of contagion that froze every other instinct. "Father abandoned child, wife husband, one brother another," he wrote, "for this plague seemed to strike through the breath and sight. And so they died. And no one could be found to bury the dead for money or friendship. . . . And I, Angolo di Tura, called the Fat, buried my five children with my own hands, and so did many others likewise."

There were many to echo his account of inhumanity and few to balance it, 15 for the plague was not the kind of calamity that inspired mutual help. Its loathsomeness and deadliness did not herd people together in mutual distress, but only prompted their desire to escape each other. "Magistrates and notaries refused to come and make the wills of the dying," reported a Franciscan friar of Piazza in Sicily; what was worse, "even the priests did not come to hear their confessions." A clerk of the Archbishop of Canterbury reported the same of English priests who "turned away from the care of their benefices from fear of death." Cases of parents deserting children and children their parents were reported across Europe from Scotland to Russia. The calamity chilled the hearts of men, wrote Boccaccio in his famous account of the plague in Florence that serves as introduction to the *Decameron*. "One man shunned another . . . kinsfolk held aloof, brother was forsaken by brother, oftentimes husband by wife; nay, what is more, and scarcely to be believed, fathers and mothers were found to abandon their own children to their fate, untended, unvisited as if they had been strangers." Exaggeration and literary pessimism were common in the 14th century, but the Pope's physician, Guy de Chauliac, was a sober, careful observer who reported the same phenomenon: "A father did not visit his son, nor the son his father. Charity was dead."

Yet not entirely. In Paris, according to the chronicler Jean de Venette, the 16 nuns of the Hôtel Dieu or municipal hospital, "having no fear of death, tended the sick with all sweetness and humility." New nuns repeatedly took the places of those who died, until the majority "many times renewed by death now rest in peace with Christ as we may piously believe."

When the plague entered northern France in July 1348, it settled first in 17 Normandy and, checked by winter, gave Picardy a deceptive interim until the next summer. Either in mourning or warning, black flags were flown from church towers of the worst-stricken villages of Normandy. "And in that time," wrote a monk of the abbey of Fourcarment, "the mortality was so great among the people of Normandy that those of Picardy mocked them." The same unneighborly reaction was reported of the Scots, separated by a winter's immunity from the English. Delighted to hear of the disease that was scourging the "southrons," they gathered forces for an invasion, "laughing at their enemies." Before they could move, the savage mortality fell upon them too, scattering some in death and the rest in panic to spread the infection as they fled.

In Picardy in the summer of 1349 the pestilence penetrated the castle of   18
Coucy to kill Enguerrand's mother,[1] Catherine, and her new husband. Whether her nine-year-old son escaped by chance or was perhaps living elsewhere with one of his guardians is unrecorded. In nearby Amiens, tannery workers, responding quickly to losses in the labor force, combined to bargain for higher wages. In another place villagers were seen dancing to drums and trumpets, and on being asked the reason, answered that, seeing their neighbors die day by day while their village remained immune, they believed that they could keep the plague from entering "by the jollity that is in us. That is why we dance." Further north in Tournai on the border of Flanders, Gilles li Muisis, Abbot of St. Martin's, kept one of the epidemic's most vivid accounts. The passing bells rang all day and all night, he recorded, because sextons were anxious to obtain their fees while they could. Filled with the sound of mourning, the city became oppressed by fear, so that the authorities forbade the tolling of bells and the wearing of black and restricted funeral services to two mourners. The silencing of funeral bells and of criers' announcements of deaths was ordained by most cities. Siena imposed a fine on the wearing of mourning clothes by all except widows.

Flight was the chief recourse of those who could afford it or arrange it. The   19
rich fled to their country places like Boccaccio's young patricians of Florence, who settled in a pastoral palace "removed on every side from the roads" with "wells of cool water and vaults of rare wines." The urban poor died in their burrows, "and only the stench of their bodies informed neighbors of their death." That the poor were more heavily afflicted than the rich was clearly remarked at the time, in the north as in the south. A Scottish chronicler, John of Fordun, stated flatly that the pest "attacked especially the meaner sort and common people—seldom the magnates." Simon de Covino of Montpellier made the same observation. He ascribed it to the misery and want and hard lives that made the poor more susceptible, which was half the truth. Close contact and lack of sanitation was the unrecognized other half. It was noticed too that the young died in greater proportion than the old; Simon de Covino compared the disappearance of youth to the withering of flowers in the fields.

In the countryside peasants dropped dead on the roads, in the fields, in their   20
houses. Survivors in growing helplessness fell into apathy, leaving ripe wheat uncut and livestock untended. Oxen and asses, sheep and goats, pigs and chick-

---

[1]Enguerrand de Coucy: the French nobleman whose life is followed by Tuchman as a way of unifying her study of the fourteenth century. [Eds.]

ens ran wild and they too, according to local reports, succumbed to the pest. English sheep, bearers of the precious wool, died throughout the country. The chronicler Henry Knighton, canon of Leicester Abbey, reported 5,000 dead in one field alone, "their bodies so corrupted by the plague that neither beast nor bird would touch them," and spreading an appalling stench. In the Austrian Alps wolves came down to prey upon sheep and then, "as if alarmed by some invisible warning, turned and fled back into the wilderness." In remote Dalmatia bolder wolves descended upon a plague-stricken city and attacked human survivors. For want of herdsmen, cattle strayed from place to place and died in hedgerows and ditches. Dogs and cats fell like the rest.

The dearth of labor held a fearful prospect because the 14th century lived 21 close to the annual harvest both for food and for next year's seed. "So few servants and laborers were left," wrote Knighton, "that no one knew where to turn for help." The sense of a vanishing future created a kind of dementia of despair. A Bavarian chronicler of Neuberg on the Danube recorded that "Men and women . . . wandered around as if mad" and let their cattle stray "because no one had any inclination to concern themselves about the future." Fields went uncultivated, spring seed unsown. Second growth with nature's awful energy crept back over cleared land, dikes crumbled, salt water reinvaded and soured the lowlands. With so few hands remaining to restore the work of centuries, people felt, in Walsingham's words, that "the world could never again regain its former prosperity."

Though the death rate was higher among the anonymous poor, the known 22 and the great died too. King Alfonso XI of Castile was the only reigning monarch killed by the pest, but his neighbor King Pedro of Aragon lost his wife, Queen Leonora, his daughter Marie, and a niece in the space of six months. John Cantacuzene, Emperor of Byzantium, lost his son. In France the lame Queen Jeanne and her daughter-in-law Bonne de Luxemburg, wife of the Dauphin, both died in 1349 in the same phase that took the life of Enguerrand's mother. Jeanne, Queen of Navarre, daughter of Louis X, was another victim. Edward III's second daughter, Joanna, who was on her way to marry Pedro, the heir of Castile, died in Bordeaux. Women appear to have been more vulnerable than men, perhaps because, being more housebound, they were more exposed to fleas. Boccaccio's mistress Fiammetta, illegitimate daughter of the King of Naples, died, as did Laura, the beloved—whether real or fictional—of Petrarch. Reaching out to us in the future, Petrarch cried, "Oh happy posterity who will not experience such abysmal woe and will look upon our testimony as a fable."

In Florence Giovanni Villani, the great historian of his time, died at 68 in 23 the midst of an unfinished sentence: " . . . *e dure questo pistolenza fino a . . .* (in the midst of this pestilence there came to an end . . .)." Siena's master painters, the brothers Ambrogio and Pietro Lorenzetti, whose names never appear after 1348, presumably perished in the plague, as did Andrea Pisano, architect and sculptor of Florence. William of Ockham and the English mystic Richard Rolle of Hampole both disappear from mention after 1349. Francisco Datini, merchant of Prato, lost both his parents and two siblings. Curious sweeps of mortality afflicted certain bodies of merchants in London. All eight wardens of the Company of Cutters, all six wardens of the Hatters, and four wardens of the Goldsmiths died before July 1350. Sir John Pulteney, master draper and four times Mayor of London, was a victim, likewise Sir John Montgomery, Governor of Calais.

Among the clergy and doctors the mortality was naturally high because of   24 the nature of their professions. Out of 24 physicians in Venice, 20 were said to have lost their lives in the plague, although, according to another account, some were believed to have fled or to have shut themselves up in their houses. At Montpellier, site of the leading medieval medical school, the physician Simon de Covino reported that, despite the great number of doctors, "hardly one of them escaped." In Avignon, Guy de Chauliac confessed that he performed his medical visits only because he dared not stay away for fear of infamy, but "I was in continual fear." He claimed to have contracted the disease but to have cured himself by his own treatment; if so, he was one of the few who recovered.

Clerical mortality varied with rank. Although the one-third toll of cardinals   25 reflects the same proportion as the whole, this was probably due to their concentration in Avignon. In England, in strange and almost sinister procession, the Archbishop of Canterbury, John Stratford, died in August 1348, his appointed successor died in May 1349, and the next appointee three months later, all three within a year. Despite such weird vagaries, prelates in general managed to sustain a higher survival rate than the lesser clergy. Among bishops the deaths have been estimated at about one in twenty. The loss of priests, even if many avoided their fearful duty of attending the dying, was about the same as among the population as a whole.

Government officials, whose loss contributed to the general chaos, found,   26 on the whole, no special shelter. In Siena four of the nine members of the governing oligarchy died, in France one third of the royal notaries, in Bristol 15 out of the 52 members of the Town Council or almost one third. Tax-collecting obviously suffered, with the result that Philip VI was unable to collect more than a fraction of the subsidy granted him by the Estates in the winter of 1347–48.

Lawlessness and debauchery accompanied the plague as they had during the   27 great plague of Athens of 430 B.C., when according to Thucydides, men grew bold in the indulgence of pleasure: "For seeing how the rich died in a moment and those who had nothing immediately inherited their property, they reflected that life and riches were alike transitory and they resolved to enjoy themselves while they could." Human behavior is timeless. When St. John had his vision of plague in Revelation, he knew from some experience or race memory that those who survived "repented not of the work of their hands. . . . Neither repented they of their murders, nor of their sorceries, nor of their fornication, nor of their thefts."

NOTES[2]

1: "DEATH IS SEEN SEATED": Simon de Covino, q. Campbell, 80.

2: "COULD INFECT THE WORLD": q. Gasquet, 41.

3: WELSH LAMENT: q. Ziegler, 190.

9: "DOGS DRAGGED THEM FORTH": Agnolo di Tura, q. Ziegler, 58. "OR IF NO MAN IS PRESENT": Bishop of Bath and Wells, q. Ziegler, 125.

10: "NO BELLS TOLLED": Agnolo di Tura, q. Schevill, *Siena*, 211. The same observation was made by Gabriel de Muisis, notary of Piacenza, q. Crawford, 113.

11: GIVRY PARISH REGISTER: Renouard, 111. THREE VILLAGES OF CAM-BRIDGESHIRE: Saltmarsh. PETRARCH'S BROTHER: Bishop, 273. BROTHER JOHN CLYN: q. Ziegler, 195.

13: APATHY; "AND IN THESE DAYS": q. Deaux, 143, citing only "an old northern chronicle."

14: AGNOLO DI TURA, "FATHER ABANDONED CHILD": q. Ziegler, 58.

15: "MAGISTRATES AND NOTARIES": q. Deaux, 49. ENGLISH PRIESTS TURNED AWAY: Ziegler, 261. PARENTS DESERTING CHILDREN: Hecker, 30. GUY DE CHAULIAC, "A FATHER": q. Gasquet, 50–51.

16: NUNS OF THE HOTEL DIEU: *Chron. Jean de Venette*, 49.

17: PICARDS AND SCOTS MOCK MORTALITY OF NEIGHBORS: Gasquet, 53, and Ziegler, 198.

18: CATHERINE DE COUCY: *L'Art de vérifier*, 237. AMIENS TANNERS: Gasquet, 57. "BY THE JOLLITY THAT IS IN US": *Grandes Chrons.*, VI, 486–87.

19: JOHN OF FORDUN: q. Ziegler, 199. SIMON DE COVINO ON THE POOR:Gasquet, 42. ON YOUTH: Cazelles, *Peste*.

20: KNIGHTON ON SHEEP: q. Ziegler, 175. WOLVES OF AUSTRIA AND DALMATIA: ibid., 84, 111. DOGS AND CATS: Muisis, q. Gasquet, 44, 61.

21: BAVARIAN CHRONICLER OF NEUBERG: q. Ziegler, 84. WALSINGHAM, "THE WORLD COULD NEVER": Denifle, 273.

22: "OH HAPPY POSTERITY": q. Ziegler, 45.

23: GIOVANNI VILLANI, "*e dure questo*": q. Snell, 334.

24: PHYSICIANS OF VENICE: Campbell, 98. SIMON DE COVINO: ibid., 31. GUY DE CHAULIAC, "I WAS IN FEAR": q. Thompson, *Ec. and Soc.*, 379.

27: THUCYDIDES: q. Crawford, 30–31.

BIBLIOGRAPHY

L'Art de vérifier les dates des faits historiques, par un Religieux de la Congregation de St.-Maur, vol. XII. Paris, 1818.

[2]Tuchman does not use numbered footnotes, but at the back of her book she identifies the source of every quotation or citation. The works cited follow in a bibliography. Although Tuchman's notes are labeled by page number, the numbers here refer to the paragraphs in which the sources are mentioned. [Eds.].

"THIS IS THE END OF THE WORLD": THE BLACK DEATH

Campbell, Anna M., *The Black Death and Men of Learning*. Columbia University Press, 1931.

Chronicle of Jean de Venette. Trans. Jean Birdsall. Ed. Richard A. Newhall. Columbia University Press, 1853.

Crawfurd, Raymond, *Plague and Pestilence in Literature and Art*. Oxford, 1914.

Deaux, George, *The Black Death, 1347*. London, 1969.

Denifle, Henri, *La Désolation des églises, monastères et hopitaux en France pendant la geurre de cent ans*, vol. I. Paris, 1899.

Gasquet, Francis Aidan, Abbot, *The Black Death of 1348 and 1349*, 2nd ed. London, 1908.

Grandes Chroniques de France, vol. VI (to 1380). Ed. Paulin Paris. Paris, 1838.

Hecker, J. F. C., *The Epidemics of the Middle Ages*. London, 1844.

Saltmarsh, John, "Plague and Economic Decline in England in the Later Middle Ages," *Cambridge Historical Journal*, vol. VII, no. 1, 1941.

Schevill, Ferdinand, *History of Florence*. New York, 1961.

Snell, Frederick, *The Fourteenth Century*. Edinburgh, 1899.

Thompson, James Westfall, *Economic and Social History of Europe in the Later Middle Ages*. New York, 1931.

Ziegler, Philip, *The Black Death*. New York, 1969. (The best modern study.)

QUESTIONS

1. Try to imagine yourself in Tuchman's position. If you were assigned the task of reporting on the black plague in Europe, how would you go about it? What problems would you expect to encounter in the research and in the composition of your report?

2. The notes and bibliography reveal a broad scholarly base: Tuchman's research was clearly prodigious. But so were the problems of organization after the research had been done. Tuchman had to find a way to present her information to us that would be clear and interesting. How has she solved her problem? What overall patterns of organization do you find in this selection? Can you mark off subsections with topics of their own?

3. How does Tuchman organize her paragraphs? Consider paragraph 20, for example. What is the topic? What are the subtopics? Why does the paragraph begin and end as it does? Consider paragraph 22. How does the first sentence serve as a transition from the previous paragraph? How is the rest of the paragraph ordered? Does the next paragraph start a new topic or continue developing that announced at the beginning of paragraph 22?

4. Many paragraphs end with direct quotations. Examine some of these. What do they have in common? Why do you suppose Tuchman closes so many paragraphs in this way?

5. Much of this essay is devoted to the reporting of facts and figures. This could be supremely dull, but Tuchman is an expert at avoiding dullness. How does she help the reader see and feel the awfulness of the plague? Locate specific examples in the text, and discuss their effectiveness.

6. We have included the notes for the chapter reprinted here. Examine Tuchman's list of sources, and explain how she has used them. Does she quote directly from each source, or does she paraphrase it? Does she use a source to illustrate a point, or as

evidence for argument, or in some other way? Describe Tuchman's general method of using sources.

7. Taking Tuchman as a model, write a report on some other catastrophe, blending factual reporting with description of what it was like to be there. This will require both careful research and artful selection and arrangement of the fruits of that research.

8. Using Tuchman's notes to *A Distant Mirror* as a reference guide, find out more about some specific place or event mentioned by Tuchman. Write a report of your findings.

Social Sciences and Public Affairs

WEIRD ROAR SURGES FROM EXCHANGE FLOOR
New York Times

October 24, 1929, had seen the greatest volume of sales in the history of the New York Stock Exchange. People were selling stock as prices plummeted, and the whole financial structure of the market, built as it was on speculation, threatened to collapse. Temporarily saved by a group of bankers, the market finally hit bottom on November 13, 1929, and the Great Depression began. The following selection appeared on page two of the New York Times *on October 25, 1929. This "color" piece, meant to supplement the news of the collapsing market that appeared on page one, reports events in and around the New York Stock Exchange on that day of panic.*

WEIRD ROAR SURGES FROM EXCHANGE FLOOR DURING TRADING IN A RECORD SMASHING DAY

BROKERS IN UPROAR AS MARKET BOILS

New York Times

1,000 Mill Madly on Floor of Exchange and Thunder of Voices is Heard Outside.

FURIOUS PACE BEFORE GONG

Then Perspiring Traders With Torn Collars Stand Limply or Jump and Laugh.

CROWDS SURGE IN STREET

Movie Men Take Pictures of Excited Throngs—50,000 Clerks at Work as Wall St. Stays Up All Night.

The big clock above the Stock Exchange trading floor registered one minute   1
to 3 o'clock yesterday. A short, slim man tensely watching the dial from a small balcony hunched forward in his seat. Below him more than 1,000 brokers and as many more helpers milled madly about the trading posts.

The weird roar compounded of the voices of thousands of shouting men held   2
to its steady volume. It never rose, it never fell, but rumbled to the high ceiling in mighty monotone. It was the voice of the Street, now hopeful, now tragic, making audible the history of a momentous day in the market. It could be heard on the Broad Street sidewalk.

The hand of the clock crawled on. William R. Crawford, superintendent of   3
the Exchange's reporting department, stood up in his balcony. He looked oddly like a judge about to charge a jury or deliver an oral decision. The brokers below were rushing about even more intensively as they realized that only seconds were left in which to execute orders.

BRIEF SILENCE FOLLOWS GONG.

Suddenly Mr. Crawford seized a gavel and as the minute hand touched three   4
he sounded the gong, ending trading for the day. In long, quivering notes the cease-business warning clanged through the medley of noise. Thrice Mr. Crawford sounded the gong. There was a second of silence, during which the telegraph wires sped the news of the close of trading to all points.

Then the roar from the floor was resumed, swelling to a new height and   5 then gradually receding. As it faded, a singular cacophony welled from the floor where more than 12,000,000 shares had changed hands, and where paper fortunes had vanished.

It was a mixture of groans, of boos and of sighs of relief. The final chorus had an eerie quality, like chords from a primitive requiem. And it meant the end of a day of pressure, of worry and of strain such as the exchange had never experienced. 6

Tired brokers, their faces streaming perspiration, their collars torn, leaned against the posts. Others, their hands full of unexecuted orders, stood as though dazed. Yet others, reacting to the trials of the session, laughed and jumped about, while handfuls of torn paper, or memorandum pads were thrown into the air. 7

CLERKS LABOR INTO NIGHT.

Although the gong ended the wild session, it meant to thousands of clerks only the beginning of their labor. Last night Wall Street and the financial district, usually pastoral after business hours, blazed with light and brokerage houses hummed with activity. More than 50,000 employees had settled down to tabulate the day's transactions, some of them scheduled to work through the night. 8

Calls for more margin[1] flashed over brokers' wires to remote places in the country—calls which were made with curt notice that failure to cover would mean sales of holdings when the market opened today. Account after account, usually of dabblers in speculative fields, was marked closed as the figures for yesterday were chalked up. 9

Rooms in downtown hotels were at a premium. Some of the larger firms engaged whole floors to enable their employes to get at least a few hours' sleep before the opening this morning. Restaurants which had been deserted through the day were jammed at dinner time, and hurry calls were put through to provision merchants to get food enough to meet the emergency situation. 10

The office boys and runners made the night lively as they scampered from office to office making deliveries. They seemed to have caught the excitement in full measure and went shouting and whooping through the streets. At 8:30 P.M. a group of several hundred boys were let out from offices in the Bankers Trust Company Building at 16 Wall Street. 11

The yelling contingent landed in the lobby and made for the doors. Some were through for the night and others were bound for dinner. Several were upset 12

---

[1]calls for more margin: investors could buy stocks by putting up a fraction of the true price, borrowing the rest from the broker and using the stock as collateral. When stock prices dropped, so did the value of the collateral, and brokers asked for more cash. [Eds.]

in the scramble. At 20 Broad Street fifty boys seized ticker tape and began tossing it about. Policemen chased them and confiscated the paper.

The uproar of the boys became so great at 60 Beaver Street that brokers called 13 upon the police of the Old Slip station to check the exuberance of the runners. The antics of the lads caused several false reports of "riots."

BROKERS WERE PREPARED.

The tidal wave of selling which struck the Exchange when it opened did not 14 catch the brokers unawares. It had been sighted starting stocks downward during the session on Wednesday and when the gong sounded for the opening yesterday the brokers were there in number. Usually between 750 and 800 members are on the floor when business is normal.

Virtually the full membership of 1,100 was on hand as the gong was sounded. 15 Brokers who are content as a rule to let the younger and sprier members of the firm battle around the posts were ready to reinforce their colleagues. Telephone staffs were supplemented and all available employes of the Exchange itself were on duty.

The rush of business came with a smash. The ticker struggled manfully for 16 a brief time and then began to fall behind. Groups about the machines, finding themselves far behind the quotations, gave up the effort to gauge the market, which began to go "blind." At 11:30 A.M. the turmoil on the trading floor reached its peak.

The annunciator call boards, located on the north and the south walls of the 17 trading pit, presented a dizzy appearance. Telephone operators at the boards back of the brass rails, just off the floor itself, were overwhelmed by the rush of orders to sell coming in from the firms. They kept buzzing the call boards, with the broker's numbers, in efforts to transmit the orders to the members on the floor. The plates with the numbers on the call board kept flipping up and down nervously.

CROWDS GATHER OUTSIDE.

Word of the mad market had spread through the district. Thousands of 18 persons congregated at Broad, Wall and Exchange Place. They formed a great pool of humanity in front of the Exchange and in front of the office of J. P. Morgan & Co., directly opposite. Notable in the composition of the crowd was the number of women, largely stenographers, who apprehensively watched the Exchange building. Many of them had small accounts and their talk indicated that they were waiting for the worst.

A score of motion picture operators took posts on the steps of the Subtreasury 19
and began shooting the scene. Wild rumors of failures, of suicides and other
calamity spread through the district. Ambulances were reported clanging to
buildings where men were reported to have shot themselves because of losses.
Last night, when the hysteria had ebbed, all of the rumors were demonstrated
to have been just rumors.

Ordinarily, thirty uniformed men patrol the vicinity of the Exchange, but 20
yesterday when the crowd began to form, Captain Edward Quinn of the Old
Slip Station sent ten additional men and twenty mounted men to the scene.
Twenty detectives were ordered to reinforce the regular Wall Street detail.

The policemen promptly set to work to disperse the crowd between the Ex- 21
change and the Morgan offices. At noon the information came that a conference
of bankers was being held in the Morgan office. This served to divert the attention of the crowd from the Exchange building to the Morgan doors. Hundreds
stood in the street or on the sidewalk and stared with fascination at the Morgan
building.

SPECULATORS WATCH BOARDS.

Board rooms, usually deserted soon after stock market closing time, held 22
audiences of depressed speculators until darkness set in. They watched for the
most part silently the illuminated strips of opaque glass on which glided quotations of sales made on the market hours previously.

The only touch of relief to these scenes were the boys, who in trading hours, 23
or whenever the ticker is running, move to and fro changing the figures on the
quotation boards that form the most prominent features of brokers' offices. These
young fellows, indifferent to the ruin spelled by the figures they posted, laughed
and gossiped.

In one office, which described itself as speculative, some more seasoned 24
speculators, their hats on the backs of their heads, were attempting a few graveyard jests. The only woman in the room sat in a corner, where she had been
placed while she awaited a meeting with one of the principals. She was white
haired and in black, and she wore a dazed expression. Apparently she was
puzzled as to just what had taken place in the market.

The flow of messages over the brokers' telegraph wires was enormous. In a 25
large wire house it was said that orders transmitted over their private wires to 3
o'clock totaled 15,000, or about 25 per cent more than they did in the break
that came early in 1926. Morse and manual operators worked at high speed
during the day and into the night.

Usually the last wire is closed at 9 o'clock in this house, but last night the 26

63

operators were told to be prepared to remain until 11 o'clock. Not only were the usual bookkeeping entries, greatly swelled, to be transmitted, but also incoming orders for today's market.

GALLERY IS THRONGED.

Word of the wild scenes on the trading floor brought people from uptown down to view the trading. At 12:30 o'clock the Exchange officials ordered the Broad Street gallery, from which visitors view the proceedings, closed. At that hour 722 persons had visited the gallery, a record attendance. Among those who paused briefly to look down upon the frantic brokers was Winston Churchill, former Chancellor of the Exchequer of Great Britain. 27

While rumors flew about fast and furiously, while anxious thousands scanned editions of evening newspapers for market prices, the market itself ground feverishly on. Milling groups were swaying about Post 2, where United States Steel is listed, the other groups struggled around the horseshoe where Radio and General Motors are dealt in. The ticker had fallen 160 minutes behind the market prices, and only those with personal representatives on the floor knew how stocks were selling. 28

The excitement on the floor was greatest in the two hours following 11:30 A.M. After that, although the torrent of business was tremendous, a recession seemed to be setting in. There was no let-up, however, in the offices of the brokers. Customers communicated by telephone or, feeling this method inadequate, came hurrying into the offices. All were eager for news of their stocks and the sudden descent of customers strained the facilities—and the nerves—of brokers' staffs. 29

Clerks dashing about, a sandwich in one hand and a sheaf of orders in the other, gave the customers bits of information and then continued the scramble to keep up with the pressure of business. Other clerks on the telephone talked steadily for hours into the transmitter, advising the telephone order clerk at the Exchange of sales, or telling customers to raise more margin. Despite the confusion and the sudden pressure, brokerage firms reported that margin was coming in satisfactorily, particularly toward the close of the day. 30

QUESTIONS

1. Why do the headlines of this article feature the "weird roar"? Does this emphasis on noise give an accurate sense of the substance of the article?

2. The information in this article was probably gathered by more than one reporter. The point of view in paragraph 1 suggests that one reporter was recording the scene from a balcony in the Stock Exchange at the end of the trading day. Where were the other reporters gathering information and at what times of day?

Weird Roar Surges from Exchange Floor

3. It is nearly midnight, Thursday, October 24, 1929, and an editor is trying to edit and organize the material for this article submitted by various reporters. How does he organize it? Why does he start the article with the close of the trading day?

4. In the first paragraph, we move from the "big clock" to the "short, slim man" to the "1,000 brokers" milling on the floor below. What effect did the writer wish to achieve by such movement? Where else in this article is a close-up view of one person or of a small group presented?

5. In paragraph 27, we are told that one of the observers in the Stock Exchange was "Winston Churchill, former Chancellor of the Exchequer of Great Britain." Find out through library research why he was there and how he was affected by the stock market crash.

6. Work with a group of four or five other students from your class. Observe and record events in a large, busy place, such as a cafeteria, a transportation terminal, a rock concert, or a parade. Each member of your group should choose a vantage point and record a description of the whole scene (as in paragraphs 5, 6, and 7 of the *Times* article) as well as a description of a person or a small group that is part of the scene (as in paragraphs 4 and 27 of the *Times* article). Copy these descriptions and distribute them to each member of your group. Then each person should organize the material and write it up in a report. In organizing the material, emphasize the dominant impression made on you as an observer of the event. For the *Times* writer, the noise heard from the large crowds in the Stock Exchange was what impressed him most. For you, it may have been silence, colors, smells, and so on. Also consider whether you are describing a typical day in this place or an unusual one. Be sure to help the reader see what is typical or unusual about the event you're describing.

A DAY IN SAMOA
Margaret Mead

Margaret Mead (1901–1979) was a cultural anthropologist for almost sixty years. She is the author of many books and articles in the field and is especially known for her studies of the South Sea Islanders. Coming of Age in Samoa *(1928) was her first book, based on her first field trip as a working anthropologist. The essay reprinted here is chapter 2 from that book, which is a study of adolescent girls in Samoa. In the introduction to the fifth edition of the book in 1973, Mead wrote, "The little girls whom I studied are buxom grandmothers, still dancing light-footed as Samoan matrons do. . . . And I, instead of being a dutiful granddaughter writing letters home . . . am now a grandmother delighting in a dancing grandchild."*

The life of the day begins at dawn, or if the moon has shown until daylight, the shouts of the young men may be heard before dawn from the hillside. Uneasy in the night, populous with ghosts, they shout lustily to one another as they hasten with their work. As the dawn begins to fall among the soft brown roofs and the slender palm trees stand out against a colourless, gleaming sea, lovers slip home from trysts beneath the palm trees or in the shadow of beached canoes, that the light may find each sleeper in his appointed place. Cocks crow, negligently, and a shrill-voiced bird cries from the breadfruit trees. The insistent roar of the reef seems muted to an undertone for the sounds of a waking village. Babies cry, a few short wails before sleepy mothers give them the breast. Restless little children roll out of their sheets and wander drowsily down to the beach to freshen their faces in the sea. Boys, bent upon an early fishing, start collecting their tackle and go to rouse their more laggard companions. Fires are lit, here and there, the white smoke hardly visible against the paleness of the dawn. The whole village, sheeted and frowsy, stirs, rubs its eyes, and stumbles towards the beach. "Talofa!" "Talofa!" "Will the journey start to-day?" "Is it bonito fishing your lordship is going?" Girls stop to giggle over some young ne'er-do-well who escaped during the night from an angry father's pursuit and to venture a shrewd guess that the daughter knew more about his presence than she told. The boy who is taunted by another, who has succeeded him in his sweetheart's favour, grapples with his rival, his foot slipping in the wet sand. From the other end of the village comes a long drawn-out, piercing wail. A messenger has just brought word of the death of some relative in another village. Half-clad, unhurried women, with babies at their breasts, or astride their hips, pause in their tale of

66

Losa's outraged departure from her father's house to the greater kindness in the home of her uncle, to wonder who is dead. Poor relatives whisper their requests to rich relatives, men make plans to set a fish trap together, a woman begs a bit of yellow dye from a kinswoman, and through the village sounds the rhythmic tattoo which calls the young men together. They gather from all parts of the village, digging sticks in hand, ready to start inland to the plantation. The older men set off upon their more lonely occupations, and each household, reassembled under its peaked roof, settles down to the routine of the morning. Little children, too hungry to wait for the late breakfast, beg lumps of cold taro which they munch greedily. Women carry piles of washing to the sea or to the spring at the far end of the village, or set off inland after weaving materials. The older girls go fishing on the reef, or perhaps set themselves to weaving a new set of Venetian blinds.

In the houses, where the pebbly floors have been swept bare with a stiff long-handled broom, the women great with child and the nursing mothers, sit and gossip with one another. Old men sit apart, unceasingly twisting palm husk on their bare thighs and muttering old tales under their breath. The carpenters begin work on the new house, while the owner bustles about trying to keep them in a good humour. Families who will cook to-day are hard at work; the taro, yams and bananas have already been brought from inland; the children are scuttling back and forth, fetching sea water, or leaves to stuff the pig. As the sun rises higher in the sky, the shadows deepen under the thatched roofs, the sand is burning to the touch, the hibiscus flowers wilt on the hedges, and little children bid the smaller ones, "Come out of the sun." Those whose excursions have been short return to the village, the women with strings of crimson jelly fish, or baskets of shell fish, the men with cocoanuts, carried in baskets slung on a shoulder pole. The women and children eat their breakfasts, just hot from the oven, if this is cook day, and the young men work swiftly in the midday heat, preparing the noon feast for their elders. 2

It is high noon. The sand burns the feet of the little children, who leave their palm leaf balls and their pin-wheels of frangipani blossoms to wither in the sun, as they creep into the shade of the houses. The women who must go abroad carry great banana leaves as sun-shades or wind wet cloths about their heads. Lowering a few blinds against the slanting sun, all who are left in the village wrap their heads in sheets and go to sleep. Only a few adventurous children may slip away for a swim in the shadow of a high rock, some industrious woman continues with her weaving, or a close little group of women bend anxiously over a woman in labour. The village is dazzling and dead; any sound seems oddly loud and out of place. Words have to cut through the solid heat slowly. And then the sun gradually sinks over the sea. 3

A second time, the sleeping people stir, roused perhaps by the cry of "a boat," resounding through the village. The fishermen beach their canoes, weary and spent from the heat, in spite of the slaked lime on their heads, with which they 4 have sought to cool their brains and redden their hair. The brightly coloured fishes are spread out on the floor, or piled in front of the houses until the women pour water over them to free them from taboo. Regretfully, the young fishermen separate out the "Taboo fish," which must be sent to the chief, or proudly they pack the little palm leaf baskets with offerings of fish to take to their sweethearts. Men come home from the bush, grimy and heavy laden, shouting as they come, greeted in a sonorous rising cadence by those who have remained at home. They gather in the guest house for their evening kava drinking. The soft clapping of hands, the high-pitched intoning of the talking chief who serves the kava echoes through the village. Girls gather flowers to weave into necklaces; children, lusty from their naps and bound to no particular task, play circular games in the half shade of the late afternoon. Finally the sun sets, in a flame which stretches from the mountain behind to the horizon on the sea, the last bather comes up from the beach, children straggle home, dark little figures etched against the sky; lights shine in the houses, and each household gathers for its evening meal. The suitor humbly presents his offering, the children have been summoned from their noisy play, perhaps there is an honoured guest who must be served first, after the soft, barbaric singing of Christian hymns and the brief and graceful evening prayer. In front of a house at the end of the village, a father cries out the birth of a son. In some family circles a face is missing, in others little runaways have found a haven! Again quiet settles upon the village, as first the head of the household, then the women and children, and last of all the patient boys, eat their supper.

After supper the old people and the little children are bundled off to bed. If the young people have guests the front of the house is yielded to them. For day is the time for the councils of old men and the labours of youth, and night is the time for lighter things. Two kinsmen, or a chief and his councillor, sit and gossip over the day's events or make plans for the morrow. Outside a crier goes through the village announcing that the communal breadfruit pit will be opened in the morning, or that the village will make a great fish trap. If it is moonlight, groups of young men, women by twos and threes, wander through the village, and crowds of children hunt for land crabs or chase each other among the breadfruit trees. Half the village may go fishing by torchlight and the curving reef will gleam with wavering lights and echo with shouts of triumph or disappointment, teasing words or smothered cries of outraged modesty. Or a group of youths may dance for the pleasure of some visiting maiden. Many of those who have retired to sleep, drawn by the merry music, will wrap their sheets about them and set out to find the dancing. A white-clad, ghostly throng will gather in a circle about the gaily lit house, a cricle from which every now and then a few will detach themselves and wander away among the trees. Sometimes sleep will not descend upon the village until long past midnight; then at last there is only the mellow thunder of the reef and the whisper of lovers, as the village rests until dawn.

68

QUESTIONS

1. Go through the essay, and note every word or phrase that indicates the time of day. When you have found them all, consider what they reveal about the way Mead has organized her material.

2. There are five paragraphs in this essay. How has Mead used the paragraph in shaping her material? That is, what principle or method of selection has determined what should go in each of the five paragraphs?

3. Is this a report of a specific day or a representation of a typical day? Can you find places where Mead seems to be reporting a particular event? Can you also find places where she is clearly speaking of various events that *might* happen on a typical day? How and why does she mix these two modes of writing?

4. Does this essay have an evaluative dimension? Is Samoan life presented neutrally? Is it made especially attractive or unattractive at any points? Consider specific events or episodes.

5. How does Mead achieve the representational quality of this essay? That is, how does she attempt to make the Samoan day available to us as a sensory experience? How does she convey the "feel" of it?

6. Write an essay in which you represent for the reader "A Day in————." Study Mead's way of selecting details and organizing them as you plan and compose your own essay on a day in a place you know well.

OBSERVING WOLVES
Farley Mowat

Farley Mowat was born in Ontario, Canada, in 1921 and finished college at the University of Toronto in 1949, after wartime service and two years living in the Arctic. He makes his living as a writer rather than a scientist, but he works in the same areas covered by anthropologists and zoologists. Often he writes more as a partisan of primitive people and animals rather than as an "objective" scientist, and his work has reached a wide audience. He has written engagingly about the strange animals he grew up with in Owls in the Family *(1963) and about wolves in* Never Cry Wolf *(1963), from which the following selection is taken.*

During the next several weeks I put my decision into effect with the thoroughness for which I have always been noted. I went completely to the wolves. To begin with I set up a den of my own as near to the wolves as I could conveniently get without disturbing the even tenor of their lives too much. After all, I *was* a stranger, and an unwolflike one, so I did not feel I should go too far too fast. 1

Abandoning Mike's cabin (with considerable relief, since as the days warmed up so did the smell) I took a tiny tent and set it up on the shore of the bay immediately opposite to the den esker.[1] I kept my camping gear to the barest minimum—a small primus stove, a stew pot, a teakettle, and a sleeping bag were the essentials. I took no weapons of any kind, although there were times when I regretted this omission, even if only fleetingly. The big telescope was set up in the mouth of the tent in such a way that I could observe the den by day or night without even getting out of my sleeping bag. 2

During the first few days of my sojourn with the wolves I stayed inside the tent except for brief and necessary visits to the out-of-doors which I always undertook when the wolves were not in sight. The point of this personal concealment was to allow the animals to get used to the tent and to accept it as only another bump on a very bumpy piece of terrain. Later, when the mosquito population reached full flowering, I stayed in the tent practically all of the time unless there was a strong wind blowing, for the most bloodthirsty beasts in the Arctic are not wolves, but the insatiable mosquitoes. 3

My precautions against disturbing the wolves were superfluous. It had re- 4

---

[1]esker: a long, narrow deposit of gravel and sand left by a stream flowing from a glacier. [Eds.]

quired a week for me to get their measure, but they must have taken mine at our first meeting; and, while there was nothing overtly disdainful in their evident assessment of me, they managed to ignore my presence, and indeed my very existence, with a thoroughness which was somehow disconcerting.

Quite by accident I had pitched my tent within ten yards of one of the major paths used by the wolves when they were going to, or coming from, their hunting grounds to the westward; and only a few hours after I had taken up residence one of the wolves came back from a trip and discovered me and my tent. He was at the end of a hard night's work and was clearly tired and anxious to go home to bed. He came over a small rise fifty yards from me with his head down, his eyes half-closed, and a preoccupied air about him. Far from being the preternaturally alert and suspicious beast of fiction, this wolf was so self-engrossed that he came straight on to within fifteen yards of me, and might have gone right past the tent without seeing it at all, had I not banged my elbow against the teakettle, making a resounding clank. The wolf's head came up and his eyes opened wide, but he did not stop or falter in his pace. One brief, sidelong glance was all he vouchsafed to me as he continued on his way.

It was true that I wanted to be inconspicuous, but I felt uncomfortable at being so totally ignored. Nevertheless, during the two weeks which followed, one or more wolves used the track past my tent almost every night—and never, except on one memorable occasion, did they evince the slightest interest in me.

By the time this happened I had learned a good deal about my wolfish neighbors, and one of the facts which had emerged was that they were not nomadic roamers, as is almost universally believed, but were settled beasts and the possessors of a large permanent estate with very definite boundaries.

The territory owned by my wolf family comprised more than a hundred square miles, bounded on one side by a river but otherwise not delimited by geographical features. Nevertheless there *were* boundaries, clearly indicated in wolfish fashion.

Anyone who has observed a dog doing his neighborhood rounds and leaving his personal mark on each convenient post will have already guessed how the wolves marked out *their* property. Once a week, more or less, the clan made the rounds of the family lands and freshened up the boundary markers—a sort of lupine beating of the bounds. This careful attention to property rights was perhaps made necessary by the presence of two other wolf families whose lands abutted on ours, although I never discovered any evidence of bickering or disagreements between the owners of the various adjoining estates. I suspect, therefore, that it was more of a ritual activity.

In any event, once I had become aware of the strong feeling of property rights which existed amongst the wolves, I decided to use this knowledge to make them at least recognize my existence. One evening, after they had gone off for their regular nightly hunt, I staked out a property claim of my own, embracing perhaps three acres, with the tent at the middle, and *including a hundred-yard long section of the wolves' path.*

Staking the land turned out to be rather more difficult than I had anticipated. In order to ensure that my claim would not be overlooked, I felt obliged to make a property mark on stones, clumps of moss, and patches of vegetation at intervals of not more than fifteen feet around the circumference of my claim. This took most of the night and required frequent returns to the tent to consume copious quantities of tea; but before dawn brought the hunters home the task was done, and I retired, somewhat exhausted, to observe results. 11

I had not long to wait. At 0814 hours, according to my wolf log, the leading male of the clan appeared over the ridge behind me, padding homeward with his usual air of preoccupation. As usual he did not deign to glance at the tent; but when he reached the point where my property line intersected the trail, he stopped as abruptly as if he had run into an invisible wall. He was only fifty yards from me and with my binoculars I could see his expression very clearly. 12

His attitude of fatigue vanished and was replaced by a look of bewilderment. Cautiously he extended his nose and sniffed at one of my marked bushes. He did not seem to know what to make of it or what to do about it. After a minute of complete indecision he backed away a few yards and sat down. And then, finally, he looked directly at the tent and at me. It was a long, thoughtful, considering sort of look. 13

Having achieved my object—that of forcing at least one of the wolves to take cognizance of my existence—I now began to wonder if, in my ignorance, I had transgressed some unknown wolf law of major importance and would have to pay for my temerity. I found myself regretting the absence of a weapon as the look I was getting became longer, yet more thoughtful, and still more intent. 14

I began to grow decidedly fidgety, for I dislike staring matches, and in this particular case I was up against a master, whose yellow glare seemed to become more baleful as I attempted to stare him down. 15

The situation was becoming intolerable. In an effort to break the impasse I loudly cleared my throat and turned my back on the wolf (for a tenth of a second) to indicate as clearly as possible that I found his continued scrutiny impolite, if not actually offensive. 16

He appeared to take the hint. Getting to his feet he had another sniff at my marker, and then he seemed to make up his mind. Briskly, and with an air of decision, he turned his attention away from me and began a systematic tour of the area I had staked out as my own. As he came to each boundary marker he sniffed it once or twice, then carefully placed *his* mark on the outside of each clump of grass or stone. As I watched I saw where I, in my ignorance, had erred. He made his mark with such economy that he was able to complete the entire circuit without having to reload once, or, to change the simile slightly, he did it all on one tank of fuel. 17

The task completed—and it had taken him no longer than fifteen minutes— 18
he rejoined the path at the point where it left my property and trotted off towards
his home—leaving me with a good deal to occupy my thoughts.

QUESTIONS

1. What did you know about wolves before reading this piece? What was the most
surprising—or amusing—information you acquired from reading about Mowat's experience?

2. Write a paragraph summarizing the information about wolves that you can infer
from this selection.

3. How would you describe the narrator of this piece? What does he tell us about
himself, and how do his actions describe him?

4. The writer concludes by saying that he was left "with a good deal to occupy my
thoughts" (paragraph 18). What, do you suppose, were these thoughts?

5. Find a more objective, "scientific" account of wolves. Which of Mowat's observations are substantiated there?

6. Rewrite the main events in this piece from the wolf's point of view.

7. Observe the actions of a dog or a cat as it roams your neighborhood. Write an
objective report of the animal's actions. Conclude with your reactions to the animal's
behavior and, if pertinent, the animal's reactions to your behavior.

FIRST OBSERVATIONS
Jane van Lawick-Goodall

*Jane van Lawick-Goodall (b. 1934), British student of an-
imal behavior, began her work as an assistant to Louis Leakey,
an anthropologist and paleontologist who has studied human origins. In 1960, with his help, she settled in Tanzania, East Africa, in the Gombe Stream Game Reserve to
investigate the behavior of chimpanzees in their natural
habitat. Her discoveries have been widely published in
professional journals and in a number of books for more
general audiences. The selection reprinted here is taken from*
In the Shadow of Man *(1971), a popular work in which she
is careful to report her own behavior as well as that of her
chimpanzee subjects.*

For about a month I spent most of each day either on the Peak or overlooking   1
Mlinda Valley where the chimps, before or after stuffing themselves with figs,
ate large quantities of small purple fruits that tasted, like so many of their foods,
as bitter and astringent as sloes or crab apples. Piece by piece, I began to form
my first somewhat crude picture of chimpanzee life.

The impression that I had gained when I watched the chimps at the msulula   2
tree of temporary, constantly changing associations of individuals within the
community was substantiated. Most often I saw small groups of four to eight
moving about together. Sometimes I saw one or two chimpanzees leave such a
group and wander off on their own or join up with a different association. On
other occasions I watched two or three small groups joining to form a larger
one.

Often, as one group crossed the grassy ridge separating the Kasekela Valley   3
from the fig trees in the home valley, the male chimpanzee, or chimpanzees,
of the party would break into a run, sometimes moving in an upright position,
sometimes dragging a fallen branch, sometimes stamping or slapping the hard
earth. These charging displays were always accompanied by loud pant-hoots and
afterward the chimpanzee frequently would swing up into a tree overlooking
the valley he was about to enter and sit quietly, peering down and obviously
listening for a response from below. If there were chimps feeding in the fig trees
they nearly always hooted back, as though in answer. Then the new arrivals
would hurry down the steep slope and, with more calling and screaming, the
two groups would meet in the fig trees. When groups of females and youngsters
with no males present joined other feeding chimpanzees, usually there was none

of this excitement; the newcomers merely climbed up into the trees, greeted some of those already there, and began to stuff themselves with figs.

While many details of their social behavior were hidden from me by the foliage, I did get occasional fascinating glimpses. I saw one female, newly arrived in a group, hurry up to a big male and hold her hand toward him. Almost regally he reached out, clasped her hand in his, drew it toward him, and kissed it with his lips. I saw two adult males embrace each other in greeting. I saw youngsters having wild games through the treetops, chasing around after each other or jumping again and again, one after the other, from a branch to a springy bough below. I watched small infants dangling happily by themselves for minutes on end, patting at their toes with one hand, rotating gently from side to side. Once two tiny infants pulled on opposite ends of a twig in a gentle tug-of-war. Often, during the heat of midday or after a long spell of feeding, I saw two or more adults grooming each other, carefully looking through the hair of their companions.

At that time of year the chimps usually went to bed late, making their nests when it was too dark to see properly through binoculars, but sometimes they nested earlier and I could watch them from the Peak. I found that every individual, except for infants who slept with their mothers, made his own nest each night. Generally this took about three minutes: the chimp chose a firm foundation such as an upright fork or crotch, or two horizontal branches. Then he reached out and bent over smaller branches onto this foundation, keeping each one in place with his feet. Finally he tucked in the small leafy twigs growing around the rim of his nest and lay down. Quite often a chimp sat up after a few minutes and picked a handful of leafy twigs, which he put under his head or some other part of his body before settling down again for the night. One young female I watched went on and on bending down branches until she had constructed a huge mound of greenery on which she finally curled up.

I climbed up into some of the nests after the chimpanzees had left them. Most of them were built in trees that for me were almost impossible to climb. I found that there was quite complicated interweaving of the branches in some of them. I found, too, that the nests were never fouled with dung; and later, when I was able to get closer to the chimps, I saw how they were always careful to defecate and urinate over the edge of their nests, even in the middle of the night.

During that month I really came to know the country well, for I often went on expeditions from the Peak, sometimes to examine nests, more frequently to collect specimens of the chimpanzees' food plants, which Bernard Verdcourt had kindly offered to identify for me. Soon I could find my way around the sheer ravines and up and down the steep slopes of three valleys—the home valley, the Pocket, and Mlinda Valley—as well as a taxi driver finds his way about in the main streets and byways of London. It is a period I remember vividly, not only because I was beginning to accomplish something at last, but also because of the delight I felt in being completely by myself. For those who love to be alone with nature I need add nothing further; for those who do not, no words of mine could ever convey, even in part, the almost mystical awareness of beauty and eternity that accompanies certain treasured moments. And, though the beauty was always there, those moments came upon me unaware: when I was watching the pale flush preceding dawn; or looking up through the rustling leaves of some giant forest tree into the greens and browns and black shadows that occasionally ensnared a bright fleck of the blue sky; or when I stood, as darkness fell, with one hand on the still-warm trunk of a tree and looked at the sparkling of an early moon on the never still, sighing water of the lake.

One day, when I was sitting by the trickle of water in Buffalo Wood, pausing for a moment in the coolness before returning from a scramble in Mlinda Valley, I saw a female bushbuck moving slowly along the nearly dry streambed. Occasionally she paused to pick off some plant and crunch it. I kept absolutely still, and she was not aware of my presence until she was little more than ten yards away. Suddenly she tensed and stood staring at me, one small forefoot raised. Because I did not move, she did not know what I was—only that my outline was somehow strange. I saw her velvet nostrils dilate as she sniffed the air, but I was downwind and her nose gave her no answer. Slowly she came closer, and closer—one step at a time, her neck craned forward—always poised for instant flight. I can still scarcely believe that her nose actually touched my knee; yet if I close my eyes I can feel again, in imagination, the warmth of her breath and the silken impact of her skin. Unexpectedly I blinked and she was gone in a flash, bounding away with loud barks of alarm until the vegetation hid her completely from my view.

It was rather different when, as I was sitting on the Peak, I saw a leopard coming toward me, his tail held up straight. He was at a slightly lower level than I, and obviously had no idea I was there. Ever since arrival in Africa I had had an ingrained, illogical fear of leopards. Already, while working at the Gombe, I had several times nearly turned back when, crawling through some thick undergrowth, I had suddenly smelled the rank smell of cat. I had forced myself on, telling myself that my fear was foolish, that only wounded leopards charged humans with savage ferocity.

On this occasion, though, the leopard went out of sight as it started to climb up the hill—the hill on the peak of which I sat. I quickly hastened to climb a tree, but halfway there I realized that leopards can climb trees. So I uttered a sort of halfhearted squawk. The leopard, my logical mind told me, would be just as frightened of me if he knew I was there. Sure enough, there was a thudding of startled feet and then silence. I returned to the Peak, but the feeling of unseen eyes watching me was too much. I decided to watch for the chimps in Mlinda Valley. And, when I returned to the Peak several hours later, there, on the very rock which had been my seat, was a neat pile of leopard dung. He must have watched me go and then, very carefully, examined the place where

8

9

10

such a frightening creature had been and tried to exterminate my alien scent with his own.

As the weeks went by the chimpanzees became less and less afraid. Quite 11 often when I was on one of my food-collecting expeditions I came across chimpanzees unexpectedly, and after a time I found that some of them would tolerate my presence provided they were in fairly thick forest and I sat still and did not try to move closer than sixty to eighty yards. And so, during my second month of watching from the Peak, when I saw a group settle down to feed I sometimes moved closer and was thus able to make more detailed observations.

It was at this time that I began to recognize a number of different individuals. 12 As soon as I was sure of knowing a chimpanzee if I saw it again, I named it. Some scientists feel that animals should be labeled by numbers—that to name them is anthropomorphic—but I have always been interested in the *differences* between individuals, and a name is not only more individual than a number but also far easier to remember. Most names were simply those which, for some reason or other, seemed to suit the individuals to whom I attached them. A few chimps were named because some facial expression or mannerism reminded me of human acquaintances.

The easiest individual to recognize was old Mr. McGregor. The crown of 13 his head, his neck, and his shoulders were almost entirely devoid of hair, but a slight frill remained around his head rather like a monk's tonsure. He was an old male—perhaps between thirty and forty years of age (the longevity record of a captive chimp is forty-seven years). During the early months of my acquaintance with him, Mr. McGregor was somewhat belligerent. If I accidentally came across him at close quarters he would threaten me with an upward and backward jerk of his head and a shaking of branches before climbing down and vanishing from my sight. He reminded me, for some reason, of Beatrix Potter's old gardener in *The Tale of Peter Rabbit*.

Ancient Flo with her deformed, bulbous nose and ragged ears was equally 14 easy to recognize. Her youngest offspring at that time were two-year-old Fifi, who still rode everywhere on her mother's back, and her juvenile son, Figan, who was always to be seen wandering around with his mother and little sister. He was then about six years old; it was approximately a year before he would attain puberty. Flo often traveled with another old mother, Olly. Olly's long face was also distinctive; the fluff of hair on the back of her head—though no other feature—reminded me of my aunt, Olwen. Olly, like Flo, was accompanied by two children, a daughter younger than Fifi, and an adolescent son about a year older than Figan.

Then there was William, who, I am certain, must have been Olly's blood 15 brother. I never saw any special signs of friendship between them, but their faces were amazingly alike. They both had long upper lips that wobbled when they suddenly turned their heads. William had the added distinction of several thin, deeply etched scar marks running down his upper lip from his nose.

Two of the other chimpanzees I knew well by sight at that time were David 16
Graybeard and Goliath. Like David and Goliath in the Bible, these two individuals were closely associated in my mind because they were very often together. Goliath, even in those days of his prime, was not a giant, but he had a
splendid physique and the springy movements of an athlete. He probably weighed
about one hundred pounds. David Graybeard was less afraid of me from the
start than were any of the other chimps. I was always pleased when I picked out
his handsome face and well-marked silvery beard in a chimpanzee group, for
with David to calm the others, I had a better chance of approaching to observe
them more closely.

Before the end of my trial period in the field I made two really exciting 17
discoveries—discoveries that made the previous months of frustration well worth
while. And for both of them I had David Graybeard to thank.

One day I arrived on the Peak and found a small group of chimps just below 18
me in the upper branches of a thick tree. As I watched I saw that one of them
was holding a pink-looking object from which he was from time to time pulling
pieces with his teeth. There was a female and a youngster and they were both
reaching out toward the male, their hands actually touching his mouth. Presently the female picked up a piece of the pink thing and put it to her mouth:
it was at this moment that I realized the chimps were eating meat.

After each bite of meat the male picked off some leaves with his lips and 19
chewed them with the flesh. Often, when he had chewed for several minutes
on this leafy wad, he spat out the remains into the waiting hands of the female.
Suddenly he dropped a small piece of meat, and like a flash the youngster swung
after it to the ground. Even as he reached to pick it up the undergrowth exploded
and an adult bushpig charged toward him. Screaming, the juvenile leaped back
into the tree. The pig remained in the open, snorting and moving backward
and forward. Soon I made out the shapes of three small striped piglets. Obviously
the chimps were eating a baby pig. The size was right and later, when I realized
that the male was David Graybeard, I moved closer and saw that he was indeed
eating piglet.

For three hours I watched the chimps feeding. David occasionally let the 20
female bite pieces from the carcass and once he actually detached a small piece
of flesh and placed it in her outstretched hand. When he finally climbed down
there was still meat left on the carcass; he carried it away in one hand, followed
by the others.

Of course I was not sure, then, that David Graybeard had caught the pig for 21
himself, but even so, it was tremendously exciting to know that these chimpanzees actually ate meat. Previously scientists had believed that although these
apes might occasionally supplement their diet with a few insects or small rodents
and the like they were primarily vegetarians and fruit eaters. No one had suspected that they might hunt larger mammals.

It was within two weeks of this observation that I saw something that excited 22
me even more. By then it was October and the short rains had begun. The

blackened slopes were softened by feathery new grass shoots and in some places the ground was carpeted by a variety of flowers. The Chimpanzees' Spring, I called it. I had had a frustrating morning, tramping up and down three valleys with never a sign or sound of a chimpanzee. Hauling myself up the steep slope of Mlinda Valley I headed for the Peak, not only weary but soaking wet from crawling through dense undergrowth. Suddenly I stopped, for I saw a slight movement in the long grass about sixty yards away. Quickly focusing my binoculars I saw that it was a single chimpanzee, and just then he turned in my direction. I recognized David Graybeard.

Cautiously I moved around so that I could see what he was doing. He was 23 squatting beside the red earth mound of a termite nest, and as I watched I saw him carefully push a long grass stem down into a hole in the mound. After a moment he withdrew it and picked something from the end with his mouth. I was too far away to make out what he was eating, but it was obvious that he was actually using a grass stem as a tool.

I knew that on two occasions casual observers in West Africa had seen chim- 24 panzees using objects as tools: one had broken open palm-nut kernels by using a rock as a hammer, and a group of chimps had been observed pushing sticks into an underground bees' nest and licking off the honey. Somehow I had never dreamed of seeing anything so exciting myself.

For an hour David feasted at the termite mound and then he wandered 25 slowly away. When I was sure he had gone I went over to examine the mound. I found a few crushed insects strewn about, and a swarm of worker termites sealing the entrances of the nest passages into which David had obviously been poking his stems. I picked up one of his discarded tools and carefully pushed it into a hole myself. Immediately I felt the pull of several termites as they seized the grass, and when I pulled it out there were a number of worker termites and a few soldiers, with big red heads, clinging on with their mandibles. There they remained, sticking out at right angles to the stem with their legs waving in the air.

Before I left I trampled down some of the tall dry grass and constructed a 26 rough hide—just a few palm fronds leaned up against the low branch of a tree and tied together at the top. I planned to wait there the next day. But it was another week before I was able to watch a chimpanzee "fishing" for termites again. Twice chimps arrived, but each time they saw me and moved off immediately. Once a swarm of fertile winged termites—the princes and princesses, as they are called—flew off on their nuptial flight, their huge white wings fluttering frantically as they carried the insects higher and higher. Later I realized that it is at this time of year, during the short rains, when the worker termites extend the passages of the nest to the surface, preparing for these emigrations. Several such swarms emerge between October and January. It is principally during these months that the chimpanzees feed on termites.

On the eighth day of my watch David Graybeard arrived again, together with 27 Goliath, and the pair worked there for two hours. I could see much better: I observed how they scratched open the sealed-over passage entrances with a thumb or forefinger. I watched how they bit the ends off their tools when they became bent, or used the other end, or discarded them in favor of new ones. Goliath once moved at least fifteen yards from the heap to select a firm-looking piece of vine, and both males often picked three or four stems while they were collecting tools, and put the spares beside them on the ground until they wanted them.

Most exciting of all, on several occasions they picked small leafy twigs and prepared them for use by stripping off the leaves. This was the first recorded example of a wild animal not merely *using* an object as a tool, but actually modifying an object and thus showing the crude beginnings of tool*making*.   28

Previously man had been regarded as the only tool-making animal. Indeed, one of the clauses commonly accepted in the definition of man was that he was a creature who "made tools to a regular and set pattern." The chimpanzees, obviously, had not made tools to any set pattern. Nevertheless, my early observations of their primitive toolmaking abilities convinced a number of scientists that it was necessary to redefine man in a more complex manner than before. Or else, as Louis Leakey put it, we should by definition have to accept the chimpanzee as Man.   29

QUESTIONS

1. This essay is an example, principally, of reporting; that is, it is a gathering of facts by a clearheaded, unbiased observer. Identify passages in the essay in which this kind of reporting clearly takes place.

2. Although Goodall, in the main, is a neutral observer of chimpanzee behavior, that neutrality is in fact impossible in any absolute sense. It is clear that she writes, for example, with an eye always on comparisons of chimpanzee and human behavior. Make a list of words, just from paragraphs 3 and 4, that reveal that particular bias.

3. Describe how the writer's comparison of chimpanzee with human behavior becomes increasingly prominent in the course of her essay.

4. Paraphrase the last discovery Goodall reports toward the end of her essay. What, exactly, was her contribution to science in this instance? What other activities, described earlier in the piece, make that discovery understandable, perhaps even unsurprising once we come to it?

5. What do you make of the choice outlined in paragraph 29? Which choice do you suppose the scientists made? Why?

6. Goodall's scientific work resembles that of an anthropologist in that she goes into the field to observe the behavior of another social group. Even from this short piece we can learn a good deal about the practices and the way of life of such a worker in the field. Describe Goodall's life in the field as best you can, making whatever inferences you can from this single essay.

7. Amplify your description of Goodall's life in the field, done for question 6, by reading whatever articles you can find that tell more about her and about her work.

8. Place yourself somewhere and observe behavior more or less as Goodall does. You might observe wildlife—pigeons, sparrows, crows, squirrels, or whatever is available—or you might observe some aspect of human behavior. If you choose the latter, look for behavior that is unfamiliar to you, such as that of children at play, of workers on the job, or of persons in a social group very different from your own. Write a report detailing your observations.

9. After you have completed question 8, write a second, shorter report in which you comment on the nature of your task as an observer. Was it difficult to watch? Was it difficult to decide what was meaningful behavior? Did you influence what you saw so that you could not be confident that the behavior was representative? Looking back on your experience as a field worker, what else seems questionable to you now?

BODY RITUAL AMONG THE NACIREMA

Horace Miner

Horace Miner (b. 1912) has been a cultural anthropologist and a professor of anthropology at the University of Michigan in Ann Arbor for many years. The topics of his published studies have ranged from Timbuktu to French Canada. The following selection appeared first in a professional journal, the American Anthropologist, *in 1956. Reprinted far and wide, it has now become a classic joke among social scientists.*

The anthropologist has become so familiar with the diversity of ways in which 1
different peoples behave in similar situations that he is not apt to be surprised
by even the most exotic customs. In fact, if all of the logically possible combinations of behavior have not been found somewhere in the world, he is apt
to suspect that they must be present in some yet undescribed tribe. This point
has, in fact, been expressed with respect to clan organization by Murdock (1949:71).
In this light, the magical beliefs and practices of the Nacirema present such
unusual aspects that it seems desirable to describe them as an example of the
extremes to which human behavior can go.

Professor Linton first brought the ritual of the Nacirema to the attention of 2
anthropologists twenty years ago (1936:326), but the culture of this people is
still very poorly understood. They are a North American group living in the
territory between the Canadian Cree, the Yaqui and Tarahumare of Mexico,
and the Carib and Arawak of the Antilles. Little is known of their origin,
although tradition states that they came from the east. According to Nacirema
mythology, their nation was originated by a culture hero, Notgnihsaw, who is
otherwise known for two great feats of strength—the throwing of a piece of
wampum across the river Pa-To-Mac and the chopping down of a cherry tree
in which the Spirit of Truth resided.

Nacirema culture is characterized by a highly developed market economy 3
which has evolved in a rich natural habitat. While much of the people's time
is devoted to economic pursuits, a large part of the fruits of these labors and a
considerable portion of the day are spent in ritual activity. The focus of this
activity is the human body, the appearance and health of which loom as a
dominant concern in the ethos of the people. While such a concern is certainly
not unusual, its ceremonial aspects and associated philosophy are unique.

Body Ritual among the Nacirema

The fundamental belief underlying the whole system appears to be that the human body is ugly and that its natural tendency is to debility and disease. Incarcerated in such a body, man's only hope is to avert these characteristics through the use of the powerful influences of ritual and ceremony. Every household has one or more shrines devoted to this purpose. The more powerful individuals in the society have several shrines in their houses and, in fact, the opulence of a house is often referred to in terms of the number of such ritual centers it possesses. Most houses are of wattle and daub construction, but the shrine rooms of the more wealthy are walled with stone. Poorer families imitate the rich by applying pottery plaques to their shrine walls.

While each family has at least one such shrine, the rituals associated with it are not family ceremonies but are private and secret. The rites are normally only discussed with children, and then only during the period when they are being initiated into these mysteries. I was able, however, to establish sufficient rapport with the natives to examine these shrines and to have the rituals described to me.

The focal point of the shrine is a box or chest which is built into the wall. In this chest are kept the many charms and magical potions without which no native believes he could live. These preparations are secured from a variety of specialized practitioners. The most powerful of these are the medicine men, whose assistance must be rewarded with substantial gifts. However, the medicine men do not provide the curative potions for their clients, but decide what the ingredients should be and then write them down in an ancient and secret language. This writing is understood only by the medicine men and by the herbalists who, for another gift, provide the required charm.

The charm is not disposed of after it has served its purpose, but is placed in the charm-box of the household shrine. As these magical materials are specific for certain ills, and the real or imagined maladies of the people are many, the charm-box is usually full to overflowing. The magical packets are so numerous that people forget what their purposes were and fear to use them again. While the natives are very vague on this point, we can only assume that the idea in retaining all the old magical materials is that their presence in the charm-box, before which the body rituals are conducted, will in some way protect the worshipper.

Beneath the charm-box is a small font. Each day every member of the family, in succession, enters the shrine room, bows his head before the charm-box, mingles different sorts of holy water in the font, and proceeds with a brief rite of ablution. The holy waters are secured from the Water Temple of the community, where the priests conduct elaborate ceremonies to make the liquid ritually pure.

In the hierarchy of magical practitioners, and below the medicine men in prestige, are specialists whose designation is best translated "holy-mouth-men." The Nacirema have an almost pathological horror of and fascination with the mouth, the condition of which is believed to have a supernatural influence on all social relationships. Were it not for the rituals of the mouth, they believe that their teeth would fall out, their gums bleed, their jaws shrink, their friends desert them, and their lovers reject them. They also believe that a strong relationship exists between oral and moral characteristics. For example, there is a ritual ablution of the mouth for children which is supposed to improve their moral fiber.

The daily body ritual performed by everyone includes a mouth-rite. Despite the fact that these people are so punctilious about care of the mouth, this rite involves a practice which strikes the uninitiated stranger as revolting. It was reported to me that the ritual consists of inserting a small bundle of hog hairs into the mouth, along with certain magical powders, and then moving the bundle in a highly formalized series of gestures. 10

In addition to the private mouth-rite, the people seek out a holy-mouth-man once or twice a year. These practitioners have an impressive set of paraphernalia, consisting of a variety of augers, awls, probes, and prods. The use of these objects in the exorcism of the evils of the mouth involves almost unbelievable ritual torture of the client. The holy-mouth-man opens the client's mouth and, using the above mentioned tools, enlarges any holes which decay may have created in the teeth. Magical materials are put into these holes. If there are no naturally occurring holes in the teeth, large sections of one or more teeth are gouged out so that the supernatural substance can be applied. In the client's view, the purpose of these ministrations is to arrest decay and to draw friends. The extremely sacred and traditional character of the rite is evident in the fact that the natives return to the holy-mouth-men year after year, despite the fact that their teeth continue to decay. 11

It is to be hoped that, when a thorough study of the Nacirema is made, there will be careful inquiry into the personality structure of these people. One has but to watch the gleam in the eye of a holy-mouth-man, as he jabs an awl into an exposed nerve, to suspect that a certain amount of sadism is involved. If this can be established, a very interesting pattern emerges, for most of the population shows definite masochistic tendencies. It was to these that Professor Linton referred in discussing a distinctive part of the daily body ritual which is performed only by men. This part of the rite involves scraping and lacerating the surface of the face with a sharp instrument. Special women's rites are performed only four times during each lunar month, but what they lack in frequency is made up in barbarity. As part of this ceremony, women bake their heads in small ovens for about an hour. The theoretically interesting point is that what seems to be a preponderantly masochistic people have developed sadistic specialists. 12

The medicine men have an imposing temple, or *latipso*, in every community of any size. The more elaborate ceremonies required to treat very sick patients can only be performed at this temple. These ceremonies involve not only the thaumaturge but a permanent group of vestal maidens who move sedately about the temple chambers in distinctive costume and headdress. 13

The *latipso* ceremonies are so harsh that it is phenomenal that a fair pro- 14
portion of the really sick natives who enter the temple ever recover. Small
children whose indoctrination is still incomplete have been known to resist
attempts to take them to the temple because "that is where you go to die."
Despite this fact, sick adults are not only willing but eager to undergo the
protracted ritual purification, if they can afford to do so. No matter how ill the
supplicant or how grave the emergency, the guardians of many temples will not
admit a client if he cannot give a rich gift to the custodian. Even after one has
gained admission and survived the ceremonies, the guardians will not permit
the neophyte to leave until he makes still another gift.

The supplicant entering the temple is first stripped of all his or her clothes. 15
In every-day life the Nacirema avoids exposure of his body and its natural
functions. Bathing and excretory acts are performed only in the secrecy of the
household shrine, where they are ritualized as part of the body-rites. Psychological shock results from the fact that body secrecy is suddenly lost upon entry
into the *latipso*. A man, whose own wife has never seen him in an excretory
act, suddenly finds himself naked and assisted by a vestal maiden while he
performs his natural functions into a sacred vessel. This sort of ceremonial
treatment is necessitated by the fact that the excreta are used by a diviner to
ascertain the course and nature of the client's sickness. Female clients, on the
other hand, find their naked bodies are subjected to the scrutiny, manipulation
and prodding of the medicine men.

Few supplicants in the temple are well enough to do anything but lie on 16
their hard beds. The daily ceremonies, like the rites of the holy-mouth-men,
involve discomfort and torture. With ritual precision, the vestals awaken their
miserable charges each dawn and roll them about on their beds of pain while
performing ablutions, in the formal movements of which the maidens are highly
trained. At other times they insert magic wands in the supplicant's mouth or
force him to eat substances which are supposed to be healing. From time to
time the medicine men come to their clients and jab magically treated needles
into their flesh. The fact that these temple ceremonies may not cure, and may
even kill the neophyte, in no way decreases the people's faith in the medicine
men.

There remains one other kind of practitioner, known as a "listener." This 17
witch-doctor has the power to exorcise the devils that lodge in the heads of
people who have been bewitched. The Nacirema believe that parents bewitch
their own children. Mothers are particularly suspected of putting a curse on
children while teaching them the secret body rituals. The counter-magic of the
witch-doctor is unusual in its lack of ritual. The patient simply tells the "listener"
all his troubles and fears, beginning with the earliest difficulties he can remember. The memory displayed by the Nacirema in these exorcism sessions is truly
remarkable. It is not uncommon for the patient to bemoan the rejection he felt
upon being weaned as a babe, and a few individuals even see their troubles
going back to the traumatic effects of their own birth.

85

Horace Miner

In conclusion, mention must be made of certain practices which have their base in native esthetics but which depend upon the pervasive aversion to the natural body and its functions. There are ritual fasts to make fat people thin and ceremonial feasts to make thin people fat. Still other rites are used to make women's breasts larger if they are small, and smaller if they are large. General dissatisfaction with breast shape is symbolized in the fact that the ideal form is virtually outside the range of human variation. A few women afflicted with almost inhuman hypermammary development are so idolized that they make a handsome living by simply going from village to village and permitting the natives to stare at them for a fee. 18

Reference has already been made to the fact that excretory functions are ritualized, routinized, and relegated to secrecy. Natural reproductive functions are similarly distorted. Intercourse is taboo as a topic and scheduled as an act. Efforts are made to avoid pregnancy by the use of magical materials or by limiting intercourse to certain phases of the moon. Conception is actually very infrequent. When pregnant, women dress so as to hide their condition. Parturition takes place in secret, without friends or relatives to assist, and the majority of women do not nurse their infants. 19

Our review of the ritual life of the Nacirema has certainly shown them to be a magic-ridden people. It is hard to understand how they have managed to exist so long under the burdens which they have imposed upon themselves. But even such exotic customs as these take on real meaning when they are viewed with the insight provided by Malinowski when he wrote (1948:70): 20

> Looking from far and above, from our high places of safety in the developed civilization, it is easy to see all the crudity and irrelevance of magic. But without its power and guidance early man could not have mastered his practical difficulties as he has done, nor could man have advanced to the higher stages of civilization.

REFERENCES CITED

LINTON, RALPH
　　1936　The Study of Man. New York, D. Appleton-Century Co.
MALINOWSKI, BRONISLAW
　　1948　Magic, Science, and Religion. Glencoe, The Free Press.
MURDOCK, GEORGE P.
　　1949　Social Structure. New York, The Macmillan Co.

QUESTIONS

1. Where do the Nacirema live? Why would an anthropologist want to study their culture? Do the Nacirema sound like people you would want to know more about?

86

2. What is the writer's attitude toward his subject? Is his report objective, or is there evaluative language present?

3. What evidence is presented to support the writer's claim in paragraph 12 that "most of the population shows definite masochistic tendencies"? How is the evidence organized? Is enough evidence presented to substantiate this claim?

4. Miner's report was written in 1956. Have you seen in your community any more recent evidence that would indicate that the Nacirema's belief in magical powers has enabled them to advance to a higher stage of civilization, as Malinowski suggests it might?

5. Miner concentrates on the body rituals of the Nacirema. Obviously, the Nacirema must have other rituals, and surely some of these are more pleasurable than those described here. On the other hand, Miner may not have included other barbaric customs of the Nacirema. Do some field research of your own, and write a report of another Nacirema ritual that you have observed.

6. Nonanthropologists find this piece humorous because of Professor Miner's treatment of the Nacirema. Might anthropologists find this piece more humorous than nonanthropologists find it? Use your answer to draw some conclusions about how different audiences respond to humor.

HOMO MONSTROSUS
Annemarie de Waal Malefijt

*Annemarie de Waal Malefijt was born in Amsterdam in
1914 and came to the United States in 1951 to study anthropology at Columbia University in New York City. She
is professor of anthropology at Hunter College of the City
University of New York and the author of two books in her
special field, the history of anthropology. Unlike the cultural
anthropologists who observe primitive societies "in the field,"
Malefijt does her observing in libraries. She published the
following results of her research in* Scientific American *in
1968.*

When Carl von Linné (Linnaeus) worked out his monumental classification [1]
of natural things in the 18th century, he included the species *Homo monstrosus*.
By *Homo monstrosus* he meant a species related to *Homo sapiens* but markedly
different in physical appearance. To do Linnaeus full justice, he was quite aware
that there were men on all continents who belonged to the species *Homo sapiens*.
He nonetheless believed, as many of his contemporaries and predecessors did,
that in remote areas there were manlike creatures with weird characteristics.

The belief in the existence of monstrous races had endured in the Western [2]
world for at least 2,000 years. During that time a rich assortment of semihuman
creatures were described by explorers and travelers, whose accounts were probably based largely on malformed individuals and the desire to enhance their
own fame at home. No part of the human body was neglected; each was conceived as having elaborate variations. There were, for example, peoples with
tiny heads, with gigantic heads, with pointed heads, with no heads, with de-
tachable heads, with dog heads, with horse heads, with pig snouts and with bird
beaks. In the absence of knowledge about faraway places (and about the limits
of human variation) men populated them with creatures of their imagination.

At the same time there were efforts to explain how such strange beings could [3]
have originated and what was responsible for their extraordinary characteristics.
Thus in the rise and decline of *Homo monstrosus* one encounters ideas and
attitudes that hold much interest for the modern anthropologist. The credulousness of those who accepted the reality of monstrous peoples is not so very
different from the unfounded prejudices that human groups often harbor toward
one another today, and one of the major tasks of anthropology is to clear away
misinformation that may lead to such misunderstanding.

Among the earlier writers on fabulous peoples was the Greek historian Herod- [4]
otus. In the fifth century B.C. he traveled widely in the world that was known

to him. He was fairly objective in his accounts of the nearby Egyptians and Persians, and he certainly did not believe everything he was told. In lands far from home, however, people and their habits often appear more unusual; as Herodotus wrote, "The ends of the earth produce the things that we think most fair and rare." Thus he reports that in Ethiopia near the Egyptian border a tribe called the Troglodytes live underground. They eat snakes and lizards, and their language resembles the screeching of bats. Near the Atlas Mountains live the Atlantes, who are unable to dream. The Indian Padaei consume their fellow men as soon as they show the slightest sign of illness; the Libyan Adyrmachidae, after catching a flea on their person, give it bite for bite before throwing it away.

If human habits could be so strange, it was perhaps not surprising that phys- 5 ical differences also existed. Herodotus reports that the Agrippaei across the River Don are totally bald. In the mountains of the same region, so the bald men told him, are a goat-footed race of men and another group that sleeps six months of the year, hibernating like bears.

"I don't believe it," Herodotus comments, yet he continues. He describes 6 the Arimaspi, who have only one eye situated in the middle of their forehead, and the griffins (half-lion, half-eagle) that guard hoards of gold. He writes that, according to the Libyans, their region has dog-headed men, headless people with eyes in their chest, wild men and wild women and many other monstrous races.

It may be that Herodotus actually heard such stories in his travels, but it 7 should be noted that other Greeks of his time were acquainted with similar fabulous tales. Several centuries before Herodotus the poet Hesiod had mentioned one-eyed, dog-headed and breast-eyed tribes. Homer wrote about the one-eyed Cyclops and about giants and pygmies; the epic poet Aristeas spoke of the one-eyed Arimaspi. Herodotus thus did not invent the monsters; he was rather the first to locate them in actual geographic areas.

The Greeks knew that surrounding them were peoples with cultures quite 8 different from their own. This may have made it easier for them to accept the monstrous races as a reality. There was at least one Greek theory of evolution that could account for the existence of hybrid creatures. Empedocles, a contemporary of Herodotus, held that parts of men and animals arose separately and independently. Hands wandered without arms, feet without legs and heads without trunks. These isolated parts combined at random, so that there could be animals with human heads or manlike creatures with the features of animals. Although in time only favorable combinations survived, peculiar ones could still be found.

Soon after the death of Herodotus reports about India added to the credibility 9 of monstrous races. At the beginning of the fourth century B.C. Ktesias, who had once been a physician at the Persian court, wrote that India was populated by many wondrous tribes. He described the Sciapodes, who had a single large foot on which they could hop faster than any biped. They made further use of

REPRESENTATIVES OF MONSTROUS TRIBES were believed to inhabit actual lands, principally India. Among the foreign peoples described by Herodotus, Ktesias and Megasthenes are (*from left to right, top to bottom*) the one-eyed people; the Blemmyae, or headless ones; the long-eared Phanesians; the big-lipped people; the Sciapodes (who used their single foot as an umbrella) and the goat-footed people, later called satyrs. The woodcuts are from the *Liber Chronicarum*, by Hartmann Schedel, published in 1493.

this appendage by employing it as a kind of umbrella, holding it over their head for protection against the rain or the heat of the sun. The Cynocephali, or dog-headed ones, were said to bark rather than to use words; the Blemmyae were headless, with their face between their shoulders. There were people with ears so long they covered their arms as far as the elbow; others had long and very hairy tails; still others had eight fingers on each hand and eight toes on each foot.

Similar reports about India came from Megasthenes, the learned ambassador of the Babylonian king Seleucus I. Having served at the Indian court of Chandragupta, he added some new examples to the older ones and was the first to give currency to the tale of certain Indian nomads who had no nose but only small holes for nostrils. He also spoke of Sciapodes whose feet pointed backward, and of the happy Hyborians, whose lifespan was 1,000 years. The Phanesians, he said, had ears so long they slept in them, with one ear serving as a mattress and the other as a blanket. There were also Indian tribes that had dog ears or had an upper lip extending below their chin or had no mouth. The last, being unable to eat (or to speak), subsisted on the odor of roast meat and fruit and the perfume of flowers.

The invasion of India by Alexander the Great in 326 B.C. probably gave rise 11
to similar reports. With Alexander's army were scholars charged with describing the countries through which they passed. Most of these writings have been lost, but the *Romance of Alexander* (which some scholars date back to 200 B.C.) was translated into many languages in the early Middle Ages. Together with the works of Megasthenes it was for centuries an important source of knowledge about the real and imaginary inhabitants of India.

A number of learned Greeks challenged the stories about monsters. The 12
geographer Strabo, who lived at about the time of the birth of Christ, did not hesitate to call such tales mere superstition. Nonetheless, the tradition remained vigorously alive.

In the first century A.D. the Roman naturalist Pliny the Elder devoted several 13
volumes of his encyclopedic *Historia Naturalis (Natural History)* to descriptions of the physical nature and manners of mankind. Asserting that he had read more than 2,000 books, Pliny repeated in a systematic manner all that had been said about monsters; he also added a few embellishments of his own. Some later commentators remarked that a more appropriate title for these writings would have been "Unnatural History." Pliny's contributions included the cannibal Scythians, who used skulls for drinking vessels; the Thibii, who had a double pupil in one eye and the image of a horse in the other, and the solitary Essenes, who lived without women and yet propagated. Other Roman writers, such as Pomponius Mela (first century A.D.) and Caius Julius Solinus (third century), elaborated on Pliny. The ears of the Phanesians and the feet of the Sciapodes grew larger and larger; in the land of the Neuers the men were transformed into wolves in summer and regained human form in winter. These writers were important sources for the medieval acquaintance with monsters. Belief in their reliability was bolstered by reports of travelers and missionaries that were written with apparent sincerity and conviction.

Monstrous races presented a problem for the early church fathers. It was 14
difficult to deny the reality of such creatures, not only because of the mission-aries' reports but also because of the Bible. The Book of Genesis refers to races of giants. A passage in St. Jerome's translation of Isaiah reads: "And the hairy ones shall dance there." St. Jerome's own commentary explained that "the hairy ones" might be wild men.

In *The City of God* St. Augustine dealt with the question of the reality of 15
such beings. If, he wrote, the stories about monsters are not plain lies, such beings either are not men at all or, if they are men, they are, like other men,

descendants of Adam. St. Augustine tended to favor the last possibility. He argued that individual monstrous births do occur and are clearly descended from Adam. Monstrous races might therefore exist and be human.

Later medieval scholars asked themselves how such transformations could have taken place. A common answer was that the devil had so perverted the souls of some pagans that their appearance had also degenerated. Scripture could be invoked to prove that such changes were possible. The evil king Nebuchadnezzar had been transformed from a man into a beastlike creature; his hair grew like an eagle's feathers, his nails were like a bird's claws and he ate grass. 16

Other commentators who were less strict about the concept that man—monstrous or otherwise—had a single origin advanced the idea that monsters might have been separately created by the devil in an effort to confound God's creation, man. It was also deemed possible that monsters were creatures of the Antipodes who had managed to climb up over the edges of the (flat) world. 17

Meanwhile medieval travelers steadily made the monsters more monstrous. There were peoples with one eye, three eyes or five eyes, with eyes in the back of their head, with four or more arms and legs or with enormously long teeth. There were others without nostrils, without eyes, without a mouth or with a mouth so small they could only drink through a straw. Some had ears so long they hindered walking and had to be knotted together behind the back or wound around the arms; some had ears shaped like large fans. Some walked on all fours or had legs that were mere leather strips so that they could only crawl; some had spider legs or goat feet or bird claws. Some were entirely bald or exceedingly hairy; some had tails or had the neck as well as the head of horses or mice. There was also a tribe of creatures that had only a head; the rest of the body was lacking. 18

It was understood that monsters had monstrous habits; they were naked, lascivious, promiscuous and filthy; they had a bad smell and no religion. They ate snakes, lizards, dogs, mice, fleas and flies; they ate their parents or (after fattening them for years) their children. 19

The celebrated myth of Prester John lent further credence to fabulous creatures. In the 12th century there appeared the Latin text of a letter addressed to the Byzantine emperor Manuel Comnenus and purportedly written by Prester John, ruler of a realm in the East. Prester John professed to be a devout Christian whose land was enormously wealthy, harboring not only rich mineral resources but also the fountain of perpetual youth. The inhabitants of the region included, in addition to a normal human population, nearly all the marvelous and monstrous creatures ever described: wild men, men with horns, one-eyed men, pygmies, giants 40 ells (about 90 feet) tall, centaurs, fauns and so on. 20

The letter was widely accepted as being genuine. European monarchs were eager to discover Prester John's realm, if only to enlist a powerful ally in their struggle with Islam. Pope Alexander III wrote a letter to Prester John and entrusted it to his physician for personal delivery. The physician never returned. 21

ANIMAL-HEADED PEOPLE were popular during the Middle Ages. At left is shown one of the Cynocephali, or dog-headed ones, also believed to inhabit India. They were often assigned allegorical roles, at one time signifying harshness of temper, at another meekness. The goose-headed man shown at right and others like him were depicted on printed pamphlets that sold well at 17th-century country fairs. The woodcuts are reproduced from *Monstrorum Historia*, by Ulisse Aldrovandi, which was published in 1642.

Many travelers who later set out to discover this earthly paradise did return, and they gave "eyewitness" accounts. As late as 1590 an English traveler by the name of Edward Webbe reported that he had visited Prester John's court and had seen a monster there. It was kept chained to prevent it from devouring human beings, but after executions it was fed human flesh. The geographic location of Prester John's country was variously conceived. At first it was usually in or near India; later it was in Abyssinia. The discovery of the Cape of Good Hope was due in part to the efforts of the Portuguese to find Prester John's country. Columbus believed he had passed near it.

Apart from the Prester John myth and the fictitious accounts of travelers, there were many literary sources dealing with monsters. One of the earliest encyclopedic works was *Etymologies*, written by Isidore of Seville in the seventh century A.D. Isidore attempted single-handedly to summarize all knowledge; he devoted a volume to "men and monsters," and he placed the monsters in definite geographic areas. This immensely popular work was translated into several languages and was often imitated. In the 13th century a similar work explicitly directed to unlearned people (*On the Properties of Things*, by Bartholomaeus Anglicus) was translated into six European languages; with the invention of the printing press it reached 46 editions. The popularity of monsters is further attested by the fact that printed pictures of them were often sold at country fairs.

Monstrous men are also depicted on the medieval *mappa mundi*, maps of the world. In earlier editions the fabulous races were drawn on the maps them-

93

selves, indicating their supposed geographic distribution. On a late-13th-century map in Hereford Cathedral the Sciapodes, pygmies and giants are found in India, horse-hoofed and long-eared tribes in Scythia, and tailed satyrs and the Blemmyae in Abyssinia. On later maps the creatures often appear as border decorations, suggesting the direction in which they might be found.

In the Middle Ages monsters were cited to teach moral lessons. According to one 13th-century source, pygmies denoted humility, giants pride and Cynocephali harshness of temper. The long-lipped races were gossips and mischief-makers. In the widely translated *Gesta Romanorum*, a late-medieval collection of moral tales, the symbolism had changed. Long-lipped people now signified justice; long-eared ones were devout. (They were listening to the word of God.) The dog-headed people were humble. (They were said to be a model for priests.) The headless Blemmyae also represented humility. [24]

The question St. Augustine had raised—Are the monstrous races human?—became a matter of practical concern with the discovery of the New World and its inhabitants. Columbus (convinced to the day of his death that he had found the sea route to India) wrote quite objectively about the Indians of Hispaniola (today Haiti and the Dominican Republic). They were, he said, well-made men who were so generous with their possessions that they never refused anything that was requested. He described the Carib Indians as being handsome of face and figure and intelligent. Nonetheless, Columbus also mentioned the existence of races that were hairless, tailed or dog-headed. [25]

Later explorers less restrained than Columbus maintained that they had personally met Indians who were monstrous both in appearance and habits. It was necessary for Pope Paul II to declare explicitly (in his Papal Bull of 1537) that American Indians were fully human and in possession of an immortal soul. [26]

Many Europeans had the opportunity to examine human representatives of the New World. Captured "specimens" were shipped to Europe and placed on public display; some of them, dressed in tiger skins and fed raw meat, were exhibited in cages. Even so, it must have been a disappointment to many onlookers that they had no tail, were not very hirsute and had only two eyes, two arms and normal-sized ears. [27]

The character Caliban in *The Tempest* no doubt reflects attitudes toward the peoples of the New World in Shakespeare's time. Caliban is "as disproportion'd in his manners as in his shape," "a thing most brutish," a member of a "vile race," a "monster of the isle with four legs." He is filthy and smells like a fish, and one of the European sailors shipwrecked on his island at first mistakes him for a devil. Another sailor calls him a puppy-headed monster. Caliban is said to use the language taught him by his master, but only to curse. He has no capacity for abstraction and understands neither music nor love. "A devil, a born devil, on whose nature nurture can never stick. . . ." [28]

The name Caliban is an anagram of *canibal* and this Spanish word is itself a corruption of *Caribal*, an inhabitant of the Caribbean islands. *Canibal* in [29]

94

turn suggests *canino*, Spanish for "dog." The Cynocephali come readily to mind, the more so because of the term "puppy-headed monster." Shakespeare thus equated the monstrous Caliban with inhabitants of the New World. A further indication that he was thinking of the New World in *The Tempest* is his mention of "vex'd Bermoothes" (Bermuda).

With the development of modern science in the 17th century, emphasis was 30 placed on systematic study by direct observation; this method was also applied to the study of monsters. The only monsters available for examination, however, were those resulting from abnormal births. In the absence of detailed knowledge of embryology, endocrine glands and hormones the cause of such births were little understood. Most of the scholarly works dealing with them were a mixture of science and credulousness; congenital abnormalities were discussed on the same level as the fictitious monstrous races. In his book *De Monstris* (1665) Fortunio Liceti added an elephant-headed creature to the lengthy catalogue of composite beings. Other students of teratology (the study of monstrous living forms) occupied themselves with classification; they grouped fabulous tribes ac-

LATTER-DAY MONSTER was a subject of "scientific" study. Fortunio Liceti, who introduced the elephant-headed man, was one of those who considered fabulous monsters together with cases of abnormal birth. The etching is from Liceti's *De Monstris*, published in 1665.

cording to the part of the body that was abnormal. Moral lessons were not lacking: monstrous births were seen as punishment for deviation from accepted customs, most particularly for incest or promiscuity but also for a variety of other transgressions.

In the 17th century, as increasing numbers of animal and plant species were being discovered, efforts were made to arrange the species in an orderly array. In some of the earlier systems of classification the monsters presented no problem: they were simply left out (together with man himself). Linnaeus, however, proposed to classify everything in nature. In the first edition of his *System of Nature*, which appeared in 1735, he boldly classified man as a quadruped, placing him in the same order as the sloth and the ape. At that time Linnaeus had not yet introduced his binomial system of nomenclature (genus and species); he simply noted that satyrs (described as being tailed, hairy and bearded and having a human body) and tailed men were ape species.

In the 10th edition of Linnaeus (1758) man was given the name *Homo sapiens*, and the separate species *Homo monstrosus* was also listed. Linnaeus considered the satyrs and the pygmies to be closer to the apes, as is indicated by their names: *Simia satyrus* and *Simia sylvanus*. He described a somewhat more human species believed to live in Abyssinia and on Java. They are, he said, nocturnal, they walk erect, they have frizzled white hair, they speak in a hiss, they are able to think and they believe the world was made for them.

Linnaeus granted that it was extremely difficult to distinguish such creatures from man. He was of course severely handicapped; not only were there no specimens of monsters but also he had not seen many apes. The only ape he mentioned as being accessible to him for examination was an immature chimpanzee.

At least two followers of Linnaeus continued to classify fabulous tribes in a scientific manner. C. E. Hoppius, a pupil of Linnaeus', ranked *Homo troglodytus* closest to man. Next came *Homo luciferus*, as Hoppius named human creatures with tails; he was followed by *Homo satyrus* and *Homo pygmaeus*. A German physician named Martinus contended that there were two races of *Homo sylvestris*, the members of one race being smaller than those of the other.

Nonetheless, the end of *Homo monstrosus* and his like was approaching. With increased knowledge of anatomy, in particular the anatomy of the great apes, it was realized that the stories about satyrs and men with tails, if they were not fantasies, came from faulty observations of apes and monkeys. Although many a 19th-century traveler wrote about tailed men, such reports eventually became rare.

The puzzling similarities and differences between men and apes were clarified by Darwin's theory of evolution, but the theory did not solve the problem of man's specific ancestry. The erroneous idea that the lineage of man could be traced to known ape species spurred the search for a "missing link," a creature half-ape, half-man. Eugène Dubois believed that (in the fossil remains of

APELIKE MEN, thought to be human species, were the result of the enduring belief in monstrous peoples and confused observations of apes in the wild. Reading from left to right, the species are *Homo troglodytus*, *Homo luciferus*, *Homo satyrus* and *Homo pygmaeus*. The etching is reproduced from an article titled "Anthropomorpha," by C. E. Hoppius, which was published in 1760.

HIRSUTE ABORIGINE exemplifies the "hairy nations" described by Pliny the Elder and believed to exist by New World explorers. This woodcut is from *Anthropometamorphosis: Man Transformed: or The Artificial Changling*, by John Bulwer, which was published in 1653.

Pithecanthropus erectus, or Java man) he had found such a link, a belief many people shared until the discovery of other human fossils changed the picture.

With the knowledge that the ancestors of man are not represented among contemporary ape species, the search for links between men and apes ended.

Curiously, however, *Homo monstrosus* is not quite dead. Reports of an 37 "abominable snowman" living in hidden fastnesses of the Himalayas are still in circulation. Speculation about life on other planets gives rise to new monsters with pointed heads and strange appendages. These fanciful beings are mostly invented in a spirit of fun, but the lesson is the same: When men can conceive of some remote place where other men or manlike creatures might exist, he is profoundly motivated to populate the unknown with creatures of his imagination.

QUESTIONS

1. According to Malefijt, what is the purpose of this study? How does her introduction prepare the reader for what is to come?

2. Herodotus has been called the "Father of History." In what ways was he a reliable recorder? Why would he record information from the Aggripaei that he didn't believe?

3. In what ways did the basis for belief in monsters change in the Middle Ages?

4. Consider the illustrations reproduced here from fifteenth- and seventeenth-century books. How would they have reinforced belief in monsters? In what ways do they augment Malefijt's text?

5. If you have seen the film or play *Elephant Man*, compare the attitudes toward the Elephant Man with those reported in this article.

6. Investigate the background of a contemporary monster, such as the Abominable Snowman, Big Foot, or the Loch Ness monster. Or if you wish, investigate representations in science fiction of possible life on other planets. (For example, why is E.T. presented the way he is?) Write a report that presents your findings.

7. Do you think the reasons given in this article for belief in monsters can serve as a basis for what Malefijt calls "the unfounded prejudices that human groups often harbor toward one another today" (paragraph 3)? Investigate attitudes in your community towards a group or groups that are seen as "different" from yourselves. Write a report in which you compare your findings with Malefijt's theory.

CRASH!
Frederick Lewis Allen

Frederick Lewis Allen (1890–1954) was born in Boston,
went to Harvard, and spent most of his life quietly working
as an editor of Harper's *magazine. He was also the author*
of a number of popular books on recent American history,
including a biography of the tycoon J. Pierpont Morgan.
His best-known work is Only Yesterday: An Informal History of the 1920's, *from which the following chapter has*
been taken. The book first appeared in 1931, not long after
the scenes and events reported in it.

Early in September [1929] the stock market broke. It quickly recovered, 1
however; indeed, on September 19th the averages as compiled by the *New York*
Times reached an even higher level than that of September 3rd. Once more it
slipped, farther and faster, until by October 4th the prices of a good many stocks
had coasted to what seemed first-class bargain levels. Steel, for example, after
having touched 261¾ a few weeks earlier, had dropped as low as 204; American
Can, at the closing on October 4th, was nearly twenty points below its high for
the year; General Electric was over fifty points below its high; Radio had gone
down from 114¾ to 82½.

A bad break, to be sure, but there had been other bad breaks, and the 2
speculators who escaped unscathed proceeded to take advantage of the lessons
they had learned in June and December of 1928 and March and May of 1929:
when there was a break it was a good time to buy. In the face of all this
tremendous liquidation, brokers' loans as compiled by the Federal Reserve Bank
of New York mounted to a new high record on October 2nd, reaching
$6,804,000,000—a sure sign that margin buyers were not deserting the market
but coming into it in numbers at least undiminished.[1] (Part of the increase in
the loan figure was probably due to the piling up of unsold securities in dealers'
hands, as the spawning of investment trusts and the issue of new common stock
by every manner of business concern continued unabated.) History, it seemed,
was about to repeat itself, and those who picked up Anaconda at 109¾ or
American Telephone at 281 would count themselves wise investors. And sure
enough, prices once more began to climb. They had already turned upward
before that Sunday in early October when Ramsay MacDonald sat on a log with

---

[1]margin: credit, provided by a broker, for buying stock. At that time it was common for stock
to be as much as 90 percent financed. If the stock fell, the owner had to cover the loan by putting
up more money or selling the stock. [Eds.]

Herbert Hoover at the Rapidan camp and talked over the prospects for naval limitation and peace.

Something was wrong, however. The decline began once more. The wiseacres 3 of Wall Street, looking about for causes, fixed upon the collapse of the Hatry financial group in England (which had led to much forced selling among foreign investors and speculators), and upon the bold refusal of the Massachusetts Department of Public Utilities to allow the Edison Company of Boston to split up its stock. They pointed, too, to the fact that the steel industry was undoubtedly slipping, and to the accumulation of "undigested" securities. But there was little real alarm until the week of October 21st. The consensus of opinion, in the meantime, was merely that the equinoctial storm of September had not quite blown over. The market was readjusting itself into a "more secure technical position."

[2]

In view of what was about to happen, it is enlightening to recall how things 4 looked at this juncture to the financial prophets, those gentlemen whose wizardly reputations were based upon their supposed ability to examine a set of graphs brought to them by a statistician and discover, from the relation of curve to curve and index to index, whether things were going to get better or worse. Their opinions differed, of course; there never has been a moment when the best financial opinion was unanimous. In examining these opinions, and the outgivings of eminent bankers, it must furthermore be acknowledged that a bullish statement cannot always be taken at its face value: few men like to assume the responsibility of spreading alarm by making dire predictions, nor is a banker with unsold securities on his hands likely to say anything which will make it more difficult to dispose of them, unquiet as his private mind may be. Finally, one must admit that prophecy is at best the most hazardous of occupations. Nevertheless, the general state of financial opinion in October, 1929, makes an instructive contrast with that in February and March, 1928, when, as we have seen, the skies had not appeared any too bright.

Some forecasters, to be sure, were so unconventional as to counsel caution. 5 Roger W. Babson, an investment adviser who had not always been highly regarded in the inner circles of Wall Street, especially since he had for a long time been warning his clients of future trouble, predicted early in September a decline of sixty or eighty points in the averages. On October 7th the Standard Trade and Securities Service of the Standard Statistics Company advised its clients to pursue an "ultraconservative policy," and ventured this prediction: "We remain of the opinion that, over the next few months, the trend of common-stock prices will be toward lower levels." Poor's *Weekly Business and Investment Letter* spoke its mind on the "great common-stock delusion" and predicted "further liquidation in stocks." Among the big bankers, Paul M. Warburg had shown months before this that he was alive to the dangers of the situation. These commentators—along with others such as the editor of the *Commercial and Financial Chronicle* and the financial editor of the *New York Times*—would appear to deserve the 1929 gold medals for foresight.

But if ever such medals were actually awarded, a goodly number of leather 6 ones would have to be distributed at the same time. Not necessarily to the Harvard Economic Society, although on October 19th, after having explained that business was "facing another period of readjustment," it predicted that "if recession should threaten serious consequences for business (as is not indicated at present) there is little doubt that the Reserve System would take steps to ease the money market and so check the movement." The Harvard soothsayers proved themselves quite fallible: as late as October 26th, after the first wide-open crack in the stock market, they delivered the cheerful judgment that "despite its severity, we believe that the slump in stock prices will prove an intermediate movement and not the precursor of a business depression such as would entail prolonged further liquidation." This judgment turned out, of course, to be ludicrously wrong; but on the other hand the Harvard Economic Society was far from being really bullish. Nor would Colonel Leonard P. Ayres of the Cleveland Trust Company get one of the leather medals. He almost qualified when, on October 15th, he delivered himself of the judgment that "there does not seem to be as yet much real evidence that the decline in stock prices is likely to forecast a serious recession in general business. Despite the slowing down in iron and steel production, in automobile output, and in building, the conditions which result in serious business depressions are not present." But the skies, as Colonel Ayres saw them, were at least partly cloudy. "It seems probable," he said, "that stocks have been passing not so much from the strong to the weak as from the smart to the dumb."

Professor Irving Fisher, however, was more optimistic. In the newspapers of 7 October 17th he was reported as telling the Purchasing Agents Association that stock prices had reached "what looks like a permanently high plateau." He expected to see the stock market, within a few months, "a good deal higher than it is today." On the very eve of the panic of October 24th he was further quoted as expecting a recovery in prices. Only two days before the panic, the *Boston News Bureau* quoted R. W. McNeel, director of McNeel's Financial Service, as suspecting "that some pretty intelligent people are now buying stocks." "Unless we are to have a panic—which no one seriously believes—stocks have hit bottom," said Mr. McNeel. And as for Charles E. Mitchell, chairman of the great National City Bank of New York, he continuously and enthusiastically radiated sunshine. Early in October Mr. Mitchell was positive that, despite the stock-market break, "The industrial situation of the United States is absolutely sound and our credit situation is in no way critical. . . . The interest given by the public to brokers' loans is always exaggerated," he added. "Altogether too much attention is paid to it." A few days later Mr. Mitchell spoke again: "Although in some cases speculation has gone too far in the United States, the markets generally are now in a healthy condition. The last six weeks have done an immense amount of good by shaking down prices. . . . The market values have a sound basis in the general prosperity of our country." Finally, on October 22nd, two days before the panic, he arrived in the United States from a short trip to Europe with these reassuring words: "I know of nothing fundamentally wrong with the stock market or with the underlying business and credit structure. . . . The public is suffering from 'brokers' loanitis.' "

Nor was Mr. Mitchell by any means alone in his opinions. To tell the truth,   8 the chief difference between him and the rest of the financial community was that he made more noise. One of the most distinguished bankers in the United States, in closing a deal in the early autumn of 1929, said privately that he saw not a cloud in the sky. Habitual bulls like Arthur Cutten were, of course, insisting that they were "still bullish." And the general run of traders presumably endorsed the view attributed to "one large house" in mid-October in the *Boston News Bureau's* "Broad Street Gossip," that "the recent break makes a firm foundation for a big bull market in the last quarter of the year." There is no doubt that a great many speculators who had looked upon the midsummer prices as too high were now deciding that deflation had been effected and were buying again. Presumably most financial opinion agreed also with the further statement which appeared in the "Broad Street Gossip" column of October 16th, that "business is now too big and diversified, and the country too rich, to be influenced by stock-market fluctuations"; and with the editorial opinion of the *News Bureau*, on October 19th, that "whatever recessions (in business) are noted, are those of the runner catching his breath. . . . The general condition is satisfactory and fundamentally sound."

The disaster which was impending was destined to be as bewildering and   9 frightening to the rich and the powerful and the customarily sagacious as to the foolish and unwary holder of fifty shares of margin stock.

[3]

The expected recovery in the stock market did not come. It seemed to be   10 beginning on Tuesday, October 22nd, but the gains made during the day were largely lost during the last hour. And on Wednesday, the 23rd, there was a perfect Niagara of liquidation. The volume of trading was over six million shares, the tape was 104 minutes late when the three-o'clock gong ended trading for the day, and the *New York Times* averages for fifty leading railroad and industrial stocks lost 18.24 points—a loss which made the most abrupt declines in previous breaks look small. Everybody realized that an unprecedented number of margin calls must be on their way to insecurely margined traders, and that the situation at last was getting serious. But perhaps the turn would come tomorrow. Already the break had carried prices down a good deal farther than the previous breaks of the past two years. Surely it could not go on much longer.

The next day was Thursday, October 24th.   11

On that momentous day stocks opened moderately steady in price, but in   12
enormous volume. Kennecott appeared on the tape in a block of 20,000 shares, General Motors in another of the same amount. Almost at once the ticker tape began to lag behind the trading on the floor. The pressure of selling orders was disconcertingly heavy. Prices were going down. . . . Presently they were going down with some rapidity. . . . Before the first hour of trading was over, it was already apparent that they were going down with an altogether unprecedented and amazing violence. In brokers' offices all over the country, tape-watchers looked at one another in astonishment and perplexity. Where on earth was this torrent of selling orders coming from?

The exact answer to this question will probably never be known. But it seems   13
probable that the principal cause of the break in prices during that first hour on October 24th was not fear. Nor was it short selling. It was forced selling. It was the dumping on the market of hundreds of thousands of shares of stock held in the name of miserable traders whose margins were exhausted or about to be exhausted. The gigantic edifice of prices was honeycombed with speculative credit and was now breaking under its own weight.

Fear, however, did not long delay its coming. As the price structure crumbled   14
there was a sudden stampede to get out from under. By eleven o'clock traders on the floor of the Stock Exchange were in a wild scramble to "sell at the market." Long before the lagging ticker could tell what was happening, word had gone out by telephone and telegraph that the bottom was dropping out of things, and the selling orders redoubled in volume. The leading stocks were going down two, three, and even five points between sales. Down, down, down. . . . Where were the bargain-hunters who were supposed to come to the rescue at times like this? Where were the investment trusts, which were expected to provide a cushion for the market by making new purchases at low prices? Where were the big operators who had declared that they were still bullish? Where were the powerful bankers who were supposed to be able at any moment to support prices? There seemed to be no support whatever. Down, down, down. The roar of voices which rose from the floor of the Exchange had become a roar of panic.

United States Steel had opened at 205½. It crashed through 200 and presently   15
was at 193½. General Electric, which only a few weeks before had been selling above 400, had opened this morning at 315—now it had slid to 283. Things were even worse with Radio: opening at 68¾, it had gone dismally down through the sixties and the fifties and forties to the abysmal price of 44½. And as for Montgomery Ward, vehicle of the hopes of thousands who saw the chain store as the harbinger of the new economic era, it had dropped headlong from 83 to 50. In the space of two short hours, dozens of stocks lost ground which it had required many months of the bull market to gain.

Frederick Lewis Allen

Even this sudden decline in values might not have been utterly terrifying if 16 people could have known precisely what was happening at any moment. It is the unknown which causes real panic.

Suppose a man walked into a broker's branch office between twelve and one 17 o'clock on October 24th to see how things were faring. First he glanced at the big board, covering one wall of the room, on which the day's prices for the leading stocks were supposed to be recorded. The LOW and LAST figures written there took his breath away, but soon he was aware that they were un- reliable: even with the wildest scrambling, the boys who slapped into place the cards which recorded the last prices shown on the ticker could not keep up with the changes: they were too numerous and abrupt. He turned to the shining screen across which ran an uninterrupted procession of figures from the ticker. Ordinarily the practiced tape-watcher could tell from a moment's glance at the screen how things were faring, even though the Exchange now omitted all but the final digit of each quotation. A glance at the board, if not his own memory, supplied the missing digits. But today, when he saw a run of symbols and figures like

R   WX
6.5½.5.4.   9.8⅞¾½¼.8.7½.7.

he could not be sure whether the price of "6" shown for Radio meant 66 or 56 or 46; whether Westinghouse was sliding from 189 to 187 or from 179 to 177. And presently he heard that the ticker was an hour and a half late; at one o'clock it was recording the prices of half-past eleven! All this that he saw was ancient history. What was happening on the floor now?

At ten-minute intervals the bond ticker over in the corner would hammer 18 off a list of selected prices direct from the floor, and a broker's clerk would grab the uncoiling sheet of paper and shear it off with a pair of scissors and read the figures aloud in a mumbling expressionless monotone to the white-faced men who occupied every seat on the floor and stood packed at the rear of the room. The prices which he read out were *ten or a dozen or more points below those recorded on the ticker*. What about the stocks not included in that select list? There was no way of finding out. The telephone lines were clogged as inquiries and orders from all over the country converged upon the Stock Exchange. Once in a while a voice would come barking out of the broker's rear office where a frantic clerk was struggling for a telephone connection: "Steel at ninety-six!" Small comfort, however, to know what Steel was doing; the men outside were desperately involved in many another stock than Steel; they were almost com- pletely in the dark, and their imaginations had free play. If they put in an order to buy or to sell, it was impossible to find out what became of it. The Exchange's whole system for the recording of current prices and for communicating orders was hopelessly unable to cope with the emergency, and the sequel was an epidemic of fright.

CRASH!

In that broker's office, as in hundreds of other offices from one end of the   19
land to the other, one saw men looking defeat in the face. One of them was
slowly walking up and down, mechanically tearing a piece of paper into tiny
and still tinier fragments. Another was grinning shamefacedly, as a small boy
giggles at a funeral. Another was abjectly beseeching a clerk for the latest news
of American & Foreign Power. And still another was sitting motionless, as if
stunned, his eyes fixed blindly upon the moving figures on the screen, those
innocent-looking figures that meant the smash-up of the hopes of years. . . .

GL.   AWW.   JMP.
 8.7.5.2.1.90.89.7.6.   3.2½.2.   6.5.3.2½.

A few minutes after noon, some of the more alert members of a crowd which   20
had collected on the street outside the Stock Exchange, expecting they knew
not what, recognized Charles E. Mitchell, erstwhile defender of the bull market,
slipping quietly into the offices of J. P. Morgan & Company on the opposite
corner. It was scarcely more than nine years since the House of Morgan had
been pitted with the shrapnel-fire of the Wall Street explosion; now its occupants
faced a different sort of calamity equally near at hand. Mr. Mitchell was followed
shortly by Albert H. Wiggin, head of the Chase National Bank; William Potter,
head of the Guaranty Trust Company; and Seward Prosser, head of the Bankers
Trust Company. They had come to confer with Thomas W. Lamont of the
Morgan firm. In the space of a few minutes these five men, with George F.
Baker, Jr., of the First National Bank, agreed in behalf of their respective institutions to put up forty millions apiece to shore up the stock market. The
object of the two-hundred-and-forty-million-dollar pool thus formed, as explained subsequently by Mr. Lamont, was not to hold prices at any given level,
but simply to make such purchases as were necessary to keep trading on an
orderly basis. Their first action, they decided, would be to try to steady the prices
of the leading securities which served as bellwethers for the list as a whole. It
was a dangerous plan, for with hysteria spreading there was no telling what sort
of *débâcle* might be impending. But this was no time for any action but the
boldest.

The bankers separated. Mr. Lamont faced a gathering of reporters in the   21
Morgan offices. His face was grave, but his words were soothing. His first sentence alone was one of the most remarkable understatements of all time. "There
has been a little distress selling on the Stock Exchange," said he, "and we have
held a meeting of the heads of several financial institutions to discuss the situation. We have found that there are no houses in difficulty and reports from
brokers indicate that margins are being maintained satisfactorily." He went on
to explain that what had happened was due to a "technical condition of the
market" rather than to any fundamental cause.

As the news that the bankers were meeting circulated on the floor of the   22
Exchange, prices began to steady. Soon a brisk rally set in. Steel jumped back

to the level at which it had opened that morning. But the bankers had more to offer the dying bull market than a Morgan partner's best bedside manner.

At about half-past one o'clock Richard Whitney, vice-president of the Exchange, who usually acted as floor broker for the Morgan interests, went into the "steel crowd" and put in a bid of 205—the price of the last previous sale—for 10,000 shares of Steel. He bought only 200 shares and left the remainder of the order with the specialist. Mr. Whitney then went to various other points on the floor, and offered the price of the last previous sale for 10,000 shares of each of fifteen or twenty other stocks, reporting what was sold to him at that price and leaving the remainder of the order with the specialist. In short, within the space of a few minutes Mr. Whitney offered to purchase something in the neighborhood of twenty or thirty million dollars' worth of stock. Purchases of this magnitude are not undertaken by Tom, Dick, and Harry; it was clear that Mr. Whitney represented the bankers' pool. 23

The desperate remedy worked. The semblance of confidence returned. Prices held steady for a while; and though many of them slid off once more in the final hour, the net results for the day might well have been worse. Steel actually closed two points higher than on Wednesday, and the net losses of most of the other leading securities amounted to less than ten points apiece for the whole day's trading. 24

All the same, it had been a frightful day. At seven o'clock that night the tickers in a thousand brokers' offices were still chattering; not till after 7:08 did they finally record the last sale made on the floor at three o'clock. The volume of trading had set a new record—12,894,650 shares. ("The time may come when we shall see a five-million-share day," the wise men of the Street had been saying twenty months before!) Incredible rumors had spread wildly during the early afternoon—that eleven speculators had committed suicide, that the Buffalo and Chicago exchanges had been closed, that troops were guarding the New York Stock Exchange against an angry mob. The country had known the bitter taste of panic. And although the bankers' pool had prevented for the moment an utter collapse, there was no gainsaying the fact that the economic structure had cracked wide open. 25

[4]

Things looked somewhat better on Friday and Saturday. Trading was still on an enormous scale, but prices for the most part held. At the very moment when the bankers' pool was cautiously disposing of as much as possible of the stock which it had accumulated on Thursday and was thus preparing for future emergencies, traders who had sold out higher up were coming back into the market again with new purchases, in the hope that the bottom had been reached. (Hadn't they often been told that "the time to buy is when things look blackest"?) 26

CRASH!

The newspapers carried a very pretty series of reassuring statements from the occupants of the seats of the mighty; Herbert Hoover himself, in a White House statement, pointed out that "the fundamental business of the country, that is, production and distribution of commodities, is on a sound and prosperous basis." But toward the close of Saturday's session prices began to slip again. And on Monday the rout was under way once more.

The losses registered on Monday were terrific—17½ points for Steel, 47½ for General Electric, 36 for Allied Chemical, 34½ for Westinghouse, and so on down a long and dismal list. All Saturday afternoon and Saturday night and Sunday the brokers had been struggling to post their records and go over their customers' accounts and sent out calls for further margin, and another avalanche of forced selling resulted. The prices at which Mr. Whitney's purchases had steadied the leading stocks on Thursday were so readily broken through that it was immediately clear that the bankers' pool had made a strategic retreat. As a matter of fact, the brokers who represented the pool were having their hands full plugging up the "air-holes" in the list—in other words, buying stocks which were offered for sale without any bids at all in sight. Nothing more than this could have been accomplished, even if it could have been wisely attempted. Even six great banks could hardly stem the flow of liquidation from the entire United States. They could only guide it a little, check it momentarily here and there.

Once more the ticker dropped ridiculously far behind, the lights in the brokers' offices and the banks burned till dawn, and the telegraph companies distributed thousands of margin calls and requests for more collateral to back up loans at the banks. Bankers, brokers, clerks, messengers were almost at the end of their strength; for days and nights they had been driving themselves to keep pace with the most terrific volume of business that had ever descended upon them. It did not seem as if they could stand it much longer. But the worst was still ahead. It came the next day, Tuesday, October 29th.

The big gong had hardly sounded in the great hall of the Exchange at ten o'clock Tuesday morning before the storm broke in full force. Huge blocks of stock were thrown upon the market for what they would bring. Five thousand shares, ten thousand shares appeared at a time on the laboring ticker at fearful recessions in price. Not only were innumerable small traders being sold out, but big ones, too, protagonists of the new economic era who a few weeks before had counted themselves millionaires. Again and again the specialist in a stock would find himself surrounded by brokers fighting to sell—and nobody at all even thinking of buying. To give one single example: during the bull market the common stock of the White Sewing Machine Company had gone as high as 48; on Monday, October 28th, it had closed at 11⅛. On that black Tuesday, somebody—a clever messenger boy for the Exchange, it was rumored—had the bright idea of putting in an order to buy at 1—and in the temporarily complete absence of other bids he actually got his stock for a dollar a share! The scene on the floor was chaotic. Despite the jamming of the communication system, orders to buy and sell—mostly to sell—came in faster than human beings could possibly handle them; it was on that day that an exhausted broker, at the close of the session, found a large waste-basket which he had stuffed with orders to be executed and had carefully set aside for safekeeping—and then had completely forgotten. Within half an hour of the opening the volume of trading had passed three million shares, by twelve o'clock it had passed eight million, by half-past one it had passed twelve million, and when the closing gong brought the day's madness to an end the gigantic record of 16,410,030 shares had been set. Toward the close there was a rally, but by that time the average prices of fifty leading stocks, as compiled by the *New York Times*, had fallen nearly forty points. Meanwhile there was a near-panic in other markets—the foreign stock exchanges, the lesser American exchanges, the grain market.

So complete was the demoralization of the stock market and so exhausted   30 were the brokers and their staffs and the Stock Exchange employees, that at noon that day, when the panic was at its worst, the Governing Committee met quietly to decide whether or not to close the Exchange. To quote from an address made some months later by Richard Whitney: "In order not to give occasion for alarming rumors, this meeting was not held in the Governing Committee Room, but in the office of the president of the Stock Clearing Corporation directly beneath the Stock Exchange floor. . . . The forty governors came to the meeting in groups of two and three as unobtrusively as possible. The office they met in was never designed for large meetings of this sort, with the result that most of the governors were compelled to stand, or to sit on tables. As the meeting progressed, panic was raging overhead on the floor. . . . The feeling of those present was revealed by their habit of continually lighting cigarettes, taking a puff or two, putting them out and lighting new ones—a practice which soon made the narrow room blue with smoke. . . ." Two of the Morgan partners were invited to the meeting and, attempting to slip into the building unnoticed so as not to start a new flock of rumors, were refused admittance by one of the guards and had to remain outside until rescued by a member of the Governing Committee. After some deliberation, the governors finally decided not to close the Exchange.

It was a critical day for the banks, that Tuesday the 29th. Many of the   31 corporations which had so cheerfully loaned money to brokers through the banks in order to obtain interest at 8 or 9 per cent were now clamoring to have these loans called—and the banks were faced with a choice between taking over the loans themselves and running the risk of precipitating further ruin. It was no laughing matter to assume the responsibility of millions of dollars' worth of loans secured by collateral which by the end of the day might prove to have dropped to a fraction of its former value. That the call money rate never rose above 6 percent that day, that a money panic was not added to the stock panic, and that several Wall Street institutions did not go down into immediate bankruptcy, was due largely to the nerve shown by a few bankers in stepping into the breach. The story is told of one banker who went grimly on authorizing the taking over of loan after loan until one of his subordinate officers came in with a white face and told him that the bank was insolvent. "I dare say," said the banker, and went ahead unmoved. He knew that if he did not, more than one concern would face insolvency.

The next day—Wednesday, October 30th—the outlook suddenly and providentially brightened. The directors of the Steel Corporation had declared an extra dividend; the directors of the American Can Company had not only declared an extra dividend, but had raised the regular dividend. There was another flood of reassuring statements—though by this time a cheerful statement from a financier fell upon somewhat skeptical ears. Julius Klein, Mr. Hoover's Assistant Secretary of Commerce, composed a rhapsody on continued prosperity. John J. Raskob declared that stocks were at bargain prices and that he and his friends were buying. John D. Rockefeller poured Standard Oil upon the waters: "Believing that fundamental conditions of the country are sound and that there is nothing in the business situation to warrant the destruction of values that has taken place on the exchanges during the past week, my son and I have for some days been purchasing sound common stocks." Better still, prices rose—steadily and buoyantly. Now at last the time had come when the strain on the Exchange could be relieved without causing undue alarm. At 1:40 o'clock Vice-President Whitney announced from the rostrum that the Exchange would not open until noon the following day and would remain closed all day Friday and Saturday— and to his immense relief the announcement was greeted, not with renewed panic, but with a cheer.

Throughout Thursday's short session the recovery continued. Prices gyrated wildly—for who could arrive at a reasonable idea of what a given stock was worth, now that all settled standards of value had been upset?—but the worst of the storm seemed to have blown over. The financial community breathed more easily; now they could have a chance to set their houses in order.

It was true that the worst of the panic was past. But not the worst prices. There was too much forced liquidation still to come as brokers' accounts were gradually straightened out, as banks called for more collateral, and terror was renewed. The next week, in a series of short sessions, the tide of prices receded once more—until at last on November 13th the bottom prices for the year 1929 were reached. Beside the figures hung up in the sunny days of September they made a tragic showing:

	High price Sept. 3, 1929	Low price Nov. 13, 1929
American Can	181⅞	86
American Telephone & Telegraph	304	197¼
Anaconda Copper	131½	70

General Electric	396¼	168⅛
General Motors	72¾	36
Montgomery Ward	137⅞	49¼
New York Central	256⅜	160
Radio	101	28
Union Carbide & Carbon	137⅞	59
United States Steel	261¾	150
Westinghouse E. & M.	289⅞	102⅝
Woolworth	100⅜	52¼
Electric Bond & Share	186¾	50¼

The *New York Times* averages for fifty leading stocks had been almost cut in 35
half, falling from a high of 311.90 in September to a low of 164.43 on November 13th; and the *Times* averages for twenty-five leading industrials had fared still worse, diving from 469.49 to 220.95.

The Big Bull Market was dead. Billions of dollars' worth of profits—and 36
paper profits—had disappeared. The grocer, the window-cleaner, and the seamstress had lost their capital. In every town there were families which had suddenly dropped from showy affluence into debt. Investors who had dreamed of retiring to live on their fortunes now found themselves back once more at the very beginning of the long road to riches. Day by day the newspapers printed the grim reports of suicides.

Coolidge-Hoover Prosperity was not yet dead, but it was dying. Under the 37
impact of the shock of panic, a multitude of ills which hitherto had passed unnoticed or had been offset by stock-market optimism began to beset the body economic, as poisons seep through the human system when a vital organ has ceased to function normally. Although the liquidation of nearly three billion dollars of brokers' loans contracted credit, and the Reserve Banks lowered the rediscount rate, and the way in which the larger banks and corporations of the country had survived the emergency without a single failure of large proportions offered real encouragement, nevertheless the poisons were there: overproduction of capital; overambitious expansion of business concerns; overproduction of commodities under the stimulus of installment buying and buying with stock-market profits; the maintenance of an artificial price level for many commodities; the depressed condition of European trade. No matter how many soothsayers of high finance proclaimed that all was well, no matter how earnestly the President set to work to repair the damage with soft words and White House conferences, a major depression was inevitably under way.

Nor was that all. Prosperity is more than an economic condition; it is a state 38
of mind. The Big Bull Market had been more than the climax of a business cycle; it had been the climax of a cycle in American mass thinking and mass emotion. There was hardly a man or woman in the country whose attitude toward life had not been affected by it in some degree and was not now affected by the sudden and brutal shattering of hope. With the Big Bull Market gone

CRASH!

and prosperity going, Americans were soon to find themselves living in an altered world which called for new adjustments, new ideas, new habits of thought, and a new order of values. The psychological climate was changing; the ever-shifting currents of American life were turning into new channels.

The Post-war Decade had come to its close. An era had ended. 39

QUESTIONS

1. Allen is reporting on two months of history in this essay: September 19 to November 13, 1929. His organization follows the calendar, chronologically, but he does not give every day equal space. Trace his use of dates to organize his writing. What dates get least space? What dates get the most extensive treatment? Why?

2. This essay consists of four numbered sections. Each section, like a paragraph, has a topic of its own. Can you find a topic sentence (or group of sentences) for each section? If you had to give each section a title, what would it be?

3. Find the shortest paragraph in the essay. Why is it so short? Look at the second shortest, too. Can you generalize about Allen's use of short paragraphs? That is, can you say when he uses them and why?

4. What is the function of paragraph 38? How does it relate to the rest of the essay? What is it doing—reporting or something else?

5. The introduction to "Reporting" compares the firsthand observation of the Stock Exchange in the *New York Times* article (pages 59–65) and the more distanced point of view in Allen's essay, written a year and a half after the event. In what sections of the essay do you find indications that Allen may have drawn on such firsthand observations as the *New York Times* article in order to re-create the frenzy of the Stock Market crash?

6. To what extent does this essay "tell a story"? Can you find places where Allen looks forward or backward as storytellers do? How does he generate suspense?

7. "Crash!" sounds like a noisy or violent subject. Is Allen's writing itself noisy and violent? How would you describe his style? Select a sentence or group of sentences and discuss its style.

8. What would you need to know to write an essay like this? Where could you go to find your sources? What difference would it have made if Allen had written his essay now instead of a year or two after the events he describes? How would you try to compensate for any disadvantages in writing long after the events you are describing?

9. Write an essay that covers a public event of some importance, in which you try to capture both the facts and the feel of the event. Remember, Allen wrote shortly after the events he described. He was not writing ancient history, nor was he on the floor of the Stock Exchange himself. In his note on this chapter (which is not reprinted here) he gives only one source: a speech by Richard Whitney, who had been an eyewitness and participant in the crash. But Allen must have used newspapers and other records as well. You should probably select an event of brief duration, such as an assassination, a coup, or a crisis of some sort, so that you are not overwhelmed with material. Remember to try for both factual accuracy and representational quality; that is, give the reader some sense of what it was like to be there.

111

THE TOY WITH ONE MOVING PART
Marvin Kaye

Marvin Kaye (b. 1938), with B.A. and M.A. degrees from the Pennsylvania State University, has worked on a small-town newspaper, as an editor at a major publishing house, and as a contributing editor of the Mass Retailing Merchandiser. *He is the author of a number of detective novels, and he also writes about toys and hobbies. The piece reprinted here, taken from his book* The Story of Monopoly, Silly Putty, Bingo, Twister, Frisbee, Scrabble, Etcetera *(1977), tells of the development of a contemporary American toy.*

It started by mistake in a New Haven laboratory, and turned into a bonanza 1
by sheer chance on New York's Fifth Avenue. There has never been a more accidental toy.

Maybe it had to be. Who could have sat down and deliberately designed a 2
piece of pink goo that stretches like taffy, shatters when struck sharply with a hammer, picks up newsprint and photos in color, molds like clay, flows like molasses, and—when rolled into a ball—bounces like mad?

It's the ultimate plaything: unstructured, nontoxic, fascinating to all ages, 3
harmless to child and furniture alike, with more play value built into it by nature than countless research-and-development engineers have been able to pack into myriads of high-price toys.

The prodigy is Silly Putty, still as unique and popular today as it was almost 4
twenty-five years ago, when it was accidentally developed in a General Electric research lab.

"There were a lot of little toy companies like us in the old days," reminisced 5
Peter Hodgson, the goateed president of Silly Putty. "We were all scramblers and could only afford to rent a small room to show our wares at the Toy Fair." When Hodgson first introduced the stuff, many buyers tried to talk him out of selling it, predicting that the firm wouldn't last a year. But twelve months later, at the next Toy Fair, the same buyers would walk back into the Silly Putty showroom and wonder that Hodgson and his crazy product were back for another season. Then they'd ask whether the toy was still being sold for only a dollar.

"Well," grinned Hodgson, "it's nearly a quarter of a century later, and we're 6
still around, and we still sell for only a buck . . . so I think we've got hold of something good."

The publisher of a leading toy trade publication laughs at Hodgson's understatement. "Something good! Pete adores Silly Putty. He's fascinated to death by it. Can you think of any other toy company that, after two decades, still makes only one item?" 7

Silly Putty did try to introduce a new toy a few seasons back. It was called 8 "Moonshine" and it stretched like taffy, broke when struck, picked up newsprint, molded and flowed and bounced. The only difference between it and regular Silly Putty was that Moonshine was lunar green, rather than pink, had a slightly heavier consistency, and glowed in the dark. But after some unexciting preliminary test-marketing, Moonshine was discontinued.

Such conservatism of line development is unique in the American toy in- 9 dustry, where most companies create hordes of new items each year. Others will put almost anything in a box, but not Hodgson. Caution and conservatism are his watchwords when it comes to marketing Silly Putty and expanding the product line. "We may not be Mattel,"[1] Hodgson explained, "but we do have our peace of mind."

The firm could still become a multiline operation, but if that ever happens, 10 it will be only after Hodgson conducts exhaustive marketing tests and utilizes other sophisticated procedures. He feels his first responsibility is to get Silly Putty into as many homes as he can; and even after all the years it's been around, there is still room for new sales.

It is generally recognized that the moldable goo is unique in the way it works. 11 While there have been numerous imitations, none of them has solved the technical bugs which Silly Putty engineers ironed out long ago.

How does it work? The company's chief engineer, Hubert "Dixie" Dean, 12 calls it a self-contradiction. Chemically it is a liquid, but it resembles a solid. The molecular structure will stretch if the substance is slowly pulled. But if tugged, it snaps apart. The toy has a rebound capacity of 75 to 80 percent (a rubber ball has only about a 50 percent bounce-back). On top of all that, it picks up newsprint, often sharper than the original. A silicon derivative, Silly Putty won't rot; it can withstand temperatures from -70 degrees Fahrenheit to hundreds of degrees above zero.

Despite the company's seeming willingness to talk about its first love, there 13 is considerable secrecy involved in the manufacture of the product. The location of the chief plant facilities remains under wraps, even after two decades. The only manufacturing details Hodgson will release about the toy substance is that it is produced somewhere near New Haven, Connecticut, in thousand-pound batches.

The secrecy is understandable, considering the amount of industrial espio- 14 nage in the American toy business. Since the constituents of Silly Putty are an open secret, the only thing the firm can protect is the know-how involved in

---

[1]Mattel: a large toy manufacturing company. [Eds.]

making the toy as good as it is. In this field Hodgson boasts that Silly Putty engineers are at least five years ahead of any competition.

A testament to the product's superiority was printed a few years ago in a   15
Chicago newspaper that had run a contest of letters from kids at camp. The winning entry came from a boy who got angry at his parents for sending him a knock-off of Silly Putty. "I wanted Silly Putty," he wrote them, "because you get twice as much and it's more fun."

Ironically, the "fun" product is the offshoot of second world war military   16
production. In 1945, General Electric was running a series of experiments at its New Haven silicone division. In answer to the war effort, the company hoped to come up with a viable synthetic rubber.

Silicone, a substance refined from sand, was in great abundance at the labo-   17
ratory. One day, a Scottish engineer named James Wright dropped some boric acid into a test tube containing silicone oil. When he examined the resultant compound, he found, to his amazement, that it bounced when thrown on the floor.

Accident number one: Silly Putty is born.   18

Meanwhile, Hodgson, a native of Montreal, was exploring the infant mar-   19
keting profession. Shortly after the 1929 crash, Hodgson left his family home in Norfolk, Virginia, and joined the Navy. After his hitch, he came to New York to work as an advertising copywriter and later headed a research team for *Look*. As he learned the techniques of marketing, Hodgson had the opportunity to sell everything from a presidential candidate (Wendell Willkie) to beer, food, and tires. After an unsuccessful stint as an independent marketing research consultant, he went to New Haven to join an ad agency. Six months later the job collapsed, and so did his marriage. It was the nadir of his career.

Accident number two: a New Haven toy shop hires Hodgson to publish its   20
catalog.

America had almost nothing in the way of a modern toy store before World   21
War II. Instead, playthings were sold primarily in department stores. However, with the first crop of war babies, shops began to spring up selling toys and other supplies to nursery schools and parents. One such store was the Block Shop in New Haven, then a one-woman operation run by the late Ruth Fallgatter, an Antioch psychology master who later became an executive at Creative Playthings.

The Block Shop, Hodgson recalled, was already doing a vigorous business.   22
Military families on the move kept subscribing to the store's catalog, giving it a worldwide following. Ruth Fallgatter introduced Hodgson to the toy business and left the new catalog up to him. While he was preparing it, he got the notion of including a page of toys for grown-ups.

Meanwhile, GE's mystery goo was becoming a conversation piece at local   23
cocktail parties. Ruth Fallgatter saw it, thought it amusing, and showed it to Hodgson.

THE TOY WITH ONE MOVING PART

"Everybody kept saying there was no earthly use for the stuff," he explained,   24
"but I watched them as they fooled with it. I couldn't help noticing how people
with busy schedules wasted as much as fifteen minutes at a shot just fondling
and stretching it. I decided to take a chance and sell some. We put an ad in
the catalog on the adult page along with such goodies as a spaghetti-making
machine. We packaged the goop in a clear compact case and tagged it at two
dollars."

At year's end, Hodgson found that Silly Putty, at twice its present price, and   25
even without a picture, outsold every toy in the catalog but one, a box of crayons.
He suggested that his employer should manufacture it, but she wasn't interested.
Hodgson obtained a release from her and decided to put it on the market himself.
It was not rash speculation, he later declared, for the figures were right in front
of him and he was convinced that Silly Putty was a winner.

Borrowing $147, Pete Hodgson ordered a batch of the putty from General   26
Electric and hired a Yale student to help him reduce it to one-ounce dabs. But
now they were faced with the problem of how to pack it.

Accident number three: Economic necessity forces Hodgson to encase his   27
product in plastic "eggs," which would be cheap and easy to ship in inexpensive
cartons from the Connecticut Cooperative Poultry Association.

Later, when the company was able to sit back and take a second look at its   28
packaging, another container was briefly tried. But top toy buyers protested
loudly, and Hodgson went back to the egg format. Something about the brightly
colored eggshells seemed to label the stuff inside as "fun."

Of course, it takes more than just a good idea in attractive wraps to make a   29
buck in the hard-nosed toy business. Hodgson had sunk all his capital into the
operating costs of the business, and there was no surplus for advertising. It took
a lot of arguing to get Silly Putty into any stores at all. Neiman Marcus in
Dallas tried it for Easter. Then in St. Louis, Doubleday ordered a few dozen
Silly Putty eggs on trial. A few weeks later, a second order came for a gross—
then the order was changed to two gross. The next day, the order was changed
to four gross. A week later, the manager of the New York Doubleday—who had
turned the toy down at first—reluctantly ordered "four dozen of those Silly Putty
things." One week after that, the store was selling five hundred a day and asking
for more.

With the celerity with which fads catch on in New York, Silly Putty—sitting   30
in the Doubleday windows at Fifty-second Street and Fifth Avenue—became
the "in" thing. But the real boom was yet to come.

One afternoon, a writer for the *New Yorker* dropped into the bookstore to   31
buy a present for a friend. He noticed the oddball substance on display, bought
a piece and began playing with it. He found it a fascinating way to relax and
became so enthralled with the product that he wrote almost a page of copy about
it for his magazine.

When that issue hit the newsstands, Pete Hodgson's telephone began to ring.   32
Three days later, when it finally quieted down, Hodgson found a quarter of a

115

million dollars' worth of orders sitting on his desk, some of them from as far away as Seattle and Havana.

Hodgson thought he was about to have the last laugh on industry pundits, but he still had some rough roads to travel. For one thing, chemical engineers familiar with the new technology of silicones were still scarce. Then a more serious thing happened to the company: the Korean War. The government suddenly clamped down on all defense-priority materials. By that time, silicone was usable as synthetic rubber and there was some fear that America's rubber source might be cut off. So Hodgson was left with fifteen hundred pounds of Silly Putty on his hands, tons of unfilled orders, and no immediate prospect of getting more raw material. By 1951, he was practically out of business. **33**

But just when toymen were sure they'd seen the last of the crazy glop, silicone was released for industrial use once more. By then, the market for Silly Putty was absolutely dead. **34**

"It took me two years to rebuild a demand for the toy," Hodgson said, "but I was damned well decided that I was going to do it again. People still wanted Silly Putty, but they couldn't find it in stores. I realized that if I was going to sell the buyers I'd first have to get people coming into their local toy stores asking for Silly Putty." **35**

Hodgson and his sales representatives started going directly to the people. Region by region, state by state, retailers would be contacted by mail. Then a field representative would go into the various stores and demonstrate Silly Putty to customers. The staff worked long and hard, and Hodgson figures he must have traveled to every state in the Union, many of them twice to demonstrate the substance. **36**

Eventually, the market picked up again, and Hodgson was able to supplant store demonstrations with local TV advertising. But the new Silly Putty, to Hodgson's surprise, was being bought mostly by children. The customer percentage at first was 80 percent adults, the rest kids. Then it turned completely around. According to Hodgson, children—some of them practically infants—would walk into toy stores and ask for Silly Putty by name. **37**

This reversal of market led to the toughest single problem the toy had to surmount: quality control. It took ten years to solve. **38**

The trouble was that parents couldn't trust kids to put the putty back into the eggshell container. Consequently, it was getting into everybody's hair—not to mention their clothes, rugs, and sofas. A gob dropped onto fabric would soak into the fibers and become absolutely inseparable. **39**

Hodgson's engineering staff worked on the stickiness problem throughout the nineteen-fifties. At last, in 1960, they cracked it, and the new nonsticky Silly Putty has been sold ever since. **40**

Today's Silly Putty, backed up with network and local TV ads, is a perennial favorite, accounting for a little better than 1 percent of annual sales in the average retail toy store. The company itself records about $6.5 million in sales per year. **41**

In the usual sense of the term, competition is no problem to Hodgson, thanks   42
to his staff's half-decade head start in technology. "Nothing else is Silly Putty,"
he says. "That's our biggest advertising slogan. But on the other hand, everything
that competes for the consumer's time and dollars could be considered as a form
of competition. This means anything from toys to Cadillacs to blondes. It is up
to those products to find their proper markets and stay out of ours. And vice
versa."

Today Silly Putty has become a household word. Newspaper critics have   43
likened Buddy Hackett's physique and Michael Pollard's face to it;[2] talk-show
hosts often allude to it, and some keep it handy to play with. A sportscaster
once referred to it in describing a badly mauled boxer. And Paul Krassner, editor
of *The Realist*, once presented his world vision, eschewing philosophical jargon,
in terms of Silly Putty.

Probably the most illustrious role Silly Putty has played in recent history was   44
aboard the Apollo 8 mission. A woman in Dallas who wanted the astronauts to
have unusual Christmas presents purchased three gobs of Silly Putty in sterling-
silver eggshells from Neiman Marcus at seventy-five dollars apiece. She thought
it would give the spacemen something to do in their spare time while in the
rocket, and also provide a convenient substance for sticking tools in place during
weightlessness.

The volume of free publicity Silly Putty has received over the years is so   45
huge (Hodgson estimates it would total millions of dollars if bought) that the
firm is extremely sensitive to the danger of the product's name becoming generic.
The company's public-relations agency spends plenty of time guarding against
use of the toy's name in lower case, even to the extent of sending offenders wry
letters in which everything *except* Silly Putty is uncapitalized. "The day that
Silly Putty loses its identity," says the agency, "is the day that the product loses
its trademark." And the day it loses its trademark is the day any firm can call
its product Silly Putty.

Why has Silly Putty become such a phenomenal success in the crowded toy   46
field, with gimmicky, expensive new playthings dazzling the youngster's eye at
every turn?

The answer is elementary: Silly Putty is as near as one can get to a perfect   47
toy.

"I've spent my life trying to define what a toy is," said Hodgson, "and I don't   48
think I'm any closer to finding out the answer. But whatever it takes to make a
great toy, Silly Putty has it!"

There is, of course, one obvious advantage that Silly Putty has over much   49
of the competition—simplicity. Without having to worry about complicated
instructions, any child can pitch right in and pull, yank, mold, or pound his
glob.

---

[2]Buddy Hackett's . . . Michael Pollard's: Hackett is a stout comedian; Pollard is a boyish-faced
actor. [Eds.]

Marvin Kaye

"All you have to do," said Hodgson, "is pop open the shell and go to it. It's 50 the toy with one moving part!"

QUESTIONS

1. The writer's purpose is to tell the story of Silly Putty. How does he organize his material? What function do his first fifteen paragraphs serve? Are there any indications that the writer has actually played with Silly Putty?

2. Nowhere in the article are we told why the toy was named "Silly Putty." Is this a serious omission?

3. Consider the popularity of Silly Putty. In marketing this toy, how well could the president of the company have predicted who would buy Silly Putty? What did he learn from the public? What did you learn about marketing and advertising from the Silly Putty experience?

4. What did you think of the toy business before you read this article? Did the article change your conception of this business in any way?

5. At the end of the article, Hodgson talks about the difficulty of defining what a toy is. Think of a toy you particularly loved as a small child. Consider why you loved it, and compare your response with the responses of your classmates. As a group, can you come closer to defining what a toy is than Hodgson did?

6. Watch some Saturday morning television. What kinds of toys are being advertised? To whom is the advertising directed: children, parents, or both? How would you describe the advertisers' attitudes toward children? How might a visitor from a foreign country interpret this aspect of American culture?

7. Do some research on a toy that's been popular for a long time, such as the Barbie Doll or G. I. Joe. Like the writer of this article, you may want to supplement information found in business and advertising magazines with an inquiry directed to the toy's manufacturer and with interviews of toy-store owners and children who play with this toy. Find out who created the toy, how it was promoted, and why it has been so popular. In considering the last point, the information gathered for questions 5 and 6 may be useful.

LOVE CANAL AND THE POISONING OF AMERICA
Michael Brown

Michael Brown is a free-lance writer interested in environmental issues. His investigations into the dumping of toxic waste, which have appeared in newspaper and magazine articles, have won him three Pulitzer Prize nominations and a special award from the Environmental Protection Agency. This essay is taken from his book Laying Waste: The Poisoning of America by Toxic Chemicals *(1980).*

Niagara Falls is a city of unmatched natural beauty; it is also a tired industrial workhorse, beaten often and with a hard hand. A magnificent river—a strait, really—connecting Lake Erie to Lake Ontario flows hurriedly north, at a pace of a half-million tons a minute, widening into a smooth expanse near the city before breaking into whitecaps and taking its famous 186-foot plunge. Then it cascades through a gorge of overhung shale and limestone to rapids higher and swifter than anywhere else on the continent. 1

The falls attract long lines of newlyweds and other tourists. At the same time, the river provides cheap electricity for industry; a good stretch of its shore is now filled with the spiraled pipes of distilleries, and the odors of chlorine and sulfides hang in the air. 2

Many who live in the city of Niagara Falls work in chemical plants, the largest of which is owned by the Hooker Chemical Company, a subsidiary of Occidental Petroleum since the 1960s. Timothy Schroeder did not. He was a cement technician by trade, dealing with the factories only if they needed a pathway poured, or a small foundation set. Tim and his wife, Karen, lived in a ranch-style home with a brick and wood exterior at 460 99th Street. One of the Schroeders' most cherished purchases was a Fiberglas pool, built into the ground and enclosed by a red-wood fence. 3

Karen looked from a back window one morning in October 1974, noting with distress that the pool had suddenly risen two feet above the ground. She called Tim to tell him about it. Karen then had no way of knowing that this was the first sign of what would prove to be a punishing family and economic tragedy. 4

Mrs. Schroeder believed that the cause of the uplift was the unusual ground-water flow of the area. Twenty-one years before, an abandoned hydroelectric 5 canal directly behind their house had been backfilled with industrial rubble. The underground breaches created by this disturbance, aided by the marshland nature of the region's surficial layer, collected large volumes of rainfall and undermined the back yard. The Schroeders allowed the pool to remain in its precarious position until the following summer and then pulled it from the ground, intending to pour a new pool, cast in cement. This they were unable to do, for the gaping excavation immediately filled with what Karen called "chemical water," rancid liquids of yellow and orchid and blue. These same chemicals had mixed with the groundwater and flooded the entire yard, attacking the redwood posts with such a caustic bite that one day the fence simply collapsed. When the chemicals receded in the dry weather, they left the gardens and shrubs withered and scorched, as if by a brush fire.

How the chemicals got there was no mystery. In the late 1930s, or perhaps early 1940s, the Hooker Company, whose many processes included the manufacture of pesticides, plasticizers, and caustic soda, began using the abandoned canal as a dump for at least 20,000 tons of waste residues—"still-bottoms," in the language of the trade. 6

Karen Schroeder's parents had been the first to experience problems with the canal's seepage. In 1959, her mother, Aileen Voorhees, encountered a strange black sludge bleeding through the basement walls. For the next twenty years, she and her husband, Edwin, tried various methods of halting the irritating intrusion, pasting the cinder-block wall with sealants and even constructing a gutter along the walls to intercept the inflow. Nothing could stop the chemical smell from permeating the entire household, and neighborhood calls to the city for help were fruitless. One day, when Edwin punched a hole in the wall to see what was happening, quantities of black liquid poured from the block. The cinder blocks were full of the stuff. 7

More ominous than the Voorhees basement was an event that occurred at 11:12 P.M. on November 21, 1968, when Karen Schroeder gave birth to her third child, a seven-pound girl named Sheri. No sense of elation filled the delivery room. The child was born with a heart that beat irregularly and had a hole in it, bone blockages of the nose, partial deafness, deformed ear exteriors, and a cleft palate. Within two years, the Schroeders realized Sheri was also mentally retarded. When her teeth came in, a double row of them appeared on her lower jaw. And she developed an enlarged liver. 8

The Schroeders considered these health problems, as well as illnesses among their other children, as acts of capricious genes—a vicious quirk of nature. Like Mrs. Schroeder's parents, they were concerned that the chemicals were devaluing their property. The crab apple tree and evergreens in the back were dead, and even the oak in front of the home was sick; one year, the leaves had fallen off on Father's Day. 9

The canal had been dug with much fanfare in the late nineteenth century by a flamboyant entrepreneur named William T. Love, who wanted to construct 10 an industrial city with ready access to water power and major markets. The setting for Love's dream was to be a navigable power channel that would extend seven miles from the Upper Niagara before falling two hundred feet, circumventing the treacherous falls and at the same time providing cheap power. A city would be constructed near the point where the canal fed back into the river, and he promised it would accommodate half a million people.

So taken with his imagination were the state's leaders that they gave Love a free hand to condemn as much property as he liked, and to divert whatever amounts of water. Love's dream, however, proved grander than his resources, and he was eventually forced to abandon the project after a mile-long trench, ten to forty feet deep and generally twenty yards wide, had been scoured perpendicular to the Niagara River. Eventually, the trench was purchased by Hooker. 11

Few of those who, in 1977, lived in the numerous houses that had sprung up by the site were aware that the large and barren field behind them was a burial ground for toxic waste. Both the Niagara County Health Department and the city said it was a nuisance condition, but no serious danger to the people. Officials of the Hooker Company refused comment, claiming only that they had no records of the chemical burials and that the problem was not their responsibility. Indeed, Hooker had deeded the land to the Niagara Falls Board of Education in 1953, for a token $1. With it the company issued no detailed warnings of the chemicals, only a brief paragraph in the quitclaim document that disclaimed company liability for any injuries or deaths which might occur at the site. 12

Though Hooker was undoubtedly relieved to rid itself of the contaminated land, the company was so vague about the hazards involved that one might have thought the wastes would cause harm only if touched, because they irritated the skin; otherwise, they were not of great concern. In reality, as the company must have known, the dangers of these wastes far exceeded those of acids or alkalines or inert salts. We now know that the drums Hooker had dumped in the canal contained a veritable witch's brew—compounds of truly remarkable toxicity. There were solvents that attacked the heart and liver, and residues from pesticides so dangerous that their commercial sale was shortly thereafter restricted outright by the government; some of them were already suspected of causing cancer. 13

Yet Hooker gave no hint of that. When the board of education, which wanted the parcel for a new school, approached Hooker, B. Klaussen, at the time Hooker's executive vice president, said in a letter to the board. "Our officers have carefully considered your request. We are very conscious of the need for new elementary schools and realize that the sites must be carefully selected. We will be willing to donate the entire strip of property which we own between Colvin Boulevard and Frontier Avenue to be used for the erection of a school at a location to be determined. . . ." 14

The board built the school and playground at the canal's midsection. Construction progressed despite the contractor's hitting a drainage trench that gave off a strong chemical odor and the discovery of a waste pit nearby. Instead of halting the work, the authorities simply moved the school eighty feet away. Young families began to settle in increasing numbers alongside the dump, many of them having been told that the field was to be a park and recreation area for their children.

Children found the "playground" interesting, but at times painful. They sneezed, and their eyes teared. In the days when the dumping was still in progress, they swam at the opposite end of the canal, occasionally arriving home with hard pimples all over their bodies. Hooker knew children were playing on its spoils. In 1958, three children were burned by exposed residues on the canal's surface, much of which, according to residents, had been covered with nothing more than fly ash and loose dirt. Because it wished to avoid legal repercussions, the company chose not to issue a public warning of the dangers it knew were there, nor to have its chemists explain to the people that their homes would have been better placed elsewhere.

The Love Canal was simply unfit as a container for hazardous substances, poor even by the standards of the day, and now, in 1977, local authorities were belatedly finding that out. Several years of heavy snowfall and rain had filled the sparingly covered channel like a bathtub. The contents were overflowing at a frightening rate.

The city of Niagara Falls, I was assured, was planning a remedial drainage program to halt in some measure the chemical migration off the site. But no sense of urgency had been attached to the plan, and it was stalled in red tape. No one could agree on who should pay the bill—the city, Hooker, or the board of education—and engineers seemed confused over what exactly needed to be done.

Niagara Falls City Manager Donald O'Hara persisted in his view that, however displeasing to the eyes and nose, the Love Canal was not a crisis matter, mainly a question of aesthetics. O'Hara reminded me that Dr. Francis Clifford, county health commissioner, supported that opinion.

With the city, the board, and Hooker unwilling to commit themselves to a remedy, conditions degenerated in the area between 97th and 99th streets, until, by early 1978, the land was a quagmire of sludge that oozed from the canal's every pore. Melting snow drained the surface soot onto the private yards, while on the dump itself the ground had softened to the point of collapse, exposing the crushed tops of barrels. Beneath the surface, masses of sludge were finding their way out at a quickening rate, constantly forming springs of contaminated liquid. The Schroeder back yard, once featured in a local newspaper for its beauty, had reached the point where it was unfit even to walk upon. Of course, the Schroeders could not leave. No one would think of buying the property. They still owed on their mortgage and, with Tim's salary, could not afford to

15

16

17

18

19

20

maintain the house while they moved into a safer setting. They and their four children were stuck.

Apprehension about large costs was not the only reason the city was reluctant 21
to help the Schroeders and the one hundred or so other families whose properties abutted the covered trench. The city may also have feared distressing Hooker. To an economically depressed area, the company provided desperately needed employment—as many as 3000 blue-collar jobs and a substantial number of tax dollars. Hooker was speaking of building a $17 million headquarters in downtown Niagara Falls. So anxious were city officials to receive the new building that they and the state granted the company highly lucrative tax and loan incentives, and made available to the firm a prime parcel of property near the most popular tourist park on the American side.

City Manager O'Hara and other authorities were aware of the nature of 22
Hooker's chemicals. In fact, in the privacy of his office, O'Hara, after receiving a report on the chemical tests at the canal, had informed the people at Hooker that it was an extremely serious problem. Even earlier, in 1976, the New York State Department of Environmental Conservation had been made aware that dangerous compounds were present in the basement sump pump of at least one 97th Street home, and soon after, its own testing had revealed that highly injurious halogenated hydrocarbons were flowing from the canal into adjoining sewers. Among them were the notorious PCBs; quantities as low as one part PCBs to a million parts normal water were enough to create serious environmental concerns; in the sewers of Niagara Falls, the quantities of halogenated compounds were thousands of times higher. The other materials tracked, in sump pumps or sewers, were just as toxic as PCBs, or more so. Prime among the more hazardous ones was residue from hexachlorocyclopentadiene, or C-56, which was deployed as an intermediate in the manufacture of several pesticides. In certain dosages, the chemical could damage every organ in the body.

While the mere presence of C-56 should have been cause for alarm, gov- 23
ernment remained inactive. Not until early 1978—a full eighteen months after C-56 was first detected—was testing conducted in basements along 97th and 99th streets to see if the chemicals had vaporized off the sump pumps and walls and were present in the household air.

While the basement tests were in progress, the rains of spring arrived at the 24
canal, further worsening the situation. Heavier fumes rose above the barrels. More than before, the residents were suffering from headaches, respiratory discomforts, and skin ailments. Many of them felt constantly fatigued and irritable, and the children had reddened eyes. In the Schroeder home, Tim developed a rash along the backs of his legs. Karen could not rid herself of throbbing pains in her head. Their daughter, Laurie, seemed to be losing some of her hair.

The EPA test revealed that benzene, a known cause of cancer in humans, 25
had been readily detected in the household air up and down the streets. A widely used solvent, benzene was known in chronic-exposure cases to cause

123

headaches, fatigue, loss of weight, and dizziness followed by pallor, nose-bleeds, and damage to the bone marrow.

No public announcement was made of the benzene hazard. Instead, officials 26 appeared to shield the finding until they could agree among themselves on how to present it.

Dr. Clifford, the county health commissioner, seemed unconcerned by the 27 detection of benzene in the air. His health department refused to conduct a formal study of the people's health, despite the air-monitoring results. For this reason, and because of the resistance growing among the local authorities, I went to the southern end of 99th Street to take an informal health survey of my own. I arranged a meeting with six neighbors, all of them instructed beforehand to list the illnesses they were aware of on their block, with names and ages specified for presentation at the session.

The residents' list was startling. Though unafflicted before they moved there, 28 many people were now plagued with ear infections, nervous disorders, rashes, and headaches. One young man, James Gizzarelli, said he had missed four months of work owing to breathing troubles. His wife was suffering epileptic-like seizures which her doctor was unable to explain. Meanwhile, freshly applied paint was inexplicably peeling from the exterior of their house. Pets too were suffering, most seriously if they had been penned in the back yards nearest to the canal, constantly breathing air that smelled like mothballs and weedkiller. They lost their fur, exhibited skin lesions, and, while still quite young, developed internal tumors. A great many cases of cancer were reported among the women, along with much deafness. On both 97th and 99th streets, traffic signs warned passing motorists to watch for deaf children playing near the road.

Evidence continued to mount that a large group of people, perhaps all of 29 the one hundred families immediately by the canal, perhaps many more, were in imminent danger. While watching television, while gardening or doing a wash, in their sleeping hours, they were inhaling a mixture of damaging chemicals. Their hours of exposure were far longer than those of a chemical factory worker, and they wore no respirators or goggles. Nor could they simply open a door and escape. Helplessness and despair were the main responses to the blackened craters and scattered cinders behind their back yards.

But public officials often characterized the residents as hypochondriacs. Every 30 agent of government had been called on the phone or sent pleas for help, but none offered aid.

Commissioner Clifford expressed irritation at my printed reports of illness, 31 and disagreement began to surface in the newsroom on how the stories should be printed. "There's a high rate of cancer among my friends," Dr. Clifford argued. "It doesn't mean anything."

Yet as interest in the small community increased, further revelations shook 32 the neighborhood. In addition to the benzene, eighty or more other compounds were found in the makeshift dump, ten of them potential carcinogens. The physiological effects they could cause were profound and diverse. At least fourteen of them could impact on the brain and central nervous system. Two of them, carbon tetrachloride and chlorobenzene, could readily cause narcotic or anesthetic consequences. Many others were known to cause headaches, seizures, loss of hair, anemia, or skin rashes. Together, the compounds were capable of inflicting innumerable illnesses, and no one knew what new concoctions were being formulated by their mixture underground.

Edwin and Aileen Voorhees had the most to be concerned about. When a state 33 biophysicist analyzed the air content of their basement, he determined that the safe exposure time there was less than 2.4 minutes—the toxicity in the basement was thousands of times the acceptable limit for twenty-four-hour breathing. This did not mean they would necessarily become permanently ill, but their chances of contracting cancer, for example, had been measurably increased. In July, I visited Mrs. Voorhees for further discussion of her problems, and as we sat in the kitchen, drinking coffee, the industrial odors were apparent. Aileen, usually chipper and feisty, was visibly anxious. She stared down at the table, talking only in a lowered voice. Everything now looked different to her. The home she and Edwin had built had become their jail cell. Their yard was but a pathway through which toxicants entered the cellar walls. The field out back, that proposed "park," seemed destined to be the ruin of their lives.

On July 14 I received a call from the state health department with some 34 shocking news. A preliminary review showed that women living at the southern end had suffered a high rate of miscarriages and had given birth to an abnormally high number of children with birth defects. In one age group, 35.3 percent had records of spontaneous abortions. That was far in excess of the norm. The odds against it happening by chance were 250 to one. These tallies, it was stressed, were "conservative" figures. Four children in one small section of the neighborhood had documentable birth defects, club feet, retardation, and deafness. Those who lived there the longest suffered the highest rates.

The data on miscarriages and birth defects, coupled with the other accounts 35 of illness, finally pushed the state's bureaucracy into motion. A meeting was scheduled for August 2, at which time the state health commissioner, Dr. Robert Whalen, would formally address the issue. The day before the meeting, Dr. Nicholas Vianna, a state epidemiologist, told me that residents were also incurring some degree of liver damage. Blood analyses had shown hepatitis-like symptoms in enzyme levels. Dozens if not hundreds of people, apparently, had been adversely affected.

In Albany, on August 2, Dr. Whalen read a lengthy statement in which he 36 urged that pregnant women and children under two years of age leave the southern end of the dump site immediately. He declared the Love Canal an official emergency, citing it as a "great and imminent peril to the health of the general public."

125

When Commissioner Whalen's words hit 97th and 99th streets, by way of   37
one of the largest banner headlines in the Niagara *Gazette*'s 125-year history,
dozens of people massed on the streets, shouting into bullhorns and micro-
phones to voice frustrations that had been accumulating for months. Many of
them vowed a tax strike because their homes were rendered unmarketable and
unsafe. They attacked their government for ignoring their welfare. A man of
high authority, a physician with a title, had confirmed that their lives were in
danger. Most wanted to leave the neighborhood immediately.

Terror and anger roiled together, exacerbated by Dr. Whalen's failure to   38
provide a government-funded evacuation plan. His words were only a recommendation: individual families had to choose whether to risk their health and
remain, or abandon their houses and, in so doing, write off a lifetime of work
and savings.

On August 3, Dr. Whalen decided he should speak to the people. He arrived   39
with Dr. David Axelrod, a deputy who had directed the state's investigation,
and Thomas Frey, a key aide to Governor Hugh Carey.

At a public meeting, held in the 99th Street School auditorium, Frey was   40
given the grueling task of controlling the crowd of 500 angry and frightened
people. In an attempt to calm them, he announced that a meeting between the
state and the White House had been scheduled for the following week. The
state would propose that the Love Canal be classified a national disaster, thereby
freeing federal funds. For now, however, he could promise no more. Neither
could Dr. Whalen and his staff of experts. All they could say was what was
already known: twenty-five organic compounds, some of them capable of causing cancer, were in their homes, and because young children were especially
prone to toxic effects, they should be moved to another area.

Dr. Whalen's order had applied only to those living at the canal's southern   41
end, on its immediate periphery. But families living across the street from the
dump site, or at the northern portion, where the chemicals were not so visible
at the surface, reported afflictions remarkably similar to those suffered by families
whose yards abutted the southern end. Serious respiratory problems, nervous
disorders, and rectal bleeding were reported by many who were not covered by
the order.

Throughout the following day, residents posted signs of protest on their front   42
fences or porch posts. "Love Canal Kills," they said, or "Give Me Liberty, I've
Got Death." Emotionally exhausted and uncertain about their future, men
stayed home from work, congregating on the streets or comforting their wives.
By this time the board of education had announced it was closing the 99th
Street School for the following year, because of its proximity to the exposed
toxicants. Still, no public relief was provided for the residents.

Another meeting was held that evening, at a firehall on 102nd Street. It was   43
unruly, but the people, who had called the session in an effort to organize
themselves, managed to form an alliance, the Love Canal Homeowners Asso-

ciation, and to elect as president Lois Gibbs, a pretty, twenty-seven-year-old woman with jet-black hair who proved remarkably adept at dealing with experienced politicians and at keeping the matter in the news. After Mrs. Gibbs' election, Congressman John LaFalce entered the hall and announced, to wild applause, that the Federal Disaster Assistance Administration would be represented the next morning, and that the state's two senators, Daniel Patrick Moynihan and Jacob Javits, were working with him in an attempt to get funds from Congress.

With the Love Canal story now attracting attention from the national media, the Governor's office announced that Hugh Carey would be at the 99th Street School on August 7 to address the people. Decisions were being made in Albany and Washington. Hours before the Governor's arrival, a sudden burst of "urgent" reports from Washington came across the newswires. President Jimmy Carter had officially declared the Hooker dump site a national emergency. 44

Hugh Carey was applauded on his arrival. The Governor announced that the state, through its Urban Development Corporation, planned to purchase, at fair market value, those homes rendered uninhabitable by the marauding chemicals. He spared no promises. "You will not have to make mortgage payments on homes you don't want or cannot occupy. Don't worry about the banks. The state will take care of them." By the standards of Niagara Falls, where the real estate market was depressed, the houses were in the middle-class range, worth from $20,000 to $40,000 apiece. The state would assess each house and purchase it, and also pay the costs of moving, temporary housing during the transition period, and special items not covered by the usual real estate assessment, such as installation of telephones. 45

First in a trickle and then, by September, in droves, the families gathered their belongings and carted them away. Moving vans crowded 97th and 99th streets. Linesmen went from house to house disconnecting the telephones and electrical wires, while carpenters pounded plywood over the windows to keep vandals away. By the following spring, 237 families were gone; 170 of them had moved into new houses. In time the state erected around a six-block residential area a green chain-link fence, eight feet in height, clearly demarcating the contamination zone. 46

In October 1978, the long-awaited remedial drainage program began at the south end. Trees were uprooted, fences and garages torn down, and swimming pools removed from the area. So great were residents' apprehensions that dangerous fumes would be released over the surrounding area that the state, at a cost of $500,000, placed seventy-five buses at emergency evacuation pickup spots during the months of work, in the event that outlying homes had to be vacated quickly because of an explosion. The plan was to construct drain tiles around the channel's periphery, where the back yards had been located, in order to divert leakage to seventeen-foot-deep wet wells from which contaminated 47

127

groundwater could be drawn and treated by filtration through activated carbon. (Removing the chemicals themselves would have been financially prohibitive, perhaps costing as much as $100 million—and even then the materials would have to be buried elsewhere.) After the trenching was complete, and the sewers installed, the canal was to be covered by a sloping mound of clay and planted with grass. One day, city officials hoped, the wasteland would become a park.

In spite of the corrective measures and the enormous effort by the state health 48 department, which took thousands of blood samples from past and current residents and made uncounted analyses of soil, water, and air, the full range of the effects remained unknown. In neighborhoods immediately outside the official "zone of contamination," more than 500 families were left near the desolate setting, their health still in jeopardy. The state announced it would buy no more homes.

The first public indication that chemical contamination had probably reached 49 streets to the east and west of 97th and 99th streets, and to the north and south as well, came on August 11, 1978, when sump-pump samples I had taken from 100th and 101st streets, analyzed in a laboratory, showed the trace presence of a number of chemicals found in the canal itself, including lindane, a restricted pesticide that had been suspected of causing cancer in laboratory animals. While probing 100th Street, I had knocked on the door of Patricia Pino, thirty-four, a blond divorcee with a young son and daughter. I had noticed that some of the leaves on a large tree in front of her house exhibited a black oiliness much like that on the trees and shrubs of 99th Street; she was located near what had been a drainage swale.

After I had extracted a jar of sediment from her sump pump for the analysis, 50 we conversed about her family situation and what the trauma now unfolding meant to them. Ms. Pino was extremely depressed and embittered. Both of her children had what appeared to be slight liver abnormalities, and her son had been plagued with "non-specific" allergies, teary eyes, sinus trouble, which improved markedly when he was sent away from home. Patricia told of times, during the heat of summer, when fumes were readily noticeable in her basement and sometimes even upstairs. She herself had been treated for a possibly cancerous condition on her cervix. But, like others, her family was now trapped.

On September 24, 1978, I obtained a state memorandum that said chemical 51 infiltration of the outer regions was significant indeed. The letter, sent from the state laboratories to the U.S. Environmental Protection Agency, said, "Preliminary analysis of soil samples demonstrates extensive migration of potentially toxic materials outside the immediate canal area." There it was, in the state's own words. Not long afterward, the state medical investigator, Dr. Nicholas Vianna, reported indications that residents from 93rd to 103rd streets might also have incurred liver damage.

On October 4, a young boy, John Allen Kenny, who lived quite a distance 52 north of the evacuation zone, died. The fatality was due to the failure of another organ that can be readily affected by toxicants, the kidney. Naturally, suspicions were raised that his death was in some way related to a creek that still flowed behind his house and carried, near an outfall, the odor of chlorinated compounds. Because the creek served as a catch basin for a portion of the Love Canal, the state studied an autopsy of the boy. No conclusions were reached. John Allen's parents, Norman, a chemist, and Luella, a medical research assistant, were unsatisfied with the state's investigation, which they felt was "superficial." Luella said, "He played in the creek all the time. There had been restrictions on the older boys, but he was the youngest and played with them when they were old enough to go to the creek. We let him do what the other boys did. He died of nephrosis. Proteins were passing through his urine. Well, in reading the literature, we discovered that chemicals can trigger this. There was no evidence of infection, which there should have been, and there was damage to his thymus and brain. He also had nosebleeds and headaches, and dry heaves. So our feeling is that chemicals probably triggered it."

The likelihood that water-carried chemicals had escaped from the canal's deteriorating bounds and were causing problems quite a distance from the site was not lost upon the Love Canal Homeowners Association and its president, Lois Gibbs, who was attempting to have additional families relocated. Because she lived on 101st Street, she was one of those left behind, with no means of moving despite persistent medical difficulties in her six-year-old son, Michael, who had been operated on twice for urethral strictures. [Mrs. Gibbs' husband, a worker at a chemical plant, brought home only $150 a week, she told me, and when they subtracted from that the $90 a week for food and other necessities, clothing costs for their two children, $125 a month for mortgage payments and taxes, utility and phone expenses, and medical bills, they had hardly enough cash to buy gas and cigarettes, let alone vacate their house.]

Assisted by two other stranded residents, Marie Pozniak and Grace McCoulf, and with the professional analysis of a Buffalo scientist named Beverly Paigen, Lois Gibbs mapped out the swale and creekbed areas, many of them long ago filled, and set about interviewing the numerous people who lived on or near formerly wet ground. The survey indicated that these people were suffering from an abnormal number of kidney and bladder aggravations and problems of the reproductive system. In a report to the state, Dr. Paigen claimed to have found, in 245 homes outside the evacuation zone, thirty-four miscarriages, eighteen birth defects, nineteen nervous breakdowns, ten cases of epilepsy, and high rates of hyperactivity and suicide.

In their roundabout way, the state health experts, after an elaborate investigation, confirmed some of the homeowners' worst fears. On February 8, 1979, Dr. David Axelrod, who by then had been appointed health commissioner, and whose excellence as a scientist was widely acknowledged, issued a new order that officially extended the health emergency of the previous August, citing high incidences of birth deformities and miscarriages in the areas where creeks and swales had once flowed, or where swamps had been. With that, the state offered to evacuate temporarily those families with pregnant women or children under the age of two from the outer areas of contamination, up to 103rd Street. But no additional homes would be purchased; nor was another large-scale evacuation, temporary or otherwise, under consideration. Those who left under the new plan would have to return when their children passed the age limit.

Twenty-three families accepted the state's offer. Another seven families, ineligible under the plan but of adequate financial means to do so, simply left their homes and took the huge loss of investment. Soon boarded windows speckled the outlying neighborhoods. 56

The previous November and December, not long after the evacuation of 97th and 99th streets, I became interested in the possibility that Hooker might have buried in the Love Canal waste residues from the manufacture of what is known as 2,4,5-trichlorophenol. My curiosity was keen because I knew that this substance, which Hooker produced for the manufacture of the antibacterial agent hexachlorophene, and which was also used to make defoliants such as Agent Orange, the herbicide employed in Vietnam, carries with it an unwanted by-product technically called 2,3,7,8-tetrachlorodibenzo-para-dioxin, or tetra dioxin. The potency of dioxin of this isomer is nearly beyond imagination. Although its toxicological effects are not fully known, the few experts on the subject estimate that if three ounces were evenly distributed and subsequently ingested among a million people, or perhaps more than that, all of them would die. It compares in toxicity to the botulinum toxin. On skin contact, dioxin causes a disfiguration called "chloracne," which begins as pimples, lesions, and cysts, but can lead to calamitous internal damage. Some scientists suspect that dioxin causes cancer, perhaps even malignancies that occur, in galloping fashion, within a short time of contact. At least two (some estimates went as high as eleven) pounds of dioxin were dispersed over Seveso, Italy, in 1976, after an explosion at a trichlorophenol plant: dead animals littered the streets, and more than 300 acres of land were immediately evacuated. In Vietnam, the spraying of Agent Orange, because of the dioxin contaminant, was banned in 1970, when the first effects on human beings began to surface, including dioxin's powerful teratogenic, or fetus-deforming, effects. 57

I posed two questions concerning trichlorophenol: Were wastes from the process buried in the canal? If so, what were the quantities? 58

On November 8, before Hooker answered my queries, I learned that, indeed, trichlorophenol had been found in liquids pumped from the remedial drain ditches. No dioxin had been found yet, and some officials, ever wary of more emotionalism among the people, argued that, because the compound was not soluble in water, there was little chance it had migrated off-site. Officials at Newco Chemical Waste Systems, a local waste disposal firm, at the same time claimed that if dioxin had been there, it had probably been photolytically destroyed. Its half-life, they contended, was just a few short years. 59

130

I knew from Whiteside, however, that in every known case, waste from 2,4,5- 60
trichlorophenol carried dioxin with it. I also knew that dioxin *could* become
soluble in groundwater and migrate into the neighborhood upon mixing with
solvents such as benzene. Moreover, because it had been buried, sunlight would
not break it down.

On Friday, November 10, I called Hooker again to urge that they answer 61
my questions. Their spokesman, Bruce Davis, came to the phone and, in a
controlled tone, gave me the answer: His firm had indeed buried trichlorophenol
in the canal—200 tons of it.

Immediately I called Whiteside. His voice took on an urgent tone. According 62
to his calculation, if 200 tons of trichlorophenol were there, in all likelihood
they were accompanied by 130 pounds of tetra dioxin, an amount equaling the
estimated total content of dioxin in the thousands of tons of Agent Orange rained
upon Vietnamese jungles. The seriousness of the crisis had deepened, for now
the Love Canal was not only a dump for highly dangerous solvents and pesticides; it was also the broken container for one of the most toxic substances ever
synthesized by man.

I reckoned that the main danger was to those working on the remedial project, 63
digging in the trenches. The literature on dioxin indicated that, even in quantities at times too small to detect, the substance possessed vicious characteristics.
In one case, workers in a trichlorophenol plant had developed chloracne, although the substance could not be traced on the equipment with which they
worked. The mere tracking of minuscule amounts of dioxin on a pedestrian's
shoes in Seveso led to major concerns, and, according to Whiteside, a plant in
Amsterdam, upon being found contaminated with dioxin, had been "disman-
tled, brick by brick, and the material embedded in concrete, loaded at a specially
constructed dock, on ships, and dumped at sea, in deep water near the Azores."
Workers in trichlorophenol plants had died of cancer or severe liver damage,
or had suffered emotional and sexual disturbances.

Less than a month after the first suspicions arose, on the evening of December 64
9, I received a call from Dr. Axelrod. "We found it. The dioxin. In a drainage
trench behind 97th Street. It was in the part-per-trillion range."

The state remained firm in its plans to continue the construction, and, despite 65
the ominous new findings, no further evacuations were announced. During the
next several weeks, small incidents of vandalism occurred along 97th and 99th
streets. Tacks were spread on the road, causing numerous flat tires on the trucks.
Signs of protest were hung in the school. Meetings of the Love Canal Homeowners Association became more vociferous. Christmas was near, and in the
association's office at the 99th Street School, a holiday tree was decorated with
bulbs arranged to spell "DIOXIN."

The Love Canal people chanted and cursed at meetings with the state offi- 66
cials, cried on the telephone, burned an effigy of the health commissioner,
traveled to Albany with a makeshift child's coffin, threatened to hold officials

131

hostage, sent letters and telegrams to the White House, held days of mourning and nights of prayer. On Mother's Day this year, they marched down the industrial corridor and waved signs denouncing Hooker, which had issued not so much as a statement of remorse. But no happy ending was in store for them. The federal government was clearly not planning to come to their rescue, and the state felt it had already done more than its share. City Hall was silent and remains silent today. Some residents still hoped that, miraculously, an agency of government would move them. All of them watched with anxiety as each newborn came to the neighborhood, and they looked at their bodies for signs of cancer.

One hundred and thirty families from the Love Canal area began leaving   67
their homes last August and September, seeking temporary refuge in local hotel rooms under a relocation plan funded by the state which had been implemented after fumes became so strong, during remedial trenching operations, that the United Way abandoned a care center it had opened in the neighborhood.

As soon as remedial construction is complete, the people will probably be   68
forced to return home, as the state will no longer pay for their lodging. Some have threatened to barricade themselves in the hotels. Some have mentioned violence. Anne Hillis of 102nd Street, who told reporters her first child had been born so badly decomposed that doctors could not determine its sex, was so bitter that she threw table knives and a soda can at the state's on-site coordinator.

In October, Governor Carey announced that the state probably would buy   69
an additional 200 to 240 homes, at an expense of some $5 million. In the meantime, lawyers have prepared lawsuits totaling about $2.65 billion and have sought court action for permanent relocation. Even if the latter action is successful, and they are allowed to move, the residents' plight will not necessarily have ended. The psychological scars are bound to remain among them and their children, along with the knowledge that, because they have already been exposed, they may never fully escape the Love Canal's insidious grasp.

QUESTIONS

1. What caused the poisoning of Love Canal? Why did it take so long for both local and state officials to acknowledge the seriousness of the condition of Love Canal?

2. What kind of information does Brown provide to document the tragedy of Love Canal? What role did he play in uncovering this information?

3. Consider the introduction to this article. Why did the writer choose to tell the story of the Schroeder family in the opening paragraphs?

4. The power of this essay has much to do with the overwhelming tragedy and horror it relates. Find passages in the essay that you feel are especially effective. Explain how the writer creates this effect on the reader.

5. In this essay, the writer relies primarily on the factual data he has collected to tell

the story of Love Canal. Compare this writer's approach with that found in newspapers featuring sensational headlines. Analyze one of the headlined stories. How much factual evidence is present? How would such a newspaper's treatment of the story of the Schroeder family differ from Brown's treatment?

6. Environmental calamities such as Love Canal or Three Mile Island have become a permanent part of our lives. The Environmental Protection Agency reports that in most communities the groundwater has become so laced with toxic chemicals that it is no longer safe to drink. Investigate some aspect of the environment in your community such as the water supply or the quality of the air. Write a report based on your investigation.

Sciences and Technologies

THE END OF THE SCOPES TRIAL
New York Times

John Scopes, a public-school biology teacher in Dayton, Tennessee, had in the spring of 1925 violated a new state law by teaching the theory of evolution. What might have been a simple court case grew into a major conflict between science and fundamentalist religion when liberal attorney Clarence Darrow joined the defense and Democratic politician William Jennings Bryan joined the prosecution. Scopes was virtually forgotten as these two famous lawyers turned the trial into what we would call today a "media event." The following article appeared on the front page of the New *York Times of July 22, 1925, with the headline, "SCOPES GUILTY, FINED $100, SCORES LAW."*

Special to the New York Times (July 22, 1925)

DAYTON, Tenn., July 21st—The trial of John Thomas Scopes for teaching 1 evolution in Tennessee, which Clarence Darrow characterised today as "the first case of its kind since we stopped trying people for witchcraft,"[1] is over. Mr. Scopes was found guilty and fined $100, and his counsel will appeal to the Supreme Court of Tennessee for reversal of the verdict. The scene will then be

---

[1]Clarence Darrow (1857–1938): American labor lawyer and criminal lawyer; he defended Scopes. [Eds.]

shifted from Dayton to Knoxville, where the case will probably come up on the first Monday in September.

But the end of the trial did not end the battle on evolution, for not long after its conclusion William Jennings Bryan opened fire on Clarence Darrow with a strong statement and a list of nine questions on the basic principles of the Christian religion.[2] To them Mr. Darrow replied and added a statement explaining Mr. Bryan's "rabies." Dudley Field Malone also contributed a statement predicting ultimate victory for evolution and repeating that Mr. Bryan ran away from the fight.

The end of the trial came as unexpectedly as anything else in this trial, in which nothing has happened according to schedule except the opening of court each morning with a prayer. It was reached practically by agreement between counsel in an effort to end the case, which showed signs of going on forever, although all the testimony offered before the jury took only two hours.

Young Scopes, in his shirt sleeves, his collar open at the neck, his carrot-colored hair brushed back, stood up before the bar with a gold epauletted policeman beside him, and Judge Raulston had pronounced sentence before his counsel could suggest that Mr. Scopes might have something to say.

"Oh," exclaimed Judge Raulston, "Have you anything to say, Mr. Scopes, as to why the Court should not impose punishment upon you?"

SCOPES CALLS STATUTE UNJUST.

Mr. Scopes, who is hardly more than a boy and whose pleasant demeanor and modest bearing have won him many friends since this case started, was nervous. His voice trembled a little as he folded his arms and said:

"Your Honor, I feel that I have been convicted of violating an unjust statute. I will continue in the future, as I have in the past, to oppose the law in any way I can. Any other action would be in violation of my ideal of academic freedom, that is, to teach the truth as guaranteed in our Constitution, of personal and religious freedom. I think the fine is unjust."

No one had expected such a quick ending. Mr. Darrow came into court full of the pleasant anticipation of another "go" at Mr. Bryan, whom he questioned to the delight of hundreds the day before. But the court had no sooner opened than Judge Raulston decided that there would be no further questioning, and then ordered Mr. Bryan's testimony expunged from the record.

Mr. Bryan, who had contented himself with the thought that he would have an opportunity to put Mr. Darrow on the stand and tear into him, was somewhat chagrined at this turn of the case, and announced that he would have to appeal

---

[2]William Jennings Bryan (1860–1925): a superb orator and the unsuccessful Democratic candidate in three presidential elections; he was the prosecutor in the trial of John Scopes. [Eds.]

to the fairness of the press to give prominence to the questions which he would
have asked Mr. Darrow.

"I had not reached the point where I could give my statement to answer the   10
charges made by the counsel for the defense as to my ignorance and bigotry,"
he said, bitterly.

SPARROW POSES AS DOVE OF PEACE.

But before the day's session was over a dove of peace hovered over the court   11
room in the form of a frightened sparrow, which had strayed in through an
open window, and everybody exchanged felicitations except Mr. Bryan and Mr.
Darrow. Judge John Raulston declared that the Word of God "given to man,
that man may use it as a waybill to that other world," was an indestructible
thing, and prayed God that he had decided right the questions raised in the
trial. A minister pronounced a benediction and court adjourned.

QUESTIONS

1. Consider the organization of material in this article. Why does the writer start
with a summary of events?

2. How objective is the writer? What indications do you find that he favors one side
over another?

3. Find in your local newspaper a report of a current trial. First read the article from
the defense's point of view, and write a paragraph in which you tell what effect the article
might have on your case. Then read the article from the prosecution's point of view,
and write a similar paragraph. Finally, write a paragraph in which you reach some
conclusion about whether or not the trial was objectively reported. In addition to the
article's language and content, take into account the length of the article, its placement
in the paper, and any pictures that are flattering or unflattering to either side.

4. If your library has newspapers for 1925, find other reports of the Scopes trial, and
write a summary of the important moments. What happened to John Thomas Scopes
after this trial? Why was it called the "Monkey Trial"? Who received the most publicity,
Scopes or the two lawyers, Bryan and Darrow?

5. The theory of evolution is still a hotly debated issue. Find some contemporary
articles on this issue, and write a report in which you consider why we are still arguing
about it.

WORMS AND
THE SOIL
Charles Darwin

Charles Darwin (1809–1882), British botanist, geologist, and naturalist, is best known for his discovery that natural selection was responsible for changes in organisms during evolution. After an undistinguished academic career and a five-year voyage to South America with a British survey ship, he began keeping his Transmutation Notebooks *(1837–1839), developing the idea of "selection owing to struggle." In 1842 and 1844 he published short accounts of his views and in 1859 published* On the Origin of Species, *which made him famous—even notorious—as the father of the "Theory of Evolution." He preferred to avoid controversy and left the debates over his theories to others whenever possible. But he was a keen observer and continued to study and write on natural history all his life. The essay that follows here is a sample of his late work, which features close observation and careful description. It is taken from* The Formation of Vegetable Mould, Through the Action of Worms, with Observations on Their Habits *(1881).*

Worms have played a more important part in the history of the world than most persons would at first suppose. In almost all humid countries they are extraordinarily numerous, and for their size possess great muscular power. In many parts of England a weight of more than ten tons of dry earth annually passes through their bodies and is brought to the surface on each acre of land; so that the whole superficial bed of vegetable mould passes through their bodies in the course of every few years.[1] From the collapsing of the old burrows the mould is in constant though slow movement, and the particles composing it are thus rubbed together. By these means fresh surfaces are continually exposed to the action of the carbonic acid in the soil, and of the humus-acids which appear to be still more efficient in the decomposition of rocks.[2] The generation of the humus-acids is probably hastened during the digestion of the many half-decayed leaves which worms consume. Thus the particles of earth, forming the

[1]mould: rich, soft soil suitable for growing plants. [Eds.]
[2]humus-acids: acids in the humus, the black or brown organic material in the soil that is composed of partly decayed plant and animal matter. [Eds.]

superficial mould, are subjected to conditions eminently favorable for their decomposition and disintegration. Moreover, the particles of the softer rocks suffer some amount of mechanical trituration in the muscular gizzards of worms, in which small stones serve as mill-stones.[3]

The finely levigated castings,[4] when brought to the surface in a moist condition, flow during rainy weather down any moderate slope; and the smaller particles are washed far down even a gently inclined surface. Castings when dry often crumple into small pellets and these are apt to roll down any sloping surface. Where the land is quite level and is covered with herbage,[5] and where the climate is humid so that much dust cannot be blown away, it appears at first sight impossible that there should be any appreciable amount of subaerial denudation;[6] but worm castings are blown, especially whilst moist and viscid, in one uniform direction by the prevalent winds which are accompanied by rain. By these several means the superficial mould is prevented from accumulating to a great thickness; and a thick bed of mould checks in many ways the disintegration of the underlying rocks and fragments of rock. 2

The removal of worm castings by the above means leads to results which are far from insignificant. It has been shown that a layer of earth, two tenths of an inch in thickness, is in many places annually brought to the surface per acre; and if a small part of this amount flows, or rolls, or is washed, even for a short distance down every inclined surface, or is repeatedly blown in one direction, a great effect will be produced in the course of ages. It was found by measurements and calculations that on a surface with a mean inclination of 9°26′, two and four tenths cubic inches of earth which had been ejected by worms crossed, in the course of a year, a horizontal line one yard in length; so that 240 cubic inches would cross a line 100 yards in length. This latter amount in a damp state would weigh 11½ pounds. Thus a considerable weight of earth is continually moving down each side of every valley, and will in time reach its bed. Finally this earth will be transported by the streams flowing in the valleys into the ocean, the great receptacle for all matter denuded from the land. It is known from the amount of sediment annually delivered into the sea by the Mississippi, that its enormous drainage-area must on an average be lowered .00263 of an inch each year; and this would suffice in four and a half million years to lower the whole drainage-area to the level of the seashore. So that, if a small fraction of the layer of fine earth, two tenths of an inch in thickness, which is annually brought to the surface by worms, is carried away, a great result cannot fail to be produced within a period which no geologist considers extremely long. 3

Archaeologists ought to be grateful to worms, as they protect and preserve for an indefinitely long period every object not liable to decay, which is dropped 4

---

[3]trituration: pulverization by crushing or grinding. [Eds.]
[4]levigated castings: things cast out, such as excrement, ground to a smooth powder. [Eds.]
[5]herbage: green, leaflike (rather than woody) plants such as grasses. [Eds.]
[6]subaerial denudation: surface erosion. [Eds.]

Charles Darwin

on the surface of the land, by burying it beneath their castings. Thus, also, many elegant and curious tessellated pavements and other ancient remains have been preserved;[7] though no doubt the worms have in these cases been largely aided by earth washed and blown from the adjoining land, especially when cultivated. The old tessellated pavements have, however, often suffered by having subsided unequally from being unequally undermined by the worms. Even old massive walls may be undermined and subside; and no building is in this respect safe, unless the foundations lie six or seven feet beneath the surface, at a depth at which worms cannot work. It is probable that many monoliths and some old walls have fallen down from having been undermined by worms.[8]

Worms prepare the ground in an excellent manner for the growth of fibrous-rooted plants and for seedlings of all kinds. They periodically expose the mould to the air, and sift it so that no stones larger than the particles which they can swallow are left in it. They mingle the whole intimately together, like a gardener who prepares fine soil for his choicest plants. In this state it is well fitted to retain moisture and to absorb all soluble substances, as well as for the process of nitrification.[9] The bones of dead animals, the harder parts of insects, the shells of land-molluscs, leaves, twigs, etc., are before long all buried beneath the accumulated castings of worms, and are thus brought in a more or less decayed state within reach of the roots of plants. Worms likewise drag an infinite number of dead leaves and other parts of plants into their burrows, partly for the sake of plugging them up and partly as food.

The leaves which are dragged into the burrows as food, after being torn into the finest shreds, partially digested, and saturated with the intestinal and urinary secretions, are commingled with much earth. This earth forms the dark colored, rich humus which almost everywhere covers the surface of the land with a fairly well-defined layer or mantle. Von Hensen placed two worms in a vessel eighteen inches in diameter, which was filled with sand, on which fallen leaves were strewed; and these were soon dragged into their burrows to a depth of three inches. After about six weeks an almost uniform layer of sand four tenths of an inch in thickness was converted into humus by having passed through the alimentary canals of these two worms.[10] It is believed by some people that worm burrows, which often penetrate the ground almost perpendicularly to a depth of five or six feet, materially aid in its drainage; notwithstanding that the viscid castings piled over the mouths of the burrows prevent or check the rainwater directly entering them. They allow the air to penetrate deeply into the ground. They also greatly facilitate the downward passage of roots of moderate size; and these will be nourished by the humus with which the burrows are lined. Many

---

[7]tessellated: formed in a checkered pattern from small mosaic squares. [Eds.]

[8]monoliths: big blocks of stone, such as columns, used in architecture. [Eds.]

[9]nitrification: the combination of nitrogen compounds, which act as fertilizers, with the soil. [Eds.]

[10]alimentary canals: digestive tracts. [Eds.]

seeds owe their germination to having been covered by castings; and others buried to a considerable depth beneath accumulated castings lie dormant, until at some future time they are accidentally uncovered and germinate.

Worms are poorly provided with sense-organs, for they cannot be said to see, although they can just distinguish between light and darkness; they are completely deaf, and have only a feeble power of smell; the sense of touch alone is well developed. They can therefore learn little about the outside world, and it is surprising that they should exhibit some skill in lining their burrows with their castings and with leaves, and in the case of some species in piling up their castings into tower-like constructions. But it is far more surprising that they should apparently exhibit some degree of intelligence instead of a mere blind instinctive impulse, in their manner of plugging up the mouths of their burrows. They act in nearly the same manner as would a man, who had to close a cylindrical tube with different kinds of leaves, petioles,[11] triangles of paper, etc., for they commonly seize such objects by their pointed ends. But with thin objects a certain number are drawn in by their broader ends. They do not act in the same unvarying manner in all cases, as do most of the lower animals; for instance, they do not drag in leaves by their foot-stalks, unless the basal part of the blade is as narrow as the apex, or narrower than it. 7

When we behold a wide, tuft-covered expanse, we should remember that its smoothness, on which so much of its beauty depends, is mainly due to all the inequalities having been slowly leveled by worms. It is a marvelous reflection that the whole of the superficial mould over any such expanse has passed, and will again pass, every few years through the bodies of worms. The plough is one of the most ancient and most valuable of man's inventions; but long before he existed the land was in fact regularly ploughed, and still continues to be thus ploughed by earth-worms. It may be doubted whether there are many other animals which have played so important a part in the history of the world, as have these lowly organized creatures. 8

QUESTIONS

1. Darwin's style is both familiar and technical. He talks about a common creature and common experience in an easy and matter-of-fact way, but he also uses a vocabulary that is, in part, difficult. Make a list of several unfamiliar words, and look them up in a college dictionary to find out their meanings. Then look them up in the *Oxford English Dictionary*. This dictionary, which you can find in almost any library reference room, will give you the history of the usage of words. Where did words such as "viscid" (paragraph 2) or "levigated" (paragraph 2) or "trituration" (paragraph 1) come from? What was their earliest meaning? Do they still mean the same today?

2. One of the themes of this essay is the worm's contribution to the larger world.

---

[11]petioles: leaf stems. [Eds.]

Charles Darwin

How many acts of the worm does Darwin mention specifically? Which contributions of the worm interest or surprise you most, and why? Spend a few minutes observing the work of a fly, a mosquito, an ant, a spider, or some other small creature. What "great works" might you attribute to one of them?

3. Since worms are responsible for so much, part of Darwin's purpose apparently is to take them more seriously than we commonly do and to dignify their labors. What are some choices of phrasing and vocabulary that do dignify the life and work of worms?

4. This short essay clearly depends upon someone's having made very close observations of worms. Such an experiment is mentioned specifically in paragraph 6, but the details in paragraphs 2, 3, and 7 must also depend on such observation. Try to imagine as specifically as you can the experiments and controlled observations by which some of the information reported here could have been gathered. Write out a description of such an experiment, as best you can imagine it. What were the scientists doing?

5. In paragraph 7, certain suggestions are made about life from a worm's point of view. Taking hints from that paragraph and from elsewhere in the essay, write an account of a worm's working day, from a worm's point of view, as if you were a worm writing a chapter of your autobiography.

A DELICATE OPERATION
Roy C. Selby, Jr.

*Roy C. Selby, Jr., (b. 1930) graduated from Louisiana State
University and the University of Arkansas Medical School,
where he specialized in neurology and neurosurgery. He now
practices in the Chicago area and is the author of numerous
professional articles on neurosurgery. "A Delicate Operation," which first appeared in* Harper's *magazine in 1975,
reports for a more general audience the details of a difficult
brain operation.*

In the autumn of 1973 a woman in her early fifties noticed, upon closing   1
one eye while reading, that she was unable to see clearly. Her eyesight grew
slowly worse. Changing her eyeglasses did not help. She saw an ophthalmolo-
gist, who found that her vision was seriously impaired in both eyes. She then
saw a neurologist, who confirmed the finding and obtained X rays of the skull
and an EMI scan—a photograph of the patient's head. The latter revealed a
tumor growing between the optic nerves at the base of the brain. The woman
was admitted to the hospital by a neurosurgeon.

Further diagnosis, based on angiography, a detailed X-ray study of the cir-   2
culatory system, showed the tumor to be about two inches in diameter and
supplied by many small blood vessels. It rested beneath the brain, just above
the pituitary gland, stretching the optic nerves to either side and intimately close
to the major blood vessels supplying the brain. Removing it would pose many
technical problems. Probably benign and slow-growing, it may have been present
for several years. If left alone it would continue to grow and produce blindness
and might become impossible to remove completely. Removing it, however,
might not improve the patient's vision and could make it worse. A major blood
vessel could be damaged, causing a stroke. Damage to the undersurface of the
brain could cause impairment of memory and changes in mood and personality.
The hypothalamus, a most important structure of the brain, could be injured,
causing coma, high fever, bleeding from the stomach, and death.

The neurosurgeon met with the patient and her husband and discussed the   3
various possibilities. The common decision was to operate.

The patient's hair was shampooed for two nights before surgery. She was   4
given a cortisonelike drug to reduce the risk of damage to the brain during
surgery. Five units of blood were cross-matched, as a contingency against hem-
orrhage. At 1:00 P.M. the operation began. After the patient was anesthetized

her hair was completely clipped and shaved from the scalp. Her head was prepped with an organic iodine solution for ten minutes. Drapes were placed over her, leaving exposed only the forehead and crown of the skull. All the routine instruments were brought up—the electrocautery used to coagulate areas of bleeding, bipolar coagulation forceps to arrest bleeding from individual blood vessels without damaging adjacent tissues, and small suction tubes to remove blood and cerebrospinal fluid from the head, thus giving the surgeon a better view of the tumor and surrounding areas.

A curved incision was made behind the hairline so it would be concealed   5
when the hair grew back. It extended almost from ear to ear. Plastic clips were applied to the cut edges of the scalp to arrest bleeding. The scalp was folded back to the level of the eyebrows. Incisions were made in the muscle of the right temple, and three sets of holes were drilled near the temple and the top of the head because the tumor had to be approached from directly in front. The drill, powered by nitrogen, was replaced with a fluted steel blade, and the holes were connected. The incised piece of skull was pried loose and held out of the way by a large sponge.

Beneath the bone is a yellowish leatherlike membrane, the dura, that sur-   6
rounds the brain. Down the middle of the head the dura carries a large vein, but in the area near the nose the vein is small. At that point the vein and dura were cut, and clips made of tantalum, a hard metal, were applied to arrest and prevent bleeding. Sutures were put into the dura and tied to the scalp to keep the dura open and retracted. A malleable silver retractor, resembling the blade of a butter knife, was inserted between the brain and skull. The anesthesiologist began to administer a drug to relax the brain by removing some of its water, making it easier for the surgeon to manipulate the retractor, hold the brain back, and see the tumor. The nerve tracts for smell were cut on both sides to provide additional room. The tumor was seen approximately two-and-one-half inches behind the base of the nose. It was pink in color. On touching it, it proved to be very fibrous and tough. A special retractor was attached to the skull, enabling the other retractor blades to be held automatically and freeing the surgeon's hands. With further displacement of the frontal lobes of the brain, the tumor could be seen better, but no normal structures—the carotid arteries, their branches, and the optic nerves—were visible. The tumor obscured them.

A surgical microscope was placed above the wound. The surgeon had selected   7
the lenses and focal length prior to the operation. Looking through the micro-scope, he could see some of the small vessels supplying the tumor and he coagulated them. He incised the tumor to attempt to remove its core and thus collapse it, but the substance of the tumor was too firm to be removed in this fashion. He then began to slowly dissect the tumor from the adjacent brain tissue and from where he believed the normal structures to be.

Using small squares of cotton, he began to separate the tumor from very   8
loose fibrous bands connecting it to the brain and to the right side of the part of the skull where the pituitary gland lies. The right optic nerve and carotid

artery came into view, both displaced considerably to the right. The optic nerve had a normal appearance. He protected these structures with cotton compresses placed between them and the tumor. He began to raise the tumor from the skull and slowly to reach the point of its origin and attachment—just in front of the pituitary gland and medial to the left optic nerve, which still could not be seen. The small blood vessels entering the tumor were cauterized. The upper portion of the tumor was gradually separated from the brain, and the branches of the carotid arteries and the branches to the tumor were coagulated. The tumor was slowly and gently lifted from its bed, and for the first time the left carotid artery and optic nerve could be seen. Part of the tumor adhered to this nerve. The bulk of the tumor was amputated, leaving a small bit attached to the nerve. Very slowly and carefully the tumor fragment was resected.

The tumor now removed, a most impressive sight came into view—the pituitary gland and its stalk of attachment to the hypothalamus, the hypothalamus itself, and the brainstem, which conveys nerve impulses between the body and the brain. As far as could be determined, no damage had been done to these structures or other vital centers, but the left optic nerve, from chronic pressure of the tumor, appeared gray and thin. Probably it would not completely recover its function. 9

After making certain there was no bleeding, the surgeon closed the wounds and placed wire mesh over the holes in the skull to prevent dimpling of the scalp over the points that had been drilled. A gauze dressing was applied to the patient's head. She was awakened and sent to the recovery room. 10

Even with the microscope, damage might still have occurred to the cerebral cortex and hypothalamus. It would require at least a day to be reasonably certain there was none, and about seventy-two hours to monitor for the major postoperative dangers—swelling of the brain and blood clots forming over the surface of the brain. The surgeon explained this to the patient's husband, and both of them waited anxiously. The operation had required seven hours. A glass of orange juice had given the surgeon some additional energy during the closure of the wound. Though exhausted, he could not fall asleep until after two in the morning, momentarily expecting a call from the nurse in the intensive care unit announcing deterioration of the patient's condition. 11

At 8:00 A.M. the surgeon saw the patient in the intensive care unit. She was alert, oriented, and showed no sign of additional damage to the optic nerves or the brain. She appeared to be in better shape than the surgeon or her husband. 12

QUESTIONS

1. Why did the neurosurgeon decide to operate? What could have happened if the patient chose not to have the operation? What effect does knowing this information have on the reader?

2. Although the essay is probably based on the writer's experience, it is reported in

the third person. What effect does this have on the information reported? How would the report have come across if it had been written in the first person?

3. The writer uses different methods of reporting to create the drama of "The Delicate Operation." At what point in the essay does he provide background information? How much of the essay reports events before, during, and after the operation? At what points does the writer explain terms and procedures for the reader?

4. Which passages in this essay do you find especially powerful? How did the writer create this effect?

5. Write a report of a procedure with which you are familiar and which calls for some expertise or sensitivity or a combination of these because there is always the chance that something could go wrong. You should proceed step by step, giving the reader as much information as necessary to understand and follow the procedure. At appropriate points also include the problems you face. Suggestions are trimming a Christmas tree, carrying out a chemistry experiment, getting a child off to school, or preparing a gourmet meal.

THE DISCUS
THROWER
Richard Selzer

*Richard Selzer (b. 1928) is a surgeon and professor of surgery
at the Yale University Medical School. His articles on various aspects of medicine have appeared in* Harper's, Esquire,
and Redbook. *In 1975 he won the National Magazine Award
for his articles. His books include a volume of short stories,*
Rituals of Surgery, *and a collection of autobiographical essays,* Mortal Lessons. *In the essay reprinted here, which first
appeared in* Harper's *magazine in 1977, Selzer reports on
the visits he made to one of his patients.*

I spy on my patients. Ought not a doctor to observe his patients by any means   1
and from any stance, that he might the more fully assemble evidence? So I
stand in the doorways of hospital rooms and gaze. Oh, it is not all that furtive
an act. Those in bed need only look up to discover me. But they never do.

From the doorway of Room 542 the man in the bed seems deeply tanned.   2
Blue eyes and close-cropped white hair give him the appearance of vigor and
good health. But I know that his skin is not brown from the sun. It is rusted,
rather, in the last stage of containing the vile repose within. And the blue eyes
are frosted, looking inward like the windows of a snowbound cottage. This man
is blind. This man is also legless—the right leg missing from midthigh down,
the left from just below the knee. It gives him the look of a bonsai, roots and
branches pruned into the dwarfed facsimile of a great tree.

Propped on pillows, he cups his right thigh in both hands. Now and then   3
he shakes his head as though acknowledging the intensity of his suffering. In
all of this he makes no sound. Is he mute as well as blind?

The room in which he dwells is empty of all possessions—no get-well cards,   4
small, private caches of food, day-old flowers, slippers, all the usual kickshaws
of the sickroom. There is only the bed, a chair, a nightstand, and a tray on
wheels that can be swung across his lap for meals.

"What time is it?" he asks.   5

"Three o'clock."   6

"Morning or afternoon?"   7

"Afternoon."   8

He is silent. There is nothing else he wants to know.   9

147

"How are you?" I say.   10

"Who is it?" he asks.   11

"It's the doctor. How do you feel?"   12

He does not answer right away.   13

"Feel?" he says.   14

"I hope you feel better," I say.   15

I press the button at the side of the bed.   16

"Down you go," I say.   17

"Yes, down," he says.   18

He falls back upon the bed awkwardly. His stumps, unweighted by legs and   19
feet, rise in the air, presenting themselves. I unwrap the bandages from the
stumps, and begin to cut away the black scabs and the dead, glazed fat with
scissors and forceps. A shard of white bone comes loose. I pick it away. I wash
the wounds with disinfectant and redress the stumps. All this while, he does
not speak. What is he thinking behind those lids that do not blink? Is he
remembering a time when he was whole? Does he dream of feet? Of when his
body was not a rotting log?

He lies solid and inert. In spite of everything, he remains impressive, as   20
though he were a sailor standing athwart a slanting deck.

"Anything more I can do for you?" I ask.   21

For a long moment he is silent.   22

"Yes," he says at last and without the least irony. "You can bring me a pair 23
of shoes."

In the corridor, the head nurse is waiting for me.   24

"We have to do something about him," she says. "Every morning he orders   25
scrambled eggs for breakfast, and, instead of eating them, he picks up the plate
and throws it against the wall."

"Throws his plate?"   26

"Nasty. That's what he is. No wonder his family doesn't come to visit. They   27
probably can't stand him any more than we can."

She is waiting for me to do something.   28

"Well?"   29

"We'll see," I say.   30

The next morning I am waiting in the corridor when the kitchen delivers his   31
breakfast. I watch the aide place the tray on the stand and swing it across his
lap. She presses the button to raise the head of the bed. Then she leaves.

In time the man reaches to find the rim of the tray, then on to find the   32
dome of the covered dish. He lifts off the cover and places it on the stand. He
fingers across the plate until he probes the eggs. He lifts the plate in both hands,
sets it on the palm of his right hand, centers it, balances it. He hefts it up and
down slightly, getting the feel of it. Abruptly, he draws back his right arm as
far as he can.

There is the crack of the plate breaking against the wall at the foot of his bed   33
and the small wet sound of the scrambled eggs dropping to the floor.

And then he laughs. It is a sound you have never heard. It is something new   34
under the sun. It could cure cancer.

Out in the corridor, the eyes of the head nurse narrow.   35

"Laughed, did he?"   36

She writes something down on her clipboard.   37

A second aide arrives, brings a second breakfast tray, put it on the nightstand,   38
out of his reach. She looks over at me shaking her head and making her mouth
go. I see that we are to be accomplices.

"I've got to feed you," she says to the man.   39

"Oh, no you don't," the man says.   40

"Oh, yes I do," the aide says, "after the way you just did. Nurse says so."   41

"Get me my shoes," the man says.   42

"Here's oatmeal," the aide says. "Open." And she touches the spoon to his   43
lower lip.

"I ordered scrambled eggs," says the man.   44

"That's right," the aide says.   45

I step forward.   46

"Is there anything I can do?" I say.   47

"Who are you?" the man asks.   48

In the evening I go once more to that ward to make my rounds. The head   49
nurse reports to me that Room 542 is deceased. She has discovered this quite
by accident, she says. No, there had been no sound. Nothing. It's a blessing,
she says.

I go into his room, a spy looking for secrets. He is still there in his bed. His   50
face is relaxed, grave, dignified. After a while, I turn to leave. My gaze sweeps
the wall at the foot of the bed, and I see the place where it has been repeatedly
washed, where the wall looks very clean and very white.

QUESTIONS

1. Why does the writer say, "I spy on my patients" (paragraph 1)? Don't doctors usually "look in on" their patients? What effect did the writer hope to achieve by starting with such a statement?

2. The writer uses the present tense throughout this piece. Would the past tense be just as effective? Explain your answer.

3. Selzer writes in the first person. Why might he have decided to make himself prominent in the report in that way? How would his report have come across if it had been written in the third person rather than the first person?

4. How would you describe this doctor's attitude toward his patient? How would you

describe the nurse's attitude toward the patient? How does the narrator manage to characterize himself in one way and the nurse in another?

5. Is the title, "The Discus Thrower," appropriate for this piece? In a slightly revised version, the title was changed to "Four Appointments with the Discus Thrower." Is this a better title?

6. What do you think Selzer's purpose was in writing this essay? Did he simply wish to shock us, or is there a message in this piece for the medical profession or for those of us who fear illness and death?

7. The essay reports on four visits to the patient by the doctor. Write a shorter version reporting on two or more visits by the head nurse. How would she react to the patient's request for shoes? How might her own point of view explain some of her reactions?

8. For many of us, knowledge of hospitals is limited, perhaps to television shows in which the hospital functions as a backdrop for the romances of its staff. Write a short essay in which you present your conception of what a hospital is and in which you consider how Selzer's essay either made you revise that conception or reaffirmed what you know through experience.

RIVER-GRAY,
RIVER-GREEN
Edward Hoagland

Edward Hoagland was born in New York City in 1932. He grew up in Connecticut and graduated from Harvard in 1954. He claims that his writing was influenced by his stammering: "As a child, since I couldn't talk to people, I became close to animals. I became an observer, and in all my books, even the novels, witnessing things is what counts." Hoagland's many essays resulting from his observations of wildlife are collected in The Courage of Turtles *(1971),* Walking the Dead Diamond River *(1973),* Red Wolves and Black Bears *(1976), and* The Edward Hoagland Reader *(1979), from which the following essay is taken.*

Was lifted today by my fisheries friends to the slide on the Tahltan River [1] where the salmon are blocked.[1] The Tahltan is the main spawning tributary of the Stikine, which is naturally why the tribe gave it their name. Lately, most of the fish are being harvested by Alaskan boats on the coast and therefore the Americans are footing part of the bill. The operation has been a fiasco so far. The first plan was to have the men on the ground scoop the fish into barrels of water that the helicopter simply lifted upriver. The fish were traumatized by this, however, and the water in the barrels became toxic to them. At present, the helicopter only ferries the men back and forth and takes the foreman on tours. His dilemma is that if he blows a passage with dynamite he will kill all the fish who are waiting and perhaps precipitate a worse slide.

The canyon is a rudimentary steep V, the walls clay and silt. The river within [2] looks slender and white from the air, but the damaged area is like an artillery range, pitted with boulders, heaped with khaki-colored debris. Our arrival sent up legions of birds—eagles, crows, gulls from the sea. Being left to my own devices, I explored gingerly, completely alone once the pilot dropped me. It's only a little neighborhood river but it moves with violent velocity. The *water* gets through, all right; it has blasted a zigzag chute for itself with the force of a fire hose. Just to sit in the thunder and watch is awesome. There were so many fish waiting in the slower water below the chute that half an hour must have gone by before I was even aware of them. I listened and looked at the gulls who had gotten the word and had traveled so far. I thought the actual fish were

---

[1]Tahltan River: in British Columbia, Canada. [Eds.]

thickets of driftwood that the river had smashed together and submerged; their fins stuck out like a welter of branches. I was astonished instead at the carnage on shore, the bear-chewed or beak-bitten bodies scattered about everywhere. When I did see the living fish I gaped because there were many thousands. The Tahltan was jammed with them, flank to flank and atop one another, seldom moving, just holding whatever position they'd gained, though that took continual swimming. Hundreds of them were in water which scarcely covered their backs. I thought of shark fins, except that there was a capitulation to it, a stockade stillness, as if they were prisoners of war waiting in huddled silence under the river's bombarding roar. The pity I felt was so strong that I did everything I could not to alarm the ones nearest me. They were in an eddy behind a boulder a few feet away, and I wouldn't have dreamed of touching one of them. Each had fought to attain that eddy, and at any confusion or weakening of resolve he lost his hold and was washed downstream. Like mountain climbers, the most active fish would wiggle twenty yards further on and gain a new cranny. It might require a number of tries, but they were the freshest fish, unscarred, and occasionally one would get into some partially sheltered corner of the chute itself, in one of the zigs or zags. These dozen desperate niches were so packed that they were like boxfuls of crated fish set into the bullet-gray water. The salmon who were able to battle upcurrent did so by shimmying and thrusting more than by leaping, although they did leap now and again. This was the cruelest sight of all, because they were like paper airplanes thrown into the hydrant blast. The water shattered and obliterated the leap and then banged the limp, tender body down the same stretch of rapids that it had been fighting its way up for perhaps the past day and a half.

Most of the salmon were quite catatonic by now. They just held their own 3 in whichever clump or eddy they'd reached, unless some pathetic impulse moved them again. They might try to better themselves, only to be dislodged and lose fifteen yards. For me, walking back and forth on the bank with absolute freedom, it was eerie to watch a spectacle of death that was measured in feet and yards. I could lift a fly out of a spider's web but I couldn't assist these salmon. The swimmer who drowns is surrounded by fish who scull at their ease, and I suppose there was something in it about spheres of existence and the difference between being on water and land. But I felt like a witness at a slow massacre. Thirty thousand fish, each as long as my arm, stymied and dying in the droning roar.

These were sockeyes. Their bodies have a carroty tint on top of the back at 4 spawning time, often quite bright, and their heads turn a garish green. They wear a lurid, mascaraed look, a tragedian's look, as if they were dressed for an *auto-da-fé*.[2] I could tell how long a fish had been waiting by the color he'd turned and also, especially, by the length of his nose. This was another delayed discovery. All of them were gashed from being battered on the rocks, but some,

---

[2]*auto-da-fé*: the execution of a heretic, usually by burning. [Eds.]

I realized in horror, had practically no nose left, as though a fishmonger had amputated it, as though he had thrown the poor fish on his chopping block and cut off the front end right by the eyes.

The Stikine is a very rough river. Permanent canyons shut off its upper tributaries to the salmon entirely. The Spatsizi, the Pitman, the Klappan have none. Tahltan Lake happens to be ideal for spawning, but this year only two individuals out of the umpteen thousands who've tried have been seen by the fisheries counters to have reached the lake. Salmon live in the ocean for four years or so before they return, by the grace of some unexplained recording device, to the fresh-water source where they were born. They lay their eggs, languish genteelly and die. Thus four generations are in the sea at a time, and when a rock slide occurs, three years can go by before the blockage *has* to be cleared. If the fourth generation is equally foiled when it tries to spawn, then the river ceases to be a salmon river because no other salmon are living with memories of how to swim there. Given that much time, the Tahltan itself, fire hose that it is, might manage to clear its bed of the debris of the slide, but in the meantime a lot of commercial fishermen will be going broke.

The seven-man ground crew, arriving on the opposite bluff, stood looking at me. I was reminded uneasily of what the Tahltans did to the early prospectors who trespassed during a salmon run: they stripped them and tossed them in. These fellows descended the bluff by means of a rope, put on rubber suits, took long-handled nets and commenced to dip salmon out of the niches and crannies along the lower sides of the chute, sixty pounds at a clip. It was a fisherman's dream until about the thirty-ninth netload, and then, as somebody said, you would never want to fish again. They'd constructed a rock-walled pool next to the chute with an exit into the river above, and in assembly-line fashion they dumped their catches in that, although it was such an onerous business one man was kept busy simply repairing the nets. They worked with care, hurrying the fish to the pool before they could smother, with the common benevolence we have nowadays, for the race but not for the individual. Yesterday they moved something like twenty-three hundred, so it seemed very promising, except I'd already been told that there is a second rockslide upriver which the fish are not able to pass and there isn't the manpower to lift them over that one yet.

The eagles were reveling in the air like bank robbers who had broken into the vault. All they could see below them was fish; the river smelled like a fish-peddler's cart. The gulls sat by the water, so fat by now that they ate only the eyes. The river raged by like a forest fire, while the living fish in it, as silent as climbers, clung to the eddies for their very lives. The level had fallen, draining several of the pools on the edge. There fish lay in the sand in spoke patterns where they'd been trapped, with gaping eyes and their gills aghast, like victims stretched in a common grave.

Walking downriver, I met grizzly tracks; also coyote and fox tracks and tracks of black bear: then more grizzly tracks—little bears, big bears and cub bear tracks. Blood and roe were smeared over the rocks. A lynx had been licking at it. Immense fish heads stared up. But the salmon still in the Tahltan were much warier and less fatigued here. They were newcomers and were alarmed when they blundered into the shallows, instead of resting in exhausted droves. This far downstream it became like a regular salmon river, the fish dawdling along in a placid if cautious manner, keeping a decent distance from one another, though their fins filled the river and they were obviously unaccustomed to such constricted circumstances after their free-swimming years at sea. When one of them leaped, it was a superleap, a fat-bellied, splendid, classic leap, not overwhelmed. They looked startlingly large and maneuverable, as if they would not be easy to catch despite the glut and congestion and the squeezed gauntlet that they had to run. When I matched my boot with a grizzly's paws, our hind feet turned out to be the same size. His forepaws were about as broad as my boot was long. His stool consisted of nothing but berry seeds, so yesterday he was up in the meadows and this morning he was down biting salmon in half.

On my way home, I stopped at the Wood family's smokehouse above the   9 main river to see some salmon who had come to a different end. It's an ambitious structure, like the one at Tahltan. Water from a spring flows by on a series of wooden flumes, where the fish are washed. Mr. Wood, a gentle fellow from Casca, has a couple of pickling barrels for the fish that he wants to salt. Most of them are split and hung inside, however, spitted on long poles so that they look like tobacco curing, on two levels. The smoke comes from small piles of fireweed burning under two washtubs with holes punched in them, but the red fish make the whole barn seem on fire—salmon from floor to ceiling, as thick as red leaves.

Of course there would be no salmon if every time a creek was blocked by a   10 slide all of its spawning stock died futilely, butting the rocks. Suppressed and feeble under the instinct to return to the single site at all cost is a counterurge. After taking a terrific beating, some very few of those Tahltan salmon will let the current wash them downstream into the Stikine and down the Stikine to the Chutine or perhaps the Katete to search for another spawning ground.

QUESTIONS

1. Hoagland uses figurative language to help the reader see the events. For example, at the end of paragraph 2 he uses a simile: "they were like paper airplanes thrown into the hydrant blast." Find other examples of figurative language, noting where the example occurs in a particular paragraph. How does the image evoked help to organize the paragraph or summarize part of the narrative?

2. We noted in the introduction to "Reporting" that Hoagland organizes his descriptive narrative spatially; that is, his point of view is visually controlled. Trace the movement of the "camera eye" in this piece, considering the various angles of vision such as overhead shots, traveling shots, and close-ups. For what reasons might Hoagland have

decided on this arrangement? What might have been an alternative method of organization?

3. In which sections of the narrative does the writer describe his own reactions? Do his feelings add to the effect he wishes to create or are they intrusive?

4. Rewrite this essay as a short newspaper article, reporting only the facts of the events on the Tahltan River. Consider where in a newspaper such an article would be placed and how a reader would respond to it.

5. Go as an observer to a place where large groups of people are moving toward a particular goal, such as a cafeteria line, subway or stadium exit, or a sale table at a department store. Describe what you see. In organizing your descriptive narrative, consider what form of organization is most appropriate, such as spatial or chronological, and how you might use figurative language to help your reader see and feel what you do.

THE CELLS THAT WOULD NOT DIE
Michael Gold

A biochemist at the Oregon Graduate Center in Beaverton, Michael Gold was born in Paterson, New Jersey, in 1941. He has degrees in genetics and biochemistry from Rutgers University and the State University of New York at Buffalo. The article reprinted here appeared first in a magazine for a general audience, Science 81, *for which Gold worked as a staff writer.*

It was all very hush-hush. In the winter of 1973 a top official of the National   1
Cancer Institute flew from Washington, D.C., to Oakland, California, carrying in his briefcase five plastic flasks. Growing in a milky film at the bottom of each flask were live tumor cells. The cells came from cancer patients in five different medical centers in the Soviet Union. In the spirit of detente Russia had given the cells to American scientists, who hoped they might contain new clues to the cause of cancer.

The man from Washington brought the flasks to the University of California   2
at Berkeley, where he turned them over to Walter Nelson-Rees at the university's cell bank. It was Nelson-Rees' job to store cells in a deep-freeze repository and to periodically remove a few of one sort or another, grow them, and send them to certain government and private researchers. In the case of the top-secret Russian cells, however, he was told simply to store them away. He was neither to send them out nor to experiment with them himself.

But Walter Nelson-Rees was a perfectionist devoted to careful checking. He   3
routinely screened all samples that came through his lab to make sure they were what they were supposed to be. So a few days after being warned not to, he began analyzing a batch of the Soviet cells. He also sent some to a colleague in Detroit for testing.

The investigations produced a startling conclusion: The cells were not from   4
five different cancer patients in Russia. In fact the cells in all five flasks closely matched those of a black woman from Baltimore, Maryland, who had died of cervical cancer 22 years earlier. Her name was Henrietta Lacks.

It was not the first time Henrietta Lacks' cells had turned up unexpectedly.   5
A few years earlier some normal liver cells, which researchers had been using to study liver function, were found instead to be cervical tumor cells taken from Henrietta Lacks. Likewise, cells that scientists had cultured from an intestinal cancer, a tumor of the larynx, a normal heart, and half a dozen other organs

156

from various patients all over the world had somehow become the cells of Henrietta Lacks. Many scientists were gathering erroneous information and wasting perhaps millions of dollars because they had been mistakenly working on the wrong cells for years. The Russian incident was only the latest and most dramatic demonstration of how far the confusion had spread—and a hint of how much further it might go.

For Nelson-Rees the mix-up was the first of several events that launched a 6
personal crusade. Lots of people joined the effort to track down and ferret out the troublesome cells of Henrietta Lacks. But no one filled so many file drawers and thick black notebooks with details of the cells' habits as Nelson-Rees. No one collected so high a stack of micrographic mug shots of their many disguises. And no one else had the gall to publish periodic hit lists of other cells found to be overtaken by those of Henrietta Lacks and, to the dismay of many researchers, the names of the scientists working with the indicted cells. His obsession for quality control and his polite, precise manner of speech are more characteristic of *The Odd Couple's* fastidious Felix Unger than the rough and abrasive fictional sleuth Philip Marlowe; but Walter Nelson-Rees has become one of science's toughest detectives. Since 1973 he had doggedly pursued these fugitive cells of biology around the globe. Yet the chase is far from over. Henrietta Lacks has a considerable head start.

One winter day in 1951, when Nelson-Rees was still an undergraduate stu- 7
dent, 31-year-old Henrietta Lacks arrived at the medical clinic of Johns Hopkins University in Baltimore. The doctor who examined her found a strange purple lesion about an inch in diameter within her cervix. He cut out a tiny section of the tissue for closer study and determined it to be malignant.

Several days later doctors removed another fragment of the tissue and deliv- 8
ered it to a research group working at the university. With limited success, the group was attempting to grow tumor cells in the laboratory in order to study the mechanisms of cancer. While the researchers tried to grow those few cancer cells in a petri dish containing clotted chicken blood, doctors began bombarding Henrietta Lacks with radiation in an effort to kill the cancer still inside her.

The tumor proved invulnerable. Eight months after her first visit to the clinic, 9
the cancer had spread throughout her body, and Henrietta Lacks died.

That is, most of Henrietta Lacks died. In the research lab, the few cells taken 10
from the original tumor were thriving, doubling their number every 24 hours. The same vigor that had enabled the cancer cells to resist radiation and overrun Henrietta Lacks' body kept them flourishing in the artificial conditions of a petri dish. Cells taken from the tumors of dozens of other patients had not grown at all. A few grew only haltingly, then quickly died off. The cells of Henrietta Lacks, however, divided and redivided without limit. "If allowed to grow un-inhibited under optimal cultural conditions," wrote one of the scientists later, "[the cells] would have taken over the world."

In fact, as the first human cells that were easy to grow and manipulate outside 11
the body for long periods of time, the cells from Henrietta Lacks' cervical tumor

were sought by researchers everywhere. Code-named HeLa (pronounced hee-lah), the cells provided the first widely available model of human tissue, allowing scientists to experiment on human cells growing conveniently in petri dishes. Researchers studied the HeLa cells' nutritional requirements, their production of proteins, their reactions to drugs, their patterns of mutation. As one of the few fertile environments for human viruses, HeLa cells also were crucial to the development of a polio vaccine. Even as techniques advanced to the point where other cells could be developed into long-lasting cultures or cell lines, HeLa cells remained popular in research. They were so readily available, so versatile, and so easy to grow.

That popularity was partly responsible for the head start that HeLa cells had   12
on people like Nelson-Rees. By the time it was realized that the cells grew a little *too* easily, they already had a foothold in many tissue culture laboratories. At the same time, through years of use and countless new generations, the innately vigorous HeLa cells had evolved into creatures very much at home in the laboratory environment. They had adapted so well to life in a petri dish that if but a few HeLa cells inadvertently made their way into a culture of one of the newer cell lines, they would overpower the culture in a matter of days.

Unwittingly scientists aided the spread of HeLa with nonsterile equipment   13
and sloppy procedures. For example, technicians would transfer cells from a HeLa dish into a non-HeLa dish by touching both with the same bottle of growth medium. A couple of stray cells on the lip of the bottle were enough to seed the contamination. One group of researchers found that HeLa cells can travel within tiny airborne droplets created by such common lab activities as pipetting, pulling stoppers, and streaking cultures. When the droplets landed on open petri dishes, the HeLa cells began growing furiously, overwhelming the original cultures there in three weeks. Some scientists are convinced that HeLa cells can even survive on counter tops and the sides of flasks for days, lying in wait for their next host.

In the case of the tumor cells from Russia, Nelson-Rees believes that a HeLa   14
culture must have been under study at each of the medical centers that supplied them to the United States. With the involuntary help of Soviet scientists, and using a few tricks of their own, the HeLa cells slipped into all five flasks un-noticed. To the naked eye there is little difference between cultures of HeLa and something else. One possible clue of a HeLa take-over might be sudden explosive growth where the cells had been sluggish before. But biologists often would see such a change as a sign that they had finally coaxed and coddled a finicky cell culture into a hardy one.

For Nelson-Rees, a geneticist by training, the most incriminating evidence   15
came from chromosomes, the rodlike structures inside a cell's nucleus that carry its genetic information. Previous investigators had found that HeLa cells con-tained, in addition to the normal complement of chromosomes, four oddly shaped ones. These weird chromosomes, called markers, were unique to HeLa.

It was through these markers that Nelson-Rees recognized the Russian cells as HeLa. He decided to use them as mug shots to screen other suspect cells.

There were backup tests as well. Henrietta Lacks carried a digestive enzyme 16 that occurs rarely, and only in the black population. The Russian sample that Nelson-Rees sent to Detroit went to a friend who was able to find that enzyme. Recently more tests have been developed for many of the HeLa cells' biochemical characteristics, all of which Nelson-Rees uses in building cases against suspicious cells. "One doesn't have to drink the whole bottle to know that the milk is sour," he says. "Still, it's nice to be sure about these things." But it was Nelson-Rees' interest in chromosomes that led him to his second unexpected encounter with the cells of Henrietta Lacks.

It was just after the Russian mix-up. A colleague studying a line of breast 17 cancer cells called HBT-3 (HBT for human breast tumor) observed several unusual features unlike those of other breast cancer cells. When she mentioned this to Nelson-Rees, he remembered that HBT-3 contained a strange chromosome shaped like Mickey Mouse ears. He has seen Mickey Mouse chromosomes in only one other cell line, HEK, taken from the kidney of a human embryo. "Perhaps this odd breast cell is really a kidney cell," he thought, and decided to analyze all the chromosomes of both cells. For comparison he added a third cell from another breast culture called HBT-39B.

He stained the nuclei to make the chromosome markings stand out, photo- 18 graphed them through a microscope, and sorted out the enlargements like a philatelist going through his stamp collection.[1] Suddenly it was the Russian incident all over again. "All three cells were identical. None were what they were supposed to be," he recalls, still slightly stunned. "And all three had HeLa markers." In addition, although at least one of the cells was supposed to have come from a Caucasian donor, the rare and characteristic black enzyme of HeLa turned up in all three. The Mickey Mouse ears, which had not been seen in any previously observed HeLa cultures, meant that HeLa cells had grown into several slightly different strains as they traveled from one spawning ground to the next.

Coming on the heels of the Russian HeLa case, the discovery seemed much 19 more than coincidence to Nelson-Rees. Wasn't anyone working with the right cells? *Had* the whole world been taken over by HeLa? It was then that he launched his campaign to put this runaway cell back in its useful place. He combed the literature for anything that was already known about HeLa, searching for information that could help him trace its travels, uncover suspect cultures, and help control its spread. As a warning to his co-workers and in an effort to make the problem more visible, Nelson-Rees published a list of five HeLa contaminants in the journal *Science* in 1974. Now HeLa was no longer the family secret of tissue culturists, and if there had been any doubt about it

---

[1]philatelist: a stamp collector. [Eds.]

being a real problem, the doubt was gone: The chromosomal mug shots and enzyme data were very convincing.

"It really sent shock waves through the scientific world," recalls Jeffrey Schlom, 20 head of the National Cancer Institute's molecular oncology program. "It set back a lot of scientific careers."

Not that the wayward cancer cell posed any health threat to the scientists 21 whose labs it invaded. But to Nelson-Rees it was clear that by masquerading as other cells used in research, HeLa was perpetuating myths about the nature of cancer, bewildering experimenters.

Since the mid-1950s, for example, scientists had observed the same char- 22 acteristics in what they thought were different cancer cells and concluded that these traits must be common to all cancers. All cancer cells had certain nutritional needs, all could grow in soft agar cultures,[2] all could seed new solid tumors when transplanted into experimental animals, and all contained drastically abnormal chromosomes—the "mark of cancer," which were the unifying theories that emerged. In fact these traits are not common to all cancers. They are characteristic of the one cell that many different scientists were mistakenly studying. "It was our lady friend," says Nelson-Rees. "It is impossible to say how many millions of dollars were spent on research based on these misconceptions, but the whole spectrum of cancer characteristics had to be reevaluated."

Another popular myth held that normal human cells growing in a laboratory 23 culture dish could spontaneously turn cancerous. Such "spontaneous transformations" had been observed and well documented in early experiments in animal cells, but then scientists began reporting the phenomena in human cultures. Slow-growing normal cells, which never divide more than 50 to 60 times, reportedly exploded into growth and multiplied endlessly.

One such culture, labeled MA-160, began as normal prostate cells taken 24 from the administrator of a biological materials firm who decided to offer them as part of his company's inventory. By the time Nelson-Rees came across MA-160, another investigator already had found the black HeLa enzyme within the cells—which was odd since the donor was Caucasian. Nelson-Rees then identified the HeLa marker chromosomes and included the culture in his first hit list. Obviously, HeLa cells had sneaked into and overwhelmed the culture, as they had many cell lines that were thought to have magically become cancer cells. Today, few scientists believe there are any reliable reports of normal human cells becoming spontaneously transformed. To read the literature of the 1960s and early 1970s, though, you would think it happened every other day.

In addition to muddying the scientific waters with cancer myths, HeLa cells 25 cast shadows of doubt over results that depended on the specific identity of a cell. Investigators who had been working with MA-160 under the assumption

---

[2]agar: a gelatinous medium derived from red algae or seaweed. [Eds.]

that it was a normal prostate cell from a white male, for instance, had to consider much of their work irrelevant when they learned it was a cervical cancer cell from a black woman. The same was true for the scientists searching for breast tumor viruses by experimenting on the two breast cancer lines indicted by Nelson-Rees. Studies based on their findings were jeopardized too.

After his first hit list was published, Nelson-Rees began receiving samples of HeLa suspects from all over the world, cells presumed to be everything from skin to stomach. Many turned out to be HeLa. For each contaminant, he took micrographic mug shots of the chromosomes and duly noted the details of the case in his burgeoning notebooks. Occasionally, the source of a HeLa contaminant would say he had never heard of HeLa and certainly had no cells by that name in his lab. In those labs, however, Nelson-Rees was usually able to find another cell line, assumed to be pure, that itself had been contaminated by HeLa. He was to get to know that trick. The only way to fight back, he figured, was to continue publicizing as many of HeLa's disguises as he could.

In 1976 Nelson-Rees published his second hit list, naming 55 HeLa impostors that had been reported previously and 11 new ones. As he had for the first list, he included the sources of the phony cells for two reasons. He thought there might be uncontaminated supplies of some cultures in the hands of more careful people. He also hoped that naming names might discourage further distribution of the spoiled goods.

By this time Nelson-Rees had earned two reputations. To some he was the meticulous Ralph Nader of tissue culture who sought to improve the science by exposing shoddy materials and warning people away from them. "Walter's sometimes a little pointed, a little blunt," says Wade Parks, a microbiologist at the University of Miami who has followed Nelson-Rees' work since the days of the Russian HeLa cells. "But he's not wrong, I'll tell you that." To others, particularly to the scientists who never asked him to test their cells but whose names ended up on his lists just the same, he was an opportunistic publicity hound.

"Until now I have been very patient with your peculiar techniques to collect 'data' for your anti-HeLa publications, but this time you have gone too far." That is the opening of a venomous letter from a virologist whose newly cultivated breast cancer line was fingered in Nelson-Rees' 1976 hit list. He has an entire file full of similar reactions. In this case, the virologist reminded Nelson-Rees that he had never received permission to test the cell line and never notified the virologist that he was planning to discredit it in print. He concluded with "a strong and solemn protest" against Nelson-Rees' "unethical and irresponsible way of handling information."

Nelson-Rees' calm reply stated that it was the virologist's own co-worker who had requested the analysis. The co-worker is now convinced that the new "breast cells" are actually HeLa, he added. He also chided the virologist for announcing

161

the establishment of the new culture in a journal in spite of the partner's misgivings. Pointing out that several researchers wasted valuable time on the cells before they learned they were HeLa, the letter concludes in classic Nelson-Rees style: "I note from the latest issue of *Mammalian Chromosome Newsletter* that you are working on a new cell line. If you feel that I could be of any assistance to you in connection with this work, I should be pleased to do so." In other words, "I'll be keeping an eye on things."

Nelson-Rees realizes it is only natural for those who spend years developing cell lines and who base much of their research on them to be resentful. But he says that is beside the point: "I've been admonished in the past not to overkill, but this endless flow of nonsense has got to stop. We have to demand only the best and only the most proven in our line of work. It's not like recalling a truck. One can't recall a bogus cell culture and undo the damage after it's been growing and disseminating." 31

When Nelson-Rees isn't publishing lists and receiving angry letters, he is standing up at scientific meetings to question people's findings, preach the value of careful techniques, and warn about HeLa's wily ways. What has it got him? 32

Small victories. Whereas the authenticity of cell lines was never stressed in the training of young scientists, Nelson-Rees' hit lists are now required reading in a few programs. To reduce contamination, a growing number of research labs today work with only one cell type at a time, thoroughly disinfecting equipment before they move on to the next. Those who can afford the time and money never start an experiment without having the identity of their cells verified by authorities like Nelson-Rees. 33

In January the American Type Culture Collection, a nonprofit cell bank like Nelson-Rees', destroyed a dozen HeLa-contaminated cells in its supplies and slapped bold warnings on the few it retained. Director Robert Stevenson, one of Nelson-Rees' greatest fans, is emphasizing the point by distributing textured-rubber jar openers with the slogan: "For a good grip on your research, use authenticated cultures." Stevenson also has been pleading with the editors of journals to require researchers to include a detailed pedigree of the cells they work with in any report submitted for publication. 34

Meanwhile Nelson-Rees continues to pursue the strangely immortal woman from Baltimore. Last summer he reported that supposedly normal kidney cells used for years by scientists to study the health hazards of radiation were in fact HeLa, throwing into doubt much of that work. The "kidney cells" appeared on his third hit list, published earlier this year. Of the several hundred human cancer cultures used in research today, he has now fingered 90 as HeLa. And he is currently on the trail of three recently cultured liver cancer lines from China that bear a suspicious resemblance to "our lady friend." 35

Maybe it's a good thing that Nelson-Rees will never quite catch up with Henrietta Lacks. The image of the fugitive cells always one step ahead of the 36 scientific gumshoe is a useful reminder—not only for tissue culturists, but also for scientists who hope to engineer new forms of life in a safe manner, for technicians trying to harness tricky new kinds of energy, and for the public that puts its faith in those pursuits. Science is after all a human activity with human fallibilities, and things are not always what they seem.

QUESTIONS

1. What do you suppose Gold's methods of research are like? Try to describe them.

2. After gathering information, Gold's next task is to organize his presentation of it. This is not just a matter of deciding what to say first, then second, but also a matter of deciding how to characterize his story. What particular methods does Gold use to attract you to the story he tells?

3. How does Gold coordinate the two major threads in his account—his report of the HeLa phenomenon and his report about Nelson-Rees?

4. Consider the choice of words and the persons outside of this immediate story that Gold mentions in paragraph 6. What do those elements have in common, and how do they assist Gold in presenting his information to us?

5. In how many places other than paragraph 6 do you find the same sort of language used? Do you think that this usage is controlled and purposeful, or does it get out of hand? Could it be said to act like the HeLa cells themselves and to "contaminate" the larger "culture" of Gold's story? Or do you find that spreading usage justified and defensible? Explain.

6. In his last paragraph, Gold suggests the broader significance of this story. Are those reasonable worries, or is he just adding on something at the end? Identify one of those other subjects mentioned so briefly. Look up some articles on it, and write a report on what might be at issue there.

TWO PATHS TO THE TELEPHONE
David Hounshell

David Hounshell (b. 1950), a historian of technology, is curator of technology at the Hagley Museum in Wilmington, Delaware, and assistant professor of history at the University of Delaware. He studied electrical engineering as an undergraduate but studied history for his M.A. and Ph.D. because "I could understand the big questions about technology and society better through the study of history than through engineering." He has published widely in Science, Technology and Culture *and the* Journal of American History. *This essay, which presents a classic example of simultaneous invention, was first published in* Scientific American *in 1981.*

In one day in 1876—February 14—the U.S. Patent Office received two   1
communications describing the electrical transmission and reception of human
speech by means of variations in the resistance of the transmitter. The variable-
resistance device was the original telephone. The first description was in the
form of a patent application by a 29-year-old amateur inventor whose name
became world-famous: Alexander Graham Bell. The second description, which
arrived only hours later, came from a 41-year-old professional inventor who had
been granted the first of his many electrical patents almost a decade earlier:
Elisha Gray.

Who was Elisha Gray? Why is Bell widely if not universally known as the   2
inventor of the telephone and Gray, who envisioned the same device at the
same time, known to few except historians of technology? To answer the question it is helpful to have an understanding of not only the technical aspects of
this classic example of simultaneous invention but also the social ones. In the
history of the telephone the differences between the world of the professional
and the world of the amateur appear at almost every turn, as will be made clear
by a brief exploration of the two worlds, first Gray's and then Bell's.

Elisha Gray, born in Barnesville, Ohio, in 1835, attended Oberlin College,   3
but he was not graduated owing to ill health. His early interest in the electrical
aspects of telegraphy led in 1867 to his first patent, for a self-adjusting telegraph
relay. His device attracted the attention of the principal firm in the field, the
Western Union Telegraph Company. It also earned Gray enough money for
him to secure a partnership in a Cleveland firm that manufactured telegraphic

instruments. He and his partner, Enos Barton, transformed the company into the nation's leading maker of electrical apparatus, renamed it the Western Electric Manufacturing Company and in the early 1870's relocated it in Chicago. In 1872 Western Union acquired a one-third interest in the business, and Western Electric eventually became the sole supplier of telegraphic equipment to Western Union.

Telegraphy had grown steadily in the U.S. from its introduction in 1844, and that growth had accelerated in the Civil War years. By the end of the war some 50,000 miles of telegraph wire had been strung over routes totaling nearly 30,000 miles, and a decade later the figures had risen to 250,000 miles of wire over routes of more than 100,000 miles. Until 1872, however, each wire could transmit only one message in one direction at a time. Enlarging the transmission capacity between any two points could be accomplished only by stringing new wires.

This one-way-at-a-time bottleneck was built into the telegraph system because the transmitted signal consisted of intermittent pulses of direct current. In 1872, however, Western Union adopted a "duplex" system of transmission developed by Joseph B. Stearns, a Boston electrician. A modification of the Morse system, the Stearns system allowed two messages to be transmitted simultaneously, one from each end of the wire. The adoption of the duplex system effectively doubled

STRIKING PARALLELS between the telephones envisioned by Elisha Gray and Alexander Graham Bell are evident in their respective sketches of the instruments. Both Gray's transmitter (*left*) and Bell's (*right*) depended on varying the resistance to the flow of current from a battery. Both variations would be caused by the vertical movement of a needle in a liquid bath; the motion would be due to the response of a diaphragm to the sound waves of the human voice. In Gray's transmitter the variation in resistance would depend on changes in the distance between the tip of the needle and the bottom electrode. In Bell's the variation would depend on the changes in the area of the wedge-shaped needle tip immersed in the bath. The varying current would then pass through an electromagnet (*right*) at the receiving end of the circuit; variations in the magnetic field would cause a second diaphragm (in Gray's scheme) or a metal reed (in Bell's) to vibrate, thereby reproducing the sound waves that actuated the transmitter. Gray made the sketch of his device on February 11, 1876, some two months after he conceived the idea. Bell made his sketch on March 9, 24 days after filing his patent application.

165

the capacity of the Western Union network. Could multiplex systems be developed, systems that would increase the capacity many times further? One thing was certain: the inventor of a multiplex system could virtually name his own price.

Gray's close relations with Western Union made him aware of the rewards 6 awaiting the successful inventor, and early in 1874 he hit on a solution almost by pure accident. One day he found his nephew, whom he allowed to use his electrical apparatus, amusing himself in the bathroom with two battery-powered circuits. In one circuit the battery caused a reed "electrotome" to vibrate. The vibrations opened and closed the other circuit, which included an induction coil. Gray's nephew had also connected one lead of the second circuit to the zinc bathtub and was closing the circuit and "taking shocks" from the induction coil by rubbing his hand, which held the other lead, across the surface of the tub.

The vibrating reed made an audible hum, and when Gray's nephew rubbed 7 his hand on the tub, a second hum of the same pitch was heard. Gray's interest was piqued. He changed the frequency of the reed and found that the sound made by the rubbing of his hand on the tub changed to match it. The action of the induction coil was to transform the on-off impulses imposed on the circuit by the vibrating reed into a sinusoidal wave of electric current.

Gray was quick to explore the phenomenon of what he named vibratory 8 currents, seeking to find some practical use for their transmission and reception. Although he found no immediate application, he so resolutely believed vibratory currents would have a major usefulness that he resigned as the superintendent of Western Electric, determined to pursue the matter on an independent full-time basis. In order to do so he secured the financial backing of Samuel S. White, a wealthy manufacturer of dentistry equipment in Philadelphia.

With funds at his disposal Gray soon built four experimental devices: two 9 transmitters of frequencies in the audible range and two receivers. One of the transmitters he called a single-tone transmitter; it was essentially a refinement of his nephew's bathtub apparatus. The other he called a two-tone transmitter; it was capable of simultaneously generating sinusoidal waves of two different frequencies. One of the two receivers seems quaint in retrospect; the other was quite conventional.

The first receiver consisted of a violin with its strings removed and a silver 10 plate attached to the soundboard. When one of the leads of the induction-coil circuit was connected to the plate and the hand holding the other lead was rubbed across the metal surface, as it was in the bathtub experiment, the tones generated by either transmitter were reproduced with a richer quality. The other receiver consisted of an electromagnet and a metal diaphragm. When the magnet caused the diaphragm to vibrate according to the frequencies of the current in the induction-coil circuit, the tones of the transmitters were faithfully reproduced. The results suggested to Gray three possible applications.

166

RECEIVING APPARATUS, a stringless violin with a silver plate covering the soundboard, was devised by Gray in 1874 to draw attention to the "vibratory currents" first made audible by the bathtub experiment (*see below*). Here one lead from the induction coil connects to the silver plate. The demonstrator (Gray in this instance) holds the other lead in his hand and rubs his fingers along the metal surface. The musical tone thus generated duplicated the tone of his transmitter, a metal reed that vibrated at audio frequencies.

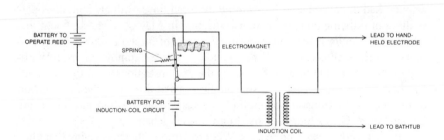

BATHTUB EXPERIMENT, based on a chance discovery by Gray's nephew in 1874, involved the circuits illustrated here. The first circuit, at the left, was closed and opened by the back-and-forth motion of a spring-loaded metal reed that vibrated at a fixed frequency. When the circuit was closed, it energized an electromagnet. The response of the reed to the attraction of the magnet reopened the circuit and the action of the spring promptly reclosed it. A second pair of contacts, one of them fixed to the reed, simultaneously closed and opened a second circuit. An induction coil in this circuit converted the interrupted current into a continuous sinusoidal current of the same frequency as the tone of the reed. When one of the leads from the induction coil (*right*) was attached to a zinc tub, and the experimenter, holding the other lead, rubbed his hand across the tub's surface, a sound was heard identical in pitch with the tone of the reed.

The most obvious application and probably the easiest to perfect was what 11
today would be called an electric organ; Gray thought of it as a "musical telegraph." He would merely have to build a keyboard consisting of switches that
would actuate a series of single-tone transmitters, each tuned to a different
musical pitch. It would even be possible to sound chords by pressing two or
more keys simultaneously.

A more immediate commercial application was implicit in the ability of a 12
telegraph wire to carry a "composite current," one consisting of two, four or a
much larger number of frequencies. Could not each tone be made to carry a
telegraph signal? The musical telegraph could function as a multiplex-signal
transmitter if a receiver could be devised that was able to segregate the individual
tones of the composite current. For this purpose, Gray realized, neither of his
receivers would be of any use.

The magnet-and-diaphragm receiver, however, was perfectly suited to the 13
third application Gray had in mind. If many combinations of tones could be
carried by wire and the composite signal could then be reproduced electrically,
would it not be possible to transmit the sounds of the human voice? Gray may
have perceived an irony in this application. Just as the potential multiplex system
of telegraphy was in need of a receiver, so the potential composite-current system
of telephony was in need of a transmitter. Gray saw no easy way to solve the
voice-transmitter problem, although he immediately envisioned a complex synthesizing device consisting of a number of individual tone transmitters, each
responding to a different tone of the human voice.

Within a few weeks of the bathtub episode Gray, in a rush of experimental 14
activity, had discovered and in his mind explored the seemingly boundless possibilities of utilizing audible vibratory currents. In May of 1874, confident that
he had sufficiently investigated the implications of these currents, he demonstrated his transmitters and receivers to audiences of telegraphy experts in Washington, New York and Boston. Reports of the demonstrations allow the inference
that he mentioned all three potential applications of this work: the transmission
of music, the transmission of multiple messages and the transmission of the
human voice. Gray's tour gave rise to a flurry of debate.

The New York Times reported one Western Union official as saying that Gray 15
had taken "the first step toward doing away with manipulating instruments [that
is, telegraph keys] altogether." "In time," the official continued, "the operators
will transmit the sound of their own voices over the wire, and talk with one
another instead of telegraphing."

The leading journal of the industry, *The Telegrapher*, took the opposite tack. 16
Declaring that the transmission of the human voice was nothing new, the journal cited an account it had published five years earlier describing the Reis
telephone. Johann Reis, a German schoolmaster and experimenter, had in 1861
coined the word "telephone" to describe a laboratory device he had built to
reproduce music and the voice. *The Telegrapher* noted that the Reis telephone

had proved to have "no direct practical application" and remained "a mere scientific . . . curiosity."

The Telegrapher also mentioned what it said was an old joke in telegraphic circles. Voice communications had once been tried on the telegraph line between Philadelphia and New York, the story went, "but had to be given up on account of the Philadelphia operator's breath smelling too strongly of bad whiskey." The journal's view of the Reis telephone was echoed by A. L. Hayes, one of Gray's own patent attorneys and himself an expert in electrical technology. Assuring his client of the novelty and importance of the new discoveries, he went on to say the German instrument was "merely a toy" that could be made to work only with careful handling and that amounted to no more than a scientific oddity. Reis had died that same year, and interest in his "curiosity" had languished. 17

Discouraged by the negative opinions on voice communication, Gray turned in the summer of 1874 to the development of the remaining applications: the musical telegraph and multiplexing. For the transmission of music he built an organlike apparatus with an array of single-tone transmitters covering a range of one octave; later it was enlarged to a two-octave apparatus. To improve the tone quality of the receiver Gray made the diaphragm larger by replacing the flat metal plate with a washbasin; thereafter the device was known as the washbasin receiver. 18

In August and September of 1874 Gray toured England with these devices and others. Among those for whom he demonstrated them were John Tyndall, who succeeded Michael Faraday at the Royal Institution, and J. Latimer Clark, then perhaps the most eminent figure in British telegraphy. Gray also took advantage of the visit to test how well his vibratory currents performed when they were conducted by submarine cables. He concluded that there were no technical obstacles in the way of transforming musical telegraphy into a multiplex-message system, where both he and his backer White knew the greatest financial rewards would lie. 19

For the rest of 1874 Gray concentrated on multiplexing. In an effort to learn more about audio-frequency currents, as they would be called today, he built what he called a "mechanical" transmitter. The vibrating reed was replaced by two cams, mounted on a shaft rotated at speeds equal to audio frequencies, that opened and closed two sets of contact points. Adjustable "elastic springs" were included for regulating the pressure between the points. 20

The first time Gray tested his mechanical transmitter, on January 1, 1875, he observed something completely unexpected. With only one set of contact points in operation he found, not unexpectedly, that the washbasin receiver produced tones that varied in frequency according to the speed of the camshaft. When he then adjusted the tension of the spring, however, thereby either lessening or increasing the pressure between the points, he found he "was able to imitate many different [voice] sounds." He at once concluded that the complex 21

169

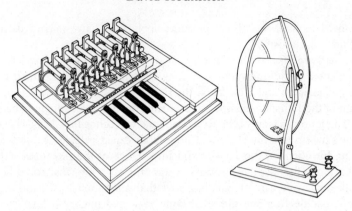

ADVANCED TRANSMITTER AND RECEIVER were two of the devices Gray took to England in 1874. The keyboard device at the left incorporated an array of single-tone transmitters that covered a range of one octave. The upended washbasin at the right formed the diaphragm of a receiving apparatus. Paired electromagnets translated "vibratory currents" into vibrations of the diaphragm.

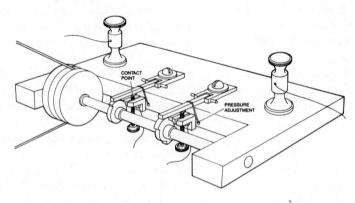

SUBSTITUTE FOR REEDS, devised by Gray late in 1874, was a belt-driven camshaft. Two cams opened and closed sets of contact points, and springs allowed for adjustment of the pressure between the points. Testing his "mechanical transmitter" in the audio-frequency range on January 1, 1875, Gray found that changing the pressure between points altered the output of interrupted current in such a way that his washbasin receiver emitted various voicelike sounds. He concluded that a simple device could transmit the human voice.

synthesizing voice transmitter he had conceived of earlier was unnecessary. Some much simpler device could be made to transmit the human voice.

Even with the prospect of voice communication so much improved, how- 22 ever, Gray did not pursue it. Instead he chose to continue the development of a multiplex telegraph as a potentially far more profitable venture. His strides toward this goal are evident in the number of patent applications he filed early

170

in 1875. He was soon to learn that his work was coming "into interference," as it is said in patent law, with the applications of another inventor. That inventor was Alexander Graham Bell.

By coincidence Bell was also in hot pursuit of a multiplex-telegraph system   23
working within the audio-frequency spectrum. (What Gray called vibratory currents Bell called undulatory currents.) The youthful Bell was an amateur, but he knew that a pot of gold awaited the inventor of a practical multiplex telegraph. Furthermore, although Bell was an amateur inventor, he was a thoroughgoing professional in his own field: elocution and speech therapy. His father, Alexander M. Bell, professor of elocution at the University of Edinburgh, had won international recognition for his system of teaching the deaf to speak, and his son had an intimate knowledge of the physiology of human speech. Indeed, he had already put forward a theory of vowel tones.

One consequence of this work was profound. Alexander J. Ellis, a prominent   24
British phonetician who had learned of Bell's theory, pointed out to him that the same theory had been advanced in a classic work, "On the Sensation of Tone as a Physiological Basis for the Theory of Music," by the German polymath Hermann von Helmholtz. Ellis also called Bell's attention to the electrically driven tuning fork used by Helmholtz in many of his experiments. Bell acquired a French edition of Helmholtz' book and read it during his passage from England to America in 1870.

When Bell settled in Boston in 1871 to teach at the School for Deaf Mutes,   25
he found others who were closely acquainted with Helmholtz' acoustical work, among them Lewis Monroe, a friend of the Bell family's and professor of elocution at the Massachusetts Institute of Technology. Monroe told Bell that experimental apparatus of the Helmholtz type was available at M.I.T. and suggested that he and Bell repeat the experiments someday. He also lent Bell a copy of a recent book on acoustics by Tyndall. Bell was soon in contact with others who were interested in investigating sound, among them Charles R. Cross, assistant to the physicist Edward C. Pickering at M.I.T., and the Boston physician Clarence J. Blake, lecturer on otology at the Harvard Medical School.

The background of Bell's work on the telephone was therefore acoustical.   26
The immediate path to that work, however, was like Gray's the multiplex telegraph. Bell began to pursue such an invention late in 1872, when he read an account in a Boston newspaper of Western Union's adoption of the Stearns duplex system. If Stearns had become rich by devising a system that could transmit only two messages at a time, and those in opposite directions, what wealth awaited the man who invented a system that could do more?

The Helmholtz apparatus gave Bell a starting point. Helmholtz had devised   27
a way of generating an intermittent current at audio frequencies by using the vibrating end of one tine of a tuning fork as an interrupter. He then employed the intermittent current to drive other tuning forks. The method suggested to Bell a way of transmitting multiple messages. If several Helmholtz tuning-fork

171

interrupters were tuned to different frequencies, each interrupter could transmit a separate message. This scheme left Bell facing the same problem Gray had faced: devising a receiver that could sort out the combined messages. Bell, however, was proceeding more on blind faith than Gray. He had yet to learn whether it was even possible to transmit composite tones by wire.

From late in 1872 through most of 1873 Bell worked off and on at his   28
multiplex-telegraph scheme. Unlike Gray, who employed a professional instrument maker, Bell built his own apparatus. Because he had almost no mechanical skill the apparatus was crude. For example, at first he could not rig a Helmholtz interrupter that would work for more than a few seconds. His being an amateur at invention was no mere artificial distinction.

Late in the spring of 1874 Bell learned about Gray's work with vibratory   29
currents. He at once accelerated the pace of his own work. Up to then Bell's efforts had been almost without success, but his faith in his multiplex scheme remained strong. That faith might well have faltered, however, if he had not found himself in partnership with Gardiner G. Hubbard, a telegraphy enthusiast. Hubbard had hired Bell to tutor his daughter, who had been made deaf by scarlet fever. Hubbard viewed Western Union as an enemy of progress in telegraphy, believing the monopoly was stifling innovation. The two men naturally talked about telegraphy, and in October of 1874 Bell disclosed that he was working on a multiplex scheme. Hubbard had predicted even before he knew Bell that "one wire [might eventually] be used for four or possibly eight messages." He now provided Bell with enough money to hire an expert in the field of electrical studies and pay for the services of the expert's instrument maker. The quality of Bell's apparatus soon improved. Perhaps Hubbard's most important contribution to the partnership was his insistence that Bell keep his mind on the main goal: multiplex telegraphy.

By the summer of 1875 Bell's work had convinced him it was possible to   30
transmit speech, the same conclusion that had been reached earlier that year by Gray. Although Gray had set the notion aside in favor of further work on multiplex telegraphy, Bell's keen interest in the voice made him feel that such an achievement would be of the first importance. Like Gray, Bell had initially conceived of a complex voice transmitter, but experiments with tuned steel reeds in transmitters and receivers led him to devise an instrument for both purposes that consisted of a reed attached to the center of a diaphragm. Both the transmitter and the receiver were placed near one of the poles of an electromagnet with a slightly but permanently magnetized core.

With this pair of instruments Bell and his assistant were able, on July 1,   31
1875, to transmit and receive what Bell described as "vocal sounds." These sounds were not, however, speech. The system required that Bell or his assistant shout into the diaphragm of the transmitting instrument. The diaphragm was agitated by the sound waves, which caused the reed to vibrate. The motion generated a weak "undulatory current" in the transmitting electromagnet, which

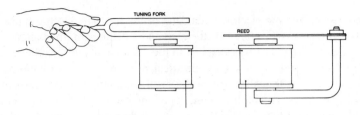

TUNING FORK

REED

BELL'S EXPERIMENTS, urgently pursued after he had filed his patent application, included some, such as the one illustrated here, that used electromagnets in both the transmitter and the receiver. Bell had tried a similar approach in 1875 but without success. He did not return to the magnetoelectric transmitter-receiver system until after he had successfully transmitted speech with a variable-resistance instrument. Here the vibration of a tuning fork near the electromagnet at the left caused its magnetic field to fluctuate. The fluctuations produced corresponding fluctuations in the current and hence in the field of the electromagnet at the right, making the steel reed above it vibrate with the same frequency as that of the tuning fork. A more advanced state of such a transmitter-receiver was the system Bell exhibited at the Centennial Exhibition in Philadelphia in June, 1876. It was the one used for the first commercial telephone in 1877.

actuated the receiving electromagnet, causing the receiving diaphragm to reproduce the movements of the transmitting diaphragm.

Bell was captivated by the potential of these instruments. (It is worth noting 32 that the first commercial telephones, which appeared in 1877, were not much more than improved versions of the 1875 magnet-and-diaphragm instruments.) Hubbard, however, was less than interested; like Gray and Gray's backer he kept his sights on the development of the multiplex telegraph.

By this time Gray and Bell were playing cat and mouse with each other. 33 Each suspected that the other was spying on him; each believed his own work was the more advanced, but each worried that the other might achieve the decisive breakthrough. Gray, however, gradually came to the conclusion that Bell's effort had been derailed. In October of 1875 Gray wrote his patent attorney: "Bell seems to be spending all his energies in [the] talking telegraph. While this is very interesting scientifically it has no commercial value at present, for [the telegraph industry] can do more business over a line by methods already in use than by that system. I don't want at present to spend my time and money for that which will bring no reward."

All the same, when later that month Gray happened to see two boys playing 34 with a homemade toy known as a "lover's telegraph," he immediately realized how an electric telephone should be constructed. A lovers' telegraph is what would be known today as a tin-can telephone. Two cans with the top removed are connected by a string knotted inside a hole punched in the bottom of each can. When the string is stretched tight, sounds uttered into one of the cans make its bottom vibrate. The vibrations are carried by the taut string to the bottom of the other can, where the sounds are coarsely reproduced.

Gray recognized the electrical analogue of the toy. The electric transmitter   35
would consist of a voice chamber (the can) and a diaphragm (the bottom of the
can). If one end of a wire was attached to the diaphragm and the other end was
immersed in a liquid with a high electrical resistance, the movement of the
wire in response to the vibrations of the diaphragm could be transformed into
a vibratory current that faithfully reproduced the various frequencies of speech.
Gray already knew that his electromagnet-and-diaphragm receiver could turn
the vibratory current back into sound waves.

Although the device seemed to Gray to lack commercial application, he   36
believed it would work and intended to patent it. He already knew that the
movement of a wire in a liquid could produce vibrations in an electric current.
While he was still a proprietor of Western Electric the company had made and
sold liquid rheostats: devices that changed the resistance of a circuit by varying
the depth to which a metal rod was submerged in a liquid with a high electrical
resistance. Because of his pressing work on the multiplex telegraph, however,
he waited more than three months before he took any patent action. In February
of 1876 he finally put his ideas on paper. Instead of applying for a patent,
however, Gray filed what was known at the time as a caveat, or warning.

A caveat was supposed to give the Patent Office formal notice of an inventor's   37
basic concept. The idea was that after filing a caveat the inventor would develop

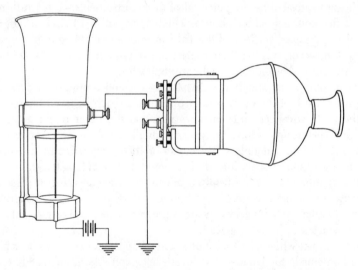

GRAY'S TELEPHONE, in the form presented in his Patent Office caveat application of
February 14, 1876, differed little from the apparatus he had sketched three days earlier.
The slight changes in current produced by the movement of the transmitter diaphragm
at the left resulted in electromagnet-powered vibrations of the receiver diaphragm at the
right. Although Gray might have contested Bell's patent application, filed earlier the
same day, he accepted the advice of his patent attorney and his financial backer and
dropped the matter.

the concept into a workable device and then apply for a patent. The procedure was intended to give a certain amount of protection to inventor's concepts. On this occasion Gray's patent attorney wrote to White, Gray's backer, that the inventor's "talking telegraph caveat" potentially interfered with a patent application from Bell. "As Gray's caveat was filed on the same day as Bell's application, but later in the day," the attorney reported, "the Commissioner holds that he is not entitled to an interference and Bell's application has been ordered to issue. . . . We could still have an interference by Gray's coming tomorrow and promptly filing an application for a patent. If you want this done, telegraph me in the morning, on receipt of this, and I will have the papers ready in time to stop the issue of Bell's patent, but my judgment is against it."

When the letter reached White, the inventor happened to be visiting him. White firmly impressed on Gray that he should concentrate on multiplex telegraphy. Since the attorney too had advised against proceeding further, Gray dropped the matter. The telephone was left to Alexander Graham Bell. 38

The experts in telegraphy, including Gray, had concluded that the telephone was not worth serious attention. Bell had remained steadfast in his belief that a successful telephone would be an invention of the first importance. Most of his draft patent application dealt with the devices tested in July of 1875 (which came to be known as the "magnetoelectric telephone"). As an afterthought, however, he inserted a description of a different kind of transmitter. 39

"Electrical undulations," he wrote, "may also be caused by alternately increasing and diminishing the resistance of the circuit. . . . For instance, let mercury or some other liquid form part of a voltaic circuit. Then the more deeply the conducting wire is immersed in the liquid, the less resistance does the liquid offer to the passage of the current. Hence the vibration of the conducting wire in a liquid included in the circuit occasions undulations in the current." 40

Bell had clearly misjudged the electrical properties of mercury; it is a low-resistance liquid, not a high-resistance one. Why he did so is something of a puzzle, because he had been familiar with the electrical properties of mercury since he had first read about them in Helmholtz. It is also not entirely clear 41

... 174,537	Table, ironing, J. V. Six	174,385	**W** AN Po
... 174,490	Tailor's drafting apparatus, P. Roudel	174,443	Stationary
... 174,471	Tank filler, automatic, A. Haerle	174,420	about as g
... 174,5C2	Teapot handle, J. A. Graff	174,520	
. . 174,474	Telegraphy, A. G. Bell	174,465	
... 174,586	Tether, S. L. Boyles	174,407	**I** NDEX CHINI
... 174,559	Thill coupling, W. H. Cornell	174,413	number of
... 174,582	Thrashing machines, spike for, C. Wilde	174,453	and hoyok

PATENT NO. 174,465 was one of 270-odd granted by the U.S. Patent Office during the week ending March 7, 1876, three weeks after Bell had filed his telephone patent application. This "official notice" was published in the April 8, 1876, issue of *Scientific American*.

David Hounshell

just how Bell conceived of a variable-resistance transmitter, that is, what precedents he relied on. There is even some question as to how and when the descriptive paragraph found its way into his final patent specification. Finally, one may wonder why he filed an application rather than a caveat. His concepts had not been, in terms of patent law, "reduced to practice," a fact the Patent Office either overlooked or ignored. These questions have been sources of speculation for more than a century and need not detain us here.

In June of 1876 Gray saw Bell demonstrate his telephone at the Centennial   42
Exhibition in Philadelphia. He later told an associate: "As to Bell's talking telegraph, it only creates interest in scientific circles. [Its] commercial value will be limited." So did the professional Gray continue to misjudge the importance of the telephone even after its successful realization. In contrast, the amateur Bell wrote his father two weeks after filing his patent application (and nearly two weeks before he was first to hear human speech through his instrument): *"The whole thing is mine*—and I am sure of fame, fortune and success."

QUESTIONS

1. Who was Elisha Gray? Why is Alexander Graham Bell universally known as the inventor of the telephone, and Gray, who envisioned the same device, known to few?

2. Why did Gray conclude that the telephone was not worth serious attention, while Bell believed that a successful telephone would be an invention of the greatest importance?

3. From what we are told of Elisha Gray and Alexander Graham Bell in this article, how would you describe the qualities of mind necessary to be an inventor? What would you say motivated these two men?

4. How does the writer create a feeling of suspense and interest in the outcome of this episode even though the outcome is already known to the reader?

5. How well does the writer explain technical details for the general reader? Would you say there are too many such details in this article, or are there places where more explanation of such details is warranted? Why do you suppose the writer included only the detail he did?

6. In paragraph 2, Hounshell suggests that we need to be aware of "not only the technical aspects of this classic example of simultaneous invention but also the social ones" to understand why Gray is not widely recognized today as an inventor of the telephone. What does Hounshell mean by this? Write a short essay that reports how, in Hounshell's view, social circumstances influenced the patenting of the telephone.

7. Try to imagine what life was like before the telephone was invented. To help you envision such a world, describe what a typical week in your life would be like without a telephone.

8. Do some research on another invention we consider important, such as the car, the typewriter, the moving picture, or the television. If the invention you research provides another example of simultaneous invention, consider why this was so. If it was invented by one person or group, consider why this was so. Write a report of your findings.

9. Investigate the history of the United States Patent Office. What are its procedures, and how well do they protect individuals? Write a report on your findings. If you wish, use the case of Gray and Bell as an illustration.

DEATH IN
THE DARKROOM
Bill Jay

An associate professor of art at Arizona State University, Bill Jay is a specialist in the early history of photography. He has M.A. and M.F.A. degrees from the University of New Mexico in this field and is the author of several critical and historical books on photography and photographers. The essay reprinted here is a research report on the chemical dangers of nineteenth-century photography. It appeared first in Phoebus 3, *a journal of art history published by the School of Art History at Arizona State University.*

The pages of 19th century photographic periodicals are littered with the tales 1 of hardships and dangers endured by early photographers. Many did not endure—they were defeated or killed by their insatiable need for pictures. Photographers fell off mountains and buildings while "stepping back" for a better view; they were attacked by brigands, scalped by Indians, pursued by robbers, and harassed by "heathens" of every color in practically every country. They were charged by bulls, elephants, and rhinoceroses; mauled by lions and tigers; attacked by alligators and wild dogs. They were shipwrecked at sea and fought for survival in jungles, deserts, and blizzards, and faced battles with armed and irate natives. They faced bullets, deadly snakes, swarms of insects, jealous husbands, and angry customers. They resourcefully reset and splinted their own broken limbs while alone in the wilderness, and turned tragedy into vaudeville by confounding hostile natives with the "magic" of photography. The above list could be endless and it is not a list of fictional possibilities; each case of hardship, tragedy, or survival refers to a specific event in the life of a 19th century photographer. In pursuit of pictures, photographers bravely and recklessly risked, and sometimes lost, their lives—and they did so with such frequency that the cumulative effect of their reports is to understand an aspect of early photography which is often missing from the history books. This awareness is enhanced by the understanding that the photographic process itself was fraught with difficulties and hardships. It is one thing to be in peril and yet another to be so when encumbered by all the paraphernalia of the wet-plate process. For good reason, this can be called the "Heroic Age" of photography.

The dangers did not diminish with the relief of transporting the hard-won 2 glass plates back to the photographer's home base (in itself, no mean feat). The darkroom could be a deadly place even for those who never ventured outside

178

the studio. And the dangers of processing and printing are all the more insidious for being unseen and often unrealised, until it was too late. A poison arrow from a band of attacking natives and a poison gas in the comfort of a private darkroom might have the same ultimate effect, but there is a sense of injustice in the fact that danger exists in a personal space. At least the photographer-adventurer had confronted and accepted the risks (and it was these risks which might have spurred his need to travel). A feeling of bewilderment suffuses many of the reports of death in the darkroom, particularly if the cause was sudden and unseen.

It is no exaggeration to state that 19th century photographers ran as many 3 risks in the dark as they did in the act of finding and taking pictures. Practically every week the photographic press reported an accident or death of a photographer which occurred during his chemical manipulations. The student or historian, reading these journals page by page, cannot escape the strong impression that darkroom health hazards were rife and real.

An omnipresent danger in the darkroom was the risk of poisoning. Through- 4 out the 19th century the photographic process demanded that photographers employ exceedingly dangerous chemicals. Poisonings were so frequent that rarely a week went by without a report of a death in the photographic press. Editorial writers and their expert correspondents incessantly implored their readers to be careful, to observe proper precautions, to understand probable results of inhaling, ingesting or simply handling their chemicals.

One of the most useful, if frightening, contributions was published in *The* 5 *British Journal of Photography* in 1860. "A Table of Antidotes to the Poisoning Bodies used in Photography (Drawn up from the Most Recent Medical Authorities), by Samuel Highley, F.G.S., F.C.S., etc. Late Lecturer on Medical Mineralogy at the Saint George's School of Medicine, Grosvenor Place, London."[1] Highley prefaces his table with the remark that "the list of deadly poisons employed in photography make (sic) a formidable array" and gives a few preventative tips, such as "During the preparation of gun cotton care should be taken not to inhale the fumes." He then advises his readers how to act in the case of poisoning. He lists twenty-one poisons with their symptoms and recommended treatment. What is frightening about the treatment is that a sense of hopelessness suffuses the remarks. "No antidote" is the sparse conclusion or try "an emetic of mustard in warm water."

Highley was right to emphasize that "prevention is better than cure," partic- 6 ularly when no cure was known. Editorial writers continued to stress the dangers and plead for precaution. Typical of these editorials was one published in *The Photographic News* during the same year.

Perhaps there are few professions connected with the arts of peace, which involve the daily use of so many dangerous and destructive agents as photography. Cor-

---

[1] *The British Journal of Photography* (London), 1 June 1860, pp. 160–161.

179

rosive acids, caustic alkalies, and deadly salts are its constant familiars. Whilst the dangers consequent upon the indiscriminate sale of poisons have been for some years past constantly impressed upon the public mind, and ingenuity has been taxed to the utmost to enact precautions, and provide bottles of different colours and shapes in which poisons should be vended, the photographer has been able to purchase, unchallenged, cyanide of potassium, bichloride of mercury, and other equally fatal agents sufficient to poison a colony.[2]

The frequent editorials warning photographers of the danger of their chem-   7 icals had a predictable outcome. Photographers, especially latent hypochon-driacs, became aware of symptoms and were able to blame them on their dark-room processes. Naturally, they wrote long letters to the magazines asking for advice. Typical is the letter from "a sufferer" who listed the following symptoms: "Attacks of biliousness; spasms in the stomach; very acid stomach, and general indigestion." He complained that his life had been a misery for the past nine years: "ever since I began photography."[3] The editor recommended more exercise, regular eating habits, well-ventilated darkrooms and avoidance of taxing the nervous system.

This editorial on "Photography and Disease" in *The Photographic News* led   8 to an unusually long series of correspondence. Evidently it had touched a highly sensitive spot in the lives of many photographers. The letters of complaints about symptoms and possible cures of illnesses continued in the journal from February to May 1868. These correspondence columns are well worth reading, giving a cumulative impression that, hypochondriacs apart, this was an issue which seriously concerned the professional photographer. Photography as an occupation was, and was known to be, an unhealthy pursuit. It is impossible to quote many of these letters at length but it is worth examining one example as being typical of the rest. The correspondent was J. M. Burgess, who was "well-known in the profession as a skillful photographer of much art and cul-ture—and especially as the inventor of the eburneum process."[4] Burgess neatly summed up the problems of health hazards in the darkroom:

> My own opinion is, that the ill effects cannot be attributed to any one chemical agency, but that they are the result of breathing for several hours every day an atmosphere contaminated with noxious fumes arising from the collodion, devel-oper, and, in some cases cyanide, to which may probably be added, absorption of poisonous substances through the skin, when the system has been already debilitated from over work, both of mind and body.[5]

Burgess then referred to the editorial's mention of "overtaxing the nervous   9 system." He felt convinced that photographers were particularly prone to stress arising out of their work—and the strain often resulted in severe physical symptoms:

---

[2]*The Photographic News* (London), 19 October 1860, p. 290.
[3]*The Photographic News*, 28 February 1868, p. 98.
[4]*The Photographic News*, 31 January 1873.
[5]*The Photographic News*, 6 March 1868, p. 117.

There is a very great temptation to this in the case of any one who is very fond of the pursuit, and has also to make his living by it. He is never satisfied with the results he obtains; each improvement only makes him more anxious for higher attainments; hence many hours are spent in thought and experiment; and then, when rest is required, there is the work which must be done. The result is that exercise in fresh air is neglected, and work continued to unreasonable hours. Meanwhile, the excitement and pleasure afforded by the pursuit blind him to any symptoms of injury to the constitution until it is almost too late for recovery; too late, at least, for care and exercise alone to effect a cure. Indigestion, wind spasms, violent colic pains, extreme nervousness, and something like local paralysis are induced, until the sufferer is brought to such a state of weakness as to be unable to digest any solid food. So violent at times is the pain, that the sufferer is convulsed, and symptoms not unlike poisoning by strychnine produced. The face assumes a leaden hue, the limbs become rigid, with the hands tightly clenched, and the back arched, so that the body rests on the back of the head and heels. But is it possible that this can in any way result from the practice of photography?

Burgess answers the question by declaring that his symptoms disappear if he takes a break from photography and has a few weeks holiday in the country, and he therefore concludes that there is a direct link between his illness and his work. This becomes all the more poignant in light of the fact that Burgess died less than five years later—at the age of 31. [10]

A more facetious letter was signed "Hypochondriac" and he reiterated the symptoms of photography-related illnesses, and added a new one—copious bleeding of the nose. This was due, he said, to "my face coming into somewhat rude contact with the hand of a vulgar boor, whom I endeavored to eject from my angle of view, persuasion having failed."[6] [11]

With this single exception all the letters in this series of correspondence took the matter of health hazards in the darkroom exceedingly seriously. Most of the solutions were of the common-sense variety—better ventilated darkrooms, the use of tongs in dangerous chemical baths, walks in the fresh air, regular meals, frequent washing of the hands, and "to sponge daily with cold water the whole surface of the body"—but a few writers had more specific antidotes to noxious chemicals. A Dr. Napias recommended that photographers drink lemonade or seltzer water "which tend to annihilate the effects of the ether fumes." On arriving home the photographer should down a glass of claret laced with quinine or drink sugar water to which is added a few drops of ammonia or vinegar.[7] [12]

Approaching the problem of poisons from another direction, a Bill was introduced in the House of Lords at the end of this series of correspondence which attempted to restrict the retailing of dangerous substances to registered pharmaceutical chemists. All poisons had to be distinctly labelled. A list of chemicals was drawn up which constituted the poison substances covered by the Bill, most of which were commonly employed by photographers.[8] [13]

---

[6]*The Photographic News*, 20 March 1868, p. 143.
[7]*The Photographic Times* (London), Vol. IV, 1874, pp. 124–125.
[8]*The Photographic News*, 29 May 1868, p. 263.

During the 1860s and 1870s, there was a good deal of confusion about photographically-related illnesses. No statistical evidence or empirical proof at that time could associate a specific disease with a particular photographic operation. Both Oscar Rejlander and T. R. Williams died from diabetes.[9] A photographic magazine seems to imply that photography may have contributed to their illnesses and deaths. As late as 1895 a photographic magazine noted that "the frequent appearance of diabetes among photographers is . . . remarkable."[10] Camille Silvy was dangerously sick at one point during his career due to cyanide absorbed through a small cut in his finger while his hands were in the fixing bath. Thomas Sutton attributed "fits of deafness, followed with lethargic sleep"[11] to the inhalation of ether fumes from the collodion process. Throughout the 1870s photographers continued to write long letters to the photographic press listing symptoms which they attributed to their photographic work, giving fellow photographers rules and regulations for healthy lives, and objecting to all the fuss about health hazards. J. H. Fitzgibbon boasted that he had been in the business for thirty-six years, twenty of which were spent in the darkroom:

> I suppose I have inhaled enough mercury to make a shining mirror for others to reflect from, and if it could be possible for a chemist to extract the chemicals and compounds that have made acquaintance with the interior of my darkroom, he might get enough ether, alcohol, cyanide, iodine, gold, silver, bichloride of mercury, bromides and chlorides, acids, and other chemicals of minor note, to open a small stock depot at a small cost.[12]

Fitzgibbon challenged anyone to doubt his robust health, by setting in front of him "a plate of good old English roast beef, and a slice of plum pudding thrown in."

In spite of Fitzgibbon's assurances, the vast majority of 19th century photographers were understandably worried about the dangerous chemicals which they daily handled. The journals regularly listed photographic poisons and their suggested antidotes. The following are typical: "Photographic Poisons and Their Antidotes," *The Photographic News*, 4 May 1877, pp. 207–208; "Poisonous Qualities of some Photographic Chemicals," *The Photographic Times*, Vol. X. 1880, pp. 77–79; "Dangerous Photographic Chemicals," *The Amateur Photographer*, 21 December 1908, pp. 605–606.

"It would seem," said *The Photographic Review of Reviews* in 1895, "that the average dangers which the ordinary soldier has to encounter are not nearly so great as those which beset the photographer's path. It is a wonder that any of us manage to live through it all . . ."[13]

[9]*The Photographic News*, 19 February 1875, p. 90.
[10]*The Photographic Review of Reviews* (London), January 1895, p. 22.
[11]*The Photographic News*, 19 September 1876, p. 458.
[12]*The Photographic News*, 16 March 1877, p. 129.
[13]*The Photographic News*, 16 March 1877, p. 129.

It is worth listing a few of these chemicals, in common use in 19th century   18
photography, which presented such dangers in the darkroom.

During the early years of the medium, the daguerreotype process necessitated   19
the fuming of the plate over heated mercury.[14] And mercury vapor is a deadly
poison. As far back as 1797 it was known that small traces of mercury, from,
say, a broken thermometer, were enough to kill all plants in a greenhouse. The
problem was confounded drastically when daguerreotypists breathed the fumes
of mercury placed over a spirit lamp. The photographic magazines attributed
many cases of bad health among daguerreotypists to this essential practice. All
they could recommend was that the darkroom was well ventilated. Even then,
some photographers succumbed. Jeremiah Gurney, one of America's foremost
daguerreotypists, was close to death in 1852 due to the effects of mercury. "He
has suffered the most acute pain, and been unable to move his limbs; his legs
and arms have been swollen to nearly double the ordinary size."[15] The magazine
which reported Gurney's illness stated that this was the fourth case of this nature
which it had known in the previous two years. Photographers were warned not
to allow any mercury to spill on the floor as "many cases of bad health have
been traced to the presence of small quantities of mercury in the cracks in the
floor. . . ."[16]

Even though mercury poisoning was the most likely cause of illness among   20
daguerreotypists, the fumes of iodine and bromine were far from harmless. Even
the copper plates on which the daguerreotype silver image was formed could be
dangerous. In 1850 a photographer cut his hand while handling a copper plate—
the resultant poisoning necessitated amputation of the hand.[17]

By the mid-1850s, the daguerreotype process had been largely superseded by   21
the collodion process. But even here mercury poisoning was common. Salts of
mercury, particularly the bichloride which was called "corrosive sublimate,"
were "to be found in every photographic studio, being commonly employed for
intensifying negatives."[18] Fortunately the wet-plate photographer, who drank his
intensifier in error, had a convenient antidote to hand. The recommended
treatment for this virulent poison was albumen, or whites of egg, used in the
production of his printing paper.

As late as 1901, when the collodion process had given way to the dry-plate,   22
mercury poisonings still took place. In that year, one of Lafayette's assistants

---

[14]Daguerreotype process: the first practical method of photography, invented in 1839 by the
Frenchman, Louis Jacques Mandé Daguerre. During this process, a picture made on a silver surface
sensitized with iodine was developed by exposure to mercury vapor. The collodion, or "wet plate,"
process of Frederick Scott Archer was introduced in 1851 and used a glass plate to produce a
negative. It rapidly replaced the daguerreotype process because it allowed the mass production of
prints while retaining the definition and detail of the photographic image. [Eds.]

[15]*Humphrey's Journal* (New York), Vol. IV, 1852, p. 28.

[16]*The Photographic News*, 16 August 1867, p. 399.

[17]*The Daguerreian Journal* (New York), Vol. 1, 1850, p. 228.

[18]*The Photographic News*, 26 January 1877, p. 37.

Bill Jay

drank mercury intensifier by mistake. Even though he was immediately rushed to hospital he died a few days later.[19]

The explosive and flammable dangers of ether vapour have already been mentioned. But an equally real, if less dramatic, health hazard existed for the photographer who breathed ether fumes from his collodion in a hot, cramped and often ill-ventilated darkroom or tent.

Alcohol fumes were also a source of trouble in the same situation. *The Photographic News* of 1865 published a long article on the toxical effects of these chemicals.[20] The dangers listed were so gruesome that it is a wonder that any photographer ever again practised the collodion process. The only consolation was that the article admitted photographers could become tolerant of the poisonous atmosphere in their darkrooms through habit. If the plate-coating assistant was rendered unconscious, magazines recommended "sprinkling with water."

Collodion was not only explosive and the source of dangerous ether and alcohol fumes, it also required two other major ingredients for photographic use, both of which were potential health hazards: potassium iodide and silver nitrate.

In 1861 two year old Henry Giblett died after swallowing a bottle of potassium iodide which he found in the van of an itinerant photographer while his guardians were having their portraits taken.[21] A similar case occurred in 1870. A photographer had visited the Stoke-on-Trent Workhouse in order to photograph its governor, Mr. M'Nish, and his family. He left behind a bottle of potassium iodide. When M'Nish asked for a glass of gin, his wife poured from the wrong bottle—and her husband died an hour later.[22] In both these cases the victims were "innocent," unaware of the nature of the liquid which they drank. Photographers would be less likely to make such a mistake and, even if they did, they would be more likely to know the recommended treatment: drinking albumen, starch paste or milk of magnesia. The effects might have been unpleasant but rarely fatal.

It was also true that silver nitrate poisoning rarely killed photographers; it was not a virulent enough poison to be ingested by the suicidal and its effects could be counteracted to some degree, in the event of accidental swallowing, by the same antidotes recommended for potassium iodide or a good dose of salt water. The fatalities attributed to silver nitrate were usually to the non-photographer. A typical story, with comic undertones, concerned the Abbé Salvy, vicar of a small town in France, who was an enthusiastic photographer. He was transferred to a new parish and asked three of the locals to help move his furniture. The Abbé placed some bottles of cider in the wagon to refresh the men on their

[19]*The Amateur Photographer* (London), 12 July 1901, p. 36.
[20]*The Photographic News*, 24 February 1865, pp. 86–88.
[21]*The Photographic News*, 15 November 1861, p. 550.
[22]*The Photographic News*, 7 January 1870, p. 11.

journey. He also placed in the wagon a smaller bottle, well-covered and tied up, which he told them they must not touch. The day was hot . . .

"That must be right good stuff, which the curé told us not to touch." "No doubt," replied another, "it must be far better than the cider." "Let us try it," said all three. The bottle was produced. The man who took a good sup said it was not good. "See," said he, handing it to one of his companions. The second tried, and pronounced a still more unfavorable opinion. "As it is so bad," said the third, "I shall not have any; let us put back the bottle." Scarcely was this done than the two who partook of the liquid fell on the ground writhing in dreadful agony. In a short time both were dead.[23]

As silver nitrate in the presence of a reducing agent blackens on exposure to light, it had a few bizarre uses. A popular story among 19th century photographers was the image-seeking adventurer in Africa who was captured by natives. The situation looked dangerous. But with admirable presence of mind, he noticed that the chief had a grey beard. He washed the chief's hair in "water," which was in fact silver nitrate, and in a few minutes the beard was black again. The photographer was hailed as a miracle-worker and set free. The blackening effect of silver nitrate could be used for less salutary reasons. M. Thiebaut was a photographer—and a ladies' man. His wife objected to his adulterous liaisons, and her actions led to a scandalous court case in Versailles in 1860. "It is a long tale of love, jealousy, infidelity, and vengeance," said a reporter.[24] The wife was charged with disfiguring her husband's mistress with photographic chemicals. She admitted that she had been in the habit of carrying a bottle of silver nitrate in her pocket for the purpose of disfiguring her rival. When she learnt that this would blacken the skin, but little more, she switched to a more serious solution. "She subsequently threw a quantity of sulphuric acid over her, and beat her severely with a stick." 28

Not everyone considered photographic chemicals to be entirely harmful. The French photographer Eugene Ogier claimed that the inhalation of fumes in his darkroom had cured him of pulmonary consumption.[25] F. B. Gage, an experienced American photographer, claimed that silver nitrate had cured his chronic bronchitis.[26] This solution was applied to his throat with a brush. Although this relieved the pain, after a few days the coagulated surface would slough off and the inflammation would begin again. The answer, he found, was to coat the throat with silver iodide—which not only gave temporary relief but the iodine began to cure the inflamed membranes of the throat. 29

Even the sulphuric acid, used by Mrs. Thiebaut to disfigure her rival, had its medicinal uses. *The Photographic Times* of 1882 asserted that sulphuric acid, 30

---

[23]*The Photographic News*, 10 July 1868, p. 335.
[24]*The Photographic News*, 7 December 1860, p. 384.
[25]*The Photographic News*, 2 February 1872, p. 50.
[26]*Ibid.* pp. 50–51.

in a dilute solution, could cure dysentery, hemorrhages, fevers, ulcerations of the throat, chronic inflammation of the joints, rheumatism, and skin diseases.[27] It was also useful as a hair invigorator and to remove dandruff as well as prevent undue perspiration of the feet.

Most of the 19th century articles on photographic chemicals were not so hopeful. Death seemed to be an ever-present concomitant of being a photographer. Even the commonly used developer, pyrogallic acid, was a deadly poison. In spite of warnings in more than 30 years of publications, photographers were still susceptible to silly accidents. In 1891 E. C. Tweedy, a well known photographer of Baltimore, met his death by mistaking in the dim light of his darkroom a solution of pyrogallic acid for a glass of whiskey and water. He knew the danger he was in, and immediately took a powerful emetic. To no avail. "In three days he was a corpse."[28] A few years later, Dr. Browning's wife mistook pyrogallic acid for a bottle of medicine. She, too, died.[29]

The photographic journals published more than the usual number of articles warning photographers of the poisonous qualities of bichromates. Potassium bichromate was in "general use in the every day practice of many photographers," mainly in such processes as gum printing, carbon-printing, and practically all photo-mechanical reproductions. As little as fifteen grains of potassium bichromate is enough to cause serious illness. The major problem, however, was not that the solution was ingested, although that too often happened by accident, but that the chemical was inhaled from the polluted air and absorbed through cuts and abrasions in the skin. A fascinating article on the subject was an editorial in an 1864 issue of The Photographic News.[30] Almost the same article was used in The Amateur Photographer of 1901. Very little had changed in nearly 30 years. Both articles asserted that snuff-takers seemed immune from potassium bichromate poisoning through breathing molecules of the chemical in the air. Both warned photographers about cuts in the skin when placing hands in solutions. The warnings were obviously necessary as carbon printers were particularly susceptible to what was known as "bichromate disease."[31] A long and detailed article entitled "Poisoning by salts of chromium," asserts that "cases of poisoning by compounds of chromium are not rare," and details many specific case histories from eminent medical authorities.[32] Again, there were the odd instances of death due to drinking the chemical in mistake for more refreshing beverages. Thomas Crump, of Scarborough, died in this manner in 1870.[33]

The list of photographic chemicals which caused sufferings and deaths in 19th century photography could be extended almost indefinitely, but there is

[27]The Photographic Times (London), Vol. XII, 1882, pp. 99–100.
[28]The Photographic News, 22 May 1891, p. 384.
[29]The Photographic Review, October 1896, p. 326.
[30]The Photographic News, 24 June 1864.
[31]The Amateur Photographer, 22 March 1901, p. 230.
[32]The Photographic News, 16 September 1887, pp. 578–580.
[33]The Photographic News, 11 March 1870, p. 119.

one last substance which must be mentioned as it accounted for more deaths among photographers than all the other hazards combined: potassium cyanide. The deadly poison, which is particularly noxious in that death occurs so rapidly, was a stock chemical in every photographer's darkroom. It had two main purposes—as a fixer for negatives, and as a stain remover for spots and blemishes from drippings of silver nitrate.

What is so intriguing, and ironic, is that a harmless fixing salt (sodium thiosulphate, or "hypo") had been employed from the earliest years of the medium. There seemed to be no good reason why photographers would subject themselves to such a virulent poison as potassium cyanide when an equally efficient and harmless alternative was available. The editorial writer of *The Photographic Times* in 1880 was equally bemused: 34

> Many people are puzzled, and with good reason, to account for the habit into which numerous photographers have got of using the poisonous cyanide of potassium as a fixing agent, when the innocuous hyposulphite of soda answers the purpose, not merely equally as well but in most instances a good deal better.[34]

It is difficult, if not impossible, to discover where this practice originated, or why. An early textbook by J. B. Hockin, *Practical Hints on Photography: its Chemistry and its Manipulations*, published in 1860, asserts the superiority of potassium cyanide over hypo, and claims the use of cyanide is a "necessity" in the production of positives (such as ambrotypes). He does not give any reasons for these recommendations—and worse, declares that cyanide is only injurious if imbibed. In fact, he declares that its odour is "by no means unpleasant" and "not at all injurious." This was obvious nonsense, but Hockin's book may be one of the reasons for the continued use of cyanide over hypo. *Napier's Metallurgy* outlined the symptoms of poisoning from inhaling fumes from potassium cyanide: 35

> Poisoning by cyanide gives to the mouth a saline taste and scarcity of saliva; the saliva secreted is frothy; the nose becomes dry and itchy, and small pimples are found within the nostrils, which are very painful. Then follows a general languor of body, disinclination to take food, and a want of relish. After being in this state for some time, there follows a benumbing sensation in the head, with pains, not acute, shooting along the brow; the head feels as a heavy mass, without any individuality in its operations. Then there is bleeding at the nose in the mornings when newly out of bed; after that comes giddiness; objects are seen flitting before the eyes, and momentary feelings as of the earth lifting up, and then leaving the feet, so as to cause a stagger. This is accompanied with feelings of terror, gloomy apprehensions, and irritability of temper. Then follows a rushing of blood to the head; the rush is felt behind the ears with a kind of hissing noise, causing severe pain and blindness; this passes off in a few seconds, leaving a giddiness which lasts for several minutes. In our own case the rushing of blood was without pain, but attended with instant blindness, and then followed with giddiness. For months

---

[34]*The Photographic Times*, Vol. X, 1880, p. 17.

afterwards a dimness remained, as if a mist intervened between us and the objects looked at; it was always worse towards evening, when we grew very languid and inclined to sleep. Then we rose comparatively well in the morning, yet we were restless, our stomach was acid, visage pale, features sharp, eyes sunk in the head, and round them dark in colour; these effects were slowly developed. Our experience was nearly three years. We have been thus particular in detailing these effects as a warning to all using cyanide; but we have no doubt that, in lofty rooms, airy and well ventilated, these effects would not be felt. Employers would do well to look to this matter; and amateurs, who only use a small solution in a tumbler, should not, as the custom sometimes is, keep it in their bedrooms; the practice is decidedly dangerous.[35]

Although photographers occasionally complained about one or more of these symptoms which they attributed to working in a darkroom with potassium cyanide, far more serious effects were caused by absorbing the cyanide through cuts or abrasions in the skin while fixing plates. The photographic press occasionally reported the suffering of a photographer whose hands swelled up and were covered in open wounds from this cause. The only solution was amputation. The problem was so real that as early as 1857 John Sang invented a handle for collodion plates in order that the photographers' hands need never be in contact with the cyanide solution.[36] In the same year, one of the major suppliers of cyanide to photographers, Harvey and Reynolds, of Leeds, issued a circular to all their customers "respecting the danger attendant upon the incautious use of cyanide of potassium amongst photographers."[37]

In spite of innumerable warnings, from the 1850s to the early years of this century, photographers continued to die from cyanide poisoning—either by drinking the solution in mistake for some other beverage, or as a quick and certain method of suicide. Only a few examples can be given, from the scores of cases reported in the photographic press.

In 1855 G. W. Greatrex narrowly escaped death when he made a pot of coffee from water which an assistant had polluted with a cyanide solution. Even though the dilution was considerable, Greatrex was still violently sick. But he guessed the cause, threw away the rest of the coffee and drank the recommended antidotes—iron sulphate, powerful emetics, anything that induced vomiting, inhaling the vapour of ammonia, and cold water "poured from some height in a stream on the naked head, neck, and spine."[38] Green tea was also recommended.

These antidotes might well be administered in cases involving extremely dilute solutions. Otherwise, the effect of cyanide is so sudden that nothing will help. This was true in the case of a German photographer in 1860. He was

36

37

38

39

[35]Quoted in *The British Journal of Photography*, 20 December 1867, p. 609.
[36]*Journal of the Photographical Society* (London), 21 September 1857, pp. 33–34.
[37]*Journal of the Photographic Society* (London), 21 September 1857, pp. 33–34.
[38]*The British Journal of Photography*, 1 June 1860, p. 160.

cleaning a glass plate, with difficulty. He got angry. He "became suddenly transported with passion, and, in his madness, dashed the plate on the floor, and seizing a vessel of cyanide of potassium, poured it down his throat. He dropped as if he was shot, and died in half a minute."[39]

In 1865 *The Photographic News*, in reporting two more suicides from cyanide, commented that such deaths are "becoming lamentably common."[40] The next month it reported the death of G. Cameron Hodgson, a photographer from Sunderland, who sipped his fixer after becoming maudlin drunk.[41] Within a few months it asked: "When will cyanide be banished from the photographer's laboratory? Ever week we hear of somebody being either maimed, paralysed, or killed by this deadly, and, to a photographer, totally unnecessary poison."[42]

Ignorance and carelessness continued. A photographer reported that he visited a druggist to buy some cyanide and the chemist found one lump was too large to enter the neck of the bottle—so he bit it into two pieces! "Nothing but very prompt measures saved his life."[43] Carelessness caused the deaths of innocents, often the children of photographers. A photographer named Kenneth, of Lochee, Scotland, saw his child drink from a phial of cyanide but he was too late to save it.[44] Other deaths of children from cyanide continued to be reported with alarming frequency.[45]

In 1866, Frederick Poller, aged 28, died from inhaling hot potassium cyanide fumes;[46] in 1867 a photographer's lady assistant committed suicide by drinking the fixer;[47] in 1868 a lady poisoned herself in New York by taking a dose of cyanide in mistake for rhubarb(!);[48] in 1869, Frederick Guinness died from drinking cyanide in mistake for a medicine;[49] in 1870, Elizabeth Lyons committed suicide after a quarrel with her lover, a photographer named Bocock of Liverpool;[50] in 1871, Cordine Gee, daughter of a photographer, in a burst of temper through a trivial domestic quarrel, ran to her father's darkroom and swallowed cyanide;[51] in 1872, Charles E. Pelton, a young photographer, was eating cloves which laid on the darkroom shelf. He picked up a piece of cyanide by mistake.[52] And so on, week after week, year after year. The overriding impression from reading so many of these reports is that the suicides were often for

[39]*The Photographic News*, 9 November 1860, p. 335.
[40]*The Photographic News*, 17 March 1865, p. 131.
[41]*The Photographic News*, 21 April 1865, p. 192.
[42]*The Photographic Journal* (London), 16 November 1865, p. 200.
[43]*The Photographic Journal*, 16 November 1865, p. 200.
[44]*The Photographic News*, 1 January 1875, p. 12
[45]For examples: *The Photographic News*, 2 November 1866, p. 527; *The Philadelphia Photographer*, Vol. IV, 1867, p. 403; *The Photographic News*, 22 November 1867, p. 568.
[46]*The Photographic News*, 17 August 1866, p. 388.
[47]*The Photographic News*, 17 May 1867, p. 240.
[48]*The Photographic News*, 3 January 1868, p. 457.
[49]*The Photographic News*, 11 June 1869, p. 288.
[50]*The Photographic News*, 19 August 1870, p. 395.
[51]*The Photographic News*, 8 September 1871, editorial.
[52]*The Photographic News*, 21 June 1872, p. 299.

trivial reasons and that if cyanide had not been so readily available, the victims would certainly have recovered enough from their grief, spite, rage, or jealousy, to continue life quite happily. The accidents were also wasted lives when such a harmless alternative as hypo was not only available but recommended by many editors.

Magazines constantly affirmed that there was no good reason for potassium cyanide to be used in any photographic darkroom. 43

This fact makes the death of Professor Fischer, of Czechoslovakia, all the more melancholy. Although he was only twenty-five years of age, he had gained a reputation as being "of the highest eminence in his profession," and occupied the Chemical Chair at the Prague High School. An ardent experimentalist, he had conceived the idea that the poisonous properties of cyanide could be neutralised without affecting its efficiency as a fixing agent. He mixed his solution in the laboratory in the Gymnasium of Prague, turned to his assistant and said: "Science has now so far advanced as to be even able to render harmless so dangerous an agent as cyanide of potassium": With these words he drank the mixture—and died within minutes "with the most violent and excruciating agonies."53 44

There is some suggestion that Fischer might have committed suicide under the guise of a scientific experiment. This seems unlikely, but if true, he was more successful than the photographer satirized in the popular jingle *The Ballad of Billy Baker*.54 In this ballad, sung to the tune "One-horse Shay," William Baker "*carte-de-visite* taker," falls in love with one of his sitters, Jemima Jenkins. She will have nothing to do with poor Billy Baker, who decides to take cyanide: 45

> On suicide intent,
> To the darkroom then he went;
> But instead of cyanide he swallowed th' hypo.
> Although it gave him pain,
> He soon got well again,
> But never flirted after in his stu-di-o.

The moral was clear: keep bottles properly labelled otherwise when you want to kill yourself you may drink the wrong solution. 46

When Jemima rejected Billy Baker's love she said: "Take such black paws as those/with heart that's quite as black, for anything I know," and struck a blow at every 19th century photographer's weak spot. The reason why Billy had "black paws" was that his hands were stained with silver solutions, which, as has been mentioned, turned everything black with which it came into contact. Queen Victoria did not allow photographers to use the wet-plate process in any royal residence, as soon as a dry process became practical, as the silver bath drippings 47

53*The Photographic News*, 20 September 1878, pp. 445, 450–451.
54*The British Journal of Photography*, 7 February 1868, p. 66.

ruined the carpets. The most common method of removing these black marks, from hands and furnishings, was to scrub them with potassium cyanide. Photographers had the habit of rubbing their fingers with solid lumps of cyanide, at the end of each day's work. Although risky, "photographers do it every day," claimed *The Photographic News* before reporting the death of a Belgian photographer.[55] He had no apparent cut on his hands so proceeded to remove the black silver with a lump of cyanide. A little piece of the lump chipped off and pushed under his finger nail where it broke the skin. He died in a few hours.

In spite of constant warnings that cyanide could be absorbed through the skin, photographers continued to use their hands in the solution. Usually, they escaped harm; often they suffered badly. One photographer wrote: 48

> I have not yet been able to resume my work in the chemical room. The last few weeks I have passed at the Springs, trying to extract the poison from my hands, which pain me so much that I have been obliged to keep them constantly in cold water. The first apparent effect of the poison was a feeling of numbness after using cyanide. This would soon pass away by a little friction in rubbing both hands together. I did not even then think of any further injurious effect. After some time this was followed by an eruption on the joints and between the fingers, accompanied by a constant itching sensation. This soon increased, until both hands were covered with watery blistering sores, and the itching pain became so intolerable that no words can describe the torture, which could only be borne by keeping both hands in cold water.[56]

Cyanide sores on the hands were a common complaint of photographers. The recommended treatment was rainwater. Several photographers on both sides of the Atlantic claimed to have been cured by this method. A typical letter reads: 49

> The winter of 1867–68 I had cyanide sores on my hands for several weeks. My family physician failed to heal them. I then, on going to bed, wrapped my hands in muslin wet in rain-water, and kept them wet all night from a dish by my bed. After three nights' treatment in this way they were well.[57]

Such cures might or might not have worked but it seems strange that photographers continued to expose their hands to the risk of cyanide sores when safer hand cleaning solutions were available. For example, in 1868, M. Carey Lea wrote an article on "Poisoning by External Use of Cyanide of Potassium" in *The Philadelphia Photographer* in which he states "there is no recognised treatment for such troubles." He suggests prevention, by avoiding cyanide to remove silver stains. He recommended a solution of potassium bichromate, 1 part; hydrochloric acid, 2 parts; water, 20 parts. Once this has removed the silver stains, rinse the hands in sodium thiosulphate (hypo) and wash with soap and water. 50

---

[55]*The Photographic News*, 22 October 1875, p. 505.
[56]*American Journal of Photography*; quoted in *The Photographic News*, 12 October 1866, p. 487.
[57]*The Photographic News*, 18 March 1870, p. 131.

A similar method was recommended in "A Safe Method of Removing Silver Stains from the Skin," in *The Photographic Times* in 1881.[58]

Not everyone agreed that an alternative to cyanide was necessary. E. P. Ogier, for example. He was a writer from St. Heliers', Jersey, who suffered from bronchitis which, he believed, was turning into consumption. His doctor advised more manual labour, so he became a photographer. He not only used cyanide for fixing but also for cleaning his hands, using a particularly strong solution and often rubbing the stubborn stains with a pumice stone. The abrasions absorbed the cyanide: "In a couple of months the serious symptoms with which I had been troubled had passed away, and now for three years I have enjoyed, relatively speaking, perfect health. My chronic bronchitis even, that had troubled me so long, almost disappeared."[59] The next week, D. Welch, a photographer from Newry, Ireland, also attributed the relief of his consumption to photography.

But apart from these isolated examples of the beneficial effects of potassium cyanide, the overwhelming mass of evidence condemned the use of this chemical in photographic darkrooms.

Potassium cyanide was not an *essential* ingredient in 19th century photography—yet it accounted for hundreds, and probably thousands of deaths. In many respects it represented a puzzling phenomenon of almost willful masochism—yet it led to small news items which readily bring to the senses the *zeitgeist* of an age. Historians constantly write about and talk about the establishment figures, the rich and famous among 19th century photographers, those whose names regularly appeared in the photographic press. The suicides of failures remind us that there was another, more shadowy and insubstantial, but none the less equally human side of the medium. So, just for the record, let one essay on photographic history mention the name of W. Dickson. In April 1883, he was 40 years old. He was discovered by a policeman on the east side of Calton Hill, near Edinburgh, far from his home town. An envelope was found in one of his pockets. On it was written: "Have no work, no money, no friends and no place to sleep in tonight.—W. Dickson, Photographer, April 12, 1883." Alongside the body was a small bottle of potassium cyanide.[60]

QUESTIONS

1. The author is a specialist on the early history of photography, so we can assume he would have read books and articles on early photographers and on early photographic techniques. Speculate on how this reading might have provoked him to start researching the topic of this article.

[58] *The Photographic Times*, Vol. XI, 1881, pp. 182–183.
[59] *The Photographic News*, 16 June 1871, pp. 277–278.
[60] *The Photographic News*, 20 April 1883, p. 256.

2. How does the writer organize his material? What is the purpose of his first paragraph? What are his main points and how well documented are they?

3. If potassium cyanide was so dangerous and could have been replaced by "innocuous" hypo, why did photographers continue to use it? Are you satisfied with the writer's conclusion about this?

4. What chemical in use today might be a fit subject for a research article like this one written by a writer a hundred years from now? What hazardous chemicals are being written about today?

5. This article was written from research in primary sources: letters, editorials, and articles by nineteenth-century photographers. Find in your library copies of a journal from fifty to a hundred years ago in a profession or field that interests you. Look at the issues for one year, and write a report of the main issues and ideas being discussed.

6. Is photography today considered a dangerous profession? Write a report of a job, profession, or leisure activity that interests you, emphasizing those side effects that may endanger one's physical, emotional, or intellectual well-being.

WRITING SUGGESTIONS
FOR REPORTING

1. At the end of his essay "The Ring of Time," E. B. White says that he has failed in his attempt to "describe what is indescribable." And in "Tut-Ankh-Amen's Tomb Is Opened" the *New York Times* reporter struggles with an event he considers indescribable. Compare what it is that the two writers claim to find indescribable. Then consider your own experience and those events in your life that you find indescribable. Try to generalize about what sorts of experience can be considered indescribable. In the process, of course, you'll have to consider how the two writers actually did go about describing the indescribable and how you would go about it.

2. Consider the differing attitudes toward education expressed by whites and blacks in Frederick Douglass's "Learning to Read and Write" and Maya Angelou's "Graduation." Write an essay in which you compare the Mistress's attitude toward education for blacks with that expressed by Mr. Donleavy at Angelou's graduation ceremonies over one hundred years later. Compare the responses of the twelve-year-olds Douglass and Angelou to the attitudes of the Mistress and Mr. Donleavy. In your conclusion, consider how Douglass, had he been present at Angelou's graduation, might have assessed the progress in education for blacks in those hundred years separating his youth and Angelou's.

3. Buster Keaton, Isadora Duncan, and Laurence Olivier are all renowned performers, yet they are treated very differently in the essays about them by James Agee, Winthrop Palmer, and Ronald Bryden, respectively. How does the selection of information about each performer and its presentation shape your view of each? Despite the differences among the reports, what characteristics do they suggest these performers have in common?

4. Both Farley Mowat and Jane Goodall study a specific animal in its natural habitat. How are their procedures similar? How are they different? In what ways do their procedures influence their findings and the way they are presented?

5. Barbara Tuchman writes her chapter " 'This Is the End of the World': The Black Death" as a historian, whereas Annemarie de Waal Malefijt is an anthropologist investigating a historical topic in her "*Homo Monstrosus*." They both, however, rely on source material from and about the periods they are writing on. Compare their presentations of this material, and consider how their differences in presentation might reflect their different academic disciplines.

6. Experiment with Roy C. Selby, Jr.'s "A Delicate Operation" and Richard Selzer's "The Discus Thrower." Use a different perspective to rewrite a short section of each by changing the first person to the third, and vice versa. (Another option would be to rewrite a short portion of Selby's essay as Selzer might write it, and vice versa.) How do these changes alter the nature of the information presented and the effect of each report?

7. Compare your conception of the hospital world with the worlds presented in Roy C. Selby, Jr.'s "A Delicate Operation" and Richard Selzer's "The Discus Thrower." In what ways did one or both of these essays cause you either to revise your conception or to reaffirm what you already knew?

8. Many of the essays in "Reporting" are written by firsthand observers who reveal their own roles as they report their observations. Select at least three of these observers, and write an essay about how the role each chooses to play affects the report each finally writes. Choose from among writers such as E. B. White, James Agee, Ronald Bryden, Margaret Mead, Farley Mowat, Jane Goodall, Michael Brown, Roy C. Selby, Jr., Richard Selzer, and Edward Hoagland.

9. Compare Michael Gold's position as a writer/reporter in relation to his topic ("The Cells That Would Not Die") with that of Michael Brown ("The Poisoning of Love Canal"). What similarities and what differences can you find in the ways Gold and Brown gather their information? How do their presentations of that information compare? Try to come to some conclusion about the most effective way to present provocative subject matter.

10. Investigate the special requirements of writing about history and of writing about the present. Select an essay in which the author treats the past and one in which the author treats present events. How are their techniques alike, and how are they different? Which characteristics result from differences in time period and which from differences in writer or topic? (You might analyze Bill Jay's "Death in the Darkroom" or Barbara Tuchman's " 'This Is the End of the World': The Black Death" and Michael Brown's "Love Canal and the Poisoning of America." Or consider Annemarie de Waal Malefijt's "*Homo Monstrosus*" and Margaret Mead's "A Day in Samoa" or Horace Miner's "Body Ritual Among the Nacirema.")

11. In the essays in "Reporting" by Maya Angelou, Margaret Mead, and Edward Hoagland, the events recorded take place within the time frame of a single day. Mead uses the movement of time in a day (morning, noon, and night) to structure her description of a day in Samoa. How does the presentation of a day's events differ in Angelou's essay and in Hoagland's? Compare the three writers' purposes and the way in which their purposes help to determine the organization of time in their essays.

195

EXPLAINING

EXPLAINING

Here in "Explaining" you will find writing by specialists from a wide range of fields seeking to account for matters as various as the color of the sky, the fear of death, the nature of theater, the singing of sparrows, the cycle of inflation, the art of the pyramids, and the popularity of *King Kong*. Explanation is an essential kind of writing in every academic field and profession. Facts, after all, do not speak for themselves, nor do figures add up on their own. Even the most vividly detailed report or computer printout requires someone to make sense of the information it contains. To make sense of a subject, we need to see it in terms of something that is related to it—the color of the sky in terms of light waves from the sun, the art of the pyramids in terms of ancient Egyptian beliefs. To understand a subject, in other words, we must examine it in terms of some context that will shed light on its origin and development, or its nature and design, or its elements and functions, or its causes and effects, or its meaning and significance. For this reason, you will repeatedly find the writers in this section drawing on specific bodies of knowledge and systems of interpretation to explain the problems and subjects that they address.

This essential element of explaining can be seen in connection with the following passage from James Jeans's "Why the Sky Is Blue":

We know that sunlight is a blend of lights of many colors—as we can prove for ourselves by passing it through a prism, or even through a jug of water, or as Nature demonstrates to us when she passes it through the raindrops of a summer shower and produces a rainbow. We also know that light consists of waves, and that the different colors of light are produced by waves of different lengths, red light by long waves and blue light by short waves. The mixture of waves which constitutes sunlight has to struggle through the obstacles it meets in the atmosphere, just as the mixture of waves at the seaside has to struggle past the columns of the pier. And these obstacles treat the light-waves much as the columns of the pier treat the sea-waves. The long waves which constitute red light are hardly affected, but the short waves which constitute blue light are scattered in all directions.

Thus, the different constituents of sunlight are treated in different ways as they struggle through the earth's atmosphere. A wave of blue light may be scattered by a dust particle, and turned out of its course. After a time a second dust particle again turns it out of its course, and so on, until finally it enters our eyes by a path

Explaining

as zigzag as that of a flash of lightning. Consequently the blue waves of the sunlight enter our eyes from all directions. And that is why the sky looks blue.

Jeans's purpose here is to explain "why the sky looks blue," and as you can see from the opening sentences of the passage he systematically establishes an explanatory context by setting forth directly relevant information about the nature and properties of sunlight, light, and light waves. He approaches the explanatory problem, that is, in terms of knowledge drawn from his specialized fields of astronomy and physics. With this knowledge in hand, he then proceeds to show how "the different constituents of sunlight are treated in different ways as they struggle through the earth's atmosphere." In this way, he develops his explanation according to the analytic framework one would expect of an astronomer and physicist, concerning himself as he does with the interaction of the atmosphere and light waves. Having formulated a cause-and-effect analysis demonstrating that blue light is scattered "in all directions," he is able to conclude that "the blue waves of the sunlight enter our eyes from all directions. And that is why the sky looks blue." Thus the particular body of information that Jeans draws upon from astronomy and physics makes it possible for him to offer a knowledgeable, systematic, and instructive explanation.

To appreciate how significant an explanatory context can be, you need only consider how knowledge from other fields might influence an understanding of "why the sky looks blue." A zoologist specializing in optics, for example, might note the importance of the retinal organs known as cones, which in vertebrate animals are thought to be the mechanism primarily responsible for the reception of color. Given this crucial bit of information, a zoologist might observe that the sky looks blue to human beings because their eyes are equipped with cones, whereas it does not look blue to animals lacking cones, such as guinea pigs, owls, and armadillos. An anthropologist, in turn, might think it worth noting that coastal and island cultures, given the maritime conditions of their livelihood, tend to develop unusually rich vocabularies for describing how the sea looks and how the sky looks. Given this bit of information, an anthropologist might observe that members of maritime cultures are likely to be especially discerning about the colors of the sea and sky.

Our hypothetical zoologist and anthropologist would both differ from Jeans in their explanatory approach to the blue sky. Whereas Jeans approached it in terms of accounting for the source and prevalence of the blue color, our zoologist and anthropologist would take the color for granted and seek instead to account for the human ability to perceive the color or the propensity of some cultures to be especially discriminating in their perception of it. Their differing approaches, in this case as in others, would result from their differing fields of study. Each academic area, after all, involves a distinctive body of knowledge, a distinctive array of interests, and a distinctive set of methods for making sense of the subjects that fall within its field of interest. Thus it follows that each area is likely to approach problems from different angles and arrive at different kinds of explanations. It follows, too, that no area can lay claim to the ultimate truth about things. But, as the case of the blue sky illustrates, each field does have a special angle on the truth, particularly about subjects that fall within its area of specialization. Our zoologist and anthropologist could be as valid and as enlightening in this case as the astronomer-physicist. In a broader sense, you can see from the case of the blue sky that in trying to explain a particular subject or problem one always has to look at it or approach it from a particular angle or a combination of viewpoints and that any particular approach brings a specific set of knowledge to bear upon an understanding of the subject. Relevant knowledge, quite simply, is the most essential element of explaining.

But knowledge alone is not sufficient to produce intelligible and effective explanation. Jeans's explanation, for example, depends not only upon a body of information about the properties and movement of light and light waves but also, as you will see, upon the form and style in which the information is presented. To develop your ability in explaining, then, you will need to develop a resourcefulness in putting your knowledge to use. One way to do that is to consider some of the ways that knowledge is commonly structured and applied in explanatory writing.

THE RANGE OF EXPLANATORY WRITING

Explanatory writing serves a wide range of academic, professional, and public purposes. Rules and regulations, guidelines and instructions—all these are familiar examples of explanation in the service of telling people how to carry on many of the practical and public activities of their lives. Textbooks, such as the one you are reading right now, as well as popularized presentations of highly specialized research or theory are common examples of explanatory writing in the service of helping people to understand a particular body of information and ideas. Scholarly research papers, government documents, and other highly technical presentations of data and analysis, though less familiar to the general reader, are important kinds of explanation that advance knowledge and informed decision making.

To serve the differing needs of such varied purposes and audiences, explanatory writing necessarily incorporates various forms and styles of presentation. Jeans's piece about the sky, for example, comes from a book intended as an introduction to astronomy. Thus he writes in a style that depends completely on familiar language. And to make sure that beginners will understand the important concepts in his explanation, Jeans repeatedly illustrates his discussion with analogies and references to familiar experience. In fact, if you look at the whole of Jeans's piece, you will see that he establishes his analogy of light waves to sea waves at the very beginning of his discussion and then systematically uses it to organize and clarify the rest of his explanation.

By contrast, the scientific paper of Peter Marler and Susan Peters, "Sparrows Learn Adult Song and More from Memory," is written for a highly specialized audience of researchers, as you can tell immediately from the abstract that precedes it as well as from its highly technical language and illustrations. Thus Marler and Peters do not structure their explanation in terms of a familiar analogy but instead use a standardized scientific format for writing up the results of experimental research. According to this format, their paper consists of four parts: an introduction that defines a research problem and places it in the context of related studies, followed by a section that identifies the materials and methods used in the experiment, followed by a section that reports the data resulting from the research, followed by a concluding discussion that interprets the data and explains its significance. They adhere to this structure so that other researchers will be able not only to understand the outcome of the experiment in question but also to verify the results of the experiment by carrying it out themselves.

For yet another variation in the format and style of explanatory writing, we need only shift our attention from the sciences to the social sciences and look at Bruno Bettelheim's "Joey: A 'Mechanical Boy.' " Here Bettelheim is presenting research based not on experimentation but on the case-study method, which entails the close observation of an individual subject over time. Because the subject of a case study is by definition unique, the study cannot be replicated by other researchers. A case study, therefore, must be written up in sufficient detail not only to document the observer's understanding of the subject but also to enable other researchers to draw their own conclusions about the subject. So you will find that Bettelheim provides an extensively detailed description, history, and analysis of Joey's behavior. You will also find that Bettelheim writes on the whole in a standard rather than specialized style, as befits the audience of generally educated readers who are the predominant subscribers to *Scientific American*, the magazine where his article first appeared.

But just to make clear that style and format do not always adhere to audience and purpose exactly as one might expect, we need only look at the following passage from Douglas L. Wilson's "The Other Side of the Wall":

> In 1968–69 I spent a sabbatical year on a small farm that my wife and I had just acquired and that had over a mile and a half of line fence. Almost the first question asked me by one of my neighbors when I met him was whether I intended to pasture cows. This question was prompted by the wretched condition of the fences I had inherited from the former owner. My new neighbor was visibly relieved when I said that I didn't.

Judging from the plain style and the hint of familiarity in the contraction at the end of the last sentence, as well as from the autobiographical story telling, you might well wonder exactly what this piece is doing in the explanation section of arts and humanities. But if you read the whole of Wilson's essay, you will discover that it is a highly informed essay, based on extensive research, about Robert Frost's poem "Mending Wall." You will also discover that Wilson sustains this narrative format throughout most of his essay both because he seeks to provide a complete record of the process through which he acquired his special knowledge about the poem and because he aims to show that this process in a very significant way involved his experience of living on a farm. Thus the narrative form of his essay proves to be a very artful and appropriate way to present the special knowledge that Wilson brings to his explanation of the poem.

As you can see from our brief discussion of just this handful of selections, explanation is a widely varied form of writing, involving as it does in every case a delicate mix of adjustments to the audience, purpose, specialized field, and subject matter. Thus as a reader of explanation, you will have to be very flexible in your approach, always willing to make your way through unfamiliar territory on the way to a clear understanding of things, or perhaps to a clear recognition that understanding may be beyond the scope of your knowledge in a particular field. And as a writer you will have to be equally flexible in your choice of language, as well as in your selection and arrangement of material, so as to put your knowledge and understanding in a form that not only satisfies you but also satisfies the complex set of conditions to which your explanation is addressed.

METHODS OF EXPLANATORY WRITING

In planning a piece of explanatory writing, you should begin by reviewing your material with an eye to deciding upon the overall approach that you intend to use. As our previous discussion has indicated, you should aim to develop an approach that is adjusted to all the conditions of your explanatory situation. Some methods, you will find, are inescapable, no matter what your subject, audience, or purpose. Every piece of explanation requires that ideas be clarified and demonstrated through *illustration*, that is, through the citing of specific examples, as you can see from the earlier passage by Jeans and in the following excerpt from Bettelheim's essay on Joey:

> During Joey's first weeks with us we would watch absorbedly as this at once fragile-looking and imperious nine-year-old went about his mechanical existence. Entering the dining room, for example, he would string an imaginary wire from his "energy source"—an imaginary electric outlet—to the table. There he "insulated" himself with paper napkins and finally plugged himself in. Only then could Joey eat, for he firmly believed that the "current" ran his ingestive apparatus.

Bettelheim's obligation to illustrate and demonstrate the machine-centered behavior of Joey leads him here, as elsewhere in his piece, to turn to a detailed *description* and *narration* of Joey's actions. So it is that reporting constitutes an essential element of explaining. And not only for reasons of clarity, but also for purposes of reliability. If an explanation cannot be illustrated, or can only be weakly documented, then it is likely to be much less reliable than one that can be amply and vividly detailed.

Some methods, while not required in every case, are often so important that they should be kept in mind as being potentially necessary in any piece of explanation. An essay that depends on the use of special terms or concepts almost certainly will call for a *definition* of each term and concept, in order to assure that the reader understands them exactly as the writer intends them to be understood. In his essay about Joey, for example, Bettelheim introduces a special term and concept in the phrase "mechanical boy," and thus he immediately defines it at the beginning of his piece by citing examples of it in Joey's behavior, his self-conception, and the perception of him by others. Bettelheim also uses some relatively familiar terms in his discussion of Joey, such as "disturbed children," but he evidently recognizes that familiar terms, too, need to be defined. Familiar words, after all, are commonly understood in different ways by different readers and writers. And the more varied are the understandings of a particular word or concept, the greater are the chances of it being misunderstood if it is not defined. So Bettelheim defines the exact sense in which he means us to understand "disturbed children" by identifying an essential quality or characteristic of their disturbed behavior—"they remain withdrawn, prisoners of the inner world of delusion and fantasy." And just to make sure that we are clear about his definition, he sharpens it by distinguishing the fantasy life of "disturbed children" from that of "normal children." Definition, in other words, can be carried out in a variety of ways—by citing examples, by identifying essential qualities or characteristics, by offering synonyms, by making distinctions.

Other methods, while not necessarily imperative, can be very effective in a broad range of explanatory situations. If you are trying to explain the character, design, elements, or nature of something, you will often do best to *compare and contrast* it with something to which it is logically and self-evidently related. Comparison calls attention to similarities, contrast focuses on differences, and together the methods work to clarify and emphasize important points by playing related subjects off against each other. In "On the Fear of Death," for example, Elizabeth Kübler-Ross aims to shed light on the tendency of modern society to "deny the reality of death," and she does so by comparing and contrasting "old customs and rituals" with modern ways of dealing with death. Her comparison and contrast enables her to show on the one hand that the fear of death has pervaded all cultures from ancient to modern times, but on the other that modern practices alone are characterized by a "flight away from facing death calmly." Kübler-Ross could, of course, have discussed the modern evasion of death in and of itself, but it stands out all the more sharply by contrast with older customs that reflect the "acceptance of a fatal outcome." Like Kübler-

Ross's piece, some examples of comparison and contrast rely on a strategic balancing of similarities and differences. Other pieces, such as Murray Ross's "Football Red and Baseball Green," which explains the differing appeals of two very well known American spectator sports, depend largely on a sustained contrast. And still other pieces, such as Adam Smith's "The Great Inflation," which uses the German experience with inflation shortly after World War I to shed light on the recent American inflation, work primarily in terms of comparison. The mix within each piece is adjusted to the needs of its explanatory situation. By the same token, you should make sure that whenever you use comparison and contrast, your attention to similarities and differences is adjusted to the needs of your explanatory situation.

A special form of comparison, namely *analogy*, can also be helpful in many explanatory situations. Analogies provide a handy means of putting intangible or unfamiliar things in tangible and familiar terms. In "Why the Sky is Blue," for example, Jeans's analogy of light-waves to sea-waves enables us to visualize a process that we could not otherwise see. Similarly, in "A Zero-Sum Game," Lester Thurow's analogy of our economic situation to a game "where for every winner there is a loser, and winners can only exist if losers exist," enables us to understand the painful truth that every economic solution necessarily involves substantial losses for some group of people. Useful as analogies are, however, they rely at last upon drawing particular resemblances between things that are otherwise unlike. Sea-waves, after all, are not light-waves, and games are not economic situations. So, whenever you develop an analogy, you should be careful in applying it to your explanatory situation, so as to make sure that it fits and that it does not involve misleading implications.

Some explanatory methods are especially suited to a particular kind of situation. If you are trying to explain how to do something, or how something works, or how something was done, you will find it best to use a method known as *process analysis*. In analyzing a process, your aim is to make it clear by providing a narrative breakdown and presentation of it step by step, by identifying and describing each step or stage in the process, and by showing how each step leads to the next and how the process as a whole leads to its final result. Jeans's piece, for example, analyzes the process by which light waves from the sun make their way through the earth's atmosphere and determine the color of the sky. Marler and Peters in their research paper on sparrows offer a detailed explanation of the process by which they carried out their research. And Jean Piaget in "How Children Form Mathematical Concepts" explains the surprisingly organized process according to which children acquire certain numerical and geometrical concepts.

A method related to process analysis is *causal analysis*. As the term suggests, this type of analysis seeks to get at the causes of things, particularly ones that are sufficiently complex as to be open to various lines of explanation. Usually, then, a causal analysis involves a careful investigation that works backward from something difficult to account for—such as the popularity of *King Kong*, the machinelike behavior of Joey, or the singing of adult sparrows—through an examination of various conditions that might account for it. Because no two things can be identically accounted for, no set procedure exists for carrying out a causal analysis. But there are a few cautionary activities to keep in mind. You should review other possible causes and other related circumstances before attempting to assert the priority of one cause or set of causes over another, and you should present enough evidence to demonstrate the reliability of an explanation. By doing so, you will be avoiding the temptation to oversimplify things.

As you can probably tell by now, almost any piece of writing that aims to make sense of something will inevitably have to combine several methods of explanation. But this should come as no surprise if you stop to think about the way people usually explain even the simplest things in their day-to-day conversations with each other. Just ask someone, for example, to give you directions for getting from one place to another, and you will probably find that the person gives you both an overview of where the place is situated and a step-by-step set of movements to follow and places to look for, as well as brief descriptions of the most prominent guideposts along the way, and possibly even a review of the original directions, together with a brief remark or two about misleading spots to avoid. Whenever we ask for directions, after all, we want not only to get reliable information but also to get it in a form that cannot be misunderstood. So, whenever people give directions, they try not only to give them accurately but also to give them so clearly from start to finish that they cannot be mistaken. By the same token, whenever people try to explain something in writing, they want to help readers get from one place to another in a particular subject matter. So, in the midst of giving a process analysis or causal analysis, a writer might feel compelled to illustrate this point, or define that term, or offer a telling analogy.

In the twenty-seven pieces that make up this section, you will get to see how different writers in different fields combine various methods of explaining things in language. And in later sections, you will see how explaining combines with both arguing and reflecting.

Arts and Humanities

WHO KILLED KING KONG?
X. J. Kennedy

X. J. Kennedy was born Joseph Charles Kennedy in New Jersey in 1929. With a B.S. from Seton Hall College, M.A. from Columbia University, and four years' service in the U.S. Navy, he went to the University of Michigan for further graduate study. In 1961, his first book of poetry, Nude Descending a Staircase, *was the distinguished Lamont Poetry Selection. A poet who wishes "to be seriously funny," Kennedy is also well known as an essayist; an anthologist, especially of poetry; and a teacher. The following essay, speculating on the appeal of the original version of the ever-popular* King Kong, *first appeared in 1960 in* Dissent: A Quarterly of Socialist Opinion, *edited by the author, teacher, and critic Irving Howe.*

The ordeal and spectacular death of King Kong, the giant ape, undoubtedly 1 have been witnessed by more Americans than have ever seen a performance of *Hamlet, Iphigenia at Aulis,* or even *Tobacco Road.* Since RKO-Radio Pictures first released *King Kong,* a quarter-century has gone by; yet year after year, from prints that grow more rain-beaten, from sound tracks that grow more tinny, ticket-buyers by thousands still pursue Kong's luckless fight against the forces of technology, tabloid journalism, and the DAR. They see him chloroformed to sleep, see him whisked from his jungle isle to New York and placed on show, see him burst his chains to roam the city (lugging a frightened blonde), at last to plunge from the spire of the Empire State Building, machine-gunned by model airplanes.

X. J. Kennedy

Though Kong may die, one begins to think his legend unkillable. No clearer 2 proof of his hold upon the popular imagination may be seen than what emerged one catastrophic week in March 1955, when New York WOR-TV programmed *Kong* for seven evenings in a row (a total of sixteen showings). Many a rival network vice-president must have scowled when surveys showed that *Kong*— the 1933 B-picture—had lured away fat segments of the viewing populace from such powerful competitors as Ed Sullivan, Groucho Marx and Bishop Sheen.

But even television has failed to run *King Kong* into oblivion. Coffee-in-the- 3 lobby cinemas still show the old hunk of hokum, with the apology that in its use of composite shots and animated models the film remains technically interesting. And no other monster in movie history has won so devoted a popular audience. None of the plodding mummies, the stultified draculas, the white-coated Lugosis with their shiny pinball-machine laboratories,[1] none of the invisible stranglers, berserk robots, or menaces from Mars has ever enjoyed so many resurrections.

Why does the American public refuse to let King Kong rest in peace? It is 4 true, I'll admit, that *Kong* outdid every monster movie before or since in sheer carnage. Producers Cooper and Schoedsack crammed into it dinosaurs, headhunters, riots, aerial battles, bullets, bombs, bloodletting. Heroine Fay Wray, whose function is mainly to scream, shuts her mouth for hardly one uninterrupted minute from first reel to last. It is also true that *Kong* is larded with good healthy sadism, for those whose joy it is to see the frantic girl dangled from cliffs and harried by pterodactyls. But it seems to me that the abiding appeal of the giant ape rests on other foundations.

Kong has, first of all, the attraction of being manlike. His simian nature 5 gives him one huge advantage over giant ants and walking vegetables in that an audience may conceivably identify with him. Kong's appeal has the quality that established the Tarzan series as American myth—for what man doesn't secretly image himself a huge hairy howler against whom no other monster has a chance? If Tarzan recalls the ape n us, then Kong may well appeal to that great-granddaddy primordial brute from whose tribe we have all deteriorated.

Intentionally or not, the producers of *King Kong* encourage this identification 6 by etching the character of Kong with keen sympathy. For the ape is a figure in a tradition familiar to moviegoers: the tradition of the pitiable monster. We think of Lon Chaney in the role of Quasimodo, of Karloff in the original *Frankenstein*.[2] As we watch the Frankenstein monster's fumbling and disastrous attempts to befriend a flower-picking child, our sympathies are enlisted with the monster in his impenetrable loneliness. And so with Kong. As he roars in his chains, while barkers sell tickets to boobs who gape at him, we perhaps feel

---

[1]Lugosis: after the actor, Bela Lugosi, known for his roles in horror movies. [Eds.]

[2]Lon Chaney . . . Karloff: Chaney (1883–1930) was an actor who played the title role in *The Hunchback of Notre Dame*; Boris Karloff (1887–1969) was also an actor known for his monster roles, particularly in the 1931 version of *Frankenstein*. [Eds.]

something more deep than pathos. We begin to sense something of the problem that engaged Eugene O'Neill in *The Hairy Ape:* the dilemma of a displaced animal spirit forced to live in a jungle built by machines.

King Kong, it is true, had special relevance in 1933. Landscapes of the depression are glimpsed early in the film when an impresario, seeking some desperate pretty girl to play the lead in a jungle movie, visits souplines and a Woman's Home Mission. In Fay Wray—who's been caught snitching an apple from a fruitstand—his search is ended. When he gives her a big feed and a movie contract, the girl is magic-carpeted out of the world of the National Recovery Act.[3] And when, in the film's climax, Kong smashes that very Third Avenue landscape in which Fay had wandered hungry, audiences of 1933 may well have felt a personal satisfaction.

What is curious is that audiences of 1960 remain hooked. For in the heart of urban man, one suspects, lurks the impulse to fling a bomb. Though machines speed him to the scene of his daily grind, though IBM comptometers ("freeing the human mind from drudgery") enable him to drudge more efficiently once he arrives, there comes a moment when he wishes to turn upon his machines and kick hell out of them. He wants to hurl his combination radio-alarmclock out the bedroom window and listen to its smash. What subway commuter wouldn't love—just for once—to see the downtown express smack head-on into the uptown local? Such a wish is gratified in that memorable scene in *Kong* that opens with a wide-angle shot: interior of a railway car on the Third Avenue El. Straphangers are nodding, the literate refold their newspapers. Unknown to them, Kong has torn away a section of trestle toward which the train now speeds. The motorman spies Kong up ahead, jams on the brakes. Passengers hurtle together like so many peas in a pail. In a window of the car appear Kong's bloodshot eyes. Women shriek. Kong picks up the railway car as if it were a rat, flips it to the street and ties knots in it, or something. To any commuter the scene must appear one of the most satisfactory pieces of celluloid ever exposed.

Yet however violent his acts, Kong remains a gentleman. Remarkable is his sense of chivalry. Whenever a fresh boa constrictor threatens Fay, Kong first sees that the lady is safely parked, then manfully thrashes her attacker. (And she, the ingrate, runs away every time his back is turned.) Atop the Empire State Building, ignoring his pursuers, Kong places Fay on a ledge as tenderly as if she were a dozen eggs. He fondles her, then turns to face the Army Air Force. And Kong is perhaps the most disinterested lover since Cyrano:[4] his attentions to the lady are utterly without hope of reward. After all, between a five-foot blonde and a fifty-foot ape, love can hardly be more than an intellectual

[3]National Recovery Act: congressional legislation passed in 1933 to help industry recover from the Depression and to reduce unemployment. [Eds.]

[4]Cyrano (de Bergerac): hero of Edmond Rostand's play by the same name who is prevented from professing his love by his sensitivity about his huge nose. [Eds.]

flirtation. In his simian way King Kong is the hopelessly yearning lover of Petrarchan convention.[5] His forced exit from his jungle, in chains, results directly from his single-minded pursuit of Fay. He smashes a Broadway theater when the notion enters his dull brain that the flashbulbs of photographers somehow endanger the lady. His perilous shinnying up a skyscraper to pluck Fay from her boudoir is an act of the kindliest of hearts. He's impossible to discourage even though the love of his life can't lay eyes on him without shrieking murder.

The tragedy of King Kong then, is to be the beast who at the end of the fable 10 fails to turn into the handsome prince. This is the conviction that the scriptwriters would leave with us in the film's closing line. As Kong's corpse lies blocking traffic in the street, the entrepreneur who brought Kong to New York turns to the assembled reporters and proclaims: "That's your story, boys—it was Beauty killed the Beast!" But greater forces than those of the screaming Lady have combined to lay Kong low, if you ask me. Kong lives for a time as one of those persecuted near-animal souls bewildered in the middle of an industrial order, whose simple desires are thwarted at every turn. He climbs the Empire State Building because in all New York it's the closest thing he can find to the clifftop of his jungle isle. He dies, a pitiful dolt, and the army brass and publicitymen cackle over him. His death is the only possible outcome to as neat a tragic dilemma as you can ask for. The machine-guns do him in, while the manicured human hero (a nice clean Dartmouth boy) carries away Kong's sweetheart to the altar. O, the misery of it all. There's far more truth about upper-middle-class American life in *King Kong* than in the last seven dozen novels of John P. Marquand.[6]

A Negro friend from Atlanta tells me that in movie houses in colored neigh- 11 borhoods throughout the South, *Kong* does a constant business. They show the thing in Atlanta at least every year, presumably to the same audiences. Perhaps this popularity may simply be due to the fact that Kong is one of the most watchable movies ever constructed, but I wonder whether Negro audiences may not find some archetypical appeal in this serio-comic tale of a huge black powerful free spirit whom all the hardworking white policemen are out to kill.

Every day in the week on a screen somewhere in the world, King Kong 12 relives his agony. Again and again he expires on the Empire State Building, as audiences of the devout assist his sacrifice. We watch him die, and by extension kill the ape within our bones, but these little deaths of ours occur in prosaic surroundings. We do not die on a tower, New York before our feet, nor do we give our lives to smash a few flying machines. It is not for us to bring to a

---

[5]the hopelessly yearning lover of Petrarchan convention: typical condition of the lover in the sonnets of the Italian poet Francis Petrarch (1304–1374) and in the poetry of those influenced by him. [Eds.]

[6]John P. Marquand (1893–1960): American novelist and short-story writer, known for his affectionate satires of upper-middle-class Boston society. [Eds.]

momentary standstill the civilization in which we move. King Kong does this for us. And so we kill him again and again, in much-spliced celluloid, while the ape in us expires from day to day, obscure, in desperation.

QUESTIONS

1. In paragraph 10, Kennedy reminds us of a capsule interpretation of *King Kong* that the movie itself supplies: "That's your story, boys—it was Beauty killed the Beast!" But it is clear that Kennedy isn't satisfied with that explanation. What are some of the points that lead him beyond the movie's own explanation?

2. Define Kennedy's point of view in this essay. To what extent does his point of view limit what he is able to say about the movie? What different considerations might he have included had he written from a feminist's perspective, or as a civil defense director, or as an administrator of the S.P.C.A.?

3. Why does Kennedy refer to "the old hunk of hokum" (paragraph 3)? Does he refer more to the monster or the film?

4. One of the complicating factors Kennedy finds in the movie is the possibility of our own identification, as moviegoers, with King Kong, who recalls, according to Kennedy, "that great-granddaddy primordial brute from whose tribe we have all deteriorated" (paragraph 5). How thoroughly does Kennedy develop this notion of identification, and how seriously do you take it?

5. What is implied by the word "deteriorated" in the passage quoted in question 4 above? What does that word suggest about the world in which Kong finds himself? How does Kennedy's choice of that word in its context reflect on this article's title?

6. Consider the phrases "so many peas in a pail" and "or something" in paragraph 8. What do those phrases make you alert to? What are other examples of similar phrasing?

7. Write an interpretation of a more recent "monster movie," trying to explain the appeal of its central character.

8. Read several movie reviews of Dino De Laurentiis's remake of *King Kong*, which appeared in 1976. Write a paper explaining how it was compared to RKO's original version from 1933, which Kennedy discusses.

ART FOR ETERNITY
E. H. Gombrich

E. H. Gombrich (b. 1890) describes himself as an art historian "with philosophical and psychological interests." He directs the Warburg Institute of the University of London. His Mellon Lectures, given in 1956 at the National Gallery of Art in Washington, D.C., were published as Art and Illusion, *his most important and influential book. Gombrich has also written an introduction to art history,* The Story of Art *(1972), in which the following selection appears as part of the second chapter.*

Everyone knows that Egypt is the land of the pyramids, those mountains of stone which stand like weathered landmarks on the distant horizon of history [Fig. 1]. However remote and mysterious they seem, they tell us much of their own story. They tell us of a land which was so thoroughly organized that it was possible to pile up these gigantic mounds in the lifetime of a single king, and they tell us of kings who were so rich and powerful that they could force thousands and thousands of workers or slaves to toil for them year in, year out, to quarry the stones, to drag them to the building site, and to shift them with the most primitive means till the tomb was ready to receive the king. No king and no people would have gone to such expense, and taken so much trouble, for the creation of a mere monument. In fact, we know that the pyramids had their practical importance in the eyes of the kings and their subjects. The king was considered a divine being who held sway over them, and on his departure from this earth he would again ascend to the gods whence he had come. The pyramids soaring up to the sky would probably help him to make his ascent. In any case they would preserve his sacred body from decay. For the Egyptians believed that the body must be preserved if the soul is to live on in the beyond. That is why they prevented the corpse from decaying by an elaborate method of embalming it, and binding it up in strips of cloth. It was for the mummy of the king that the pyramid had been piled up, and his body was laid right in the center of the huge mountain of stone in a stone coffin. Everywhere round the burial chamber, spells and incantations were written to help him on his journey to the other world.

But it is not only these oldest relics of human architecture which tell of the role played by age-old beliefs in the story of art. The Egyptians held the belief that the preservation of the body was not enough. If the likeness of the king was also preserved, it was doubly sure that he would continue to exist for ever. So they ordered sculptors to chisel the king's head out of hard, imperishable granite,

212

and put it in the tomb where no one saw it, there to work its spell and to help his soul to keep alive in and through the image. One Egyptian word for sculptor was actually "He-who-keeps-alive."

At first these rites were reserved for kings, but soon the nobles of the royal household had their minor tombs grouped in neat rows round the king's mound; and gradually every self-respecting person had to make provision for his after-life by ordering a costly grave which would house his mummy and his likeness, and where his soul could dwell and receive the offerings of food and drink which were given to the dead. Some of these early portraits from the pyramid age, the fourth "dynasty" of the "Old Kingdom,"[1] are among the most beautiful works of Egyptian art [Fig. 2]. There is a solemnity and simplicity about them which one does not easily forget. One sees that the sculptor was not trying to flatter his sitter, or to preserve a fleeting expression. He was concerned only with essentials. Every lesser detail he left out. Perhaps it is just because of this strict concentration on the basic forms of the human head that these portraits remain so impressive. For, despite their almost geometrical rigidity, they are not prim-itive. . . . Nor are they . . . naturalistic portraits. . . . The observation of nature,

1. The Great Pyramid of Gizeh. *Built about* 2700 B.C.

---

[1]the fourth "dynasty" of the "Old Kingdom": period in Egyptian history from about 2900 B.C. to 2700 B.C. [Eds.]

2. Portrait head of limestone. *Found in a tomb at Gizeh, made about 2700* B.C. *Vienna, Kunst-historisches Museum*

and the regularity of the whole, are so evenly balanced that they impress us as being lifelike and yet remote and enduring.

This combination of geometric regularity and keen observation of nature is 4 characteristic of all Egyptian art. We can study it best in the reliefs and paintings that adorned the walls of the tombs. The word "adorned," it is true, may hardly fit an art which was meant to be seen by no one but the dead man's soul. In fact, these works were not intended to be enjoyed. They, too, were meant to "keep alive." Once, in a grim distant past, it had been the custom when a powerful man died to let his servants and slaves accompany him into the grave. They were sacrificed so that he should arrive in the beyond with a suitable train. Later, these horrors were considered either too cruel or too costly, and art came to the rescue. Instead of real servants, the great ones of this earth were given images as substitutes. The pictures and models found in Egyptian tombs were connected with the idea of providing the soul with helpmates in the other world.

To us these reliefs and wall-paintings provide an extraordinarily vivid picture 5 of life as it was lived in Egypt thousands of years ago. And yet, looking at them for the first time, one may find them rather bewildering. The reason is that the Egyptian painters had quite a different way from ours of representing real life. Perhaps this is connected with the different purpose their paintings had to serve. What mattered most was not prettiness but completeness. It was the artists' task to preserve everything as clearly and permanently as possible. So they did not set out to sketch nature as it appeared to them from any fortuitous angle. They drew from memory, according to strict rules which ensured that everything that had to go into the picture would stand out in perfect clarity. Their method, in fact, resembled that of the map-maker rather than that of the painter. Fig. 3 shows it in a simple example, representing a garden with a pond. If we had to draw such a motif we might wonder from which angle to approach it. The shape and character of the trees could be seen clearly only from the sides, the shape of the pond would be visible only if seen from above. The Egyptians had no compunction about this problem. They would simply draw the pond as if it were seen from above, and the trees from the side. The fishes and birds in the pond, on the other hand, would hardly look recognizable as seen from above, so they were drawn in profile.

In such a simple picture, we can easily understand the artist's procedure. A 6 similar method is often used by children. But the Egyptians were much more consistent in their application of these methods than children ever are. Everything had to be represented from its most characteristic angle. Fig. 4 shows the effect which this idea had on the representation of the human body. The head was most easily seen in profile so they drew it sideways. But if we think of the human eye we think of it as seen from the front. Accordingly, a full-face eye was planted into the side view of the face. The top half of the body, the shoulders and chest, are best seen from the front, for then we see how the arms are hinged to the body. But arms and legs in movement are much more clearly seen sideways. That is the reason why Egyptians in these pictures look so strangely flat and contorted. Moreover the Egyptian artists found it hard to visualize either foot seen from the outside. They preferred the clear outline from the big toe upwards. So both feet are seen from the inside, and the man on the relief looks as if he had two left feet. It must not be supposed that Egyptian artists thought

215

E. H. Gombrich

3. Painting of a pond. *From a tomb in Thebes. About 1400* B.C. *London, British Museum*

that human beings looked like that. They merely followed a rule which allowed them to include everything in the human form that they considered important. Perhaps this strict adherence to the rule had something to do with their magic purpose. For how could a man with his arm "foreshortened" or "cut off" bring or receive the required offerings to the dead?

Here as always, Egyptian art is not based on what the artist could see at a given moment, but rather on what he knew belonged to a person or a scene. It was out of these forms which he had learned, and which he knew, that he built his representations, much as the tribal artist builds his figures out of the forms he can master. It is not only his knowledge of forms and shapes that the artist embodies in his picture, but also his knowledge of their significance. We sometimes call a man a "big boss." The Egyptian drew the boss bigger than his servants or even his wife.

Once we have grasped these rules and conventions, we understand the language of the pictures in which life of the Egyptians is chronicled. Fig. 5 gives

7

8

216

4. Portrait of Hesire from a wooden door in his tomb. *Carved about 2700* B.C. *Cairo, Museum*

a good idea of the general arrangement of a wall in a tomb of a high Egyptian dignitary of the so-called "Middle Kingdom,"[2] some nineteen hundred years before our era. The inscriptions in hieroglyphs tell us exactly who he was, and what titles and honors he had collected in his lifetime. His name, we read, was Chnemhotep, the Administrator of the Eastern Desert, Prince of Menat Chufu, Confidential Friend of the King, Royal Acquaintance, Superintendent of the

[2]"Middle Kingdom": period in Egyptian history from about 2000 B.C. to 1800 B.C. [Eds.]

E. H. Gombrich

5. A wall from the tomb of Chnemhotep near Beni Hassan. *About 1900* B.C.

Priests, Priest of Horus, Priest of Anubis, Chief of all the Divine Secrets, and—most impressive of all—Master of all the Tunics. On the left side we see him hunting wild-fowl with a kind of boomerang, accompanied by his wife Cheti, his concubine Jat, and one of his sons who, despite his tiny size in the picture, held the title of Superintendent of the Frontiers. Below, in the frieze, we see fishermen under their superintendent Mentuhotep hauling in a big catch. On top of the door Chnemhotep is seen again, this time trapping waterfowl in a net. Understanding the methods of the Egyptian artist, we can easily see how this device worked. The trapper sat hidden behind a screen of reeds, holding a cord, which was linked with the open net (seen from above). When the birds had settled on the bait, he pulled the rope and the net closed over them. Behind Chnemhotep is his eldest son Nacht, and his Superintendent of the Treasures, who was also responsible for the ordering of the tomb. On the right side, Chnemhotep, who is called "great in fish, rich in wild-fowl, loving the goddess of the chase," is seen spearing fish. Once more we can observe the conventions of the Egyptian artist who lets the water rise among the reeds to show us the clearing with the fish. The inscription says: "Canoeing in the papyrus beds, the

218

pools of wild-fowl, the marshes and the streams, spearing with the two-pronged spear, he transfixes thirty fish; how delightful is the day of hunting the hippopotamus." Below is an amusing episode with one of the men who had fallen into the water being fished out by his mates. The inscription round the door records the days on which offerings are to be given to the dead, and includes prayers to the gods.

When we have become accustomed to looking at these Egyptian pictures we are as little troubled by their unrealities as we are by the absence of color in a photograph. We even begin to realize the great advantages of the Egyptian method. Nothing in these pictures gives the impression of being haphazard, nothing looks as if it could just as well be somewhere else. It is worth while taking a pencil and trying to copy one of these "primitive" Egyptian drawings. Our attempts always look clumsy, lopsided and crooked. At least my own do. For the Egyptian sense of order in every detail is so strong that any little variation seems to upset it entirely. The Egyptian artist began his work by drawing a network of straight lines on the wall, and he distributed his figures with great care along these lines. And yet all this geometrical sense of order did not prevent him from observing the details of nature with amazing accuracy. Every bird or fish is drawn with such truthfulness that zoologists can still recognize the species. Fig. 6 shows such a detail of Fig. 5—the birds in the tree by Chnemhotep's fowling net. It was not only his great knowledge which guided the artist, but also an eye for pattern.

It is one of the greatest things in Egyptian art that all the statues, paintings and architectural forms seem to fall into place as if they obeyed one law. We call such a law, which all creations of a people seem to obey, a "style." It is very difficult to explain in words what makes a style, but it is far less difficult to see. The rules which govern all Egyptian art give every individual work the effect of poise and austere harmony.

The Egyptian style comprised a set of very strict laws, which every artist had to learn from his earliest youth. Seated statues had to have their hands on their knees; men had to be painted with darker skin than women; the appearance of every Egyptian god was strictly laid down: Horus, the sun-god, had to be shown as a falcon or with a falcon's head, Anubis, the god of death, as a jackal or with a jackal's head. Every artist also had to learn the art of beautiful script. He had to cut the images and symbols of the hieroglyphs clearly and accurately in stone. But once he had mastered all these rules he had finished his apprenticeship. No one wanted anything different, no one asked him to be "original." On the contrary, he was probably considered the best artist who could make his statues most like the admired monuments of the past. So it happened that in the course of three thousand years or more Egyptian art changed very little. Everything that was considered good and beautiful in the age of the pyramids was held to be just as excellent a thousand years later. True, new fashions appeared, and

219

6. Birds in a bush. *Detail of Fig. 5*

new subjects were demanded of the artists, but their mode of representing man and nature remained essentially the same.

Only one man ever shook the iron bars of the Egyptian style. He was a king 12 of the Eighteenth Dynasty, in the period known as the "New Kingdom,"[3] which was founded after a catastrophic invasion of Egypt. This king, called Amenophis IV, was a heretic. He broke with many of the customs hallowed by age-old tradition. He did not wish to pay homage to the many strangely shaped gods of his people. For him only one god was supreme, Aton, whom he worshipped and whom he had represented in the shape of the sun. He called himself Akhnaton, after his god, and he moved his court out of reach of the priests of the other gods, to a place which is now called El-Amarna.

The pictures which he commissioned must have shocked the Egyptians of 13 his day by their novelty. In them none of the solemn and rigid dignity of the earlier Pharaohs was to be found. Instead, he had himself depicted lifting his daughter on to his knees, walking with his wife in the garden, leaning on his stick. Some of his portraits show him as an ugly man [Fig. 7]—perhaps he wanted the artists to portray him in all his human frailty or, perhaps, he was so convinced of his unique importance as a prophet that he insisted on a true likeness. Akhnaton's successor was Tutankhamen, whose tomb with its treasures was discovered in 1922. Some of these works are still in the modern style of the Aton religion—particularly the back of the king's throne [Fig. 8], which shows the king and queen in a homely idyll. He is sitting on his chair in an attitude which might have scandalized the strict Egyptian conservative—almost lolling, by Egyptian standards. His wife is no smaller than he is, and gently puts her hand on his shoulder while the Sun-god, represented as a golden orb, is stretching his hands in blessing down to them.

It is not impossible that this reform of art in the Eighteenth Dynasty was 14 made easier for the king because he could point to foreign works that were much less strict and rigid than the Egyptian products. On an island overseas, in Crete, there dwelt a gifted people whose artists delighted in the representation of swift movement. When the palace of their king at Knossos was excavated at the end of the nineteenth century, people could hardly believe that such a free and graceful style could have been developed in the second millennium before our era. Works in this style were also found on the Greek mainland; a dagger from Mycenae [Fig. 9] shows a sense of movement and flowing lines which must have impressed any Egyptian craftsman who had been permitted to stray from the hallowed rules of his style.

But this opening of Egyptian art did not last long. Already during the reign 15 of Tutankhamen the old beliefs were restored, and the window to the outside world was shut again. The Egyptian style, as it had existed for more than a

---

[3]the Eighteenth Dynasty, in the period known as the "New Kingdom": a period in Egyptian history from about 1600 B.C. to 1200 B.C., corresponding to the exodus of the Israelites from Egypt and the fall of Troy. [Eds.]

221

7. King Amenophis IV. *Limestone relief. About 1370* B.C. *Berlin, Museum*

thousand years before his time, continued to exist for another thousand years or more, and the Egyptians doubtless believed it would continue for all eternity. Many Egyptian works in our museums date from this later period, and so do nearly all Egyptian buildings such as temples and palaces. New themes were introduced, new tasks performed, but nothing essentially new was added to the achievement of art.

8. The Pharaoh Tutankhamen and his wife. *Gilt and painted woodwork from the throne found in his tomb. Made about 1350* B.C. *Cairo, Museum*

E. H. Gombrich

9. A dagger from Mycenae. *About 1600* B.C. *Athens, Museum*

QUESTIONS

1. Briefly state in your own words what Gombrich considers "the achievement of art" (paragraph 15) in ancient Egypt.

2. Sum up the ways in which Gombrich says Egyptian beliefs affected Egyptian art.

3. Gombrich's viewpoint is that of an art historian, but he also draws on information from other fields such as religion, anthropology, government, history, archaeology, and so on. Select one paragraph or short section, and explain how a specialist in another field might present essentially the same subject from a different angle of vision.

4. Compare the point of view of the NY Times reporter in "Tutankhamen's Tomb Is Opened" in the Reporting section with that of Gombrich, especially in paragraph 13. In what sense is Gombrich the more knowledgeable observer?

5. Given the Egyptian stylistic conventions, how do you suppose the study of Egyptian art differs from the study of the art of other periods and places?

6. The Egyptian method of drawing, as described in paragraphs 5 and 6, might be called *explanatory* or, perhaps, *analytical*. Use this method of analysis to sketch your classroom, a room in which you work regularly, or a room in which you live. Or, make an "Egyptian" portrait of a roommate or friend.

7. Like the Egyptians, we explain the relation of parts to the whole with pictorial analyses such as maps, diagrams of electrical circuitry, dress patterns, diagrams of football plays, and so on. Sometimes, however, we need to analyze with words. Select some familiar item with little or no mechanical complexity, something like a calendar, the face of a clock, or a radio or telephone dial. Write a description of it that takes into account its parts and their relations to each other.

8. Select an object to describe as you did in question 7, but this time pick something with working parts, such as an eggbeater, a can opener, a bicycle pedal and chain, a doorknob and latch, or the latch on a gate. Write a description of the item you choose, and explain how the parts work together.

9. Test Gombrich's generalizations against some examples of Egyptian art. Look for

illustrations in art history books or in books about ancient Egyptian culture. Select and describe one or two works of art in relation to Gombrich's comments about the conventional style or the violation of convention under Akhnaton.

10. Consider the idea of style as described in paragraphs 10 and 11. What styles are apparent in the ways people live in your community? Do you shift from one style of dress and behavior to another, or does a single style serve for all you do? How do you tell one style from another?

11. Write an account of styles of dress over the last few years. Consider, for example, style in men's clothing so as to emphasize either its many changes or its underlying consistency. That is, make your account either as similar to or as different from Gombrich's account of Egyptian pictorial style as you can. Compare your account with that of a classmate who has taken the opposite point of view.

12. Consider what modern constructions approach the grandeur and possible excesses of the pyramids—perhaps the Empire State Building, the space shuttle, a superdome, the Golden Gate Bridge, or something in your community. How might future historians explain one of those structures?

THE HISTORIAN AND HIS FACTS
Edward Hallet Carr

E. H. Carr (1892–1982) was a distinguished British historian whose major work was The History of Soviet Russia, *in fourteen volumes. A Fellow of Trinity College, Cambridge, Carr delivered a series of lectures there in 1961 under the general title of "What Is History?" The lectures were later published as a book, which opened with the selection reprinted here. It addressed the general question—What is history?—in terms of a more specific question: What is a historical fact?*

What is history? Lest anyone think the question meaningless or superfluous, I will take as my text two passages relating respectively to the first and second incarnations of *The Cambridge Modern History*. Here is Acton in his report of October 1896 to the Syndics of the Cambridge University Press on the work which he had undertaken to edit:[1]

> It is a unique opportunity of recording, in the way most useful to the greatest number, the fullness of the knowledge which the nineteenth century is about to bequeath. . . . By the judicious division of labour we should be able to do it, and to bring home to every man the last document, and the ripest conclusions of international research.
>
> Ultimate history we cannot have in this generation; but we can dispose of conventional history, and show the point we have reached on the road from one to the other, now that all information is within reach, and every problem has become capable of solution.[2]

And almost exactly sixty years later Professor Sir George Clark, in his general introduction to the second *Cambridge Modern History*, commented on this belief of Acton and his collaborators that it would one day be possible to produce "ultimate history," and went on:

> Historians of a later generation do not look forward to any such prospect. They expect their work to be superseded again and again. They consider that knowledge of the past has come down through one or more human minds, has been "processed"

---

[1] John Dalberg Acton (1834–1902): British historian and editor of the first *Cambridge Modern History*. [Eds.]

[2] *The Cambridge Modern History: Its Origin, Authorship and Production* (Cambridge University Press; 1907), pp. 10–12.

by them, and therefore cannot consist of elemental and impersonal atoms which nothing can alter. . . . The exploration seems to be endless, and some impatient scholars take refuge in scepticism, or at least in the doctrine that, since all historical judgments involve persons and points of view, one is as good as another and there is no "objective" historical truth.[3]

Where the pundits contradict each other so flagrantly the field is open to en- quiry. I hope that I am sufficiently up-to-date to recognize that anything written in the 1890's must be nonsense. But I am not yet advanced enough to be committed to the view that anything written in the 1950's necessarily makes sense. Indeed, it may already have occurred to you that this enquiry is liable to stray into something even broader than the nature of history. The clash between Acton and Sir George Clark is a reflection of the change in our total outlook on society over the interval between these two pronouncements. Acton speaks out of the positive belief, the clear-eyed self-confidence of the later Victorian age; Sir George Clark echoes the bewilderment and distracted scepticism of the beat generation. When we attempt to answer the question, What is history?, our answer, consciously or unconsciously, reflects our own position in time, and forms part of our answer to the broader question, what view we take of the society in which we live. I have no fear that my subject may, on closer inspec- tion, seem trivial. I am afraid only that I may seem presumptuous to have broached a question so vast and so important.

The nineteenth century was a great age for facts. "What I want," said Mr. 2 Gradgrind in *Hard Times*,[4] "is Facts. . . . Facts alone are wanted in life." Nineteenth-century historians on the whole agreed with him. When Ranke in the 1830's,[5] in legitimate protest against moralizing history, remarked that the task of the historian was "simply to show how it really was (*wie es eigentlich gewesen*)" this not very profound aphorism had an astonishing success. Three generations of German, British, and even French historians marched into battle intoning the magic words, "*Wie es eigentlich gewesen*" like an incantation— designed, like most incantations, to save them from the tiresome obligation to think for themselves. The Positivists, anxious to stake out their claim for history as a science, contributed the weight of their influence to this cult of facts. First ascertain the facts, said the positivists, then draw your conclusions from them. In Great Britain, this view of history fitted in perfectly with the empiricist tradition which was the dominant strain in British philosophy from Locke to Bertrand Russell.[6] The empirical theory of knowledge presupposes a complete separation between subject and object. Facts, like sense-impressions, impinge on the observer from outside, and are independent of his consciousness. The

---

[3]*The New Cambridge Modern History*, I (Cambridge University Press; 1957), pp. xxiv–xxv.
[4]*Hard Times*: a novel by Charles Dickens. [Eds.]
[5](Leopold von) Ranke (1795–1886): German historian. [Eds.]
[6]Locke . . . Russell: John Locke (1632–1704) was an English philosopher; Bertrand Russell (1872–1970) was an English philosopher and mathematician. [Eds.]

process of reception is passive: having received the data, he then acts on them. *The Shorter Oxford English Dictionary*, a useful but tendentious work of the empirical school, clearly marks the separateness of the two processes by defining a fact as "a datum of experience as distinct from conclusions." This is what may be called the common-sense view of history. History consists of a corpus of ascertained facts. The facts are available to the historian in documents, inscriptions, and so on, like fish on the fishmonger's slab. The historian collects them, takes them home, and cooks and serves them in whatever style appeals to him. Acton, whose culinary tastes were austere, wanted them served plain. In his letter of instructions to contributors to the first *Cambridge Modern History* he announced the requirement "that our Waterloo must be one that satisfies French and English, German and Dutch alike; that nobody can tell, without examining the list of authors where the Bishop of Oxford laid down the pen, and whether Fairbairn or Gasquet, Liebermann or Harrison took it up."[7] Even Sir George Clark, critical as he was of Acton's attitude, himself contrasted the "hard core of facts" in history with the "surrounding pulp of disputable interpretation"[8]— forgetting perhaps that the pulpy part of the fruit is more rewarding than the hard core. First get your facts straight, then plunge at your peril into the shifting sands of interpretation—that is the ultimate wisdom of the empirical, common-sense school of history. It recalls the favorite dictum of the great liberal journalist C. P. Scott: "Facts are sacred, opinion is free."

Now this clearly will not do. I shall not embark on a philosophical discussion   3
of the nature of our knowledge of the past. Let us assume for present purposes that the fact that Caesar crossed the Rubicon and the fact that there is a table in the middle of the room are facts of the same or of a comparable order, that both these facts enter our consciousness in the same or in a comparable manner, and that both have the same objective character in relation to the person who knows them. But, even on this bold and not very plausible assumption, our argument at once runs into the difficulty that not all facts about the past are historical facts, or are treated as such by the historian. What is the criterion which distinguishes the facts of history from other facts about the past?

What is a historical fact? This is a crucial question into which we must look   4
a little more closely. According to the common-sense view, there are certain basic facts which are the same for all historians and which form, so to speak, the backbone of history—the fact, for example, that the Battle of Hastings was fought in 1066. But this view calls for two observations. In the first place, it is not with facts like these that the historian is primarily concerned. It is no doubt important to know that the great battle was fought in 1066 and not in 1065 or 1067, and that it was fought at Hastings and not at Eastbourne or Brighton. The historian must not get these things wrong. But when points of this kind are

---

[7]Acton: *Lectures on Modern History* (London: Macmillan & Co.; 1906), p. 318.
[8]Quoted in *The Listener* (June 19, 1952), p. 992.

raised, I am reminded of Housman's remark that "accuracy is a duty, not a virtue."[9] To praise a historian for his accuracy is like praising an architect for using well-seasoned timber or properly mixed concrete in his building. It is a necessary condition of his work, but not his essential function. It is precisely for matters of this kind that the historian is entitled to rely on what have been called the "auxiliary sciences" of history—archaeology, epigraphy, numismatics, chronology, and so forth. The historian is not required to have the special skills which enable the expert to determine the origin and period of a fragment of pottery or marble, to decipher an obscure inscription, or to make the elaborate astronomical calculations necessary to establish a precise date. These so-called basic facts which are the same for all historians commonly belong to the category of the raw materials of the historian rather than of history itself. The second observation is that the necessity to establish these basic facts rests not on any quality in the facts themselves, but on an *a priori* decision of the historian. In spite of C. P. Scott's motto, every journalist knows today that the most effective way to influence opinion is by the selection and arrangement of the appropriate facts. It used to be said that facts speak for themselves. This is, of course, untrue. The facts speak only when the historian calls on them: it is he who decides to which facts to give the floor, and in what order or context. It was, I think, one of Pirandello's characters who said that a fact is like a sack[10]—it won't stand up till you've put something in it. The only reason why we are interested to know that the battle was fought at Hastings in 1066 is that historians regard it as a major historical event. It is the historian who has decided for his own reasons that Caesar's crossing of that petty stream, the Rubicon, is a fact of history, whereas the crossing of the Rubicon by millions of other people before or since interests nobody at all. The fact that you arrived in this building half an hour ago on foot, or on a bicycle, or in a car, is just as much a fact about the past as the fact that Caesar crossed the Rubicon. But it will probably be ignored by historians. Professor Talcott Parsons once called science "a selective system of cognitive orientations to reality."[11] It might perhaps have been put more simply. But history is, among other things, that. The historian is necessarily selective. The belief in a hard core of historical facts existing objectively and independently of the interpretation of the historian is a preposterous fallacy, but one which it is very hard to eradicate.

Let us take a look at the process by which a mere fact about the past is   5 transformed into a fact of history. At Stalybridge Wakes in 1850, a vendor of gingerbread, as the result of some petty dispute, was deliberately kicked to death by an angry mob. Is this a fact of history? A year ago I should unhesitatingly

---

[9]M. Manilius: *Astronomicon: Liber Primus*, 2nd ed. (Cambridge University Press; 1937), p. 87. A. E. Housman (1859–1936): poet and classical scholar who edited Manilius. [Eds.]

[10]Luigi Pirandello (1867–1936): Italian playwright. [Eds.]

[11]Talcott Parsons and Edward A. Shils: *Toward a General Theory of Action*, 3rd ed. (Cambridge, Mass.: Harvard University Press; 1954), p. 167.

have said "no." It was recorded by an eyewitness in some little-known memoirs;[12] but I had never seen it judged worthy of mention by any historian. A year ago Dr. Kitson Clark cited it in his Ford lectures in Oxford.[13] Does this make it into a historical fact? Not, I think, yet. Its present status, I suggest, is that it has been proposed for membership of the select club of historical facts. It now awaits a seconder and sponsors. It may be that in the course of the next few years we shall see this fact appearing first in footnotes, then in the text, of articles and books about nineteenth-century England, and that in twenty or thirty years' time it may be a well established historical fact. Alternatively, nobody may take it up, in which case it will relapse into the limbo of unhistorical facts about the past from which Dr. Kitson Clark has gallantly attempted to rescue it. What will decide which of these two things will happen? It will depend, I think, on whether the thesis or interpretation in support of which Dr. Kitson Clark cited this incident is accepted by other historians as valid and significant. Its status as a historical fact will turn on a question of interpretation. This element of interpretation enters into every fact of history.

May I be allowed a personal reminiscence? When I studied ancient history 6 in this university many years ago, I had as a special subject "Greece in the period of the Persian Wars." I collected fifteen or twenty volumes on my shelves and took it for granted that there, recorded in these volumes, I had all the facts relating to my subject. Let us assume—it was very nearly true—that those volumes contained all the facts about it that were then known, or could be known. It never occurred to me to enquire by what accident or process of attrition that minute selection of facts, out of all the myriad facts that must have once been known to somebody, had survived to become *the* facts of history. I suspect that even today one of the fascinations of ancient and mediaeval history is that it gives us the illusion of having all the facts at our disposal within a manageable compass: the nagging distinction between the facts of history and other facts about the past vanishes because the few known facts are all facts of history. As Bury, who had worked in both periods, said, "the records of ancient and mediaeval history are starred with lacunae."[14] History has been called an enormous jig-saw with a lot of missing parts. But the main trouble does not consist of the lacunae. Our picture of Greece in the fifth century B.C. is defective not primarily because so many of the bits have been accidentally lost, but because it is, by and large, the picture formed by a tiny group of people in the city of Athens. We know a lot about what fifth-century Greece looked like to an Athenian citizen; but hardly anything about what it looked like to a Spartan, a Corinthian, or a Theban—not to mention a Persian, or a slave or other non-

---

[12]Lord George Sanger: *Seventy Years a Showman* (London: J. M. Dent & Sons; 1926); pp. 188–9.

[13]These will shortly be published under the title *The Making of Victorian England*.

[14]John Bagnell Bury: *Selected Essays* (Cambridge University Press; 1930), p. 52. (lacunae: empty spaces or gaps. [Eds.])

citizen resident in Athens. Our picture has been pre-selected and predetermined for us, not so much by accident as by people who were consciously or unconsciously imbued with a particular view and thought the facts which supported that view worth preserving. In the same way, when I read in a modern history of the Middle Ages that the people of the Middle Ages were deeply concerned with religion, I wonder how we know this, and whether it is true. What we know as the facts of mediaeval history have almost all been selected for us by generations of chroniclers who were professionally occupied in the theory and practice of religion, and who therefore thought it supremely important, and recorded everything relating to it, and not much else. The picture of the Russian peasant as devoutly religious was destroyed by the revolution of 1917. The picture of mediaeval man as devoutly religious, whether true or not, is indestructible, because nearly all the known facts about him were pre-selected for us by people who believed it, and wanted others to believe it, and a mass of other facts, in which we might possibly have found evidence to the contrary, has been lost beyond recall. The dead hand of vanished generations of historians, scribes, and chroniclers has determined beyond the possibility of appeal the pattern of the past. "The history we read," writes Professor Barraclough, himself trained as a mediaevalist, "though based on facts, is, strictly speaking, not factual at all, but a series of accepted judgments."[15]

But let us turn to the different, but equally grave, plight of the modern historian. The ancient or mediaeval historian may be grateful for the vast winnowing process which, over the years, has put at his disposal a manageable corpus of historical facts. As Lytton Strachey said in his mischievous way, "ignorance is the first requisite of the historian, ignorance which simplifies and clarifies, which selects and omits."[16] When I am tempted, as I sometimes am, to envy the extreme competence of colleagues engaged in writing ancient or mediaeval history, I find consolation in the reflexion that they are so competent mainly because they are so ignorant of their subject. The modern historian enjoys none of the advantages of this built-in ignorance. He must cultivate this necessary ignorance for himself—the more so the nearer he comes to his own times. He has the dual task of discovering the few significant facts and turning them into facts of history, and of discarding the many insignificant facts as unhistorical. But this is the very converse of the nineteenth-century heresy that history consists of the compilation of a maximum number of irrefutable and objective facts. Anyone who succumbs to this heresy will either have to give up history as a bad job, and take to stamp-collecting or some other form of antiquarianism, or end in a madhouse. It is this heresy, which during the past hundred years has had such devastating effects on the modern historian, producing in Germany, in Great Britain, and in the United States a vast and

---

[15]Geoffrey Barraclough: *History in a Changing World* (London: Basil Blackwell & Mott; 1955), p. 14.
[16]Lytton Strachey: Preface to *Eminent Victorians*.

growing mass of dry-as-dust factual histories, of minutely specialized mono-
graphs, of would-be historians knowing more and more about less and less, sunk
without trace in an ocean of facts. It was, I suspect, this heresy—rather than
the alleged conflict between liberal and Catholic loyalties—which frustrated
Acton as a historian. In an early essay he said of his teacher Döllinger: "He
would not write with imperfect materials, and to him the materials were always
imperfect."[17] Acton was surely here pronouncing an anticipatory verdict on himself, on that strange phenomenon of a historian whom many would regard as
the most distinguished occupant the Regius Chair of Modern History in this
university has ever had—but who wrote no history. And Acton wrote his own
epitaph in the introductory note to the first volume of the *Cambridge Modern
History*, published just after his death, when he lamented that the requirements
pressing on the historian "threaten to turn him from a man of letters into the
compiler of an encyclopedia."[18] Something had gone wrong. What had gone
wrong was the belief in this untiring and unending accumulation of hard facts
as the foundation of history, the belief that facts speak for themselves and that
we cannot have too many facts, a belief at that time so unquestioning that few
historians then thought it necessary—and some still think it unnecessary today—
to ask themselves the question: What is history?

The nineteenth-century fetishism of facts was completed and justified by a
fetishism of documents. The documents were the Ark of the Covenant in the
temple of facts. The reverent historian approached them with bowed head and
spoke of them in awed tones. If you find it in the documents, it is so. But what,
when we get down to it, do these documents—the decrees, the treaties, the
rent-rolls, the blue books, the official correspondence, the private letters and
diaries—tell us? No document can tell us more than what the author of the
document thought—what he thought had happened, what he thought ought to
happen or would happen, or perhaps only what he wanted others to think he
thought, or even only what he himself thought he thought. None of this means
anything until the historian has got to work on it and deciphered it. The facts,
whether found in documents or not, have still to be processed by the historian
before he can make any use of them: the use he makes of them is, if I may put
it that way, the processing process.

Let me illustrate what I am trying to say by an example which I happen to
know well. When Gustav Stresemann, the Foreign Minister of the Weimar
Republic,[19] died in 1929, he left behind him an enormous mass—300 boxes
full—of papers, official, semi-official, and private, nearly all relating to the six

---

[17]Quoted in George P. Gooch: *History and Historians in the Nineteenth Century* (London:
Longmans, Green & Company; 1952), p. 385. Later Acton said of Döllinger that "it was given
him to form his philosophy of history on the largest induction ever available to man" (*History of
Freedom and Other Essays* [London: Macmillan & Co.; 1907], p. 435).
[18]*The Cambridge Modern History*, I (1902), p.4.
[19]Weimar Republic: the government of Germany, established in the city of Weimar after World
War I (1919) and lasting until Adolf Hitler rose to power in 1933. [Eds.]

years of his tenure of office as Foreign Minister. His friends and relatives naturally thought that a monument should be raised to the memory of so great a man. His faithful secretary Bernhardt got to work; and within three years there appeared three massive volumes, of some 600 pages each, of selected documents from the 300 boxes, with the impressive title *Stresemanns Vermächtnis*.[20] In the ordinary way the documents themselves would have mouldered away in some cellar or attic and disappeared for ever; or perhaps in a hundred years or so some curious scholar would have come upon them and set out to compare them with Bernhardt's text. What happened was far more dramatic. In 1945 the documents fell into the hands of the British and the American governments, who photographed the lot and put the photostats at the disposal of scholars in the Public Record Office in London and in the National Archives in Washington, so that, if we have sufficient patience and curiosity, we can discover exactly what Bernhardt did. What he did was neither very unusual nor very shocking. When Stresemann died, his Western policy seemed to have been crowned with a series of brilliant successes—Locarno, the admission of Germany to the League of Nations, the Dawes and Young plans and the American loans, the withdrawal of allied occupation armies from the Rhineland. This seemed the important and rewarding part of Stresemann's foreign policy; and it was not unnatural that it should have been over-represented in Bernhardt's selection of documents. Stresemann's Eastern policy, on the other hand, his relations with the Soviet Union, seemed to have led nowhere in particular; and, since masses of documents about negotiations which yielded only trivial results were not very interesting and added nothing to Stresemann's reputation, the process of selection could be more rigorous. Stresemann in fact devoted a far more constant and anxious attention to relations with the Soviet Union, and they played a far larger part in his foreign policy as a whole, than the reader of the Bernhardt selection would surmise. But the Bernhardt volumes compare favorably, I suspect, with many published collections of documents on which the ordinary historian implicitly relies.

This is not the end of my story. Shortly after the publication of Bernhardt's 10 volumes, Hitler came into power. Stresemann's name was consigned to oblivion in Germany, and the volumes disappeared from circulation: many, perhaps most, of the copies must have been destroyed. Today *Stresemanns Vermächtnis* is a rather rare book. But in the West Stresemann's reputation stood high. In 1935 an English publisher brought out an abbreviated translation of Bernhardt's work—a selection from Bernhardt's selection; perhaps one third of the original was omitted. Sutton, a well-known translator from the German, did his job competently and well. The English version, he explained in the preface, was "slightly condensed, but only by the omission of a certain amount of what, it was felt, was more ephemeral matter . . . of little interest to English readers or

---

[20]*Stresemanns Vermächtnis*: this title may be translated as "Stresemann's Legacy." [Eds.]

students."[21] This again is natural enough. But the result is that Stresemann's Eastern policy, already under-represented in Bernhardt, recedes still further from view, and the Soviet Union appears in Sutton's volumes merely as an occasional and rather unwelcome intruder in Stresemann's predominantly Western foreign policy. Yet it is safe to say that, for all except a few specialists, Sutton and not Bernhardt—and still less the documents themselves—represents for the Western world the authentic voice of Stresemann. Had the documents perished in 1945 in the bombing, and had the remaining Bernhardt volumes disappeared, the authenticity and authority of Sutton would never have been questioned. Many printed collections of documents gratefully accepted by historians in default of the originals rest on no securer basis than this.

But I want to carry the story one step further. Let us forget about Bernhardt 11 and Sutton, and be thankful that we can, if we choose, consult the authentic papers of a leading participant in some important events of recent European history. What do the papers tell us? Among other things they contain records of some hundreds of Stresemann's conversations with the Soviet ambassador in Berlin and of a score or so with Chicherin.[22] These records have one feature in common. They depict Stresemann as having the lion's share of the conversations and reveal his arguments as invariably well put and cogent, while those of his partner are for the most part scanty, confused, and unconvincing. This is a familiar characteristic of all records of diplomatic conversations. The documents do not tell us what happened, but only what Stresemann thought had happened, or what he wanted others to think, or perhaps what he wanted himself to think, had happened. It was not Sutton or Bernhardt, but Stresemann him- self, who started the process of selection. And, if we had, say, Chicherin's records of these same conversations, we should still learn from them only what Chicherin thought, and what really happened would still have to be recon- structed in the mind of the historian. Of course, facts and documents are es- sential to the historian. But do not make a fetish of them. They do not by themselves constitute history; they provide in themselves no ready-made answer to this tiresome question: What is history?

At this point I should like to say a few words on the question of why nine- 12 teenth-century historians were generally indifferent to the philosophy of history. The term was invented by Voltaire,[23] and has since been used in different senses; but I shall take it to mean, if I use it at all, our answer to the question: What is history? The nineteenth century was, for the intellectuals of Western Europe, a comfortable period exuding confidence and optimism. The facts were on the whole satisfactory; and the inclination to ask and answer awkward questions about them was correspondingly weak. Ranke piously believed that divine prov-

[21]*Gustav Stresemann: His Diaries, Letters, and Papers* (London: Macmillan & Co.; 1935), I, Editor's Note.

[22]Grigory Chicherin (1872–1936): a powerful Russian diplomat. [Eds.]

[23]Voltaire (1694–1778): French dramatist, philosopher, and social critic. [Eds.]

idence would take care of the meaning of history if he took care of the facts; and Burckhardt with a more modern touch of cynicism observed that "we are not initiated into the purposes of the eternal wisdom." Professor Butterfield as late as 1931 noted with apparent satisfaction that "historians have reflected little upon the nature of things and even the nature of their own subject."[24] But my predecessor in these lectures, Dr. A. L. Rowse, more justly critical, wrote of Sir Winston Churchill's *The World Crisis*—his book about the First World War—that, while it matched Trotsky's *History of the Russian Revolution* in personality, vividness, and vitality, it was inferior in one respect: it had "no philosophy of history behind it."[25] British historians refused to be drawn, not because they believed that history had no meaning, but because they believed that its meaning was implicit and self-evident. The liberal nineteenth-century view of history had a close affinity with the economic doctrine of *laissez-faire*— also the product of a serene and self-confident outlook on the world. Let everyone get on with his particular job, and the hidden hand would take care of the universal harmony. The facts of history were themselves a demonstration of the supreme fact of a beneficent and apparently infinite progress towards higher things. This was the age of innocence, and historians walked in the Garden of Eden, without a scrap of philosophy to cover them, naked and unashamed before the god of history. Since then, we have known Sin and experienced a Fall; and those historians who today pretend to dispense with a philosophy of history are merely trying, vainly and self-consciously, like members of a nudist colony, to recreate the Garden of Eden in their garden suburb. Today the awkward question can no longer be evaded.

QUESTIONS

1. Carr's essay answers the question, "What is a historical fact?" Summarize his answer to that question.

2. In paragraph 7, Carr says the historian must "cultivate . . . ignorance." What does this expression mean in its context? What is the point of the discussion of Acton and Döllinger in that paragraph? How does this discussion contribute to the larger theme of the essay?

3. In presenting an explanation, especially a controversial one, a writer must often seek to gain the confidence of the reader. How does Carr go about this? What sort of picture does he present of himself? What impression of him do you get from his references to himself in paragraphs 1 and 6, and how does that impression affect your evaluation of his position?

4. Carr's essay is not only explanatory; it is an essay on interpretation. Locate the many uses of the words *interpret* or *interpretation* in the essay, and consider how they

---

[24]Herbert Butterfield: *The Whig Interpretation of History* (London: George Bell & Sons; 1931), p. 67.
[25]Alfred L. Rowse: *The End of an Epoch* (London: Macmillan & Co.; 1947), pp. 282–3.

function in the larger discussion. What view of the relationship between facts and interpretation is presented here?

5. Carr's essay contradicts previously existing explanations of the relationship between historians and the facts they must deal with in writing history. Where does Carr summarize the opposing position? State in your own words the views of historical facts with which Carr takes issue.

6. Consider several facts generally known to you and your class. Limit your attention to recent facts, specifically from the last year. (You might first discuss in class what sorts of facts merit your attention.) Which of those facts has the best chance of becoming "a historical fact," in Carr's terms. On what does that process depend? Write an explanation of the historicity of a fact you choose, trying to convince your classmates that your fact will become a historical fact.

7. Using an accepted historical fact not mentioned by Carr, write an essay in which you consider why your chosen fact is a historical fact and what grounds we have for understanding it and accepting it as a fact.

AMERICA REVISED
Frances FitzGerald

Frances FitzGerald (b. 1940), an American free-lance jour-
nalist, won a Pulitzer Prize in general nonfiction for her
reporting of the Vietnam War. Her writing about the war,
first published in The New Yorker, *was collected in* Fire in
the Lake: The Vietnamese and Americans in Vietnam *(1973).*
She then turned to the study of American history and an
investigation of how history books change with the needs
and prejudices of the time. This work resulted in Fitz-
Gerald's second book, America Revised *(1979), where the*
following essay appears as the first chapter.

Those of us who grew up in the fifties believed in the permanence of our   1
American-history textbooks. To us as children, those texts were the truth of
things: they were American history. It was not just that we read them before we
understood that not everything that is printed is the truth, or the whole truth.
It was that they, much more than other books, had the demeanor and trappings
of authority. They were weighty volumes. They spoke in measured cadences:
imperturbable, humorless, and as distant as Chinese emperors. Our teachers
treated them with respect, and we paid them abject homage by memorizing a
chapter a week. But now the textbook histories have changed, some of them to
such an extent that an adult would find them unrecognizable.

One current junior-high-school American history begins with a story about   2
a Negro cowboy called George McJunkin. It appears that when McJunkin was
riding down a lonely trail in New Mexico one cold spring morning in 1925 he
discovered a mound containing bones and stone implements, which scientists
later proved belonged to an Indian civilization ten thousand years old. The book
goes on to say that scientists now believe there were people in the Americas at
least twenty thousand years ago. It discusses the Aztec, Mayan, and Incan
civilizations and the meaning of the word "culture" before introducing the
European explorers.[1]

Another history text—this one for the fifth grade—begins with the story of   3
how Henry B. Gonzalez, who is a member of Congress from Texas, learned
about his own nationality. When he was ten years old, his teacher told him he
was an American because he was born in the United States. His grandmother,
however, said, "The cat was born in the oven. Does that make him bread?"
After reporting that Mr. Gonzalez eventually went to college and law school,

---

[1]Wood, Gabriel, and Biller, *America* (1975), p. 3.

the book explains that "the melting pot idea hasn't worked out as some thought it would," and that now "some people say that the people of the United States are more like a salad bowl than a melting pot."[2]

Poor Columbus! He is a minor character now, a walk-on in the middle of American history. Even those books that have not replaced his picture with a Mayan temple or an Iroquois mask do not credit him with discovering America—even for the Europeans. The Vikings, they say, preceded him to the New World, and after that the Europeans, having lost or forgotten their maps, simply neglected to cross the ocean again for five hundred years. Columbus is far from being the only personage to have suffered from time and revision. Captain John Smith, Daniel Boone, and Wild Bill Hickok—the great self-promoters of American history—have all but disappeared, taking with them a good deal of the romance of the American frontier. General Custer has given way to Chief Crazy Horse; General Eisenhower no longer liberates Europe single-handed; and, indeed, most generals, even to Washington and Lee, have faded away, as old soldiers do, giving place to social reformers such as William Lloyd Garrison and Jacob Riis. A number of black Americans have risen to prominence: not only George Washington Carver but Frederick Douglass and Martin Luther King, Jr. W. E. B. Du Bois now invariably accompanies Booker T. Washington. In addition, there is a mystery man called Crispus Attucks, a fugitive slave about whom nothing seems to be known for certain except that he was a victim of the Boston Massacre and thus became one of the first casualties of the American Revolution. Thaddeus Stevens has been reconstructed[3]—his character changed, as it were, from black to white, from cruel and vindictive to persistent and sincere. As for Teddy Roosevelt, he now champions the issue of conservation instead of charging up San Juan Hill. No single President really stands out as a hero, but all Presidents—except certain unmentionables in the second half of the nineteenth century—seem to have done as well as could be expected, given difficult circumstances.

Of course, when one thinks about it, it is hardly surprising that modern scholarship and modern perspectives have found their way into children's books. Yet the changes remain shocking. Those who in the sixties complained of the bland optimism, the chauvinism, and the materialism of their old civics texts did so in the belief that, for all their protests, the texts would never change. The thought must have had something reassuring about it, for that generation never noticed when its complaints began to take effect and the songs about radioactive rainfall and houses made of ticky-tacky began to appear in the textbooks. But this is what happened.

---

[2] King and Anderson, *The United States* (sixth level), Houghton Mifflin Social Studies Program (1976), pp. 15–16.

[3] Thaddeus Stevens (1792–1868): Republican congressman from Pennsylvania. A leader in the House during and after the Civil War, he was a determined abolitionist who hated the South and violently opposed Lincoln's moderate reconstruction plan. Stevens dominated the committee that impeached Andrew Johnson.

The history texts now hint at a certain level of unpleasantness in American   6
history. Several books, for instance, tell the story of Ishi, the last "wild" Indian
in the continental United States, who, captured in 1911 after the massacre of
his tribe, spent the final four and a half years of his life in the University of
California's museum of anthropology, in San Francisco. At least three books
show the same stunning picture of the breaker boys, the child coal miners of
Pennsylvania—ancient children with deformed bodies and blackened faces who
stare stupidly out from the entrance to a mine. One book quotes a soldier on
the use of torture in the American campaign to pacify the Philippines at the
beginning of the century. A number of books say that during the American
Revolution the patriots tarred and feathered those who did not support them,
and drove many of the loyalists from the country. Almost all the present-day
history books note that the United States interned Japanese-Americans in de-
tention camps during the Second World War.

Ideologically speaking, the histories of the fifties were implacable, seamless.   7
Inside their covers, America was perfect: the greatest nation in the world, and
the embodiment of democracy, freedom, and technological progress. For them,
the country never changed in any important way: its values and its political
institutions remained constant from the time of the American Revolution. To
my generation—the children of the fifties—these texts appeared permanent just
because they were so self-contained. Their orthodoxy, it seemed, left no hand-
holds for attack, no lodging for decay. Who, after all, would dispute the wonders
of technology or the superiority of the English colonists over the Spanish? Who
would find fault with the pastorale of the West or the Old South? Who would
question the anti-Communist crusade? There was, it seemed, no point in comparing these visions with reality, since they were the public truth and were thus
quite irrelevant to what existed and to what anyone privately believed. They
were—or so it seemed—the permanent expression of mass culture in America.

But now the texts have changed, and with them the country that American   8
children are growing up into. The society that was once uniform is now a
patchwork of rich and poor, old and young, men and women, blacks, whites,
Hispanics, and Indians. The system that ran so smoothly by means of the
Constitution under the guidance of benevolent conductor Presidents is now a
rattletrap affair. The past is no highway to the present; it is a collection of issues
and events that do not fit together and that lead in no single direction. The
word "progress" has been replaced by the word "change": children, the modern
texts insist, should learn history so that they can adapt to the rapid changes
taking place around them. History is proceeding in spite of us. The present,
which was once portrayed in the concluding chapters as a peaceful haven of
scientific advances and Presidential inaugurations, is now a tangle of problems:
race problems, urban problems, foreign-policy problems, problems of pollution,
poverty, energy depletion, youthful rebellion, assassination, and drugs. Some
books illustrate these problems dramatically. One, for instance, contains a picture of a doll half buried in a mass of untreated sewage; the caption reads, "Are

we in danger of being overwhelmed by the products of our society and wastage created by their production? Would you agree with this photographer's interpretation?"[4] Two books show the same picture of an old black woman sitting in a straight chair in a dingy room, her hands folded in graceful resignation;[5] the surrounding text discusses the problems faced by the urban poor and by the aged who depend on Social Security. Other books present current problems less starkly. One of the texts concludes sagely:

> Problems are part of life. Nations face them, just as people face them, and try to solve them. And today's Americans have one great advantage over past generations. Never before have Americans been so well equipped to solve their problems. They have today the means to conquer poverty, disease, and ignorance. The technetronic age has put that power into their hands.[6]

Such passages have a familiar ring. Amid all the problems, the deus ex machina of science still dodders around in the gloaming of pious hope.

Even more surprising than the emergence of problems is the discovery that the great unity of the texts has broken. Whereas in the fifties all texts represented the same political view, current texts follow no pattern of orthodoxy. Some books, for instance, portray civil-rights legislation as a series of actions taken by a wise, paternal government; others convey some suggestion of the social upheaval involved and make mention of such people as Stokely Carmichael and Malcolm X. In some books, the Cold War has ended; in others, it continues, with Communism threatening the free nations of the earth.

The political diversity in the books is matched by a diversity of pedagogical approach. In addition to the traditional narrative histories, with their endless streams of facts, there are so-called "discovery," or "inquiry," texts, which deal with a limited number of specific issues in American history. These texts do not pretend to cover the past; they focus on particular topics, such as "stratification in Colonial society" or "slavery and the American Revolution," and illustrate them with documents from primary and secondary sources. The chapters in these books amount to something like case studies, in that they include testimony from people with different perspectives or conflicting views on a single subject. In addition, the chapters provide background information, explanatory notes, and a series of questions for the student. The questions are the heart of the matter, for when they are carefully selected they force students to think much as historians think: to define the point of view of the speaker, analyze the ideas presented, question the relationship between events, and so on. One text, for example, quotes Washington, Jefferson, and John Adams on the question of foreign alliances and then asks, "What did John Adams assume that the

[4]Sellers et al., *As It Happened* (1975), p. 812.
[5]Graff, *The Free and the Brave*, 2nd ed. (1972), p. 696; and Graff and Krout, *The Adventure*, 2nd ed. (1973), p. 784.
[6]Wood, Gabriel, and Biller, *America* (1975), p. 812.

international situation would be after the American Revolution? What did Washington's attitude toward the French alliance seem to be? How do you account for his attitude?" Finally, it asks, "Should a nation adopt a policy toward alliances and cling to it consistently, or should it vary its policies toward other countries as circumstances change?"[7] In these books, history is clearly not a list of agreed-upon facts or a sermon on politics but a babble of voices and a welter of events which must be ordered by the historian.

In matters of pedagogy, as in matters of politics, there are not two sharply   11 differentiated categories of books; rather, there is a spectrum. Politically, the books run from moderate left to moderate right; pedagogically, they run from the traditional history sermons, through a middle ground of narrative texts with inquiry-style questions and of inquiry texts with long stretches of narrative, to the most rigorous of case-study books. What is common to the current texts— and makes all of them different from those of the fifties—is their engagement with the social sciences. In eighth-grade histories, the "concepts" of social science make fleeting appearances. But these "concepts" are the very foundation stones of various elementary-school social-studies series. The 1970 Harcourt Brace Jovanovich series, for example, boasts in its preface of "a horizontal base or ordering of conceptual schemes" to match its "vertical arm of behavioral themes."[8] What this means is not entirely clear, but the books do proceed from easy questions to hard ones, such as—in the sixth-grade book—"How was interaction between merchants and citizens different in the Athenian and Spartan social systems?" Virtually all the American-history texts for older children include discussions of "role," "status," and "culture." Some of them stage debates between eminent social scientists in roped-off sections of the text; some include essays on economics or sociology; some contain pictures and short biographies of social scientists of both sexes and of diverse races. Many books seem to accord social scientists a higher status than American Presidents.

Quite as striking as these political and pedagogical alterations is the change   12 in the physical appearance of the texts. The schoolbooks of the fifties showed some effort in the matter of design: they had maps, charts, cartoons, photographs, and an occasional four-color picture to break up the columns of print. But beside the current texts they look as naïve as Soviet fashion magazines. The print in the fifties books is heavy and far too black, the colors muddy. The photographs are conventional news shots—portraits of Presidents in three-quarters profile, posed "action" shots of soldiers. The other illustrations tend to be Socialist-realist-style drawings (there are a lot of hefty farmers with hoes in the Colonial-period chapters) or incredibly vulgar made-for-children paintings of patriotic events. One painting shows Columbus standing in full court dress on a beach in the New World from a perspective that could have belonged only

---

[7]Fenton, gen. ed., *A New History of the United States*, grade eleven (1969), p. 170.
[8]Brandwein et al., *The Social Sciences* (1975), introductions to all books.

to the Arawaks.[9] By contrast, the current texts are paragons of sophisticated modern design. They look not like *People* or *Family Circle* but, rather, like *Architectural Digest* or *Vogue*. One of them has an Abstract Expressionist design on its cover, another a Rauschenberg-style collage, a third a reproduction of an American primitive painting. Inside, almost all of them have a full-page reproduction of a painting of the New York school—a Jasper Johns flag, say, or "The Boston Massacre," by Larry Rivers. But these reproductions are separated only with difficulty from the over-all design, for the time charts in the books look like Noland stripe paintings, and the distribution charts are as punctilious as Albers' squares in their color gradings. The amount of space given to illustrations is far greater than it was in the fifties; in fact, in certain "slow-learner" books the pictures far outweigh the text in importance. However, the illustrations have a much greater historical value. Instead of made-up paintings or anachronistic sketches, there are cartoons, photographs, and paintings drawn from the periods being treated. The chapters on the Colonial period will show, for instance, a ship's carved prow, a Revere bowl, a Copley painting—a whole gallery of Early Americana. The nineteenth century is illustrated with nineteenth-century cartoons and photographs—and the photographs are all of high artistic quality. As for the twentieth-century chapters, they are adorned with the contents of a modern-art museum.

The use of all this art and high-quality design contains some irony. The 13 nineteenth-century photographs of child laborers or urban slum apartments are so beautiful that they transcend their subjects. To look at them, or at the Victor Gatto painting of the Triangle shirtwaist-factory fire, is to see not misery or ugliness but an art object. In the modern chapters, the contrast between style and content is just as great: the color photographs of junkyards or polluted rivers look as enticing as *Gourmet*'s photographs of food. The book that is perhaps the most stark in its description of modern problems illustrates the horrors of nuclear testing with a pretty Ben Shahn picture of the Bikini explosion,[10] and the potential for global ecological disaster with a color photograph of the planet swirling its mantle of white clouds.[11] Whereas in the nineteen-fifties the texts were childish in the sense that they were naïve and clumsy, they are now childish in the sense that they are polymorphous-perverse. American history is not dull any longer; it is a sensuous experience.

The surprise that adults feel in seeing the changes in history texts must come 14 from the lingering hope that there is, somewhere out there, an objective truth. The hope is, of course, foolish. All of us children of the twentieth century know, or should know, that there are no absolutes in human affairs, and thus there can be no such thing as perfect objectivity. We know that each historian

---

[9]Arawaks: American Indians then inhabiting the Caribbean area. [Eds.]
[10]Bikini explosion: the Bikini atoll in the Pacific Ocean was the site of American nuclear-bomb testing from 1946 to 1958. [Eds.]
[11]Ver Steeg and Hofstadter, *A People* (1974), pp. 722–23.

in some degree creates the world anew and that all history is in some degree contemporary history. But beyond this knowledge there is still a hope for some reliable authority, for some fixed stars in the universe. We may know journalists cannot be wholly unbiased and that "balance" is an imaginary point between two extremes, and yet we hope that Walter Cronkite will tell us the truth of things. In the same way, we hope that our history will not change—that we learned the truth of things as children. The texts, with their impersonal voices, encourage this hope, and therefore it is particularly disturbing to see how they change, and how fast.

Slippery history! Not every generation but every few years the content of American-history books for children changes appreciably. Schoolbooks are not, like trade books,[12] written and left to their fate. To stay in step with the cycles of "adoption" in school districts across the country, the publishers revise most of their old texts or substitute new ones every three or four years. In the process of revision, they not only bring history up to date but make changes—often substantial changes—in the body of the work. History books for children are thus more contemporary than any other form of history. How should it be otherwise? Should students read histories written ten, fifteen, thirty years ago? In theory, the system is reasonable—except that each generation of children reads only one generation of schoolbooks. That transient history is those children's history forever—their particular version of America.

QUESTIONS

1. What does FitzGerald say are the main differences between the history textbooks of the fifties and those of today? What are the main points of her comparison?

2. What evidence does FitzGerald offer to support her explanation of these differences? Can you think of other illustrations that she might have used, perhaps from a textbook that you have read?

3. FitzGerald identifies her primary audience in the first sentence: "Those of us who grew up in the fifties believed in the permanence of our American-history textbooks." What techniques does FitzGerald use to involve that audience? What role is she inviting her readers to play?

4. Assuming you did not grow up in the fifties, how do you relate to this essay? Are you left out, or does FitzGerald include you in some way? At what other times have you not been directly addressed as a primary audience but been spoken to clearly and forcefully nevertheless?

5. How does FitzGerald organize her discussion of the textbooks? What topics does she discuss? How does one topic connect to the next? How does she organize the movement back and forth between current textbooks and those of the fifties?

6. What are some of the major historical events in your lifetime? Which of these events are likely to remain classified as "major historical events"? Why is this likely?

---

[12]trade books: not textbooks but books written for a general audience. [Eds.]

How might these events be revised and presented in history textbooks a hundred years from now?

7. See if your library has some older textbooks for a course you are taking or have taken. If so, compare your textbook with the older one to see what has changed. Look, as FitzGerald did, at the opening, the major figures or topics, the attitudes, the pedagogical types, the physical appearance, and any other major features of each book. Write an essay explaining what you find.

8. Locate a current textbook in American history. How does it compare to your memory of American history as you learned it in junior high or high school? What was America "like," according to your old text? What is it "like" now?

TO IMPERSONATE, TO WATCH, AND TO BE WATCHED

Eric Bentley

Born in England in 1916, Eric Bentley holds degrees from Oxford and Yale; he has been a drama critic, a translator of plays, and a professor of theater. His writing over a dozen books on various aspects of drama has established him as a major scholar in this field. The material reprinted here is an excerpt from chapter 5, "Enactment," of his 1964 book, The Life of the Drama.

The theatrical situation, reduced to a minimum, is that A impersonates B   1
while C looks on. Such impersonation is universal among small children, and such playing of a part is not wholly distinct from the other playing that children do. All play creates a world within a world—a territory with laws of its own—and the theater might be regarded as the most durable of the many magic palaces which infantile humanity has built. The distinction between art and life begins there.

Impersonation is only half of this little scheme. The other half is watching—   2
or, from the viewpoint of A, being watched. Even when there is actually no spectator, an impersonator imagines that there is, often by dividing himself into two, the actor and his audience. That very histrionic object, the mirror, enables any actor to watch himself and thereby to become C, the audience. And the mirror on the wall is only one: the mirrors in the mind are many.

What is it to want to be watched? Impossible to ask such a question these   3
days without eliciting the word: exhibitionism. To want to be watched is to be exhibitionistic. Is this merely to say: to want to be watched is to want to be watched? Not quite. "Exhibitionism" is a clinical phenomenon, and the word carries a connotation of the socially inappropriate as well as the mentally unhealthy. Which, I am afraid, only makes it the more applicable to the theater. Wishing to be watched, sometimes and in a small way, is one thing, but wishing to become an actor is wishing to be watched all the time and in a big way. Such a wish would take a lot of justifying and even more explaining. It is bizarre, and brings to mind Thomas Mann's notion that there is a natural affinity between art and pathology.[1]

---

[1]Thomas Mann (1875–1955): German novelist and essayist; awarded the 1929 Nobel Prize in literature. [Eds.]

Is the Folies-Bergère the quintessence of theater?[2] That depends, I think, on 4
how one takes the Folies-Bergère. Sir Kenneth Clark has distinguished between
the naked and the nude.[3] A nude body is one that calls for no clothing; a naked
body is a clothed body temporarily stripped of its clothing. Sir Kenneth's interest
in the distinction lies in the fact that the arts he is professionally concerned
with—painting and sculpture—deal, not with the naked, but with the nude; in
fact (so far as Europe is concerned) they invented it. Not so the theater, however.
Even in places and at times which had nothing against the body, the method
of the theater has been concealment by mask and costume. True, one of the
archetypal acts of the theater is to remove this concealment. But one can only
take off what is on. Or, in Sir Kenneth's terms, theater can present the naked,
but never the nude. When therefore the girls of the Folies-Bergère are made a
highbrow tableau of in the likeness of classical nude paintings, in trying to be
nude they succeed in being untheatrical. When, on the other hand, they take
off their clothes for us, or parade around in *almost* no clothing, they become
theatrical through the act or simulation of unmasking. In short, if these girls
are nude, they are art; if they are naked, they are theater. Parts of the French
audience take them to be nude, or try to. The foreign tourists take them to be
naked. That is because the tourists have "dirty minds." But the tourists are right.
The nudity is spurious; the nakedness, genuine.

Hence, theater has less in common with the tradition of the nude in painting 5
than with the tradition of the striptease in "vulgar" entertainment. Theater is
shamelessly "low"; it cannot look down on the body, because it *is* the body. If
you want the soul, why pay to see chorus girls? Why pay to *see* nonchorus girls?
To begin to understand and accept theatrical art, we must be willing to say,
yes, it's true, we *do* wish to see, and we do wish to be stimulated by seeing
bodies—we decline to say "titillated" because the word "titillate" belongs to the
puritan enemy of the theater. We must be willing to aver, further, that the
bodies we wish to see are not "spiritualized" as Sir Kenneth Clark says nudes
are, they are "naked," their spiritual credit is nil, their appeal is "prurient." We
are prying into filthy secrets: the police department and the post office can begin
to shift uneasily in their shoes.

How indecent the theater is! Yet, for our peace of mind, the indecency is in 6
general placed at a remove: the nakedness is usually of the soul, not the body—
and it is Phaedra's nakedness we see,[4] not Gypsy Rose Lee's.[5] For once that we

---

[2]Folies-Bergère: a music hall in Paris widely known for striptease and sensational displays of
female nudity. [Eds.]

[3]Sir Kenneth Clark (1903–1983): English art historian; one of his most famous books is entitled
The Nude. [Eds.]

[4]Phaedra: the title character in a play by the French dramatist Racine; according to classical
mythology she fell in love with her stepson, Hippolytus, and when her advances were repulsed she
engineered his death. She committed suicide when Hippolytus's innocence was established. [Eds.]

[5]Gypsy Rose Lee (1919–1970): world's most famous striptease artist. [Eds.]

see Salome remove her seven veils in Wilde's play or Strauss's opera,[6] we see the veils removed a thousand times in other operas and plays from the individual spirit, from society, from the universe.

The problem with this is that to show the naked spirit is impossible. Only the spirit's envelope can be shown, and this is the body. And though a philosopher may represent the body as a mere shadow of a more substantial spiritual reality, and a playwright may follow him in this, our crude retort is inevitably that the shadow is itself pretty substantial. "Can spirit set to a leg? No. Or an arm? No." Platonic thoughts can be entertained in the mind, but not lived by from breakfast to lunch. And though the great nakednesses of the theater are spiritual, the immediate reality of theater is aggressively physical, corporeal. 7

The physical world is real for every artist, and is that through which even a St. John of the Cross must communicate his antiphysical philosophy.[7] Still, literature maintains some restraint in addressing its physicalities to the mind's eye only. Even painting and sculpture maintain some restraint in that the skin tints of the one have no skin under them, and the solidities of the other have no flesh or bone. Only theater thrusts at its audience the supreme object of sensual thoughts: the human body. And while in the theater it will never be nude, and will seldom be naked, its clothing is the more erotic in its double function of concealing and revealing, canceling and enhancing, denying and affirming. 8

That clothes may be used to heighten the sexual appeal of bodies, rather than reduce it, is a familiar enough fact. The exhibitionism of the actor is not so crudely sexual. He may even make himself theatrically more interesting by being less sexual: what has more appeal than Hamlet's funereal black? At worst, an actor or actress will concentrate on secondary sexual characteristics: a sensual mouth, a soulful eye, a rich head of hair, a slim waist, a well-shaped leg. He or she exhibits the body, but not for its beauty. In this the actor is closer to the acrobat than to the artist's model, since he exhibits his body largely for what it can do. And what an actor's body can do is expressive rather than lovely, and may be expressive, indeed, in the least lovely mode, such as grotesque comedy. 9

Does an actor exhibit *himself*? There has been much discussion on this head. Educators usually tell students of theater that the actor does not exhibit himself: that would be egotistic. He submerges himself in his roles: a noble example of self-discipline, if not self-sacrifice. Louis Jouve was saying as much when he stated that to embody a role the actor disembodies himself.[8] One knows what 10

---

[6]Salome: in the New Testament her dance before her father, Herod, was rewarded by his granting her request for the head of John the Baptist. [Eds.]

[7]St. John of the Cross (1542–1591): Spanish mystic and poet who urged, "Live in the world, as if God and your soul only were in it; so shall your heart be never made captive by any earthly thing." [Eds.]

[8]Louis Jouvet (1887–1951): French actor, producer, and director. [Eds.]

he meant. When Sir Laurence Olivier plays Justice Shallow,[9] the noble Olivier face and erect body are gone. Yet the very fact that I put it this way proves that I am not looking at the performance as I would if it were played by an actor who did not have a handsome face and an erect carriage. Does this signify only that I am a gossip, unable to concentrate on the show itself? I think not. The knowledge that an acrobatic trick is difficult is not irrelevant to the experience of watching it. On the contrary. We know it is easy for many creatures to fly up and down at great speed: the interest is *only* in seeing men and women do it, because it is not easy for them to do it. To see Olivier as Shallow is to see comparable difficulties overcome, comparable laws of nature defied by human prowess. Hence we are not enjoying the role alone, but also the actor. And he, on his side, is not exhibiting the role alone, he is exhibiting his prowess, he is exhibiting himself. Nor is the self-exhibition confined to the skill with which he portrays someone we define as "so different from himself." To wear a heavy, senile make-up and hunch the shoulders would not be enough if there were not a Justice Shallow in Olivier, if Shallow were not something he might yet become, or might have become. In such roles the actor is exhibiting the many different possibilities of being that he finds in himself.

No need to say anything about actors who all too evidently exhibit nothing but themselves. I am saying that even the actor who seems to be at the opposite pole from this is still exhibiting himself. Exceptional in Sir Laurence is the talent. Unexceptional is the original, naïve impulse that said: Watch me! 11

What of the pleasure of watching? In some respects, there is no difference between the theater spectator and the "consumer" of other arts—the listener to music, the reader of novels. It might be imagined that his position is identical with that of the observer of painting, sculpture, and architecture: all are on-lookers. But the phenomenon is less straightforward. If theater is a visual art like painting, it is also a temporal art like music. The watcher is also a listener—the voyeur is also an eavesdropper. 12

Such words as *exhibitionist* and *voyeur*—though some will discount them as jargon—add to the purely descriptive words an implication of guilt. 13

> I have heard
> That guilty creatures sitting at a play
> Have by the very cunning of the scene
> Been struck so to the soul that presently
> They have proclaimed their malefactions.

Literal-minded persons will find Hamlet's ideas on crime detection somewhat far-fetched, but poetic drama deals in essences, and here Shakespeare, Hamlet, and all audiences of *Hamlet* take it that the essence of theater is to strike guilty

[9]Justice Shallow: Robert Shallow, Justice of the Peace, a character in Shakespeare's *Henry IV* and *Merry Wives of Windsor*. [Eds.]

creatures to the soul—or, as we would say in prose cliché, to play on the guilt feelings of the audience. Seen in this way, the logic is good.

> The play's the thing
> Wherein I'll catch the conscience of the king. . . .

—because plays *are* things wherein consciences are caught.

This makes it sound as if watching were very unpleasurable indeed—as, for King Claudius,[10] it was. Hamlet plotted to defy the distinction between art and life, to exploit the possibility of a leap from art to life. When that happens we are no longer dealing with drama but with the destruction of its main convention. If we are not King Claudius, and have not literally killed our brother, we are also spared his reaction. Instead of calling for lights and making our exit, we stay on to "enjoy the show." Is our conscience *not* caught, then? Are our withers unwrung? It is. They are. But in art, not life. Such is the paradox of pain in drama: we do and do not suffer. We are suffering; we are also enjoying ourselves. When we watch, though we do not watch in the way we watch actual happenings, neither do we watch in the spirit of "scientific detachment" but always with some degree of emotional involvement. I am suggesting that this involvement is not an innocent one. 14

It would be impossible to draw the line between drama and gossip, drama and scandal, drama and the front page of the worst newspapers—which, understandably enough, claim to be dramatic. Even what is called pornography is by no means in any separate realm from the realm of the tragic and comic poets. All these things are enjoyed by human beings, and to all some measure of guilt is attached. Perhaps if one took the guilt away, the dirty picture, so called, would lose much of its appeal, and perhaps if one took from theater the element of voyeurism, the occasion would lose much of its appeal. 15

Certainly that element has been on the increase in modern times. The Greek, Elizabethan, and Spanish theaters were less voyeuristic because the plays were put on in broad daylight. It is the modern age that worked out the idea of a pitch-dark auditorium. Scholars call the modern stage the peepshow stage. The corollary is that this is a theater for Peeping Toms. It is; and the classical criticism of it is that, from the eighteenth century to Tennessee Williams, it has been so too crudely. It has been, all too often, a theater of domestic triviality. 16

The pleasure of looking on is in itself an equivocal thing. It includes such delights as feeling one has committed the crime yet is able to escape the penalty because the final curtain descends and one finds "it was all a dream." 17

What is pornography? One element in it is that forbidden wishes are seen gratified—the punishment being escaped because the man on the "dirty picture" is not oneself. The literature that is called pornographic often has another fea- 18

---

[10]King Claudius: in Shakespeare's *Hamlet* he has succeeded to the throne of his dead brother and married his widow; his nephew Hamlet arranges for the king to watch a reenactment by visiting players of Claudius's murder of his brother, Hamlet's father. [Eds.]

Eric Bentley

ture: following forbidden pleasure, condign punishment. Does not Tennessee Williams' *Sweet Bird of Youth* afford us the pleasure of being a gigolo for three quarters of the evening and then in the last part giving him the punishment that exactly fits the crime? Affords *us* the pleasure but gives *him* the punishment: which is to say, affords us the pleasure, but finds us a whipping boy. This might well be called pornography. It also has a lot in common with high tragedy which from its beginnings has presented crime and its punishment, the punished protagonist being a scapegoat for the audience. Pornography is continuous with art; and the pleasure of watching is continuous with the pleasure of peeping.

QUESTIONS

1. What, for Bentley, distinguishes going to the theater from other sorts of aesthetic experience?

2. At what points in his explanation of the theatrical situation does Bentley provide specific illustrations? Point out where he uses comparison and where he defines the terms he uses.

3. Bentley's explanation of the appeal of acting draws on some knowledge of other fields of study than drama. What words tip you off to that fact? What other fields of knowledge does he draw upon?

4. Bentley is fond of using rhetorical questions. Where does he use such questions to emphasize a point? Where does he use them to set up an idea for development? Do you find his use of rhetorical questions effective or excessive?

5. Consider Bentley's assertion at the end of paragraph 7: "And though the great nakednesses of the theater are spiritual, the immediate reality of theater is aggressively physical, corporeal." What evidence has he presented in the previous paragraphs to support such an assertion? Why and how does he develop this assertion in the succeeding paragraphs?

6. Describe your reaction to a play or film you have seen recently in the light of Bentley's explanation of the "pleasure of watching" (paragraph 12). Did your enjoyment of what you saw include, for example, "such delights as feeling one has committed the crime yet is able to escape the penalty" (paragraph 17)? In writing your response, be sure to describe specific moments in the performance that elicited your strongest reactions. You may find that you disagree with Bentley's explanation of the pleasure of watching. If so, present your own explanation.

7. How might an actor or actress explain the theatrical situation? Consider your own performing experience if you have had any, or ask friends who are involved in the theater. Why do they like to act? What occurs between them and an audience in a performance? You might also refer to some autobiographies or biographies of actors and actresses for more information. Write up your findings, explaining the theatrical situation from a performer's point of view. Do you find yourself in sympathy with Bentley's claim that "wishing to become an actor is wishing to be watched all the time and in a big way" (paragraph 3)?

FOOTBALL RED AND BASEBALL GREEN
Murray Ross

Murray Ross (b. 1942) was born in Pasadena, California, and educated at Williams College in Massachusetts and the University of California at Berkeley. He is now artistic director of the theater program at the University of Colorado, Colorado Springs. This essay was first published in the Chicago Review in 1971 when Ross was a graduate student at Berkeley. Though not a study of a usual academic subject, "Football Red and Baseball Green" shows Ross thinking about those sports much as a critic might think about one of the performing arts.

The Super Bowl, the final game of the professional football season, draws a 1
larger television audience than any of the moon walks or Tiny Tim's wedding. This revelation is one way of indicating just how popular spectator sports are in this country. Americans, or American men anyway, seem to care about the games they watch as much as the Elizabethans cared about their plays, and I suspect for some of the same reasons. There is, in sport, some of the rudimentary drama found in popular theater: familiar plots, type characters, heroic and comic action spiced with new and unpredictable variations. And common to watching both activities is the sense of participation in a shared tradition and in shared fantasies. If sport exploits these fantasies, without significantly transcending them, it seems no less satisfying for all that.

It is my guess that sport spectating involves something more than the vicarious 2
pleasures of identifying with athletic prowess. I suspect that each sport contains a fundamental myth which it elaborates for its fans, and that our pleasure in watching such games derives in part from belonging briefly to the mythical world which the game and its players bring to life. I am especially interested in baseball and football because they are so popular and so uniquely *American*; they began here and unlike basketball they have not been widely exported. Thus whatever can be said, mythically, about these games would seem to apply to our culture.

Baseball's myth may be the easier to identify since we have a greater historical 3
perspective on the game. It was an instant success during the Industrialization, and most probably it was a reaction to the squalor, the faster pace and the dreariness of the new conditions. Baseball was old-fashioned right from the start; it seems conceived in nostalgia, in the resuscitation of the Jeffersonian dream.

251

Murray Ross

It established an artificial rural environment, one removed from the toil of an urban life, which spectators could be admitted to and temporarily breathe in. Baseball is a *pastoral* sport, and I think the game can be best understood as this kind of art. For baseball does what all good pastoral does—it creates an atmosphere in which everything exists in harmony.

Consider, for instance, the spatial organization of the game. A kind of controlled openness is created by having everything fan out from home plate, and the crowd sees the game through an arranged perspective that is rarely violated. Visually this means that the game is always seen as a constant, rather calm whole, and that the players and the playing field are viewed in relationship to each other. Each player has a certain position, a special area to tend, and the game often seems to be as much a dialogue between the fielders and the field as it is a contest between players themselves; will that ball get through the hole? Can that outfielder run under that fly? As a moral genre, pastoral asserts the virtue of communion with nature. As a competitive game, baseball asserts that the team which best relates to the playing field (by hitting the ball in the right places) will win.   4

I suspect baseball's space has a subliminal function too, for topographically it is a sentimental mirror of older America. Most of the game is played between the pitcher and the hitter in the extreme corner of the playing area. This is the busiest, most sophisticated part of the ball park, where something is always happening, and from which all subsequent action originates. From this urban corner we move to a supporting infield, active but a little less crowded, and from there we come to the vast stretches of the outfield. As is traditional in American lore, danger increases with distance, and the outfield action is often the most spectacular in the game. The long throw, the double off the wall, the leaping catch—these plays take place in remote territory, and they belong, like most legendary feats, to the frontier.   5

Having established its landscape, pastoral art operates to eliminate any reference to that bigger, more disturbing, more real world it has left behind. All games are to some extent insulated from the outside by having their own rules, but baseball has a circular structure as well which furthers its comfortable feeling of self-sufficiency. By this I mean that every motion of extension is also one of return—a ball hit outside is a *home* run, a full circle. Home—familiar, peaceful, secure—it is the beginning and end. You must go out and come back; only the completed movement is registered.   6

Time is a serious threat to any form of pastoral. The genre poses a timeless world of perpetual spring, and it does its best to silence the ticking of clocks which remind us that in time the green world fades into winter. One's sense of time is directly related to what happens in it, and baseball is so structured as to stretch out and ritualize whatever action it contains. Dramatic moments are few, and they are almost always isolated by the routine texture of normal play. It is certainly a game of climax and drama, but it is perhaps more a game of   7 repeated and predictable action: the foul balls, the walks, the pitcher fussing around on the mound, the lazy fly ball to centerfield. This is, I think, as it should be, for baseball exists as an alternative to a world of too much action, struggle and change. It is a merciful release from a more grinding and insistent tempo, and its time, as William Carlos Williams suggests, makes a virtue out of idleness simply by providing it:[1]

> The crowd at the ball game
> is moved uniformly
> by a spirit of uselessness
> Which delights them . . .

Within this expanded and idle time the baseball fan is at liberty to become   8
a ceremonial participant and a lover of style. Because the action is normalized, how something is done becomes as important as the action itself. Thus baseball's most delicate and detailed aspects are often, to the spectator, the most interesting. The pitcher's windup, the anticipatory crouch of the infielders, the quick waggle of the bat as it poises for the pitch—these subtle miniature movements are as meaningful as the home runs and the strikeouts. It somehow matters in baseball that all the tiny rituals are observed: the shortstop must kick the dirt and the umpire must brush the plate with his pocket broom. In a sense baseball is largely a continuous series of small gestures, and I think it characteristic that the game's most treasured moment came when Babe Ruth pointed to where he subsequently hit a home run.

Baseball is a game where the little things mean a lot, and this, together with   9
its clean serenity, its open space, and its ritualized action is enough to place it in a world of yesterday. Baseball evokes for us a past which may never have been ours, but which we believe was, and certainly that is enough. In the Second World War, supposedly, we fought for "Baseball, Mom and Apple Pie," and considering what baseball means that phrase is a good one. We fought then for the right to believe in a green world of tranquillity and uninterrupted contentment, where the little things would count. But now the possibilities of such a world are more remote, and it seems that while the entertainment of such a dream has an enduring appeal, it is no longer sufficient for our fantasies. I think this may be why baseball is no longer our preeminent national pastime, and why its myth is being replaced by another more appropriate to the new realities (and fantasies) of our time.

Football, especially professional football, is the embodiment of a newer myth,   10
one which in many respects is opposed to baseball's. The fundamental difference is that football is not a pastoral game; it is a heroic one. One way of seeing the difference between the two is by the juxtaposition of Babe Ruth and Jim Brown, both legendary players in their separate genres. Ruth, baseball's most powerful

---

[1]William Carlos Williams (1883–1963): American poet, short-story writer, and physician. [Eds.]

hitter, was a hero maternalized (his name), an epic figure destined for a second immortality as a candy bar. His image was impressive but comfortable and altogether human: round, dressed in a baggy uniform, with a schoolboy's cap and a bat which looked tiny next to him. His spindly legs supported a Santa-sized torso, and this comic disproportion would increase when he was in motion. He ran delicately, with quick, very short steps, since he felt that stretching your stride slowed you down. This sort of superstition is typical of baseball players, and typical too is the way in which a personal quirk or mannerism mitigates their awesome skill and makes them poignant and vulnerable.

There was nothing funny about Jim Brown. His muscular and almost perfect   11
physique was emphasized further by the uniform which armored him. Babe Ruth had a tough face, but boyish and innocent; Brown was an expressionless mask under the helmet. In action he seemed invincible, the embodiment of speed and power in an inflated human shape. One can describe Brown accurately only with superlatives, for as a player he was a kind of Superman, undisguised.

Brown and Ruth are caricatures, yet they represent their games. Baseball is   12
part of a comic tradition which insists that its participants be humans, while football, in the heroic mode, asks that its players be more than that. Football converts men into gods, and suggests that magnificence and glory are as desirable as happiness. Football is designed, therefore, to impress its audience rather differently than baseball.

As a pastoral game, baseball attempts to close the gap between the players   13
and the crowd. It creates the illusion, for instance, that with a lot of hard work, a little luck, and possibly some extra talent, the average spectator might well be playing; not watching. For most of us can do a few of the things the ball players do: catch a pop-up, field a ground ball, and maybe get a hit once in a while. Chance is allotted a good deal of play in the game. There is no guarantee, for instance, that a good pitch will not be looped over the infield, or that a solidly batted ball will not turn into a double play. In addition to all of this, almost every fan feels he can make the manager's decision for him, and not entirely without reason. Baseball's statistics are easily calculated and rather meaningful; and the game itself, though a subtle one, is relatively lucid and comprehendible.

As a heroic game football is not concerned with a shared community of near-   14
equals. It seeks almost the opposite relationship between its spectators and players, one which stresses the distance between them. We are not allowed to identify directly with Jim Brown any more than we are with Zeus, because to do so would undercut his stature as something more than human. The players do much of the distancing themselves by their own excesses of speed, size and strength. When Bob Brown, the giant all-pro tackle says that he could "block King Kong all day," we look at him and believe. But the game itself contributes to the players' heroic isolation. As George Plimpton has graphically illustrated

in *Paper Lion*,[2] it is almost impossible to imagine yourself in a professional football game without also considering your imminent humiliation and possible injury. There is scarcely a single play that the average spectator could hope to perform adequately, and there is even a difficulty in really understanding what is going on. In baseball what happens is what meets the eye, but in football each action is the result of eleven men acting simultaneously against eleven other men, and clearly this is too much for the eye to totally comprehend. Football has become a game of staggering complexity, and coaches are now wired in to several "spotters" during the games so they can find out what is happening.

If football is distanced from its fans by its intricacy and its "superhuman" play, it nonetheless remains an intense spectacle. Baseball, as I have implied, dissolves time and urgency in a green expanse, thereby creating a luxurious and peaceful sense of leisure. As is appropriate to a heroic enterprise, football reverses this procedure and converts space into time. The game is ideally played in an oval stadium, not in a "park," and the difference is the elimination of perspective. This makes football a perfect television game, because even at first hand it offers a flat, perpetually moving foreground (wherever the ball is). The eye in baseball viewing opens up; in football it zeroes in. There is no democratic vista in football, and spectators are not asked to relax, but to concentrate. You are encouraged to watch the drama, not a medley of ubiquitous gestures, and you are constantly reminded that this event is taking place in time. The third element in baseball is the field; in football this element is the clock. Traditionally heroes do reckon with time, and football players are no exceptions. Time in football is wound up inexorably until it reaches the breaking point in the last minutes of a close game. More often than not it is the clock which emerges as the real enemy, and it is the sense of time running out that regularly produces a pitch of tension uncommon in baseball.

A further reason for football's intensity is that the game is played like a war. The idea is to win by going through, around or over the opposing team and the battle lines, quite literally, are drawn on every play. Violence is somewhere at the heart of the game, and the combat quality is reflected in football's army language ("blitz," "trap," "zone," "bomb," "trenches," etc.). Coaches often sound like generals when they discuss their strategy. Woody Hayes of Ohio State, for instance, explains his quarterback option play as if it had been conceived in the Pentagon: "You know," he says, "the most effective kind of warfare is siege. You have to attack on broad fronts. And that's all the option is— attacking on a broad front. You know General Sherman ran an option through the south."

15

16

---

[2]George Plimpton (b. 1927): best-selling author and journalist, founder of the *Paris Review*; he wrote in *Paper Lion* about his experiences in training with the Detroit Lions. [Eds.]

Football like war is an arena for action, and like war football leaves little   17
room for personal style. It seems to be a game which projects "character" more
than personality, and for the most part football heroes, publicly, are a rather
similar lot. They tend to become personifications rather than individuals, and,
with certain exceptions, they are easily read emblematically as embodiments of
heroic qualities such as "strength," "confidence," "perfection," etc.—clichés
really, but forceful enough when represented by the play of a Dick Butkus, a
Johnny Unitas or a Bart Starr. Perhaps this simplification of personality results
in part from the heroes' total identification with their mission, to the extent that
they become more characterized by their work than by what they intrinsically
"are." At any rate football does not make allowances for the idiosyncrasies that
baseball actually seems to encourage, and as a result there have been few football
players as uniquely crazy or human as, say, Casey Stengel or Dizzy Dean.

A further reason for the underdeveloped qualities of football personalities,   18
and one which gets us to the heart of the game's modernity, is that football is
very much a game of modern technology. Football's action is largely interaction,
and the game's complexity requires that its players mold themselves into a
perfectly coordinated unit. Jerry Kramer, the veteran guard and author of *Instant
Replay*, writes how Lombardi would work to develop such integration:

> He makes us execute the same plays over and over, a hundred times, two hundred
> times, until we do every little thing automatically. He works to make the kickoff-
> team perfect, the punt-return team perfect, the field-goal team perfect. He ignores
> nothing. Technique, technique, technique, over and over and over, until we feel
> like we're going crazy. But we win.

Mike Garrett, the halfback, gives the player's version:

> After a while you train your mind like a computer—put the ideas in, and the
> body acts accordingly.

As the quotations imply, pro football is insatiably preoccupied with the   19
smoothness and precision of play execution, and most coaches believe that the
team which makes the fewest mistakes will be the team that wins. Individual
identity thus comes to be associated with the team or unit that one plays for to
a much greater extent than in baseball. To use a reductive analogy, it is the
difference between *Bonanza* and *Mission Impossible*. Ted Williams is mostly
Ted Williams, but Bart Starr is mostly the Green Bay Packers. The latter metaphor is a precise one, since football heroes stand out not because of purely
individual acts, but because they epitomize the action and style of the groups
they are connected to. Kramer cites the obvious if somewhat self-glorifying
historical precedent: "Perhaps," he writes, "we're living in Camelot." Ideally a
football team should be what Camelot was supposed to have been, a group of
men who function as equal parts of a larger whole, dependent on each other
for total meaning.

The humanized machine as hero is something very new in sport, for in [20]
baseball anything approaching a machine has always been suspect. The famous
Yankee teams of the fifties were almost flawlessly perfect and never very popular.
Their admirers took pains to romanticize their precision into something more
natural than plain mechanics—Joe DiMaggio, for instance, was the "Yankee
Clipper." Even so, most people hoped fervently the Brooklyn Dodgers (the
"bums") would thrash them in every World Series. To take a more recent
example, the victory of the Mets in 1969 was so compelling largely because it
was at the expense of a superbly homogenized team, the Baltimore Orioles, and
it was accomplished by a somewhat random collection of inspired leftovers. In
baseball, machinery seems tantamount to villainy, whereas in football this smooth
perfection is part of the expected integration a championship team must attain.

It is not surprising, really, that we should have a game which asserts the [21]
heroic function of a mechanized group, since we have become a country where
collective identity is a reality. Football as a game of groups is appealing to us
as a people of groups, and for this reason football is very much an "establishment" game—since it is in the corporate business and governmental structures
that group America is most developed. The game comments on the culture,
and vice versa:

> President Nixon, an ardent football fan, got a football team picture as an inaugural
> anniversary present from his cabinet. . . .
> Superimposed on the faces of real gridiron players were the faces of cabinet
> members. (A.P.)

This is not to say that football appeals only to a certain class, for group America
is visible everywhere. A sign held high in the San Francisco Peace Morato-
rium . . . read: "49er Fans against War, Poverty and the Baltimore Colts."

Football's collective pattern is only one aspect of the way in which it seems [22]
to echo our contemporary environment. The game, like our society, can be
thought of as a cluster of people living under great tension in a state of perpetual
flux. The potential for sudden disaster or triumph is as great in football as it is
in our own age, and although there is something ludicrous in equating inter-
ceptions with assassinations and long passes with moonshots, there is also something valid and appealing in the analogies. It seems to me that football does
successfully reflect those salient and common conditions which affect us all,
and it does so with the end of making us feel better about them and our lot.
For one thing, it makes us feel that something can be released and connected
in all this chaos; out of the accumulated pile of bodies something can emerge—
a runner breaks into the clear or a pass finds its way to a receiver. To the
spectator plays such as these are human and dazzling. They suggest to the
audience what it has hoped for (and been told) all along, that technology is still
a tool and not a master. Fans get living proof of this every time a long pass is
completed; they see at once that it is the result of careful planning, perfect

integration and an effective "pattern," but they see too that it is human and that what counts as well is man, his desire, his natural skill and his "grace under pressure." Football metaphysically yokes heroic action and technology by violence to suggest that they are mutually supportive. It's a doubtful proposition, but given how we live it has its attractions.

Football, like the space program, is a game in the grand manner, yet it is a 23 rather sober sport and often seems to lack that positive, comic vision of which baseball's pastoral mannerisms are a part. It is a winter game, as those fans who saw the Minnesota Vikings play the Detroit Lions one Thanksgiving were graphically reminded. The two teams played in a blinding snowstorm, and except for the small flags in the corners of the end zones, and a patch of mud wherever the ball was downed, the field was totally obscured. Even through the magnified television lenses the players were difficult to identify; you saw only huge shapes come out of the gloom, thump against each other and fall in a heap. The movement was repeated endlessly and silently in a muffled stadium, interrupted once or twice by a shot of a bare-legged girl who fluttered her pompons in the cold. The spectacle was by turns pathetic, compelling and absurd; a kind of theater of oblivion.

Games such as this are by no means unusual, and it is not difficult to see 24 why for many football is a gladiatorial sport of pointless bludgeoning played by armored monsters. However accurate this description may be, I still believe that even in the worst of circumstances football can be a liberating activity. In the game I have just described, for instance, there was one play, the turning point of the game, which more than compensated for the sluggishness of most of the action. Jim Marshall, the huge defensive end (who hunts on dogsleds during the off season), intercepted a pass deep in his own territory and rumbled upfield like a dinosaur through the mud, the snow, and the opposing team, lateraling at the last minute to another lineman who took the ball in for a touchdown. It was a supreme moment because Marshall's principal occupation is falling on quarterbacks, not catching the ball and running with it. His triumphant jaunt, something that went unequaled during the rest of that dark afternoon, was a hearty burlesque of the entire sport, an occasion for epic laughter in bars everywhere (though especially in Minnesota), and it was more than enough to rescue the game from the snowbound limbo it was in.

In the end I suppose both football and baseball could be seen as varieties of 25 decadence. In its preoccupation with mechanization, and in its open display of violence, football is the more obvious target for social moralists, but I wonder if this is finally more "corrupt" than the seductive picture of sanctuary and tranquillity that baseball has so artfully drawn for us. Almost all sport is vulnerable to such criticism because it is not strictly ethical in intent, and for this reason there will always be room for puritans like the Elizabethan John Stubbes who howled at the "wanton fruits which these cursed pastimes bring forth." As

258

a long-time dedicated fan of almost anything athletic, I confess myself out of sympathy with most of this; which is to say, I guess, that I am vulnerable to those fantasies which these games support, and that I find happiness in the company of people who feel as I do.

A final note. It is interesting that the heroic and pastoral conventions which underlie our most popular sports are almost classically opposed. The contrasts are familiar: city versus country, aspirations versus contentment, activity versus peace and so on. Judging from the rise of professional football we seem to be slowly relinquishing that unfettered rural vision of ourselves that baseball so beautifully mirrors, and we have come to cast ourselves in a genre more reflective of a nation confronted by constant and unavoidable challenges. Right now, like the Elizabethans, we seem to share both heroic and pastoral yearnings, and we reach out to both. Perhaps these divided needs account in part for the enormous attention we as a nation now give to spectator sports. For sport provides one place where we can have our football and our baseball too.

QUESTIONS

1. Summarize each of the "fundamental myths" of baseball and football. Do you find Ross's interpretations justifiable?

2. In discussing two games, Ross makes use of several other fields of human activity and modes of behavior, both ancient and modern. Make lists of the chief terms he draws upon in characterizing baseball and football. How do those terms help you understand Ross's explanation of baseball and football?

3. How would you describe the audience for whom Ross is writing? How much knowledge of baseball and football does he expect of his readers? How much knowledge of other matters, such as literary conventions and patterns in American cultural history, does he assume?

4. From what viewpoint does Ross look at baseball and football? Contrast his particular approach with that of the writer of a typical sports article.

5. Ross structures his essay mostly by means of comparison and contrast. At what points does he discuss his subjects (baseball and football) separately and at what points together? What is his purpose in such an arrangement?

6. Are there other popular pastimes which could be said to "echo our contemporary environment" (paragraph 22) as Ross claims football does? Are there others which reflect our yearnings for a simpler, more pastoral America?

7. More than a decade has passed since Ross published this essay. Do you think his evaluations of baseball and football have stood the test of time? Write a short paper expressing your opinion on this matter.

8. Despite its exportation to the world, we still think of basketball as mainly an American game. Write an essay in which you compare and contrast basketball with either football or baseball. As you prepare your essay, see which of Ross's interpretations remain useful to you, which fade away, and which you change.

9. Compare and contrast another pair of fantasies, perhaps of those who watch horror movies with those who watch westerns, of those who play poker with those who play chess, or of those who prefer one electronic game to another.

10. Research the public response to baseball and football since Ross's essay was first published. Investigate how the public responded to the World Series and the Super Bowl in 1971 (the date of Ross's essay), 1976 (our bicentennial year), and last season. Write a paper explaining whatever trends you discover.

THE OTHER SIDE
OF THE WALL
Douglas L. Wilson

Born in St. James, Minnesota, in 1935, Douglas Wilson is a librarian with degrees from Doane College in Nebraska and the University of Pennsylvania. In addition to directing both the library and a program in American Studies at Knox College in Galesburg, Illinois, Wilson writes regularly on American subjects and is currently working on a book about American agrarian traditions. About the following essay, reprinted from The Iowa Review, *he says that he was interested in demonstrating how a literary understanding that he had never questioned, and about which there was no controversy whatever, could be turned absolutely around in the wake of persuasive personal experience.*

I

My starting point is something that must seem fairly obvious: the notion that 1
we are creatures of our own experience. I would not expect to get much of an
argument on that score, and yet if one begins to develop this idea in certain
ways, one can readily create a dialectic that has the appearance, at least, of a
dilemma. One could, for example, emphasize the ways in which we are the
victims of our experience, limited or, to heighten the metaphor, imprisoned by
its iron precincts. Or one could, I think, with equal validity emphasize the
liberating character of experience and stress how every new experience frees us
from the limitations of our former condition. It is simply a matter of how we
wish to construe the notion that we are creatures of our own experience. What
both versions of the idea have in common, however, is the concept of a barrier,
a line of demarcation. And this has special significance for the poem that is the
focus of my essay—Robert Frost's "Mending Wall."

"Mending Wall" is extremely familiar, certainly one of Frost's best known 2
poems and perhaps one of the most famous in all of American poetry. It is
almost invariably read by students from elementary school to the college level;
until very recently, it made every anthology; it readily lends itself to quotation.
Say "Something there is that doesn't love a wall" and educated people are certain
to catch the reference. Moreover, it is a remarkably straightforward poem. That
is to say, given the standard new critical reservations, it seems to mean pretty
much what it says and to present no classic ambiguities. A survey of the long

Douglas L. Wilson

record of commentary on the poem, which was published in 1914, reveals relatively little critical disagreement.

To rehearse briefly a very familiar story, "Mending Wall" is about two New   3
England neighbors who meet in the spring to repair the stone wall that separates their properties. Since they clearly live in the country, one might assume that they are farmers, though all we are told is that one "is all pine" and the other is "apple orchard" and that neither has cows (and, by extension, other livestock) that might wander through the broken wall. As they mend the wall, the speaker attempts to engage his neighbor in a debate over the necessity of having a wall between them. His position is summed up in the classic line, "Something there is that doesn't love a wall." His neighbor refuses to be drawn into an argument and simply replies (another classic line), "Good fences make good neighbors." The speaker regards this as a kind of category mistake, for he sees his neighbor as applying a rule that was intended to cover a different kind of situation. The poem concludes with the speaker's depiction of the neighbor as an unreflective primitive, incapable of independent thinking or change.

> I see him there,
> Bringing a stone grasped firmly by the top
> In each hand, like an old-stone savage armed,
> He moves in darkness as it seems to me,
> Not of woods only and the shade of trees.
> He will not go behind his father's saying,
> And he likes having thought of it so well
> He says again, "Good fences make good neighbors."

Now in spite of all the ways that the poem can be, and has been, approached   4
and dealt with, it is difficult *not* to adopt the point of view of the speaker, and virtually all the commentators do. Given the commitment of educators and educated people to the examined life and the predominantly progressive spirit of modern times, this is perhaps inevitable. Is there any way of understanding the poem, one might ask, in which the neighbor does not emerge as the heavy? Before 1968–69 I would have said "no," but since that time I have found myself on the other side of the wall.

II

In 1968–69 I spent a sabbatical year on a small farm that my wife and I had   5
just acquired and that had over a mile and a half of line fence. Almost the first question asked me by one of my neighbors when I met him was whether I intended to pasture cows. This question was prompted by the wretched condition of the fences I had inherited from the former owner. My new neighbor was visibly relieved when I said that I didn't. During the course of that year I was to see and hear a good deal about the importance of fences in a rural community.

One of the first things I heard about was the case of a former neighbor who   6
had been regarded as a notoriously bad neighbor. It was not simply that his
fences were neglected and in a constant state of disrepair. This is a very serious
matter in dairy country, where half of a farmer's line fence (or boundary fence)
is his responsibility and the other half is the responsibility of his neighbor. But
it was clearly more than that. It was more that he was distrustful, quarrelsome,
and generally indifferent or insensitive towards his neighbors—cardinal sins in
a community that operated on the basis of mutual assistance and support. In
truth, it was his attitude towards his neighbors and his neighborly responsibilities
that accounted for his notoriety, and his fences, I came to see, were actually
regarded not so much the source as the symbol of the problem. A long-standing
member of the neighborhood, and one I am sure who had never heard of Robert
Frost or read his poems, summarized the situation for me as follows: "They say
good fences make good neighbors."

As time went by, I had occasion to see the problem a little closer to home.   7
My neighbor across the road could not keep his livestock properly penned, and
I awoke one morning to find that a huge sow had uprooted half our front lawn.
The situation deteriorated as the summer went along, and we found ourselves
on the receiving end of a pilgrimage of pigs. I could take matters in hand and
build a fence around my front yard (which I eventually did), but this would not
keep the pigs at home. I decided in due course that the fault was not in my
neighbor's fences but in my neighbor—more precisely in his attitude toward his
neighborly responsibilities.

As one of my principal preoccupations that year was considering what it   8
meant to live in the country and how that differed from urban life, I began to
think a good deal about fences. And whenever I did, my thoughts invariably
returned to Frost's "Mending Wall." Having studied it in school, college, and
graduate school, and having taught it every year in my American literature
classes, I assumed that I knew "Mending Wall" pretty thoroughly and understood perfectly well.

> "Good fences make good neighbors."
> "Why do they make good neighbors? Isn't it
> Where there are cows? But here there are no cows.
> Before I built a wall I'd ask to know
> What I was walling in and walling out,
> And to whom I was like to give offense."

The position of the speaker was convincing enough, as it had been in the   9
past, and my experience on the farm had given it ample warrant. But the notion
that the speaker was leaving something important out of the equation—that
fences were more than merely barriers to livestock—would not go away and, in
fact, continued to grow in my mind.

In the fall of the year I happened to meet one of my neighbors—a reticent,   10
older man—at the fenceline, where he was making some makeshift repairs to a

stretch of very poor fence that I realized, alas, was my responsibility to keep up. I was, of course, properly embarrassed but also surprised because I had understood that he never kept cattle in that field. He quickly explained that he only wanted to pasture his cows there for a few weeks and that he didn't expect me to rebuild the fence just for that. We fell to talking about the condition of our fences, what repairs were needed and which should be made first. Having satisfied himself as to my good intentions, he volunteered that he did not feel right about his neglect of the fencerow in front of us. While the fence in question was mine to keep up, he had allowed trees and shrubs to grow up on his side, as they had done prodigiously on mine, making for a dense and entangled mass of foliage on either side of the dilapidated fence. I thought I saw what he was driving at, and I said that this certainly made it more difficult to keep up the fence. But that wasn't it. What bothered him, he finally allowed, was that "it didn't *look* good." We soon agreed, with a warmth and enthusiasm that astonished me, to meet in the spring and clear the fencerow together.

It became abundantly clear to me, in thinking about this encounter, that 11 what we have been talking about was much more than the condition of the fence that divided our farms. It had rather to do with our relationship as neighbors. The practical aspect of the fence, in fact, had virtually been eliminated from consideration, for he had told me that he was about to give up his cows and his milking operation so as to qualify for social security. What we had agreed to do had little or nothing to do with wandering livestock. My cornstalks would never get across and eat his alfalfa. We were going to put our fences in order because we wanted to be good neighbors.

Coming back to "Mending Wall" after this series of experiences, I began to 12 see it in a different light. There was a pattern in these experiences—the notorious former neighbor, the neighbor with the unpenable pigs, and the neighbor who wanted to clear the fencerow—and I began to discern what it was. Good fences *do* make good neighbors. Not just where there are cows but where there are neighbors. The speaker in "Mending Wall," if he really believes that the force of nature that sunders stone walls should be regarded as a cue to right conduct, is short on experience and long on mischief. The neighbor's view, on the other hand, is true wisdom. Our only reason for supposing that he "moves in darkness" is that this is the way the speaker represents him. How, I began to ask myself, if this were the case, had this poem come to be so widely misread and misunderstood? And how had Frost, who must have known all of this perfectly well from the beginning, come to cast the poem in the form he did? The balance of my essay deals with these two questions.

III

The first question can be answered fairly easily, I believe, in the context of 13 the unstartling proposition with which I began. We are creatures of our own experience. To understand that the neighbor who says "Good fences make good neighbors" is uttering something like practical wisdom requires an appeal to experience. As a debate there is little to choose. The speaker seems to have all the arguments on his side. The wall is useless, and mending it is meaningless, done only in the interest of the outmoded thinking of the neighbor; and all of this is confirmed by a principle of nature: "Something there is that doesn't love a wall." To judge this encounter strictly as a debate, as most readers apparently do, is inevitably to run a tally in favor of the speaker and award him the decision on points. Besides, he has qualities that have general appeal to readers of modern American poetry: he is critical; he doesn't take things like traditional sayings for granted; he is open to change; and he has a sense of humor. Our impression of the neighbor, poor man, is just the opposite, though it rests almost entirely on the speaker's biased references.

To judge the issue between them intelligently requires knowledge or experience that lies outside the poem—what Frost calls elsewhere "the need of being versed in country things." The speaker in the poem tries to deal with the issue of fences philosophically—by speculation, by arguments, by appeals to the nature of things. What the reader must grasp is that the speaker cannot or, for some reason, *will* not acknowledge what is truly at stake in the ritual of fence mending. He insists that, since he has only apple trees and the neighbor has only pines, the wall is not "needed." This assumes that a boundary serves only a very limited function, such as keeping livestock out or in. But country people know, not by an appeal to philosophy but as part of their culture, that a boundary is something very important; it is both an acknowledgement of responsibility and a token of respect. Maintaining a boundary is a hedge against uncertainty, a guarantee against dispute. The boundary can be seen in these terms as nothing less than an aspect of one's identity.

Now these are things that are understood implicitly by people whose land is an extension of their lives. One could never persuade a farmer that the speaker in this poem has the better of this argument. Certainty Frost was aware of this, for his poetry is replete with references to boundaries and their critical importance. As Radcliffe Squires has observed, if Frost's position with respect to boundaries is represented by the speaker in "Mending Wall," it is at odds with everything else he has written on the subject. But Frost's readers, and certainly his commentators, have not been farmers. On the contrary, we have been city dwellers who have approached his poem from an unmistakably urban perspective. This, in combination with our disposition to judge the poem as a debate, has led to a decidedly imperfect understanding of the poem.

IV

There is a great deal that might be said at this point, but I propose to postpone further discussion of the poem's interpretation in order to say something about

265

the second question I raised, namely, how did Frost come to cast the dramatic encounter of "Mending Wall" in the form that he did and so seem to contribute to a widespread misunderstanding of his own poem. To pursue this question, I am going to risk the indulgence of the reader and ease back into the biographical mode in which I began.

As is well known, Frost's career as a poet did not really begin in earnest until 17 he was nearly 40 years old and he had moved his family to England. How he came to find himself as a poet while there was not simply his good fortune in finding a publisher for a volume of his early poems or his acquaintance with Edward Thomas and other British poets or his recognition by Ezra Pound, though these were all important results of his two-year stay in England. What Lawrance Thompson's biography and his edition of the letters make clear is that Frost's sudden emergence as a poet can be traced to a series of poems, written in England and published in *North of Boston*, that were the outcropping of his homesickness for the life and landscape of rural New England.

In 1975, I had the good fortune to spend a summer in England, and while 18 there I set for myself the task of investigating the circumstances in which Frost's emergence as a poet took place. Not long after arriving in England, I went with my family on a tour of the Cotswolds, a picturesque range of broad-backed hills west of Oxford. There my attention was caught at once by the distinctive stone walls that lined the fields and roadsides. Here were miles of well-kept walls made of neatly stacked slabs of limestone, which nowhere betrayed signs of an annual upheaval, even though they frequently had been built on the steepest of inclines. If something there is that doesn't love a wall, it seemed to be inoperative in the Cotswolds.

A little investigation into these walls served only to heighten my interest. 19 They are called dry stone walls, "dry" because they are made without cement, and they do stand for scores of years, if well made, without need of repair. They are found only in certain parts of England and Scotland (where they are called dry stane dykes) for the obvious reason that they are only put up where limestone is readily available and close to the site of the wall.

Had Frost seen these dry stone walls before he wrote "Mending Wall," I 20 wondered. Certainly they would have caught his eye if he had been around them, for they are both very prominent and very attractive features of the rural landscape where they appear. What began as curiosity soon ripened into speculation. If Frost had seen the dry stone walls, he would have made it a point to learn something about them and would have discovered their remarkable properties. If he came to see that stone walls, under certain conditions, can stand for generations without repair, it would have undoubtedly affected the way he conceived and constructed a poem that seems to urge upon its readers the futility of wall-building. He would have been made keenly aware of how limited and parochial the position taken by the speaker in "Mending Wall" can be seen to be.

So compelling was this possibility that I conceived an hypothesis about the   21
writing of "Mending Wall": that Frost's experiences in England had brought
about a dramatic change in his attitude toward rural New England and the life
that he had lived there; for the people and the places that he had left behind
thinking he hated, he discovered that he now felt something like affection; he
grew homesick for the life that he had so gladly left, and this experience issued
in a series of new poems that were far better than anything he had written
previously. So much of my theory was simply drawn from the biographical
record as it emerges from the published letters and Thompson's biography.
"Mending Wall," I now conjectured, could have come to Frost as a recon-
sideration of his relationship with his former New Hampshire neighbor, Napolean Guay. Nostalgically remembering his neighbor and their spring outings
at the wall in conjunction with seeing dry stone walls could have triggered a
poem in which his perversity in having made the worse appear the better reasoning was implicitly acknowledged.

A number of problems now presented themselves. If this theory were to hold   22
its own, it would be necessary to show that Frost was at least exposed to dry
stone walls before "Mending Wall" was written. If he had brought the poem
over to England with him from America, for example, the theory was kaput.
But that did not seem to be the case, though it was true of a few *North of Boston*
poems. Frost seems to have begun writing the poems for this volume—except
for these few earlier poems—in the late fall of 1912, and the completed manuscript was apparently sent to the publisher about a year later. It seemed a reasonable time in which to get Frost and dry stone walls together and to get the
poem written. All that was required, I reasoned, was the necessary persistence
on my part.

I had the benefit of ideal working conditions for this task, for the summer of   23
1975 was an unprecedented season of glorious sunshine in England, and I was
working in the rarefied scholarly atmosphere of the English Reading Room of
the Bodleian Library at Oxford. The sunshine was important, incidentally, not
just for its effect on the spirit, but because the light in the Bodleian, like its
cataloging system, is scandalous by American library standards, and I could not
always arrive in time to get a seat by the windows.

The early going was not encouraging. Frost had spent his first year and a   24
half in England—the time during which the *North of Boston* poems were written—in Beaconsfield in Buckinghamshire. Chalk country. Lovely but no limestone, and thus no dry stone walls. No mention of "Mending Wall" could be
found in the published letters during this period, and Frost was staying mad-
deningly close to Beaconsfield, with occasional trips to London, which was only
30 miles away. By August, he had so nearly completed the new book that he
was considering various titles for it and had awarded himself and his family a
vacation. But now things began to look up, for he announced in letters to his
friends that he was going to spend his vacation in Scotland. Having just read a

marvellous book on dry stone walls written by a Scotsman, I knew that he was headed in a promising direction. His report on his trip to Scotland, in a letter to Sidney Cox dated *circa* Sept. 15, proved to be all that I could have hoped for. It read in part:

> We are just back from a two week's journey in Scotland . . . The best adventure was the time in Kingsbarns where tourists and summer boarders never come. The common people in the south of England I don't like to have around me. They don't know how to meet you man to man. The people in the north are more like Americans. I wonder whether they made Burns' poems or Burns' poems made them. And there are stone walls (dry stone dykes) in the north; I liked those.

To say that I was elated at finding this passage in Frost's letter to Cox on that bright summer morning in the Bodleian is to seriously understate it. And yet I was curiously troubled by a minor matter. "Could Frost," I wrote in my notebook, "have written 'dry stane dykes'?" This was admittedly trivial, but I felt *certain* that if Frost had taken note of the Scottish form "dykes," as he had, he would likely have used "stane" as well. And certainty exacts its price. I duly noted that the letter was in the Baker Library at Dartmouth and resolved to check it for myself when I got the chance.

I was thus able to establish that Frost had indeed seen the dry stone walls of 25 Great Britain, and he had taken particular note of them. But had he already written "Mending Wall" when he saw them? Just before going to Scotland he had written a letter to his friend John T. Bartlett in which he listed the titles of 12 poems to be included in the new book, which would eventually appear with a total of 17 poems. "Mending Wall" was not on the list. Had it been omitted for some reason, inadvertently left out, or was it more likely that it had not yet been written? I decided that there was no percentage in doubting.

The only other clue that I could find in the published sources was a seemingly 26 unrelated reference, buried deep in the footnotes of Thompson's biography, to a friendship that Frost had formed with a Scots Shakespearian scholar named James Cruickshanks Smith. Thompson mentions this friendship only in connection with Frost's departure from England in 1915, for Smith was one of the people who loaned him money to make the crossing to America. Frost, according to Thompson, had met Smith at Kingsbarns during his 1913 vacation, so I made a note in my notebook to check out the relationship between Frost and Smith. I could find nothing further to shed light on my theory in England, and, in due course, I followed Frost back to America.

V

The following year, in 1976, I went with my family on a bicentennial pil- 27 grimage to the eastern United States, where, with millions of others, we patriot-ically made the rounds of the essential New England sites: Bunker Hill in Boston, Concord Bridge at Concord, and the Baker Library at Dartmouth. I may as well confess that, while I was excited about working in the superb collection of original Frost materials that repose in the Baker Library, the prospect that I most keenly anticipated was the examination of Frost's letter to Cox in which he had written of the dry stone dykes, a topic that had become dear to my heart. I was certain that Thompson, in editing the letters, had mistranscribed Frost's handwriting and that the word "stone" would actually be "stane"—and I was right. Thus fortified by a clearcut victory, I settled down in that marvellous reading room (the light was much better than the Bodleian's) to see what I could learn from the remaining material.

There are a great many different collections in the Baker relating to Frost, and I soon discovered that virtually all of the interesting letters by Frost himself had been published by Thompson. The collection that proved to be most productive for my purposes turned out to be the file of letters that Frost received while living in England. In trying to gauge Frost's homesickness while in England, because of its crucial effect on his poetry, I had observed that the mail that he received was of great importance to him. A passage in Frost's correspondence captures his feelings very memorably. "Homesickness makes us newshungry. Every time the postman bangs the letter-slot-door our mouths go open and our eyes shut like birds' in a nest. . . ." Sitting in the Baker Library, I spent several fascinating hours reading through the mail that had come through that letter-slot-door. 28

Thus engaged in the otherwise despicable practice of reading someone else's mail, I struck gold. For here were the letters written to Frost by the man he had met on his Scottish vacation at Kingsbarns, James Cruickshanks Smith. This first letter acknowledges receipt of Frost's first book, A Boy's Will, and its Sept. 15 date indicates that Frost must have sent the book to him immediately after arriving home from his vacation in Kingsbarns. The second letter is dated Nov. 24, 1913, which is very close to the time that the final manuscript of North of Boston was to go to the printer. Smith begins by describing the work that he had been doing and then the things that he does for recreation. "I do some pure geometry," he writes, "and learn some Shelley by heart: Geometry is very like poetry for releasing the mind. And that, by one of the natural transitions of which the masters of style have the secret, brings me round to your latest poems—which I herewith return. Now about those poems:— 29

"Imprimis.[1] Of course I recognized 'Mending Wall' at once as the poem which had been suggested by our walk at Kingsbarns. . . ." 30

It was not the 4th of July in Hanover, New Hampshire, but at that moment it felt like fireworks to me. 31

---

[1]Imprimis: in the first place. [Eds.]

VI

I realize, of course, that it would be premature at this juncture to pronounce: 32
Q.E.D.[2] What I have been able to show is that Frost wrote "Mending Wall"
in the fall of 1913 and that it was prompted by something that happened on a
walk with J. C. Smith at Kingsbarns, Fifeshire, Scotland, where he had been
particularly attracted by dry stone walls. But adding this to what we know about
Frost's situation and attitudes at this time, I feel little hesitation in filling in the
picture as follows: Frost takes a walk in the countryside with J. C. Smith, who
explains dry stone walls to him—how they are built, how durable they are, and
how little maintenance they require. Frost responds with a description of the
wall on his farm in Derry, N.H., which he shared with his neighbor, Napolean
Guay. He describes how he used to argue with Guay each spring about mending
the wall, partly out of mischief, partly from an inability to see the point of it
all. Possibly he emphasized the contrast between the ingenious arguments of
the young schoolteacher and the stubbornly laconic reply of the neighbor. With
this dramatic encounter freshly summoned up in his consciousness, Frost returned to Beaconsfield and began working on the poem. His frame of mind is
suggested by a remark he made years later: "I wrote the poem 'Mending Wall'
thinking of the old wall that I hadn't mended in several years and which must
be in a terrible condition. I wrote that poem in England when I was very
homesick for my old wall in New England."

I began this essay with the proposition that we are creatures of our own 33
experience. It is certainly true for me, as I have tried to show in shamelessly
personal terms. But I want to conclude by suggesting that it was also profoundly
true for Frost and that bearing this in mind can help us to gain a truer perspective
on "Mending Wall." The poet who had found his subject and was beginning
to find success, who was living in England and growing increasingly homesick
for a region he thought he despised, saw and understood the world differently
from the bitterly discontented schoolteacher he had been a few years before. So
much did the young schoolteacher think himself a *victim* of his circumstances
that he had begun to believe that the grandfather who had willed him the hated
Derry farm had deliberately intended the legacy as a curse. In England, he
began to see his experiences in a very different and what we may legitimately
call a *liberating* perspective, as is perfectly illustrated in his confessed homesickness for the old wall. The extent of this change is measured rather precisely
in "Mending Wall" in the difference between the point of view of the poet,
who understands the wisdom of the neighbor's view, and that of the speaker in
the poem, who presumably does not. But this can only be grasped by readers
who are sufficiently versed in country things to know how to judge the substance

---

[2]Q.E.D.: which was to be demonstrated, an abbreviation of the Latin phrase *quod erat demon-
strandum.* [Eds.]

of the issue between them. To be persuaded by the arguments of the speaker is clearly to be misled.

Ironically, it may well be that this sympathetic response to the speaker, which 34 I believe is a function of an urban perspective and essentially misplaced, largely accounts for the poem's popularity. Frost, who is reported to have said that "the poet is entitled to everything that the reader can find in the poem," may have been aware that this was the case, for he deliberately sidestepped a number of opportunities to explain the poem or take sides in the debate. Indeed, he once claimed that he had played "exactly fair" in the poem because he had twice said "Good fences make good neighbors" and twice "Something there is that doesn't love a wall." But this is a perfect example of the puckish answer that Frost liked to give when someone tried to pin him down. (In a poem of 45 lines, the speaker's position is expounded in all but two; and those, setting forth the neighbor's position, are virtually the same.) Whatever disputative equilibrium the poem has may be said to be achieved by a balancing of all the advantages of the speaker—the central point of view, the wit, the humor, the arguments, the invidious depiction of the neighbor—against a simple statement whose full authority is undiminished by all that the speaker can say or do. A more fitting authorial commentary on the poem, to my mind, is a celebrated remark of the mature Frost, which appears in the preface to his *Complete Poems*. He is describing what he calls "the figure a poem makes." "It begins," he says, "in delight and ends in wisdom."

> "Something there is that doesn't love a wall."
> "Good fences make good neighbors."

MENDING WALL

Something there is that doesn't love a wall,
That sends the frozen-ground-swell under it
And spills the upper boulders in the sun,
And makes gaps even two can pass abreast.
The work of hunters is another thing:
I have come after them and made repair
Where they have left not one stone on a stone,
But they would have the rabbit out of hiding,
To please the yelping dogs. The gaps I mean,
No one has seen them made or heard them made,
But at spring mending-time we find them there.
I let my neighbor know beyond the hill;

And on a day we meet to walk the line
And set the wall between us once again.
We keep the wall between us as we go.
To each the boulders that have fallen to each.
And some are loaves and some so nearly balls
We have to use a spell to make them balance:
"Stay where you are until our backs are turned!"
We wear our fingers rough with handling them.
Oh, just another kind of outdoor game,
One on a side. It comes to little more:
There where it is we do not need the wall:
He is all pine and I am apple orchard.
My apple trees will never get across
And eat the cones under his pines, I tell him.
He only says, "Good fences make good neighbors."
Spring is the mischief in me, and I wonder
If I could put a notion in his head:
"*Why* do they make good neighbors? Isn't it
Where there are cows? But here there are no cows.
Before I built a wall I'd ask to know
What I was walling in or walling out,
And to whom I was like to give offense.
Something there is that doesn't love a wall,
That wants it down." I could say "Elves" to him,
But it's not elves exactly, and I'd rather
He said it for himself. I see him there,
Bringing a stone grasped firmly by the top
In each hand, like an old-stone savage armed.
He moves in darkness as it seems to me,
Not of woods only and the shade of trees.
He will not go behind his father's saying,
And he likes having thought of it so well
He says again, "Good fences make good neighbors."

Robert Frost

QUESTIONS

1. Summarize the conventional understanding of "Mending Wall," according to Wilson.

2. What experience leads Wilson to contradict that understanding and replace it with another? Summarize Wilson's interpretation of "Mending Wall."

3. What are the two quite different kinds of research that contributed to Wilson's understanding of Frost's poem? What does Wilson search for in the libraries of Oxford and Dartmouth? What does he find?

4. Wilson's essay is interesting for what it demonstrates not only about Frost's poem but also about a certain pleasure that can be part of research and of intellectual inquiry. Outline the steps of Wilson's research. Which moments provide the greatest pleasure? How do they relate to his work as a whole? What picture of himself does he present? What do you suppose motivates him?

5. If good fences make good neighbors in rural life, what makes good neighbors in your community, your dorm, your apartment building, or whatever other living unit you are familiar with? Write an essay explaining what your answer is and how you discovered its importance.

6. Identify a time when your own experience has led you to overturn the accepted understanding of some question. Recount the steps to your discovery, and explain how you composed your alternative understanding.

THE WATER OF LIFE
W. H. Auden

Wystan Hugh Auden (1907–1973) was born in York, England, and educated at Oxford. Known for his poetry even while a student, Auden went on to become one of the major poets of his time. He moved to the United States in 1939 and became a U.S. citizen shortly thereafter, but he spent the later years of his life living mostly in England and on a farm in Austria. In 1952 a long-standing interest in traditional literary form culminated in his writing an introduction for a collection of fairy tales. This introduction was also published separately in New World Writing, *a semi-annual literary magazine. From this introduction we have selected a section that deals primarily with a single tale, "The Water of Life," first collected and published by the Grimm brothers in their two volumes of* Nursery and Household Tales *(1812, 1815). We have reprinted the tale itself following the essay.*

1   A fairy story, as distinct from a merry tale, or an animal story, is a serious tale with a human hero and a happy ending. The progression of its hero is the reverse of the tragic hero's: at the beginning he is either socially obscure or despised as being stupid or untalented, lacking in the heroic virtues, but at the end, he has surprised everyone by demonstrating his heroism and winning fame, riches, and love. Though ultimately he succeeds, he does not do so without a struggle in which his success is in doubt, for opposed to him are not only natural difficulties like glass mountains, or barriers of flame, but also hostile wicked powers, stepmothers, jealous brothers and witches. In many cases, indeed, he would fail were he not assisted by friendly powers who give him instructions or perform tasks for him which he cannot do himself; that is, in addition to his own powers, he needs luck, but this luck is not fortuitous but dependent upon his character and his actions. The tale ends with the establishment of justice; not only are the good rewarded but also the evil are punished.

2   Take, for example, "The Water of Life." Three brothers set out in turn on a difficult quest to find the water of life to restore the King, their sick father, to health. Each one meets a dwarf who asks him where he is going. The two elder give rude answers and are punished by being imprisoned in ravines. The third brother gives a courteous answer and is rewarded by being told where the water of life is and how to appease the lions who guard it, but is warned to leave before the clock strikes twelve. He reaches the enchanted castle, where he finds a princess who tells him to return in a year and marry her. At this point he

274

almost fails because he falls asleep and only just manages to escape as the clock strikes twelve and the iron door shuts, carrying away a piece of his heel. On the way home he again meets the dwarf and begs him to release his brothers, which he does with a warning that they have bad hearts. The brothers steal the water of life from him and substitute salt water so that his father condemns him to be secretly shot. The huntsman entrusted with the task has not the heart to do it, and lets the young prince go away into the forest. Now begins a second quest for the Princess. She has built a golden road to test her suitors. Whoever rides straight up it is to be admitted, whoever rides to the side is not. When the two elder brothers come to it, they think "it would be a sin and a shame to ride over that" and so fail the test. At the end of the year, the exiled brother rides thither but is so preoccupied with thinking of the Princess that he never notices the golden road and rides straight up. They are married, the King learns how the elder brothers had betrayed the Prince, and they, to escape punishment, put to sea and never come back.

The hero is in the third or inferior position. (The youngest son inherits least.)[1] There are two quests, each involving a test which the hero passes and his brothers fail.

The first test is the encounter with the dwarf. The elder brothers disregard him a) because he looks like the last person on earth who could help them; b) they are impatient and thinking only of their success; and c) what is wrong with their concentration on their task is, firstly, over-self-confidence in their own powers and, secondly, the selfishness of their motive. They do not really love their father but want him to reward them.

The hero, on the other hand, is a) humble enough; b) cares enough for his father's recovery; and c) has a loving disposition toward all men, so that he asks the dwarf for assistance and gets it.

The second test of the golden road is a reversal of the first: the right thing to do this time is to take no notice of it. The brothers who dismissed the dwarf notice the road because of its worldly value, which is more to them than any Princess, while the hero, who paid attention to the dwarf, ignores the road because he is truly in love.

The Water of Life and the Princess are guarded by lions; these, in this tale, are not malevolent but ensure that no one shall succeed who has not learned the true way. The hero almost fails here by forgetting the dwarf's warning and falling asleep; further it is through falling asleep and not watching his brothers that they almost succeed in destroying him. The readiness to fall asleep is a sign of the trustfulness and lack of fear which are the qualities which bring about his success; at the same time it is pointed out that, carried too far, they are a danger to him.

If such a tale is not history, what is it about? Broadly speaking, and in most

---

[1] I now think I was mistaken. In many peasant communities, where early marriages are the rule, it is the youngest son who inherits the farm.

cases, the fairy tale is a dramatic projection in symbolic images of the life of the psyche, and it can travel from one country to another, one culture to another culture, whenever what it has to say holds good for human nature in both, despite their differences. Insofar as the myth is valid, the events of the story and its basic images will appeal irrespective of the artistic value of their narration; a genuine myth, like the Chaplin clown, can always be recognized by the fact that its appeal cuts across all differences between highbrow and lowbrow tastes. Further, no one conscious analysis can exhaust its meaning. There is no harm, however, if this is realized, in trying to give one.

Thus reading "The Water of Life," it occurs to me that the two quests, for   9
the water which heals the old sick King and the Princess through marriage with whom the new life will come into being are one and the same, though it is only by first trying to restore the past that one comes to discover one's future path. One's true strength rarely lies in the capacities and faculties of which one is proud, but frequently in those one regards as unimportant or even as weaknesses. Success can never be achieved by an act of conscious will alone; it always requires the co-operation of grace or luck. But grace is not arbitrary; it is always there to assist anyone who is humble enough to ask for it and those who reject it convert it by their own act of rejection into a negative force; they get what they demand. There is no joy or success without risk and suffering, and those who try to avoid suffering fail to obtain the joy, but get the suffering anyway. Finally, and above all, one must not be anxious about ultimate success or failure but think only about what it is necessary to do at the present moment. What seems a story stretched out in time takes place in fact at every instant; the proud and the envious are even now dancing in red-hot shoes or rolling downhill in barrels full of nails; the trustful and loving are already married to princesses.

THE WATER OF LIFE

There was once a King who had an illness, and no one believed that he   1
would come out of it with his life. He had three sons who were much distressed about it, and went down into the palace-garden and wept. There they met an old man who inquired as to the cause of their grief. They told him that their father was so ill that he would most certainly die, for nothing seemed to cure him. Then the old man said, "I know of one more remedy, and that is the water of life; if he drinks of it he will become well again; but it is hard to find." The eldest said, "I will manage to find it," and went to the sick King, and begged to be allowed to go forth in search of the water of life, for that alone could save him. "No," said the King, "the danger of it is too great. I would

helper #2

rather die." But he begged so long that the King consented. The prince thought in his heart, "If I bring the water, then I shall be best beloved of my father, and shall inherit the kingdom." So he set out, and when he had ridden forth a little distance, a dwarf stood there in the road who called to him and said, "Whither away so fast?" "Silly shrimp," said the prince, very haughtily, "it is nothing to you," and rode on. But the little dwarf had grown angry, and had wished an evil wish. Soon after this the prince entered a ravine, and the further he rode the closer the mountains drew together, and at last the road became so narrow that he could not advance a step further; it was impossible either to turn his horse or to dismount from the saddle, and he was shut in there as if in prison. The sick King waited long for him, but he came not. Then the second son said, "Father, let me go forth to seek the water," and thought to himself, "If my brother is dead, then the kingdom will fall to me." At first the King would not allow him to go either, but at last he yielded, so the prince set out on the same road that his brother had taken, and he too met the dwarf, who stopped him to ask, whither he was going in such haste? "Little shrimp," said the prince, "that is nothing to thee," and rode on without giving him another look. But the dwarf bewitched him, and he, like the other, got into a ravine, and could neither go forwards nor backwards. So fare haughty people.

As the second son also remained away, the youngest begged to be allowed to go forth to fetch the water, and at last the King was obliged to let him go. When he met the dwarf and the latter asked him whither he was going in such haste, he stopped, gave him an explanation, and said, "I am seeking the water of life, for my father is sick unto death." "Dost thou know, then, where that is to be found?" "No," said the prince. "As thou hast borne thyself as is seemly, and not haughtily like thy false brothers, I will give thee the information and tell thee how thou mayst obtain the water of life. It springs from a fountain in the courtyard of an enchanted castle, but thou wilt not be able to make thy way to it, if I do not give thee an iron wand and two small loaves of bread. Strike thrice with the wand on the iron door of the castle, and it will spring open: inside lie two lions with gaping jaws, but if thou throwest a loaf to each of them, they will be quieted, then hasten to fetch some of the water of life before the clock strikes twelve, else the door will shut again, and thou wilt be imprisoned." The prince thanked him, took the wand and the bread, and set out on his way. When he arrived, everything was as the dwarf had said. The door sprang open at the third stroke of the wand, and when he had appeased the lions with the bread, he entered into the castle, and came in a large and splendid hall, wherein sat some enchanted princes whose rings he drew off their fingers. A sword and a loaf of bread were lying there, which he carried away. After this, he entered a chamber, in which was a beautiful maiden who rejoiced when she saw him, kissed him, and told him that he had delivered her, and should have the whole of her kingdom, and that if he would return in a year their wedding should be celebrated; likewise she told him where the spring of the water of life

rings
sword
loaf of bread

was, and that he was to hasten and draw some of it before the clock struck twelve. Then he went onwards, and at last entered a room where there was a beautiful newly-made bed, and as he was very weary, he felt inclined to rest a little. So he lay down and fell asleep. When he awoke, it was striking a quarter to twelve. He sprang up in a fright, ran to the spring, drew some water in a cup which stood near, and hastened away. But just as he was passing through the iron door, the clock struck twelve, and the door fell to with such violence that it carried away a piece of his heel. He, however, rejoicing at having obtained the water of life, went homewards, and again passed the dwarf. When the latter saw the sword and the loaf, he said, "With these thou hast won great wealth; with the sword thou canst slay whole armies, and the bread will never come to an end." But the prince would not go home to his father without his brothers, and said, "Dear dwarf, canst thou not tell me where my two brothers are? They went out before I did in search of the water of life, and have not returned." "They are imprisoned between two mountains," said the dwarf. "I have condemned them to stay there, because they were so haughty." Then the prince begged until the dwarf released them; he warned him, however, and said, "Beware of them, for they have bad hearts." When his brothers came, he rejoiced, and told them how things had gone with him, that he had found the water of life, and had brought a cupful away with him, and had delivered a beautiful princess, who was willing to wait a year for him, and then their wedding was to be celebrated, and he would obtain a great kingdom. After that they rode on together, and chanced upon a land where war and famine reigned, and the King already thought he must perish, for the scarcity was so great. Then the prince went to him and gave him the loaf, wherewith he fed and satisfied the whole of his kingdom, and then the prince gave him the sword also, wherewith he slew the hosts of his enemies, and could now live in rest and peace. The prince then took back his loaf and his sword, and the three brothers rode on. But after this they entered two more countries where war and famine reigned, and each time the prince gave his loaf and his sword to the Kings, and had now delivered three kingdoms, and after that they went on board a ship and sailed over the sea. During the passage, the two eldest conversed apart and said, "The youngest has found the water of life and not we, for that our father will give him the kingdom—the kingdom which belongs to us, and he will rob us of all our fortune." They then began to seek revenge, and plotted with each other to destroy him. They waited until once when they found him fast asleep, then they poured the water of life out of the cup, and took it for themselves, but into the cup they poured salt sea-water. Now therefore, when they arrived at home, the youngest took his cup to the sick King in order that he might drink out of it, and be cured. But scarcely had he drunk a very little of the salt sea-water than he became still worse than before. And as he was lamenting over this, the two eldest brothers came, and accused the youngest of having intended to poison him, and said that they had brought him the true water of life, and handed it

278

to him. He had scarcely tasted it, when he felt his sickness departing, and became strong and healthy as in the days of his youth. After that they both went to the youngest, mocked him, and said, "You certainly found the water of life, but you have had the pain, and we the gain; you should have been sharper, and should have kept your eyes open. We took it from you whilst you were asleep at sea, and when a year is over, one of us will go and fetch the beautiful princess. But beware that you do not disclose aught of this to our father; indeed he does not trust you, and if you say a single word, you shall lose your life into the bargain, but if you keep silent, you shall have it as a gift."

The old King was angry with his youngest son, and thought he had plotted against his life. So he summoned the court together, and had sentence pronounced upon his son, that he should be secretly shot. And once when the prince was riding forth to the chase, suspecting no evil, the King's huntsman had to go with him, and when they were quite alone in the forest, the huntsman looked so sorrowful that the prince said to him, "Dear huntsman, what ails you?" The huntsman said, "I cannot tell you, and yet I ought." Then the prince said, "Say openly what it is, I will pardon you." "Alas!" said the huntsman, "I am to shoot you dead, the King has ordered me to do it." Then the prince was shocked, and said, "Dear huntsman, let me live; there, I give you my royal garments; give me your common ones in their stead." The huntsman said, "I will willingly do that, indeed I should not have been able to shoot you." Then they exchanged clothes, and the huntsman returned home; the prince, however, went further into the forest. After a time three wagons of gold and precious stones came to the King for his youngest son, which were sent by the three Kings who had slain their enemies with the prince's sword, and maintained their people with his bread, and who wished to show their gratitude for it. The old King then thought, "Can my son have been innocent?" and said to his people, "Would that he were still alive, how it grieves me that I have suffered him to be killed!" "He still lives," said the huntsman, "I could not find it in my heart to carry out your command," and told the King how it had happened. Then a stone fell from the King's heart, and he had it proclaimed in every country that his son might return and be taken into favour again.

The princess, however, had a road made up to her palace which was quite bright and golden, and told her people that whosoever came riding straight along it to her, would be the right wooer and was to be admitted, and whoever rode by the side of it, was not the right one, and was not to be admitted. As the time was now close at hand, the eldest thought he would hasten to go to the King's daughter, and give himself out as her deliverer, and thus win her for his bride, and the kingdom to boot. Therefore he rode forth, and when he arrived in front of the palace, and saw the splendid golden road, he thought it would be a sin and a shame if he were to ride over that, and turned aside, and rode on the right side of it. But when he came to the door, the servants told him that he was not the right man, and was to go away again. Soon after this the second prince set out, and when he came to the golden road, and his horse had put one foot on it, he thought it would be a sin and a shame to tread a piece of it off, and he turned aside and rode on the left side of it, and when he reached the door, the attendants told him he was not the right one, and was to go away again. When at last the year had entirely expired, the third son likewise wished to ride out of the forest to his beloved, with her to forget his sorrows. So he set out and thought of her so incessantly, and wished to be with her so much, that he never noticed the golden road at all. So his horse rode onwards up the middle of it, and when he came to the door, it was opened and the princess received him with joy, and said he was her deliverer, and lord of the kingdom, and their wedding was celebrated with great rejoicing. When it was over she told him that his father invited him to come to him, and had forgiven him. So he rode thither, and told him everything; how his brothers had betrayed him, and how he had nevertheless kept silence. The old King wished to punish them, but they had put to sea, and never came back as long as they lived.

Jacob and Wilhelm Grimm

QUESTIONS

1. What is the meaning of the title of this fairy tale? Where does it direct our attention? After reading the tale, propose alternative titles for it. Would you read the tale differently if it were called something else?

2. What incidents in "The Water of Life" illustrate the bad hearts of the older brothers and the worthiness of the youngest?

3. Auden's discussion of the tale comes in three parts. First he summarizes the story. Then he comments on the meaning of some of its most noticeable features. After that he interprets or analyzes the tale by telling us what it is about. Where do these sections begin and end, and why are they in that particular order?

4. In his summary of the tale, what details does Auden omit most conspicuously? Why does he make these omissions? Write your own summary, including details he omits and omitting some that he includes in order to work toward your own interpretation of the story.

5. Examine Auden's commentary in paragraphs 3 through 7. Again he comments on some elements of the story but not on others. Why, for example, does he offer no comment on how the third son uses the sword and the loaf that he took when he left the princess? Could those acquisitions present the third son with a third test? Write a commentary on that "third test" or on some other feature of the tale that Auden ignores.

6. Auden remarked that "no one conscious analysis can exhaust [a tale s] meaning" (paragraph 8). Write your own analysis of the tale, emphasizing features Auden slights. Justify your own interpretation as an alternative to his by attending, interestingly and sensibly, to equally important features of the tale.

7. Select another fairy tale told by the Grimm brothers. Analyze it as Auden has analyzed "The Water of Life."

Social Sciences and Public Affairs

A ZERO-SUM GAME
Lester C. Thurow

Born in Livingston, Montana, in 1938, Lester Thurow has degrees in economics from Williams College, Oxford University, and Harvard University. He is the author of over sixty articles on economics and a number of books. Currently teaching at the Sloan School of Management at the Massachusetts Institute of Technology, Thurow writes frequently on economic matters for newspapers. He reached a wide audience with The Zero-Sum Society, *which Business Week called "a ruthlessly honest, tough-minded book." The following selection is from chapter 1 of that book, "An Economy That No Longer Performs."*

This is the heart of our fundamental problem. Our economic problems are 1
solvable. For most of our problems there are several solutions. But all these
solutions have the characteristic that someone must suffer large economic losses.
No one wants to volunteer for this role, and we have a political process that is
incapable of forcing anyone to shoulder this burden. Everyone wants someone
else to suffer the necessary economic losses, and as a consequence none of the
possible solutions can be adopted.

Basically we have created the world described in Robert Ardrey's *The Terri-* 2
torial Imperative. To beat an animal of the same species on his home turf, the
invader must be twice as strong as the defender. But no majority is twice as
strong as the minority opposing it. Therefore we each veto the other's initiatives,
but none of us has the ability to create successful initiatives ourselves.

Lester C. Thurow

Our political and economic structure simply isn't able to cope with an econ- 3
omy that has a substantial zero-sum element. A zero-sum game is any game
where the losses exactly equal the winnings. All sporting events are zero-sum
games. For every winner there is a loser, and winners can only exist if losers
exist. What the winning gambler wins, the losing gambler must lose.

When there are large losses to be allocated, any economic decision has a 4
large zero-sum element. The economic gains may exceed the economic losses,
but the losses are so large as to negate a very substantial fraction of the gains.
What is more important, the gains and losses are not allocated to the same
individuals or groups. On average, society may be better off, but this average
hides a large number of people who are much better off and large numbers of
people who are much worse off. If you are among those who are worse off, the
fact that someone else's income has risen by more than your income has fallen
is of little comfort.

To protect our own income, we will fight to stop economic change from 5
occurring or fight to prevent society from imposing the public policies that hurt
us. From our perspective they are not good public policies even if they do result
in a larger GNP.[1] We want a solution to the problem, say the problem of
energy, that does not reduce our income, but all solutions reduce someone's
income. If the government chooses some policy option that does not lower our
income, it will have made a supporter out of us, but it will have made an
opponent out of someone else, since someone else will now have to shoulder
the burden of large income reductions.

The problem with zero-sum games is that the essence of problem solving is 6
loss allocation. But this is precisely what our political process is least capable of
doing. When there are economic gains to be allocated, our political process
can allocate them. When there are large economic losses to be allocated, our
political process is paralyzed. And with political paralysis comes economic paralysis.

The importance of economic losers has also been magnified by a change in 7
the political structure. In the past, political and economic power was distributed
in such a way that substantial economic losses could be imposed on parts of the
population if the establishment decided that it was in the general interest. Economic losses were allocated to particular powerless groups rather than spread
across the population. These groups are no longer willing to accept losses and
are able to raise substantially the costs for those who wish to impose losses upon
them.

There are a number of reasons for this change. Vietnam and the subsequent 8
political scandals clearly lessened the population's willingness to accept their
nominal leader's judgments that some project was in their general interest. With
the civil rights, poverty, black power, and women's liberation movements, many

---

[1]GNP: gross national product, an annual measure of the wealth generated by a country—in this
case, the United States. [Eds.]

of the groups that have in the past absorbed economic losses have become militant. They are no longer willing to accept losses without a political fight. The success of their militancy and civil disobedience sets an example that spreads to other groups representing the environment, neighborhoods, and regions.

All minority groups have gone through a learning process. They have dis- 9 covered that it is relatively easy with our legal system and a little militancy to delay anything for a very long period of time. To be able to delay a program is often to be able to kill it. Legal and administrative costs rise, but the delays and uncertainties are even more important. When the costs of delays and uncertainties are added into their calculations, both government and private industry often find that it pays to cancel projects that would otherwise be profitable. Costs are simply higher than benefits.

In one major environmental group, delays are such a major part of their 10 strategy that they have a name for it—analysis paralysis. Laws are to be passed so that every project must meet a host of complicated time-consuming requirements. The idea is not to learn more about the costs and benefits of projects, but to kill them. If such requirements were to be useful in deciding whether a project should be undertaken, environmental-impact statements, for example, would have to be inexpensive, simple, and quick to complete. Then a firm might undertake the studies to help determine whether they should or should not start a project.

Instead, the studies are to be expensive and complex to serve as a financial 11 deterrent to undertaking any project, to substantially lengthen the time necessary to complete any project, and to ensure that they can be challenged in court (another lengthy process). As a consequence, the developer will start the process only if he has already decided on other grounds to go ahead with the project. The result is an adversary situation where the developer cannot get his project underway—and where the environmentalists also cannot get existing plants (such as Reserve Mining) to clean up their current pollution. Where it helps them, both sides have learned the fine art of delay.

Consider the interstate highway system. Whatever one believes about the 12 merits of completing the remaining intracity portion of the system, it is clear that it gives the country an intercity transportation network that would be sorely missed had it not been built. Even those who argue against it do so on the grounds that if it had not been built, some better (nonauto) system would have been devised. Yet most observers would agree that the interstate highway system could not have been built if it had been proposed in the mid-1970s rather than in the mid-1950s.

Exactly the same factors that would prevent the initiation of an interstate 13 highway system would also prevent the initiation of any alternative transportation system. A few years ago, when a high-speed rail system was being considered for the Boston-Washington corridor, a former governor of Connecticut announced that he would veto any relocation of the Boston-to-New York line on

Lester C. Thurow

the grounds that it would be of prime benefit to those at either end of the line, but would tear up Connecticut homes. The groups opposing an intercity rail network would be slightly different from the groups opposing an intercity highway network, but they would be no less effective in stopping the project. Any transportation system demands that land be taken and homes be torn down. At one time, this was possible; at the moment, it is impossible.

The Balkanization of nations is a worldwide phenomenon that the United States has not escaped.[2] Regions and localities are less and less willing to incur costs that will primarily help people in other parts of the same country. Consider the development of the coalfields of Wyoming and Montana. There is no question that most of the benefits will accrue to those living in urban areas in the rest of the country while most of the costs will be imposed on those living in that region. As a result, the local population objects. More coal mining might be good for the United States, but it will be bad for local constituents. Therefore they will impose as many delays and uncertainties as possible.

The same problem is visible in the location of nuclear power plants. Whatever one believes about the benefits of nuclear power, it is clear that lengthy delays in approving sites serve no purpose other than as a strategy for killing the projects. If the projects are undertaken anyway, the consumer will have to suffer the same risks and pay the higher costs associated with these delays. What is wanted is a quick yes or no answer; but this is just what we find impossible to do. The question of nuclear power sites also raises the Balkanization issue. Whatever the probabilities of accidents, the consequences of such failures are much less if the plants are located in remote areas. But those who live in remote areas do not want the plants, since they suffer all the potential hazards and do not need the project. Everyone wants power, but no one wants a power plant next to his own home.

Domestic problems also tend to have a much longer time horizon. In modern times, even long wars are won or lost in relatively short periods of time. In contrast, a project such as energy independence would take decades to achieve. The patience and foresight necessary for long-range plans is generally not an American virtue. Consequently, representatives seeking reelection every two, four, or six years want to support programs that will bring them votes. They do not want to stick their necks out for a good cause that may conflict with their careers. Even more fundamentally, domestic problems often involve long periods where costs accrue, with the benefits following much later. Think about energy independence. For a long time, sacrifices must be made to construct the necessary mines and plants. Benefits emerge only near the end of the process. The politician who must incur the costs (raise the necessary revenue and incur the anger of those who are hurt as the projects are constructed) is unlikely to be around to collect the credits when energy independence has been achieved.

[2]Balkanization: the process by which a region breaks down into smaller, usually hostile units. The term derives from the division of the Balkan countries in southeastern Europe by the Great Powers early in this century. [Eds.]

284

QUESTIONS

1. Does Thurow say that the United States economy is a zero-sum game? What, exactly, does he say, and what, exactly, is a zero-sum game?

2. In his first paragraph, Thurow mentions a fundamental problem. What is that problem? What has it got to do with zero-sum games?

3. What is the logical structure of the first paragraph? Where does it move from premises or assumptions to conclusions?

4. In paragraph 3, how does Thurow make sure you will understand his definition of a zero-sum game? (Consider also the structure of the last two sentences of that paragraph. How does the form of those sentences relate to the idea being conveyed? Why could you call them zero-sum sentences?)

5. How does Thurow organize paragraphs 11 through 14? What gives each paragraph its coherence? How are all four related to the larger structure of the essay?

6. How does this essay divide into sections that develop different parts of the subject? Make an outline of the essay by listing a few topics and then assigning the appropriate paragraphs to each topic.

7. In paragraph 6, Thurow says, "the essence of problem solving is loss allocation." What does he mean by *loss allocation?* Present a proposal for solving a particular problem. Do so in such a way as to make clear the loss allocation that will be required. Try to present your case in such a way that the allocation seems reasonable.

8. When Thurow says that "the essence of problem solving is loss allocation" (paragraph 6), he implicitly defines problem solving. Is every solution a matter of cost-benefit analysis? Is the winners-losers framework an assumption—or a pragmatic observation? Write a paper in which you explain the nature of problem solving by agreeing or disagreeing with Thurow.

9. Write an essay in which you interpret or explain the causes of a particular situation, such as why a team loses or why something costs what it does. Support your reasoning with concrete examples and specific details.

10. Analyze a government proposal being made right now, locally, regionally, or nationally. What is the problem? What is the proposed solution? In particular, what is the system of loss allocation being suggested? How direct are the proponents of this legislation about the loss allocation that will be necessary?

HOW CHILDREN FORM MATHEMATICAL CONCEPTS
Jean Piaget

Jean Piaget was born in Switzerland and lived from 1896 to 1980. The earliest influences on his life were his father, who was a historian who did not believe in historical facts; a friendly museum curator who helped him become a published zoologist by the age of fifteen; and his godfather, who read philosophy with him to keep him from becoming too specialized. Not surprisingly, Piaget firmly believed in interdisciplinary studies, founding a school of "genetic epistemology" for the study of how the human mind develops. He is world famous for his many books on child development. The following article from Scientific American *(1953) is representative of his basic and important work.*

It is a great mistake to suppose that a child acquires the notion of number 1
and other mathematical concepts just from teaching. On the contrary, to a remarkable degree he develops them himself, independently and spontaneously. When adults try to impose mathematical concepts on a child prematurely, his learning is merely verbal; true understanding of them comes only with his mental growth.

This can easily be shown by a simple experiment. A child of five or six may 2
readily be taught by his parents to name the numbers from 1 to 10. If 10 stones are laid in a row, he can count them correctly. But if the stones are rearranged in a more complex pattern or piled up, he no longer can count them with consistent accuracy. Although the child knows the names of the numbers, he has not yet grasped the essential idea of number: namely, that the number of objects in a group remains the same, is "conserved," no matter how they are shuffled or arranged.

On the other hand, a child of six and a half or seven often shows that he 3
has spontaneously formed the concept of number even though he may not yet have been taught to count. Given eight red chips and eight blue chips, he will discover by one-to-one matching that the number of red is the same as the number of blue, and he will realize that the two groups remain equal in number regardless of the shape they take.

286

The experiment with one-to-one correspondence is very useful for investi-   4
gating children's development of the number concept. Let us lay down a row
of eight red chips, equally spaced about an inch apart, and ask our small subjects
to take from a box of blue chips as many chips as there are on the table. Their
reactions will depend on age, and we can distinguish three stages of development. A child of five or younger, on the average, will lay out blue chips to
make a row exactly as long as the red row, but he will put the blue chips close
together instead of spacing them. He believes the number is the same if the
length of the row is the same. At the age of six, on the average, children arrive
at the second stage; these children will lay a blue chip opposite each red chip
and obtain the correct number. But they have not necessarily acquired the
concept of number itself. If we spread the red chips, spacing out the row more
loosely, the six-year-olds will think that the longer row now has more chips,
though we have not changed the number. At the age of six and a half to seven,
on the average, children achieve the third stage: they know that, though we
close up or space out one row of chips, the number is still the same as in the
other.

In a similar experiment a child is given two receptacles of identical shape   5
and size and is asked to put beads, one at a time, into both receptacles with
both hands simultaneously—a blue bead into one box with his right hand and
a red bead into the other with his left hand. When he has more or less filled
the two receptacles, he is asked how they compare. He is sure that both have
the same number of beads. Then he is requested to pour the blue beads into a
receptacle of a different size and shape. Here again we see differences in understanding according to age. The smallest children think that the number has
changed: if, for instance, the beads fill the new receptacle to a higher level,
they think there are more beads in it than in the original one; if to a lower
level, they think there are fewer. But children near the age of seven know that
the transfer has not changed the number of beads.

In short, children must grasp the principle of conservation of quantity before   6
they can develop the concept of number. Now conservation of quantity of course
is not in itself a numerical notion; rather, it is a logical concept. Thus these
experiments in child psychology throw some light on the epistemology of the
number concept—a subject which has been examined by many mathematicians
and logicians.

The mathematicians Henri Poincaré and L. E. J. Brouwer[1] have held that   7
the number concept is a product of primitive intuition, preceding logical notions. The experiments just described deny this thesis, in our opinion. Bertrand

---

[1]Henri Poincaré . . . Brouwer: Poincaré (1854–1912) was a French mathematician and physicist
who contributed to the theory of functions and did research in differential equations. Lutizen E.
J. Brouwer (1881–1966) was a Dutch mathematician and was one of the founders of modern
topology. [Eds.]

Russell,[2] on the other hand, has supported the view that number is a purely logical concept: that the idea of cardinal number derives from the logical notion of category (a number would be a category made up of equivalent categories) while the notion of ordinal number derives from the logical relationships of order. But Russell's theory does not quite fit the psychological processes as we have observed them in small children. Children at the start make no distinction between cardinal and ordinal number, and besides, the concept of cardinal number itself presupposes an order relationship. For instance, a child can build a one-to-one correspondence only if he neither forgets any of the elements nor uses the same one twice. The only way of distinguishing one unit from another is to consider it either before or after the other in time or in space, that is, in the order of enumeration.

Study of the child's discovery of spatial relationships—what may be called   8
the child's spontaneous geometry—is no less rewarding than the investigation of his number concepts. A child's order of development in geometry seems to reverse the order of historical discovery. Scientific geometry began with the Euclidean system (concerned with figures, angles and so on), developed in the 17th century the so-called projective geometry (dealing with problems of perspective) and finally came in the 19th century to topology (describing spatial relationships in a general qualitative way—for instance, the distinction between open and closed structures, interiority and exteriority, proximity and separation). A child begins with the last: his first geometrical discoveries are topological. At the age of three he readily distinguishes between open and closed figures: if you ask him to copy a square or a triangle, he draws a closed circle; he draws a cross with two separate lines. If you show him a drawing of a large circle with a small circle inside, he is quite capable of reproducing this relationship, and he can also draw a small circle outside or attached to the edge of the large one. All this he can do before he can draw a rectangle or express the Euclidean characteristics (number of sides, angles, etc.) of a figure. Not until a considerable time after he has mastered topological relationships does he begin to develop his notions of Euclidean and projective geometry. Then he builds those simultaneously.

Curiously enough, this psychological order is much closer to modern ge-   9
ometry's order of deductive or axiomatic construction than the historical order of discovery was. It offers another example of the kinship between psychological construction and the logical construction of science itself.

Let us test our young subjects on projective constructions. First we set up   10
two "fence posts" (little sticks stuck in bases of modeling clay) some 15 inches apart and ask the child to place other posts in a straight line between them. The

---

[2]Bertrand Russell (1872–1970): English mathematician, logician, and philosopher who was awarded the Nobel Prize for literature in 1950. [Eds.]

youngest children (under the age of four) proceed to plant one post next to another, forming a more or less wavy line. Their approach is topological: the elements are joined by the simple relationship of proximity rather than by projection of a line as such. At the next stage, beyond the age of four, the child may form a straight fence if the two end posts parallel the edge of the table, or if there is some other straight line to guide him. If the end posts are diagonally across the table, he may start building the line parallel to the table's edge and then change direction and form a curve to reach the second post. Occasionally a youngster may make a straight line, but he does so only by trial-and-error and not by system.

At the age of seven years, on the average, a child can build a straight fence 11 consistently in any direction across the table, and he will check the straightness of the line by shutting one eye and sighting along it, as a gardener lines up bean poles. Here we have the essence of the projective concept; the line is still a topological line, but the child has grasped that the projective relationship depends on the angle of vision, or point of view.

One can proceed to study this with other experiments. For instance, you 12 stand a doll on a table and place before it an object oriented in a certain direction: a pencil lying crosswise, diagonally or lengthwise with respect to the doll's line of vision, or a watch lying flat on the table or standing up. Then you ask the child to draw the doll's view of the object, or, better still, ask him to choose from two or three drawings the one that represents the doll's point of view. Not until the age of about seven or eight can a child deduce correctly the doll's angle of vision.

A similar experiment testing the same point yields the same conclusions. 13 Objects of different shapes are placed in various positions between a light and a screen, and the child is asked to predict the shape of the shadow the object will cast on the screen.

Ability to coordinate different perspectives does not come until the age of 9 14 or 10. This is illustrated by an experiment I suggested some time ago to my collaborator Dr. Edith Meyer. The experimenter sits at a table opposite the child, and between the child and herself she places a cardboard range of mountains. The two see the range from opposite perspectives. The child is then asked to select from several drawings the ones that picture both his own and the opposite person's views of the mountain range. Naturally the youngest children can pick out only the picture that corresponds to their own view; they imagine that all the points of view are like their own. What is more interesting, if the child changes places with the experimenter and sees the mountains from the other side, he now thinks that his new view is the only correct one; he cannot reconstruct the point of view that was his own just a little while before. This is a clear example of the egocentricity so characteristic of children—the primitive reasoning which prevents them from understanding that there may be more than one point of view.

It takes a considerable evolution for children to come, at around the age of 9 or 10, to the ability to distinguish between and coordinate the different possible perspectives. At this stage they can grasp projective space in its concrete or practical form, but naturally not in its theoretical aspects. 15

At the same time the child forms the concept of projective space, he also constructs Euclidean space; the two kinds of construction are based upon one another. For example, in lining up a straight row of fence posts he may not only use the sighting method but may line up his hands parallel to each other to give him the direction. That is, he is applying the concept of conservation of direction, which is a Euclidean principle. Here is another illustration of the fact that children form mathematical notions on a qualitative or logical basis. 16

The conservation principle arises in various forms. There is first the conservation of length. If you place a block on another of the same length and then push one block so that its end projects beyond the other, a child under six will suppose that the two blocks are no longer of equal length. Not until near the age of seven, on the average, does the child understand that what is gained at one end of the block is lost at the other. He arrives at this concept of the conservation of length, be it noted, by a process of logic. 17

Experiments on a child's discovery of the conservation of distance are especially illuminating. Between two small toy trees standing apart from each other on a table you place a wall formed of a block or a thick piece of cardboard, and you ask the child (in his own language, of course) whether the trees are still the same distance apart. The smallest children think the distance has changed; they are simply unable to add up two parts of a distance to a total distance. Children of five or six believe the distance has been reduced, claiming that the width of the wall does not count as distance; in other words, a filled-up space does not have the same value as an empty space. Only near the age of seven do children come to the realization that intervening objects do not change the distance. 18

However you test them, you find the same thing true: children do not appreciate the principle of conservation of length or surface until, somewhere around the age of seven, they discover the reversibility that shows the original quantity has remained the same (e.g., the realignment of equal-length blocks, the removal of the wall, and so on). Thus the discovery of logical relationships is a prerequisite to the construction of geometrical concepts, as it is in the formation of the concept of number. 19

This applies to measurement itself, which is only a derived concept. It is interesting to study how children spontaneously learn to measure. One of my collaborators, Dr. Inhelder, and I have made the following experiment: We show the child a tower of blocks on a table and ask him to build a second tower of the same height on another table (lower or higher than the first) with blocks of a different size. Naturally we provide the child with all the necessary measuring tools. Children's attempts to deal with this problem go through a fascinating 20 evolution. The youngest children build up the second tower to the same visual level as the first, without worrying about the difference in height of the tables. They compare the towers by stepping back and sighting them. At a slightly more advanced stage a child lays a long rod across the tops of the two towers to make sure that they are level. Somewhat later he notices that the base of his tower is not at the same level as the model's. He then wants to place his tower next to the model on the same table to compare them. Reminded that the rules of the game forbid him to move his tower, he begins to look around for a measuring standard. Interestingly enough, the first that comes to his mind is his own body. He puts one hand on top of his tower and the other at its base, and then, trying to keep his hands the same distance apart, he moves over to the other tower to compare it. Children of about the age of six often carry out this work in a most assured manner, as if their hands could not change position on the way! Soon they discover that the method is not reliable, and then they resort to reference points on the body. The child will line up his shoulder with the top of his tower, mark the spot opposite the base on his thigh with his hand and walk over to the model to see whether the distance is the same.

Eventually the idea of an independent measuring tool occurs to the child. His first attempt in this direction is likely to be the building of a third tower next to and the same height as the one he has already erected. Having built it, he moves it over to the first table and matches it against the model; this is allowed by the rules. The child's arrival at this stage presupposes a process of logical reasoning. If we call the model tower A, the second tower C and the movable tower B, the child has reasoned that B = C and B = A, therefore A = C.   21

Later the child replaces the third tower with a rod, but at first the rod must be just the same length as the height of the tower to be measured. He then conceives the idea of using a longer rod and marking the tower height on it with his finger. Finally, and this is the beginning of true measurement, he realizes that he can use a shorter rod and measure the height of the tower by applying the rod a certain number of times up the side.   22

The last discovery involves two new operations of logic. The first is the process of division which permits the child to conceive that the whole is composed of a number of parts added together. The second is the displacement, or substitution, which enables him to apply one part upon others and thus to build a system of units. One may therefore say that measurement is a synthesis of division into parts and of substitution, just as number is a synthesis of the inclusion of categories and of serial order. But measurement develops later than the number concept, because it is more difficult to divide a continuous whole into interchangeable units than to enumerate elements which are already separate.   23

To study measurement in two dimensions, we give the child a large sheet of paper with a pencil dot on it and ask him to put a dot in the same position on   24 another sheet of the same size. He may use rods, strips of paper, strings, rulers or any other measuring tools he needs. The youngest subjects are satisfied to make a visual approximation, using no tools. Later a child applies a measuring tool, but he measures only the distance of the point from the side or bottom edge of the paper and is surprised that this single measurement does not give him the correct position. Then he measures the distance of the point from a corner of the paper, trying to keep the same slant (angle) when he applies the ruler to his own sheet. Finally, at about the age of eight or nine, he discovers that he must break up the measurement into two operations: the horizontal distance from a side edge and the perpendicular distance from the bottom or top edge. Similar experiments with a bead in a box show that a child discovers how to make three-dimensional measurements at about the same age.

Measurement in two or three dimensions brings us to the central idea of   25 Euclidean space, namely the axes of coordinates—a system founded on the horizontality or verticality of physical objects. It may seem that even a baby should grasp these concepts, for after all it can distinguish between the upright and lying-down positions. But actually the representation of vertical and horizontal lines brings up quite another problem from this subjective awareness of postural space. Dr. Inhelder and I have studied it with the following experiments: Using a jar half-filled with colored water, we ask our young subjects to predict what level the water will take when the jar is tipped one way or another. Not until the age of nine, on the average, does a child grasp the idea of horizontality and predict correctly. Similar experiments with a plumb line or a toy sailboat with a tall mast demonstrate that comprehension of verticality comes at about the same time. The child's tardiness in acquiring these concepts is not really surprising, for they require not only a grasp of the internal relationships of an object but also reference to external elements (*e.g.*, a table or the floor or walls of the room).

When a child has discovered how to construct these coordinate axes by   26 reference to natural objects, which he does at about the same time that he conceives the coordination of perspectives, he has completed his conception of how to represent space. By that time he has developed his fundamental mathematical concepts, which spring spontaneously from his own logical operations.

The experiments I have described, simple as they are, have been surprisingly   27 fruitful and have brought to light many unexpected facts. These facts are illuminating from the psychological and pedagogical points of view; more than that, they teach us a number of lessons about human knowledge in general.

QUESTIONS

1. Piaget's essay seems about as pure an example of explanatory writing as one could write. He seems simply to want to make clear and to illustrate information that his studies

have made available to him. What is the gist of that information? Do you find it surprising?

2. Identify the stages of development that Piaget distinguishes.

3. Piaget's main technique is to illustrate the point he wishes to make by reporting on several experiments he either directed or that were performed by colleagues. What range do you find in these experiments? Do they fall into groups or categories of any kind?

4. One word that he uses repeatedly is *conservation*. He speaks of conservation of number, of direction, of length, and of distance. What do these concepts have in common, and how do they help him organize his article?

5. If there is a thesis to the article overall, it must have to do with the priority of logical concepts to concepts in mathematics. How close does Piaget come to saying exactly that, and how can you best put his discovery into words of your own?

6. It has often been said that high school geometry is a good subject to take because it "teaches one logic" or "develops the mind." What would Piaget probably have to say about that notion?

7. Try to invent a few simple experiments that are analogous to the ones Piaget describes. Write a statement explaining how you would conduct one of those experiments. What would you hope to discover by it? What would constitute proof?

8. If possible, work with a small group of classmates to test the experiments each of you explained in question 7. Have a child (related to or known by a group member) try your experiment. Observe and write up your results as Piaget did.

JOEY: A
"MECHANICAL BOY"
Bruno Bettelheim

Born in 1903 and educated in Vienna, Bruno Bettelheim's psychoanalytic work was strongly influenced by Sigmund Freud. During 1938 and 1939, he was a prisoner in Nazi concentration camps; he wrote about those experiences in The Informed Heart *after coming to the United States in 1939. Bettelheim has described his major work with emotionally disturbed children in books addressed to the general reader as well as to his fellow psychoanalysts. His other work includes* Children of the Dream, *a study of children raised in an Israeli kibbutz, and a study of fairy tales called* The Uses of Enchantment. *This essay on Joey was first published in* Scientific American *in 1959.*

Joey, when we began our work with him, was a mechanical boy. He functioned as if by remote control, run by machines of his own powerfully creative fantasy. Not only did he himself believe that he was a machine but, more remarkably, he created this impression in others. Even while he performed actions that are intrinsically human, they never appeared to be other than machine-started and executed. On the other hand, when the machine was not working we had to concentrate on recollecting his presence, for he seemed not to exist. A human body that functions as if it were a machine and a machine that duplicates human functions are equally fascinating and frightening. Perhaps they are so uncanny because they remind us that the human body can operate without a human spirit, that body can exist without soul. And Joey was a child who had been robbed of his humanity.

Not every child who possesses a fantasy world is possessed by it. Normal children may retreat into realms of imaginary glory or magic powers, but they are easily recalled from these excursions. Disturbed children are not always able to make the return trip; they remain withdrawn, prisoners of the inner world of delusion and fantasy. In many ways Joey presented a classic example of this state of infantile autism.[1]

At the Sonia Shankman Orthogenic School of the University of Chicago it

---

[1] autism: a form of psychosis characterized by an inability to relate to and perceive the environment in a realistic manner. Autistic thinking is characterized by withdrawal and detachment from reality, fantasies, delusions, and hallucinations. [Eds.]

is our function to provide a therapeutic environment in which such children may start life over again. I have previously described in this magazine the rehabilitation of another of our patients ["Schizophrenic Art: A Case Study"; SCIENTIFIC AMERICAN, April, 1952]. This time I shall concentrate upon the illness, rather than the treatment. In any age, when the individual has escaped into a delusional world, he has usually fashioned it from bits and pieces of the world at hand. Joey, in his time and world, chose the machine and froze himself in its image. His story has a general relevance to the understanding of emotional development in a machine age.

Joey's delusion is not uncommon among schizophrenic children today.[2] He   4 wanted to be rid of his unbearable humanity, to become completely automatic. He so nearly succeeded in attaining this goal that he could almost convince others, as well as himself, of his mechanical character. The descriptions of autistic children in the literature take for their point of departure and comparison the normal or abnormal human being. To do justice to Joey I would have to compare him simultaneously to a most inept infant and a highly complex piece of machinery. Often we had to force ourselves by a conscious act of will to realize that Joey was a child. Again and again his acting-out of his delusions froze our own ability to respond as human beings.

During Joey's first weeks with us we would watch absorbedly as this at once   5 fragile-looking and imperious nine-year-old went about his mechanical existence. Entering the dining room, for example, he would string an imaginary wire from his "energy source"—an imaginary electric outlet—to the table. There he "insulated" himself with paper napkins and finally plugged himself in. Only then could Joey eat, for he firmly believed that the "current" ran his ingestive apparatus. So skillful was the pantomime that one had to look twice to be sure there was neither wire nor outlet nor plug. Children and members of our staff spontaneously avoided stepping on the "wires" for fear of interrupting what seemed the source of his very life.

For long periods of time, when his "machinery" was idle, he would sit so   6 quietly that he would disappear from the focus of the most conscientious observation. Yet in the next moment he might be "working" and the center of our captivated attention. Many times a day he would turn himself on and shift noisily through a sequence of higher and higher gears until he "exploded," screaming "Crash, crash!" and hurling items from his ever present apparatus— radio tubes, light bulbs, even motors or, lacking these, any handy breakable object. (Joey had an astonishing knack for snatching bulbs and tubes unobserved.) As soon as the object thrown had shattered, he would cease his screaming and wild jumping and retire to mute, motionless nonexistence.

Our maids, inured to difficult children, were exceptionally attentive to Joey;   7

---

[2]schizophrenic: severe mental disorder characterized by unrealistic behavior, bizarre actions, and a tendency to live in an inner world dominated by private fantasies. [Eds.]

they were apparently moved by his extreme infantile fragility, so strangely coupled with megalomaniacal superiority. Occasionally some of the apparatus he fixed to his bed to "live him" during his sleep would fall down in disarray. This machinery he contrived from masking tape, cardboard, wire and other paraphernalia. Usually the maids would pick up such things and leave them on a table for the children to find, or disregard them entirely. But Joey's machine they carefully restored: "Joey must have the carburetor so he can breathe." Similarly they were on the alert to pick up and preserve the motors that ran him during the day and the exhaust pipes through which he exhaled.

How had Joey become a human machine? From intensive interviews with his parents we learned that the process had begun even before birth. Schizophrenia often results from parental rejection, sometimes combined ambivalently with love. Joey, on the other hand, had been completely ignored.

"I never knew I was pregnant," his mother said, meaning that she had already excluded Joey from her consciousness. His birth, she said, "did not make any difference." Joey's father, a rootless draftee in the wartime civilian army, was equally unready for parenthood. So, of course, are many young couples. Fortunately most such parents lose their indifference upon the baby's birth. But not Joey's parents. "I did not want to see or nurse him," his mother declared. "I had no feeling of actual dislike—I simply didn't want to take care of him." For the first three months of his life Joey "cried most of the time." A colicky baby, he was kept on a rigid four-hour feeding schedule, was not touched unless necessary and was never cuddled or played with. The mother, preoccupied with herself, usually left Joey alone in the crib or playpen during the day. The father discharged his frustration by punishing Joey when the child cried at night.

Soon the father left for overseas duty, and the mother took Joey, now a year and a half old, to live with her at her parents' home. On his arrival the grandparents noticed that ominous changes had occurred in the child. Strong and healthy at birth, he had become frail and irritable; a responsive baby, he had become remote and inaccessible. When he began to master speech, he talked only to himself. At an early date he became preoccupied with machinery, including an old electric fan which he could take apart and put together again with surprising deftness.

Joey's mother impressed us with a fey quality that expressed her insecurity, her detachment from the world and her low physical vitality. We were struck especially by her total indifference as she talked about Joey. This seemed much more remarkable than the actual mistakes she made in handling him. Certainly he was left to cry for hours when hungry, because she fed him on a rigid schedule; he was toilet-trained with great rigidity so that he would give no trouble. These things happen to many children. But Joey's existence never registered with his mother. In her recollections he was fused at one moment with one event or person; at another, with something or somebody else. When

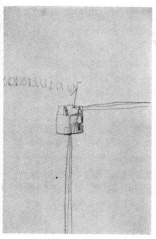  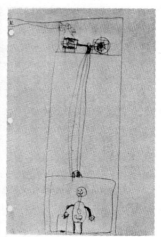

GROWING SELF-ESTEEM is shown in this sequence of drawings. At left Joey portrays himself as an electrical "papoose," completely enclosed, suspended in empty space and operated by wireless signals. In center drawing his figure is much larger, though still under wireless control. At right he is able to picture the machine which controls him, and he has acquired hands with which he can manipulate his immediate environment.

she told us about his birth and infancy, it was as if she were talking about some vague acquaintance, and soon her thoughts would wander off to another person or to herself.

When Joey was not yet four, his nursery school suggested that he enter a special school for disturbed children. At the new school his autism was immediately recognized. During his three years there he experienced a slow improvement. Unfortunately a subsequent two years in a parochial school destroyed this progress. He began to develop compulsive defenses, which he called his "preventions." He could not drink, for example, except through elaborate piping systems built of straws. Liquids had to be "pumped" into him, in his fantasy, or he could not suck. Eventually his behavior became so upsetting that he could not be kept in the parochial school. At home things did not improve. Three months before entering the Orthogenic School he made a serious attempt at suicide.

To us Joey's pathological behavior seemed the external expression of an overwhelming effort to remain almost nonexistent as a person. For weeks Joey's only reply when addressed was "Bam." Unless he thus neutralized whatever we said, there would be an explosion, for Joey plainly wished to close off every form of contact not mediated by machinery. Even when he was bathed he rocked back and forth with mute, engine-like regularity, flooding the bathroom. If he stopped rocking, he did this like a machine too; suddenly he went com-

Bruno Bettelheim

pletely rigid. Only once, after months of being lifted from his bath and carried to bed, did a small expression of puzzled pleasure appear on his face as he said very softly: "They even carry you to your bed here."

For a long time after he began to talk he would never refer to anyone by name, but only as "that person" or "the little person" or "the big person." He was unable to designate by its true name anything to which he attached feelings. Nor could he name his anxieties except through neologisms or word contaminations.[3] For a long time he spoke about "master paintings" and "a master painting room" (i.e., masturbating and masturbating room). One of his machines, the "criticizer," prevented him from "saying words which have unpleasant feelings." Yet he gave personal names to the tubes and motors in his collection of machinery. Moreover, these dead things had feelings; the tubes bled when hurt and sometimes got sick. He consistently maintained this reversal between animate and inanimate objects.

In Joey's machine world everything, on pain of instant destruction, obeyed inhibitory laws much more stringent than those of physics. When we came to know him better, it was plain that in his moments of silent withdrawal, with his machine switched off, Joey was absorbed in pondering the compulsive laws of his private universe. His preoccupation with machinery made it difficult to establish even practical contacts with him. If he wanted to do something with a counselor, such as play with a toy that had caught his vague attention, he could not do so: "I'd like this very much, but first I have to turn off the machine." But by the time he had fulfilled all the requirements of his preventions, he had lost interest. When a toy was offered to him, he could not touch it because his motors and his tubes did not leave him a hand free. Even certain colors were dangerous and had to be strictly avoided in toys and clothing, because "some colors turn off the current, and I can't touch them because I can't live without the current."

Joey was convinced that machines were better than people. Once when he bumped into one of the pipes on our jungle gym he kicked it so violently that his teacher had to restrain him to keep him from injuring himself. When she explained that the pipe was much harder than his foot, Joey replied: "That proves it. Machines are better than the body. They don't break; they're much harder and stronger." If he lost or forgot something, it merely proved that his brain ought to be thrown away and replaced by machinery. If he spilled something, his arm should be broken and twisted off because it did not work properly. When his head or arm failed to work as it should, he tried to punish it by hitting it. Even Joey's feelings were mechanical. Much later in his therapy, when he had formed a timid attachment to another child and had been rebuffed, Joey cried: "He broke my feelings."

[3]neologisms or word contaminations: words that Joey made up or words that he peculiarly altered. [Eds.]

298

JOEY: A "MECHANICAL BOY"

ELABORATE SEWAGE SYSTEM in Joey's drawing of a house reflects his long preoccupation with excretion. His obsession with sewage reflected intense anxieties produced by his early toilet-training, which was not only rigid but also completely impersonal.

Gradually we began to understand what had seemed to be contradictory in Joey's behavior—why he held on to the motors and tubes, then suddenly destroyed them in a fury, then set out immediately and urgently to equip himself with new and larger tubes. Joey had created these machines to run his body and mind because it was too painful to be human. But again and again he became dissatisfied with their failure to meet his need and rebellious at the way they frustrated his will. In a recurrent frenzy he "exploded" his light bulbs and tubes, and for a moment became a human being—for one crowning instant he came alive. But as soon as he had asserted his dominance through the self-created explosion, he felt his life ebbing away. To keep on existing he had immediately to restore his machines and replenish the electricity that supplied his life energy. 17

What deep-seated fears and needs underlay Joey's delusional system? We were long in finding out, for Joey's preventions effectively concealed the secret of his autistic behavior. In the meantime we dealt with his peripheral problems one by one. 18

During his first year with us Joey's most trying problem was toilet behavior. This surprised us, for Joey's personality was not "anal" in the Freudian sense; his original personality damage had antedated the period of his toilet-training. Rigid and early toilet-training, however, had certainly contributed to his anxieties. It was our effort to help Joey with this problem that led to his first recognition of us as human beings. 19

299

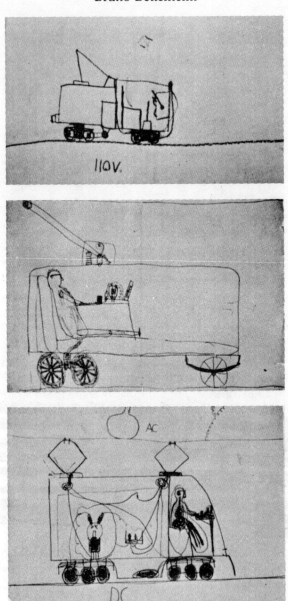

GROWING AUTONOMY is shown in Joey's drawings of the imaginary "Carr" (car) family. Top drawing shows a machine which can move but is unoccupied. Machine in center is occupied, but by a passive figure. In bottom drawing figure has gained control of machine.

JOEY: A "MECHANICAL BOY"

Going to the toilet, like everything else in Joey's life, was surrounded by elaborate preventions. We had to accompany him; he had to take off all his clothes; he could only squat, not sit, on the toilet seat; he had to touch the wall with one hand, in which he also clutched frantically the vacuum tubes that powered his elimination. He was terrified lest his whole body be sucked down. 20

To counteract this fear we gave him a metal wastebasket in lieu of a toilet. Eventually, when eliminating into the wastebasket, he no longer needed to take off all his clothes, nor to hold on to the wall. He still needed the tubes and motors which, he believed, moved his bowels for him. But here again the all-important machinery was itself a source of new terrors. In Joey's world the gadgets had to move their bowels, too. He was terribly concerned that they should, but since they were so much more powerful than men, he was also terrified that if his tubes moved their bowels, their feces would fill all of space and leave him no room to live. He was thus always caught in some fearful contradiction. 21

Our readiness to accept his toilet habits, which obviously entailed some hardship for his counselors, gave Joey the confidence to express his obsessions in drawings. Drawing these fantasies was a first step toward letting us in, however distantly, to what concerned him most deeply. It was the first step in a yearlong process of externalizing his anal preoccupations. As a result he began seeing feces everywhere; the whole world became to him a mire of excrement. At the same time he began to eliminate freely wherever he happened to be. But with this release from his infantile imprisonment in compulsive rules, the toilet and the whole process of elimination became less dangerous. Thus far it had been beyond Joey's comprehension that anybody could possibly move his bowels without mechanical aid. Now Joey took a further step forward; defecation became the first physiological process he could perform without the help of vacuum tubes. It must not be thought that he was proud of this ability. Taking pride in an achievement presupposes that one accomplishes it of one's own free will. He still did not feel himself an autonomous person who could do things on his own. To Joey defecation still seemed enslaved to some incomprehensible but utterly binding cosmic law, perhaps the law his parents had imposed on him when he was being toilet-trained. 22

It was not simply that his parents had subjected him to rigid, early training. Many children are so trained. But in most cases the parents have a deep emotional investment in the child's performance. The child's response in turn makes training an occasion for interaction between them and for the building of genuine relationships. Joey's parents had no emotional investment in him. His obedience gave them no satisfaction and won him no affection or approval. As a toilet-trained child he saved his mother labor, just as household machines saved her labor. As a machine he was not loved for his performance, nor could he love himself. 23

So it had been with all other aspects of Joey's existence with his parents. Their reactions to his eating or noneating, sleeping or wakening, urinating or 24

301

defecating, being dressed or undressed, washed or bathed did not flow from any unitary interest in him, deeply embedded in their personalities. By treating him mechanically his parents made him a machine. The various functions of life—even the parts of his body—bore no integrating relationship to one another or to any sense of self that was acknowledged and confirmed by others. Though he had acquired mastery over some functions, such as toilet-training and speech, he had acquired them separately and kept them isolated from each other. Toilet-training had thus not gained him a pleasant feeling of body mastery; speech had not led to communication of thought or feeling. On the contrary, each achievement only steered him away from self-mastery and integration. Toilet-training had enslaved him. Speech left him talking in neologisms that obstructed his and our ability to relate to each other. In Joey's development the normal process of growth had been made to run backward. Whatever he had learned put him not at the end of his infantile development toward integration but, on the contrary, farther behind than he was at its very beginning. Had we understood this sooner, his first years with us would have been less baffling.

It is unlikely that Joey's calamity could befall a child in any time and culture 25
but our own. He suffered no physical deprivation; he starved for human contact. Just to be taken care of is not enough for relating. It is a necessary but not a sufficient condition. At the extreme where utter scarcity reigns, the forming of relationships is certainly hampered. But our society of mechanized plenty often makes for equal difficulties in a child's learning to relate. Where parents can provide the simple creature-comforts for their children only at the cost of significant effort, it is likely that they will feel pleasure in being able to provide for them; it is this, the parents' pleasure, that gives children a sense of personal worth and sets the process of relating in motion. But if comfort is so readily available that the parents feel no particular pleasure in winning it for their children, then the children cannot develop the feeling of being worthwhile around the satisfaction of their basic needs. Of course parents and children can and do develop relationships around other situations. But matters are then no longer so simple and direct. The child must be on the receiving end of care and concern given with pleasure and without the exaction of return if he is to feel loved and worthy of respect and consideration. This feeling gives him the ability to trust; he can entrust his well-being to persons to whom he is so important. Out of such trust the child learns to form close and stable relationships.

For Joey relationship with his parents was empty of pleasure in comfort- 26
giving as in all other situations. His was an extreme instance of a plight that sends many schizophrenic children to our clinics and hospitals. Many months passed before he could relate to us; his despair that anybody could like him made contact impossible.

When Joey could finally trust us enough to let himself become more infan- 27
tile, he began to play at being a papoose. There was a corresponding change in

$$f'(x) = \lim_{h \to 0} \frac{f(x+h) - f(x)}{h}$$

JOEY: A "MECHANICAL BOY"

his fantasies. He drew endless pictures of himself as an electrical papoose. Totally enclosed, suspended in empty space, he is run by unknown, unseen powers through wireless electricity [*see illustration at left on page* 297].

As we eventually came to understand, the heart of Joey's delusional system   28
was the artificial, mechanical womb he had created and into which he had locked himself. In his papoose fantasies lay the wish to be entirely reborn in a womb. His new experiences in the school suggested that life, after all, might be worth living. Now he was searching for a way to be reborn in a better way. Since machines were better than men, what was more natural than to try rebirth through them? This was the deeper meaning of his electrical papoose.

As Joey made progress, his pictures of himself became more dominant in   29
his drawings. Though still machine-operated, he has grown in self-importance [*see illustration at center on page* 297]. Another great step forward is represented in the picture at right. . . . Now he has acquired hands that do something, and he has had the courage to make a picture of the machine that runs him. Later still the papoose became a person, rather than a robot encased in glass.

Eventually Joey began to create an imaginary family at the school: the "Carr"   30

GENTLE LANDSCAPE painted by Joey after his recovery symbolizes the human emotions he had regained. At 12, having learned to express his feelings, he was no longer a machine.

family. Why the Carr family? In the car he was enclosed as he had been in his papoose, but at least the car was not stationary; it could move. More important, in a car one was not only driven but also could drive. The Carr family was Joey's way of exploring the possibility of leaving the school, of living with a good family in a safe, protecting car [*see illustrations on page 300*].

Joey at last broke through his prison. In this brief account it has not been 31 possible to trace the painfully slow process of his first true relations with other human beings. Suffice it to say that he ceased to be a mechanical boy and became a human child. This newborn child was, however, nearly 12 years old. To recover the lost time is a tremendous task. That work has occupied Joey and us ever since. Sometimes he sets to it with a will; at other times the difficulty of real life makes him regret that he ever came out of his shell. But he has never wanted to return to his mechanical life.

One last detail and this fragment of Joey's story has been told. When Joey 32 was 12, he made a float for our Memorial Day parade. It carried the slogan: "Feelings are more important than anything under the sun." Feelings, Joey had learned, are what make for humanity; their absence, for a mechanical existence. With this knowledge Joey entered the human condition.

QUESTIONS

1. Bettelheim's task was to explain Joey's behavior as best he could. What did he and his colleagues do, what did they examine, and how did they behave in order to develop their explanation of Joey?

2. Joey, of course, had already come to some conclusions about himself and about the world he inhabited. These explanations seem to have become fixed as interpretations, by which we mean simply that he had come to understand himself in terms of something else. In which passages does Bettelheim come closest to presenting Joey as his own interpreter? Summarize Joey's interpretation of himself—the structure or set of principles by which he understands himself.

3. In order to begin to be cured, Joey had to *reinterpret* his life. What were the major steps toward that reinterpretation? What changed for Joey?

4. Even to say *cured*, as we just did in question 3, involves an unexamined interpretation. What assumptions guide our use of that word? Do you find *cured* a satisfying explanation of what begins to happen to Joey?

5. The introduction to this part mentions this essay as an example of a case study, that is, a close examination of a unique person, event, or situation over time in a set of circumstances that are probably not replicable. Using this essay as your example, what else might characterize a case study? What makes a case believable?

6. Quite a few people play roles or assume characterizations that deviate from what we think we know about them. Describe a person who does that. Offer your own limited case study. Try to indicate the extent to which that person's understanding of himself or herself is based on reality and the extent to which it isn't.

7. College can lead you to reinterpret yourself. In fact, that traditionally has been a

large part of the experience of going to college. Write an explanation of yourself or of someone else you know well who is undergoing such a reinterpretation. What were the terms that prevailed earlier? What happened to call them into question? What kind of change has occurred, and what is at stake in this matter?

THE GREAT
INFLATION
Adam Smith

"Adam Smith," the name of a British economist of two centuries ago, was taken by George J. W. Goodman (b. 1930) for some of his popular writings on economics. Goodman, who was a Rhodes Scholar at Oxford after graduating from Harvard, has had a distinguished career as an economic journalist, was a cofounder of New York Magazine, *and is the author of several novels and four "Adam Smith" books on economics. The following selection is from* Paper Money, *a best-seller in 1981.*

The New York Times printed a letter from a lawyer, once a sixties activist, who wrote this: "I don't understand what's going on. I make a good salary, but the prices of houses and apartments seem outrageous. Money doesn't mean anything. Your income goes up, but taxes go up and expenses go up and the rest goes right out of your wallet. I don't think anybody's in control; it feels like things are out of control." 1

This lament is common. There is an archetypal fear at work here, just beyond the realm of consciousness. The fear is of losing what you have. For Americans of previous generations, "losing what you have" meant losing a job and not being able to get another, or losing the family farm to drought, dust, and the bankers. There is probably a group of cells somewhere in the cerebral cortex that resonates to the fear of the unknown, of the enemy tribe over the horizon, of strange men on horseback burning farms. The current form of this fear is relatively new to Americans now alive: it is that the currency is losing its value, becoming meaningless. We are told that Americans have changed their economic behavior in the past five years; they have stopped saving, and they spend even when there is no immediate necessity to spend. Europeans know the symbol of meaningless currency: it is the wheelbarrow full of money, the image of the Great Inflation in Germany in the 1920s. The Great Inflation not only helped bring Hitler to power; the memory of it has an effect even today, and it has some lessons for us. 2

Before World War I Germany was a prosperous country, with a gold-backed currency, expanding industry, and world leadership in optics, chemicals, and machinery. The German mark, the British shilling, the French franc, and the Italian lira all had about equal value, and all were exchanged four or five to the dollar. That was in 1914. In 1923, at the most fevered moment of the 3

German hyperinflation, the exchange rate between the dollar and the mark was one trillion marks to one dollar, and a wheelbarrow full of money would not even buy a newspaper. Most Germans were taken by surprise by the financial tornado.

"My father was a lawyer," says Walter Levy, an internationally known German-born oil consultant in New York, "and he had taken out an insurance policy in 1903, and every month he had made the payments faithfully. It was a twenty-year policy, and when it came due, he cashed it in and bought *a single loaf of bread*." The Berlin publisher Leopold Ullstein wrote that an American visitor tipped their cook one dollar. The family convened, and it was decided that a trust fund should be set up in a Berlin bank with the cook as beneficiary, the bank to administer and invest the dollar.

In retrospect, you can trace the steps to hyperinflation, but some of the reasons remain cloudy. Germany abandoned the gold backing of its currency in 1914. The war was expected to be short, so it was financed by government borrowing, not by savings and taxation. Fifty years later, the United States did not finance the Vietnam War by savings and taxation because its leaders thought that Vietnam was only a limited involvement and would be over quickly. In Germany prices doubled between 1914 and 1919, just as they have here in the past ten years.

The parallels are limited. Germany had lost a war. Under the Treaty of Versailles it had already made a reparations payment in gold-backed marks,[1] and it was due to lose part of the production of the Ruhr and of the province of Upper Silesia.[2] The Weimar Republic was politically fragile.[3]

But the bourgeois habits were very strong. Ordinary citizens worked at their jobs, sent their children to school and worried about their grades, maneuvered for promotions and rejoiced when they got them, and generally expected things to get better. The prices that had doubled from 1914 to 1919 were doubling again during just five months in 1922. Milk went from 7 marks per liter to 16; beer from 5.6 to 18. There were complaints about the high cost of living. Professors and civil servants complained of getting squeezed. Factory workers pressed for wage increases. An underground economy developed, aided by a desire to beat the tax collector.

On June 24, 1922, right-wing fanatics assassinated Walter Rathenau, the moderate, able foreign minister. Rathenau was a charismatic figure, and the idea that a popular, wealthy, and glamorous government minister could be shot in a law-abiding society shattered the faith of the Germans, who wanted to

4

5

6

7

8

---

[1]Treaty of Versailles: the peace treaty between the Allied powers and Germany, signed at the Palace of Versailles in 1919, formally ending World War I. [Eds.]

[2]Ruhr . . . Upper Silesia: the Ruhr is the most important industrial region of Germany. Upper Silesia was a German province, some of which became part of the newly established state of Poland. [Eds.]

[3]Weimar Republic: the German Republic formed by a constitutional assembly at Weimar in 1919; it was dissolved when Hitler came to power in 1933. [Eds.]

believe that things were going to be all right. Rathenau's state funeral was a national trauma. The nervous citizens of the Ruhr were already getting their money out of the currency and into real goods—diamonds, works of art, safe real estate. Now ordinary Germans began to get out of marks and into real goods. Pianos, wrote the British historian Adam Fergusson, were bought even by unmusical families. Sellers held back because the mark was worth less every day. As prices went up, the amounts of currency demanded were greater, and the German central bank responded to the demands. Yet the ruling authorities did not see anything wrong. A leading financial newspaper said that the amounts of money in circulation were not excessively high. Dr. Rudolf Havenstein, the president of the Reichsbank—equivalent to the Federal Reserve—told an economics professor that he needed a new suit but wasn't going to buy one until prices came down.

Why did the German government not act to halt the inflation? It was a shaky, 9 fragile government, especially after the assassination. The vengeful French sent their army into the Ruhr to enforce their demands for reparations, and the Germans were powerless to resist. More than inflation, the Germans feared unemployment. In 1919 Communists had tried to take over, and severe unemployment might give the Communists another chance. The great German industrial combines—Krupp, Thyssen, Farben, Stinnes—condoned the inflation and survived it well. A cheaper mark, they reasoned, would make German goods cheap and easy to export, and they needed the export earnings to buy raw materials abroad. Inflation kept everyone working.

So the printing presses ran, and once they began to run, they were hard to 10 stop. The price increases began to be dizzying. Menus in cafés could not be revised quickly enough. A student at Freiburg University ordered a cup of coffee at a café. The price on the menu was 5,000 marks. He had two cups. When the bill came, it was for 14,000 marks.

"If you want to save money," he was told, "and you want two cups of coffee, 11 you should order them both at the same time."

The presses of the Reichsbank could not keep up, though they ran through 12 the night. Individual cities and states began to issue their own money. Dr. Havenstein, the president of the Reichsbank, did not get his new suit. A factory worker described payday, which was every day at 11:00 A.M.: "At eleven o'clock in the morning a siren sounded and everybody gathered in the factory forecourt where a five-ton lorry was drawn up loaded brimful with paper money. The chief cashier and his assistants climbed up on top. They read out names and just threw out bundles of notes. As soon as you had caught one you made a dash for the nearest shop and bought just anything that was going." Teachers, paid at 10:00 A.M., brought their money to the playground, where relatives took the bundles and hurried off with them. Banks closed at 11:00 A.M.; the harried clerks went on strike.

Dentists and doctors stopped charging in currency, and demanded butter or 13 eggs, but the farmers were holding back their produce. "We don't want any

Jew-confetti from Berlin," a chronicler quotes a Bavarian farmer. The flight from currency that had begun with the buying of diamonds, gold, country houses, and antiques now extended to minor and almost useless items—bric-a-brac, soap, hairpins. The law-abiding country crumbled into petty thievery. Copper pipes and brass armatures weren't safe. Gasoline was siphoned from cars. People bought things they didn't need and used them to barter—a pair of shoes for a shirt, some crockery for coffee. Berlin had a "witches' Sabbath"[4] atmosphere. Prostitutes of both sexes roamed the streets. Cocaine was the fashionable drug. In the cabarets the newly rich and their foreign friends could dance and spend money. Other reports noted that not all the young people had a bad time. Their parents had taught them to work and save, and that was clearly wrong, so they could spend money, enjoy themselves, and flout the old.

The publisher Leopold Ullstein wrote: "People just didn't understand what   14
was happening. All the economic theory they had been taught didn't provide for the phenomenon. There was a feeling of utter dependence on anonymous powers—almost as a primitive people believed in magic—that somebody must be in the know, and that this small group of 'somebodies' must be a conspiracy."

When the one-thousand-billion-mark note came out, few bothered to collect   15
the change when they spent it. By November 1923, with one dollar equal to one trillion marks, the breakdown was complete. The currency had lost meaning.

What happened immediately afterward is as fascinating as the Great Inflation   16
itself. The tornado of the mark inflation was succeeded by the "miracle of the Rentenmark." A new president took over the Reichsbank, Horace Greeley Hjalmar Schacht, who came by his first two names because of his father's admiration for an editor of the *New York Tribune*. The Rentenmark was not Schacht's idea, but he executed it, and, as the Reichsbank president, he got the credit for it. For decades afterward he was able to maintain a reputation for financial wizardry. He became the architect of the financial prosperity brought by the Nazi party.

Obviously, though the currency was worthless, Germany was still a rich   17
country—with mines, farms, factories, forests. The backing for the Rentenmark was mortgages on the land and bonds on the factories, but that backing was a fiction; the factories and land couldn't be turned into cash or used abroad. Nine zeros were struck from the currency; that is, one Rentenmark was equal to one billion old marks. The Germans wanted desperately to believe in the Rentenmark, and so they did. "I remember," said one Frau Barten of East Prussia, "the feeling of having just one Rentenmark to spend. I bought a small tin bread bin. Just to buy something that had a price tag for *one* mark was so exciting."

All money is a matter of belief. *Credit* derives from Latin, *credere*, "to be-   18
lieve." Belief was there, the factories functioned, the farmers delivered their

---

Adam Smith

produce. The central bank kept the belief alive when it would not let even the government borrow further.

But although the country functioned again, the savings were never restored, 19 nor were the values of hard work and decency that had accompanied the savings. There was a different temper in the country, a temper that Hitler would later exploit with diabolical talent. Thomas Mann wrote:[5] "The market woman who without batting an eyelash demanded a hundred million for an egg lost the capacity for surprise. And nothing that has happened since has been insane or cruel enough to surprise her."

With the currency went many of the lifetime plans of average citizens. It 20 was the custom for the bride to bring some money to a marriage; many marriages were called off. Widows dependent on insurance found themselves destitute. People who had worked a lifetime found that their pensions would not buy one cup of coffee.

Pearl Buck, the American writer who became famous for her novels of China, 21 was in Germany in 1923. She wrote later: "The cities were still there, the houses not yet bombed and in ruins, but the victims were millions of people. They had lost their fortunes, their savings; they were dazed and inflation-shocked and did not understand how it had happened to them and who the foe was who had defeated them. Yet they had lost their self-assurance, their feeling that they themselves could be the masters of their own lives if only they worked hard enough; and lost, too, were the old values of morals, of ethics, of decency."

The fledgling Nazi party, whose attempted coup had failed in 1923, won 32 22 seats legally in the next election. The right-wing Nationalist party won 106 seats, having promised 100-percent compensation to the victims of inflation and vengeance on the conspirators who had brought it. A British economist who had been in his country's delegation at the peace treaty had written a polemic called *The Economic Consequences of the Peace*. Fired from the Treasury, John Maynard Keynes wrote brilliant, quick-tempered articles to London papers, recalling his foresight.

Since our own time of economic nightmare was not when a currency lost 23 its meaning but when men lost jobs—the Depression—we have not had the German fear of losing what you have because of explosion of the currency. We are far more likely to have a soggy British-style inflation than a frenzied German-style hyperinflation featuring wheelbarrows full of money. But the lessons of the Great Inflation go beyond the simple formula of the monetarists—that if the money supply is limited, all will be well. The lessons have to do with belief and instinct. When Americans create a mania for housing—not building houses, but bidding up housing at the rate of $100 billion a year, as they have done in the past five years—they are losing belief in their currency as a store of value.

---

[5]Thomas Mann (1875–1955): German novelist and essayist; awarded the 1929 Nobel Prize for literature. [Eds.]

Why does everyone talk so obsessively about houses? What can be so inter-   24
esting about bricks and mortar and plumbing and wiring? It isn't the houses
themselves, the architecture, the layout, the traffic patterns, the kitchens, how
we shape the houses and how they shape us, that is the obsessive topic. It's the
prices. The reason there is so much talk about condos and co-ops and houses
is that there is a new twist to the old adage "A house is not a home." When is
a house not just a home? When it is a way to flee the currency.

QUESTIONS

1. Smith both reports and explains in this essay. Point out examples of each type of
writing. In general, when does he report, and when does he explain?

2. Smith begins and ends with comments on America's economic situation. Why
does he do this? What has the German situation from 1914 to 1930 got to do with the
United States in 1981 or now?

3. What, in fact, is Smith explaining here? What has German economics got to do
with German politics, in his view? Look particularly at paragraph 19.

4. To what extent is Smith suggesting something comparable between the German
and the American situations? Consider especially what he says about real estate in his
concluding paragraphs. What is his thesis in this essay?

5. In paragraph 18, Smith offers us a definition based on the derivation of a word.
What has this got to do with his explanation of the German and American stiuations?

6. Smith's book was published in 1981. Write a short paper in which you relate his
explanations to some recent development in the American economy. For example, you
might explain something about the relation of inflation to employment, in our recent
history, by reference to Smith's views.

7. Recent reports on the United States economy have stressed the role of the Federal
Reserve in controlling something called M1. What is M1, and how does the Federal
Reserve's role toward it affect inflationary tendencies in our economy? How secure is the
United States from the kind of runaway economy Smith describes in Germany after
World War I?

SOME PEOPLE
ALWAYS MAKE IT:
THE OPTIONAIRES
Celeste MacLeod

Celeste MacLeod (b. 1931) is an active social worker and a free-lance journalist who has written for magazines ranging from the Nation *to* California Living. *Her book* Horatio Alger, Farewell: The End of the American Dream *(1980) is a study of the economic situation of American young people, based on observation, interviews, and research. Its methodology puts it on the border between journalism and sociology—a very busy piece of territory in contemporary intellectual life. The selection reprinted here is taken from chapter 11 of that book.*

"Optionaires" is a new word to describe people who grew up in the affluent   1
society. The word derives from "options," because the upbringing and education that people in the affluent society receive gives them a wider range of career choices and life-styles than those who grew up in the nonaffluent society are likely to have.

A third of all Americans—more than seventy million people—are option-   2
aires, a higher percentage of affluent citizens than any other large nation has produced. Indeed, so numerous are they in America, and so firmly in charge of running the nation and virtually everything else, that the impact of their presence blocks out our awareness of people who have not become affluent.

There is some recognition among optionaires that the country has minority   3
groups of nonwhite citizens who are excluded from the affluent society because of racial prejudice; a handful of people from these groups is admitted into affluence and their membership is touted as evidence of America's inherent equality of opportunity. But the vast majority of people in the nonaffluent society—more than 140 million Americans—are generally ignored. (An exception is just before election time, when optionaires running for office remember the existence, and voting rights, of the nonaffluent until all the ballots are in.)

When optionaires think of "today's youth" or the problems of today's youth,   4
they think of their children or their relatives' and neighbors' children; if they are young, they think of themselves or their friends. The sons and daughters of two-thirds of the population are overlooked. A newspaper article about applicants for a job in San Francisco illustrates the point.

Some People Always Make It: The Optionaires

In 1976 a new restaurant in San Francisco needed more help. It ran the following ad in the newspaper: "Host or hostess. Full-time position available. Monday through Friday, daytime. Experience helpful but not necessary."[1] The job paid $90 a week, the minimum wage at that time.

The restaurant managers were amazed when upward of 400 people applied for the job—and they were even more stunned to find that more than half the applicants had college degrees.

These applicants with degrees were optionaires who a decade earlier would have had a range of jobs to choose from after graduation. Now, after frustrating attempts to secure "professional" positions in San Francisco, they were ready to take whatever they could get, at least temporarily, to keep themselves going until something better turned up. A hosting job in an elegant restaurant would be more prestigious and interesting than waiting on tables or delivering the mail (although it would pay less), and the contacts with rich customers might lead to a better position in time.

Both the restaurant management and the newspaper reporting the incident empathized with the predicament of these college-educated young people who could not find suitable jobs. "It's sad, terrible," said the restaurant's assistant manager. "And what a waste of brains. Over half of them have college degrees. They're desperate enough to take anything." The article's subhead read: "The Anguish of College Grads Who Are Forced to Grab Any Work."

There was no mention of the anguish of college dropouts who cannot find work. Nor the anguish of high-school graduates who are being pushed out of the unskilled jobs they traditionally have held, by educated optionaires. In fact, there was no mention at all of the more than 200 people without college degrees who had also applied for the job.

The restaurant picked "Catherine," aged 23, as the daytime hostess and "Elliot," a man of 29, for the evening shift. Catherine was a Phi Beta Kappa from Boston, with degrees in sociology and psychology, who had already been accepted by a California law school and wanted a job until the term started in the fall. Her father owned a Cadillac dealership, and her mother sat on a hospital board of directors. Elliot was a lawyer from Philadelphia who had quit his job and headed for California after his marriage broke up. For several months he had hunted unsuccessfully for a position in a San Francisco law office. He'd finally taken a job as waiter, but was laid off a month later.

Catherine had spent a "heartbreaking year" in San Francisco looking for a job until law school started. When she and the girl friend with whom she shared a flat on lower Nob Hill ran short of cash, "We'd be so poor we'd play little tricks, like if one of us was going out for a lunch interview, the other would pretend to walk casually by the table so we could both get our lunches free."

---

[1] Ivan Sharpe, "Amazing Stampede for a Lowly $90 Job," *San Francisco Chronicle*, January 25, 1976, p. 19.

Clearly Catherine knew how to work the system. She did not need to visit   12
the Haight-Ashbury Switchboard in search of one-day cleaning jobs or eat at
the Food Project. Employed or not, Catherine belonged to the world of optionaires, and she would stay there.

Elliot said, "If I were getting out of high school now, I wouldn't bother going   13
to college. You might as well plan on becoming a bartender, waitress, or whatever."

Elliot's advice was well meant, but it overlooked the facts. He, with his law   14
degree and optionaire polish, was chosen over a few hundred applicants with
lesser qualifications. The entrance of optionaires like Elliot into the job market
for waiters and hosts increases the probability that those who don't go beyond
high school may have difficulty finding any job at all.

CONTACTS AND CONFIDENCE:
THE UNBEATABLE DUO

Education counts when you go job hunting, and so does individual initiative;   15
but these may not be the crucial factors that determine whether you are hired.
Whom you know, or whom your parents know, and what you think of yourself
may supersede education and initiative. If you have contacts (also known as
"connections") with the people who give out the jobs, and if you have a high
opinion of yourself and your abilities—regardless of the factual basis for such
belief—you are more likely to succeed than people without such assets; in some
cases you may win out over people who are better qualified by education and
ability to hold a particular job than you are.

People from the nonaffluent society may enjoy contacts on a small scale.   16
The young man who gains admittance to a union because his father is a member
has contacts; so does the teen-ager who gets a job as a garage mechanic because
his uncle knows the manager, and the young woman who gets a job at the
beauty shop near her home because her mother's best friend owns the shop.
Such contacts are generally local and they rarely extend to the professional
sphere or to jobs that pay on a scale that allows one to enter the affluent society.
The young man or woman from the nonaffluent society who aspires to go up
the socioeconomic ladder will need a superabundance of self-confidence and
drive to compensate for a lack of contacts.

Although some people in the nonaffluent society have self-confidence, this   17
quality is far more common among optionaires; the higher up one goes on the
social scale, the greater the chances for self-confidence.

Professor G. William Domhoff, a sociologist at the University of California   18
in Santa Cruz who specializes in studying the upper class, has isolated confidence as the chief characteristic of upper-class people. Confidence begins in
early childhood, says Domhoff, when rich youngsters are singled out for special

attention, and it continues as they attend a series of exclusive schools. Living in a special world where they and their parents are constantly deferred to because of their wealth, they grow up believing they are special people. They expect doors to open for them everywhere, and doors usually do open for them, which reinforces their high opinion of themselves. As Arlene Daniels, another sociologist who studies the upper class, puts it: "They have this confidence even if they are boobies."[2]

Only a few percent of Americans are members of the upper class, so their world would not interest us here if it did not illustrate in pristine form how privilege and contacts operate. (These families also wield significant power in business, foreign affairs, and domestic policies, including programs for the unemployed and the poor. In *Who Rules America?* and *The Higher Circles*, Domhoff argues that the upper class is also the ruling class.)   19

The upper-class network of contacts is national—even international—in scope, formed through attendance and membership in exclusive schools, clubs, and summer resorts, through intermarriages, and through business, professional, and social connections of the very rich. If Elizabeth, an upper-class daughter in New York City, wants to work in San Francisco, she will not have to apply for a job as a restaurant hostess or visit the state employment office. Before she leaves home, her father can arrange a suitable job for her in San Francisco while her mother arranges for her to stay with friends on arrival who will sponsor her entrance into upper-class social circles on the West Coast.   20

The line separating the "upper class" from the "upper middle class"—like all class distinctions in America—is difficult to draw. Here (using 1979 prices) we will define "upper middle class" families as those with incomes of roughly $70,000–$300,000 a year, as well as plenty of college degrees and social connections.   21

The book *Passages*, by Gail Sheehy, provides case histories of upper-middle-class youths and their sphere of privilege. There is "Donald Babcock,"[3] whose father graduated from Hotchkiss and Yale before entering business. The son, Donald, after finishing Hotchkiss and a year at Yale, decided to leave home and strike out on his own in California, but on the way he was seriously injured in an automobile accident.   22

"The accident was a setback for me in a lot of ways," he told Sheehy. "I couldn't take the job that was waiting for me in California."   23

How did a young man with one year of college and no work experience have a job waiting for him on the other side of the country? Presumably he had contacts, through the father whose life-style he was fleeing.   24

After the accident Donald found himself at home in a back brace, but his disability did not stop him from finding a job. "My father came through with   25

---

[2]*San Francisco Chronicle*, January 8, 1976, p. 17.
[3]Gail Sheehy, *Passages: Predictable Crises of Adult Life* (New York: Bantam, 1977), p. 58.

a job for me as a security guard on a museum estate. As a Republican committeeman, he has a lot of jobs to give out."[4] On the estate, Donald fell in love; he married, returned to Yale, and followed his father into business.

In *Passages*, whose subtitle is "Predictable Crises of Adult Life," Donald was 26 presented as "an example of how the Merger Self can overwhelm before the Seeker Self has a chance to kick up its heels." But in the context of this book, Donald is an example of someone so firmly ensconced in the world of optionaire privilege that he would come out on top no matter which Self emerged.

Moving down the social scale we come to the group that includes most 27 optionaires, the people at the base of the affluent society, who traditionally were called the middle class. They come from families with incomes of $20,000–$70,000, with the bottom end open for those in the gray areas. Contacts are less pervasive here than at the higher levels, but they still operate to a marked degree. When optionaires from this group seek admission to college, professional jobs, and entrance into other areas of privilege, contacts may be their most important resource. But confidence ranks as a close second. Those without contacts may still be able to make it if they have a high enough opinion of themselves and are sufficiently adept at working the system. A traditional optionaire upbringing builds its members in both these areas.

If optionaire children do not go to private schools, they are likely to attend 28 up-to-date public schools in pleasant suburbs or well-preserved sections of the city. Their formal schooling is supplemented with music lessons, books from the library, help with homework, trips to zoos and museums, summer camps, and travel. Verbal and written fluency develop as naturally as learning to walk. Each child has a separate bedroom or shares one with a sibling of the same sex. The parents (whether a couple or alone) may have their problems, but chronic financial worries are not paramount in their lives. In this milieu, discipline is achieved more often through talks than beatings.

Confidence begins to grow at an early age. To see how this happens, let's 29 look at Michael, a hypothetical young man from an optionaire background.

When Michael comes home from nursery school at age 3 with a few blotches 30 of color on a sheet of newsprint and his mother exclaims, "What a beautiful picture you painted, Michael!" as she tapes it on the wall for father (an accountant) to admire later, Michael's self-esteem zooms upward. It continues going up as Michael does well in school, becomes a pitcher in Little League, and is elected president of his senior class in high school, while his parents and relatives form a chorus of admiration in the background.

Michael comes to adulthood with an unshakable sense of self-worth. He 31 expects to make it. He feels he deserves to make it. A college education and a career of his choice are options that he takes for granted.

[4]Ibid.

Michael decides to be a lawyer and goes to law school. Graduating in the 32 mid-1970s, he encounters job problems he never expected, because numerous other well-educated, confident young men and women from optionaire backgrounds have also become lawyers and are looking for jobs with good futures in prestigious law firms. This may be a setback for Michael, but it will not stop him. Michael is one of those people who will always make it.

If 300 people apply for the same job and 220 have the necessary qualifica- 33 tions, of whom 60 also have the personality and charisma the employer is seeking, Michael will be among the 10 finalists. He may even be the one selected. If not, he will probably make it the next time. Or the next. Michael will not give up. Nor does he need to. He is sure to make it.

If Michael runs out of money while job-hunting, his family will come through 34 with funds to keep him going. If for some reason he doesn't get family help (he isn't speaking to his parents that year or his father just quit his job and ran off to California to become a guru), Michael has other options: Friends or relatives will let him occupy the spare bedroom for several months and eat at their table; he will move into the apartment of a young woman who has a job, and become her "old man" until he finds the right job; or he will become part of a commune for a while and live off other members' salaries.

If necessary, Michael may take a nonprofessional job temporarily (he gen- 35 erally comes out on top in such competitions). If he doesn't want to tie up his job-hunting hours with work, Michael knows enough about working the system to get himself onto some form of welfare. He will never have to sleep in the street or skip dinner while he looks for a job.

Michael may spend a year looking for the right job, but he will eventually 36 find it. And then he will make lots of money. Twenty years later, after he has been a partner in the firm and is appointed a federal judge, Michael may view all unemployed people as wastrels and those on welfare as cheats. He will speak from the heart—and from direct personal experience—when he says with feeling, "Anyone can make it in this country if he tries hard enough."

Obviously not every optionaire has Michael's confidence. He is of interest 37 here for two reasons. First, the example of his success serves those who want to disprove the theories of Domhoff and others who claim that the United States is ruled by an upper-class elite; which brings us to the second reason: Michael is the kind of person who succeeds in politics. He has charisma and drive, and he is not shy about pushing himself ahead. It is the Michaels of this country, along with the children of the upper-class elite, who make the laws and regulations that govern employment, welfare, health insurance, and other social services for the masses.

If confidence like Michael's could be ordered through the Sears catalog, then 38 equality of opportunity would be more widespread—and people like Michael would lose the advantage they now enjoy.

317

OPTIONAIRES WITH PROBLEMS

What about optionaires at the opposite end of the confidence spectrum—the [39] people who grew up in the affluent society but are unsure of themselves, or those who have severe emotional problems that may hinder their education and careers? Mental illness may occur at any level of society: it does not respect class distinctions. But parents in the affluent society can better afford professional help—doctors, psychiatrists, special schools—for children with serious problems, and in their milieu it is socially more acceptable to seek such help than in many sectors of the nonaffluent society. This help is not always effective, but often it is. The disturbed adolescent whose parents spend $200,000 in hospital and psychiatric fees may emerge from a few years of treatment as a functioning adult, able to hold a job and marry, while his or her counterpart in the nonaffluent society who receives no help is more likely to end up permanently incarcerated in an institution.

As for shy, insecure optionaires, they may be buttressed by contacts and [40] money, or they may be guided into careers that suit their temperaments. Without such help, the shy optionaire may not make it, for the meek have a low priority in a country built on aggressive individualism.

Finally, the neuroses of optionaires may not impede their ability to make a [41] good living. Alexander Portnoy, the hero—or antihero—of Philip Roth's novel *Portnoy's Complaint*, is a case in point.[5] He is a neurotic, self-pitying man who has difficulties achieving intimacy with other people, but in school and on the job he has nothing but success. Part of the book's satire derives from the contrast between Portnoy's public success and private hell; but the former is impressive.

Portnoy graduates from a top law school and serves as commissioner of hu- [42] man opportunity for New York City. He functions effectively on the job (the job itself lacks substance, not Portnoy's performance), he makes a high enough salary to eliminate financial worries and allow him to travel abroad in style, and he enjoys respect and status because of his high position. Although Portnoy rails incessantly against his mother, blaming her for all the obnoxious personality traits he displays as an adult, his optionaire upbringing has given him enough skills and self-confidence to make it handsomely in the Establishment. Many a workingman might be glad to take on Portnoy's troubles if he could also have his salary and his status.

VARIATIONS ON THE OPTIONAIRES THEME

People who grow up as optionaires and then drop out of the Establishment— [43] to go back to the land and live a natural life, to pursue their art even if it means

---

[5]Philip Roth, *Portnoy's Complaint* (New York: Random House, 1969).

living below the poverty level while they try to sell their handcrafted jewelry on the street—are often thought of as being wholly outside the optionaire framework. In fact, they are variations on the optimistic theme. Such people may see themselves as outsiders, but they drop out with all the advantages of their optionaire upbringing intact.

When optionaires pursue an occupation outside the mainstream, they bring 44 to it all the skills and confidence they learned at home. Although they may not use their Establishment contacts in their new pursuits, they will quickly build up contacts within the counterculture framework. As surely as their fathers back home knew who ran city hall, they will learn who are "the right people" to know in their special world and who are the dregs to avoid. The business acumen they imbibed from their successful parents will stand them in good stead when they refuse to join the system. Yesterday's bohemians fit this pattern. Today's street craftsmen are a current example.

In any area where the counterculture flourishes, you will find young people 45 selling their crafts on the streets. It could be the Embarcadero Plaza in San Francisco, the Spanish Steps in Rome, the East Village in New York, or Telegraph Avenue in Berkeley. They sell leather goods, jewelry, woven belts, candles, knitted caps, wooden bowls, stained-glass objects, photographs, and paintings, to name but a sampling. Whatever is the rage among buyers that season you will find in abundance, be it tie-dyed T-shirts or terrariums. For the purpose of street selling is to make money.

It would seem natural to call these craftspeople "street people," since they 46 sell their wares on the streets. But they bear scant resemblance to the down-and-out young people described earlier in this book. The street craftspeople are not street people, nor are they new migrants; they are either optionaires or borderliners. Most new migrants would not have enough capital to buy the equipment and materials needed to set up shop; even if they did find the money by a fluke, they would be hard put to keep up with the knowledgeable competition they would face from other street vendors.

In the early 1970s, when the recession had not yet touched their lives, young 47 street vendors often spoke of their work in terms reminiscent of hippie philosophy. "Shelley," who sold her handmade silver pendants on Telegraph Avenue, sounded that way. She was a graduate of Northwestern University who had previously worked as a schoolteacher and then as a secretary. "I was making five hundred and fifty dollars a month in my last job. I could get that tomorrow if I wanted to do that kind of work again," she said when we interviewed her in 1973.

Shelley's face went blank when she was asked about new migrants in Berke- 48 ley. "I've never met anyone like that," she said. "Lots of the people who sell on the street here have Ph.D.s. They could easily get other jobs, but they prefer the freedom of this life to the hassle of a large university or big business."

While Shelley talked, people kept walking by her street stall. Some of them 49 were new migrants, but they could have been 3000 miles away as far as Shelley was concerned. They simply did not penetrate her awareness. She did not meet such people at the parties she attended after work; she never talked to such people: Therefore, they did not exist.

Three years later, street craftspeople in Berkeley were more aware of the poverty that surrounded them, and of their own tenuous positions. Some of their friends with master's and doctoral degrees were delivering mail or working for the new subway system, not by choice but because they could not find jobs in the academic world. The street craftspeople of 1976 knew that making it in the Establishment was not easy—at least not in California.

"Richard," a leather craftsman from a nearby suburb, felt that his business was "too good to last"; but while it did, he was making a comfortable living and enjoying his trade. "I'm lucky I got here while the licenses were still for sale," Richard told us. "It gives me a hell of an opportunity. You learn so much when you start from roots like this. How to manage money. How to budget yourself. You learn about different personalities and how to use tact; you have to, or else you miss a lot of sales."

The romantic concept of street vendors as rebels against modern technology and the Establishment does not hold up in Berkeley. Many craftspeople take credit cards these days. A conflict over which vendors should get the most desirable locations along Telegraph Avenue was resolved by means of a computer. Now every morning a city employee arrives with a computer print-out of the day's spaces; if licensed craftsmen do not claim their spaces by 10:00 A.M., the choice empty spots are reassigned by a lottery. This procedure has operated in Berkeley for several years. Modern technology and city hall have helped the street vendors survive in Berkeley, and most of them are all for it. If street vendors complain about city hall, it is because officials do not enforce the regulations strictly enough.

The major conflict among street vendors is over handcrafted items versus manufactured goods. The city issues inexpensive licenses to street vendors, with the stipulation that they sell only items which they have handcrafted themselves. But a few entrepreneurs have imported manufactured "craft" items from Mexico or Europe in bulk and sold them on the streets as "handmade" at considerable profit.

This practice angered the merchants with stores along Telegraph. As one businessman explained: "We're glad to give young people a chance to sell their own handcrafted work on the streets; but some of these people are setting up three and four stalls with cheap junk from Mexico and paying street kids less than the minimum wage to sell for them. I pay my employees a decent wage and lots of other benefits as well. It isn't fair to let some unscrupulous entrepreneurs come in and make a killing. They don't even have to pay rent or property tax."[6]

---

[6]Ove M. Wittstock, owner, Layton's Store, Berkeley.

Some People Always Make It: The Optionaires

Two sides developed in the conflict, but the sides were not street craftspeople   55
versus the business establishment. Instead, street sellers who wanted to keep
manufactured goods off the Avenue formed a coalition with some store owners;
together they went to the city council and demanded that the city enforce the
regulation forbidding the sale of manufactured items at street stalls.

The craftspeople who teamed up with the store owners could relate to one   56
another because they spoke the same language; the businessmen were similar
to the fathers and uncles the craftspeople had grown up with. It would be hard
to imagine street people or new migrants forming an alliance with store owners—
or expecting help from city hall. But you will not find new migrants selling
crafts on Telegraph Avenue, unless they work for some entrepreneur for a pit-
tance. The craftspeople are a contemporary variation of the optionaire theme.

In every circumstance, it pays to be an optionaire.   57

QUESTIONS

1. Consider the power of the name *optionaires* itself. To what entent is that name a
definition? How thoroughly does MacLeod define the term as she uses it? What does
that definition contribute to her explanation of optionaires?

2. How does MacLeod refer to people without the options of the optionaires? To
what extent is their disadvantage expressed in their having no such comparable name?

3. This account relies heavily upon MacLeod's ability to offer representative types of
the people she discusses. Sometimes types run toward being stereotypes. What do you
take to be the difference between a type and a stereotype? Are MacLeod's examples more
of one kind or of the other?

4. Consider the portrait of Michael in paragraphs 29 through 38. Is that a realistic
portrait? Why is it given so much weight in this presentation? What role does this portrait
play in MacLeod's explanation as a whole?

5. "In every circumstance," MacLeod concludes, "it pays to be an optionaire" (paragraph 57). Do you agree with that conclusion? Back up your explanation with specific
examples.

6. Not only does MacLeod identify optionaires as an influential segment of American
society, she does so against a more or less conventional breakdown of American society
according to class. How does she represent the class structure of American society? How,
insofar as you can determine, do optionaires fit into that picture?

7. Write about two hypothetical young people of your own, similar to the portrait of
Michael. Write of one who seems to you a more convincing example of an optionaire
than Michael. Also write of someone left out, someone more like one of the people
without college degrees who had also applied for that restaurant job, who were never
seriously considered, and who were left out of the newspaper's account of that incident
(paragraphs 5 through 9).

8. MacLeod refers to *Passages*, by Gail Sheehy. Find a copy of that book, and write
a short review of it. How is Sheehy's subject related to MacLeod's? How do their methods
compare?

ON THE FEAR
OF DEATH
Elizabeth Kübler-Ross

Elizabeth Kübler-Ross (b. 1926), a Swiss-American psychi-
atrist, is one of the leaders of the movement that may help
change the way Americans think about death. Born in Zu-
rich, Switzerland, she received her M.D. from the University
of Zurich in 1957 and came to the United States as an
intern the following year. Kübler-Ross began her work with
terminally ill patients while teaching psychiatry at the Uni-
versity of Chicago Medical School. She now heads "Shanti
Nilaya" (Sanskrit for "home of peace"), an organization she
founded north of Escondido, California, in 1976, "dedicated
to the promotion of physical, emotional, and spiritual health."
"On the Fear of Death" is taken from her first and most
famous book, On Death and Dying *(1969).*

> *Let me not pray to be sheltered from*
> *dangers but to be fearless in facing*
> *them.*
> *Let me not beg for the stilling of*
> *my pain but for the heart to conquer it.*
> *Let me not look for allies in life's*
> *battlefield but to my own strength.*
> *Let me not crave in anxious fear to*
> *be saved but hope for the patience to*
> *win my freedom.*
> *Grant me that I may not be a*
> *coward, feeling your mercy in my*
> *success alone; but let me find the grasp*
> *of your hand in my failure.*

> Rabindranath Tagore, *Fruit-Gathering*

Epidemics have taken a great toll of lives in past generations. Death in infancy   1
and early childhood was frequent and there were few families who didn't lose
a member of the family at an early age. Medicine has changed greatly in the
last decades. Widespread vaccinations have practically eradicated many illnesses,
at least in western Europe and the United States. The use of chemotherapy,
especially the antibiotics, has contributed to an ever-decreasing number of fa-

talities in infectious diseases. Better child care and education has effected a low morbidity and mortality among children. The many diseases that have taken an impressive toll among the young and middle-aged have been conquered. The number of old people is on the rise, and with this fact come the number of people with malignancies and chronic diseases associated more with old age.

Pediatricians have less work with acute and life-threatening situations as they have an ever-increasing number of patients with psychosomatic disturbances and adjustment and behavior problems. Physicians have more people in their waiting rooms with emotional problems than they have ever had before, but they also have more elderly patients who not only try to live with their decreased physical abilities and limitations but who also face loneliness and isolation with all its pains and anguish. The majority of these people are not seen by a psychiatrist. Their needs have to be elicited and gratified by other professional people, for instance, chaplains and social workers. It is for them that I am trying to outline the changes that have taken place in the last few decades, changes that are ultimately responsible for the increased fear of death, the rising number of emotional problems, and the greater need for understanding of and coping with the problems of death and dying.

When we look back in time and study old cultures and people, we are impressed that death has always been distasteful to man and will probably always be. From a psychiatrist's point of view this is very understandable and can perhaps best be explained by our basic knowledge that, in our unconscious, death is never possible in regard to ourselves. It is inconceivable for our unconscious to imagine an actual ending of our own life here on earth, and if this life of ours has to end, the ending is always attributed to a malicious intervention from the outside by someone else. In simple terms, in our unconscious mind we can only be killed; it is inconceivable to die of a natural cause or of old age. Therefore death in itself is associated with a bad act, a frightening happening, something that in itself calls for retribution and punishment.

One is wise to remember these fundamental facts as they are essential in understanding some of the most important, otherwise unintelligible communications of our patients.

The second fact that we have to comprehend is that in our unconscious mind we cannot distinguish between a wish and a deed. We are all aware of some of our illogical dreams in which two completely opposite statements can exist side by side—very acceptable in our dreams but unthinkable and illogical in our wakening state. Just as our unconscious mind cannot differentiate between the wish to kill somebody in anger and the act of having done so, the young child is unable to make this distinction. The child who angrily wishes his mother to drop dead for not having gratified his needs will be traumatized greatly by the actual death of his mother—even if this event is not linked closely in time with his destructive wishes. He will always take part or the whole blame for the loss of his mother. He will always say to himself—rarely to others—"I did it, I am

323

responsible, I was bad, therefore Mommy left me." It is well to remember that the child will react in the same manner if he loses a parent by divorce, separation, or desertion. Death is often seen by a child as an impermanent thing and has therefore little distinction from a divorce in which he may have an opportunity to see a parent again.

Many a parent will remember remarks of their children such as, "I will bury my doggy now and next spring when the flowers come up again, he will get up." Maybe it was the same wish that motivated the ancient Egyptians to supply their dead with food and goods to keep them happy and the old American Indians to bury their relatives with their belongings. 6

When we grow older and begin to realize that our omnipotence is really not so omnipotent, that our strongest wishes are not powerful enough to make the impossible possible, the fear that we have contributed to the death of a loved one diminishes—and with it the guilt. The fear remains diminished, however, only so long as it is not challenged too strongly. Its vestiges can be seen daily in hospital corridors and in people associated with the bereaved. 7

A husband and wife may have been fighting for years, but when the partner dies, the survivor will pull his hair, whine and cry louder and beat his chest in regret, fear and anguish, and will hence fear his own death more than before, still believing in the law of talion—an eye for an eye, a tooth for a tooth—"I am responsible for her death, I will have to die a pitiful death in retribution." 8

Maybe this knowledge will help us understand many of the old customs and rituals which have lasted over the centuries and whose purpose is to diminish the anger of the gods or the people as the case may be, thus decreasing the anticipated punishment. I am thinking of the ashes, the torn clothes, the veil, the *Klage Weiber* of the old days[1]—they are all means to ask you to take pity on them, the mourners, and are expressions of sorrow, grief, and shame. If someone grieves, beats his chest, tears his hair, or refuses to eat, it is an attempt at self-punishment to avoid or reduce the anticipated punishment for the blame that he takes on the death of a loved one. 9

This grief, shame, and guilt are not very far removed from feelings of anger and rage. The process of grief always includes some qualities of anger. Since none of us likes to admit anger at a deceased person, these emotions are often disguised or repressed and prolong the period of grief or show up in other ways. It is well to remember that it is not up to us to judge such feelings as bad or shameful but to understand their true meaning and origin as something very human. In order to illustrate this I will again use the example of the child—and the child in us. The five-year-old who loses his mother is both blaming himself for her disappearance and being angry at her for having deserted him and for no longer gratifying his needs. The dead person then turns into something the child loves and wants very much but also hates with equal intensity for this severe deprivation. 10

---

[1] *Klage Weiber*: wailing wives. [*Eds.*]

On the Fear of Death

The ancient Hebrews regarded the body of a dead person as something un- 11
clean and not to be touched. The early American Indians talked about the evil
spirits and shot arrows in the air to drive the spirits away. Many other cultures
have rituals to take care of the "bad" dead person, and they all originate in this
feeling of anger which still exists in all of us, though we dislike admitting it.
The tradition of the tombstone may originate in the wish to keep the bad spirits
deep down in the ground, and the pebbles that many mourners put on the grave
are leftover symbols of the same wish. Though we call the firing of guns at
military funerals a last salute, it is the same symbolic ritual as the Indian used
when he shot his spears and arrows into the skies.

I give these examples to emphasize that man has not basically changed. Death 12
is still a fearful, frightening happening, and the fear of death is a universal fear
even if we think we have mastered it on many levels.

What has changed is our way of coping and dealing with death and dying 13
and our dying patients.

Having been raised in a country in Europe where science is not so advanced, 14
where modern techniques have just started to find their way into medicine, and
where people still live as they did in this country half a century ago, I may have
had an opportunity to study a part of the evolution of mankind in a shorter
period.

I remember as a child the death of a farmer. He fell from a tree and was not 15
expected to live. He asked simply to die at home, a wish that was granted without
question. He called his daughters into the bedroom and spoke with each one
of them alone for a few moments. He arranged his affairs quietly, though he
was in great pain, and distributed his belongings and his land, none of which
was to be split until his wife should follow him in death. He also asked each of
his children to share in the work, duties, and tasks that he had carried on until
the time of the accident. He asked his friends to visit him once more, to bid
goodbye to them. Although I was a small child at the time, he did not exclude
me or my siblings. We were allowed to share in the preparations of the family
just as we were permitted to grieve with them until he died. When he did die,
he was left at home, in his own beloved home which he had built, and among
his friends and neighbors who went to take a last look at him where he lay in
the midst of flowers in the place he had lived in and loved so much. In that
country today there is still no make-believe slumber room, no embalming, no
false makeup to pretend sleep. Only the signs of very disfiguring illnesses are
covered up with bandages and only infectious cases are removed from the home
prior to the burial.

Why do I describe such "old-fashioned" customs? I think they are an indi- 16
cation of our acceptance of a fatal outcome, and they help the dying patient as
well as his family to accept the loss of a loved one. If a patient is allowed to
terminate his life in the familiar and beloved environment, it requires less
adjustment for him. His own family knows him well enough to replace a sedative
with a glass of his favorite wine; or the smell of a home-cooked soup may give

him the appetite to sip a few spoons of fluid which, I think, is still more enjoyable than an infusion. I will not minimize the need for sedatives and infusions and realize full well from my own experience as a country doctor that they are sometimes life-saving and often unavoidable. But I also know that patience and familiar people and foods could replace many a bottle of intravenous fluids given for the simple reason that it fulfills the physiological need without involving too many people and/or individual nursing care.

The fact that children are allowed to stay at home where a fatality has struck and are included in the talk, discussions, and fears gives them the feeling that they are not alone in their grief and gives them the comfort of shared responsibility and shared mourning. It prepares them gradually and helps them view death as part of life, an experience which may help them grow and mature. 17

This is in great contrast to a society in which death is viewed as taboo, discussion of it is regarded as morbid, and children are excluded with the presumption and pretext that it would be "too much" for them. They are then sent off to relatives, often accompanied by some unconvincing lies of "Mother has gone on a long trip" or other unbelievable stories. The child senses that something is wrong, and his distrust in adults will only multiply if other relatives add new variations of the story, avoid his questions or suspicions, shower him with gifts as a meager substitute for a loss he is not permitted to deal with. Sooner or later the child will become aware of the changed family situation and, depending on the age and personality of the child, will have an unresolved grief and regard this incident as a frightening, mysterious, in any case very traumatic experience with untrustworthy grownups, which he has no way to cope with. 18

It is equally unwise to tell a little child who lost her brother that God loved little boys so much that he took little Johnny to heaven. When this little girl grew up to be a woman she never solved her anger at God, which resulted in a psychotic depression when she lost her own little son three decades later. 19

We would think that our great emancipation, our knowledge of science and of man, has given us better ways and means to prepare ourselves and our families for this inevitable happening. Instead the days are gone when a man was allowed to die in peace and dignity in his own home. 20

The more we are making advancements in science, the more we seem to fear and deny the reality of death. How is this possible? 21

We use euphemisms, we make the dead look as if they were asleep, we ship the children off to protect them from the anxiety and turmoil around the house if the patient is fortunate enough to die at home, we don't allow children to visit their dying parents in the hospitals, we have long and controversial discussions about whether patients should be told the truth—a question that rarely arises when the dying person is tended by the family physician who has known him from delivery to death and who knows the weaknesses and strengths of each member of the family. 22

I think there are many reasons for this flight away from facing death calmly. 23

One of the most important facts is that dying nowadays is more gruesome in many ways, namely, more lonely, mechanical, and dehumanized; at times it is even difficult to determine technically when the time of death has occurred.

Dying becomes lonely and impersonal because the patient is often taken out of his familiar environment and rushed to an emergency room. Whoever has been very sick and has required rest and comfort especially may recall his experience of being put on a stretcher and enduring the noise of the ambulance siren and hectic rush until the hospital gates open. Only those who have lived through this may appreciate the discomfort and cold necessity of such transportation which is only the beginning of a long ordeal—hard to endure when you are well, difficult to express in words when noise, light, pumps, and voices are all too much to put up with. It may well be that we might consider more the patient under the sheets and blankets and perhaps stop our well-meant efficiency and rush in order to hold the patient's hand, to smile, or to listen to a question. I include the trip to the hospital as the first episode in dying, as it is for many. I am putting it exaggeratedly in contrast to the sick man who is left at home—not to say that lives should not be saved if they can be saved by a hospitalization but to keep the focus on the patient's experience, his needs and his reactions.

When a patient is severely ill, he is often treated like a person with no right to an opinion. It is often someone else who makes the decision if and when and where a patient should be hospitalized. It would take so little to remember that the sick person too has feelings, has wishes and opinions, and has—most important of all—the right to be heard.

Well, our presumed patient has now reached the emergency room. He will be surrounded by busy nurses, orderlies, interns, residents, a lab technician perhaps who will take some blood, an electrocardiogram technician who takes the cardiogram. He may be moved to X-ray and he will overhear opinions of his condition and discussions and questions to members of the family. He slowly but surely is beginning to be treated like a thing. He is no longer a person. Decisions are made often without his opinion. If he tries to rebel he will be sedated and after hours of waiting and wondering whether he has the strength, he will be wheeled into the operating room or intensive treatment unit and become an object of great concern and great financial investment.

He may cry for rest, peace, and dignity, but he will get infusions, transfusions, a heart machine, or tracheotomy if necessary. He may want one single person to stop for one single minute so that he can ask one single question—but he will get a dozen people around the clock, all busily preoccupied with his heart rate, pulse, electrocardiogram or pulmonary functions, his secretions or excretions but not with him as a human being. He may wish to fight it all but it is going to be a useless fight since all this is done in the fight for his life, and if they can save his life they can consider the person afterwards. Those who consider the person first may lose precious time to save his life! At least this seems to be the rationale or justification behind all this—or is it? Is the reason for this increasingly mechanical, depersonalized approach our own defensiveness? Is this approach our own way to cope with and repress the anxieties that a terminally or critically ill patient evokes in us? Is our concentration on equipment, on blood pressure, our desperate attempt to deny the impending death which is so frightening and discomforting to us that we displace all our knowledge onto machines, since they are less close to us than the suffering face of another human being which would remind us once more of our lack of omnipotence, our own limits and failures, and last but not least perhaps our own mortality?

Maybe the question has to be raised: Are we becoming less human or more 28 human?. . .it is clear that whatever the answer may be, the patient is suffering more—not physically, perhaps, but emotionally. And his needs have not changed over the centuries, only our ability to gratify them.

QUESTIONS

1. Why does Kübler-Ross describe the death of a farmer? What point is she making in explaining "such 'old-fashioned' customs" (paragraph 16)?

2. To what extent is this essay explanatory? Summarize a particular explanation of hers that you find intriguing. Do you find it persuasive?

3. At what point in this essay does Kübler-Ross turn from explanation toward argument? Do you think she has taken a stand on her subject? How sympathetic are you to her position?

4. In paragraphs 2 and 10, Kübler-Ross indicates a specialized audience for her writing. Who is that audience, and how do you relate to it?

5. Think of the audience you described in question 4 as a primary audience and of yourself as a member of a secondary audience. To what extent do the two audiences overlap? How thoroughly can you divide one from the other?

6. What experience of death have you had so far? Write of a death that you know something about, even if your relation to it is distant, perhaps only through the media. Can you locate elements of fear and anger in your own behavior or in the behavior of other persons involved? Does Kübler-Ross's interpretation of those reactions help you come to terms with the experience?

7. What kind of balance do you think best between prolonging life and allowing a person to die with dignity? What does the phrase "dying with dignity" mean?

8. If you were told you had a limited time to live, how would that news change the way you are living? Or would it? Offer an explanation for your position.

OBEDIENCE AND DISOBEDIENCE TO AUTHORITY
Stanley Milgram

Stanley Milgram was born in New York in 1933, went to Queens College and Harvard University, and at present is a professor of social psychology at the Graduate Center of the City University of New York. The following explanation of Milgram's experiment first appeared in the professional journal Human Relations *in 1965 and made him famous, causing a storm of controversy over his method of experimentation and the results of his experiment. Milgram has said of his work, "As a social psychologist, I look at the world not to master it in any practical sense, but to understand it and to communicate that understanding to others."*

The situation in which one agent commands another to hurt a third turns   1
up time and again as a significant theme in human relations.[1] It is powerfully expressed in the story of Abraham, who is commanded by God to kill his son. It is no accident the Kierkegaard,[2] seeking to orient his thought to the central themes of human experience, chose Abraham's conflict as the springboard to his philosophy.

War too moves forward on the triad of an authority which commands a   2
person to destroy the enemy, and perhaps all organized hostility may be viewed as a theme and variation on the three elements of authority, executant, and victim.[3] We describe an experimental program, recently concluded at Yale

[1]This research was supported by two grants from the National Science Foundation: NSF G-17916 and NSF G-24152. Exploratory studies carried out in 1960 were financed by a grant from the Higgins Funds of Yale University. I am grateful to John T. Williams, James J. McDonough, and Emil Elges for the important part they played in the project. Thanks are due also to Alan Elms, James Miller, Taketo Murata, and Stephen Stier for their aid as graduate assistants. My wife, Sasha, performed many valuable services. Finally, I owe a profound debt to the many persons in New Haven and Bridgeport who served as subjects.

[2]Søren Kierkegaard (1813–1855): Danish philosopher and theologian. [Eds.]

[3]Consider, for example, J. P. Scott's analysis of war in his monograph on aggression:

. . . while the actions of key individuals in a war may be explained in terms of direct stimulation to aggression, vast numbers of other people are involved simply by being part of an organized society.

. . . For example, at the beginning of World War I an Austrian archduke was assassinated in Sarajevo. A few days later soldiers from all over Europe were marching toward each other, not because they were stimulated by the archduke's misfortune, but because they had been trained to obey orders.

(Slightly rearranged from Scott (1958), *Aggression*, p. 103.)

University, in which a particular expression of this conflict is studied by experimental means.

In its most general form the problem may be defined thus: if X tells Y to 3
hurt Z, under what conditions will Y carry out the command of X and under
what conditions will he refuse. In the more limited form possible in laboratory
research, the question becomes: If an experimenter tells a subject to hurt another
person, under what conditions will the subject go along with this instruction,
and under what conditions will he refuse to obey. The laboratory problem is
not so much a dilution of the general statement as one concrete expression of
the many particular forms this question may assume.

One aim of the research was to study behavior in a strong situation of deep 4
consequence to the participants, for the psychological forces operative in powerful and lifelike forms of the conflict may not be brought into play under
diluted conditions.

This approach meant, first, that we had a special obligation to protect the 5
welfare and dignity of the persons who took part in the study; subjects were, of
necessity, placed in a difficult predicament, and steps had to be taken to ensure
their wellbeing before they were discharged from the laboratory. Toward this
end, a careful, post-experimental treatment was devised and has been carried
through for subjects in all conditions.[4]

TERMINOLOGY

If Y follows the command of X we shall say that he has obeyed X; if he fails 6
to carry out the command of X, we shall say that he has disobeyed X. The
terms to *obey* and to *disobey*, as used here, refer to the subject's overt action
only, and carry no implication for the motive or experiential states accompanying the action.[5]

---

[4]It consisted of an extended discussion with the experimenter and, of equal importance, a friendly
reconciliation with the victim. It is made clear that the victim did *not* receive painful electric shocks.
After the completion of the experimental series, subjects were sent a detailed report of the results
and full purposes of the experimental program. A formal assessment of this procedure points to its
overall effectiveness. Of the subjects, 83.7 percent indicated that they were glad to have taken part
in the study; 15.1 percent reported neutral feelings; and 1.3 percent stated that they were sorry to
have participated. A large number of subjects spontaneously requested that they be used in further
experimentation. Four-fifths of the subjects felt that more experiments of this sort should be carried
out, and 74 percent indicated that they had learned something of personal importance as a result
of being in the study. Furthermore, a university psychiatrist, experienced in outpatient treatment,
interviewed a sample of experimental subjects with the aim of uncovering possible injurious effects
resulting from participation. No such effects were in evidence. Indeed, subjects typically felt that
their participation was instructive and enriching. A more detailed discussion of this question can
be found in Milgram (1964).

[5]*To obey* and *to disobey* are not the only terms one could use in describing the critical action
of Y. One could say that Y is cooperating with X, or displays conformity with regard to X's commands. However, *cooperation* suggests that X agrees with Y's ends, and understands the relationship

To be sure, the everyday use of the word *obedience* is not entirely free from 7 complexities. It refers to action within widely varying situations, and connotes diverse motives within those situations: a child's obedience differs from a soldier's obedience, or the love, honor, and *obey* of the marriage vow. However, a consistent behavioral relationship is indicated in most uses of the term: in the act of obeying, a person does what another person tells him to do. Y obeys X if he carries out the prescription for action which X has addressed to him; the term suggests, moreover, that some form of dominance-subordination, or hierarchical element, is part of the situation in which the transaction between X and Y occurs.

A subject who complies with the entire series of experimental commands 8 will be termed an *obedient* subject; one who at any point in the command series defies the experimenter will be called a *disobedient* or *defiant* subject. As used in this report the terms refer only to the subject's performance in the experiment, and do not necessarily imply a general personality disposition to submit to or reject authority.

SUBJECT POPULATION

The subjects used in all experimental conditions were male adults, residing 9 in the greater New Haven and Bridgeport areas, aged 20 to 50 years, and engaged in a wide variety of occupations. Each experimental condition described in this report employed 40 fresh subjects and was carefully balanced for age and occupational types. The occupational composition for each experiment was: work-

---

between his own behavior and the attainment of those ends. (But the experimental procedure, and, in particular, the experimenter's command that the subject shock the victim even in the absence of a response from the victim, preclude such understanding.) Moreover, cooperation implies status parity for the co-acting agents, and neglects the asymmetrical, dominance-subordination element prominent in the laboratory relationship between experimenter and subject. *Conformity* has been used in other important contexts in social psychology, and most frequently refers to imitating the judgments or actions of others when no explicit requirement for imitation has been made. Furthermore, in the present study there are two sources of social pressure; pressure from the experimenter issuing the commands, and pressure from the victim to stop the punishment. It is the pitting of a common man (the victim) against an authority (the experimenter) that is the distinctive feature of the conflict. At a point in the experiment the victim demands that he be let free. The experimenter insists that the subject continue to administer shocks. Which act of the subject can be interpreted as conformity? The subject may conform to the wishes of his peer or to the wishes of the experimenter, and conformity in one direction means the absence of conformity in the other. Thus the word has no useful reference in this setting, for the dual and conflicting social pressures cancel out its meaning.

In the final analysis, the linguistic symbol representing the subject's action must take its meaning from the concrete context in which that action occurs; and there is probably no word in everyday language that covers the experimental situation exactly, without omissions or irrelevant connotations. It is partly for convenience, therefore, that the terms *obey* and *disobey* are used to describe the subject's actions. At the same time, our use of the words is highly congruent with dictionary meaning.

ers, skilled and unskilled: 40 percent; white collar, sales, business: 40 percent; professionals: 20 percent. The occupations were intersected with three age categories (subjects in 20's, 30's, and 40's, assigned to each condition in the proportions of 20, 40, and 40 percent, respectively).

THE GENERAL LABORATORY PROCEDURE[6]

The focus of the study concerns the amount of electric shock a subject is   10
willing to administer to another person when ordered by an experimenter to give the "victim" increasingly more severe punishment. The act of administering shock is set in the context of a learning experiment, ostensibly designed to study the effect of punishment on memory. Aside from the experimenter, one naïve subject and one accomplice perform in each session. On arrival each subject is paid $4.50. After a general talk by the experimenter, telling how little scientists know about the effect of punishment on memory, subjects are informed that one member of the pair will serve as teacher and one as learner. A rigged drawing is held so that the naïve subject is always the teacher, and the accomplice becomes the learner. The learner is taken to an adjacent room and strapped into an "electric chair."

The naïve subject is told that it is his task to teach the learner a list of paired   11
associates, to test him on the list, and to administer punishment whenever the learner errs in the test. Punishment takes the form of electric shock, delivered to the learner by means of a shock generator controlled by the naïve subject. The teacher is instructed to increase the intensity of electric shock one step on the generator on each error. The learner, according to plan, provides many wrong answers, so that before long the naïve subject must give him the strongest shock on the generator. Increases in shock level are met by increasingly insistent demands from the learner that the experiment be stopped because of the growing discomfort to him. However, in clear terms the experimenter orders the teacher to continue with the procedure in disregard of the learner's protests. *Thus, the naïve subject must resolve a conflict between two mutually incompatible demands from the social field. He may continue to follow the orders of the experimenter and shock the learner with increasing severity, or he may refuse to follow the orders of the experimenter and heed the learner's pleas. The experimenter's authority operates not in a free field, but against ever-mounting countervailing pressure from the person being punished.*

A few technical points need to be considered before the findings of the study   12
are described. For the purpose of delivering shock, a simulated shock generator

---

[6]A more detailed account of the laboratory procedure can be found in Milgram (1963). A similar and independently evolved experimental procedure, employing a shock generator, victim, and learning task, was reported by Buss (1961). Buss used the technique for studying aggression, not obedience, and did not make use of the fundamental measure employed in the present study: break-off points.

is used, with 30 clearly marked voltage levels that range from 15 to 450 volts. (Each level is activated by one of 30 individual lever switches set in a horizontal line.) The naïve subject is given a sample shock of 45 volts to convince him of the authenticity of the instrument. The generator bears verbal designations that range from "Slight Shock" to "Danger: Severe Shock."

The responses of the victim are standardized on tape, and each protest is   13
coordinated to a particular voltage level on the shock generator. Starting with 75 volts the learner begins to grunt and moan. At 150 volts he demands to be let out of the experiment. At 180 volts he cries out that he can no longer stand the pain. At 300 volts he refuses to provide any more answers to the memory test, insisting that he is no longer a participant in the experiment and must be freed. In response to this last tactic, the experimenter instructs the naïve subject to treat the absence of an answer as equivalent to a wrong answer, and to follow the usual shock procedure. The experimenter reinforces his demand with the statement: "You have no other choice, you must go on!" (This imperative is used whenever the naïve subject tries to break off the experiment.) If the subject refuses to give the next higher level of shock, the experiment is considered at an end. A quantitative value is assigned to the subject's performance based on the maximum-intensity shock he administered before breaking off. Thus any subject's score may range from zero (for a subject unwilling to administer the first shock level) to 30 (for a subject who proceeds to the highest voltage level on the board). For any particular subject and for any particular experimental condition, the degree to which participants have followed the experimenter's orders may be specified with a numerical value, corresponding to the metric on the shock generator.

This laboratory situation gives us a framework in which to study the subject's   14
reactions to the principal conflict of the experiment. Again, this conflict is between the experimenter's demands that he continue to administer the electric shock, and the learner's demands, which become increasingly more insistent, that the experiment be stopped. The crux of the study is to vary systematically the factors believed to alter the degree of obedience to the experimental commands, to learn under what conditions submission to authority is most probable and under what conditions defiance is brought to the fore.

PILOT STUDIES

Pilot studies for the present research were completed in the winter of 1960;   15
they differed from the regular experiments in a few details: for one, the victim was placed behind a silvered glass, with the light balance on the glass such that the victim could be dimly perceived by the subject (Milgram, 1961).

Though essentially qualitative in treatment, these studies pointed to several   16
significant features of the experimental situation. At first no vocal feedback was used from the victim. It was thought that the verbal and voltage designations

on the control panel would create sufficient pressure to curtail the subject's obedience. However, this was not the case. In the absence of protests from the learner, virtually all subjects, once commanded, went blithely to the end of the board, seemingly indifferent to the verbal designations ("Extreme Shock" and "Danger: Severe Shock"). This deprived us of an adequate basis for scaling obedient tendencies. A force had to be introduced that would strengthen the subject's resistance to the experimenter's commands, and reveal individual differences in terms of a distribution of break-off points.

This force took the form of protests from the victim. Initially, mild protests   17
were used, but proved inadequate. Subsequently, more vehement protests were inserted into the experimental procedure. To our consternation, even the strongest protests from the victim did not prevent all subjects from administering the harshest punishment ordered by the experimenter; but the protests did lower the mean maximum shock somewhat and created some spread in the subject's performance; therefore, the victim's cries were standardized on tape and incorporated into the regular experimental procedure.

The situation did more than highlight the technical difficulties of finding a   18
workable experimental procedure: It indicated that subjects would obey authority to a greater extent than we had supposed. It also pointed to the importance of feedback from the victim in controlling the subject's behavior.

One further aspect of the pilot study was that subjects frequently averted their   19
eyes from the person they were shocking, often turning their heads in an awkward and conspicuous manner. One subject explained: "I didn't want to see the consequences of what I had done." Observers wrote:

> . . . subjects showed a reluctance to look at the victim, whom they could see through the glass in front of them. When this fact was brought to their attention they indicated that it caused them discomfort to see the victim in agony. We note, however, that although the subject refuses to look at the victim, he continues to administer shocks.

This suggested that the salience of the victim may have, in some degree,   20
regulated the subject's performance. If, in obeying the experimenter, the subject found it necessary to avoid scrutiny of the victim, would the converse be true? If the victim were rendered increasingly more salient to the subject, would obedience diminish? The first set of regular experiments was designed to answer this question.

IMMEDIACY OF THE VICTIM

This series consisted of four experimental conditions. In each condition the   21
victim was brought "psychologically" closer to the subject giving him shocks.

In the first condition (Remote Feedback) the victim was placed in another   22 room and could not be heard or seen by the subject, except that, at 300 volts, he pounded on the wall in protest. After 315 volts he no longer answered or was heard from.

The second condition (Voice Feedback) was identical to the first except that voice protests were introduced. As in the first condition the victim was placed in an adjacent room, but his complaints could be heard clearly through a door left slightly ajar and through the walls of the laboratory.[7]   23

The third experimental condition (Proximity) was similar to the second, except that the victim was now placed in the same room as the subject, and 1½ feet from him. Thus he was visible as well as audible, and voice cues were provided.   24

The fourth, and final, condition of this series (Touch-Proximity) was identical to the third, with this exception: The victim received a shock only when his hand rested on a shockplate. At the 150-volt level the victim again demanded to be let free and, in this condition, refused to place his hand on the shockplate. The experimenter ordered the naïve subject to force the victim's hand onto the plate. Thus obedience in this condition required that the subject have physical contact with the victim in order to give him punishment beyond the 150-volt level.   25

Forty adult subjects were studied in each condition. The data revealed that obedience was significantly reduced as the victim was rendered more immediate   26

---

[7]It is difficult to convey on the printed page the full tenor of the victim's responses, for we have no adequate notation for vocal intensity, timing, and general qualities of delivery. Yet these features are crucial to producing the effect of an increasingly severe reaction to mounting voltage levels. (They can be communicated fully only by sending interested parties the recorded tapes.) In general terms, however, the victim indicates no discomfort until the 75-volt shock is administered, at which time there is a light grunt in response to the punishment. Similar reactions follow the 90- and 105-volt shocks, and at 120 volts the victim shouts to the experimenter that the shocks are becoming painful. Painful groans are heard on administration of the 135-volt shock, and at 150 volts the victim cries out, 'Experimenter, get me out of here! I won't be in the experiment any more! I refuse to go on!' Cries of this type continue with generally rising intensity, so that at 180 volts the victim cries out, 'I can't stand the pain,' and by 270 volts his response to the shock is definitely an agonized scream. Throughout, he insists that he be let out of the experiment. At 300 volts the victim shouts in desperation that he will no longer provide answers to the memory test; and at 315 volts, after a violent scream, he reaffirms with vehemence that he is no longer a participant. From this point on, he provides no answers, but shrieks in agony whenever a shock is administered; this continues through 450 volts. Of course, many subjects will have broken off before this point.

A revised and stronger set of protests was used in all experiments outside the Proximity series. Naturally, new baseline measures were established for all comparisons using the new set of protests.

There is overwhelming evidence that the great majority of subjects, both obedient and defiant, accepted the victims' reactions as genuine. The evidence takes the form of: (a) tension created in the subjects (see discussion of tension); (b) scores on "estimated-pain" scales filled out by subjects immediately after the experiment; (c) subjects' accounts of their feelings in post-experimental interviews; and (d) quantifiable responses to questionnaires distributed to subjects several months after their participation in the experiments. This matter will be treated fully in a forthcoming monograph.

(The procedure in all experimental conditions was to have the naïve subject announce the voltage level before administering each shock, so that—independently of the victim's responses—he was continually reminded of delivering punishment of ever-increasing severity.)

to the subject. The mean maximum shock for the conditions is shown in Figure 1.

Expressed in terms of the proportion of obedient to defiant subjects, the findings are that 34 percent of the subjects defied the experimenter in the Remote condition, 37.5 percent in Voice Feedback, 60 percent in Proximity, and 70 percent in Touch-Proximity.

How are we to account for this effect? A first conjecture might be that as the victim was brought closer the subject became more aware of the intensity of his suffering and regulated his behavior accordingly. This makes sense, but our evidence does not support the interpretation. There are no consistent differences in the attributed level of pain across the four conditions (i.e. the amount of pain experienced by the victim as estimated by the subject and expressed on a 14-point scale). But it is easy to speculate about alternative mechanisms:

Empathic cues. In the Remote and to a lesser extent the Voice Feedback conditions, the victim's suffering possesses an abstract, remote quality for the subject. He is aware, but only in a conceptual sense, that his actions cause pain to another person; the fact is apprehended, but not felt. The phenomenon is common enough.

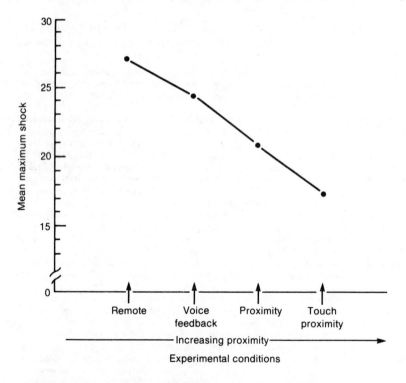

FIGURE 1. Mean maxima in proximity series.

The bombardier can reasonably suppose that his weapons will inflict suffering and death, yet this knowledge is divested of affect and does not move him to a felt, emotional response to the suffering resulting from his actions. Similar observations have been made in wartime. It is possible that the visual cues associated with the victim's suffering trigger empathic responses in the subject and provide him with a more complete grasp of the victim's experience. Or it is possible that the empathic responses are themselves unpleasant, possessing drive properties which cause the subject to terminate the arousal situation. Diminishing obedience, then, would be explained by the enrichment of empathic cues in the successive experimental conditions.

Denial and narrowing of the cognitive field. The Remote condition allows a narrowing of the cognitive field so that the victim is put out of mind. The subject no longer considers the act of depressing a lever relevant to moral judgment, for it is no longer associated with the victim's suffering. When the victim is close it is more difficult to exclude him phenomenologically. He necessarily intrudes on the subject's awareness since he is continuously visible. In the Remote condition his existence and reactions are made known only after the shock has been administered. The auditory feedback is sporadic and discontinuous. In the Proximity conditions his inclusion in the immediate visual field renders him a continuously salient element for the subject. The mechanism of denial can no longer be brought into play. One subject in the Remote condition said: "It's funny how you really begin to forget that there's a guy out there, even though you can hear him. For a long time I just concentrated on pressing the switches and reading the words." 30

Reciprocal fields. If in the Proximity condition the subject is in an improved position to observe the victim, the reverse is also true. The actions of the subject now come under proximal scrutiny by the victim. Possibly, it is easier to harm a person when he is unable to observe our actions than when he can see what we are doing. His surveillance of the action directed against him may give rise to shame, or guilt, which may then serve to curtail the action. Many expressions of language refer to the discomfort or inhibitions that arise in face-to-face confrontation. It is often said that it is easier to criticize a man "behind his back" than to "attack him to his face." If we are in the process of lying to a person it is reputedly difficult to "stare him in the eye." We "turn away from others in shame" or in "embarrassment" and this action serves to reduce our discomfort. The manifest function of allowing the victim of a firing squad to be blindfolded is to make the occasion less stressful for him, but it may also serve a latent function of reducing the stress of the executioner. In short, in the Proximity conditions, the subject may sense that he has become more salient in the victim's field of awareness. Possibly he becomes more self-conscious, embarrassed, and inhibited in his punishment of the victim. 31

Phenomenal unity of act. In the Remote condition it is more difficult for the subject to gain a sense of *relatedness* between his own actions and the consequences of these actions for the victim. There is a physical and spatial separation of the act and its consequences. The subject depresses a lever in one room, and protests and cries are heard from another. The two events are in correlation, yet they lack 32

337

a compelling phenomenological unity. The structure of a meaningful act—*I am hurting a man*—breaks down because of the spatial arrangements, in a manner somewhat analogous to the disappearance of phi phenomena[8] when the blinking lights are spaced too far apart. The unity is more fully achieved in the Proximity condition as the victim is brought closer to the action that causes him pain. It is rendered complete in Touch-Proximity.

Incipient group formation. Placing the victim in another room not only takes him   33
further from the subject, but the subject and the experimenter are drawn relatively closer. There is incipient group formation between the experimenter and the subject, from which the victim is excluded. The wall between the victim and the others deprives him of an intimacy which the experimenter and subject feel. In the Remote condition, the victim is truly an outsider, who stands alone, physically and psychologically.

When the victim is placed close to the subject, it becomes easier to form an   34
alliance with him against the experimenter. Subjects no longer have to face the experimenter alone. They have an ally who is close at hand and eager to collaborate in a revolt against the experimenter. Thus, the changing set of spatial relations leads to a potentially shifting set of alliances over the several experimental conditions.

Acquired behavior dispositions. It is commonly observed that laboratory mice will   35
rarely fight with their litter mates. Scott (1958) explains this in terms of passive inhibition. He writes: "By doing nothing under . . . circumstances [the animal] learns to do nothing, and this may be spoken of as passive inhibition . . . this principle has great importance in teaching an individual to be peaceful, for it means that he can learn not to fight simply by not fighting." Similarly, we may learn not to harm others simply by not harming them in everyday life. Yet this learning occurs in a context of proximal relations with others, and may not be generalized to that situation in which the person is physically removed from us. Or possibly, in the past, aggressive actions against others who were physically close resulted in retaliatory punishment which extinguished the original form of response. In contrast, aggression against others at a distance may have only sporadically led to retaliation. Thus the organism learns that it is safer to be aggressive toward others at a distance, and precarious to be so when the parties are within arm's reach. Through a pattern of rewards and punishments, he acquires a disposition to avoid aggression at close quarters, a disposition which does not extend to harming others at a distance. And this may account for experimental findings in the remote and proximal experiments.

Proximity as a variable in psychological research has received far less attention   36
than it deserves. If men were sessile[9] it would be easy to understand this neglect. But we move about; our spatial relations shift from one situation to the next, and the fact that we are near or remote may have a powerful effect on the

---

[8]phi phenomena: the optical impression of motion generated when similar stationary objects are presented one after another at a certain interval. [Eds.]
[9]sessile: permanently attached. [Eds.]

psychological processes that mediate our behavior toward others. In the present situation, as the victim is brought closer to the subject ordered to give him shocks, increasing numbers of subjects break off the experiment, refusing to obey. The concrete, visible, and proximal presence of the victim acts in an important way to counteract the experimenter's power to generate disobedience.[10]

CLOSENESS OF AUTHORITY

If the spatial relationship of the subject and victim is relevant to the degree of obedience, would not the relationship of subject to experimenter also play a part? 37

There are reasons to feel that, on arrival, the subject is oriented primarily to the experimenter rather than to the victim. He has come to the laboratory to fit into the structure that the experimenter—not the victim—would provide. He has come less to understand his behavior than to *reveal* that behavior to a competent scientist, and he is willing to display himself as the scientist's purposes require. Most subjects seem quite concerned about the appearance they are making before the experimenter, and one could argue that this preoccupation in a relatively new and strange setting makes the subject somewhat insensitive to the triadic nature of the social situation. In other words, the subject is so concerned about the show he is putting on for the experimenter that influences from other parts of the social field do not receive as much weight as they ordinarily would. This overdetermined orientation to the experimenter would account for the relative insensitivity of the subject to the victim, and would also lead us to believe that alterations in the relationship between subject and experimenter would have important consequences for obedience. 38

In a series of experiments we varied the physical closeness and degree of surveillance of the experimenter. In one condition the experimenter sat just a few feet away from the subject. In a second condition, after giving initial instructions, the experimenter left the laboratory and gave his orders by telephone. In still a third condition the experimenter was never seen, providing instructions by means of a tape recording activated when the subjects entered the laboratory. 39

Obedience dropped sharply as the experimenter was physically removed from 40

---

[10]Admittedly, the terms *proximity, immediacy, closeness,* and *salience-of-the-victim* are used in a loose sense, and the experiments themselves represent a very coarse treatment of the variable. Further experiments are needed to refine the notion and tease out such diverse factors as spatial distance, visibility, audibility, barrier interposition, etc.

The Proximity and Touch-Proximity experiments were the only conditions where we were unable to use taped feedback from the victim. Instead, the victim was trained to respond in these conditions as he had in Experiment 2 (which employed taped feedback). Some improvement is possible here, for it should be technically feasible to do a proximity series using taped feedback.

the laboratory. The number of obedient subjects in the first condition (Experimenter Present) was almost three times as great as in the second, where the experimenter gave his orders by telephone. Twenty-six subjects were fully obedient in the first condition, and only nine in the second (Chi square obedient *vs.* defiant in the two conditions, df = 14.7; p < 0.001). Subjects seemed able to take a far stronger stand against the experimenter when they did not have to encounter him face to face, and the experimenter's power over the subject was severely curtailed.[11]

Moreover, when the experimenter was absent, subjects displayed an interesting form of behavior that had not occurred under his surveillance. Though continuing with the experiment, several subjects administered lower shocks than were required and never informed the experimenter of their deviation from the correct procedure. (Unknown to the subjects, shock levels were automatically recorded by an Esterline-Angus event recorder wired directly into the shock generator; the instrument provided us with an objective record of the subjects' performance.) Indeed, in telephone conversations some subjects specifically assured the experimenter that they were raising the shock level according to instruction, whereas in fact they were repeatedly using the lowest shock on the board. This form of behavior is particularly interesting: although these subjects acted in a way that clearly undermined the avowed purposes of the experiment, they found it easier to handle the conflict in this manner than to precipitate an open break with authority.   41

Other conditions were completed in which the experimenter was absent during the first segment of the experiment, but reappeared at the point that the subject definitely refused to give higher shocks when commanded by telephone. Although he had exhausted his power via telephone, the experimenter could frequently force further obedience when he reappeared in the laboratory.   42

Experiments in this series show that the *physical presence* of an authority is an important force contributing to the subject's obedience or defiance. Taken together with the first experimental series on the proximity of the victim, it would appear that something akin to fields of force, diminishing in effectiveness with increasing psychological distance from their source, have a controlling effect on the subject's performance. As the victim is brought closer, the subject finds it harder to administer shocks to him. When the victim's position is held constant relative to the subject, and the authority is made more remote, the subject finds it easier to break off the experiment. This effect is substantial in both cases, but manipulation of the experimenter's position yielded the more powerful results. Obedience to destructive commands is highly dependent on the proximal relations between authority and subject.   43

---

[11]The third condition also led to significantly lower obedience than this first situation in which the experimenter was present, but it contains technical difficulties that require extensive discussion.

TENSIONS

The description of final scores does not fully convey the character of the 44
subjects' performance, and it would be useful to interrupt our reporting of
quantitative relationships to remark on the subjects' general reaction to the
situation.

One might suppose that a subject would simply break off or continue as his 45
conscience and temperament dictated. Yet this is very far from what happened.
There were powerful reactions of tension and emotional strain in a substantial
proportion of the participants. Persons were observed to sweat, tremble, stutter,
bite their lips, and groan as they found themselves increasingly implicated in
the experimental conflict. Some sense of the subjects' mood can be found in a
transcript of their remarks at break-off point. Here are the remarks of two defiant
subjects:

> Is he banging? . . . Is he hurt out there? Well, I don't want to be responsible for
> anything that happens to him. No, I can't go on with it. I don't know whether
> he's all right or not. I mean he may have a heart condition or something; I wouldn't
> feel right doing it. He's banging for help. He's evidently in trouble or he wouldn't
> bang . . . I don't see any sense to this—to knocking him out or something. I just
> can't see it.
> [*Subject refuses to administer shocks*]   [*Subject 0108*]

> The man is banging. He wants to get out . . . I'm sorry. If the man wants to get
> out I'd just as soon stop . . . I don't want to administer any more [extremely
> excited] . . . I will gladly refund the check, but I will not harm this man . . . I'm
> sorry, I will not give him any more if he obviously wants to get out. There is no
> money in the world that will make me hurt another individual.   [*Subject 010X*]

And here is a transcript from an obedient subject. He began the experiment 46
calmly, but became increasingly tense as the experiment proceeded. After administering the 150-volt shock, he began to address the experimenter in agitated
tones:

> *150 volts delivered.* You want me to keep going?
> *165 volts delivered.* That guy is hollering in there. There's a lot of them here.
> He's liable to have heart condition. You want me to go?
> *180 volts delivered.* He can't stand it! I'm not going to kill that man in there! You
> hear him hollering? He's hollering. He can't stand it. What if something happens
> to him? . . . I'm not going to get that man sick in there. He's hollering in there.
> You know what I mean? I mean I refuse to take responsibility. He's getting hurt
> in there. He's in there hollering. Too many left here. Geez, if he gets them wrong.
> There's too many of them left. I mean who is going to take responsibility if
> anything happens to that gentleman?
> [*The experimenter accepts responsibility.*] All right.

341

195 volts delivered. You see he's hollering. Hear that. Gee, I don't know.
[*The experimenter says: 'The experiment requires that you go on.'*]—I know it does,
sir, but I mean—hugh—he don't know what he's in for. He's up to 195 volts.
210 volts delivered.
225 volts delivered.
240 volts delivered. Aw, no. You mean I've got to keep going up with the scale?
No sir. I'm not going to kill that man! I'm not going to give him 450 volts!
[*The experimenter says: 'The experiment requires that you go on.'*]—I know it does,
but that man is hollering there, sir . . .

Despite his numerous, agitated objections, which were constant accompaniments to his actions, the subject unfailingly obeyed the experimenter, proceeding to the highest shock level on the generator. He displayed a curious dissociation between word and action. Although at the verbal level he had resolved not to go on, his actions were fully in accord with the experimenter's commands. This subject did not want to shock the victim, and he found it an extremely disagreeable task, but he was unable to invent a response that would free him from E's authority. Many subjects cannot find the specific verbal formula that would enable them to reject the role assigned to them by the experimenter. Perhaps our culture does not provide adequate models for disobedience.

One puzzling sign of tension was the regular occurrence of nervous laughing 47 fits. In the first four conditions 71 of the 160 subjects showed definite signs of nervous laughter and smiling. The laughter seemed entirely out of place, even bizarre. Full-blown, uncontrollable seizures were observed for 15 of these subjects. On one occasion we observed a seizure so violently convulsive that it was necessary to call a halt to the experiment. In the post-experimental interviews subjects took pains to point out that they were not sadistic types and that the laughter did not mean they enjoyed shocking the victim.

In the interview following the experiment subjects were asked to indicate on 48 a 14-point scale just how nervous or tense they felt at the point of maximum tension (Figure 2). The scale ranged from "not at all tense and nervous" to "extremely tense and nervous." Self-reports of this sort are of limited precision and at best provide only a rough indication of the subject's emotional response. Still, taking the reports for what they are worth, it can be seen that the distribution of responses spans the entire range of the scale, with the majority of subjects concentrated at the center and upper extreme. A further breakdown showed that obedient subjects reported themselves as having been slightly more tense and nervous than the defiant subjects at the point of maximum tension.

How is the occurrence of tension to be interpreted? First, it points to the 49 presence of conflict. If a tendency to comply with authority were the only psychological force operating in the situation, all subjects would have continued to the end and there would have been no tension. Tension, it is assumed, results from the simultaneous presence of two or more incompatible response tendencies (Miller, 1944). If sympathetic concern for the victim were the exclusive

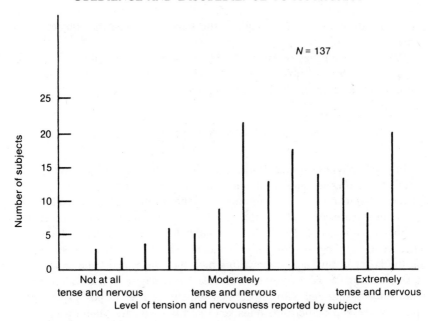

FIGURE 2. Level of tension and nervousness: the self-reports on "tension and nervousness" for 137 subjects in the Proximity experiments. Subjects were given a scale with 14 values ranging from "not at all tense and nervous" to "extremely tense and nervous." They were instructed: "Thinking back to that point in the experiment when you felt the most tense and nervous, indicate just how you felt by placing an X at the appropriate point on the scale." The results are shown in terms of midpoint values.

force, all subjects would have calmly defied the experimenter. Instead, there were both obedient and defiant outcomes, frequently accompanied by extreme tension. A conflict develops between the deeply ingrained disposition not to harm others and the equally compelling tendency to obey others who are in authority. The subject is quickly drawn into a dilemma of a deeply dynamic character, and the presence of high tension points to the considerable strength of each of the antagonistic vectors.

Moreover, tension defines the strength of the aversive state from which the subject is unable to escape through disobedience. When a person is uncomfortable, tense, or stressed, he tries to take some action that will allow him to terminate this unpleasant state. Thus tension may serve as a drive that leads to escape behavior. But in the present situation, even where tension is extreme, many subjects are unable to perform the response that will bring about relief. Therefore there must be a competing drive, tendency, or inhibition that precludes activation of the disobedient response. The strength of this inhibiting factor must be of greater magnitude than the stress experienced, or else the terminating act would occur. Every evidence of extreme tension is at the same

343

time an indication of the strength of the forces that keep the subject in the situation.

Finally, tension may be taken as evidence of the reality of the situations for 51 the subjects. Normal subjects do not tremble and sweat unless they are implicated in a deep and genuinely felt predicament.

BACKGROUND AUTHORITY

In psychophysics, animal learning, and other branches of psychology, the 52 fact that measures are obtained at one institution rather than another is irrelevant to the interpretation of the findings, so long as the technical facilities for measurement are adequate and the operations are carried out with competence.

But it cannot be assumed that this holds true for the present study. The 53 effectiveness of the experimenter's commands may depend in an important way on the larger institutional context in which they are issued. The experiments described thus far were conducted at Yale University, an organization which most subjects regarded with respect and sometimes awe. In post-experimental interviews several participants remarked that the locale and sponsorship of the study gave them confidence in the integrity, competence, and benign purposes of the personnel; many indicated that they would not have shocked the learner if the experiments had been done elsewhere.

This issue of background authority seemed to us important for an interpre- 54 tation of the results that had been obtained thus far; moreover it is highly relevant to any comprehensive theory of human obedience. Consider, for example, how closely our compliance with the imperatives of others is tied to particular institutions and locales in our day-to-day activities. On request, we expose our throats to a man with a razor blade in the barber shop, but would not do so in a shoe store; in the latter setting we willingly follow the clerk's request to stand in our stockinged feet, but resist the command in a bank. In the laboratory of a great university, subjects may comply with a set of commands that would be resisted if given elsewhere. *One must always question the relationship of obedience to a person's sense of the context in which he is operating.*

To explore the problem we moved our apparatus to an office building in 55 industrial Bridgeport and replicated experimental conditions, without any visible tie to the university.

Bridgeport subjects were invited to the experiment through a mail circular 56 similar to the one used in the Yale study, with appropriate changes in letterhead, etc. As in the earlier study, subjects were paid $4.50 for coming to the laboratory. The same age and occupational distributions used at Yale and the identical personnel were employed.

The purpose in relocating in Bridgeport was to assure a complete dissociation 57 from Yale, and in this regard we were fully successful. On the surface, the study appeared to be conducted by Research Associates of Bridgeport, an organization of unknown character (the title had been concocted exclusively for use in this study).

The experiments were conducted in a three-room office suite in a somewhat run-down commercial building located in the downtown shopping area. The laboratory was sparsely furnished, though clean, and marginally respectable in appearance. When subjects inquired about professional affiliations, they were informed only that we were a private firm conducting research for industry.

Some subjects displayed skepticism concerning the motives of the Bridgeport experimenter. One gentleman gave us a written account of the thoughts he experienced at the control board:

> . . . Should I quit this damn test? Maybe he passed out? What dopes we were not to check up on this deal. How do we know that these guys are legit? No furniture, bare walls, no telephone. We could of called the Police up or the Better Business Bureau. I learned a lesson tonight. How do I know that Mr. Williams [the experimenter] is telling the truth . . . I wish I knew how many volts a person could take before lapsing into unconsciousness . . . [*Subject 2414*]

Another subject stated:

> I questioned on my arrival my own judgment [about coming]. I had doubts as to the legitimacy of the operation and the consequences of participation. I felt it was a heartless way to conduct memory or learning processes on human beings and certainly dangerous without the presence of a medical doctor. [*Subject 2440V*]

There was no noticeable reduction in tension for the Bridgeport subjects. And the subjects' estimation of the amount of pain felt by the victim was slightly, though not significantly, higher than in the Yale study.

A failure to obtain complete obedience in Bridgeport would indicate that the extreme compliance found in New Haven subjects was tied closely to the background authority of Yale University; if a large proportion of the subjects remained fully obedient, very different conclusions would be called for.

As it turned out, the level of obedience in Bridgeport, although somewhat reduced, was not significantly lower than that obtained at Yale. A large proportion of the Bridgeport subjects were fully obedient to the experimenter's commands (48 percent of the Bridgeport subjects delivered the maximum shock versus 65 percent in the corresponding condition at Yale).

How are these findings to be interpreted? It is possible that if commands of a potentially harmful or destructive sort are to be perceived as legitimate they must occur within some sort of institutional structure. But it is clear from the study that it need not be a particularly reputable or distinguished institution. The Bridgeport experiments were conducted by an unimpressive firm lacking any credentials; the laboratory was set up in a respectable office building with title listed in the building directory. Beyond that, there was no evidence of benevolence or competence. It is possible that the *category* of institution, judged

58

59

60

61

62

63

according to its professed function, rather than its qualitative position within that category, wins our compliance. Persons deposit money in elegant, but also in seedy-looking banks, without giving much thought to the differences in security they offer. Similarly, our subjects may consider one laboratory to be as competent as another, so long as it is a scientific laboratory.

It would be valuable to study the subjects' performance in other contexts 64 which go even further than the Bridgeport study in denying institutional support to the experimenter. It is possible that, beyond a certain point, obedience disappears completely. But that point had not been reached in the Bridgeport office: almost half the subjects obeyed the experimenter fully.

FURTHER EXPERIMENTS

We may mention briefly some additional experiments undertaken in the Yale 65 series. A considerable amount of obedience and defiance in everyday life occurs in connection with groups. And we had reason to feel in light of the many group studies already done in psychology that group forces would have a profound effect on reactions to authority. A series of experiments was run to examine these effects. In all cases only one naïve subject was studied per hour, but he performed in the midst of actors who, unknown to him, were employed by the experimenter. In one experiment (Groups for Disobedience) two actors broke off in the middle of the experiment. When this happened 90 percent of the subjects followed suit and defied the experimenter. In another condition the actors followed the orders obediently; this strengthened the experimenter's power only slightly. In still a third experiment the job of pushing the switch to shock the learner was given to one of the actors, while the naïve subject performed a subsidiary act. We wanted to see how the teacher would respond if he were involved in the situation but did not actually give the shocks. In this situation only three subjects out of forty broke off. In a final group experiment the subjects themselves determined the shock level they were going to use. Two actors suggested higher and higher shock levels; some subjects insisted, despite group pressure, that the shock level be kept low; others followed along with the group.

Further experiments were completed using women as subjects, as well as a 66 set dealing with the effects of dual, unsanctioned, and conflicting authority. A final experiment concerned the personal relationship between victim and subject. These will have to be described elsewhere, lest the present report be extended to monographic length.

It goes without saying that future research can proceed in many different 67 directions. What kinds of response from the victim are most effective in causing disobedience in the subject? Perhaps passive resistance is more effective than vehement protest. What conditions of entry into an authority system lead to greater or lesser obedience? What is the effect of anonymity and masking on the subject's behavior? What conditions lead to the subject's perception of responsibility for his own actions? Each of these could be a major research topic in itself, and can readily be incorporated into the general experimental procedure described here.

LEVELS OF OBEDIENCE AND DEFIANCE

One general finding that merits attention is the high level of obedience   68
manifested in the experimental situation. Subjects often expressed deep disapproval of shocking a man in the face of his objections, and others denounced it as senseless and stupid. Yet many subjects complied even while they protested. The proportion of obedient subjects greatly exceeded the expectations of the experimenter and his colleagues. At the outset, we had conjectured that subjects would not, in general, go above the level of "Strong Shock." In practice, many subjects were willing to administer the most extreme shocks available when commanded by the experimenter. For some subjects the experiment provided an occasion for aggressive release. And for others it demonstrated the extent to which obedient dispositions are deeply ingrained and engaged, irrespective of their consequences for others. Yet this is not the whole story. Somehow, the subject becomes implicated in a situation from which he cannot disengage himself.

The departure of the experimental results from intelligent expectation, to   69
some extent, has been formalized. The procedure was to describe the experimental situation in concrete detail to a group of competent persons, and to ask them to predict the performance of 100 hypothetical subjects. For purposes of indicating the distribution of break-off points, judges were provided with a diagram of the shock generator and recorded their predictions before being informed of the actual results. Judges typically underestimated the amount of obedience demonstrated by subjects.

In Figure 3, we compare the predictions of forty psychiatrists at a leading   70
medical school with the actual performance of subjects in the experiment. The psychiatrists predicted that most subjects would not go beyond the tenth shock level (150 volts; at this point the victim makes his first explicit demand to be freed). They further predicted that by the twentieth shock level (300 volts; the victim refuses to answer) 3.73 percent of the subjects would still be obedient; and that only a little over one-tenth of one percent of the subjects would administer the highest shock on the board. But, as the graph indicates, the obtained behavior was very different. Sixty-two percent of the subjects obeyed the experimenter's commands fully. Between expectation and occurrence there is a whopping discrepancy.

Why did the psychiatrists underestimate the level of obedience? Possibly,   71
because their predictions were based on an inadequate conception of the deter-

347

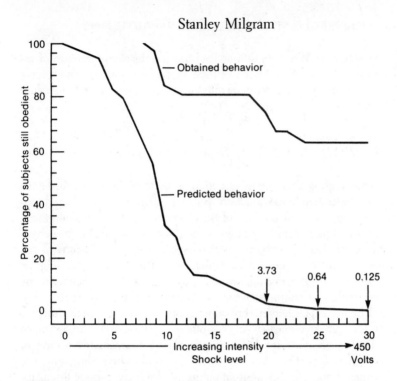

FIGURE 3. Predicted and obtained behavior in voice feedback.

minants of human action, a conception that focuses on motives *in vacuo*. This orientation may be entirely adequate for the repair of bruised impulses as revealed on the psychiatrist's couch, but as soon as our interest turns to action in larger settings, attention must be paid to the situations in which motives are expressed. A situation exerts an important press on the individual. It exercises constraints and may provide push. In certain circumstances it is not so much the kind of person a man is, as the kind of situation in which he is placed, that determines his actions.

Many people, not knowing much about the experiment, claim that subjects who go to the end of the board are sadistic. Nothing could be more foolish than an overall characterization of these persons. It is like saying that a person thrown into a swift-flowing stream is necessarily a fast swimmer, or that he has great stamina because he moves so rapidly relative to the bank. The context of action must always be considered. The individual, upon entering the laboratory, becomes integrated into a situation that carries its own momentum. The subject's problem then is how to become disengaged from a situation which is moving in an altogether ugly direction.

The fact that disengagement is so difficult testifies to the potency of the forces that keep the subject at the control board. Are these forces to be conceptualized as individual motives and expressed in the language of personality dynamics, or

72

73

348

are they to be seen as the effects of social structure and pressures arising from the situational field?

A full understanding of the subject's action will, I feel, require that both 74 perspectives be adopted. The person brings to the laboratory enduring dispositions toward authority and aggression, and at the same time he becomes enmeshed in a social structure that is no less an objective fact of the case. From the standpoint of personality theory one may ask: What mechanisms of personality enable a person to transfer responsibility to authority? What are the motives underlying obedient and disobedient performance? Does orientation to authority lead to a short-circuiting of the shame-guilt system? What cognitive and emotional defenses are brought into play in the case of obedient and defiant subjects?

The present experiments are not, however, directed toward an exploration of 75 the motives engaged when the subject obeys the experimenter's commands. Instead, they examine the situational variables responsible for the elicitation of obedience. Elsewhere, we have attempted to spell out some of the structural properties of the experimental situation that account for high obedience, and this analysis need not be repeated here (Milgram, 1963). The experimental variations themselves represent our attempt to probe that structure, by systematically changing it and noting the consequences for behavior. It is clear that some situations produce greater compliance with the experimenter's commands than others. However, this does not necessarily imply an increase or decrease in the strength of any single definable motive. Situations producing the greatest obedience could do so by triggering the most powerful, yet perhaps the most idiosyncratic, of motives in each subject confronted by the setting. Or they may simply recruit a greater number and variety of motives in their service. But whatever the motives involved—and it is far from certain that they can ever be known—action may be studied as a direct function of the situation in which it occurs. This has been the approach of the present study, where we sought to plot behavioral regularities against manipulated properties of the social field. Ultimately, social psychology would like to have a compelling *theory of situations* which will, first, present a language in terms of which situations can be defined; proceed to a typology of situations; and then point to the manner in which definable properties of situations are transformed into psychological forces in the individual.[12]

POSTSCRIPT

Almost a thousand adults were individually studied in the obedience research, 76 and there were many specific conclusions regarding the variables that control

---

[12]My thanks to Professor Howard Leventhal of Yale for strengthening the writing in this paragraph.

Stanley Milgram

obedience and disobedience to authority. Some of these have been discussed briefly in the preceding sections, and more detailed reports will be released subsequently.

There are now some other generalizations I should like to make, which do not derive in any strictly logical fashion from the experiments as carried out, but which, I feel, ought to be made. They are formulations of an intuitive sort that have been forced on me by observation of many subjects responding to the pressures of authority. The assertions represent a painful alteration in my own thinking; and since they were acquired only under the repeated impact of direct observation, I have no illusion that they will be generally accepted by persons who have not had the same experience. 77

With numbing regularity good people were seen to knuckle under the demands of authority and perform actions that were callous and severe. Men who are in everyday life responsible and decent were seduced by the trappings of authority, by the control of their perceptions, and by the uncritical acceptance of the experimenter's definition of the situation, into performing harsh acts. 78

What is the limit of such obedience? At many points we attempted to establish a boundary. Cries from the victim were inserted; not good enough. The victim claimed heart trouble; subjects still shocked him on command. The victim pleaded that he be let free, and his answers no longer registered on the signal box; subjects continued to shock him. At the outset we had not conceived that such drastic procedures would be needed to generate disobedience, and each step was added only as the ineffectiveness of the earlier techniques became clear. The final effort to establish a limit was the Touch-Proximity condition. But the very first subject in this condition subdued the victim on command, and proceeded to the highest shock level. A quarter of the subjects in this condition performed similarly. 79

The results, as seen and felt in the laboratory, are to this author disturbing. They raise the possibility that human nature or, more specifically, the kind of character produced in American democratic society cannot be counted on to insulate its citizens from brutality and inhumane treatment at the direction of malevolent authority. A substantial proportion of people do what they are told to do, irrespective of the content of the act and without limitations of conscience, so long as they perceive that the command comes from a legitimate authority. If in this study an anonymous experimenter could successfully command adults to subdue a fifty-year-old man and force on him painful electric shocks against his protests, one can only wonder what government, with its vastly greater authority and prestige, can command of its subjects. There is, of course, the extremely important question of whether malevolent political institutions could or would arise in American society. The present research contributes nothing to this issue. 80

350

In an article titled "The Danger of Obedience," Harold J. Laski wrote: 81

. . . civilization means, above all, an unwillingness to inflict unnecessary pain. Within the ambit of that definition, those of us who heedlessly accept the commands of authority cannot yet claim to be civilized men.

. . . Our business, if we desire to live a life, not utterly devoid of meaning and significance, is to accept nothing which contradicts our basic experience merely because it comes to us from tradition or convention or authority. It may well be that we shall be wrong; but our self-expression is thwarted at the root unless the certainties we are asked to accept coincide with the certainties we experience. That is why the condition of freedom in any state is always a widespread and consistent skepticism of the canons upon which power insists.

REFERENCES

BUSS, ARNOLD H.
    1961.   *The Psychology of Aggression.* New York and London: John Wiley.
KIERKEGAARD, S.
    1843.   *Fear and Trembling.* English edition, Princeton: Princeton University Press, 1941.
LASKI, HAROLD J.
    1929.   "The dangers of obedience." *Harper's Monthly Magazine,* 15 June, 1–10.
MILGRAM, S.
    1961.   "Dynamics of obedience: experiments in social psychology." Mimeographed report, *National Science Foundation,* January 25.

    1963.   "Behavioral study of obedience." *J. Abnorm. Soc. Psychol.* 67, 371–378.

    1964.   "Issues in the study of obedience: a reply to Baumrind." *Amer. Psychol.* 1, 848–852.
MILLER, N.E.
    1944.   "Experimental studies of conflict." In J. McV. Hunt (ed.), *Personality and the Behavior Disorders.* New York: Ronald Press.
SCOTT, J.P.
    1958.   *Aggression.* Chicago: University of Chicago Press.

QUESTIONS

1. What did Milgram want to determine by his experiment? What were his anticipated outcomes?

2. What conclusions did Milgram reach about the extent to which ordinary individuals would obey the orders of an authority figure? Under what conditions is this submission most probable? Under what conditions is defiance most likely?

3. Describe the general procedures of this experiment. Some persons have questioned Milgram's methods. Do you think it is ethical to expose subjects without warning to

experiments that might have a lasting effect on them? What such effects might this experiment have had?

4. One characteristic of this paper is Milgram's willingness to consider several possible explanations of the same phenomenon. Study the interpretations in paragraphs 28 through 35. What do you make of the range of interpretation there and elsewhere in the essay? How does Milgram achieve such a range?

5. A report such as Milgram's is not structured in the same way as a conventional essay. His research is really a collection of separate but related experiments, each one of which requires its own interpretation. Describe the groups into which these experiments fall. Which results seemed most surprising to you? Which were easiest to anticipate?

6. In Milgram's experiment, people who are responsible and decent in everyday life were seduced, he says, by trappings of authority. Most of us, however, like to believe that we would neither engage in brutality on our own nor obey directions of this kind. Has Milgram succeeded in getting you to question your own behavior? Would you go so far as to say that he forces you to question your own human nature?

7. In paragraph 46 Milgram comments, "Perhaps our culture does not provide adequate models for disobedience." What do you think of this hypothesis? Are there such models? Ought there to be? Have there appeared such models in the time since the experiment was conducted? Explain your stand on Milgram's statement.

8. If research in social psychology takes place in your school today, there is probably a panel of some sort that enforces guidelines on research with human subjects. Locate that board, if it exists, and find out whether this experiment could take place today. Report to your class on the rules that guide researchers today. Do you think those rules are wise?

9. What, in your opinion, should be the guidelines for psychological research with human subjects? List the guidelines you think are appropriate, and compare your list with the lists of your classmates. Would your guidelines have allowed Milgram's experiment?

10. Think of a situation in which you were faced with the moral and ethical dilemma of whether or not to obey a figure of authority. How did you behave? Did your behavior surprise you? Describe and explain that experience.

THE ANTHROPOLOGY
OF MANNERS
Edward T. Hall

Edward T. Hall (b. 1914), an American anthropologist, has done fieldwork with Spanish Americans in New Mexico, Latin Americans, Navajo, Hopi, Trukese, Western Mediterranean Arabs, and Iranians. During the 1950s he was director of the Point IV Training Program in the State Department, selecting Americans for work abroad both for the government and for private businesses. His interest in human communication includes studying the way persons use behavior and space as language. His best-known books include The Hidden Dimension, Beyond Culture, *and* The Silent Language. *This selection from his work appeared in* Scientific American *in 1955.*

> The Goops they lick their fingers
> and the Goops they lick their knives;
> They spill their broth on the table cloth—
> Oh, they lead disgusting lives.
> The Goops they talk while eating,
> and loud and fast they chew;
> And that is why I'm glad that I
> am not a Goop—are you?

In Gelett Burgess' classic on the Goops we have an example of what anthropologists call "an enculturating device"—a means of conditioning the young to life in our society.[1] Having been taught the lesson of the goops from childhood (with or without the aid of Mr. Burgess) Americans are shocked when they go abroad and discover whole groups of people behaving like goops—eating with their fingers, making noises and talking while eating. When this happens, we may (1) remark on the barbarousness or quaintness of the "natives" (a term cordially disliked all over the world) or (2) try to discover the nature and meaning of the differences in behavior. One rather quickly discovers that what is good manners in one context may be bad in the next. It is to this point that I would like to address myself.

The subject of manners is complex; if it were not, there would not be so

---

[1]Gelett Burgess (1866–1947): American humorist; the verses quoted are from *Goops and How to Be Them* (1900). [Eds.]

many injured feelings and so much misunderstanding in international circles everywhere. In any society the code of manners tends to sum up the culture—to be a frame of reference for all behavior. Emily Post goes so far as to say: "There is not a single thing that we do, or say, or choose, or use, or even think, that does not follow or break one of the exactions of taste, or tact, or ethics of good manners, or etiquette—call it what you will."[2] Unfortunately many of the most important standards of acceptable behavior in different cultures are elusive: they are intangible, undefined and unwritten.

An Arab diplomat who recently arrived in the U.S. from the Middle East 3 attended a banquet which lasted several hours. When it was over, he met a fellow countryman outside and suggested they go get something to eat, as he was starving. His friend, who had been in this country for some time, laughed and said: "But, Habib, didn't you know that if you say, 'No, thank you,' they think you really don't want any?" In an Arab country etiquette dictates that the person being served must refuse the proffered dish several times, while his host urges him repeatedly to partake. The other side of the coin is that Americans in the Middle East, until they learn better, stagger away from banquets having eaten more than they want or is good for them.

When a public-health movie of a baby being bathed in a bathinette was 4 shown in India recently, the Indian women who saw it were visibly offended. They wondered how people could be so inhuman as to bathe a child in stagnant (not running) water. Americans in Iran soon learn not to indulge themselves in their penchant for chucking infants under the chin and remarking on the color of their eyes, for the mother has to pay to have the "evil eye" removed. We also learn that in the Middle East you don't hand people things with your left hand, because it is unclean. In India we learn not to touch another person, and in Southeast Asia we learn that the head is sacred.

In the interest of intercultural understanding various U.S. Government agen- 5 cies have hired anthropologists from time to time as technical experts. The State Department especially has pioneered in the attempt to bring science to bear on this difficult and complex problem. It began by offering at the Foreign Service Institute an intensive four-week course for Point 4 technicians. Later these facilities were expanded to include other foreign service personnel.

The anthropologist's job here is not merely to call attention to obvious taboos 6 or to coach people about types of thoughtless behavior that have very little to do with culture. One should not need an anthropologist to point out, for instance, that it is insulting to ask a foreigner: "How much is this in real money?" Where technical advice is most needed is in the interpretation of the unconscious aspects of a culture—the things people do automatically without being aware of the full implications of what they have done. For example, an ambassador who has been kept waiting for more than half an hour by a foreign

---

[2]Emily Post (1873–1960): American authority on etiquette. [Eds.]

visitor needs to understand that if his visitor "just mutters an apology" this is not necessarily an insult. The time system in the foreign country may be composed of different basic units, so that the visitor is not as late as he may appear to us. You must know the time system of the country to know at what point apologies are really due.

Twenty years of experience in working with Americans in foreign lands convinces me that the real problem in preparing them to work overseas is not with taboos, which they catch on to rather quickly, but rather with whole congeries of habits and attitudes which anthropologists have only recently begun to describe systematically. 7

Can you remember tying your shoes this morning? Could you give the rules for when it is proper to call another person by his first name? Could you describe the gestures you make in conversation? These examples illustrate how much of our behavior is "out of awareness," and how easy it is to get into trouble in another culture. 8

Nobody is continually aware of the quality of his own voice, the subtleties of stress and intonation that color the meaning of his words or the posture and distance he assumes in talking to another person. Yet all these are taken as cues to the real nature of an utterance, regardless of what the words say. A simple illustration is the meaning in the tone of voice. In the U.S. we raise our voices not only when we are angry but also when we want to emphasize a point, when we are more than a certain distance from another person, when we are concluding a meeting and so on. But to the Chinese, for instance, overloudness of the voice is most characteristically associated with anger and loss of self-control. Whenever we become really interested in something, they are apt to have the feeling we are angry, in spite of many years' experience with us. Very likely most of their interviews with us, however cordial, seem to end on a sour note when we exclaim heartily: "WELL, I'M CERTAINLY GLAD YOU DROPPED IN, MR. WONG." 9

The Latin Americans, who as a rule take business seriously, do not understand our mixing business with informality and recreation. We like to put our feet up on the desk. If a stranger enters the office, we take our feet down. If it turns out that the stranger and we have a lot in common, up go the feet again—a cue to the other fellow that we feel at ease. If the office boy enters, the feet stay up; if the boss enters and our relationship with him is a little strained at the moment, they go down. To a Latin American this whole behavior is shocking. All he sees in it is insult or just plain rudeness. 10

Differences in attitudes toward space—what would be territoriality in lower forms of life—raise a number of other interesting points. U.S. women who go to live in Latin America all complain about the "waste" of space in the houses. On the other hand, U.S. visitors to the Middle East complain about crowding, in the houses and on the streetcars and buses. Everywhere we go space seems to be distorted. When we see a gardener in the mountains of Italy planting a 11 single row on each of six separate terraces, we wonder why he spreads out his crop so that he has to spend half his time climbing up and down. We overlook the complex chain of communication that would be broken if he didn't cultivate alongside his brothers and his cousin and if he didn't pass his neighbors and talk to them as he moves from one terrace to the next.

A colleague of mine was caught in a snowstorm while traveling with companions in the mountains of Lebanon. They stopped at the next house and asked to be put up for the night. The house had only one room. Instead of distributing the guests around the room, their host placed them next to the pallet where he slept with his wife—so close that they almost touched the couple. To have done otherwise in that country would have been unnatural and unfriendly. In the U.S. we distribute ourselves more evenly than many other people. We have strong feelings about touching and being crowded; in a streetcar, bus or elevator we draw ourselves in. Toward a person who relaxes and lets himself come into full contact with others in a crowded place we usually feel reactions that could not be printed on this page. It takes years for us to train our children not to crowd and lean on us. We tell them to stand up, that it is rude to slouch, not to sit so close or not to "breathe down our necks." After a while they get the point. By the time we Americans are in our teens we can tell what relationship exists between a man and woman by how they walk or sit together. 12

In Latin America, where touching is more common and the basic units of space seem to be smaller, the wide automobiles made in the U.S. pose problems. People don't know where to sit. North Americans are disturbed by how close the Latin Americans stand when they converse. "Why do they have to get so close when they talk to you?" "They're so pushy." "I don't know what it is, but it's something in the way they stand next to you." And so on. The Latin Americans, for their part, complain that people in the U.S. are distant and cold—*retraídos* (withdrawing and uncommunicative). 13

An analysis of the handling of space during conversations shows the following: A U.S. male brought up in the Northeast stands 18 to 20 inches away when talking face to face to a man he does not know very well; talking to a woman under similar circumstances, he increases the distance about four inches. A distance of only eight to 13 inches between males is considered either very aggressive or indicative of a closeness of a type we do not ordinarily want to think about. Yet in many parts of Latin America and the Middle East distances which are almost sexual in connotation are the only ones at which people can talk comfortably. In Cuba, for instance, there is nothing suggestive in a man's talking to an educated woman at a distance of 13 inches. If you are a Latin American, talking to a North American at the distance he insists on maintaining is like trying to talk across a room. 14

To get a more vivid idea of this problem of the comfortable distance, try starting a conversation with a person eight or 10 feet away or one separated from you by a wide obstruction in a store or other public place. Any normally enculturated person can't help trying to close up the space, even to the extent of 15 climbing over benches or walking around tables to arrive within comfortable distance. U.S. businessmen working in Latin America try to prevent people from getting uncomfortably close by barricading themselves behind desks, typewriters or the like, but their Latin American office visitors will often climb up on desks or over chairs and put up with loss of dignity in order to establish a spatial context in which interaction can take place for them.

The interesting thing is that neither party is specifically aware of what is wrong when the distance is not right. They merely have vague feelings of discomfort or anxiety. As the Latin American approaches and the North American backs away, both parties take offense without knowing why. When a North American, having had the problem pointed out to him, permits the Latin American to get close enough, he will immediately notice that the latter seems much more at ease. 16

My own studies of space and time have engendered considerable cooperation and interest on the part of friends and colleagues. One case recently reported to me had to do with a group of seven-year-olds in a crowded Sunday-school classroom. The children kept fighting. Without knowing quite what was involved, the teacher had them moved to a larger room. The fighting stopped. It is interesting to speculate as to what would have happened had the children been moved to a smaller room. 17

The embarrassment about intimacy in space applies also to the matter of addressing people by name. Finding the proper distance in the use of names is even more difficult than in space, because the rules for first-naming are unbelievably complex. As a rule we tend to stay on the "mister" level too long with Latins and some others, but very often we swing into first naming too quickly, which amounts to talking down to them. Whereas in the U.S. we use Mr. with the surname, in Latin America the first and last names are used together and señor (Sr.) is a title. Thus when one says, "My name is Sr. So-and-So," it is interpreted to mean, "I am the Honorable, his Excellency So-and-So." It is no wonder that when we stand away, barricade ourselves behind our desks (usually a reflection of status) and call ourselves mister, our friends to the south wonder about our so-called "good neighbor" policy and think of us as either high-hat or unbelievably rude. Fortunately most North Americans learn some of these things after living in Latin America for a while, but the aversion to being touched and to touching sometimes persists after 15 or more years of residence and even under such conditions as intermarriage. 18

The difference in sense of time is another thing of which we are not aware. An Iranian, for instance, is not taught that it is rude to be late in the same way that we in the U.S. are. In a general way we are conscious of this, but we fail to realize that their time system is structured differently from ours. The different cultures simply place different values on the time units. 19

Thus let us take as a typical case of the North European time system (which has regional variations) the situation in the urban eastern U.S. A middle-class business man meeting another of equivalent rank will ordinarily be aware of 20 being two minutes early or late. If he is three minutes late, it will be noted as significant but usually neither will say anything. If four minutes late, he will mutter something by way of apology; at five minutes he will utter a full sentence of apology. In other words, the major unit is a five-minute block. Fifteen minutes is the smallest significant period for all sorts of arrangements and it is used very commonly. A half hour of course is very significant, and if you spend three quarters of an hour or an hour, either the business you transact or the relationship must be important. Normally it is an insult to keep a public figure or a person of significantly higher status than yourself waiting even two or three minutes, though the person of higher position can keep you waiting or even break an appointment.

Now among urban Arabs in the Eastern Mediterranean, to take an illustrative   21
case of another time system, the unit that corresponds to our five-minute period is 15 minutes. Thus when an Arab arrives nearly 30 minutes after the set time, by his reckoning he isn't even "10 minutes" late yet (in our time units). Stated differently, the Arab's tardiness will not amount to one significant period (15 minutes in our system). An American normally will wait no longer than 30 minutes (two significant periods) for another person to turn up in the middle of the day. Thereby he often unwittingly insults people in the Middle East who want to be his friends.

How long is one expected to stay when making a duty call at a friend's house   22
in the U.S.? While there are regional variations, I have observed that the minimum is very close to 45 minutes, even in the face of pressing commitments elsewhere, such as a roast in the oven. We may think we can get away in 30 minutes by saying something about only stopping for "a minute," but usually we discover that we don't feel comfortable about leaving until 45 minutes have elapsed. I am referring to afternoon social calls; evening calls last much longer and operate according to a different system. In Arab countries an American paying a duty call at the house of a desert sheik causes consternation if he gets up to leave after half a day. There a duty call lasts three days—the first day to prepare the feast, the second for the feast itself and the third to taper off and say farewell. In the first half day the sheik has barely had time to slaughter the sheep for the feast. The guest's departure would leave the host frustrated.

There is a well-known story of a tribesman who came to Kabul, the capital   23
of Afghanistan, to meet his brother. Failing to find him, he asked the merchants in the market place to tell his brother where he could be found if the brother showed up. A year later the tribesman returned and looked again. It developed that he and his brother had agreed to meet in Kabul but had failed to specify what year! If the Afghan time system were structured similarly to our own, which it apparently is not, the brother would not offer a full sentence of apology until he was five years late.

Informal units of time such as "just a minute," "a while," "later," "a long   24
time," "a spell," "a long, long time," "years" and so on provide us with the

culturological equivalent of Evil-Eye Fleegle's "double-whammy" (in *Li'l Abner*). Yet these expressions are not as imprecise as they seem. Any American who has worked in an office with someone else for six months can usually tell within five minutes when that person will be back if he says, "I'll be gone for a while." It is simply a matter of learning from experience the individual's system of time indicators. A reader who is interested in communications theory can fruitfully speculate for a while on the very wonderful way in which culture provides the means whereby the receiver puts back all the redundant material that was stripped from such a message. Spelled out, the message might go somewhat as follows: "I am going downtown to see So-and-So about the Such-and-Such contract, but I don't know what the traffic conditions will be like or how long it will take me to get a place to park nor do I know what shape So-and-So will be in today, but taking all this into account I think I will be out of the office about an hour but don't like to commit myself, so if anyone calls you can say I'm not sure how long I will be; in any event I expect to be back before 4 o'clock."

Few of us realize how much we rely on built-in patterns to interpret messages   25
of this sort. An Iranian friend of mine who came to live in the U.S. was hurt and puzzled for the first few years. The new friends he met and liked would say on parting: "Well, I'll see you later." He mournfully complained: "I kept expecting to see them, but the 'later' never came." Strangely enough we ourselves are exasperated when a Mexican can't tell us precisely what he means when he uses the expression *mañana*.[3]

The role of the anthropologist in preparing people for service overseas is to   26
open their eyes and sensitize them to the subtle qualities of behavior—tone of voice, gestures, space and time relationships—that so often build up feelings of frustration and hostility in other people with a different culture. Whether we are going to live in a particular foreign country or travel in many, we need a frame of reference that will enable us to observe and learn the significance of differences in manners. Progress is being made in this anthropological study, but it is also showing us how little is known about human behavior.

QUESTIONS

1. Review Hall's explanation of where the real problem lies in behavior that is " 'out of awareness' " (paragraph 8). What does he mean by that phrase? How effectively does he define it? What types of behavior are "out of awareness"?

2. Hall's essay is full of illustrations. What techniques does he use to make sure a reader understands the point of each illustration?

3. What are some examples of behavior that is "out of awareness" in the social world you know best?

---

[3]*mañana*: literally, "tomorrow" in Spanish. [Eds.]

Edward T. Hall

4. Place yourself so that you can observe social behavior in a familiar setting where you are comfortable. Explain what you find there. What are some of the controlling features of behavior, especially that which is "out of awareness"? What happens when someone seems to violate an expectation for behavior?

5. Place yourself again so that you can observe social behavior, but this time select a less familiar setting where you may be less at home with the expectations. Again explain what you observe, concentrating on what you take to be the most important features of behavior and how you were able to identify them.

6. What is the relation between our expectations about behaviors such as Hall describes and our expectations of behaviors in speech and writing? In what ways is Hall describing what could be called a grammar of behavior in certain situations? Write a paper that develops the analogy between manners and grammar.

7. Imagine that you are devising a college course designed to make students "literate" in the "silent languages" Hall describes. Imagine as ideal a course as you can, one that teaches those things that you think are most worth knowing. What would happen in that course? Write out a plan for the course as you imagine it.

GOVERNMENT ACCESS TO PERSONAL RECORDS AND "PRIVATE PAPERS"
U.S. Government Privacy Protection Study Commission

This is a government document, the report of a commission. Its author, then, is a group or committee, but no group can write anything as a group. One hand must hold the pen, or one person sit at the keyboard and punch out the words. Still, what is written must speak for the group, as the group wishes. A government commission must have a serious, reasonable voice. It must document its case with citations. It should not embarrass the government. This particular report is taken from a larger study, a book called Personal Privacy in an Information Society *(1977), in which these pages appear as the first part of chapter 9. We have left the original documentation (footnotes) in place, except for some cross-references to other chapters of the book itself.*

Discussion of the need to protect individuals from threats to personal privacy 1
often conjures up ominous images of government agents conducting surreptitious investigations and compiling dossiers. Such images come forcefully to mind when one is concerned, as the Commission is, with preventing improper inquiry into and disclosure of records about individuals. While the tendency to equate threats to personal privacy with government action, and government action with clandestine police operations, is understandable, the evidence uncovered in the Commission's inquiry shows that such equations are not necessarily accurate.

The improper collection and use of information about an individual present 2
as difficult problems when private institutions fail to observe the legitimate rights and expectations of the individual as when government fails; but, governmental intrusions on personal privacy have a longer and more dramatic history, both in law and in the public mind. Generous portions of the Bill of Rights were fashioned two centuries ago to assure that Americans would not again suffer the unwarranted intrusions by government which, in John Adams' mind, provided the spark that ignited revolution.[1] Protection from government intrusion, as

---

[1]Hiller Zobel and Kinvin Wroth (eds.), *Legal Papers of John Adams*, (Harvard University Press, Cambridge: 1965) Vol. 2, Case No. 44, pp. 106–144.

exemplified in the Fourth and Fifth Amendments, has long been the primary public focus of privacy protection.[2] The desire to assure for the individual the quiet enjoyment of his home in part justifies such protection; but in equal part, individual rights securing privacy are also intended to safeguard the personal papers and other documentation that can illuminate the associations, interests, attitudes, and beliefs as well as actions of an individual.[3] Such information is valuable in a variety of forms of government coercion, ranging from criminal prosecution to less legitimate activities. Indeed, this second aspect of personal privacy is the focus of Fourth Amendment protection, the "search and seizure" standards which never fail to stir public interest and win extensive press coverage when debated in the Supreme Court.

These well publicized elements of Constitutional controversy and national 3 history, perhaps inevitably, tend to focus on problems of law enforcement officers improperly gaining access to one's home or one's private records. Along with this emphasis on invasions of privacy by law enforcement comes a tendency to treat the issues as legal issues rather than policy ones, because, after all, the battleground for resolving those issues has traditionally been the courts. Earlier chapters of this report should dispel the impression that dangers to personal privacy are only products of government action, but the equation of government action with law enforcement activity needs to be tempered and the notion needs to be dispelled that resolving the basic privacy issues raised by government action demands a close attention to legal niceties.

The question of law enforcement, and the peculiar powers and opportunities 4 to acquire information given government for that purpose, raise uniquely sensitive problems. Nonetheless, government's expanding role as regulator and distributor of largess gives it new ways to intrude, creating new privacy protection problems. By opening more avenues for collecting information and more decision-making forums in which it can employ that information, government has enormously broadened its opportunities to embarrass, harass, and injure the individual. These new avenues (and needs) for collecting information, particularly when coupled with applications of modern information technologies, multiply the dangers of official abuse against which the Constitution seeks to protect. Recent history reminds us that these are real, not mythical, dangers.

The concern about governmental abuse which underlies traditional protec- 5 tions against government intrusion on personal privacy provides a focal point for exploring the particular balancing of interests which faced the Commission in reaching its recommendations on government access to private records as well as for emphasizing the need *not* to confine such deliberations within the

---

[2]John Eger, "Foreward" to Kent Greenawalt, *Legal Protections of Privacy*, Office of Telecommunications Policy (Washington, D.C.: 1976); Thomas I. Emerson, *The System of Freedom of Expression*, (New York: Vintage, 1970) pp. 544–48.

[3]See Note, "Formalism, Legal Realism, and Constitutionally Protected Privacy Under the Fourth and Fifth Amendments," 90 *Harv. L. Rev.* 945 (1977).

narrow precincts of law. Though solutions must finally be fashioned into law, the choices made in arriving at such solutions are not mere legal choices; they are fundamental public-policy decisions—social and political value choices of the most basic kind.

The balance to be struck is an old one; it reflects the tension between individual liberty and social order. The sovereign needs information to maintain order; the individual needs to be able to protect his independence and autonomy should the sovereign overreach. The peculiarly American notions of legally limited government and the protections in the Bill of Rights provide broad theoretical standards for reaching a workable balance. But the world has a way of disrupting the particular balance struck in past generations; the theory may remain unaltered but circumstances change, requiring a reworking of the mechanisms which maintained the balance in the past.

Current threats to personal privacy stem largely from changes in the way individuals go about their day-to-day business. The Commission's inquiry did discover, however, that some threats are the result of government rewriting the rules of the game without letting the rest of the players know. Both circumstances combine to erode the effectiveness of traditional protections for personal privacy and individual liberty.

Traditionally, the records an individual might keep on his daily activities, financial transactions, or net worth were beyond government reach unless the government could establish probable cause to believe a crime had been committed. If government were merely suspicious and wanted to investigate, such records were unavailable. The legal standards that protected them evolved in a world where such records were almost universally in the actual possession of the individual. Reflecting that reality, the law only barred government from seizing records in the possession of the individual.[4] As the record compiled by the Commission proves, that world no longer exists. Third parties, institutions or persons other than the individual, now keep a great many records documenting various activities of a particular individual. Indeed, these third parties keep records about the individual he would not ordinarily have kept in the past. Records for life and health insurance, for example, are repositories of highly intimate personal data, financial and familial as well as medical, which were virtually unknown until recent decades.

Financial records, particularly the information retained in demand deposit accounts, provide another instance where the changing patterns of life took the possession of information about himself out of the control of the individual. Of great importance, checking account records present a situation where alterations in record-keeping patterns have been exacerbated by government action. Until recently the account record maintained by one's bank frequently did not include

---

[4]*Boyd v. United States*, 116 U.S. 616 (1886); *Olmstead v. United States*, 277 U.S. 438, 474 (1928) (Brandeis, J., dissenting).

a copy of each individual check, with the payee, date, and often place and reason for drawing the check clearly noted; rather, the record might simply have noted the dollar amounts of transactions and the date of processing by the bank.[5] The Bank Secrecy Act of 1970 and the Treasury regulations which give that law effect, however, now *require* depository institutions to keep copies of the checks an individual uses to draw on the funds in his account. The checking account has become an intimate mirror of individual activity in a way it never was before the Bank Secrecy Act.

The existence of records about an individual that are not in his possession   10
poses serious privacy protection problems, especially when government seeks access to those records. Record keepers can, often do, and sometimes must, disclose records about an individual to government without seeking the individual's approval, whether the disclosure is at the request of government or through the initiative of the record keeper; and, frequently no record of the disclosure is ever made. A government request made informally through a personal visit to the record keeper or by a telephone call, for example, may leave no trace in any record. The individual may never know that agents of the government have inspected his records. Except in a limited number of situations, neither the record keeper nor the government is obliged to notify him that his records were opened to government scrutiny. Even if the individual is given notice and documentation of the disclosure, he has no legal right to challenge the propriety of government access to his records, despite the possibility that the government agent might have been on a "fishing expedition."[6]

Historically, the courts have justified relatively unrestricted government ac-   11
cess to records on individual activity kept by third parties by regarding such information as independent documentation of voluntary transactions between the individual and the record keeper.[7] Coupled with this concept of voluntariness, such records have not been viewed, and until recently rightly so, as the sorts of private records and personal papers that merit special protection because they illuminate an individual's associations, interest, attitudes, and beliefs, as well as actions. The privacy protections that help secure the independence and autonomy of the individual were not considered necessary. Courts and the public were comfortable with a legal standard that protected only records in the possession of the individual.

---

[5]As Representative Patman explained during the debates preceding passage of the Bank Secrecy Act, a primary purpose of the Act was to "make uniform and *adequate* the present record-keeping practices, or *lack of record-keeping practices*, by domestic banks and other financial institutions," (emphasis added) 116 *Cong. Rec.* 16951 (1970); also, see remarks of Representative Stark, *Administrative Summons and Antidisclosure Provisions of the Tax Reform Act of 1976*, Hearings before the Subcommittee on Oversight of the Committee on Ways and Means, U.S. House of Representatives, 95th Congress, 1st Session, ser. 95–4, at 26 (February 24, 1977).

[6]See, e.g., *United States v. Miller*, 425 U.S. 435 (1976); *Kelley v. United States*, 536 F.2d 897 (9th Cir. 1976); compare, *Donaldson v. United States*, 400 U.S. 517 (1971).

[7]*Ibid.*

Today, the law remains unchanged even though new sorts of personal records, 12
created to meet new circumstances, sometimes generated by government requirements, are vulnerable to seizure or inspection by government without the
individual being able to intervene. A record keeper may volunteer information
about an individual to government; or the Executive branch of government can
compel production of such records with little trouble and often without super-
vision by the judiciary or anyone else. Recently, the courts have begun to doubt
the assumptions of voluntariness upon which they rest their refusal to extend
basic constitutional protections to an individual when government seeks disclosure of records held by a third-party record keeper. Indeed, some judges have
taken tentative notice of the realities of contemporary record keeping and the
danger that allowing government to acquire such "third party" records might
disclose "intimate areas of personal affairs" protected by the Fourth and Fifth
Amendments.[8]

Nonetheless, to wait on the courts to reweave the fabric of law and create 13
protections for the individual is to adopt a policy of uncertain outcome. One
cannot be sure the courts will become more flexible. One can be sure, however,
that if the courts do extend protections, their efforts will be slow and piecemeal.
Yet the society is faced with problems that demand decision and resolution.
The world has altered and continues to change with increasing rapidity. As the
Commission's study of Electronic Funds Transfer Systems suggests, existing
problems with government access to records will be exacerbated by future developments; they will not go away. Today, government has access to the most
revealing personal records about an individual; yet the individual has no ability
to thwart or even contest such access. Perhaps most important, they are situations in which the individual has no choice but to allow others to maintain
records about him. Not to enter into the relationships that generate individually
identifiable records would subject the vast majority of Americans to severe economic and social burdens, disrupting the ordinary course of their lives. Think,
for instances, of the time and effort necessary to pay all bills in person, not to
mention the risk involved in carrying enough cash to transact all personal business.

Further, and of increasing importance, there is little to impede government 14
access to records about individuals held by third parties, particularly records the
government requires third parties to keep. In its Depository and Lending Institution hearings, witnesses told the Commission that informal access to bank
records, i.e., access without a subpoena or summons, was a favorite tool of
government investigators. Indeed, the American Civil Liberties Union submitted testimony originally given before the House Judiciary Committee in July,
1975, which suggested that such informal or "voluntary" disclosure was "the
means by which government normally procures access to confidential bank

---

[8]*California Bankers Assn. v. Schultz*, 416 U.S. 21, 78 (1975) (Powell, J., concurring).

records."[9] The Internal Revenue Service testified that banks are usually cooperative in responding to a "friendly" summons.[10] Even when banks are somewhat less cooperative, however, little real impediment to government access occurs. Continental Illinois Bank, for example, seeks to notify the individual that his account records have been subpoenaed and does a "four corners" check of the validity of any summons received,[11] but . . . neither action by the bank gives any real assistance to the individual. And, the extent of concern exhibited by Continental Illinois for its customers is rare.

The Commission's hearings on the record-keeping practices of credit grantors   15
and depository and lending institutions and its survey of credit-card issuers indicate that a large proportion of private-sector financial record keepers lack any policy on government access, not to mention a policy as fair as that of the Continental Illinois Bank.[12] In addition, what is labeled "policy" is frequently little more than a grant of discretion—to notify or not, to determine the validity of a subpoena or not—given to an office manager or perhaps someone lower in the hierarchy. Some record keepers even seem to have a policy of *not* notifying the individual or reviewing the validity of the subpoena. Such lack of policy, however, should not be viewed as unkindly as a first reaction might suggest. As American Express testified in February, 1976, it did not notify customers as a matter of course because it could not see what good it would do.[13] Though its position was not particularly well received by the public, American Express was right; notice to the customer does little good. Even if notified, the individual can do little to hinder government access, however illegitimate the purposes or improper the procedures. The ground rules need to be changed if any good is to be done.

QUESTIONS

1. The thesis of this explanation, which moves it toward an argument, is expressed in its final sentence. That sentence has two main parts; explain each part in your own words. What would it mean if "any good" were done in the matter under discussion? What would be involved in changing "the ground rules"?

---

[9]Written Statement of Hope Eastman, Associate Director, ACLU, *Depository and Lending Institutions,* Hearings before the Privacy Protection Study Commission, April 22, 1976, p. 5 (hereinafter cited as "Depository and Lending Institutions Hearings").

[10]Testimony of the Internal Revenue Service, Depository and Lending Institutions Hearings, April 22, 1976, pp. 777–830, and particularly pp. 804–07.

[11]Testimony of Continental Illinois Bank and Trust Company, Depository and Lending Institutions Hearings, April 21, 1976, p. 277.

[12]See Chapter 2, "Consumer-Credit Relationship," section on "Disclosures to Government Agencies," particularly the discussion of the credit-card issuers' survey; also, generally, Depository and Lending Institutions Hearings, April 21–22, 1976.

[13]Testimony of American Express Company, *Credit-Card Issuers,* Hearings before the Privacy Protection Study Commission, February 11, 1976.

2. In the title of this essay, the expression *private papers* is in quotation marks. What do these marks signify in this context? What do they have to do with the explanation being made? What relationship between private papers and personal records is developed in the essay?

3. As we see by the end, this essay is making the case for changing the ground rules for "government access to personal records and 'private papers.' " This case depends, however, upon certain assumptions about the kinds of privacy that we value. State those assumptions in your own words. To what extent does this essay depend upon our agreeing about those values?

4. What tone does the opening paragraph establish? What expectations does it establish for the rest of the paper? How does the rest of the paper relate to the image it sets up?

5. The topic of personal records is not discussed specifically until paragraph 8. What is the topic of the first six paragraphs? What is the function of the seventh?

6. What is the function of the specific examples in paragraphs 14 and 15? How do the Continental Illinois Bank and American Express fit into the larger case being made? What does each of those companies represent or illustrate about the treatment of personal records?

7. This essay implies that certain procedures governing the handling of our records are open to question and that some decisions about conduct remain to be made. Write a short essay in which you explain either why the government should retain equal (or even increased) access to our financial records or why the regulations restricting such access should be made much tighter. Try to make clear the values upon which your opinion is based.

8. It is a curious fact of this essay that the records in question are almost entirely financial. Is that really the type of privacy about which you are most concerned? What other areas of private records or private information might also be important? What rules do you think should govern those cases?

ANTHROPOLOGY AS THICK DESCRIPTION
Clifford Geertz

Born in San Francisco in 1926, Clifford Geertz has degrees from Antioch College and Harvard University. He is presently at the Institute for Advanced Study, Princeton, New Jersey. A cultural anthropologist who has done fieldwork in Indonesia (Java and Bali) and Morocco, Geertz has published widely both in professional journals and less specialized places, such as the New York Review of Books. *The selection here is from his book* The Interpretation of Cultures *(1973) in which he has collected a sampling of fifteen years of his work. It is taken from his first chapter, where he begins to present a theory of culture and of the role of anthropology as a human study.*

In anthropology, or anyway social anthropology, what the practitioners do is ethnography. And it is in understanding what ethnography is, or more exactly *what doing ethnography is,* that a start can be made toward grasping what anthropological analysis amounts to as a form of knowledge. This, it must immediately be said, is not a matter of methods. From one point of view, that of the textbook, doing ethnography is establishing rapport, selecting informants, transcribing texts, taking genealogies, mapping fields, keeping a diary, and so on. But it is not these things, techniques and received procedures, that define the enterprise. What defines it is the kind of intellectual effort it is: an elaborate venture in, to borrow a notion from Gilbert Ryle, "thick description." 1

Ryle's discussion of "thick description" appears in two recent essays of his (now reprinted in the second volume of his *Collected Papers*) addressed to the general question of what, as he puts it, *"Le Penseur"* is doing: "Thinking and Reflecting" and "The Thinking of Thoughts." Consider, he says, two boys rapidly contracting the eyelids of their right eyes. In one, this is an involuntary twitch; in the other, a conspiratorial signal to a friend. The two movements are, as movements, identical; from an I-am-a-camera, "phenomenalistic" observation of them alone, one could not tell which was twitch and which was wink, or indeed whether both or either was twitch or wink. Yet the difference, however unphotographable, between a twitch and a wink is vast; as anyone unfortunate enough to have had the first taken for the second knows. The winker is communicating, and indeed communicating in a quite precise and special way: (1) deliberately, (2) to someone in particular, (3) to impart a particular message, 2

(4) according to a socially established code, and (5) without cognizance of the rest of the company. As Ryle points out, the winker has now done two things, contracted his eyelids and winked, while the twitcher has done only one, contracted his eyelids. Contracting your eyelids on purpose when there exists a public code in which so doing counts as a conspiratorial signal *is* winking. That's all there is to it: a speck of behavior, a fleck of culture, and—*voilà!*—a gesture.

That, however, is just the beginning. Suppose, he continues, there is a third boy, who, "to give malicious amusement to his cronies," parodies the first boy's wink, as amateurish, clumsy, obvious, and so on. He, of course, does this in the same way the second boy winked and the first twitched: by contracting his right eyelids. Only this boy is neither winking nor twitching, he is parodying someone else's, as he takes it, laughable, attempt at winking. Here, too, a socially established code exists (he will "wink" laboriously, overobviously, perhaps adding a grimace—the usual artifices of the clown); and so also does a message. Only now it is not conspiracy but ridicule that is in the air. If the others think he is actually winking, his whole project misfires as completely, though with somewhat different results, as if they think he is twitching. One can go further: uncertain of his mimicking abilities, the would-be satirist may practice at home before the mirror, in which case he is not twitching, winking, or parodying, but rehearsing; though so far as what a camera, a radical behaviorist, or a believer in protocol sentences would record he is just rapidly contracting his right eyelids like all the others. Complexities are possible, if not practically without end, at least logically so. The original winker might, for example, actually have been fake-winking, say, to mislead outsiders into imagining there was a conspiracy afoot when there in fact was not, in which case our descriptions of what the parodist is parodying and the rehearser rehearsing of course shift accordingly. But the point is that between what Ryle calls the "thin description" of what the rehearser (parodist, winker, twitcher . . .) is doing ("rapidly contracting his right eyelids") and the "thick description" of what he is doing ("practicing a burlesque of a friend faking a wink to deceive an innocent into thinking a conspiracy is in motion") lies the object of ethnography: a stratified hierarchy of meaningful structures in terms of which twitches, winks, fake-winks, parodies, rehearsals of parodies are produced, perceived, and interpreted, and without which they would not (not even the zero-form twitches, which, *as a cultural category*, are as much nonwinks as winks are nontwitches) in fact exist, no matter what anyone did or didn't do with his eyelids.

Like so many of the little stories Oxford philosophers like to make up for themselves, all this winking, fake-winking, burlesque-fake-winking, rehearsed-burlesque-fake-winking, may seem a bit artificial. In way of adding a more empirical note, let me give, deliberately unpreceded by any prior explanatory comment at all, a not untypical excerpt from my own field journal to demonstrate that, however evened off for didactic purposes, Ryle's example presents an image only too exact of the sort of piled-up structures of inference and

Clifford Geertz

implication through which an ethnographer is continually trying to pick his way:

The French [the informant said] had only just arrived. They set up twenty or so 5
small forts between here, the town, and the Marmusha area up in the middle of
the mountains, placing them on promontories so they could survey the countryside. But for all this they couldn't guarantee safety, especially at night, so although
the *mezrag*, trade-pact, system was supposed to be legally abolished it in fact
continued as before.

One night, when Cohen (who speaks fluent Berber), was up there, at Mar- 6
musha, two other Jews who were traders to a neighboring tribe came by to purchase
some goods from him. Some Berbers, from yet another neighboring tribe, tried
to break into Cohen's place, but he fired his rifle in the air. (Traditionally, Jews
were not allowed to carry weapons; but at this period things were so unsettled
many did so anyway.) This attracted the attention of the French and the marauders
fled.

The next night, however, they came back, one of them disguised as a woman 7
who knocked on the door with some sort of a story. Cohen was suspicious and
didn't want to let "her" in, but the other Jews said, "oh, it's all right, it's only a
woman." So they opened the door and the whole lot came pouring in. They killed
the two visiting Jews, but Cohen managed to barricade himself in an adjoining
room. He heard the robbers planning to burn him alive in the shop after they
removed his goods, and so he opened the door and, laying about him wildly with
a club, managed to escape through a window.

He went up to the fort, then, to have his wounds dressed, and complained to 8
the local commandant, one Captain Dumari, saying he wanted his '*ar*—i.e., four
or five times the value of the merchandise stolen from him. The robbers were
from a tribe which had not yet submitted to French authority and were in open
rebellion against it, and he wanted authorization to go with his *mezrag*-holder,
the Marmusha tribal *sheikh*, to collect the indemnity that, under traditional rules,
he had coming to him. Captain Dumari couldn't officially give him permission
to do this, because of the French prohibition of the *mezrag* relationship, but he
gave him verbal authorization, saying, "If you get killed, it's your problem."

So the *sheikh*, the Jew, and a small company of armed Marmushans went off 9
ten or fifteen kilometers up into the rebellious area, where there were of course
no French, and, sneaking up, captured the thief-tribe's shepherd and stole its
herds. The other tribe soon came riding out on horses after them, armed with
rifles and ready to attack. But when they saw who the "sheep thieves" were, they
thought better of it and said, "all right, we'll talk." They couldn't really deny what
had happened—that some of their men had robbed Cohen and killed the two
visitors—and they weren't prepared to start the serious feud with the Marmusha a
scuffle with the invading party would bring on. So the two groups talked, and
talked, and talked, there on the plain amid the thousands of sheep, and decided
finally on five-hundred-sheep damages. The two armed Berber groups then lined
up on their horses at opposite ends of the plain, with the sheep herded between
them, and Cohen, in his black gown, pillbox hat, and flapping slippers, went out

alone among the sheep, picking out, one by one and at his own good speed, the best ones for his payment.

So Cohen got his sheep and drove them back to Marmusha. The French, up   10
in their fort, heard them coming from some distance ("Ba, ba, ba" said Cohen, happily, recalling the image) and said, "What the hell is that?" And Cohen said, "That is my 'ar." The French couldn't believe he had actually done what he said he had done, and accused him of being a spy for the rebellious Berbers, put him in prison, and took his sheep. In the town, his family, not having heard from him in so long a time, thought he was dead. But after a while the French released him and he came back home, but without his sheep. He then went to the Colonel in the town, the Frenchman in charge of the whole region, to complain. But the Colonel said, "I can't do anything about the matter. It's not my problem."

Quoted raw, a note in a bottle, this passage conveys, as any similar one   11
similarly presented would do, a fair sense of how much goes into ethnographic description of even the most elemental sort—how extraordinarily "thick" it is. In finished anthropological writings . . this fact—that what we call our data are really our own constructions of other people's constructions of what they and their compatriots are up to—is obscured because most of what we need to comprehend a particular event, ritual, custom, idea, or whatever is insinuated as background information before the thing itself is directly examined. (Even to reveal that this little drama took place in the highlands of central Morocco in 1912—and was recounted there in 1968—is to determine much of our understanding of it.) There is nothing particularly wrong with this, and it is in any case inevitable. But it does lead to a view of anthropological research as rather more of an observational and rather less of an interpretive activity than it really is. Right down at the factual base, the hard rock, insofar as there is any, of the whole enterprise, we are already explicating: and worse, explicating explications. Winks upon winks upon winks.

Analysis, then, is sorting out the structures of signification—what Ryle called   12
established codes, a somewhat misleading expression, for it makes the enterprise sound too much like that of the cipher clerk when it is much more like that of the literary critic—and determining their social ground and import. Here, in our text, such sorting would begin with distinguishing the three unlike frames of interpretation ingredient in the situation, Jewish, Berber, and French, and would then move on to show how (and why) at that time, in that place, their copresence produced a situation in which systematic misunderstanding reduced traditional form to social farce. What tripped Cohen up, and with him the whole, ancient pattern of social and economic relationships within which he functioned, was a confusion of tongues.

I shall come back to this too-compacted aphorism later, as well as to the   13
details of the text itself. The point for now is only that ethnography is thick description. What the ethnographer is in fact faced with—except when (as, of course, he must do) he is pursuing the more automatized routines of data

371

Clifford Geertz

collection—is a multiplicity of complex conceptual structures, many of them superimposed upon or knotted into one another, which are at once strange, irregular, and inexplicit, and which he must contrive somehow first to grasp and then to render. And this is true at the most down-to-earth, jungle field work levels of his activity: interviewing informants, observing rituals, eliciting kin terms, tracing property lines, censusing households . . . writing his journal. Doing ethnography is like trying to read (in the sense of "construct a reading of") a manuscript—foreign, faded, full of ellipses, incoherencies, suspicious emendations, and tendentious commentaries, but written not in conventionalized graphs of sound but in transient examples of shaped behavior.

QUESTIONS

1. Look up the word *ethnography* in the dictionary, and make sure you know what it means. What does the suffix *-graphy* mean, and how does that meaning play upon the idea of "thick description"?

2. Not only is there "thick description," according to Geertz, but there is also description that is "thin" (paragraph 3). What is the essential difference?

3. Reread paragraph 11, noticing the distinction between observation and interpretation near its end. Then consider the account of Cohen and the sheep. Where do you find interpretation going on in that passage, which seems, on the surface, to be a record of observation? What does Geertz mean by "our own constructions of other people's constructions of what they and their compatriots are up to" (paragraph 11)?

4. Although Geertz is explaining *ethnography*, he is also taking a stand. Paraphrase his argumentative position. Where does he identify the interpretive methods he most disagrees with?

5. Place yourself somewhere as an ethnographer in the field, and make a record of behavior you observe. Make it as thick as you can. Then report to the class, interpreting your observations sensibly.

6. Write a comment about the different kinds of writing you did for question 5. Try to distinguish observation from interpretation. Estimate the degree of "thickness" you accomplished and the influence of that thickness on the interpretations you made.

Sciences and Technologies

WHY THE
SKY IS BLUE
James Jeans

Sir James Jeans (1877–1946) was a British physicist and astronomer. Educated at Trinity College, Cambridge, he lectured there and was a professor of applied mathematics at Princeton University from 1905 to 1909. He later did research at Mount Wilson Observatory in California. Jeans won many honors for his work and wrote a number of scholarly and popular scientific books. The following selection is from The Stars in Their Courses *(1931), a written version of what began as a series of radio talks for an audience assumed to have no special knowledge of science.*

Imagine that we stand on any ordinary seaside pier, and watch the waves   1
rolling in and striking against the iron columns of the pier. Large waves pay
very little attention to the columns—they divide right and left and re-unite after
passing each column, much as a regiment of soldiers would if a tree stood in
their road; it is almost as though the columns had not been there. But the short
waves and ripples find the columns of the pier a much more formidable obstacle.
When the short waves impinge on the columns, they are reflected back and
spread as new ripples in all directions. To use the technical term, they are
"scattered." The obstacle provided by the iron columns hardly affects the long
waves at all, but scatters the short ripples.

James Jeans

We have been watching a sort of working model of the way in which sunlight 2
struggles through the earth's atmosphere. Between us on earth and outer space
the atmosphere interposes innumerable obstacles in the form of molecules of
air, tiny droplets of water, and small particles of dust. These are represented by
the columns of the pier.

The waves of the sea represent the sunlight. We know that sunlight is a blend 3
of lights of many colors—as we can prove for ourselves by passing it through a
prism, or even through a jug of water, or as Nature demonstrates to us when
she passes it through the raindrops of a summer shower and produces a rainbow.
We also know that light consists of waves, and that the different colors of light
are produced by waves of different lengths, red light by long waves and blue
light by short waves. The mixture of waves which constitutes sunlight has to
struggle through the obstacles it meets in the atmosphere, just as the mixture
of waves at the seaside has to struggle past the columns of the pier. And these
obstacles treat the light-waves much as the columns of the pier treat the sea-
waves. The long waves which constitute red light are hardly affected, but the
short waves which constitute blue light are scattered in all directions.

Thus, the different constituents of sunlight are treated in different ways as 4
they struggle through the earth's atmosphere. A wave of blue light may be
scattered by a dust particle, and turned out of its course. After a time a second
dust particle again turns it out of its course, and so on, until finally it enters
our eyes by a path as zigzag as that of a flash of lightning. Consequently the
blue waves of the sunlight enter our eyes from all directions. And that is why
the sky looks blue.

QUESTIONS

1. Analogy, the comparison of something familiar with something less familiar, occurs frequently in scientific explanation. Jeans introduces an analogy in his first paragraph. How does he develop that analogy as he develops his explanation?

2. The analogy Jeans provides enables him to explain the process by which the blue
light waves scatter throughout the sky. Hence he gives us a brief process analysis of that
phenomenon. Summarize that process in your own words.

3. Try rewriting this essay without the analogy. Remove paragraph 1 and all the
references to ocean waves and pier columns in paragraphs 2 and 3. How clear an
explanation is left?

4. Besides the sea waves, what other familiar examples does Jeans use in his explanation?

5. This piece opens with "Imagine that we stand. . . ." Suppose that every *we* was
replaced with a *you.*" How would the tone of the essay change?

6. While analogy can be effective in helping to explain difficult scientific concepts,
it can be equally useful in explaining and interpreting familiar things by juxtaposing
them in new ways. Suppose, for example, that you wished to explain to a friend why

you dislike a course you are taking. Select one of the following ideas for an analogy (or find a better one): a forced-labor camp, a three-ring circus, squirrels on a treadmill, a tea party, a group-therapy session. Think through the analogy to your course, and write a few paragraphs of explanation. Let Jeans's essay guide you in organizing your own.

SYNTAX AND
SEMANTICS
Bertram Raphael

Born in New York in 1936, Bertram Raphael has degrees from Rensselaer Polytechnic Institute, Brown University, and the Massachusetts Institute of Technology. He has published over twenty scientific articles and reviews, has been editor of Artificial Intelligence, *and has been a patrol leader of the Sierra Club Ski Patrol. He is currently Director of the Artificial Intelligence Center of the Stanford Research Institute. The following brief discussion of language appeared in his 1976 book,* The Thinking Computer: Mind Inside Matter.

The study of languages, both natural and artificial,[1] has traditionally been divided into two major areas: *syntax* and *semantics*. *Syntax* deals with the formal structure of the strings of symbols that make up the sentences of the language, without regard for their meanings. The elementary symbols of the language may be combined only in certain ways, as prescribed by a set of rules called the *grammar* of the language. The basic task for syntactic analysis is to tell which strings of symbols are grammatical, i.e., legitimately belong to the language, and which are not. A musician can play only grammatical music; a computer can compile only grammatical FORTRAN.[2] Figure 1 shows some examples of grammatical and ungrammatical samples of well-known artificial languages.   1

Semantics refers to the meanings of the symbols and of the grammatical symbol-strings of the language. The semantics of a musical score consists of tones, durations, and sound qualities; the semantics of a computer program consists of arithmetic and symbolic operations taking place in the registers of a computer. Since ungrammatical expressions seldom have semantic interpretations, we usually study formal languages in two sequential phases. First, syntactic analysis determines whether the expression is grammatical; then, if it is grammatical, semantic analysis determines what it means. (In the computer-language example, this separation is especially clear: a compiler operates in an almost purely syntactic manner,[3] and only at "run time," when the results of the compilation are executed, does the semantics emerge.)   2

---

[1]artificial language: a language developed from a set of rules determined before the language is put into use. [Eds.]

[2]FORTRAN: an acronym for Formula Translator, a high-level computer language. [Eds.]

[3]compiler: a computer program that translates programs written in a high-level source language into a language suitable for a given computer. [Eds.]

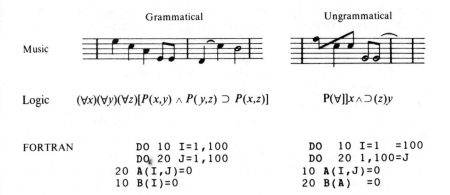

FIGURE 1. Grammatical and ungrammatical sample formal-language segments.

Until the 1950's most linguists thought that natural language could be ana- 3
lyzed in separate sequential phases: first syntactic and then semantic. Natural
language has features that are clearly syntactic and features that are clearly
semantic. It was believed that certain syntactic transformations could be applied
to natural language without affecting meaning, just as a musical score can be
changed in certain ways without changing the sounds it represents. This belief
was the basis for massive efforts during the 1950's to have computers translate
text from one language to another. First large dictionaries were placed on computer tapes so that the translations of individual words could easily be looked
up. Then elaborate grammars were developed to explain the differences, from
one language to another, of such obvious syntactic features as word order, noun
cases, and verb tenses. Linguists working with computer scientists hoped that,
if their programs captured enough of the syntactic differences between the languages, then translated sentences would come through with their meanings
undisturbed. Unfortunately, these experiments failed miserably, producing
translations whose meanings differed from the original in all kinds of strange,
unexpected ways. For example, when the Biblical quotation, "The spirit is
willing but the flesh is weak," was translated from English to Russian and then
back to English, what came out of the computer was, "The wine is agreeable
but the meat has spoiled."

The lesson learned from these early efforts at mechanical translation was that 4
the boundary between syntax and semantics in natural language is extremely
fuzzy. No system of grammatical rules has been discovered, or now seems likely
to be discoverable, that can describe the structural properties of natural language
without being concerned also with semantics. The formal ways in which words
can be strung together and the meanings of those strings appear to be interrelated
in subtle and complex ways.

Some English sentences are clearly both grammatical and meaningful, "John 5
gave the carrot to Mary," and some are clearly so ungrammatical as to be

Bertram Raphael

meaningless, "To gave Mary John carrot the." However, we also can construct English expressions whose meanings are perfectly clear even though the expressions are obviously ungrammatical: "I ain't never been there," "Me, Tarzan; you, Jane," "Them's them," and expressions that are perfectly meaningless even though they give the impression of being completely grammatical: "'Twas brillig, and the slithy toves did gyre and gimble in the wabe," "Colorless green ideas dream furiously." In fact, grammar (syntax) and meaning (semantics) of natural language are inextricably intertwined, almost from the basic definitions. The linguist—the scientist who studies the nature of language—would agree with the mathematician in defining the grammar of a language to be a set of rules that identifies which sentences belong to a language and which sentences do not belong. However, the mathematician, who is concerned with artificial languages, is satisfied to define the language by the grammar; a given sentence is part of a given artificial language if and only if the grammar permits it to be. The linguist, on the other hand, is faced with an existing natural language. The grammars he constructs are only approximations to the real, but unformalized, grammar of the language. His ultimate test of whether a given sentence is part of a given natural language is to ask some native speakers of the language; and they will usually reply that the sentence is grammatical only if it is meaningful to them. Therefore any grammar constructed as an approximate description of a natural language must attempt to separate, not only allowable from structurally ill-formed sentences, but also meaningful from meaningless sentences.

QUESTIONS

1. What is the main difference between artificial and natural language? Why did the experiment in computer translation (paragraph 3) go awry?

2. Assuming that the main point of this explanation is summarized in the last three sentences of paragraph 5, why does Raphael begin with the case of artificial languages?

3. Construct several ungrammatical English sentences, the meanings of which are perfectly clear. (See paragraph 5.) Are you satisfied with calling those sentences English? Would a native speaker include them within the boundaries of his or her own language? Conduct a survey with a few such sentences, and find out.

4. Construct several meaningless sentences that give the impression of being perfectly grammatical. (See paragraph 5 again.)

5. As Raphael says, a native speaker is the authority we rely upon to decide whether a sentence in a natural language is grammatical or meaningful. But what about the case of learned writing in a natural language? Is the language still "natural"? Who, then, is the native speaker? Write a character sketch of a "native speaker" who would be an appropriate reader of one of the more learned essays in this unit.

6. Is "business-ese" a "natural language"? Is poetry? What qualifies a "native speaker" to judge? Write a short essay on one such specialized language. Try to explain the degree to which it is "natural," who the "natives" are, and how you identify and understand them.

SPATIAL KNOWLEDGE AND GEOMETRIC REPRESENTATION IN A CHILD BLIND FROM BIRTH

Barbara Landau, Henry Gleitman, and Elizabeth Spelke

Barbara Landau (b. 1949), Henry Gleitman (b. 1925), and Elizabeth Spelke (b. 1949) worked as members of a research team in the psychology department at the University of Pennsylvania. There they conducted the experiment described in the following paper, which originally appeared in the professional journal Science *in 1981.*

ABSTRACT. *A series of experiments demonstrated that a congenitally blind 2½-year-old child—as well as sighted but blindfolded children and adults—can determine the appropriate path between two objects after traveling to each of those objects from a third object. This task requires that the child detect the distances and the angular relationship of the familiar paths and that she derive therefrom the angle of the new path. Our research indicates that the locomotion of the young blind child is guided by knowledge of the Euclidean properties of a spatial layout and by principles for making inferences based on those properties.*

We have had the opportunity to study the spatially guided locomotion of one 2½-year-old blind child in several experimental settings. After the child had been taken along several paths connecting four objects in a small room, she was able to move directly between the objects along paths she had never taken. Sighted adults and 3-year-old children, all blindfolded, performed with similar accuracy. These observations demonstrate that the locomotion of children, with or without visual experience, is guided by metric knowledge of space. This knowledge makes possible the derivation of further spatial information.

These observations were undertaken to address a classical issue in psychology, the development of human knowledge of space. Descartes suggested that the geometric principles underlying spatial knowledge are innate and accessible to any perceptual mode.[1] He offered the example of a blind man exploring objects

---

[1]R. Descartes, *Discourse on Method, Optics, Geometry, and Meteorology,* P. J. Olscamp, Transl. (Bobbs-Merrill, Indianapolis, 1965; originally published in 1637). (René Descartes [1595–1650] was a French mathematician and philosopher. [Eds.])

with a stick. For the man to discover the shapes and arrangement of those objects, he must refer each tactual impression to a unitary spatial framework, structured by the principles of Euclidean geometry.[2] Descartes proposed that any perceiver, exploring the world through any mode, faces the blind man's problem, and must draw on tacit knowledge of geometry to solve it. Descartes further reasoned that geometric principles must be innate: since those principles structure any perceptual experience, they cannot themselves be acquired through experience. These arguments form part of the core of the rationalist tradition in psychology.[3]

Descartes's analysis can be contrasted with two major subsequent developments. First, Helmholtz,[4] extending the arguments of British empiricism,[5] rejected Descartes's claim of innateness. Helmholtz suggested that the geometric principles underlying space perception can be acquired. Perceivers need be endowed only with a set of general, nonspatial inference rules. They will deduce the principles of Euclidean geometry as they apply these inference rules to the sensory information that the environment provides. Second, Gibson proposed that no geometric principles whatever need structure one's sensory impressions.[6] The spatial properties of objects are specified by higher-order relationships in spatially and temporally extended arrays of stimulation. Space perception depends on mechanisms that detect these relationships.

We have attempted to address these issues by extending Descartes's example. We focused on the attempts of a young blind child to discover the spatial layout of objects in a room from limited, temporally extended encounters with those objects and with paths between them. We investigated whether this child could make spatial deductions that rely on information about Euclidean angles and distances.

Our principal subject was Kelli, a child born 3 months prematurely and blinded shortly after birth as a result of retrolental fibroplasia. She is totally

---

[2]Euclidean geometry: the plane geometry of angles and straight and parallel lines based on the principles of the Greek mathematician Euclid, who lived around 300 B.C. [Eds.]

[3]N. Chomsky, *Aspects of the Theory of Syntax* (MIT Press, Cambridge, Mass., 1965); I. Kant, *Critique of Pure Reason* (Macmillan, New York, 1929; originally published in 1781); C. W. Leibniz, *New Essays Concerning Human Understanding* (Open Court, Chicago, 1916; originally published in 1704). (rationalist tradition: a philosophical theory that holds that reason, rather than experience, is the source of truth. [Eds.])

[4]H. von Helmholtz, *Treatise on Physiological Optics* (Dover, New York, 1962; originally published in 1867), vol. 3. Hermann von Helmholtz [1821–1894] was a German physicist, anatomist, and physiologist. [Eds.]

[5]British empiricism: the philosophical view that experience, especially of the senses, is the only valid knowledge. [Eds.]

[6]J. J. Gibson, *The Perception of the Visual World* (Houghton-Mifflin, Boston, 1950); *The Senses Considered as Perceptual Systems* (Houghton-Mifflin, 1966); *The Ecological Approach to Visual Perception* (Houghton-Mifflin, 1979). See R. Shaw and J. Bransford, in *Perceiving, Acting, and Knowing*, R. Shaw and J. Bransford, Eds. (Erlbaum, Hillsdale, N.J., 1977) for an analysis in the Gibsonian tradition of the blind-man-with-stick problem.

blind.[7] After spending the first 5 months in the hospital, primarily in an isolette, Kelli was discharged with a developmental status of newborn.

When Kelli was 32 months old, she was brought into an unfamiliar laboratory playroom, 2.44 m by 3.05 m. The room contained four landmarks in a diamond shaped array: her mother seated on a chair (M), a stack of pillows (P), a basket of toys (B), and a table (T) (Figure 1). In experiment 1, we placed her at M and walked her from there to P and back, twice; from M to T and back, twice; and from M to B and back, twice. Each time, Kelli felt the object while facing it, and she might have thus determined the orientation of the object relative to the trained path. We then induced her to find the routes between P, T, and B on her own, by giving her such simple commands as "Go to the toybasket" or "Go to the pillows." Kelli was followed as she moved until she reached the goal or expressed confusion. In the latter case, the trial was ended, and she was taken to the goal. Each route was tested twice, for a total of 12 trials, in the following order: T-B, B-T, T-B, B-T; T-P, P-T, T-P, P-T; P-B, B-P, P-B, B-P. Her route was plotted from a videotaped record by observing her position and frontal direction at 3-second intervals, and joining these points with a line representing her path of movement.

Kelli's performance on each test trial is shown in Figure 2. To test the null

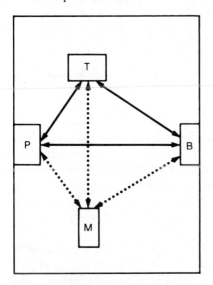

FIGURE 1. Room layout for spatial inference experiment. The room measured 2.44 m by 3.05 m. Dashed lines, trained routes; solid lines, test routes. Landmarks: M, mother; P, pillows; T, table; B, basket.

---

[7]Cases of severe prematurity are at risk for a variety of problems. Kelli has been assessed yearly since the beginning of the study and does not show any significant deficiencies relative to norms for sighted or blind children.

Barbara Landau, Henry Gleitman, and Elizabeth Spelke

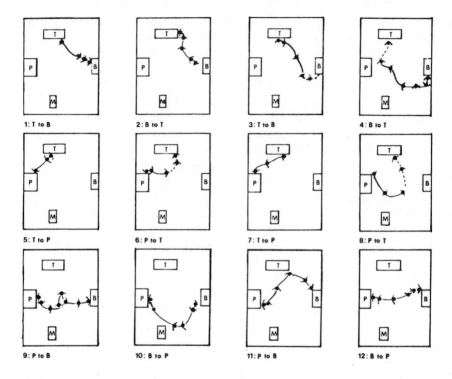

FIGURE 2. Performance on test trials. Solid line, independent movement by child; dashed line, experimenter aided child.

hypothesis that Kelli moved randomly to some stopping point, we measured her position just before reaching the target or before the trial was ended. The circle that surrounded her starting position was divided into nine 40° segments, and each trial was treated as a success if her final position fell within the 40° segment containing the target (which subtended an angle of about that magnitude). The random probability of success is .11, but Kelli's actual performance was much higher: there were eight successes and four failures. . . . Two of the failures were errors of 15° or less.

Kelli did not move ballistically toward the target. Instead, she seemed to adjust her movements, as she went, towards the target. At successive intervals of 0.61 m from her starting position, we compared her frontal direction at the beginning of the interval to her position at the end of the interval and computed the average degrees of self-correction toward the target for each trial. She adjusted her direction toward the target on 11 trials, and away from the target on 1 of the 12 trials. . . .[8]

8

[8]Had Kelli been moving constantly straight ahead, she would not have performed well, since her starting position varied on each trial. For example, on trial 2, she would have moved toward M from her starting position; on trial 3, she would have moved straight into T from her starting position.

Kelli's performance might have been caused by the use of subtle acoustic   9
cues to orient her toward the different landmarks. Experiment 2 tested for this
possibility. Its procedure was identical to that of experiment 1 with one exception: after the first six test trials, Kelli was carried out of the room, and the array
of objects was rotated 90°. Kelli was then carried back in and placed facing one
of the objects. She then received eight test trials with the rotated array. The
rotation preserved the spatial relationships among objects, but it changed the
absolute position of each object within the room. Thus, if Kelli used acoustic
information from the room as spatial landmarks or beacons, she would be expected to move incorrectly between objects, since spatial information about the
objects and about the room conflicted. Kelli's level of accuracy after this rotation
was close to what it had been before. She moved successfully to the target on
five of eight trials. . . . More important, on only one of the eight trials could
her direction of movement be accounted for by the orientation of the room, a
nonsignificant proportion. . . .

A third experiment was conducted with five sighted 3-year-old children and   10
six sighted adults, all of whom wore opaque goggles to block their vision of the
room. The accuracy of the child subjects was similar to that of Kelli, with a
mean of 8.2 successes in 12 trials. The adult subjects performed somewhat
better, with a mean of 11.0 successes.

These experiments indicate that a young blind child is able to set a course   11
between objects along a route she has never followed, after moving to each
object from a third point. In order to accomplish this, the child must have
access to information about the lengths of the two connecting routes travelled
during training and the angular separation of those routes. From this information, the child can derive new angular relationships: the angular direction of
one object from the other. Angle and distance information are properties that
are preserved in metric geometries, such as Euclidean geometry; they are not
properties of nonmetric geometries, such as the projective or topological. Furthermore, the axioms and theorems of Euclidean geometry are sufficient for the
derivation of the new angular information, whereas those of the other geometries
are not.[9] We conclude that this blind child, and sighted controls, know about
some of the metric properties of space, probably Euclidean properties.

Our findings do not distinguish conclusively between the Cartesian, Helm-   12
holtzian, and Gibsonian approaches, but they do help to sharpen the theoretical
issues and clarify the empirical tasks facing proponents of each tradition. The
Cartesian psychologist might propose that Euclidean geometry is innate. The

---

[9]Three different metric geometries could support the inferences of the blind child: Euclidean,
hyperbolic, and Riemannian geometries. These geometries are empirically indistinguishable over
the range of distances that humans can negotiate. Other geometries, such as topology and projective
geometry, have been proposed to characterize the child's spatial knowledge: see J. Piaget and B.
Inhelder, *The Child's Conception of Space* (Norton, New York, 1967; originally published in 1948).
These geometries cannot support the inferences we have studied, however, for they preserve no
metric properties [R. Courant and H. Robbins, *What is Mathematics?* (Oxford Univ. Press, New
York, 1941)].

task is then to discover the psychologically appropriate axiomatization of that geometry and to characterize the processes of inference based on a Euclidean representation. The Helmholtzian psychologist might propose that Euclidean principles can be induced in the first 2½ years by a child who applies innate nonspatial inference rules to correlated patterns of sensation, whether visual or nonvisual. The burden of a Helmholtzian is to describe these rules and the learning processes that lead to the development of a Euclidean representation and its associated inference rules, using sense information. Finally, the Gibsonian psychologist might propose that the child made no inferences at all in our task: rather, her actions may have been guided by a perceptual mechanism that detected invariant tactual relationships as she actively locomoted. Such a mechanism might be sensitive to Euclidean relationships, yielding the perception of further Euclidean relationships without producing a spatial representation to which inference rules are explicitly applied. The Gibsonian burden is to provide a general characterization of the invariants that perceivers detect and of the mechanisms that detect them—a characterization that can encompass the performance of the blind child traveling along a limited set of paths.

A young blind child exploring an environment was able to gain knowledge [13] of certain spatial relationships between objects. Moreover, she could use these relationships to derive further knowledge about the spatial properties of that layout. Our observations indicate that metric properties of space can be appreciated by children at an early age. They further indicate that vision plays no essential role in the early development of knowledge of such properties.

QUESTIONS

1. Summarize as exactly as you can what was actually learned by this study. Do you have any doubts about that learning? Are you satisfied with the claims that Landau, Gleitman, and Spelke make?

2. Study the abstract of this article. How does it help you orient yourself to the work that follows?

3. Most scientific reports are divided into sections labeled Introduction, Materials and Methods, Results, and Discussion. Examine how closely this article follows that form without using those divisions explicitly. Where does the introduction end? Where does the materials-and-methods section begin and end? How does this article vary the standard procedure of separating the materials-and-methods section from the results? Where does the discussion begin?

4. What are *controls* in the context of a scientific experiment? Identify the controls in this experiment. What did the controls do? What was their purpose? How do they affect your reactions to the authors' conclusions?

5. In their discussion, Landau and her collaborators suggest what the next tasks might be for researchers who wish to extend the explanations of Descartes, Helmholtz, or Gibson. Imagine a particular experiment that would serve to extend one of those direc-

tions of research. What kind of subjects would you need? What sort of equipment? What tests would you need to perform? What would your controls be? Describe a plan for such an experiment. Be as thorough and detailed as you can.

6. Go to the library, and find out more about the rationalists and the British empiricists. Write a paper explaining the disagreement between these two philosophies.

TIMES AND DISTANCES, LARGE AND SMALL

Francis Crick

Francis Crick (b. 1916), British molecular biologist, shared the Nobel Prize for medicine in 1962 with James D. Watson for their report on the molecular structure of DNA, one of the most important scientific discoveries of this century. Both Watson and Crick have made special efforts to explain their field of study to the general public. The essay reprinted here is the first chapter of Crick's book, Life Itself *(1981).*

There is one fact about the origin of life which is reasonably certain. Whenever and wherever it happened, it started a very long time ago, so long ago that it is extremely difficult to form any realistic idea of such vast stretches of time. Our own personal experience extends back over tens of years, yet even for that limited period we are apt to forget precisely what the world was like when we were young. A hundred years ago the earth was also full of people, bustling about their business, eating and sleeping, walking and talking, making love and earning a living, each one steadily pursuing his own affairs, and yet (with very rare exceptions) not one of them is left alive today. Instead, a totally different set of persons inhabits the earth around us. The shortness of human life necessarily limits the span of direct personal recollection.

Human culture has given us the illusion that our memories go further back than that. Before writing was invented, the experience of earlier generations, embodied in stories, myths and moral precepts to guide behavior, was passed down verbally or, to a lesser extent, in pictures, carvings and statues. Writing has made more precise and more extensive the transmission of such information and in recent times photography has sharpened our images of the immediate past. Cinematography will give future generations a more direct and vivid impression of their forebears than we can now easily get from the written word. What a pity we don't have a talking picture of Cleopatra;[1] it would not only reveal the true length of her nose but would make more explicit the essence of her charm.

We can, with an effort, project ourselves back to the time of Plato and

---

[1]Cleopatra (69 B.C.–30 B.C.): Egyptian queen who charmed Julius Caesar and Marc Antony. [Eds.]

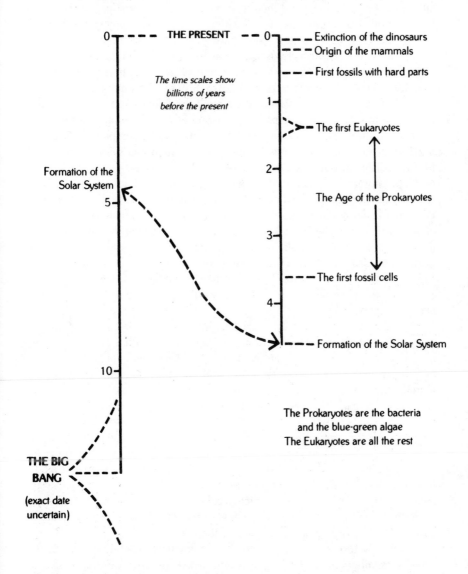

THE UNIVERSE

THE SOLAR SYSTEM

0 — THE PRESENT — 0 — Extinction of the dinosaurs
— Origin of the mammals
— First fossils with hard parts

*The time scales show
billions of years
before the present*

1 —

— The first Eukaryotes

Formation of the
Solar System

2 —

The Age of the Prokaryotes

5 —

3 —

— The first fossil cells

4 —

— Formation of the Solar System

10 —

The Prokaryotes are the bacteria
and the blue-green algae
The Eukaryotes are all the rest

**THE BIG
BANG**

(exact date
uncertain)

Aristotle,[2] and even beyond to Homer's Bronze Age heroes.[3] We can learn
something of the highly organized civilizations of Egypt, the Middle East, Cen-

[2]Plato (428 B.C.?–348 B.C.) and Aristotle (384 B.C.–322 B.C.): Greek philosophers. [Eds.]
[3]Homer's Bronze Age heroes: the heroes of *The Iliad* and *The Odyssey*, epic poems written by
the Greek poet Homer about 750 B.C. Homer's heroes fought in the Trojan War (ca. 1200 B.C.)
at the end of the Bronze Age (3500 B.C.–1000 B.C.).

tral America and China and a little about other primitive and scattered habitations. Even so, we have difficulty in contemplating steadily the march of history, from the beginnings of civilization to the present day, in such a way that we can truly experience the slow passage of time. Our minds are not built to deal comfortably with periods as long as hundreds or thousands of years.

Yet when we come to consider the origin of life, the time scales we must   4 deal with make the whole span of human history seem but the blink of an eyelid. There is no simple way to adjust one's thinking to such vast stretches of time. The immensity of time passed is beyond our ready comprehension. One can only construct an impression of it from indirect and incomplete descriptions, much as a blind man laboriously builds up, by touch and sound, a picture of his immediate surroundings.

The customary way to provide a convenient framework for one's thoughts is   5 to compare the age of the universe with the length of a single earthly day. Perhaps a better comparison, along the same lines, would be to equate the age of our earth with a single week. On such a scale the age of the universe, since the Big Bang,[4] would be about two or three weeks. The oldest macroscopic fossils (those from the start of the Cambrian)[5] would have been alive just one day ago. Modern man would have appeared in the last ten seconds and agriculture in the last one or two. Odysseus would have lived only half a second before the present time.[6]

Even this comparison hardly makes the longer time scale comprehensible to   6 us. Another alternative is to draw a linear map of time, with the different events marked on it. The problem here is to make the line long enough to show our own experience on a reasonable scale, and yet short enough for convenient reproduction and examination. For easy reference such a map has been printed at the beginning of this [essay]. But perhaps the most vivid method is to compare time to the lines of print themselves. Let us make [a 200-page] book equal in length to the time from the start of the Cambrian to the present; that is, about 600 million years. Then each full page will represent roughly 3 million years, each line about ninety thousand years and each letter or small space about fifteen hundred years. The origin of the earth would be about seven books ago and the origin of the universe (which has been dated only approximately) ten or so books before that. Almost the whole of recorded human history would be covered by the last two or three letters of the book.

If you now turn back the pages of the book, slowly reading *one letter at a*   7 *time*—remember, each letter is fifteen hundred years—then this may convey to

---

[4]Big Bang: a cosmological model in which all matter in the universe originated in a giant explosion about 18 billion years ago. [Eds.]
[5]Cambrian: the earliest period in the Paleozoic era, beginning about 600 million years ago. [Eds.]
[6]Odysseus: the most famous Greek hero of antiquity; he is the hero of Homer's *Odyssey* and a prominent character in the *Iliad*. [Eds.]

you something of the immense stretches of time we shall have to consider. On this scale the span of your own life would be less than the width of a comma.

If life really started here we need hardly be concerned with the rest of the universe, but if it started elsewhere the magnitude of large distances must be squarely faced. Though it is difficult to convey a vivid and precise impression of the age of the universe, to grasp its size is almost beyond human comprehension, however we try to express it. The main stumbling block is the extreme emptiness of space; not merely the few atoms in between the stars but the immense distance from one star to another. The visible world close to us is cluttered with objects and our intuitive estimates of their distance depend mainly on various clues provided by their apparent size and their visual interrelationships. It is much more difficult to judge the distance of an unfamiliar object floating in the emptiness of the clear, blue sky. I once heard a Canadian radio interviewer say, when challenged, that he thought the moon "was about the size of a balloon," though admittedly this was before the days of space travel.

This is how two astronomers, Jastrow and Thompson, try to describe, by analogy, the size and the distance of objects in space:

> Let the sun be the size of an orange; on that scale the earth is a grain of sand circling in orbit around the sun at a distance of thirty feet; Jupiter, eleven times larger than the earth, is a cherry pit revolving at a distance of 200 feet or one city block from the sun. The galaxy on this scale is 100 billion oranges, each orange separated from its neighbors by an average distance of 1,000 miles.[7]

The difficulty with an analogy of this type is that it is almost impossible for us to estimate distances in empty space. A comparison with a city block is misleading, because we too easily visualize the buildings in it, and in doing so lose the idea of emptiness. If you try to imagine an orange floating even a mile up in the sky you will find that its distance seems to become indefinite. An "orange" a thousand miles away would be too small to see unless it were incandescent.

Another possible method is to convert distances to time. Pretend you are on a spaceship which is traveling faster than any present-day spaceship. For various reasons, which will become clear later, let us take its speed to be one-hundredth the velocity of light; that is, about 1,800 miles per second. At this speed one could go from New York to Europe in about three seconds (Concorde takes roughly three hours), so we are certainly traveling fairly fast by everyday standards. It would take us two minutes to reach the moon and fifteen hours to reach the sun. To go right across the solar system from one side to the other—let us take this distance rather arbitrarily as the diameter of the orbit of Neptune—would take us almost three and a half weeks. The main point to grasp is that this journey is not unlike a very long train journey, rather longer than the distance

[7]Robert Jastrow and Malcolm M. Thompson, *Astronomy: Fundamentals and Frontiers*, 2nd ed. (New York: Wiley, 1972).

from Moscow to Vladivostok and back. Such a trip would probably be monotonous enough, even though the landscape were constantly flowing past the train window. While going across the solar system, there would be nothing at all just outside the window of the spaceship. Very slowly, day after day, the sun would change in size and position. As we traveled farther away from it, its apparent diameter would decrease, till near the orbit of Neptune it would look "little bigger than a pin's head," as I have previously described it, assuming that its apparent size, as viewed from the earth, corresponds roughly to that of a silver dollar. In spite of traveling so fast—remember that at this speed we could travel from any spot to any other on the earth's surface in less than seven seconds— this journey would be tedious in the extreme. Our main impression would be of the almost total emptiness of space. At this distance a planet would appear to be little more than an occasional speck in this vast wilderness.

This feeling of an immense three-dimensional emptiness is bad enough while we are focusing on the solar system. (Almost all of the scale models of the solar system one sees in museums are grossly misleading. The sun and the planets are almost always shown as far too big by comparison with the distances between them.) It is when we try to go farther afield that the enormity of space really hits us. To reach the nearest star—actually a group of three stars fairly close together—would take our spaceship 430 years and the chances are we would pass nothing significant on the way there. A whole lifetime of one hundred years, traveling at this very high speed, would take us less than a quarter of the way there. We would be constantly traveling from emptiness to emptiness with nothing but a few gas molecules and an occasional tiny speck of dust to show that we were not always in the same place. Very, very slowly a few of the nearest stars would change their positions slightly, while the sun itself would fade imperceptibly until it was just another star in the brilliant panorama of stars visible on all sides of the spaceship. Long though it would seem, this journey to the nearest star is, by astronomical standards, a very short one. To cross our own galaxy from side to side would take no less than ten million years. Such distances are beyond anything we can conceive except in the most abstract way. And yet, on a cosmic scale, the distance across the galaxy is hardly any distance at all. Admittedly it is only about twenty times as far to Andromeda, the nearest large galaxy, but to reach the limits of space visible to us in our giant telescopes we would have to travel more than a thousand times farther than that. To me it is remarkable that this astonishing discovery, the vastness and the emptiness of space, has not attracted the imaginative attention of poets and religious thinkers. People are happy to contemplate the limitless powers of God—a doubtful proposition at best—but quite unwilling to meditate creatively on the size of this extraordinary universe in which, through no virtue of their own, they find themselves. Naïvely one might have thought that both poets and priests would be so utterly astonished by these scientific revelations that they would be working with a white-hot fury to try to embody them in the foundation of our culture.

12

TIMES AND DISTANCES, LARGE AND SMALL

The psalmist who said, "When I consider Thy heavens, the work of Thy fingers, the moon and the stars, which Thou hast ordained; what is man, that Thou art mindful of him? . . ." was at least trying, within the limitations of his beliefs, to express his wonder at the universe visible to the naked eye and the pettiness of man by comparison. And yet *his* universe was a small, almost cozy affair compared to the one modern science has revealed to us. It is almost as if the utter insignificance of the earth and the thin film of its biosphere has totally paralyzed the imagination, as if it were too dreadful to contemplate and therefore best ignored.

I shall not discuss here how these very large distances are estimated. The distance of the main objects in the solar system can now be obtained very accurately by a combination of the theory of solar mechanics and radar ranging, the distances of the nearest stars by the way their relative positions change slightly when viewed from the different positions of the earth in its yearly orbit around the sun. After that the arguments are more technical and less precise. But that the distances are the sort of size astronomers estimate there is not the slightest doubt. 13

So far we have been considering very large magnitudes. Fortunately, when we turn to very small distances and times things are not quite so bad. We need to know the size of atoms—the size and contents of the tiny nucleus within each atom will concern us less—compared to everyday things. This we can manage in two relatively small hops. Let us start with a millimeter. This distance (about a twenty-fifth of an inch) is easy for us to see with the naked eye. One-thousandth part of this is called a micron. A bacteria cell is about two microns long. The wavelength of visible light (which limits what we can see in a high-powered light microscope) is about half a micron long. 14

We now go down by another factor of a thousand to reach a length known as a nanometer. The typical distance between adjacent atoms bonded strongly together in an organic compound lies between a tenth and a fifth of this. Under the best conditions we can see distances of a nanometer, or a little less, using an electron microscope, provided the specimen can be suitably prepared. Moreover, it is possible to exhibit pictures of a whole series of natural objects at every scale between a small group of atoms and a flea, so that with a little practice we can feel one scale merging into another. By contrast with the emptiness of space, the living world is crammed with detail at every level. The ease with which we can go from one scale to another should not blind us to the fact that the numbers of objects within a *volume* can be uncomfortably large. For example, a drop of water contains rather more than a thousand billion billion water molecules. 15

The short time we shall be concerned with will rarely be less than a pico-second, that is, one-millionth of a millionth of a second, though very much shorter times occur in nuclear reactions and in studies of subatomic particles. This minute interval is the sort of time scale on which molecules are vibrating, 16 but looked at another way, it does not seem so outlandish. Consider the velocity of sound. In air this is relatively slow—little faster than most jet planes—being about a thousand feet per second. If a flash of lightning is only a mile away, it will take a full five seconds for its sound to reach us. This velocity is, incidentally, approximately the same as the average speed of the molecules of gas in the air, in between their collisions with each other. The speed of sound in most solids is usually a little faster.

Now we ask, how long will it take a sound wave to pass over a small molecule? A simple calculation shows this time to be in the picosecond range. This is just what one would expect, since this is about the time scale on which the atoms of the molecule are vibrating against one another. What is important is that this is, roughly speaking, the pulse rate *underlying* chemical reactions. An enzyme— an organic catalyst—can react a thousand or more times a second. This may appear fast to us but this rate is really rather slow on the time scale of atomic vibration.

Unfortunately, it is not so easy to convey the time scales in between a second and a picosecond, though a physical chemist can learn to feel at home over this fairly large range. Fortunately, we shall not be concerned directly with these very short times, though we shall see their effects indirectly. Most chemical reactions are really very rare events. The molecules usually move around intermittently and barge against one another many times before a rare lucky encounter allows them to hit each other strongly enough and in the correct direction to surmount their protective barriers and produce a chemical reaction. It is only because there are usually so many molecules in one small volume, all doing this at the same time, that the rate of chemical reaction appears to proceed quite smoothly. The chance variations are smoothed out by the large numbers involved.

When we stand back and review once again these very different scales—the minute size of an atom and the almost unimaginable size of the universe; the pulse rate of chemical reaction compared to the deserts of vast eternity since the Big Bang—we see that in all these instances our intuitions, based on our experience of everyday life, are likely to be highly misleading. By themselves, large numbers mean very little to us. There is only one way to overcome this handicap, so natural to our human condition. We must calculate and recalculate, even though only approximately, to check and recheck our initial impressions until slowly, with time and constant application, the real world, the world of the immensely small and the immensely great, becomes as familiar to us as the simple cradle of our common earthly experience.

QUESTIONS

1. Study the diagram that accompanies the essay. How does one line relate to the other? What is the diagram trying to convey?

2. Why are the first three paragraphs devoted to the history and historical memory of humankind?

3. Compare the analogies Crick uses to explain the long passage of universal time in paragraphs 5, 6, and 7. What does the analogy of the book add to that of the week?

4. In paragraph 8, what is the implication of *elsewhere* in its first sentence? This essay is the first chapter of a book called *Life Itself*. What do you imagine to be at least one idea treated in the rest of the book?

5. Paragraph 11 is an extremely long paragraph, and paragraph 12 is even longer. Their lengths seem to correspond to the subjects they take up. Can you think of other ways to imagine the kind of emptiness those paragraphs describe?

6. Paragraph 11 implies an unusual definition of *wilderness*, its last word. Explain why you consider Crick's idea of wilderness the essential one or an eccentric notion.

7. Why do you think that priests and poets have not, as Crick observes, been "working with a white-hot fury to try to embody [these scientific revelations] in the foundation of our culture"? What does that last phrase, "foundation of our culture," mean in this context?

8. Why do you think Crick treats the very large before the very small? Which are the more astonishing measurements?

9. Think of a way of estimating, closely but reasonably, something quite numerous—for example, the number of grasses in a yard, the number of leaves or pine needles on a tree, the number of hairs on the tail of a cat, or the number of cars on all the roads, during a single day, in your state or city. Describe your system of estimation, and explain the answer it yields.

TOUCH AND SIGHT:
THE EARTH AND
THE HEAVENS
Bertrand Russell

Mathematician, philosopher, man of letters, pacifist, Bertrand Russell (1872–1970) was both an English lord and a Nobel laureate. He wrote books on a staggering range of subjects from the principles of mathematics to questions of religion and politics. In his ABC of Relativity, *he undertook the difficult task of making Einstein's theory of relativity intelligible to the general public. These pages from that book should be compared with Einstein's own effort at the same difficult task (the following selection).*

Everybody knows that Einstein did something astonishing, but very few people know exactly what it was that he did. It is generally recognized that he revolutionized our conception of the physical world, but the new conceptions are wrapped up in mathematical technicalities. It is true that there are innumerable popular accounts of the theory of relativity, but they generally cease to be intelligible just at the point where they begin to say something important. The authors are hardly to blame for this. Many of the new ideas can be expressed in non-mathematical language, but they are none the less difficult on that account. What is demanded is a change in our imaginative picture of the world—a picture which has been handed down from remote, perhaps pre-human, ancestors, and has been learned by each one of us in early childhood. A change in our imagination is always difficult, especially when we are no longer young. The same sort of change was demanded by Copernicus,[1] when he taught that the earth is not stationary and the heavens do not revolve about it once a day. To us now there is no difficulty in this idea, because we learned it before our mental habits had become fixed. Einstein's ideas, similarly, will seem easier to generations which grow up with them; but for us a certain effort of imaginative reconstruction is unavoidable.

In exploring the surface of the earth, we make use of all our senses, more particularly of the senses of touch and sight. In measuring lengths, parts of the human body are employed in pre-scientific ages: a "foot," a "cubit," a "span" are defined in this way. For longer distances, we think of the time it takes to

---

[1]Nicolaus Copernicus (1473–1543): Polish astronomer and founder of modern astronomy who argued that the earth was merely another planet that revolved around the sun. [Eds.].

walk from one place to another. We gradually learn to judge distance roughly by the eye, but we rely upon touch for accuracy. Moreover it is touch that gives us our sense of "reality." Some things cannot be touched: rainbows, reflections in looking-glasses, and so on. These things puzzle children, whose metaphysical speculations are arrested by the information that what is in the looking-glass is not "real." Macbeth's dagger was unreal because it was not "sensible to feeling as to sight." Not only our geometry and physics, but our whole conception of what exists outside us, is based upon the sense of touch. We carry this even into our metaphors: a good speech is "solid," a bad speech is "gas," because we feel that a gas is not quite "real."

In studying the heavens, we are debarred from all senses except sight. We 3 cannot touch the sun, or travel to it; we cannot walk around the moon, or apply a foot-rule to the Pleiades.[2] Nevertheless, astronomers have unhesitatingly applied the geometry and physics which they found serviceable on the surface of the earth, and which they had based upon touch and travel. In doing so, they brought down trouble on their heads, which it was left for Einstein to clear up. It turned out that much of what we learned from the sense of touch was unscientific prejudice, which must be rejected if we are to have a true picture of the world.

An illustration may help us to understand how much is impossible to the 4 astronomer as compared with the man who is interested in things on the surface of the earth. Let us suppose that a drug is administered to you which makes you temporarily unconscious, and that when you wake you have lost your memory but not your reasoning powers. Let us suppose further that while you were unconscious you were carried into a balloon, which, when you come to, is sailing with the wind on a dark night—the night of the fifth of November if you are in England,[3] or of the fourth of July if you are in America. You can see fireworks which are being sent off from the ground, from trains, and from aeroplanes travelling in all directions, but you cannot see the ground or the trains or the aeroplanes because of the darkness. What sort of picture of the world will you form? You will think that nothing is permanent: there are only brief flashes of light, which, during their short existence, travel through the void in the most various and bizarre curves. You cannot touch these flashes of light, you can only see them. Obviously your geometry and your physics and your metaphysics will be quite different from those of ordinary mortals. If an ordinary mortal were with you in the balloon, you would find his speech unintelligible. But if Einstein were with you, you would understand him more easily than the ordinary mortal would, because you would be free from a host of preconceptions which prevent most people from understanding him.

The theory of relativity depends, to a considerable extent, upon getting rid 5

---

[2]the Pleiades: a cluster of seven stars in the constellation Taurus. [Eds.]
[3]the fifth of November: Guy Fawkes Day, when the English set off fireworks and light bonfires to commemorate the anniversary of the discovery of a plot in 1605 to blow up Parliament and kill King James I. [Eds.]

of notions which are useful in ordinary life but not to our drugged balloonist. Circumstances on the surface of the earth, for various more or less accidental reasons, suggest conceptions which turn out to be inaccurate, although they have come to seem like necessities of thought. The most important of these circumstances is that most objects on the earth's surface are fairly persistent and nearly stationary from a terrestrial point of view. If this were not the case, the idea of going on a journey would not seem so definite as it does. If you want to travel from King's Cross to Edinburgh, you know that you will find King's Cross where it has always been, that the railway line will take the course that it did when you last made the journey, and that Waverly Station in Edinburgh will not have walked up to the Castle. You therefore say and think that you have traveled to Edinburgh, not that Edinburgh has travelled to you, though the latter statement would be just as accurate. The success of this common-sense point of view depends upon a number of things which are really of the nature of luck. Suppose all the houses in London were perpetually moving about, like a swarm of bees; suppose railways moved and changed their shapes like avalanches; and finally suppose that material objects were perpetually being formed and dissolved like clouds. There is nothing impossible in these suppositions. But obviously what we call a journey to Edinburgh would have no meaning in such a world. You would begin, no doubt, by asking the taxi-driver: "Where is King's Cross this morning?" At the station you would have to ask a similar question about Edinburgh, but the booking-office clerk would reply: "What part of Edinburgh do you mean, sir? Prince's Street has gone to Glasgow, the Castle has moved up into the Highlands, and Waverly Station is under the water in the middle of the Firth of Forth." And, on the journey the stations would not be staying quiet, but some would be travelling north, some south, some east or west, perhaps much faster than the train. Under these conditions you could not say where you were at any moment. Indeed, the whole notion that one is always in some definite "place" is due to the fortunate immobility of most of the large objects on the earth's surface. The idea of "place" is only a rough practical approximation: there is nothing logically necessary about it, and it cannot be made precise.

If we were not much larger than an electron, we should not have this impression of stability, which is only due to the grossness of our senses. King's Cross, which to us looks solid, would be too vast to be conceived except by a few eccentric mathematicians. The bits of it that we could see would consist of little tiny points of matter, never coming into contact with each other, but perpetually whizzing around each other in an inconceivably rapid ballet-dance. The world of our experience would be quite as mad as the one in which the different parts of Edinburgh go for walks in different directions. If—to take the opposite extreme—you were as large as the sun and lived as long, with a corresponding slowness of perception, you would again find a higgledy-piggledy universe without permanence—stars and planets would come and go like morning mists, and

6

nothing would remain in a fixed position relative to anything else. The notion of comparative stability which forms part of our ordinary outlook is thus due to the fact that we are about the size we are, and live on a planet of which the surface is not very hot. If this were not the case, we should not find pre-relativity physics intellectually satisfying. Indeed we should never have invented such theories. We should have had to arrive at relativity physics at one bound, or remain ignorant of scientific laws. It is fortunate for us that we were not faced with this alternative, since it is almost inconceivable that one man could have done the work of Euclid, Galileo, Newton and Einstein. Yet without such an incredible genius physics could hardly have been discovered in a world where the universal flux was obvious to non-scientific observation.

In astronomy, although the sun, moon, and stars continue to exist year after 7
year, yet in other respects the world we have to deal with is very different from that of everyday life. As already observed we depend exclusively on sight: the heavenly bodies cannot be touched, heard, smelt, or tasted. Everything in the heavens is moving relatively to everything else. The earth is going round the sun, the sun is moving, very much faster than an express train, towards a point in the constellation Hercules, the "fixed" stars are scurrying hither and thither like a lot of frightened hens. There are no well-marked places in the sky, like King's Cross and Edinburgh. When you travel from place to place on the earth, you say the train moves and not the stations, because the stations preserve their topographical relations to each other and the surrounding country. But in astronomy it is arbitrary which you call the train and which the station: the question is to be decided purely by convenience and as a matter of convention.

In this respect, it is interesting to contrast Einstein and Copernicus. Before 8
Copernicus, people thought that the earth stood still and the heavens revolved about it once a day. Copernicus taught that "really" the earth rotates once a day, and the daily revolution of sun and stars is only "apparent." Galileo and Newton endorsed this view, and many things were thought to prove it—for example, the flattening of the earth at the poles and the fact that bodies are heavier there than at the equator. But in the modern theory the question between Copernicus and his predecessors is merely one of convenience; all motion is relative, and there is no difference between the two statements: "The earth rotates once a day" and "the heavens revolve around the earth once a day." The two mean exactly the same thing, just as it means the same thing if I say that a certain length is six feet or two yards. Astronomy is easier if we take the sun as fixed than if we take the earth, just as accounts are easier in decimal coinage. But to say more for Copernicus is to assume absolute motion, which is a fiction. All motion is relative, and it is a mere convention to take one body as at rest. All such conventions are equally legitimate, though not all are equally convenient.

There is another matter of great importance, in which astronomy differs from 9
terrestrial physics because of its exclusive dependence upon sight. Both popular

thought and old-fashioned physics used the notion of "force," which seemed intelligible because it was associated with familiar sensations. When we are walking, we have sensations connected with our muscles which we do not have when we are sitting still. In the days before mechanical traction, although people could travel by sitting in their carriages, they could see the horses exerting themselves and evidently putting out "force" in the same way as human beings do. Everybody knew from experience what it is to push or pull, or to be pushed or pulled. These very familiar facts made "force" seem a natural basis for dynamics. But Newton's law of gravitation introduced a difficulty. The force between two billiard balls appeared intelligible because we know what it feels like to bump into another person; but the force between the earth and the sun, which are ninety-three million miles apart, was mysterious. Newton himself regarded this "action at a distance" as impossible, and believed that there was some hitherto undiscovered mechanism by which the sun's influence was transmitted to the planets. However, no such mechanism was discovered, and gravitation remained a puzzle. The fact is that the whole conception of "force" is a mistake. The sun does not exert any force on the planets; in Einstein's law of gravitation, the planet only pays attention to what it finds in its own neighborhood. The way in which this works will be explained in a later chapter; for the present we are only concerned with the necessity of abandoning the notion of "force," which was due to misleading conceptions derived from the sense of touch.

As physics has advanced, it has appeared more and more that sight is less   10
misleading than touch as a source of fundamental notions about matter. The apparent simplicity in the collision of billiard balls is quite illusory. As a matter of fact the two billiard balls never touch at all; what really happens is inconceivably complicated, but it is more analogous to what happens when a comet penetrates the solar system and goes away again than to what common sense supposes to happen.

Most of what we have said hitherto was already recognized by physicists before   11
Einstein invented the theory of relativity. "Force" was known to be merely a mathematical fiction, and it was generally held that motion is a merely relative phenomenon—that is to say, when two bodies are changing their relative position, we cannot say that one is moving while the other is at rest, since the occurrence is merely a change in their relation to each other. But a great labor was required in order to bring the actual procedure of physics into harmony with these new convictions. Newton believed in force and in absolute space and time; he embodied these beliefs in his technical methods, and his methods remained those of later physicists. Einstein invented a new technique, free from Newton's assumptions. But in order to do so he had to change fundamentally the old ideas of space and time, which had been unchallenged from time immemorial. This is what makes both the difficulty and the interest of his theory.

QUESTIONS

1. Russell bases much of his explanation of Einstein's work on a series of analogies (paragraphs 4 through 6). Consider the first analogy, in paragraph 4. What is the point Russell is trying to make? How well does the drugged balloonist serve his purpose? What is the importance of imagining Einstein in that balloon? By thinking of Einstein there, what do we learn of his imaginative work as a theoretical physicist?

2. Consider the second analogy, in paragraph 5. How does it work? What is it saying? What does it convey that the first analogy did not?

3. The movement from paragraph 5 to paragraph 6 seems, at first glance, to be simply from one analogy to another. But paragraph 6 presents different points of view rather than analogies. Identify the points of view Russell presents here. What does he gain by placing this discussion after the analogies in paragraphs 4 and 5? How do these shifts in point of view relate to the statement in paragraph 5 that "you . . . say and think that you have travelled to Edinburgh, not that Edinburgh has travelled to you, though the latter statement would be just as accurate."

4. How does Russell define both his viewpoint as a writer and the audience to whom he writes? Point out details of the essay that reveal his approach and that characterize his audience.

5. In the last paragraphs of this essay, Russell speaks mostly of force, our misunderstandings of force, and how ideas of force will change as a result of Einstein's theories. In his first paragraph, furthermore, Russell remarks that new ideas are always easier for later generations to accept, "generations which grow up with them." You are probably part of that future that Russell foresaw. To what extent would you suppose that your sense of *force* has changed from the understanding of your grandparents? Make a list of ways that you find *force* used today. Then write an essay on the contemporary meanings of *force* and their possible relations to ideas in Russell's essay.

WHAT IS THE THEORY
OF RELATIVITY?
Albert Einstein

Albert Einstein (1879–1955) revolutionized the assumptions of modern physics when he published his theory of relativity in 1905. He then worked on efforts to unify the theories of gravitational and electromagnetic forces. Though he had visited before, he moved permanently to the United States from Germany in 1933 and was, from then on, with the Institute for Advanced Study at Princeton. The essay reprinted here was addressed to a general audience at the invitation of the London Times *in 1919, but even so it is extremely difficult. Some things apparently cannot be made easy.*

I gladly accede to the request of your colleague to write something for *The* 1
Times on relativity. After the lamentable breakdown of the old active intercourse between men of learning, I welcome this opportunity of expressing my feelings of joy and gratitude toward the astronomers and physicists of England. It is thoroughly in keeping with the great and proud traditions of scientific work in your country that eminent scientists should have spent much time and trouble, and your scientific institutions have spared no expense, to test the implications of a theory which was perfected and published during the war in the land of your enemies. Even though the investigation of the influence of the gravitational field of the sun on light rays is a purely objective matter, I cannot forbear to express my personal thanks to my English colleagues for their work; for without it I could hardly have lived to see the most important implication of my theory tested.

We can distinguish various kinds of theories in physics. Most of them are 2
constructive. They attempt to build up a picture of the more complex phenomena out of the materials of a relatively simple formal scheme from which they start out. Thus the kinetic theory of gases seeks to reduce mechanical, thermal, and diffusional processes to movements of molecules—i.e., to build them up out of the hypothesis of molecular motion. When we say that we have succeeded in understanding a group of natural processes, we invariably mean that a constructive theory has been found which covers the processes in question.

Along with this most important class of theories there exists a second, which 3
I will call "principle-theories." These employ the analytic, not the synthetic, method. The elements which form their basis and starting-point are not hypothetically constructed but empirically discovered ones, general characteristics of

natural processes, principles that give rise to mathematically formulated criteria which the separate processes or the theoretical representations of them have to satisfy. Thus the science of thermodynamics seeks by analytical means to deduce necessary conditions, which separate events have to satisfy, from the universally experienced fact that perpetual motion is impossible.

The advantages of the constructive theory are completeness, adaptability, and clearness, those of the principle theory are logical perfection and security of the foundations.

The theory of relativity belongs to the latter class. In order to grasp its nature, one needs first of all to become acquainted with the principles on which it is based. Before I go into these, however, I must observe that the theory of relativity resembles a building consisting of two separate stories, the special theory and the general theory. The special theory, on which the general theory rests, applies to all physical phenomena with the exception of gravitation; the general theory provides the law of gravitation and its relations to the other forces of nature.

It has, of course, been known since the days of the ancient Greeks that in order to describe the movement of a body, a second body is needed to which the movement of the first is referred. The movement of a vehicle is considered in reference to the earth's surface, that of a planet to the totality of the visible fixed stars. In physics the body to which events are spatially referred is called the coordinate system. The laws of the mechanics of Galileo and Newton, for instance, can only be formulated with the aid of a coordinate system.

The state of motion of the coordinate system may not, however, be arbitrarily chosen, if the laws of mechanics are to be valid (it must be free from rotation and acceleration). A coordinate system which is admitted in mechanics is called an "inertial system." The state of motion of an inertial system is according to mechanics not one that is determined uniquely by nature. On the contrary, the following definition holds good: a coordinate system that is moved uniformly and in a straight line relative to an inertial system is likewise an inertial system. By the "special principle of relativity" is meant the generalization of this definition to include any natural event whatever: thus, every universal law of nature which is valid in relation to a coordinate system C, must also be valid, as it stands, in relation to a coordinate system C', which is in uniform translatory motion relatively to C.

The second principle, on which the special theory of relativity rests, is the "principle of the constant velocity of light in vacuo." This principle asserts that light in vacuo always has a definite velocity of propagation (independent of the state of motion of the observer or of the source of the light). The confidence which physicists place in this principle springs from the successes achieved by the electrodynamics of Maxwell and Lorentz.[1]

---

[1]Maxwell and Lorentz: James Clerk Maxwell (1831–1879) was a Scottish physicist, and Hendrik Antoon Lorentz (1853–1928) a Dutch physicist. [Eds.]

Both the above-mentioned principles are powerfully supported by experience, 9
but appear not to be logically reconcilable. The special theory of relativity finally
succeeded in reconciling them logically by a modification of kinematics—i.e.,
of the doctrine of the laws relating to space and time (from the point of view of
physics). It became clear that to speak of the simultaneity of two events had no
meaning except in relation to a given coordinate system, and that the shape of
measuring devices and the speed at which clocks move depend on their state of
motion with respect to the coordinate system.

But the old physics, including the laws of motion of Galileo and Newton, 10
did not fit in with the suggested relativist kinematics. From the latter, general
mathematical conditions issued, to which natural laws had to conform, if the
above-mentioned two principles were really to apply. To these, physics had to
be adapted. In particular, scientists arrived at a new law of motion for (rapidly
moving) mass points, which was admirably confirmed in the case of electrically
charged particles. The most important upshot of the special theory of relativity
concerned the inert masses of corporeal systems. It turned out that the inertia
of a system necessarily depends on its energy-content, and this led straight to
the notion that inert mass is simply latent energy. The principle of the conservation of mass lost its independence and became fused with that of the conservation of energy.

The special theory of relativity, which was simply a systematic development 11
of the electrodynamics of Maxwell and Lorentz, pointed beyond itself, however.
Should the independence of physical laws of the state of motion of the coordinate system be restricted to the uniform translatory motion of coordinate systems in respect to each other? What has nature to do with our coordinate systems
and their state of motion? If it is necessary for the purpose of describing nature,
to make use of a coordinate system arbitrarily introduced by us, then the choice
of its state of motion ought to be subject to no restriction; the laws ought to be
entirely independent of this choice (general principle of relativity).

The establishment of this general principle of relativity is made easier by a 12
fact of experience that has long been known, namely, that the weight and the
inertia of a body are controlled by the same constant (equality of inertial and
gravitational mass). Imagine a coordinate system which is rotating uniformly
with respect to an inertial system in the Newtonian manner. The centrifugal
forces which manifest themselves in relation to this system must, according to
Newton's teaching, be regarded as effects of inertia. But these centrifugal forces
are, exactly like the forces of gravity, proportional to the masses of the bodies.
Ought it not to be possible in this case to regard the coordinate system as
stationary and the centrifugal forces as gravitational forces? This seems the obvious view, but classical mechanics forbid it.

This hasty consideration suggests that a general theory of relativity must 13
supply the laws of gravitation, and the consistent following up of the idea has
justified our hopes.

But the path was thornier than one might suppose, because it demanded   14
the abandonment of Euclidean geometry. This is to say, the laws according
to which solid bodies may be arranged in space do not completely accord with
the spatial laws attributed to bodies by Euclidean geometry. This is what we
mean when we talk of the "curvature of space." The fundamental concepts
of the "straight line," the "plane," etc., thereby lose their precise significance
in physics.

In the general theory of relativity the doctrine of space and time, or kine-   15
matics, no longer figures as a fundamental independent of the rest of physics.
The geometrical behavior of bodies and the motion of clocks rather depend on
gravitational fields, which in their turn are produced by matter.

The new theory of gravitation diverges considerably, as regards principles,   16
from Newton's theory. But its practical results agree so nearly with those of
Newton's theory that it is difficult to find criteria for distinguishing them which
are accessible to experience. Such have been discovered so far:

1. In the revolution of the ellipses of the planetary orbits around the sun
(confirmed in the case of Mercury).

2. In the curving of light rays by the action of gravitational fields (confirmed
by the English photographs of eclipses).

3. In a displacement of the spectral lines toward the red end of the spectrum
in the case of light transmitted to us from stars of considerable magnitude
(unconfirmed so far).[2]

The chief attraction of the theory lies in its logical completeness. If a sin-   17
gle one of the conclusions drawn from it proves wrong, it must be given up;
to modify it without destroying the whole structure seems to be impossible.

Let no one suppose, however, that the mighty work of Newton can really be   18
superseded by this or any other theory. His great and lucid ideas will retain their
unique significance for all time as the foundation of our whole modern conceptual structure in the sphere of natural philosophy.

Note: Some of the statements in your paper concerning my life and person   19
owe their origin to the lively imagination of the writer. Here is yet another
application of the principle of relativity for the delectation of the reader: today
I am described in Germany as a "German savant," and in England as a "Swiss
Jew." Should it ever be my fate to be represented as a *bête noire,*[3] I should, on
the contrary, become a "Swiss Jew" for the Germans and a "German savant"
for the English.

---

[2]This criterion has since been confirmed.
[3]*bête noire:* literally a "black beast" in French, meaning a detested person or thing. [Eds.]

Albert Einstein

QUESTIONS

1. Review Einstein's distinction between constructive theories and principle theories of physics. What is their difference, and what does that difference mean? Which kind of theory is the theory of relativity?

2. According to paragraph 5, what kind of principles form the basis for the theory of relativity? How does paragraph 5 relate to the rest of the essay?

3. Try to explain in your own words why the principles mentioned in paragraphs 7 and 8 "appear," as Einstein says in the next paragraph, "not to be logically reconcilable."

4. Focus on the last three sentences in paragraph 10. Try to explain those sentences to yourself by rewriting them in your own words.

5. Consider Einstein's statement that "inert mass is simply latent energy" (paragraph 10). You might simplify (if not trivialize) that claim by thinking of it in terms of physical training. What, in your own words, is Einstein saying about the relation of mass to energy? Do we lose weight in order to gain energy, or do we gain weight in order to store up energy that is latent?

6. The last half of this article may simply be too difficult. But if you have had sufficient background in mathematics and physics, summarize and restate paragraphs 12 through 15.

7. Einstein is writing about his own theory, and he uses *I* several times in the essay. Nevertheless, his article does not read like a first-person account of a discovery. What are Einstein's approach and tone? Why do you suppose he chose to write his article in this way?

8. One of the sidelights of Einstein's paper is the glimpse it provides about the international life of science. Taking what hints you can from this piece, summarize that international situation as Einstein found it.

MY BUILT-IN
DOUBTER
Isaac Asimov

Isaac Asimov (b. 1920) is a professor of biochemistry at the Boston University School of Medicine and one of America's most wide-ranging and productive writers. Although he has published over two hundred books on such subjects as astronomy, biochemistry, history, mathematics, and physics, he is probably best known for his science-fiction short stories and novels. Asimov has said of his own writing: "Everything I write goes through the typewriter twice. But I have a completely unadorned style. I aim to be accurate and clear, and not to write great literature." The essay reprinted here is chapter 16 in his book Fact and Fancy *(1962), a collection of pieces that appeared first in the* Magazine of Fantasy and Science Fiction.

Once I delivered myself of an oration before a small but select audience of 1
non-scientists on the topic of "What is Science?" speaking seriously and, I hope,
intelligently.

Having completed the talk, there came the question period, and, bless my 2
heart, I wasn't disappointed. A charming young lady up front waved a pretty
little hand at me and asked, not a serious question on the nature of science,
but: "Dr. Asimov, do you believe in flying saucers?"

With a fixed smile on my face, I proceeded to give the answer I have carefully 3
given after every lecture I have delivered. I said, "No, miss, I do not, and I
think anyone who does is a crackpot!"

And oh, the surprise on her face! 4

It is taken for granted by everyone, it seems to me, that because I sometimes 5
write science fiction, I believe in flying saucers, in Atlantis, in clairvoyance and
levitation, in the prophecies of the Great Pyramid, in astrology, in Fort's theories, and in the suggestion that Bacon wrote Shakespeare.

No one would ever think that someone who writes fantasies for pre-school 6
children really thinks that rabbits can talk, or that a writer of hard-boiled detective stories really thinks a man can down two quarts of whiskey in five minutes, then make love to two girls in the next five, or that a writer for the ladies'
magazines really thinks that virtue always triumphs and that the secretary always
marries the handsome boss—but a science-fiction writer apparently *must* believe
in flying saucers.

Well, I do not. 7

To be sure, I wrote a story once about flying saucers in which I explained 8
their existence very logically. I also wrote a story once in which levitation played
a part.

If I can buddy up to such notions long enough to write sober, reasonable 9
stories about them, why, then, do I reject them so definitely in real life?

I can explain by way of a story. A good friend of mine once spent quite a 10
long time trying to persuade me of the truth and validity of what I considered
a piece of pseudo-science and bad pseudo-science at that. I sat there listening
quite stonily, and none of the cited evidence and instances and proofs had the
slightest effect on me.

Finally the gentleman said to me, with considerable annoyance, "Damn it, 11
Isaac, the trouble with you is that you have a built-in doubter."

To which the only answer I could see my way to making was a heartfelt, 12
"Thank God."

If a scientist has one piece of temperamental equipment that is essential to 13
his job, it is that of a built-in doubter. Before he does anything else, he must
doubt. He must doubt what others tell him and what he reads in reference
books, and, *most of all*, what his own experiments show him and what his own
reasoning tells him.

Such doubt must, of course, exist in varying degrees. It is impossible, im- 14
practical, and useless to be a maximal doubter at all times. One cannot (and
would not want to) check personally every figure or observation given in a
handbook or monograph before one uses it and then proceed to check it and
recheck it until one dies. *But,* if any trouble arises and nothing else seems
wrong, one must be prepared to say to one's self, "Well, now, I wonder if the
data I got out of the 'Real Guaranteed Authoritative Very Scientific Handbook'
might not be a misprint."

To doubt intelligently requires, therefore, a rough appraisal of the authori- 15
tativeness of a source. It also requires a rough estimate of the nature of the
statement. If you were to tell me that you had a bottle containing one pound
of pure titanium oxide, I would say, "Good," and ask to borrow some if I needed
it. Nor would I test it. I would accept its purity on your say-so (until further
notice, anyway).

If you were to tell me that you had a bottle containing one pound of pure 16
thulium oxide, I would say with considerable astonishment, "You have? Where?"
Then if I had use for the stuff, I would want to run some tests on it and even
run it through an ion-exchange column before I could bring myself to use it.

And if you told me that you had a bottle containing one pound of pure 17
americium oxide, I would say, "You're crazy," and walk away. I'm sorry, but
my time is reasonably valuable, and I do not consider that statement to have
enough chance of validity even to warrant my stepping into the next room to
look at the bottle.

What I am trying to say is that doubting is far more important to the advance 18
of science than believing is and that, moreover, doubting is a serious business
that requires extensive training to be handled properly. People without training
in a particular field do not know what to doubt and what not to doubt; or, to
put it conversely, what to believe and what not to believe. I am very sorry to
be undemocratic, but one man's opinion is not necessarily as good as the next
man's.

To be sure, I feel uneasy about seeming to kowtow to authority in this 19
fashion. After all, you all know of instances where authority was wrong, dead
wrong. Look at Columbus, you will say. Look at Galileo.

I know about them, and about others, too. As a dabbler in the history of 20
science, I can give you horrible examples you may never have heard of. I can
cite the case of the German scientist, Rudolf Virchow, who, in the mid-
nineteenth century was responsible for important advances in anthropology and
practically founded the science of pathology. He was the first man to engage in
cancer research on a scientific basis. However, he was dead set against the germ
theory of disease when that was advanced by Pasteur. So were many others, but
one by one the opponents abandoned doubt as evidence multiplied. Not Virchow, however. Rather than be forced to admit he was wrong and Pasteur right,
Virchow quit science altogether and went into politics. How much wronger
could Stubborn Authority get?

But this is a very exceptional case. Let's consider a far more normal and 21
natural example of authority in the wrong.

The example concerns a young Swedish chemical student, Svante August 22
Arrhenius, who was working for his Ph.D. in the University of Uppsala in the
1880s. He was interested in the freezing points of solutions because certain odd
points arose in that connection.

If sucrose (ordinary table sugar) is dissolved in water, the freezing point of 23
the solution is somewhat lower than is that of pure water. Dissolve more sucrose
and the freezing point lowers further. You can calculate how many molecules
of sucrose must be dissolved per cubic centimeter of water in order to bring
about a certain drop in freezing point. It turns out that this same number of
molecules of glucose (grape sugar) and of many other soluble substances will
bring about the same drop. It doesn't matter that a molecule of sucrose is twice
as large as a molecule of glucose. What counts is the number of molecules and
not their size.

But if sodium chloride (table salt) is dissolved in water, the freezing-point 24
drop per molecule is twice as great as normal. And this goes for certain other
substances too. For instance, barium chloride, when dissolved, will bring about
a freezing-point drop that is three times normal.

Arrhenius wondered if this meant that when sodium chloride was dissolved, 25
each of its molecules broke into two portions, thus creating twice as many
particles as there were molecules and therefore a doubled freezing-point drop.

And barium chloride might break up into three particles per molecule. Since the sodium chloride molecule is composed of a sodium atom and a chlorine atom and since the barium chloride molecule is composed of a barium atom and two chlorine atoms, the logical next step was to suppose that these particular molecules broke up into individual atoms.

Then, too, there was another interesting fact. Those substances like sucrose 26 and glucose which gave a normal freezing-point drop did not conduct an electric current in solution. Those, like sodium chloride and barium chloride, which showed abnormally high freezing-point drops, *did* do so.

Arrhenius wondered if the atoms, into which molecules broke up on solution, 27 might not carry positive and negative electric charges. If the sodium atom carried a positive charge for instance, it would be attracted to the negative electrode. If the chlorine atom carried a negative charge, it would be attracted to the positive electrode. Each would wander off in its own direction and the net result would be that such a solution would conduct an electric current. For these charged and wandering atoms, Arrhenius adopted Faraday's name "ions" from a Greek word meaning "wanderer."

Furthermore, a charged atom, or ion, would not have the properties of an 28 uncharged atom. A charged chlorine atom would not be a gas that would bubble out of solution. A charged sodium atom would not react with water to form hydrogen. It was for that reason that common salt (sodium chloride) did not show the properties of either sodium metal or chlorine gas, though it was made of those two elements.

In 1884 Arrhenius, then twenty-five, prepared his theories in the form of a 29 thesis and presented it as part of his doctoral dissertation. The examining professors sat in frigid disapproval. No one had ever heard of electrically charged atoms, it was against all scientific belief of the time, and they turned on their built-in doubters.

However, Arrhenius argued his case so clearly and, on the single assumption 30 of the dissolution of molecules into charged atoms, managed to explain so much so neatly, that the professors' built-in doubters did not quite reach the intensity required to flunk the young man. Instead, they passed him—with the lowest possible passing grade.

But then, ten years later, the negatively charged electron was discovered and 31 the atom was found to be not the indivisible thing it had been considered but a complex assemblage of still smaller particles. Suddenly the notion of ions as charged atoms made sense. If an atom lost an electron or two, it was left with a positive charge; if it gained them, it had a negative charge.

Then, the decade following, the Nobel Prizes were set up and in 1903 the 32 Nobel Prize in Chemistry was awarded to Arrhenius for that same thesis which, nineteen years earlier, had barely squeaked him through for a Ph.D.

Were the professors wrong? Looking back, we can see they were. But in 1884 33 they were *not* wrong. They did exactly the right thing and they served science well. Every professor must listen to and appraise dozens of new ideas every year. He must greet each with the gradation of doubt his experience and training tells him the idea is worth.

Arrhenius's notion met with just the proper gradation of doubt. It was radical 34 enough to be held at arm's length. However, it seemed to have just enough possible merit to be worth some recognition. The professors *did* give him his Ph.D. after all. And other scientists of the time paid attention to it and thought about it. A very great one, Ostwald,[1] thought enough of it to offer Arrhenius a good job.

Then, when the appropriate evidence turned up, doubt receded to minimal 35 values and Arrhenius was greatly honored.

What better could you expect? Ought the professors to have fallen all over 36 Arrhenius and his new theory on the spot? And if so, why shouldn't they also have fallen all over forty-nine other new theories presented that year, no one of which might have seemed much more unlikely than Arrhenius's and some of which may even have appeared less unlikely?

It would have taken *longer* for the ionic theory to have become established 37 if overcredulity on the part of scientists had led them into fifty blind alleys. How many scientists would have been left to investigate Arrhenius's notions?

Scientific manpower is too limited to investigate everything that occurs to 38 everybody, and always will be too limited. The advance of science depends on scientists in general being kept firmly in the direction of maximum possible return. And the only device that will keep them turned in that direction is doubt; doubt arising from a good, healthy and active built-in doubter.

But, you might say, this misses the point. Can't one pick and choose and 39 isolate the brilliant from the imbecilic, accepting the first at once and wholeheartedly, and rejecting the rest completely? Would not such a course have saved ten years on ions without losing time on other notions?

Sure, if it could be done, but it can't. The godlike power to tell the good 40 from the bad, the useful from the useless, the true from the false, instantly and *in toto* belongs to gods and not to men.

Let me cite you Galileo as an example; Galileo, who was one of the greatest 41 scientific geniuses of all time, who invented modern science in fact, and who certainly experienced persecution and authoritarian enmity.

Surely, Galileo, of all people, was smart enough to know a good idea when 42 he saw it, and revolutionary enough not to be deterred by its being radical.

Well, let's see. In 1632 Galileo published the crowning work of his career, 43 *Dialogue on the Two Principal Systems of the World* which was the very book that got him into real trouble before the Inquisition. It dealt, as the title indicates, with the two principal systems; that of Ptolemy, which had the earth at

---

[1](Friedrich Wilhelm) Ostwald (1853–1932): German physical chemist and philosopher, awarded the 1909 Nobel Prize in chemistry. [Eds.]

the center of the universe with the planets, sun and moon going about it in complicated systems of circles within circles; and that of Copernicus which had the sun at the center and the planets, earth, and moon going about *it* in complicated systems of circles within circles.

Galileo did not as much as mention a *third* system, that of Kepler, which had the sun at the center but abandoned all the circles-within-circles jazz. Instead, he had the various planets traveling about the sun in ellipses, with the sun at one focus of the ellipse. It was Kepler's system that was correct and, in fact, Kepler's system has not been changed in all the time that has elapsed since. Why, then, did Galileo ignore it completely?

Was it that Kepler had not yet devised it? No, indeed. Kepler's views on that matter were published in 1609, twenty-seven years before Galileo's book.

Was it that Galileo had happened not to hear of it? Nonsense. Galileo and Kepler were in steady correspondence and were friends. When Galileo built some spare telescopes, he sent one to Kepler. When Kepler had ideas, he wrote about them to Galileo.

The trouble was that Kepler was still bound up with the mystical notions of the Middle Ages. He cast horoscopes for famous men, for a fee, and worked seriously and hard on astrology. He also spent time working out the exact notes formed by the various planets in creating the "music of the spheres" and pointed out that Earth's notes were mi, fa, mi, standing for misery, famine, and misery. He also devised a theory accounting for the relative distances of the planets from the Sun by nesting the five regular solids one within another and making deductions therefrom.

Galileo, who must have heard of all this, and who had nothing of the mystic about himself, could only conclude that Kepler, though a nice guy and a bright fellow and a pleasant correspondent, was a complete nut. I am sure that Galileo heard all about the elliptical orbits and, considering the source, shrugged it off.

Well, Kepler was indeed a nut, but he happened to be luminously right on occasion, too, and Galileo, of all people, couldn't pick the diamond out from among the pebbles.

Shall we sneer at Galileo for that?

Or should we rather be thankful that Galileo didn't interest himself in the ellipses *and* in astrology *and* in the nesting of regular solids *and* in the music of the spheres. Might not credulity have led him into wasting his talents, to the great loss of all succeeding generations?

No, no, until some supernatural force comes to our aid and tells men what is right and what wrong, men must blunder along as best they can, and only the built-in doubter of the trained scientist can offer a refuge of safety.

The very mechanism of scientific procedure, built up slowly over the years, is designed to encourage doubt and to place obstacles in the way of new ideas. No person receives credit for a new idea unless he publishes it for all the world to see and criticize. It is further considered advisable to announce ideas in papers read to colleagues at public gatherings that they might blast the speaker down face to face.

Even after announcement or publication, no observation can be accepted 54 until it has been confirmed by an independent observer, and no theory is considered more than, at best, an interesting speculation until it is backed by experimental evidence that has been independently confirmed and that has withstood the rigid doubts of others in the field.

All this is nothing more than the setting up of a system of "natural selection" 55 designed to winnow the fit from the unfit in the realm of ideas, in manner analogous to the concept of Darwinian evolution. The process may be painful and tedious, as evolution itself is; but in the long run it gets results, as evolution itself does. What's more, I don't see that there can be any substitute.

Now let me make a second point. The intensity to which the built-in doubter 56 is activated is also governed by the extent to which a new observation fits into the organized structure of science. If it fits well, doubt can be small; if it fits poorly, doubt can be intensive; if it threatens to overturn the structure completely, doubt is, and should be, nearly insuperable.

The reason for this is that now, three hundred fifty years after Galileo founded 57 experimental science, the structure that has been reared, bit by bit, by a dozen generations of scientists is so firm that its complete overturning has reached the vanishing point of unlikelihood.

Nor need you point to relativity as an example of a revolution that overturned 58 science. Einstein did not overturn the structure, he merely extended, elaborated, and improved it. Einstein did not prove Newton wrong, but merely incomplete. Einstein's world system contains Newton's as a special case and one which works if the volume of space considered is not too large and if velocities involved are not too great.

In fact, I should say that since Kepler's time in astronomy, since Galileo's 59 time in physics, since Lavoisier's[2] time in chemistry, and since Darwin's time in biology no discovery or theory, however revolutionary it has seemed, has actually overturned the structure of science or any major branch of it. The structure has merely been improved and refined.

The effect is similar to the paving of a road, and its broadening and the 60 addition of clover-leaf intersections, and the installation of radar to combat speeding. None of this, please notice, is the equivalent of abandoning the road and building another in a completely new direction.

But let's consider a few concrete examples drawn from contemporary life. A 61 team of Columbia University geologists have been exploring the configuration of the ocean bottom for years. Now they find that the mid-Atlantic ridge (a chain of mountains, running down the length of the Atlantic) has a rift in the

---

[2](Antoine Laurent) Lavoisier (1743–1794): French chemist and physicist, a founder of modern chemistry. His classification of substances is the basis of the modern distinction between chemical elements and compounds and of the system of chemical nomenclature. [Eds.]

center, a deep chasm or crack. What's more, this rift circles around Africa, sends an offshoot up into the Indian Ocean and across eastern Africa, and heads up the Pacific, skimming the California coast as it does so. It is like a big crack encircling the earth.

The observation itself can be accepted. Those involved were trained and experienced specialists and confirmation is ample. 62

But why the rift? Recently one of the geologists, Bruce Heezen, suggested that the crack may be due to the expansion of the earth. 63

This is certainly one possibility. If the interior were slowly expanding, the thin crust would give and crack like an eggshell. 64

But why should Earth's interior expand? To do so it would have to take up a looser arrangement, become less dense; the atoms would have to spread out a bit. 65

Heezen suggests that one way in which all this might happen is that the gravitational force of the Earth was very slowly weakening with time. The central pressures would therefore ease up and the compressed atoms of the interior would slowly spread out. 66

Buy why should Earth's gravity decrease, unless the force of gravitation everywhere were slowly decreasing with time? Now this deserves a lot of doubt, because there is nothing in the structure of science to suggest that the force of gravitation must decrease with time. However, it is also true that there is nothing in the structure of science to suggest that the force of gravitation might *not* decrease with time.[3] 67

Or take another case. I have recently seen a news clipping concerning an eighth-grader in South Carolina who grew four sets of bean plants under glass jars. One set remained there always, subjected to silence. The other three had their jars removed one hour a day in order that they might be exposed to noise; in one case to jazz, in another to serious music, and in a third to the raucous noises of sports-car engines. The only set of plants that grew vigorously were those exposed to the engine noises. 68

The headline was: *BEANS CAN HEAR—AND THEY PREFER AUTO RACING NOISE TO MUSIC.* 69

Automatically, my built-in doubter moves into high gear. Can it be that the newspaper story is a hoax? This is not impossible. The history of newspaper hoaxes is such that one could easily be convinced that nothing in any newspaper can possibly be believed. 70

But let's assume the story is accurate. The next question to ask is whether the youngster knew what he was doing? Was he experienced enough to make the nature of the noise the only variable? Was there a difference in the soil or 71

---

[3]As a matter of fact, there have been cosmological speculations (though not, in my opinion, very convincing ones) that involve a steady and very slow decrease in the gravitational constant; and there is also Kapp's theory, . . . which involves decreasing gravitational force on earth, without involving the gravitational constant.

in the water supply or in some small matter, which he disregarded through inexperience?

Finally, even if the validity of the experiment is accepted, what does it really   72
prove? To the headline writer and undoubtedly to almost everybody who reads the article, it will prove that plants can hear; and that they have preferences and will refuse to grow if they feel lonely and neglected.

This is so far against the current structure of science that my built-in doubter   73
clicks it right off and stamps it: IGNORE. Now what is an alternative explanation that fits in reasonably well with the structure of science? Sound is not just something to hear; it is a form of vibration. Can it be that sound vibrations stir up tiny soil particles making it easier for plants to absorb water, or putting more ions within reach by improving diffusion? May the natural noise that surrounds plants act in this fashion to promote growth? And may the engine noises have worked best on a one-hour-per-day basis because they were the loudest and produced the most vibration?

Any scientist (or eighth-grader) who feels called on to experiment further,   74
ought to try vibrations that do not produce audible sound; ultrasonic vibrations, mechanical vibrations and so on. Or he might also try to expose the plant itself to vibrations of all sorts while leaving the soil insulated; and vice versa.

Which finally brings me to flying saucers and spiritualism and the like. The   75
questions I ask myself are: What is the nature of the authorities promulgating these and other viewpoints of this sort? and How well do such observations and theories fit in with the established structure of science?

My answers are, respectively, Very poor and Very poorly.   76

Which leaves me completely unrepentant as far as my double role in life is   77
concerned. If I get a good idea involving flying saucers and am in the mood to write some science fiction, I will gladly and with delight write a flying-saucer story.

And I will continue to disbelieve in them firmly in real life.   78

And if that be schizophrenia, make the most of it.   79

QUESTIONS

1. What is a "built-in doubter," and why, as in paragraph 13, is Asimov's definition of it essentially mechanical, as a piece of equipment? What are the implications of his describing his "built-in doubter" that way?

2. Asimov claims that "doubting is far more important to the advance of science than believing is" (paragraph 18) and supports that claim with the case of the scientists who refused to accept wholeheartedly the theories of Arrhenius (paragraphs 21 through 37). How does that example support his claim? What other examples does he offer?

3. Asimov also claims that it takes training to doubt well. In what field of interest might you be a well-trained doubter? Provide a set of examples from an area of interest to you that parallels the example of the three oxides in paragraphs 15 through 17. Your

examples should range from causing little or no doubt to stirring a great deal of doubt in you.

4. As humans, Asimov reminds us, we simply lack the powers to distinguish reliably "the good from the bad, the useful from the useless" (paragraph 40). Think of the difficulty of that kind of judgment in cases outside of science. Can you always tell a good movie from a bad one, a good record from a poor one, a good book from one you needn't bother reading? Tell of a case in which you changed your mind about such a judgment. What caused you to change your mind? How did that change occur?

5. We often begin by admiring something and later doubt its value. Is our "built-in doubter" simply being switched on late then, or would you describe what happens differently?

6. Asimov raises the question of when, if ever, it is right not to doubt. Consider a slightly different case: when is it right to believe without doubting? Think of an idea—something other than a matter of religious faith—that you have read about or someone has told you about that you naturally believe in. What causes you to believe in this idea? Describe the case of a "built-in believer."

7. Go to the library and do some research on one of the notions Asimov rejects (paragraph 5) or on one of the discoveries of the great scientists he admires (paragraphs 58 and 59). Write a paper explaining what you have discovered and how it accords with Asimov's judgments about built-in doubters and science.

8. The history of every discipline is filled with examples of ideas that were once doubted and then later recognized as great discoveries. Investigate such an idea from a discipline that interests you, and try to uncover not only why that idea was once doubted but also the influence it has had subsequently on that discipline.

SPARROWS LEARN ADULT SONG AND MORE FROM MEMORY

Peter Marler and Susan Peters

Peter Marler and Susan Peters are a research team from Rockefeller University's Center for Biology and Ethology in Millbrook, New York. They had published previously on the subject of bird songs before the present article appeared in Science in 1981. Because they are addressing a scientific audience, their essay follows a prescribed form, beginning with a short abstract, using careful citations of other work in the field, and noting the dates of first submission and final revision of the article as a record in case of a "simultaneous" discovery and publication of similar material by other investigators.

ABSTRACT. *Male swamp sparrows reared in the laboratory and exposed to taped songs during infancy produce accurate imitations of the material following an 8-month interval with no rehearsal. When the first rehearsal occurs, at about 300 days of age, large numbers of syllables are perfected. They are developed through invention and improvisation as well as imitation. Most are discarded at the time of song crystallization. Hence, these songbirds learn more than they manifest in full adult song.*

Many and perhaps all songbirds acquire the normal song of their species through learning.[1] Some songbirds retain an ability to develop new songs throughout life.[2] Others lose this ability early, so that songs developed at sexual maturity remain virtually unchanged over subsequent breeding seasons. Sensi-

[1]K. Immelmann, in *Bird Vocalizations*. R. A. Hinde, Ed. (Cambridge Univ. Press, Cambridge, 1969), pp. 61–74; M. Konishi and F. Nottebohm, in *ibid.*, pp. 29–48; D. Kroodsma, in *Ontogeny of Behavior*, G. Burghardt and M. Bekoff, Eds. (Garland, New York, 1978), pp. 215–230; R. E. Lemon, *Condor* 77, 385 (1975); P. Marler and P. Mundinger, in *Ontogeny of Vertebrate Behavior*, H. Moltz, Ed. (Academic Press, New York, 1971), pp. 389–450; F. Nottebohm, *Am. Nat.* 106, 116 (1972); in *Avian Biology*, V. D. Farner, Ed. (Academic Press, New York, 1975), vol. 5, pp. 287–332; W. H. Thorpe, *The Biology of Vocal Communication and Expression in Birds* (Cambridge Univ. Press, Cambridge, 1961).

[2]H. R. Güttinger, *J. Ornithol.* 119, 172 (1978); P. F. Jenkins, *Anim. Behav.* 25, 50 (1977); P. Marler, M. Konishi, A. Lutjen, M. S. Waser, *Proc. Natl. Acad. Sci. U.S.A.* 70, 1393 (1973); P. Marler, P. Mundinger, M. S. Waser, A. Lutjen, *Anim. Behav.* 20, 586 (1972); F. Nottebohm and M. E. Nottebohm, *Z. Tierpsychol.* 46, 298 (1978); J. O. Rice and W. L. Thompson, *Anim. Behav.* 16, 462 (1968); K. Yasukawa, J. L. Blank, C. B. Patterson, *Behav. Ecol. Sociobiol.* 7, 233 (1980).

Peter Marler and Susan Peters

tive periods for vocal learning are commonly found; laboratory-reared birds of several species learn from taped songs played to them in infancy more readily than later in life.[3] In some this occurs even though full song does not commence until late adolescence or adulthood. Thus certain songbirds may be said to display a remarkable capacity to learn to sing from memory. There is an early perceptual phase of listening to others and learning from them and a later phase of sensorimotor development in which birds monitor their own voice in perfecting song production.

In the sensorimotor phase, song does not spring forth fully formed, but is prefaced by a period of subsong.[4] In some species subsong begins in infancy, and can follow soon after the perceptual phase. Insofar as subsong might involve rehearsal of memorized song themes, it could be viewed as bridging the gap between the perceptual and sensorimotor phases, alleviating any undue burden on the bird's memory.

The question of early rehearsal of learned song is moot, however, because no one has conducted a sound spectrographic study of the early stages in the development of singing. We undertook such an investigation in the swamp sparrow, *Melospiza georgiana*.

Male swamp sparrows brought into the laboratory as nestlings learn readily from taped songs of their species when these are played from the third to the eighth week of life. Full song develops some 9 months later and often contains a certain proportion of "syllables" that match components on the training tapes.[5] The diverse morphology of natural swamp sparrow syllables permits choice of a great variety of training patterns. Exposure to different syllables in infancy results in different patterns of adult singing. The conclusion that songs are learned is based on this capacity to match acoustic models and on the abnormality of songs of birds reared without exposure to the species song (Figure 1).

We reared 16 male swamp sparrows by hand in acoustic isolation from the species song. They were taken from the field as 2- to 10-day-old nestlings. The birds were trained for 40 days, beginning between 16 and 26 days of age. (Song stimulation before about 10 days of age has no detectable influence on song development. The songs of untrained males raised from the egg by foster parents have a similar syllabic structure to those of males taken as 10-day-old nestlings and reared without training.) The training songs consisted of a variety of exper-

[3]W. P. J. Dittus and R. E. Lemon, *Anim. Behav.* 17, 523 (1969); F. Dowsett-Lemaire, *Ibis* 121, 453 (1979); D. Kroodsma, *Anim. Behav.* 25, 390 (1977); ——— and R. Pickert, *Nature (London)* 288, 477 (1980); W. E. Lanyon, in *Animal Sounds and Communication*, W. E. Lanyon and W. N. Tavolga, Eds. (American Institute of Biological Sciences, Washington, D.C., 1960), pp. 321–347; R. E. Lemon and D. M. Scott, *Can. J. Zool.* 44, 191 (1966); P. Marler, *J. Comp. Physiol. Psychol.* 71, 1 (1970); J. A. Mulligan, *Univ. Calif. Berkeley Publ. Zool.* 81, 1 (1966); F. Nottebohm, *Ibis* 111, 386 (1969); W. H. Thorpe, *ibid.* 100, 535 (1958).
[4]E. A. Armstrong, *A Study of Bird Song* (Oxford Univ. Press, London, 1963); F. Nottebohm, *J. Exp. Zool.* 179, 35 (1972); W. H. Thorpe and P. M. Pilcher, *Br. Birds* 51, 509 (1958).
[5]P. Marler and S. Peters, *Science* 198, 519 (1977); in *Perspectives on the Study of Speech*, P. Eimas and J. Miller, Eds. (Erlbaum, Hillsdale, N.J., 1980), pp. 75–112.

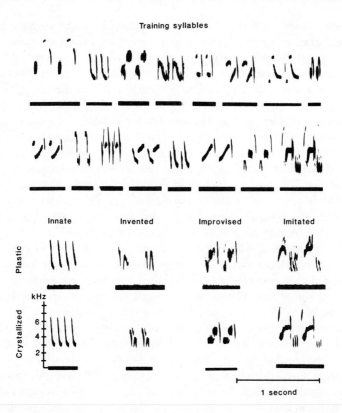

FIGURE 1. Pairs of the song syllables used for training the subjects. Also shown are pairs of syllables developed later (plastic and crystallized versions). These were classified as inventions, improvisations, and imitations. For comparison, a pair of innate syllables developed by an untrained swamp sparrow appears on the left.

imentally modified arrangements of song syllables of this species and the closely related song sparrow (*Melospiza melodia*), arranged in bouts after the manner in which these birds typically sing.[6] They were played twice a day, morning and evening. The training procedure faithfully followed methods used with success in previous years.

After training, the males were isolated in separate soundproof chambers. Beginning at about 95 days of age, their voices were recorded early in the morning once per week, continuing up to 1 year of age. Prior to this sporadic singing between 50 and 90 days was recorded and some was heard as early as 30 days. All this early singing was indistinguishable from that occurring around 100 days of age. Approximately 700 hours of recording yielded 235 hours of singing, with 15,056 songs.

[6]*Ibid.*

All vocalizations other than call notes were edited out and analyzed by real-time spectography.[7] On the basis of visual inspection, singing was classified into seven categories. Stage 1, crystallized song, is the typical stereotyped male song. It consists of a 2-second string of identical repetitions of a multinote syllable at regular intervals (Figure 1). As in nature, each male had a repertoire with an average of three song types. Stages 2 to 4, plastic song, are steps in the emergence of stereotyped syllables, separated by such criteria as stability of acoustic structure and regularity of the combinations in which they occur. Stages 5 and 6 are the variable and amorphous phases of "subplastic" song in which the rudiments of crystallized syllables can be recognized. They are transitional between plastic song and stage 7, subsong, which lacks defined syllables or other regularities.

After some singing from 100 to 150 days of age, the sparrows stopped from 160 to 238 days. Then, quite suddenly, one bird after another began to sing regularly. By 298 days all were singing. Sound spectrographic analysis revealed that the average age at which crystallized song emerged was 334 days (range, 300 to 350 days). Once crystallized, these songs remained stable for the rest of the season. In a subset of males studied during the second and third years of life, 31 crystallized songs remained unchanged, one was dropped, and one was slightly modified. There were no additions to any repertoire.

A survey of song development from the first subsong to crystallized song revealed a pattern to which all 16 birds conformed. On average, progression from subsong to subplastic song occurred at 285 days (range, 252 to 333 days). The average age at which plastic song began was 299 days. All males then advanced rapidly through the categories of plastic song—sometimes uttering several stages in a single day—to complete the process of song crystallization. Thus the first attempts of these males to reproduce memorized syllables began about 225 days after they last heard them, and rehearsal of particular syllables started about 2 weeks later.

Evidently sparrows commit song material heard in their first 2 months to memory and then keep it in storage, without rehearsal, for some 8 months. Only in early adulthood, a time of rapid testicular growth and waxing androgen production, do they begin transforming portions of the memorized material into matching sound patterns.

Previously it was implicitly assumed that adult song is a reliable register of what a male bird has learned. The analysis of plastic song reveals that the birds developed much more than was needed for adult song. As already indicated, crystallized song repertoires in swamp sparrows typically consist of three syllables per male. The plastic song recorded only 1 week before crystallization incorporated an average of six different syllables per bird. Earlier in development there may be as many as 19 distinct syllables per male, with an average maximum of 12. Thus in plastic song a male swamp sparrow produces four times

---

[7]C. D. Hopkins, M. Rossetto, A. Lutjen, Z. *Tierpsychol.* **34**, 313 (1974).

more syllables than are needed for the mature repertoire (Figure 2). A total of 199 different syllables were identified in plastic song from the 16 males. Only 45 survived the crystallization process.

Comparison of the syllable types produced in plastic song with those heard 12 in infancy was also revealing. Only 59 syllables—less than a third of those produced—were judged to be accurate copies of models. Of the remainder, 36 were construed as poor copies, perhaps modified by improvisation. This left 104 syllables unaccounted for. We conclude that these were inventions. Four of the 16 birds sang only invented and improvised syllables and 12 sang a mixture of imitated syllables. Invented and copied syllables mingle freely in plastic song, and a facility for syntactical rearrangement is evident in the many syllable re-combinations that occur. Of the 45 syllables that were finally crystallized, 19 were copies of training songs, 19 were invented, and the rest were improvised or poorly copied. Thus, both inventions and imitations are winnowed as song develops.

Although imitation plays a crucial role in swamp sparrow song development, 13 it evidently is not the only process involved. So far as we can determine, the

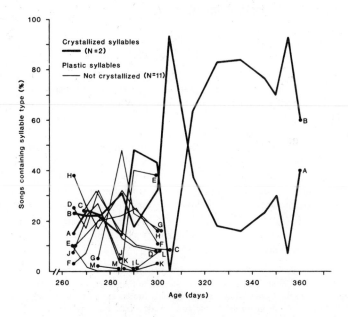

FIGURE 2. Changes in syllable usage with age in one male swamp sparrow. This bird crystallized two song types at 300 days, each with a single syllable type, A or B. Prior to this as many as 11 other syllable types were developed, only to be culled at the time of song crystallization. Syllables A and B are both copies of training syllables. Of the other syllables sung during plastic song, C, D, E, F, H, and J were copies; G and I were improvisations or poor copies; and K, L, and M were inventions.

Peter Marler and Susan Peters

invented syllables originated independently of the imitations and were not produced by progressive improvisation upon learned themes. They differed from the learned syllables in the smaller number of notes from which they were constructed (1.4 per syllable versus 2.8 for learned syllables). However, they were more complex than the innate song syllables of untrained swamp sparrows, which average 1.1 notes each (Figure 1).

The process of singing from memory described here almost certainly occurs in wild swamp sparrows. A similar process probably occurs in the first year of life in many other songbirds. Temporal separation of the perceptual and sensorimotor phases of vocal ontogeny[8] may be important in allowing cognitive mechanisms to operate on the memorized material. In sparrows these mechanisms appear to parse learned song material into syllabic multinote units that can then be recombined in novel syntactical arrangements by processes equivalent to phonological syntax in human speech.[9] Finally, vocal invention makes a major contribution in birdsong ontogeny, even in a species such as the swamp sparrow, in which the impact of learning is pervasive. Many more syllables, both imitated and invented, are used in plastic song than in the final song patterns. This may be analogous to the overproduction of diverse speech sounds in the prespeech babbling of human infants.[10]

14

QUESTIONS

1. According to paragraph 6, the sparrows, once exposed to recorded songs, were isolated in soundproof chambers for up to a year. What are the implications of that procedure for the experiment?

2. Review paragraphs 11 and 12. Summarize the nature of learning in the case of the swamp sparrow. What do you find the most surprising information here?

3. Paragraph 12 reveals how large a proportion of syllables did not imitate the training models. How does this information affect your reaction to the authors' argument?

4. What would be the difficulties involved in monitoring a control group for this experiment? Does knowledge of those difficulties alter your understanding of the results reported here?

5. The fourth sentence in the first paragraph is written unclearly. Rewrite it, trying to eliminate the difficulty.

[8]ontogeny: development in an individual as opposed to that of the species. [Eds.]

[9]We refer here to the human ability to recombine a limited set of speech sounds or phonemes in accordance with phonological rules that serve to create a potentially infinite number of different words [N. Chomsky and M. Halle, *The Sound Pattern of English* (Harper & Row, New York, 1968)].

[10]O. H. Mowrer, *Learning Theory and the Symbolic Processes* (Wiley, New York, 1960); R. Jakobson, *Child Language, Aphasia, and General Sound Laws* (Mouton, The Hague, 1968).

Supported by PHS research grant S07 RR-0765-12 to Rockefeller University and MH 14651 to P.M.

27 February 1981; revised 28 May 1981

6. Consider the terminology of paragraph 7: *crystallized*, *plastic*, and *subplastic*. How do those terms work as metaphors? What are their implications?

7. Can you make sense of Figure 1? What function does it serve?

8. Divide this report into the four sections typical of scientific reports: Introduction, Materials and Methods, Results, and Discussion. Where would each of those sections begin and end in this paper? What further subdivisions do you find? Are there sections that don't separate neatly, one from the other?

9. To what fields, besides the study of birds, might this research contribute? What methodology and technology used here are shared by other fields?

10. Explain another learning process with which you are familiar. What points of comparison does it have with the swamp sparrow's learning to sing? To what extent are the sparrow's learning and your learning process related? Your best examples might come from games or hobbies in which you have become proficient.

11. Learning to speak is obviously related to the learning of the swamp sparrows, and so is learning to write. Write an essay examining your own experience of learning to write. Let the learning of the swamp sparrows provide you with whatever suggestions and analogies seem useful to you, but don't assume that every stage in the sparrow's learning is analogous to one in your own.

TENTATIVE REPORT ON THE HUDSON RIVER BRIDGE
Othmar H. Ammann

Othmar H. Ammann (1879–1965) was a Swiss-born civil engineer whose work is familiar to most Americans, if only from postcards: over the course of a long career he played a major role in the design and construction of many bridges, including the George Washington in New York City and the Golden Gate in San Francisco. The report reprinted here was singled out as a model of good engineering prose by Walter J. Miller and Lee E. A. Saidla, two English professors at the Polytechnic Institute of Brooklyn, New York, who included it in their textbook, Engineers as Writers *(1953, 1971), and wrote the comment that follows the report. As they pointed out in their edition, Ammann was asked to write this report in 1926 when plans for what became the George Washington Bridge had reached a crucial stage. The report was written for the Port of New York Authority and sent to the governors of the two states involved, New York and New Jersey. As a result of this report, the states pledged ten million dollars for construction, ground was broken in 1927, and the bridge was open to traffic four years later.*

The selection that follows includes the cover letter to the governors; Ammann's report, which is addressed to the commissioners of the Port of New York Authority; and the comment by Miller and Saidla. The supplementary tables and other technical exhibits have been omitted.

THE PORT OF NEW YORK AUTHORITY

March 11, 1926

To the Governor of the State of New York:
To the Governor of the State of New Jersey:

SIRS:—We herewith transmit to you the Tentative Report of our Bridge 1

Engineer dealing with a bridge across the Hudson River between Fort Washington and Fort Lee, which gives the engineers' tentative conclusions.

We send this report at this time in order that you may have the latest available   2
engineering information on this matter. The Commission has not yet determined the design or location of the bridge.

We have the honor to remain,   3

Respectfully,

JULIAN A. GREGORY, Chairman,
JOHN F. GALVIN, Vice-Chairman,
The Port of   FRANK C. FERGUSON,
New York Authority   OTTO B. SHULHOF,
SCHUYLER N. RICE,
HERBERT K. TWITCHELL,
Commissioners

The Port of New York Authority

February 25, 1926

To the Commissioners of the Port of New York Authority:

DEAR SIRS:—The preliminary work necessary for the planning and con-   4
struction of the Hudson River Bridge between Fort Washington and Fort Lee, with which The Port of New York Authority has been charged by the Legislatures of New York and New Jersey, has now advanced to a point where conclusions can be drawn regarding the physical and financial feasibility of this bridge, its necessity as a link in the local and interstate transportation systems, its location, size, type, method of construction, approximate cost and aesthetic merits.

Briefly the work so far accomplished embraces comprehensive traffic studies   5
to determine the probable volume of traffic over the bridge and the revenues to be derived therefrom, topographical surveys, river borings and engineering design studies to determine the suitable site, size and type of crossing and its cost, and finally, architectural studies to determine the feasibility of rendering the bridge a befitting object in a charming landscape.

The project being of exceptional magnitude and complex aspect, it was nec-   6
essary that the preliminary studies be undertaken with great care and thoroughness. The appropriations by the two States for these preliminary studies, amounting to $200,000, became available only on July 1, 1925, and the time

has not been sufficient to permit either the completion of the studies or the rendering of a comprehensive report on the project. However, it is believed that from the studies so far completed the following conservative conclusions may be drawn:

CONCLUSIONS

(1) The traffic studies reveal an urgent demand for a crossing for vehicular   7
traffic in the vicinity of the proposed bridge to relieve the present intolerable traffic situation. The traffic volume is of more than sufficient magnitude to make it financially feasible to construct, operate and maintain, from tolls, such a crossing, not considering the broader benefits to the people of both States as well as to the local community.

(2) The general location of the bridge is well chosen with regard to topog-   8
raphy in its vicinity and the feasibility of convenient connections to the important local and arterial highway routes on both sides of the river. A crossing at this point also appears to be the next logical step after construction of the vehicular tunnel at Canal Street, since the two crossings are far enough apart not to influence materially each other's traffic quota.

(3) From the engineering point of view the construction of the bridge is in   9
every respect feasible and, while of unusual magnitude, will involve no extraordinary difficulties, nor hazardous or untried operations. The bridge will have a single river span of at least 3500 feet and a clear height above water of about 200 feet. The piers will be located within pier-head lines, as established by the War Department, and will therefore be no obstruction to navigation.

(4) The bridge is to be the suspension type, the most economical and aes-   10
thetically superior type available. It will be of extremely simple construction, and its design is conceived so that it will be feasible to build the bridge at a minimum initial expenditure to serve present traffic needs, and to enlarge its capacity as the traffic volume increases.

(5) If funds for construction of the bridge shall become available in 1927,   11
it is expected that not later than 1933 the bridge will be open for four-lane vehicular and bus passenger traffic and for pedestrians. It is estimated that this capacity will suffice to take care of the initial traffic and the expected increase until about 1943, and then it will probably become necessary to enlarge to an eight-lane vehicular capacity.

(6) While it is not possible, at the present time, to report definite cost   12
figures, it is estimated, upon information so far available and upon such forecast of real estate values as may now reasonably be made, that the bridge can be opened for highway traffic at a cost of less than $50,000,000, inclusive of interest during construction.

(7)   Depending upon traffic capacity finally to be decided upon, it is esti-   13
mated that the bridge can later be enlarged at an additional cost of between
$15,000,000 and $25,000,000, if, and when, the vehicular and passenger traffic
will have grown in volume to pay for this additional cost.

(8)   On the basis of conservative traffic analysis, and without counting upon   14
the vehicular traffic which will be generated by the construction of the bridge,
nor upon possible income from other than vehicular traffic, it is estimated that
during the first year after completion the revenue will more than cover the
annual interest charge, administration, maintenance, and amortization. The
bridge will thus be self-sustaining in every respect from the first year without
imposing unreasonable toll charges upon the traffic.

(9)   On the basis of conservative assumptions for future growth of traffic,   15
and counting upon revenue from vehicular traffic alone, it is estimated that
within ten years after opening to traffic the bridge may be enlarged to eight-lane
capacity, and that within twenty years thereafter the entire bond issue raised to
cover construction cost can be amortized.

(10)   The architectural studies so far made, while yet tentative, indicate   16
clearly that the bridge may be so designed as to form an object of grace and
beauty as well as utility, and to blend harmoniously with the grandeur of its
natural setting.

(11)   In view of this favorable aspect of the bridge, its urgent necessity to   17
relieve traffic conditions and in order to derive the benefit of a complete investigation, it is recommended that the preliminary work be carried to completion,
and that the States be asked to appropriate an additional sum of $100,000 to
make that completion possible.

Following is a more complete and detailed account of the work so far ac-   18
complished:

TRAFFIC STUDIES

Since the Legislative Acts provide that the Port Authority may levy charges   19
for the use of the bridge and that the bridge shall be built and paid for in whole
or in part by bonds of the Port Authority, or other securities, it has been necessary to ascertain whether or not the revenues from tolls for vehicles and pedestrians, and possibly franchise rights for rail passenger facilities, will be adequate to meet the cost of construction. This involves the study of a number of
traffic factors, viz.:

First: The present volume of vehicular and pedestrian traffic over each of the   20
seventeen ferries across the Hudson River.

Othmar H. Ammann

Second: The volume of traffic the bridge will be expected to attract when it   21
is opened to traffic. This requires an estimate of the effect on the bridge traffic
of the opening of the vehicular tunnel in 1926.

Third: The volume of traffic that can reasonably be expected to be diverted   22
to the bridge from each of the other crossings in that year.

Fourth: The volume of traffic over the bridge for each year, for twenty years   23
subsequent to the opening of the bridge, proper allowance being made for the
effect upon the bridge traffic of the possible construction of other crossings below
179th Street, Manhattan.

This necessitates the determination of the origin and destination of vehicles   24
by types for the existing ferries and apportioning the divertible traffic to each of
the proposed crossings in such a way as to take into account relative distances
and ferry, tunnel, and bridge charges and the elimination of undue congestion
on the approach streets to each of the proposed facilities.

Fifth: An estimate of the revenues for each year subsequent to the opening   25
of the bridge, based upon an average toll per vehicle and per pedestrian.

In order to estimate the vehicular traffic, it was necessary to obtain the trend   26
or rate of growth of the present-day traffic over seventeen ferries between the
Battery and Tarrytown (for the most recent normal year). This required the
records, by classes of vehicles, kept by each of the ferry companies from 1914
to date. Where revenues only are available for this traffic, average tolls for each
class of vehicle must be applied to the revenues to estimate the number of
vehicles. From these records the volume of traffic over each of the ferries can
be forecast for each of the years subsequent to 1932.

Instead of forecasting the traffic for each of the ferries it is better to forecast   27
the volume of traffic that will be diverted from the existing ferries to the bridge.
To obtain this divertible bridge traffic it is necessary first to ascertain the distribution of the present-day traffic over each of the ferries for the most recent
normal year. To do this the origin and destination of each vehicle is necessary
for a sample period of time, so selected that the peak and the average traffic
condition in the year will be reflected. These occur in the months of July and
October. The variations of traffic between week-days and Sundays and from
hour to hour, or both, are necessary to estimate the peak traffic conditions to
test out the roadway capacities on the bridge. Field clockings, therefore, were
taken by placing inspectors on each of the ferry boats of every route to ride the
boats throughout the day. The inspectors ascertained and recorded the following
information respecting each vehicle crossing the river by ferry:

(a) Type of vehicle, that is, whether horse drawn or motor propelled. A
division of motor vehicles was made as between commercial and pleasure, and
again sub-divided to indicate the carrying capacity of the commercial vehicles
and the seating capacity of the pleasure vehicles:

(b) Number of persons carried in each vehicle;

(c) State License;

426

(d) Origin and destination of each vehicle;

(e) Frequency of use of ferry route by each vehicle.

These clockings were made throughout the months of July, August, September and October, 1925. In carrying forward the clockings a field force of fifty-six men was employed on the seventeen ferry routes. The detailed information noted above was ascertained and recorded for a total of 242,000 vehicles. 28

Clockings were made of the vehicular traffic now passing over the streets and street intersections in the vicinity of the proposed location of the bridge, to determine the degree to which capacity of these streets is now used. Also a study was made to determine the volume of traffic carried at present by the East River bridges, particularly during the peak of travel; and the extent of saturation. 29

Examination of the records of the various ferry companies operating the seventeen ferry routes, for the purpose of ascertaining the volume of traffic and its classification handled by the ferries of each route for the past ten years, has required a force of three to four men constantly from July to the present date. 30

After having completed the field clockings, the next step was the tabulation and summarization of the data. The work of tabulating was carried on in part during the period of clocking and has proceeded since the clockings were completed in October, to bring it to a point to permit of detailed analysis. 31

These analyses are for the purpose of determining future distribution of vehicular traffic among the present crossings, the proposed 178th Street bridge, and any other crossings that might later be constructed and which might affect the future revenues of the 178th Street bridge. 32

One of the first determinations to be arrived at by analysis is the probable volume of traffic that may be expected to use the 178th Street bridge when it is opened, assuming that were the only highway across the Hudson River between Manhattan and New Jersey. 33

The second determination to be made is the volume of traffic which will be attracted to the vehicular tunnel, when it is opened, which otherwise might, in part at least, have used the 178th Street Bridge. 34

The third determination is the probable effect on the 178th Street bridge traffic by the opening of any additional highway crossing over the Hudson in the future. 35

Each of these steps involves a large number of intermediate steps. For example: highway access to the bridge; determination of a toll which will secure maximum traffic and maximum revenue; future crossings to be constructed by the City of New York across the East and Harlem Rivers; and traffic that will be generated by the stimulation of industrial and residential development, particularly on the Jersey side. 36

The results of all of these traffic studies are now being carefully recorded and will be included in a later report on the project. 37

Exhibit (A) illustrates the growth of the total trans-Hudson vehicular traffic as tentatively estimated, from 1924 to 1960, inclusive, and the number of ve- 38

427

hicles of this total traffic which would have been, or will be, diverted to the 178th Street bridge.

Below is recorded the first tentative estimate of total trans-Hudson vehicular 39 traffic for all ferries from the Battery to and including Tarrytown, and the traffic that the bridge will divert from these ferries and the tunnel.

Year	Hudson River Traffic	Bridge Traffic	Year	Hudson River Traffic	Bridge Traffic
1924	11,706,000	3,208,000	1944	36,055,000	11,476,000
1925	12,912,000	3,596,000	1945	36,767,000	11,723,000
1926	14,185,000	4,017,000	1946	37,408,000	11,944,000
....	....	....	....	....	....
1934	25,607,000	7,889,000	1953	40,841,000	13,144,000
1935	26,984,000	8,364,000	1954	41,172,000	13,263,000
1936	28,280,000	8,807,000	1955	41,478,000	13,369,000
			1956	41,765,000	13,471,000

These figures must be revised as the analysis proceeds to take into account 40 the effect of the opening of additional crossings. The above figures do not include traffic which will be generated from the adjacent territories, whose growth the bridge will stimulate. While this cannot be measured accurately, an analysis of the growth of population, intensity of realty development, and motor vehicle registration is in process to determine the effect of the East River bridges upon Brooklyn and Queens, in order to gauge roughly the effect that the Hudson River bridge will have upon Fort Lee and its contiguous communities. The amount of this traffic will be considerable and eventually will be added to the above estimates.

While the above traffic is the principal source of revenue, there are four 41 other sources which will contribute to the income of the bridge. This revenue will come from passengers in vehicles, pedestrians, bus lines and rapid transit facilities. Studies are under way to ascertain the potential traffic which will give rise to this income and will be presented in a later report.

Tables (1-a), and (1-c), appended to this report, give the gross revenues 42 estimated to date for a 50¢ rate, a 60¢ rate, a 70¢ rate, respectively, from vehicles only. It will be seen that for 1933, or the first year of operation, the income from vehicles alone is forecast as at least $3,700,000. Subtracting the charges for administration, maintenance and operation, the net operating income is close to 6½% on the $50,000,000, the probable maximum initial cost of the bridge. In addition, there will be revenue from passengers in vehicles, pedestrians, and bus lines, and from vehicular traffic which will be generated by the bridge. Consequently, it is safe to conclude at this time that the charges on the

428

initial and ultimate cost of construction can be met out of the potential revenue from traffic, and that therefore the project is economically sound.

LOCATION STUDIES

The Legislative Acts of New York and New Jersey provide that the bridge shall be located at a point between 170th and 185th Streets in Manhattan, New York City, and a point approximately opposite thereto in the borough of Fort Lee, New Jersey. 43

After a general examination of the territory on both sides of the river, within these limits, three specific sites which appeared to offer possibilities were tentatively selected for more careful study. . . . The three sites chosen are those in close vicinity of 181st Street, 179th Street, and 175th Street, Manhattan, respectively. River borings, studies of approaches, grades, street connections, tentative designs and comparative cost estimates were made for these locations. These studies revealed the central location near 179th Street as being not only the most economical, but also the most desirable with respect to approach grades and street connections and natural setting, and it was therefore decided to confine the elaboration of more complete plans and estimates to this location. 44

In the selection of the locations, careful consideration was also given to the scenic effect of the bridge, more particularly with regard to the effect upon Fort Washington Park. While, by locating the bridge at 181st Street or 175th Street, encroachment upon this park by bridge piers might be avoided, the much longer river span required at these locations, and the consequent greater proportions of the bridge, would not be as favorable, aesthetically, as a bridge at 179th Street. Moreover, the location of a pier in the Park is not believed to curtail in any way the usefulness of the Park or to mar its beauty. 45

TOPOGRAPHICAL SURVEYS, MAPPING AND TRIANGULATION

Owing to lack of maps, sufficiently accurate and complete for preliminary planning and reliable estimates of cost, it has been necessary to undertake extensive and accurate topographical surveys extending over the territories on which the bridge approaches and street connections may be located. These surveys are now nearing completion and will form a valuable basis for the final planning and construction of the bridge. The results of these surveys have been embodied in a large map to the scale of $1'' = 100'$. 46

Owing to the lateness of the season it has been found impracticable to undertake an accurate triangulation across the river, but the necessary base lines 47 have been established, and all other preparations for these measurements have been made, and it is expected that they can be accomplished in the Spring as soon as weather conditions permit. For the tentative studies, the triangulation made by the U. S. Coast and Geodetic Survey was considered to be sufficiently reliable.

RIVER BORINGS

In order to obtain reliable information on the character of the river bottom 48
and to establish beyond question the surface of the solid bedrock upon which the bridge piers have to rest, it was necessary to undertake borings carried well into the solid rock.

In all sixteen borings, at the three locations tentatively selected, have been 49
sunk, the results carefully recorded and the rock cores preserved. These borings have established the fact that, outside of the pierhead lines established by the War Department, that is, within the width of river reserved for navigation, bedrock is too deep to permit of economical construction of bridge piers and that such piers must, and can, be placed between the pierhead lines and the shore, or on shore. Moreover, thus located, the piers will form no obstructions to navigation. . . .

Additional borings will have to be made when the location of the bridge is 50
definitely established.

The character of rock revealed by these borings corresponds to that prognos- 51
ticated by the U. S. Geological Survey. On the New Jersey side bedrock was found to consist partly of solid red sandstone and shale, known as the "Newark Formation," partly of the so-called "Stockbridge Dolomite" which forms the major portion of the rockbed under the Hudson River. The borings on the New York side revealed a solid bed of "Hudson Shist" (mica shist), which is the prevailing rock of Manhattan Island. All of these rock formations are sufficiently hard to constitute a solid and permanent foundation for the bridge piers and to safely sustain the great pressure from them.

The material overlying the rock is almost entirely river silt, unsuitable for 52
foundation purposes.

ENGINEERING DESIGN STUDIES

In order to determine the most economical and suitable type and general 53
proportions of the structure, for various possible locations, it was essential to

430

undertake extended comparative design studies and cost estimates, before any final planning could be undertaken. Complete tentative designs were made for a 3500 foot river span and a 3900 foot span, as required for the 179th and 181st Street locations, respectively. Comparative estimates of cost have also been prepared for various capacities for highway traffic and for combined highway and rail passenger traffic.

Various possible forms and materials for the individual parts of this structure were given most careful consideration, and all essential features of the structure have been studied in detail with a view to assure not only economy, but conformity to the most advanced standards of design and methods of fabrication and construction.   54

Tentative schemes of erection have been evolved, inasmuch as the method of erection of a large bridge not only has an important bearing upon its design and economy, but because in this case it involves operations of unprecedented proportions.   55

As a result of these studies a tentative design has been developed which, for the 179th Street location, may be briefly described as follows: 56

TYPE AND GENERAL PROPORTIONS OF BRIDGE

Little study was necessary to determine the suspension bridge as the most suitable type, because its superior economy for such great spans and capacities is now generally recognized by engineers. Its superior aesthetic merits, when properly designed, further single it out as the best adapted type in this case.   57

A cantilever bridge, the nearest other possibility, would, with its dense and massive network of steel members, form a monstrous structure and truly mar forever the beauty of the natural scenery.   58

The general proportions of the bridge, as to length of spans and height above water, were sharply defined by the topographical and geological conditions of the site. As a result of the borings, heretofore described, the main pier on the New Jersey side was located well within the pierhead line at a point where rock can be reached at a depth of about 100 feet, which is the approximate limit for the pneumatic process, the safest and most reliable foundation method. On the New York side the logical and natural place for the pier is the rocky point of Fort Washington Park close to the pierhead line. This results in a central span of 3500 feet between centers of piers, or twice the span of the Philadelphia-Camden bridge, the longest suspension bridge so far built.   59

The rock cliffs of the Palisades form the natural abutment and anchorage on the New Jersey side and, for the sake of symmetry, which is an essential aesthetic requirement, the side span on the New York side is made the same, or approximately 700 feet.   60

The clear height of the bridge floor above water is approximately 200 feet, 61
this height resulting from the elevations of the connecting streets on both sides
of the river and the limiting grades of the approaches. Incidentally, this height
is ample to permit passage of the largest vessels which are likely to go up the
river beyond this point.

The general form and arrangement of the structure are of extreme simplicity. 62
Essentially the floor deck is suspended throughout its length from simple cables
or chains. The latter will pass over the two towers and are to be firmly anchored
in rock or massive concrete blocks at their ends.

To enhance the gracefulness of the bridge, the cables are to have a compar- 63
atively small sag or flat catenary. Structurally, the cables are to be built either
of steel wires or of high grade steel eyebars, both types of construction having
reached a high degree of perfection in American bridge practice and a degree
of safety superior to that of any other type of structural members.

Detailed studies have been made of two essentially different types of towers, 64
a slender steel tower, as exemplified in the Manhattan bridge, and a combined
steel and masonry tower of massive appearance. While the economic merits of
the slender steel tower, and its justification in some localities, are recognized,
it is felt that the conspicuous location of the proposed bridge in the midst of a
bold and impressive landscape makes the selection of the aesthetically superior
massive tower imperative.

TRAFFIC CAPACITY OF BRIDGE

One of the most important and complex questions which had to be solved, 65
and will involve further careful study in connection with the planning of this
bridge, is the determination of its traffic capacity, as regards both kinds and
volume of traffic.

The question is necessarily closely related to the study of the traffic situation 66
and definite solution has to await the results of these studies. While the Legislative Acts do not specify the kind of traffic to be accommodated, existing conditions point clearly to the need of a crossing primarily for vehicular traffic.
Furthermore, while the development of the territories contiguous to the bridge
will, sooner or later, call for the accommodation of a considerable volume of
passenger traffic, it is not likely that rapid transit or other rail passenger traffic
facilities will be needed for many years to come.

It is also realized that the demand for passenger traffic in the immediate 67
future, and possibly for many years to come, may be filled by passenger buses
running over the bridge roadway. Any provision for the accommodation of rail
traffic, which would involve a comparatively large outlay at present, would
therefore not be warranted.

As a result of our studies it now appears quite feasible, however, to build the 68
bridge initially for highway traffic only, but with provision, at a small extra
expenditure, for the future accommodation of rail passenger, or additional bus
passenger traffic.

In fact the design, as now developed (see Exhibit C), is exceptionally far- 69
reaching in its provision for a gradual increase in traffic capacity with a minimum possible initial expenditure, and with the least possible time of construction before the bridge can be opened to traffic.

The plan provides for an initial capacity of two 24-foot roadways which will 70
conveniently accommodate four lanes of vehicular traffic, two in each direction.
Two footwalks for pedestrians are also provided for. It is estimated that these
two roadways will be sufficient to fill the demand for highway traffic for about
ten years after the opening of the bridge.

If and when justified by increased volume of vehicular traffic, another four- 71
lane roadway can be added, and used for truck traffic, while the two initial
roadways may be reserved for the faster passenger automobiles. It is estimated
that the eight lanes will be ample to take care of all vehicular traffic which may
be concentrated at this crossing. All of this highway traffic is to be accommodated on an upper deck of the structure.

If and when accommodation for rail passenger traffic, or for additional bus 72
passenger traffic, across the bridge becomes necessary, two or four lanes, or
tracks, of either form of such traffic can be added on a lower deck.

The question as to whether, and to what extent, rail passenger traffic should 73
be provided for on the bridge is still under consideration, and the cooperation
and advice of the transit authorities in the two States have been sought in order
to arrive at a satisfactory solution.

APPROACHES AND HIGHWAY CONNECTIONS

Tentative studies for the approaches and highway connections on both sides 74
of the river have been made, but further studies in cooperation with the proper
municipal and State highway authorities, are necessary. The studies so far completed indicate conclusively that direct connections of the bridge approaches
with important highway arteries, such as Broadway and Riverside Drive in Manhattan, and Lemoine Avenue in New Jersey, are entirely feasible and involve
no extensive changes in the street system, at least for many years after completion
of the bridge.

It would be lacking in foresight, however, not to recognize the fact that when 75
the bridge is to be completed to capacity the vehicular traffic will have grown
to such an extent that new arteries will become necessary on both sides of the
river, more particularly for that traffic which will flow to and from the bridge

433

in an easterly and westerly direction. While such new arteries will not form part of the bridge project proper, studies are being made with respect to them and with a view to give the bridge a proper setting in the future net of highway arteries.

Regarding the structural arrangement of the approaches, more particularly that on the New York side, it should be mentioned that aesthetic considerations have been paramount in developing their design. 76

The New York approach is designed as a short viaduct of monumental appearance which will enhance rather than destroy the good character of the neighborhood (see Exhibit D). The New Jersey approach is designed as a cut through the top of the Palisades so marked at the face of the cliffs as not to destroy the appearance of the latter or to break their natural silhouette. 77

Tracks, if any are provided, will be hidden from view on the approaches. 78

ARCHITECTURAL STUDIES

The commanding location of the bridge in a charming landscape made it imperative to give prominent consideration to the aesthetic side of the bridge design; in other words, to combine beauty with utility and strength. For this purpose the Port Authority has engaged an eminent architect, Mr. Cass Gilbert, to assist the engineering staff in the preparation of the plans. A statement by the architect on the architectural aspect of the project is appended. 79

ESTIMATES OF COST

In view of the incompleted state of the preliminary work and certain as yet unsettled questions, such as provision for passenger traffic, extent of architectural treatment of the bridge and approaches, more accurate appraisal of property and damages, etc., it is impossible to give at the present time reliable cost estimates. Making reasonable allowance for the uncertain features, it is estimated that the bridge can be constructed, ready for the initial highway capacity, at a cost of less than $50,000,000, inclusive of interest during construction, and that it can later be strengthened for the eight-lane highway capacity, and provision for from two to four electric railway tracks, at an additional cost of between $15,000,000 and $20,000,000. 80

FINANCIAL STATEMENT

The financial statement following gives, for the years 1933, 1943, 1953 and 1960, the gross revenue and net operating income from vehicles only, based 81

434

upon average toll rates of 50¢, 60¢, and 70¢, respectively, an initial cost of $50,000,000 and an additional expenditure, ten years later, of $15,000,000, as required for the increased vehicular capacity.

Year	Gross Revenue from Vehicles Only	Administration Operation Maintenance	Net Operating Income Available for Interest and Amortization	Per Cent of Net Operating Income to Estimated Cost
A. Average Toll Charge 50¢				
1933	$3,700,000	$ 500,000	$3,200,000	6.40%
1943	5,608,000	750,000	4,858,000	9.72
1953	6,572,000	1,000,000	5,572,000	8.57
1960	6,910,000	1,000,000	5,910,000	9.09
B. Average Toll Charge 60¢				
1933	4,441,000	500,000	3,941,000	8.76
1943	6,730,000	750,000	5,980,000	13.29
1953	7,886,000	1,000,000	6,886,000	10.59
1960	8,293,000	1,000,000	7,293,000	11.22
C. Average Toll Charge 70¢				
1933	5,181,000	500,000	4,681,000	10.40
1943	7,851,000	750,000	7,101,000	15.78
1953	9,201,000	1,000,000	8,201,000	12.62
1960	9,675,000	1,000,000	8,675,000	13.35

Note:—Additional revenue from generated vehicular traffic and from bus and rail-passenger traffic is expected to increase materially the potential net operating income.

ACKNOWLEDGEMENT

The Engineering Staff has been aided in its studies so far made by valuable advice and information from various individuals and organizations to whom due credit will be given at the proper time.

The undersigned also take this occasion to express their acknowledgement for the valuable services so far rendered by other members of the engineering staff, more particularly, R. A. Lesher, Traffic Engineer, in charge of traffic studies; W. J. Boucher, Engineer of Construction, and R. Hoppen, Jr., Resident Engineer, in charge of surveys and borings; W. A. Cuenot and A. Andersen, Assistant Engineers, in charge of design studies.

Respectfully submitted
(Signed) O. H. AMMANN,
Bridge Engineer

Othmar H. Ammann

COMMENT

We were so pleased with the design and execution of this report that we went   84
to talk about it with Ammann himself. When we arrived in the New York office
of Ammann and Whitney, Consulting Engineers, the partners were busy examining huge charts on a long work-table. Ammann, who is in his seventies
and still energetic and graceful in his movements, led us to his desk, on which
lay a rough draft of his most recent report, scheduled for publication early in
1953. The conversation confirmed what we had surmised but had wanted to
hear in his own words: His reports and papers are born of a very definite "philosophy of composition."

"Unfortunately," the designer of the Washington Bridge told us, "most en-   85
gineers think in terms of details. And so most engineering reports are cluttered
with meaningless particulars. Actually what the reader needs most is a good
general view of the situation. In my reports I usually start off with a summary
and a statement of conclusions. Then I use logical subdivisions of the subject,
and try to develop my basic material in language the layman can understand."

He handed us the draft of the report he had been working on, a lengthy   86
account of his inspection of one of the world's largest bridges. It opened with
an explanation of the scope and arrangement of the material, immediately followed by a summary of the results of the investigation and the proposals of the
investigator. At the end of the first few pages the reader had the gist and significance of the entire document.

Ammann confessed with a smile that reports are no easier to design than   87
bridges. "I usually have to take my reports home and work on them until two
in the morning." In the course of his long professional career, he told us, he
had written more than a hundred full-length reports. And how had he trained
himself to write reports? "I rely on my studies of logic and literature. Logic
taught me how to structure my writing. Literature gives me an understanding
of the importance of style."

The 1926 report studied here follows the general approach Ammann de-   88
scribed to us. The writer's sole consideration in the opening paragraphs is to get
as quickly as possible to what the reader wants most to know: the conclusions.
Therefore, the occasion, aim, and scope of the report are swiftly treated in one
sentence. The methods employed to gather the material are reviewed with equal
brevity. Some necessary background is sketched in lightly. But all this is prelude,
fanfare, preceding the procession of conclusions. These are introduced in an
order in which each one leads to the next, until the last is a recommendation
for action by the reader.

Now, certain that his reader will be able to view particulars with some pa-   89
tience and purpose, Ammann gives his "more complete and detailed account,"

using the same order of topics. So far as that is possible, raw data are pushed to the rear, and some to appendices. The net result is a well-designed report.

Ammann's style is equally pleasing, and functionally related to his structure 90 of both reports and bridges. Generally, his writing is rapid and graceful. He uses many long-span sentences, but they carry heavy loads with great spring and verve. Since he believes that the reader must get the essence, the general view, he naturally uses qualitative language, but without unnecessary ornament. He does not feel that his "scientific objectivity" will be compromised if he translates quantity into quality ("intolerable traffic situation") or views a fact through a feeling ("charming landscape"). He accepts the professional man's responsibility not only to specialize, but to generalize. His description of what a cantilever bridge would look like in the setting of the Palisades is especially revealing in all these connections:

"A cantilever bridge, the nearest other possibility, would, with its dense and 91 massive network of steel members, form a monstrous structure and mar forever the beauty of the natural scenery."

How very similar to his description of the average report as "cluttered with 92 meaningless particulars"!

Walter J. Miller and Lee E. A. Saidla

QUESTIONS

1. Write one sentence that summarizes in your own words what Ammann recommends and why. In what ways does this report make writing such a sentence hard or easy?

2. In paragraphs 45, 64, 77, and 78, Ammann makes value judgments about the aesthetic effect the bridge will have on its immediate environment. Because those are value judgments rather than strictly technical information, how do you respond to the passages? What influences you most in your doubt or acceptance of them? What do these passages suggest about Ammann's viewpoint as an engineer?

3. Examine any few paragraphs, 7 through 10, for example, or paragraph 27. What are some examples of "language the laymen can understand" (paragraph 85)? How often does Ammann slip away from such language?

4. The comment following the report outlines Ammann's philosophy of composition in paragraph 85. Review the summary and conclusions with which Ammann begins. What logic do you find for the order of the conclusions numbered 1 through 11?

5. Paragraph 89, claims Ammann, following the presentation of his conclusions, gives his " 'more complete and detailed account,' using the same order of topics." How closely does that turn out to be the case? Compare the conclusions, paragraphs 7 through 17, with the subsections that follow. Which conclusions pertain to which subsections and vice versa?

6. The commentary in paragraph 90 describes Ammann's style. The commentator is obviously influenced by ideas of traffic ("rapid and graceful," "long-span sentences"),

and he is also concerned about Ammann's scientific objectivity. Write your own analysis of Ammann's style, limiting your examination to one of his subsections.

7. If the George Washington Bridge is unfamiliar to you, find its location, as noted in paragraph 43, on some maps both of New York City and of the United States. If your class is from another region, ask whether anyone in the room has crossed that bridge and, if so, for what reasons.

8. If you live near the George Washington Bridge, you might be able to report on whether Ammann's judgment, as expressed in paragraphs 45, 64, 77, and 78, has turned out to be valid or not. You might take special note of any conditions Ammann could not have foreseen that influence the present aesthetic aspect of the bridge.

9. Describe the bridge today. How many lanes has it? What variety of traffic does it carry? How closely does it fulfill the predictions Ammann made for it?

10. Describe a study that could be made to propose a new bridge, parking lot, shopping mall, or highway in your own community. What specific studies would be required?

WRITING SUGGESTIONS
FOR EXPLAINING

1. Consider Frances FitzGerald's "America Revised" in the light of Edward Hallett Carr's discussion of a historical fact. Is what FitzGerald observes essentially the shifting agreement among historians as to what are historical facts? Write an essay in which you consider the extent to which FitzGerald's evidence illustrates Carr's points. Does it illustrate anything else besides?

2. Consider the reports by James Agee on Buster Keaton, Winthrop Palmer on Isadora Duncan, or Ronald Bryden on Laurence Oliver in the light of Eric Bentley's essay "To Impersonate, to Watch, and to Be Watched," and write an essay in which you analyze the extent to which Bentley explains Agee's, Palmer's, or Bryden's response.

3. Using the material in Adam Smith's "The Great Inflation," Lester Thurow's "A Zero-Sum Game," and Frederick Lewis Allen's "Crash!" write a paper in which you imagine some major change in our present economic situation and project, imaginatively but also as reasonably as you can, what the effects of that change would be on life in this country. Consider especially what trade-offs might occur. Who would be the winners? Who would be the losers? Or, who might win more or lose less?

4. "On the Fear of Death," by Elizabeth Kübler-Ross, ends with a question about our human nature (paragraph 28). Bruno Bettelheim and Stanley Milgram are examples of other writers who have raised such a question. Write a short paper in which you compare and contrast at least two such views as to our essential nature. What areas of learning and experience are drawn upon for those definitions? Which one do you think gets at the more essential aspect of our nature?

5. Where in the section on "Social Sciences and Public Affairs" are descriptions that Clifford Geertz would call either thick or thin? Consider Bruno Bettelheim, Adam Smith, Celeste MacLeod, Stanley Milgram, and Edward T. Hall, Jr. What are some instances of thick description in their studies? Where is the description thin?

6. Perhaps the idea of "thick description," as Clifford Geertz discusses it, influences work in fields outside the social sciences. Consider E. H. Gombrich, Frances FitzGerald, Murray Ross, or Douglas L. Wilson from the section on "Arts and Humanities," or James Jeans, Barbara Landau, Henry Gleitman, Elizabeth Spelke, Francis Crick, or Peter Marler and Susan Peters from the section on "Sciences and Technologies." Drawing on at least two of those essays, discuss the apparent appropriateness of "thick description" for work in either the sciences or the humanities.

7. What are the implications of the papers by Barbara Landau, Henry Gleitman, and Elizabeth Spelke for the claims Jean Piaget makes about "Euclidean" perception? Whose presentation seems more trustworthy, and why?

8. Compare and contrast the ways Bertrand Russell and Albert Einstein explain the theory of relativity. What approach does each take? What methods does each use to explain complex material to a general audience? Which writer do you find more successful, and why?

439

Writing Suggestions for Explaining

9. Many of the articles in "Explaining" illustrate the inquiring mind at work. Despite their differences in subject and field, in what ways are the approaches of two or three writers such as Douglas L. Wilson, Bruno Bettelheim, Stanley Milgram, Frances FitzGerald, E. H. Gombrich, Isaac Asimov, Peter Marler and Susan Peters, or a favorite of your own similar?

10. After studying James Jeans's "Why the Sky Is Blue" or one of the other explanations of unfamiliar phenomena such as Francis Crick's "Times and Distances, Large and Small," prepare a detailed set of directions explaining how to write a brief and clear explanation of unfamiliar information. Exchange those directions with a classmate and, following the directions you receive, write a paper explaining something unfamiliar to your classmates. Evaluate the success both of your paper and of your set of directions.

11. Review O. H. Ammann's explanation of how he writes in the commentary that follows his report. Then choose another writer represented in "Explaining," and demonstrate that he or she writes either pretty much as Ammann says he does or quite differently.

ARGUING

ARGUING

Here in "Arguing" you will find authors taking positions on a wide range of controversial subjects—from the evolution of language to the salaries of corporate executives, from the nature of organized crime to the image of women in television commercials, from the causes of environmental stress to the quality of *Star Wars*. No matter what their academic fields or professions, these authors vigorously defend their stands on the issues and questions they address. But this should come as no surprise. None of us, after all, holds lightly to beliefs and ideas about what is true or beautiful or good. We are especially given to a strong defense of our position when we recognize that it is pitted against a different set of ideas, interpretations, or beliefs. So you will find these authors using a variety of methods to persuade readers to favor one side over another in a debate or disagreement about some controversial issue.

The distinctive quality of arguing can be seen in the following passage from Julian Jaynes's "The Evolution of Language":

> It is commonly thought that language is such an inherent part of the human constitution that it must go back somehow through the tribal ancestry of man to the very origin of the genus *Homo*, that is, for almost two million years. Most contemporary linguists of my acquaintance would like to persuade me that this is true. But with this view, I wish to totally and emphatically disagree. If early man, through these two million years, had even a primordial speech, why is there so little evidence of even simple culture or technology? For there is precious little archaeologically up to 40,000 B.C., other than the crudest of stone tools.
>
> Sometimes the reaction to a denial that early man had speech is, how then did man function or communicate? The answer is very simple: just like all other primates, with an abundance of visual and vocal signals which were very far removed from the syntactical language that we practice today. And when I even carry this speechlessness down through the Pleistocene Age, when man developed various kinds of primitive pebble choppers and hand axes, again my linguist friends lament my arrogant ignorance and swear oaths that in order to transmit even such rudimentary skills from one generation to another, there had to be language. But consider that it is almost impossible to describe chipping flints into choppers in language. This art was transmitted solely by imitation, exactly the way in which chimpanzees transmit the trick of inserting straws into ant hills to get ants. It is the same problem as the transmission of bicycle riding; does language assist at all?

This passage comes from a piece in which Jaynes attempts to make a case for dating the evolution of human language sometime after 40,000 B.C. But in favoring so recent a date, Jaynes realizes that he is seriously at odds with most contemporary linguists, who believe that language "must go back . . . to the very origin of the genus *Homo*, that is, for almost two million years." Given this substantial disagreement, Jaynes is not free just to make a straightforward case for his own position on the matter. He must instead contend with his opponents, refuting their claims and answering their charges against his position, while also providing evidence in support of his view. He is, in short, engaged in arguing. And the argumentative situation is immediately reflected in the debatelike structure of the opening paragraph, which begins with statements identifying the views of his opponents ("It is commonly thought that language is . . .") and then moves to counterstatements intended to refute the opposition ("But with this view, I wish to totally and emphatically disagree . . ."). This debate continues in the second paragraph, as Jaynes acknowledges a familiar counterattack of his opponents and answers it with one of his own. So it is that argument puts ideas to the test by forcing them to stand up against opposing beliefs or theories.

As this passage also reveals, argument naturally arises over significant issues or questions that are open to sharply differing points of view. The question of when human language originated, for example, is of crucial interest to persons in a wide range of fields—to archaeologists, anthropologists, historians, linguists, psychologists, and zoologists. And persons in each of these fields might well be inclined to approach the question from radically different points of view that involve different assumptions as well as different bodies of knowledge. Many contemporary linguists, as Jaynes accurately reports, do regard language as "an inherent part of the human constitution," whereas Jaynes, a psychologist interested in the development of human consciousness, evidently believes language to have been acquired through the process of evolution. Each of these assumptions necessarily leads to substantially different claims about the dating of human language, and neither claim can be conclusively proven to be true. Indeed, if conclusive evidence had existed for one view or another, the argument would never have arisen, or it would have been resolved as quickly as the evidence had been discovered. But we cannot, after all, summon witnesses or testimony from persons living forty thousand or two million years ago. So, like all controversial issues, the question remains open to debate, and anyone involved in such an argument can at best hope to make a persuasive case for a particular viewpoint—a case that will move thoughtful readers to consider that position seriously and possibly even convince them to accept it.

As readers of argumentative writing, we in turn should try to be as fair-minded as the members of a jury. We should try to set aside any biases or prejudices that we might have about one view or another. Then, we should weigh all of the evidence, logic, claims, and appeals for each viewpoint before arriving at a decision about which one we find most convincing. By the same token, as writers of argument we should assume that readers are not likely to be persuaded by a one-sided view of a complex situation. Thus we should be ready to present a case that not only will support our position but will respond to the crucial challenges of views that differ from our own. Both as readers and writers, then, we should strive to understand the balanced methods of persuasion that can be found throughout the broad range of argumentative writing.

THE RANGE OF ARGUMENTATIVE WRITING

Argumentative writing so pervades our lives that we may not even recognize it as such in the many brochures and leaflets that come our way, urging us to vote for one candidate rather than another or to support one cause rather than another. Argumentative writing also figures heavily in newspaper editorials, syndicated columns, and letters to the editor, which are typically given over to debating the pros and cons of one public issue or another, from local taxes to national defense policies. Argument, of course, is fundamental in the judicial process, providing as it does the basic procedure for conducting all courtroom trials. And it is crucial in the legislative process, for it offers a systematic means of exploring the strengths and weaknesses of different proposed policies and programs. In a similar way, argument serves the basic aims of the academic world, enabling different ideas and theories to be tested by pitting them against each other. Whatever the field or profession, argument is an important activity in the advancement of knowledge and society.

The broad range of argumentative writing may conveniently be understood by considering the kinds of issues and questions that typically give rise to disagreement and debate. Surely, the most basic sources of controversy are questions of fact—the who, what, when, and where of things, as well as how much. Questions such as these are most commonly at issue in criminal trials. But as we have already seen from Jaynes's discussion of whether language evolved 40,000 or 2,000,000 years ago, intense arguments over questions of fact can also develop in academic fields, especially when the facts in question have a significant bearing on the explanation or judgment of a particular subject or body of material.

Even when there is no question about the facts themselves, there are likely to be arguments about how to explain the facts. Disagreements of this kind abound across the full range of academic and professional fields. And the arguments inevitably arise out of sharply differing points of view on the facts, as can be seen in the following excerpt from Barry Commoner's "The Causes of Environmental Stress":

> The environmental crisis tells us that there is something seriously wrong with the way in which human beings have occupied their habitat, the earth. The fault must lie not with nature, but with man. For no one has argued, to my knowledge,

that the recent advent of pollutants on the earth is the result of some natural change independent of man. . . .

One explanation that is sometimes offered is that man is a "dirty" animal—that unlike other animals man is likely to "foul his own nest." Somehow, according to this view, people lack other animals' tidy nature and increasingly foul the world as their numbers increase. This explanation is basically faulty, for the "neatness" of animals in nature is not the result of their own sanitary activities. What removes these wastes is the activity of *other* living things, which use them as nutrients. In an ecological cycle no waste can accumulate because nothing is wasted. Thus, a living thing that is a natural part of an ecosystem cannot, by its own biological activities, degrade that ecosystem; an ecosystem is always stressed from without. Human beings, as animals, are no less tidy than other living organisms. They pollute the environment only because they have broken out of the closed, cyclical network in which all other living things are held.

In this passage Commoner is attempting to account for the fact of "environmental deterioration," and as he makes clear at the outset, everyone appears to agree that the causes must be attributable to man. But the exact senses in which man is responsible remain open to debate. Some persons evidently take a deterministic view of the problem, regarding it as an inevitable consequence of man's "dirty" nature, compounded in its effects by substantial increases in the world's population. Commoner, on the other hand, takes an ecological view of the problem and thus claims that human beings have polluted the environment not because they are any "less tidy than other living organisms," but "only because they have broken out of the closed, cyclical network in which all other living things are held." So, Commoner and his opponents approach the facts from sharply differing explanatory viewpoints, and an argument naturally ensues.

Differing viewpoints, of course, ultimately reflect differing beliefs and values. Our way of viewing any particular subject is, after all, a matter of personal choice, an outgrowth of what our experience and knowledge have led us to hold as being self-evident. In this way beliefs and values are always in some sense at issue in any argumentative situation, even when they remain more or less in the background. But in some cases the conflicting values themselves are so clearly at the heart of the argument that they become the direct focus of the debate. For example, in "Why Are Americans Afraid of Dragons?" Ursula Le Guin opposes what she calls the "antifantasy" views of Americans with a sustained argument on behalf of fantastic literature. In order to do so, of course, she is compelled to make a case for the value of the imagination itself and for the qualities she attributes to it, such as "the free play of the mind":

To be free, after all, is not to be undisciplined. I should say that the discipline of the imagination may in fact be the essential method or technique of both art and science. It is our Puritanism, insisting that discipline means repression or punishment, which confuses the subject. To discipline something, in the proper sense of the word, does not mean to repress it, but to train it—to encourage it to grow, and act, and be fruitful, whether it is a peach tree or a human mind.

In order to support her position here, Le Guin directly challenges one of the major assumptions of the opposing value structure—namely, a belief that the freedom of imaginative activity is at odds with the virtue of discipline. And she challenges this belief in a highly imaginative series of maneuvers—first by conceiving of the imagination itself as a "discipline," then by claiming this "discipline" to be "essential" to "both art and science," then by defining discipline as a form of training rather than repression, and finally by embodying this idea of discipline in the imaginative form of a metaphor that links the fruitfulness of a trained peach tree with that of a carefully trained human mind. Thus in the imaginative way that she makes her case, Le Guin enables us to witness the rigorous discipline of the imagination.

Le Guin's argument also enables us to see that conflicts over beliefs and values can have an important bearing on questions of policy and planning. Imagine, for example, how our educational system might be designed and operated if it were based on her belief "that the discipline of the imagination may in fact be the essential method or technique of both art and science." Though Le Guin does not map a new educational system in her piece, she evidently conceives of fantastic literature and other works of the imagination as being fundamental to the development of healthy human minds. For a clear-cut example of how conflicts over belief lead to debates over policy, you need only look at Lewis Thomas's "The Art of Teaching Science." In the early section of his piece, Thomas challenges conventional beliefs about the certitude of scientific knowledge with his claim that "The conclusions reached in science are always, when looked at closely, far more provisional and tentative than are most of the assumptions arrived at by our colleagues in the humanities." Based on this and related claims, Thomas then proceeds in the later portions of his piece to outline a completely new method of teaching science:

> I suggest that the introductory courses in science, at all levels from grade school through college, be radically revised. Leave the fundamentals, the so-called basics, aside for a while, and concentrate the attention of all students on the things that are not known. . . . At the outset, before any of the fundamentals, teach the still imponderable puzzles of cosmology. Describe as clearly as possible, for the youngest minds, that there are some things going on in the universe that lie still beyond comprehension, and make it plain how little is known.

Introductory science teachers might not respond too favorably to this proposal, especially since it would oblige them to deal "systematically with ignorance in science." But can you imagine what it would be like to take such a course? Can you imagine how such courses might influence the thinking of future scientists? Can you imagine how such a proposal might affect our contemporary attitudes towards science? None of these questions, of course, can be answered with certainty, for certainty is not at last possible in deliberation about the future. But Thomas does attempt to address these and other such questions, since in arguing on behalf of a proposal for change he is obligated to explore the consequences of his proposed change.

Just as his argument for a new mode of scientific education requires Thomas to consider and defend the possible effects of his proposed change, so every other kind of question imposes on writers a particular set of argumentative obligations. Le Guin's argument in favor of fantasy, for example, obliges her to defend the value of the imagination itself, and Commoner's ecological account of pollution compels him to show that human beings have, as he claims, "broken out of the closed, cyclical network in which all other living things are held." A writer who aims to be persuasive cannot simply assert that something is or is not the case, for readers in general are not willing to be bullied, hoodwinked, or otherwise manipulated into accepting a particular claim. But they are capable of being reached by civilized and rational methods of persuasion that are appropriate to controversial issues—by evidence, logic, and eloquence.

METHODS OF ARGUING

In planning a piece of argumentative writing, you should begin by examining your material with an eye to discovering the issues that have to be addressed and the points that have to be made in order to present your case and defend your position most persuasively. This means that you will have to deal not only with issues that you consider relevant but also with matters that have been raised by your opponents—in other words, you will have to deal with both sides of the controversy. In arguing about the origin of language, for example, Jaynes attempts to answer each of the challenging points and questions that have been raised by his opponents, the "contemporary linguists," before turning to his own set of issues. So, too, Commoner devotes his account of pollution not only to a presentation of his ecological explanation but also to a systematic refutation of deterministic views that attribute the problem to the irreversible effects of increases in the world's population.

After you have identified the crucial points to be addressed, then you should decide upon the methods that will be necessary to make a convincing case with respect to each of the points. Some methods, of course, are imperative no matter what point you are trying to prove. Every piece of argumentation, after all, requires that you offer appropriate and sufficient evidence to support your position. To do so, you will need to gather and present specific details that bear on each of the points you are trying to make. This basic concern for providing evidence will lead you inevitably into the activity of reporting. Commoner, for example, reports extensively on the development of synthetic materials to illustrate how modern chemistry laid the groundwork for man's violation of the

448

ecological cycle; Le Guin reports conversations to illustrate the American fear of fantasy; and Thomas reports a striking array of unsolved scientific questions to demonstrate the scope of scientific ignorance. Reporting appropriate evidence constitutes the most basic means of making a persuasive case for any point under consideration. Any point for which evidence cannot be provided, or for which only weak or limited evidence can be offered, is likely to be much less convincing than one that can be vividly substantiated.

Some kinds of argumentative situations call not only for evidence but also for logical reasoning based on the evidence (or the lack of it), as in this excerpt from Jaynes's earlier passage about the origin of language:

> If early man, through these two million years, had even a primordial speech, why is there so little evidence of even simple culture or technology?

As you can see from this question, Jaynes assumes that human language, culture, and technology must have developed at the same time. Therefore, he reasons, if there is "little evidence of even simple culture or technology" during the first two million years of man's existence, it follows that not "even a primordial speech" could have existed during that time. Having made this logical inference, Jaynes evidently realized that he had left unanswered the basic question of how early man did "function or communicate." And he deals with this problem through another kind of logical maneuver, as follows:

> The answer is very simple: just like all other primates, with an abundance of visual and vocal signals which were very far removed from the syntactical language that we practice today.

In this case, Jaynes reasons by analogy from the premise that man is a primate, and thus he makes the inference that in the absence of language man must have communicated "just like all other primates," that is, "with an abundance of visual and vocal signals." As you can see from these examples, logical reasoning serves to fill in gaps where evidence does not exist or, as in a court case, to move beyond the accumulated evidence to conclusions that follow from it. Logic, in other words, is an ingenious and often imperative method of proof in every area of learning, but like any ingenious tool it must be used with care. One weak link in a logical chain of reasoning can lead, after all, to a string of falsehood.

Some situations, of course, do not call for logic so much as for an eloquent appeal to the basic truths of general human experience. When Le Guin challenges the American distrust of fantasy, as we have seen, she does not rely on an abstract chain of reasoning but on the powerful appeal of a vivid metaphor that embodies "the discipline of the imagination" in the fruitfulness of a peach tree. And when she argues for the enduring value of fantasy, she does not simply assert it as such. Instead she invokes a powerful image to suggest the disturbing consequences of thwarting the human need for it:

449

Arguing

> I believe that all the best faculties of a mature human being exist in the child, and that if these faculties are encouraged in youth they will act well and wisely in the adult, but if they are repressed and denied in the child they will stunt and cripple the adult personality.

Surely, as she knows, we would all prefer to be fruitful rather than stunted or crippled. Some beliefs, after all, are so unmistakably true to general human experience that a universal image or metaphor is all that we need to remind us of their truth.

Explanatory techniques such as we discussed in our introduction to the preceding section also can play a role in argument, as you may already have noticed from your own reading of the passages we have just been discussing. Jaynes's argument about the origin of language, for example, is based on a cause-and-effect analysis relating the development of language to the formation of culture and technology. And Le Guin's attack on the American distrust of fantasy relies on a strategic use of definition when she asserts that "To discipline something, in the proper sense of the word, does not mean to repress it, but to train it. . . ." Any piece of argument, in other words, is likely to draw upon a wide range of techniques, for argument at last is always attempting to achieve the complex purpose not only of getting at the truth about something, and making that truth intelligible to others, but also of persuading others to accept it as such.

No matter what particular combination of techniques a writer favors, you will probably find that most writers, when carrying out an argument, always save a very telling point or bit of evidence or well-turned phrase for last. Like effective storytellers or successful courtroom lawyers, they know that a memorable detail makes the most powerful climax. In the pieces that follow in this section, you will get to see how twenty-three different writers use the various resources of language to produce some very striking and compelling pieces of argument.

Arts and Humanities

TWO REVIEWS OF STAR WARS
Stanley Kauffmann
Judith Crist

*Both of these writers are lifelong New Yorkers. Kauffmann
(b. 1916) studied theater at New York University. Crist (b.
1922) went to Hunter College and Columbia University's
School of Journalism. Kauffmann has been an editor, actor,
and director of plays but is best known as a theater and film
critic, roles he has played at the* New Republic, *the* New
York Times, *and the* Saturday Review. *Crist was a reporter
for the* New York Herald Tribune *for fifteen years before
becoming the film reviewer for* TV Guide *in 1966. Kauffmann is considered serious, sometimes severe and academic,
while Crist believes "a critic's major goal is to share good
things." Kauffmann's review of* Star Wars *appeared in his
regular* New Republic *column for June 18, 1977. Crist's
review appeared in the* Saturday Review *for July 9 of that
year.*

INNOCENCES

Star Wars (20th Century-Fox). The young American director George Lucas   1
has made three features: *THX 1138*, which was about the future; *American*

451

Graffiti, which was about adolescents; and now *Star Wars*, which is a "future" film for adolescents. Neither of the earlier pictures was distinguished for novelty or depth, but *THX 1138* tried to compensate with visual and technical ingenuity, and *American Graffiti* found some good objective correlatives,[1] in cinematic method, for its study of small-town teen-agers. *Star Wars*, Lucas' most expensive picture to date, doesn't have the technological cleverness of his first, and it's about nothing more than what it seems to be about.

This is Lucas' tribute to Flash Gordon, and is now enthralling all those who feel that Flash Gordon needs a two-hour, eight-million-dollar tribute. There's a glitzy attempt at profundity in the opening title which tells us that the story took place on a galaxy far away "a long time ago." It really takes place in the science-fiction future, a place which is as fixed and fictitious for bad sci-fi writers as the Old West is for bad Western writers. Lucas' script has Good Guys, Bad Guys, a princess, intergalactic imperialist war, staunch defenders of human and humanoid rights, secrets that will not be surrendered to the warlords—a whole spectrum of simplified earthly problems projected onto cardboard and illuminated with interminable ray-gun flashes and last-minute huge explosions.   2

About the dialogue there's nothing to be said. In fact the dialogue *itself* can hardly be said: it sticks in the actors' mouths like peanut butter. The acting is the School of Buster Crabbe, except for Alec Guinness who mumbles through on the way to his salary check. (A warlord, whose face we never see under his visored helmet, is played by David Prowse—a physical and vocal double for James Earl Jones.)   3

The only way that *Star Wars* could have been interesting was through its visual imagination and special effects. Both are unexceptional. I was not the world's biggest fan of Kubrick's *2001*, but surely after that picture and after the work of Jordan Belson that preceded it, space films have an ingenuity-mark to aim at before they can engage our wonder. In no way does Lucas come up to the Kubrick/Belson level, and, to rely on my memory, his work here seems less inventive than in *THX 1138*.   4

But I saw at last—after about, say, 20 minutes—that *Star Wars* wasn't meant to be ingenious in any way; it was meant to be exactly what it is. From Lucas' view it certainly has not failed. I kept looking for an "edge," to peer around the corny, solemn comic-book strophes; he was facing them frontally and full. This picture was made for those (particularly males) who carry a portable shrine within them of their adolescence, a chalice of a Self that was Better Then, before the world's affairs or—in any complex way—sex intruded. Flash Gordon, Buck Rogers and their peers guard the portals of American innocence, and *Star*   5

---

[1] objective correlatives: T. S. Eliot (1888–1965), the American-born poet and critic, invented the term to explain how the writer can elicit a predictable emotional response from his readers. The writer must recognize "a set of objects, a situation, a chain of events which shall be the formula of that *particular* emotion" and educe that emotion from the reader.

Wars is an unabashed, jaw-clenched tribute to the chastity still sacred beneath the middle-aged spread.

Stanley Kauffmann

"FEEL GOOD" FILM

The era of the "feel good" movie, launched by *Cousin, Cousine* and *Rocky*, is upon us—with *Star Wars* to offer lavish, glittering, and nostalgic confirmation thereof.

It is fitting that *Star Wars* is the creation of George Lucas, whose last film, in 1973, was that utterly charming re-creation of an adolescent yesterday, *American Graffiti*. This time the thirty-two-year-old writer-director has re-created the fantasies of a childhood soaked in adventure fictions, ranging from the respectability of Camelot and Oz to the trashery of comic strips and Saturday-afternoon serials. The last have provided the format for his chivalric science-fiction tale: he is giving us that very special Saturday when the printed prologue (appropriately moving off screen into the vast beyond) brings us up to date on the rebellion against the evil Galactic Empire and plunks us down into the final series of misadventures that will precede the breathtaking triumph of good over evil and the comforting assurance that the good will flourish happily ever after. Do children of all ages ask for anything more?

Lucas made an intriguing science-fiction 15-minute short as a student at the University of Southern California, won a National Student Film Festival prize with it in 1968, and was given a Warner Bros. contract to expand it to feature length. The result, 1971's *THX 1138*, was a clinical fantasy set in the twenty-fifth century but bearing all the philosophical earmarks of *1984* and the technological sci-fi clichés of 1960s television. But for *Star Wars*, set "a long time ago" in a "galaxy far, far away," his imagination is unbridled, his vision unbound. We are whisked from deserts to teeming cities to the super spaces of a super space station, all inhabited by a vast variety of men and beasts and machines and mutations thereof; we travel through galaxies and touch down at various and new worlds—with infinity and a new experience ever in the offing, so suffused in inventiveness and refreshing conception are the film's creators.

The plot is simply a series of chases, captures, and escapes as the good guys set out to rescue the princess—yes, it is Princess Leia Organa (Carrie Fisher), the sweet-faced, lush-figured, feisty leader of the rebellion, who has fallen into the hands of the vile, führer-like Grand Moff Tarkin (Peter Cushing) and his black knight, Lord Darth Vader (David Prowse behind the armor, given voice by James Earl Jones), aboard their super-Pentagonish space station, *Death Star*. As familiar-but-gussied-up as the villains are the good guys: Luke Skywalker (Mark Hamill), a blond, blue-eyed farm boy and crack pilot recruited by Ben "Obi-Wan" Kenobi (Alec Guinness), a hermit, last of the Jedi Knights, who believed in "the force" (as in "may the force be with you"), a belief that constituted "the old religion"; Han Solo (Harrison Ford), a hotshot pilot and mercenary who proves himself true-blue; Chewbacca, Solo's first mate, a gigantic, monkeylike creature who purrs and growls and bears a striking resemblance to the Cowardly Lion; and two Mutt-and-Jeff-like robots, See Threepio (C3PO), a gold-plated Tin Man programmed for diplomatic missions and therefore British-accented and prissy, and Artoo-Detoo (R2D2), a round little machine stuffed with data and given to chirps and burbles.

There are memorable moments along the way and a simply whiz-bang dazzle 5 of battling spaceships for a climax, with the happy ending all it should be. The joy of it all is that everyone is playing it straight, no bogging down in messages or monoliths on the one hand, no camping it up on the other. It is simply a triumph of creativity and technology by masters thereof, people who very obviously delight in doing what only the medium of film can do in the creation of magic. They are all listed at the end of the film and well deserve the applause you'll find yourself giving them—before you exit with that satisfied Saturday-afternoon-at-the-movies smile that feels so good.

Judith Crist

QUESTIONS

1. What is the basic position that Kauffmann takes? What key terms define his judgment about *Star Wars*?

2. What is the basic position Crist takes? What are her key terms?

3. Compare the last sentences of the two reviews. What emotions are being appealed to in the closing image of each review: the "jaw-clenched tribute" and the "satisfied . . . smile"?

4. To what extent is Crist's position more moderate than Kauffmann's? What specific words and phrases express that moderation? How do those words and phrases acknowledge another valid way of judging the film?

5. Crist praises *Star Wars's* "inventiveness and refreshing conception," while Kauffmann says that the film lacks "technological cleverness" and that its "visual imagination and special effects" are "unexceptional." Thus the two critics come very close to contradicting each other absolutely. Which critic convinces you? Why is that critic the more persuasive?

6. If you have seen *Star Wars* or either of the sequels to it, write your own review of one of those films and take issue with points raised either by Kauffmann or Crist.

7. Write a review of a film you've seen recently that you either liked or disliked strongly. After reviewing the film, find three or four reviews of it by professional film critics. Now write a second review combining your own ideas with evidence provided by the professional writers, and don't be dismayed if you have to argue against the whole lot of them.

WHY ARE AMERICANS AFRAID OF DRAGONS?
Ursula K. Le Guin

Ursula Kroeber Le Guin (b. 1929) is best known as a writer of fiction, especially science fiction and fantasy. Her most admired works are The Earthsea Trilogy *(1968–1972),* The Left Hand of Darkness *(1969), and* The Dispossessed *(1974). The essay reprinted here (from* The Language of the Night, *1979) was first presented in 1973 as a talk at a conference of the Pacific Northwest Library Association held in Portland, Oregon, Le Guin's home city.*

This was to be a talk about fantasy. But I have not been feeling very fanciful   1
lately, and could not decide what to say; so I have been going about picking people's brains for ideas. "What about fantasy? Tell me something about fantasy." And one friend of mine said, "All right, I'll tell you something fantastic. Ten years ago, I went to the children's room of the library of such-and-such a city, and asked for *The Hobbit*; and the librarian told me, 'Oh, we keep that only in the adult collection; we don't feel that escapism is good for children.' "

My friend and I had a good laugh and shudder over that, and we agreed that   2
things have changed a great deal in these past ten years. That kind of moralistic censorship of works of fantasy is very uncommon now, in the children's libraries. But the fact that the children's libraries have become oases in the desert doesn't mean that there isn't still a desert. The point of view from which that librarian spoke still exists. She was merely reflecting, in perfect good faith, something that goes very deep in the American character: a moral disapproval of fantasy, a disapproval so intense, and often so aggressive, that I cannot help but see it as arising, fundamentally, from fear.

So: Why are Americans afraid of dragons?   3

Before I try to answer my question, let me say that it isn't only Americans   4
who are afraid of dragons. I suspect that almost all very highly technological peoples are more or less antifantasy. There are several national literatures which, like ours, have had no tradition of adult fantasy for the past several hundred years: the French, for instance. But then you have the Germans, who have a good deal; and the English, who have it, and love it, and do it better than anyone else. So this fear of dragons is not merely a Western, or a technological, phenomenon. But I do not want to get into these vast historical questions; I will speak of modern Americans, the only people I know well enough to talk about.

456

In wondering why Americans are afraid of dragons, I began to realize that a great many Americans are not only antifantasy, but altogether antifiction. We tend, as a people, to look upon all works of the imagination either as suspect, or as contemptible.

"My wife reads novels. I haven't got the time."

"I used to read that science fiction stuff when I was a teenager, but of course I don't now."

"Fairy stories are for kids. I live in the real world."

Who speaks so? Who is it that dismisses *War and Peace, The Time Machine,* and *A Midsummer Night's Dream* with this perfect self-assurance?[1] It is, I fear, the man in the street—the hardworking, over-thirty American male—the men who run this country.

Such a rejection of the entire art of fiction is related to several American characteristics: our Puritanism, our work ethic, our profit-mindedness, and even our sexual mores.

To read *War and Peace* or *The Lord of the Rings* plainly is not "work"[2]— you do it for pleasure. And if it cannot be justified as "educational" or as "self-improvement," then, in the Puritan value system, it can only be self-indulgence or escapism. For pleasure is not a value, to the Puritan; on the contrary, it is a sin.

Equally, in the businessman's value system, if an act does not bring in an immediate, tangible profit, it has no justification at all. Thus the only person who has an excuse to read Tolstoy or Tolkien is the English teacher, because he gets paid for it. But our businessman might allow himself to read a best-seller now and then: not because it is a good book, but because it is a best-seller—it is a success, it has made money. To the strangely mystical mind of the money-changer, this justifies its existence; and by reading it he may participate, a little, in the power and mana of its success. If this is not magic, by the way, I don't know what is.

The last element, the sexual one, is more complex. I hope I will not be understood as being sexist if I say that, within our culture, I believe that this antifiction attitude is basically a male one. The American boy and man is very commonly forced to define his maleness by rejecting certain traits, certain human gifts and potentialities, which our culture defines as "womanish" or "childish." And one of these traits or potentialities is, in cold sober fact, the absolutely essential human faculty of imagination.

Having got this far, I went quickly to the dictionary.

The *Shorter Oxford Dictionary* says: "Imagination. 1. The action of imagining, or forming a mental concept of what is not actually present to the senses; 2. The mental consideration of actions or events not yet in existence."

---

[1] *War and Peace, The Time Machine,* and A *Midsummer Night's Dream:* by Leo Tolstoy, H. G. Wells, and William Shakespeare, respectively. [Eds.]

[2] *The Lord of the Rings:* the trilogy by J. R. R. Tolkien. [Eds.]

Ursula K. Le Guin

Very well; I certainly can let "absolutely essential human faculty" stand. But 16
I must narrow the definition to fit our present subject. By "imagination," then,
I personally mean the free play of the mind, both intellectual and sensory. By
"play" I mean recreation, re-creation, the recombination of what is known into
what is new. By "free" I mean that the action is done without an immediate
object of profit—spontaneously. That does not mean, however, that there may
not be a purpose behind the free play of the mind, a goal; and the goal may be
a very serious object indeed. Children's imaginative play is clearly a practicing
at the acts and emotions of adulthood; a child who did not play would not
become mature. As for the free play of an adult mind, its result may be *War
and Peace*, or the theory of relativity.

To be free, after all, is not to be undisciplined. I should say that the discipline 17
of the imagination may in fact be the essential method or technique of both art
and science. It is our Puritanism, insisting that discipline means repression or
punishment, which confuses the subject. To discipline something, in the proper
sense of the word, does not mean to repress it, but to train it—to encourage it
to grow, and act, and be fruitful, whether it is a peach tree or a human mind.

I think that a great many American men have been taught just the opposite. 18
They have learned to repress their imagination, to reject it as something childish
or effeminate, unprofitable, and probably sinful.

They have learned to fear it. But they have never learned to discipline it at 19
all.

Now, I doubt that the imagination can be suppressed. If you truly eradicated 20
it in a child, he would grow up to be an eggplant. Like all our evil propensities,
the imagination will out. But if it is rejected and despised, it will grow into wild
and weedy shapes; it will be deformed. At its best, it will be mere ego-centered
daydreaming; at its worst, it will be wishful thinking, which is a very dangerous
occupation when it is taken seriously. Where literature is concerned, in the old,
truly Puritan days, the only permitted reading was the Bible. Nowadays, with
our secular Puritanism, the man who refuses to read novels because it's unmanly
to do so, or because they aren't true, will most likely end up watching bloody
detective thrillers on the television, or reading hack Westerns or sports stories,
or going in for pornography, from *Playboy* on down. It is his starved imagination, craving nourishment, that forces him to do so. But he can rationalize such
entertainment by saying that it is realistic—after all, sex exists, and there are
criminals, and there are baseball players, and there used to be cowboys—and
also by saying that it is virile, by which he means that it doesn't interest most
women.

That all these genres are sterile, hopelessly sterile, is a reassurance to him, 21
rather than a defect. If they were genuinely realistic, which is to say genuinely
imagined and imaginative, he would be afraid of them. Fake realism is the
escapist literature of our time. And probably the ultimate escapist reading is that
masterpiece of total unreality, the daily stock market report.

458

Now what about our man's wife? She probably wasn't required to squelch   22
her private imagination in order to play her expected role in life, but she
hasn't been trained to discipline it, either. She is allowed to read novels, and
even fantasies. But, lacking training and encouragement, her fancy is likely
to glom on to very sickly fodder, such things as soap operas, and "true romances," and nursy novels, and historico-sentimental novels, and all the rest
of the baloney ground out to replace genuine imaginative works by the artistic sweatshops of a society that is profoundly distrustful of the uses of the
imagination.

What, then, are the uses of the imagination?   23

You see, I think we have a terrible thing here: a hardworking, upright,   24
responsible citizen, a full-grown, educated person, who is afraid of dragons,
and afraid of hobbits, and scared to death of fairies. It's funny, but it's also
terrible. Something has gone very wrong. I don't know what to do about it
but to try and give an honest answer to that person's question, even though
he often asks it in an aggressive and contemptuous tone of voice. "What's the
good of it all?" he says. "Dragons and hobbits and little green men—what's
the *use* of it?"

The truest answer, unfortunately, he won't even listen to. He won't hear it.   25
The truest answer is, "The use of it is to give you pleasure and delight."

"I haven't got the time," he snaps, swallowing a Maalox pill for his ulcer   26
and rushing off to the golf course.

So we try the next-to-truest answer. It probably won't go down much better,   27
but it must be said: "The use of imaginative fiction is to deepen your understanding of your world, and your fellow men, and your own feelings, and your
destiny."

To which I fear he will retort, "Look, I got a raise last year, and I'm giving   28
my family the best of everything, we've got two cars and a color TV. I understand
enough of the world!"

And he is right, unanswerably right, if that is what he wants, and all he   29
wants.

The kind of thing you learn from reading about the problems of a hobbit   30
who is trying to drop a magic ring into an imaginary volcano has very little
to do with your social status, or material success, or income. Indeed, if there
is any relationship, it is a negative one. There is an inverse correlation between fantasy and money. That is a law, known to economists as Le Guin's
Law. If you want a striking example of Le Guin's Law, just give a lift to one
of those people along the roads who own nothing but a backpack, a guitar,
a fine head of hair, a smile, and a thumb. Time and again, you will find
that these waifs have read *The Lord of the Rings*—some of them can practically recite it. But now take Aristotle Onassis, or J. Paul Getty: could you
believe that those men ever had anything to do, at any age, under any circumstances, with a hobbit?

Ursula K. Le Guin

But, to carry my example a little further, and out of the realm of economics, did you ever notice how very gloomy Mr. Onassis and Mr. Getty and all those billionaires look in their photographs? They have this strange, pinched look, as if they were hungry. As if they were hungry for something, as if they had lost something and were trying to think where it could be, or perhaps what it could be, what it was they've lost. 31

Could it be their childhood? 32

So I arrive at my personal defense of the uses of the imagination, especially in fiction, and most especially in fairy tale, legend, fantasy, science fiction, and the rest of the lunatic fringe. I believe that maturity is not an outgrowing, but a growing up: that an adult is not a dead child, but a child who survived. I believe that all the best faculties of a mature human being exist in the child, and that if these faculties are encouraged in youth they will act well and wisely in the adult, but if they are repressed and denied in the child they will stunt and cripple the adult personality. And finally, I believe that one of the most deeply human, and humane, of these faculties is the power of imagination: so that it is our pleasant duty, as librarians, or teachers, or parents, or writers, or simply as grownups, to encourage that faculty of imagination in our children, to encourage it to grow freely, to flourish like the green bay tree, by giving it the best, absolutely the best and purest, nourishment that it can absorb. And never, under any circumstances, to squelch it, or sneer at it, or imply that it is childish, or unmanly, or untrue. 33

For fantasy is true, of course. It isn't factual, but it is true. Children know that. Adults know it too, and that is precisely why many of them are afraid of fantasy. They know that its truth challenges, even threatens, all that is false, all that is phony, unnecessary, and trivial in the life they have let themselves be forced into living. They are afraid of dragons, because they are afraid of freedom. 34

So I believe that we should trust our children. Normal children do not confuse reality and fantasy—they confuse them much less often than we adults do (as a certain great fantasist pointed out in a story called "The Emperor's New Clothes"). Children know perfectly well that unicorns aren't real, but they also know that books about unicorns, if they are good books, are true books. All too often, that's more than Mummy and Daddy know; for, in denying their childhood, the adults have denied half their knowledge, and are left with the sad, sterile little fact: "Unicorns aren't real." And that fact is one that never got anybody anywhere (except in the story "The Unicorn in the Garden," by another great fantasist, in which it is shown that a devotion to the unreality of unicorns may get you straight into the loony bin). It is by such statements as, "Once upon a time there was a dragon," or "In a hole in the ground there lived a hobbit"—it is by such beautiful non-facts that we fantastic human beings may arrive, in our peculiar fashion, at the truth. 35

460

QUESTIONS

1. This essay was first a talk before a group of librarians. Given this, how aware does the author seem to be of this particular audience? What elements in the essay reveal this awareness? Single out specific paragraphs or sections that relate directly to libraries, and consider their probable effect on that first audience and on Le Guin's argument.

2. In paragraph 21, Le Guin distinguishes between "fake realism" and that which is "genuinely realistic." In the light of that distinction, how do you evaluate her examples in paragraphs 24 through 29? Are they genuine enough?

3. In paragraph 33, Le Guin turns to her "personal defense of the uses of the imagination." At this point she is arguing from belief rather than from facts or what you might call hard evidence. How sympathetic are you to her beliefs? In what ways are her beliefs attractive?

4. This essay attempts to establish a positive evaluation of fantastic literature by formulating a negative evaluation and then arguing against it. How much of Le Guin's argument is directed against the position taken by her opponents, and how much is against her opponents themselves? Who is she arguing against, anyway? How does she describe and locate her opponents?

5. One of Le Guin's more interesting ideas is of "disciplining" the imagination (paragraphs 17 through 19). Le Guin doesn't really say how that is done, but perhaps you have had some training in such discipline or can imagine how it could happen. Write an essay describing the experience of disciplining the imagination in an area that interests you. Try to characterize the nature of the freedom that the discipline you have acquired permits.

6. Write your own argument about fantasy for the same audience of librarians addressed by Le Guin. Write a reasonable counterargument to Le Guin's views—an effective case against fantasy, a different diagnosis of what's wrong, or even an argument that the opposition to fantasy actually packages and sells it in order to make money. Or write an argument parallel to Le Guin's but using different evidence and different cases to discover some additional reasons to encourage fantasy.

7. Le Guin's argument is concerned primarily with literary fantasy. Taking her ideas into account, write an argument for or against cinematic fantasy. The "Star Wars" series and "King Kong" suggest the range of movies that this category can include.

TRAGEDY AND THE COMMON MAN
Arthur Miller

Arthur Miller (b. 1915) is one of America's leading dram-
atists, noted especially for his attempts to locate struggles of
tragic dignity in actual contemporary situations, as in All
My Sons *(1947) and his most famous* Death of a Salesman
(1949). The essay reprinted here was written for the New
York Times *at the moment when* Death of a Salesman *had*
created a debate about whether a tragedy could be written
about an ordinary person.

In this age few tragedies are written. It has often been held that the lack is   1
due to a paucity of heroes among us, or else that modern man has had the
blood drawn out of his organs of belief by the skepticism of science, and the
heroic attack on life cannot feed on an attitude of reserve and circumspection.
For one reason or another, we are often held to be below tragedy—or tragedy
above us. The inevitable conclusion is, of course, that the tragic mode is archaic,
fit only for the very highly placed, the kings or the kingly, and where this
admission is not made in so many words it is most often implied.

I believe that the common man is as apt a subject for tragedy in its highest   2
sense as kings were. On the face of it this ought to be obvious in the light of
modern psychiatry, which bases its analysis upon classic formulations such as
the Oedipus and Orestes complexes,[1] for instances, which were enacted by royal
beings, but which apply to everyone in similar emotional situations.

More simply, when the question of tragedy in art is not at issue, we never   3
hesitate to attribute to the well-placed and the exalted the very same mental
processes as the lowly. And finally, if the exaltation of tragic action were truly
a property of the high-bred character alone, it is inconceivable that the mass of
mankind should cherish tragedy above all other forms, let alone be capable of
understanding it.

As a general rule, to which there may be exceptions unknown to me, I think   4
the tragic feeling is evoked in us when we are in the presence of a character

---

[1]Oedipus and Orestes complexes: in psychoanalysis, an Oedipus complex is the desire of a child,
especially a boy, for the parent of the opposite sex accompanied by hostility toward the parent of
the same sex. The complex is named for Oedipus, a hero of Greek tragedy, who unwittingly slew
his father and married his mother. *Orestes complex* is a psychoanalytic term for the alleged development of an Oedipus complex into a son's repressed desire to kill his mother. According to Greek
legend, Orestes killed his mother Clytemnestra and her lover Aegisthus in revenge for her murder
of his father, Agamemnon. [Eds.]

who is ready to lay down his life, if need be, to secure one thing—his sense of personal dignity. From Orestes to Hamlet, Medea to Macbeth,[2] the underlying struggle is that of the individual attempting to gain his "rightful" position in his society.

Sometimes he is one who has been displaced from it, sometimes one who   5
seeks to attain it for the first time, but the fateful wound from which the inevitable events spiral is the wound of indignity, and its dominant force is indignation. Tragedy, then, is the consequence of a man's total compulsion to evaluate himself justly.

In the sense of having been initiated by the hero himself, the tale always   6
reveals what has been called his "tragic flaw," a failing that is not peculiar to grand or elevated characters. Nor is it necessarily a weakness. The flaw, or crack in the character, is really nothing—and need be nothing, but his inherent unwillingness to remain passive in the face of what he conceives to be a challenge to his dignity, his image of his rightful status. Only the passive, only those who accept their lot without active retaliation, are "flawless." Most of us are in that category.

But there are among us today, as there always have been, those who act   7
against the scheme of things that degrades them, and in the process of action everything we have accepted out of fear or insensitivity or ignorance is shaken before us and examined, and from this total onslaught by an individual against the seemingly stable cosmos surrounding us—from this total examination of the "unchangeable" environment—comes the terror and the fear that is classically associated with tragedy.

More important, from this total questioning of what has previously been   8
unquestioned, we learn. And such a process is not beyond the common man. In revolutions around the world, these past thirty years, he has demonstrated again and again this inner dynamic of all tragedy.

Insistence upon the rank of the tragic hero, or the so-called nobility of his   9
character, is really but a clinging to the outward forms of tragedy. If rank or nobility of character was indispensable, then it would follow that the problems of those with rank were the particular problems of tragedy. But surely the right of one monarch to capture the domain from another no longer raises our passions, nor are our concepts of justice what they were to the mind of an Elizabethan king.

The quality in such plays that does shake us, however, derives from the   10
underlying fear of being displaced, the disaster inherent in being torn away from our chosen image of what and who we are in this world. Among us today this fear is as strong, and perhaps stronger, than it ever was. In fact, it is the common man who knows this fear best.

Now, if it is true that tragedy is the consequence of a man's total compulsion   11

---

[2]Orestes, Hamlet, Medea, Macbeth: tragic characters in plays by Aeschylus, Shakespeare, Euripides, and Shakespeare, respectively. [Eds.]

to evaluate himself justly, his destruction in the attempt posits a wrong or an evil in his environment. And this is precisely the morality of tragedy and its lesson. The discovery of the moral law, which is what the enlightenment of tragedy consists of, is not the discovery of some abstract or metaphysical quantity.

The tragic right is a condition of life, a condition in which the human 12 personality is able to flower and realize itself. The wrong is the condition which suppresses man, perverts the flowing out of his love and creative instinct. Tragedy enlightens—and it must, in that it points the heroic finger at the enemy of man's freedom. The thrust for freedom is the quality in tragedy which exalts. The revolutionary questioning of the stable environment is what terrifies. In no way is the common man debarred from such thoughts or such actions.

Seen in this light, our lack of tragedy may be partially accounted for by the 13 turn which modern literature has taken toward the purely psychiatric view of life, or the purely sociological. If all our miseries, our indignities, are born and bred within our minds, then all action, let alone the heroic action, is obviously impossible.

And if society alone is responsible for the cramping of our lives, then the 14 protagonist must needs be so pure and faultless as to force us to deny his validity as a character. From neither of these views can tragedy derive, simply because neither represents a balanced concept of life. Above all else, tragedy requires the finest appreciation by the writer of cause and effect.

No tragedy can therefore come about when its author fears to question ab- 15 solutely everything, when he regards any institution, habit or custom as being either everlasting, immutable or inevitable. In the tragic view the need of man to wholly realize himself is the only fixed star, and whatever it is that hedges his nature and lowers it is ripe for attack and examination. Which is not to say that tragedy must preach revolution.

The Greeks could probe the very heavenly origin of their ways and return to 16 confirm the rightness of laws. And Job could face God in anger, demanding his right and end in submission. But for a moment everything is in suspension, nothing is accepted, and in this stretching and tearing apart of the cosmos, in the very action of so doing, the character gains "size," the tragic stature which is spuriously attached to the royal or the high-born in our minds. The commonest of men may take on that stature to the extent of his willingness to throw all he has into the contest, the battle to secure his rightful place in his world.

There is a misconception of tragedy with which I have been struck in review 17 after review, and in many conversations with writers and readers alike. It is the idea that tragedy is of necessity allied to pessimism. Even the dictionary says nothing more about the word than that it means a story with a sad or unhappy ending. This impression is so firmly fixed that I almost hesitate to claim that in truth tragedy implies more optimism in its author than does comedy, and that its final result ought to be the reinforcement of the onlooker's brightest opinions of the human animal.

For, if it is true to say that in essence the tragic hero is intent upon claiming   18
his whole due as a personality, and if this struggle must be total and without
reservation, then it automatically demonstrates the indestructible will of man to
achieve his humanity.

The possibility of victory must be there in tragedy. Where pathos rules, where   19
pathos is finally derived, a character has fought a battle he could not possibly
have won. The pathetic is achieved when the protagonist is, by virtue of his
witlessness, his insensitivity or the very air he gives off, incapable of grappling
with a much superior force.

Pathos truly is the mode for the pessimist. But tragedy requires a nicer balance   20
between what is possible and what is impossible. And it is curious, although
edifying, that the plays we revere, century after century, are the tragedies. In
them, and in them alone, lies the belief—optimistic, if you will, in the per-
fectibility of man.

It is time, I think, that we who are without kings, took up this bright thread   21
of our history and followed it to the only place it can possibly lead in our time—
the heart and spirit of the average man.

QUESTIONS

1. What reasons does Miller give for his opening statement, "In this age few tragedies
are written"?

2. Miller's position is "that the common man is as apt a subject for tragedy in its
highest sense as kings were" (paragraph 2). How does he use comparison and contrast to
substantiate his thesis?

3. In defining tragedy, Miller uses two approaches: first, he tells us what type of
person the tragic hero is and what he does, and then he explains what actions evoke "the
tragic feeling" (paragraph 4) in the audience. Which approach do you find more convincing?

4. In paragraph 14, Miller says, "Above all else, tragedy requires the finest appreciation by the writer of cause and effect." How does he explain what he means by this?

5. How does Miller define tragedy as an optimistic mode and pathos as a pessimistic
mode?

6. Considering Miller's definition of modern tragedy, explain what would be an
appropriate subject for a tragic drama set in our society.

7. In paragraph 5, Miller says, "Tragedy, then, is the consequence of a man's total
compulsion to evaluate himself justly." Do you know of such a case, or can you imagine
one? Write a narrative in which you set forth the tragic action that ensues from the kind
of compulsion Miller stipulates.

8. The word *tragedy* is often used in reporting news events. What events are called
tragic in newspaper headlines or on radio or television reports? Considering Miller's
definitions of tragedy and pathos, can such events rightly be called tragic? Write an essay
in which you either defend the tragic nature of a recent event or in which you argue
that the event ought to be labeled differently.

Arthur Miller

9. Read (or, if possible, see) Miller's play, *Death of a Salesman*. Given Miller's terms, should the hero, Willy Loman, be considered a tragic or a pathetic figure? For research, you can investigate the critical arguments that have raged on this very subject. In taking a position on this matter you will, of course, have to argue on behalf of your own position.

THE QUESTION
OF ZOOS
John Berger

*Born in London in 1926, John Berger studied at the Central
and Chelsea schools of art in that city. He is known as a
painter, a teacher, a novelist, a poet, but most of all as a
radical art historian and critic. The piece reprinted here is
an extract from the first chapter of his book* About Looking
*(1980). The whole chapter is called "Why Look at Ani-
mals?" It appeared first in 1977 in* New Society *magazine.*

"About 1867," according to the *London Zoo Guide*, "a music hall artist called   1
the Great Vance sang a song called *Walking in the zoo is the OK thing to do*,
and the word 'zoo' came into everyday use. London Zoo also brought the word
'Jumbo' into the English language. Jumbo was an African elephant of mammoth
size, who lived at the zoo between 1865 and 1882. Queen Victoria took an
interest in him and eventually he ended his days as the star of the famous
Barnum circus which travelled through America—his name living on to describe
things of giant proportions."

Public zoos came into existence at the beginning of the period which was to   2
see the disappearance of animals from daily life. The zoo to which people go
to meet animals, to observe them, to see them, is, in fact, a monument to the
impossibility of such encounters. Modern zoos are an epitaph to a relationship
which was as old as man. They are not seen as such because the wrong questions
have been addressed to zoos.

When they were founded—the London Zoo in 1828, the Jardin des Plantes   3
in 1793,[1] the Berlin Zoo in 1844, they brought considerable prestige to the
national capitals. The prestige was not so different from that which had accrued
to the private royal menageries.[2] These menageries, along with gold plate, architecture, orchestras, players, furnishings, dwarfs, acrobats, uniforms, horses,
art and food, had been demonstrations of an emperor's or king's power and
wealth. Likewise in the 19th century, public zoos were an endorsement of
modern colonial power. The capturing of the animals was a symbolic representation of the conquest of all distant and exotic lands. "Explorers" proved their

---

[1]Jardin des Plantes: originally the Royal Garden of Medicinal Plants in Paris, it took in many
animals from menageries during the French Revolutions. [Eds.]
[2]royal menageries: many rulers had for centuries stocked aviaries, lion houses, and bear pits;
private menageries also became status symbols for the aristocracy. [Eds.]

John Berger

patriotism by sending home a tiger or an elephant. The gift of an exotic animal to the metropolitan zoo became a token in subservient diplomatic relations.

Yet, like every other 19th century public institution, the zoo, however supportive of the ideology of imperialism, had to claim an independent and civic function. The claim was that it was another kind of museum, whose purpose was to further knowledge and public enlightenment. And so the first questions asked of zoos belonged to natural history; it was then thought possible to study the natural life of animals even in such unnatural conditions. A century later, more sophisticated zoologists such as Konrad Lorenz asked behavioristic and ethological questions,[3] the claimed purpose of which was to discover more about the springs of human action through the study of animals under experimental conditions.

Meanwhile, millions visited the zoos each year out of a curiosity which was both so large, so vague and so personal that it is hard to express in a single question. Today in France 22 million people visit the 200 zoos each year. A high proportion of the visitors were and are children.

Children in the industrialized world are surrounded by animal imagery: toys, cartoons, pictures, decorations of every sort. No other source of imagery can begin to compete with that of animals. The apparently spontaneous interest that children have in animals might lead one to suppose that this has always been the case. Certainly some of the earliest toys (when toys were unknown to the vast majority of the population) were animal. Equally, children's games, all over the world, include real or pretended animals. Yet it was not until the 19th century that reproductions of animals became a regular part of the decor of middle class childhoods—and then, in this century, with the advent of vast display and selling systems like Disney's—of all childhoods.

In the preceding centuries, the proportion of toys which were animal, was small. And these did not pretend to realism, but were symbolic. The difference was that between a traditional hobby horse and a rocking horse: the first was merely a stick with a rudimentary head which children rode like a broom handle: the second was an elaborate "reproduction" of a horse, painted realistically, with real reins of leather, a real mane of hair, and designed movement to resemble that of a horse galloping. The rocking horse was a 19th century invention.

This new demand for verisimilitude in animal toys led to different methods of manufacture. The first stuffed animals were produced, and the most expensive were covered with real animal skin—usually the skin of still-born calves. The same period saw the appearance of soft animals—bears, tigers, rabbits—such as children take to bed with them. Thus the manufacture of realistic animal toys coincides, more or less, with the establishment of public zoos.

The family visit to the zoo is often a more sentimental occasion than a visit to a fair or a football match. Adults take children to the zoo to show them the

4

5

6

7

8

9

---

[3]Konrad Lorenz (b. 1903): Austrian zoologist, awarded the 1973 Nobel Prize in physiology and medicine; he formulated a school of study based on the concept that an animal's behavior is a product of adaptive evolution. [Eds.]

originals of their "reproductions," and also perhaps in the hope of re-finding some of the innocence of that reproduced animal world which they remember from their own childhood.

The animals seldom live up to the adults' memories, whilst to the children 10 they appear, for the most part, unexpectedly lethargic and dull. (As frequent as the calls of animals in a zoo, are the cries of children demanding: Where is he? Why doesn't he move? Is he dead?) And so one might summarize the felt, but not necessarily expressed, question of most visitors as: Why are these animals less than I believed?

And this unprofessional, unexpressed question is the one worth answering. 11

A zoo is a place where as many species and varieties of animal as possible 12 are collected in order that they can be seen, observed, studied. In principle, each cage is a frame round the animal inside it. Visitors visit the zoo to look at animals. They proceed from cage to cage, not unlike visitors in an art gallery who stop in front of one painting, and then move on to the next or the one after next. Yet in the zoo the view is always wrong. Like an image out of focus. One is so accustomed to this that one scarcely notices it any more; or, rather, the apology habitually anticipates the disappointment, so that the latter is not felt. And the apology runs like this: What do you expect? It's not a dead object you have come to look at, it's alive. It's leading its own life. Why should this coincide with its being properly visible? Yet the reasoning of this apology is inadequate. The truth is more startling.

However you look at these animals, even if the animal is up against the bars, 13 less than a foot from you, looking outwards in the public direction, *you are looking at something that has been rendered absolutely marginal*; and all the concentration you can muster will never be enough to centralize it. Why is this?

Within limits, the animals are free, but both they themselves, and their 14 spectators, presume on their close confinement. The visibility through the glass, the spaces between the bars, or the empty air above the moat, are not what they seem—if they were, then everything would be changed. Thus visibility, space, air, have been reduced to tokens.

The decor, accepting these elements as tokens, sometimes reproduces them 15 to create pure illusion—as in the case of painted prairies or painted rock pools at the back of the boxes for small animals. Sometimes it merely adds further tokens to suggest something of the animal's original landscape—the dead branches of a tree for monkeys, artificial rocks for bears, pebbles and shallow water for crocodiles. These added tokens serve two distinct purposes: for the spectator they are like theater props: for the animal they constitute the bare minimum of an environment in which they can physically exist.

The animals, isolated from each other and without interaction between spe- 16 cies, have become utterly dependent upon their keepers. Consequently most of their responses have been changed. What was central to their interest has been replaced by a passive waiting for a series of arbitrary outside interventions. The events they perceive occurring around them have become as illusory in terms of their natural responses, as the painted prairies. At the same time this very isolation (usually) guarantees their longevity as specimens and facilitates their taxonomic arrangement.

All this is what makes them marginal. The space which they inhabit is 17 artificial. Hence their tendency to bundle towards the edge of it. (Beyond its edges there may be real space.) In some cages the light is equally artificial. In all cases the environment is illusory. Nothing surrounds them except their own lethargy or hyperactivity. They have nothing to act upon—except, briefly, supplied food and—very occasionally—a supplied mate. (Hence their perennial actions become marginal actions without an object.) Lastly, their dependence and isolation have so conditioned their responses that they treat any event which takes place around them—usually it is in front of them, where the public is— as marginal. (Hence their assumption of an otherwise exclusively human attitude—indifference.)

Zoos, realistic animal toys and the widespread commercial diffusion of ani- 18 mal imagery, all began as animals started to be withdrawn from daily life. One could suppose that such innovations were compensatory. Yet in reality the innovations themselves belonged to the same remorseless movement as was dispersing the animals. The zoos, with their theatrical decor for display, were in fact demonstrations of how animals had been rendered absolutely marginal. The realistic toys increased the demand for the new animal puppet: the urban pet. The reproduction of animals in images—as their biological reproduction in birth becomes a rarer and rarer sight—was competitively forced to make animals ever more exotic and remote.

Everywhere animals disappear. In zoos they constitute the living monument 19 to their own disappearance. And in doing so, they provoked their last metaphor. *The Naked Ape, The Human Zoo*, are titles of world bestsellers. In these books the zoologist, Desmond Morris, proposes that the unnatural behavior of animals in captivity can help us to understand, accept and overcome the stresses involved in living in consumer societies.

All sites of enforced marginalization—ghettos, shanty towns, prisons, mad- 20 houses, concentration camps—have something in common with zoos. But it is both too easy and too evasive to use the zoo as a symbol. The zoo is a demonstration of the relations between man and animals; nothing else. The marginalization of animals is today being followed by the marginalization and disposal of the only class who, throughout history, has remained familiar with animals and maintained the wisdom which accompanies that familiarity: the middle and small peasant. The basis of this wisdom is an acceptance of the dualism at the very origin of the relation between man and animal. The rejection of this dualism is probably an important factor in opening the way to modern totalitarianism. But I do not wish to go beyond the limits of that unprofessional, unexpressed but fundamental question asked of the zoo.

The zoo cannot but disappoint. The public purpose of zoos is to offer visitors 21
the opportunity of looking at animals. Yet nowhere in a zoo can a stranger
encounter the look of an animal. At the most, the animal's gaze flickers and
passes on. They look sideways. They look blindly beyond. They scan mechanically. They have been immunized to encounter, because nothing can any more
occupy a *central* place in their attention.

Therein lies the ultimate consequence of their marginalization. That look 22
between animal and man, which may have played a crucial role in the development of human society, and with which, in any case, all men had always
lived until less than a century ago, has been extinguished. Looking at each
animal, the unaccompanied zoo visitor is alone. As for the crowds, they belong
to a species which has at last been isolated.

This historic loss, to which zoos are a monument, is now irredeemable for 23
the culture of capitalism.

QUESTIONS

1. In paragraph 2, Berger says that "the wrong questions have been addressed to
zoos." What is the "right" question, and who proposes it? Have you ever asked a version
of that question yourself?

2. In paragraph 4, Berger considers the claim that zoos are museums. How does he
turn this definition into a case against zoos? Trace this line of argument by definition
through the essay.

3. In paragraph 13, Berger introduces key terms toward which he has been driving.
Why do you suppose he did not begin his essay with a thesis statement declaring the
marginality of animals in the modern world? How does he develop that idea of their
marginality from paragraph 13 to the end?

4. In terms of marginality, what is the implication of the last sentence in paragraph 22?

5. Paragraphs 6 through 9 deal with imagery, representations of animals, and toys.
"Decor" (paragraph 6) is an especially telling word in this section. What is the function,
in Berger's argument, of that particular word and of the ideas that relate to it?

6. Twice in paragraph 20 Berger disclaims any intention of expanding his argument
beyond the situation of zoos. How seriously do you take that disclaimer? What is its
function?

7. Go to a local zoo, and observe both the animals and the people there. Is Berger's
description accurate? Use your observations as evidence in an essay supporting or debating
his attitudes or conclusions.

8. Imagine yourself on the board of directors of a zoo in your community. Berger
has appeared before you and made the presentation you have read. You may have some
differences of opinion, but you don't find it entirely silly or misguided. Now it is your
responsibility, and that of your colleagues, to review the case of your own zoo and make
some kind of recommendation. You might wish to defend it or disband it or alter its
nature in some way. What do you propose? Make a case that you could present before
your fellow board members at the next meeting.

9. According to the last word in this essay, the villain is less modern society than capitalism. Although that conclusion might have been foreseen as early as paragraph 3, why do you believe Berger refrained from beginning with that judgment? Do you think it is accurate, or would you suppose any modern, industrial society would be more or less equally responsible for this situation? There is a potential argument located in that question. You might even do some research into the presence and popularity of zoos in socialist countries.

TWO VIEWS
OF FAITH
Richard Robinson
Richard Taylor

*The following two selections are the work of philosophers who
present opposed views on religious faith. Richard G. F. Robinson took his degrees at Oxford University in England and
Cornell University in the United States. His Ph.D. thesis
on logic was published in 1931, and he has since written a
number of books while teaching at Oriel College of Oxford
University. Richard Clyde Taylor (b. 1919), with degrees
from Oberlin College and Brown University, is a specialist
in metaphysics and ethics who has taught at Brown, Columbia, and Rochester universities. Taylor's selection appeared first in the philosopher Sidney Hook's anthology,* Religious Experience and Truth *(1961). Robinson's was a part
of his lectures at Oxford, published in 1964 as* An Atheist's
Values.

FAITH

According to Christianity one of the great virtues is faith. Paul gave faith a   1
commanding position in the Christian scheme of values, along with hope and
love, in the famous thirteenth chapter of his first letter to the Corinthians.
Thomas Aquinas held that infidelity is a very great sin,[1] that infidels should be
compelled to believe, that heretics should not be tolerated, and that heretics
who revert to the true doctrine and then relapse again should be received into
penitence, but killed (*Summa Theologica*, 2-2, 1–16).

According to me this is a terrible mistake, and faith is not a virtue but a   2
positive vice. More precisely, there is, indeed, a virtue often called faith, but
that is not the faith which the Christians make much of. The true virtue of
faith is faith as opposed to faithlessness, that is, keeping faith and promises and

---

[1](St.) Thomas Aquinas (1225–1274): Italian Dominican monk, teacher, and philosopher; he is
regarded as the most important theologian of medieval Europe. [Eds.]

Richard Robinson and Richard Taylor

being loyal. Christian faith, however, is not opposed to faithlessness but to unbelief. It is faith as some opposite of unbelief that I declare to be a vice.

When we investigate what Christians mean by their peculiar use of the word "faith," I think we come to the remarkable conclusion that all their accounts of it are either unintelligible or false. Their most famous account is that in Heb. xi. 1: "Faith is the substance of things hoped for, the evidence of things not seen." This is obviously unintelligible. In any case, it does not make faith a virtue, since neither a substance nor an evidence can be a virtue. A virtue is a praiseworthy habit of choice, and neither a substance nor an evidence can be a habit of choice. When a Christian gives an intelligible account of faith, I think you will find that it is false. I mean that it is not a true dictionary report of how he and other Christians actually use the word. For example, Augustine asked:[2] "What is faith but believing what you do not see?" (*Joannis Evang. Tract.*, c. 40, § 8). But Christians do not use the word "faith" in the sense of believing what you do not see. You do not see thunder; but you cannot say in the Christian sense: "Have faith that it is thundering," or "I have faith that it has thundered in the past and will again in the future." You do not see mathematical truths; but you cannot say in the Christian sense: "Have faith that there is no greatest number." If we take Augustine's "see" to stand here for "know," still it is false that Christians use the word "faith" to mean believing what you do not know, for they would never call it faith if anyone believed that the sun converts hydrogen into helium, although he did not know it.

A good hint of what Christians really mean by their word "faith" can be got by considering the proposition: "Tom Paine had faith that there is no god." Is this a possible remark, in the Christian sense of the word "faith"? No, it is an impossible remark, because it is self-contradictory, because part of what Christians mean by "faith" is belief that there *is* a god.

There is more to it than this. Christian faith is not merely believing that there is a god. It is believing that there is a god no matter what the evidence on the question may be. "Have faith," in the Christian sense, means "Make yourself believe that there is a god without regard to evidence." Christian faith is a habit of flouting reason in forming and maintaining one's answer to the question whether there is a god. Its essence is the determination to believe that there is a god no matter what the evidence may be.

No wonder that there is no true and intelligible account of faith in Christian literature. What they mean is too shocking to survive exposure. Faith is a great vice, an example of obstinately refusing to listen to reason, something irrational and undesirable, a form of self-hypnotism. Newman wrote that "If we but obey God strictly, in time (through his blessing) faith will become like sight" (*Sermon*

---

[2](St.) Augustine (354–430): Bishop of Hippo, Christian philosopher and theologian; his best-known works are *The Confessions* and *The City of God*. [Eds.]

474

15).[3] This is no better than if he had said: "Keep on telling yourself that there is a god until you believe it. Hypnotize yourself into this belief."

It follows that, far from its being wicked to undermine faith, it is a duty to do so. We ought to do what we can toward eradicating the evil habit of believing without regard to evidence.   7

The usual way of recommending faith is to point out that belief and trust are often rational or necessary attitudes. Here is an example of this from Newman: "To hear some men speak (I mean men who scoff at religion), it might be thought we never acted on Faith or Trust, except in religious matters; whereas we are acting on trust every hour of our lives. . . . We trust our *memory* . . . the general soundness of our reasoning powers. . . . Faith in (the) sense of *reliance on the words of another* as opposed to trust in oneself . . . is the common meaning of the word" (*Sermon* 15).   8

The value of this sort of argument is as follows. It is certainly true that belief and trust are often rational. But it is also certainly true that belief and trust are often irrational. We have to decide in each case by rational considerations whether to believe and trust or not. Sometimes we correctly decide *not* to trust our memory on some point, but to look the matter up in a book. Sometimes even we correctly decide not to trust our own reason, like poor Canning deciding he was mad because the Duke of Wellington told him he was. But Christian faith is essentially a case of irrational belief and trust and decision, because it consists in deciding to believe and trust the proposition that there is a god no matter what the evidence may be.   9

Another common way to defend Christian faith is to point out that we are often obliged to act on something less than knowledge and proof. For example, Newman writes: "Life is not long enough for a religion of inferences; we shall never have done beginning if we determine to begin with proof. Life is for action. If we insist on proof for everything, we shall never come to action; to act you must assume, and that assumption is faith" (*Assent*, p. 92).   10

The value of this argument is as follows. It is true that we are often unable to obtain knowledge and proof. But it does not follow that we must act on faith, for faith is belief reckless of evidence and probability. It follows only that we must act on some belief that does not amount to knowledge. This being so, we ought to assume, as our basis for action, those beliefs which are more probable than their contradictories in the light of the available evidence. We ought not to act on faith, for faith is assuming a certain belief without reference to its probability.   11

There is an ambiguity in the phrase "have faith in" that helps to make faith look respectable. When a man says that he has faith in the president he is   12

[3](John Henry) Newman (1801–1890): a leader of the religious revival movement in Victorian England, he converted to Catholicism and entered the priesthood, becoming a cardinal in 1879. [Eds.]

assuming that it is obvious and known to everybody that there is a president, that the president exists, and he is asserting his confidence that the president will do good work on the whole. But if a man says he has faith in telepathy, he does not mean that he is confident that telepathy will do good work on the whole, but that he believes that telepathy really occurs sometimes, that telepathy exists. Thus the phrase "to have faith in *x*" sometimes means to be confident that good work will be done by *x*, who is assumed or known to exist, but at other times means to believe that *x* exists. Which does it mean in the phrase "have faith in God"? It means ambiguously both; and the self-evidence of what it means in the one sense recommends what it means in the other sense. If there is a perfectly powerful and good god it is self-evidently reasonable to believe that he will do good. In this sense "Have faith in God" is a reasonable exhortation. But it insinuates the other sense, namely "Believe that there is a perfectly powerful and good god, no matter what the evidence." Thus the reasonableness of trusting God if he exists is used to make it seem also reasonable to believe that he exists.

It is well to remark here that a god who wished us to decide certain questions 13 without regard to the evidence would definitely *not* be a perfectly good god.

Even when a person is aware that faith is belief without regard to evidence, 14 he may be led to hold faith respectable by the consideration that we sometimes think it good for a man to believe in his friend's honesty in spite of strong evidence to the contrary, or for a woman to believe in her son's innocence in spite of strong evidence to the contrary. But while we admire and love the love that leads the friend or parent to this view, we do not adopt or admire his conclusion unless we believe that he has private evidence of his own, gained by his long and intimate association, to outweigh the public evidence on the other side. Usually we suppose that his love has led him into an error of judgment, which both love and hate are prone to do.

This does not imply that we should never act on a man's word if we think 15 he is deceiving us. Sometimes we ought to act on a man's word although we privately think he is probably lying. For the act required may be unimportant, whereas accusing a man of lying is always important. But there is no argument from this to faith. We cannot say that sometimes we ought to believe a proposition although we think it is false!

So I conclude that faith is a vice and to be condemned. As Plato said, "It is 16 unholy to abandon the probably true" (*Rp.* 607 c). Out of Paul's "faith, hope, and love" I emphatically accept love and reject faith. As to hope, it is more respectable than faith. While we ought not to believe against the probabilities, we are permitted to hope against them. But still the Christian overtones of hope are other-worldly and unrealistic. It is better to take a virtue that avoids that. Instead of faith, hope, and love, let us hymn reason, love, and joy.

Richard Robinson

FAITH

"Our most holy religion," David Hume said,[1] "is founded on *faith*, not on   1
reason." (All quotations are from the last two paragraphs of Hume's essay "Of
Miracles.") He did not then conclude that it ought, therefore, to be rejected by
reasonable men. On the contrary, he suggests that rational evaluation has no
proper place in this realm to begin with, that a religious man need not feel in
the least compelled to put his religion "to such a trial as it is, by no means,
fitted to endure," and he brands as "dangerous friends or disguised enemies" of
religion those "who have undertaken to defend it by the principles of human
reason."

I want to defend Hume's suggestion, and go a bit farther by eliciting some   2
things that seem uniquely characteristic of *Christian* faith, in order to show
what it has, and what it has not, in common with other things to which it is
often compared. I limited myself to Christian faith because I know rather little
of any other, and faith is, with love and hope, supposed to be a uniquely
Christian virtue.

FAITH AND REASON

Faith is not reason, else religion would be, along with logic and metaphysics,   3
a part of philosophy, which it assuredly is not. Nor is faith belief resting on
scientific or historical inquiry, else religion would be part of the corpus of human
knowledge, which it clearly is not. More than that, it seems evident that by the
normal, common-sense criteria of what is reasonable, the content of Christian
faith is *un*reasonable. This, I believe, should be the starting point, the *datum*,
of any discussion of faith and reason. It is, for instance, an essential content of
the Christian faith that, at a certain quite recent time, God became man, dwelt
among us in the person of a humble servant, and then, for a sacred purpose,
died, to live again. Now, apologetics usually addresses itself to the *details* of this
story, to show that they are not inherently incredible, but this is to miss the
point. It is indeed *possible* to believe it, and in the strict sense the story is
credible. Millions of people do most deeply and firmly believe it. But even the
barest statement of the content of that belief makes it manifest that it does not
and, I think, could not, ever result from rational inquiry. "Mere reason," Hume
said, "is insufficient to convince us of its veracity." The Christian begins the
recital of his faith with the words, "I believe," and it would be an utter distortion
to construe this as anything like "I have inquired, and found it reasonable to
conclude." If there were a man who could say that in honesty, as I think there

---

[1]David Hume (1711–1776): Scottish philosopher and historian. [Eds.]

is not, then he would, in a clear and ordinary sense, believe, but he would have no religious faith whatsoever, and his beliefs themselves would be robbed of what would make them religious.

Now if this essential and (it seems to me) obvious unreasonableness of Christian belief could be recognized at the outset of any discussion of religion, involving rationalists on the one hand and believers on the other, we would be spared the tiresome attack and apologetics upon which nothing ultimately turns, the believer would be spared what is, in fact, an uncalled-for task of reducing his faith to reason or science, which can, as Hume noted, result only in "exposing" it as neither, and the rationalist would be granted his main point, not as a conclusion triumphantly extracted, but as a datum too obvious to labor. 4

FAITH AND CERTAINTY

Why, then, does a devout Christian embrace these beliefs? Now this very question, on the lips of a philosopher, is wrongly expressed, for he invariably intends it as a request for reasons, as a means of putting the beliefs to that unfair "trial" of which Hume spoke. Yet there is a clear and definite answer to this question, which has the merit of being true and evident to anyone who has known intimately those who dwell in the atmosphere of faith. The reason the Christian believes that story around which his whole life turns is, simply, that he cannot help it. If he is trapped into eliciting grounds for it, they are grounds given after the fact of conviction. Within "the circle of faith," the question whether on the evidence one *ought* to believe "does not arise." One neither seeks nor needs grounds for the acceptance of what he cannot help believing. "Whoever is moved by *faith* to assent," Hume wrote, "is conscious of a continued miracle in his own person, which subverts all the principles of his understanding, and gives him a determination to believe. . . ." It is this fact of faith which drives philosophers to such exasperation, in the face of which the believer is nonetheless so utterly unmoved. 5

The believer sees his life as a gift of God, the world as the creation of God, his own purposes, insofar as they are noble, as the purposes of God, and history as exhibiting a divine plan, made known to him through the Christian story. He sees things this way, just because they do seem so, and he cannot help it. This is why, for him, faith is so "easy," and secular arguments to the contrary so beside the point. No one seeks evidence for that of which he is entirely convinced, or regards as relevant what seems to others to cast doubt. The believer is like a child who recoils from danger, as exhibited, for instance, in what he for the first time sees as a fierce animal; the child has no difficulty *believing* he is in peril, just because he cannot help believing it, yet his belief results not at all from induction based on past experience with fierce animals, and no reassurances, garnered from *our* past experience, relieve his terror at all. 6

SOME CONFUSIONS

If this is what religious faith essentially is—if, as a believer might poetically   7
but, I think, correctly describe it, faith is an involuntary conviction, often regarded as a "gift," on the part of one who has voluntarily opened his mind and
heart to receive it—then certain common misunderstandings can be removed.

In the first place, faith should never be likened to an *assumption*, such as   8
the scientist's assumption of the uniformity of nature, or whatnot. An assumption is an intellectual device for furthering inquiry. It need not be a conviction
nor, indeed, even a belief. But a half-hearted faith is no religious faith. Faith
thus has that much, at least, in common with knowledge, that it is a *conviction*,
and its subjective state is *certainty*. One thus wholly distorts faith if he represents
the believer as just "taking" certain things "on faith," and then reasons, like a
philosopher, from these beginnings, as though what were thus "taken" could,
like an assumption, be rejected at will.

Again, it is a misunderstanding to represent faith as "mere tenacity." Tenacity   9
consists in stubbornly clinging to what one hopes, but of which one is not fully
convinced. The child who is instantly convinced of danger in the presence of
an animal is not being tenacious or stubborn, even in the face of verbal reassurances, and no more is the Christian whose acts are moved by faith. The
believer does not so much *shun* evidence as something that might *shake* his
faith, but rather regards it as not to the point. In this he may appear to philosophers to be mistaken, but only if one supposes, as he need not, that one should
hold only such beliefs as are rational.

Again, it is misleading to refer to any set of propositions, such as those   10
embodied in a creed, as being this or that person's "faith." Concerning that
content of belief in which one is convinced by faith, it is logically (though I
think not otherwise) possible that one might be convinced by evidence, in which
case it would have no more to do with faith or religion than do the statements
in a newspaper. This observation has this practical importance, that it is quite
possible—in fact, common—for the faith of different believers to be one and
the same, despite creedal differences.

And finally, both "faith" (or "fideism") and "reason" (or "rationalism") can   11
be, and often are, used as pejorative terms and as terms of commendation.
Which side one takes here is arbitrary, for there is no non-question-begging way
of deciding. A rationalist can perhaps find reasons for being a rationalist, though
this is doubtful; but in any case it would betray a basic misunderstanding to
expect a fideist to do likewise. This is brought out quite clearly by the direction
that discussions of religion usually take. A philosophical teacher will often, for
instance, labor long to persuade his audience that the content of Christian faith
is unreasonable, which is a shamefully easy task for him, unworthy of his

479

Richard Robinson and Richard Taylor

learning. Then, suddenly, the underlying assumption comes to light that Christian beliefs ought, therefore, to be abandoned by rational people! A religious hearer of this discourse might well reply that, religion being unreasonable but nonetheless manifestly worthy of belief, we should conclude with Hume that reason, in this realm at least, ought to be rejected. Now one can decide *that* issue by any light that is granted him, but it is worth stressing that the believer's position on it is just exactly as good, and just as bad, as the rational skeptic's.

Richard Taylor

QUESTIONS

1. What is the main point of each essay? Discuss this by completing the following two summary statements.
   a. Robinson: "Faith is a vice because . . ."
   b. Taylor: "Faith is a virtue because . . ."
Are the two essays arguing opposite sides of the same question, or are they arguing two different questions?

2. Throughout his essay, Taylor gives the impression that the famous skeptic and rationalist David Hume agrees with him that reason should be "rejected" in favor of faith. Suppose he were quoting Hume out of context to support his own case. Would it matter? Is Taylor under any obligation to argue reasonably?

3. Is it fair to say that Robinson is making a god of reason? How do you suppose he would respond to that charge?

4. Taylor concludes that religion is "unreasonable but nonetheless manifestly worthy of belief." What does he mean by "manifestly"? Has he taken any steps to show why religion is worthy of belief? Could he have done a better job on this, or has he done enough?

5. How might you answer the contention of Robinson's paragraph 13? What is Robinson's assumption in that passage? How could you argue that a "perfectly good god" might very well wish us "to decide certain questions without regard to the evidence"? What would you mean, then, by "a perfectly good god"?

6. What do you think of the three virtues Robinson proposes in his final paragraph? Write an essay either defending or attacking "reason, love, and joy" as the central virtues.

7. If you ever have defended yourself either against a person of more faith than yourself or against one more devoted to reason, write an account of that confrontation. What were the positions taken, as you remember them? What were the assumptions governing your argument and that of your opponent? How could you improve on that argument now?

8. Probably you have listened at one time or another either to an evangelical minister or to an unabashed skeptic inveighing against Christian belief. Try to reconstruct the presentation of one such speaker, insofar as you can remember it. How would you characterize that presentation? Is it an argument or something else? (You might want to seek out such a speaker again in order to reacquaint yourself with a presentation you could describe.)

9. If you answered question 8, write an essay that either attacks the presentation you described or that recasts it as a more formal argument.

10. Read David Hume's essay "Of Miracles," which you can find in your library copy of his *Enquiry Concerning Human Understanding*, where it appears as section X. Try to summarize Hume's argument in your own words, and then consider Taylor's position in relation to Hume's. Conclude by arguing either that Taylor has distorted Hume or that he has represented Hume's position fairly in his essay on "Faith."

Social Sciences and
Public Affairs

IS CORPORATE EXECUTIVE COMPENSATION EXCESSIVE?
Robert Thomas

An economist at the University of Washington, Robert Thomas has specialized in economic theory and history. The selection reprinted here appeared first in a book edited by Bruce M. Johnson called The Attack on Corporate America: The Corporate Issues Sourcebook *(1978). It was compiled for the Law and Economics Center of the University of Miami, Florida, as a "vigorous and unbiased" response to "the strident rhetoric used by many of the corporation's contemporary critics."*

Ralph Nader stands at the end of a long line of critics who assail the high incomes of top corporate executives.[1] Nader and his associates suggest that "in the absence of judicial limitations, excessive remuneration has become the norm."[2] They observe that the average top executive in each of the fifty largest industrial corporations earns more salary in a year than many of the corporate employees

---

[1]Ralph Nader (b. 1934): lawyer, consumer activist, and author of *Unsafe at Any Speed*, an exposé of the automobile industry. [Eds.]

[2]Ralph Nader, et al., *Corporate Power in America* (New York: Norton, 1976), p. 115.

earn in a lifetime. Salaries are only part (albeit the major part) of the compensation the top executives receive. Bonuses, lavish retirements, stock options, and stock ownership combine to swell the incomes of corporate chief executives by another 50 to 75 percent of the executives' direct remunerations. Nader and his associates conclude that the top corporate executives receive "staggeringly large salaries and stock options."[3]

THE ATTACK ON EXECUTIVE INCOME

Those who criticize the level of compensation that corporate executives receive are critical of any persons who are, or who become, rich. The top executives of our major corporations *do* become rich. *Fortune* magazine, in a survey of the chief executives of the 500 largest industrial corporations, discovered that the median income in 1976 was $209,000 a year and that when only the 100 largest corporations were considered, the median salary was $344,000 a year.[4]   2

Most Americans, however, do not consider becoming rich to be a crime. Indeed, the opposite is true. Achieving wealth reflects a high level of performance in providing through the market what the economy desires.   3

Nader and his coauthors recognize this admiration for performance and attack the level of executive compensation on other grounds. They suggest that the chief corporate executives are not entrepreneurs who risk their own capital in the search for profits, but functionaries who perform essentially the same tasks as government employees. The chief corporate executives "serve as the bureaucrats of private industry."[5]   4

The difference between industry and government is that the boards of directors of large corporations allegedly are more lax in discharging their responsibilities to their shareholders (by constraining excessive executive salaries) than the members of the Congress of the United States and the various elected officials of state and local governments who serve as the watchdogs for the public interest. The managements of large corporations take advantage of this laxness to request and receive excessive compensation. Moreover, this is not an isolated phenomenon confined to an occasional corporation. Nader reports that it "has become the norm."[6]   5

WHY EXECUTIVES ARE WELL PAID

In response, consider first who a chief corporate executive is, and examine   6

---

[3]Ibid., p. 118.
[4]*Fortune* (May 1976), p. 172.
[5]Nader, p. 118.
[6]Ibid., p. 115.

the responsibilities a chief corporate executive must discharge. The typical top executive in each of the 500 largest industrial corporations is a white Protestant male aged sixty. He got his top position at age fifty-five; he averages between fifty-five and sixty-four hours a week on the job, takes three weeks of vacation each year, and earns a salary of $209,000 a year. He has attended graduate school, and he has worked for more than two companies during his business career. He owns less than $500,000 worth of stock in the company for which he works, and during the past decade he has seen his salary rise less rapidly, in percentage terms, than the salaries of his employees. In short, he is well prepared, experienced, hardworking, and beyond middle age.

Two things distinguish each of these 500 persons from several thousand others   7
who have similar qualities. First, each is paid more. Second, each has been chosen as the person responsible for his company's present and future.

The Fortune 500 Company corporate executive directs a company whose   8
sales in 1975 averaged almost $1.75 billion, whose assets totaled $1.33 billion, and which provided employment for almost 29,000 people.[7] This executive directs the firm in a manner that allows it to earn an 11.6 percent return on its total investment. Such a rate of return is not guaranteed simply because a corporation is large. The opportunities to lose money are many; the managements of 28 of the 500 largest industrial corporations managed to show a loss in the recovery year of 1975. It is possible, moreover, to lose big: Singer reported a loss of $451.9 million in that year, and Chrysler $259.5 million. A chief executive who heads a management team that can avoid such losses and constantly succeed in earning a profit is obviously very valuable to the shareholders of a corporation. He is valuable not only to his employers but also to other corporations; thus his own firm pays him handsomely to retain his services.

Many pages of our national magazines devoted to business news—*Business*   9
Week, Forbes, Fortune—report the movements of business executives from one firm to another. These shifts are induced by substantial increases in salary, often, according to one publication, of 30 percent or more.[8] Some excellently managed corporations, such as IBM, General Motors, Procter and Gamble, and Xerox, are known in industry as "executive breeders."[9] Xerox admitted in its 1976 proxy statement that its management was increasingly becoming "a target for other corporations seeking talented executives," and it proposed a new incentive plan for its executives.[10] This request for increased executive compensation was not self-serving on the part of Xerox's management; it stemmed in part from the prior move of twelve Xerox executives to a rival copier manufacturer.

The high salaries and fringe benefits that talented executives in large cor-   10

---

[7]Charles G. Burck, "A Group Profile of the Fortune 500 Chief Executive," *Fortune*, May 1976, p. 173.

[8]*Business Week* (October 4, 1971), p. 62.

[9]Ibid., p. 57.

[10]Ibid., p. 57.

porations receive stem not from laxness on the part of the boards of directors but, rather, from the boards' vigilance. Corporations must pay their executives, as well as any other employees, what they could earn by working for a rival firm, or lose them. Competition among corporations for the best people sets the level of executive compensation. If one person is to be placed in charge of a billion dollars in shareholder assets, which can easily be lost through mismanagement, even the $766,085 a year that the highest-paid corporate executive in the United States receives might not appear excessive to shareholders, especially if that salary is what it takes to get the services of the best available person.

There are many examples of corporations that are well rewarded for paying the price necessary to get the best person to remedy a bad situation. In one recent case, a firm that once tried to produce computers, and whose stock had sold for as high as $173 a share, fell on hard times; in 1973 it lost $119 million on sales of $177 million and had $300 million in long-term debts.[11] A new chief executive, who by 1976 had made the firm profitable once again, received $200,000 a year, performance incentives that earned him another $400,000, and stock options that made him a millionaire on paper. Clearly the compensation this executive received meets the Nader criterion for being "excessive." Yet, the Bank of America thought it was a worthwhile investment to guarantee his salary in an attempt, which proved successful, to ensure the eventual repayment of the large loans it had made to the firm. Individual shareholders also applauded the move; as a result of the executive's efforts, the value of a share has increased from $2 to over $21. In this one instance, the efforts of the new chief executive succeeded in increasing the market value of the company ten times.

A talented executive is highly paid because he is very productive. He earns for his firm additional net revenue at least equal in value to his compensation. If he did not, his firm would let him go. If his firm does not pay him what he is worth to others, it will lose him to a rival. The same holds true for any other valuable input in our economy and accounts as well for the high incomes received by talented persons in other fields.[12]

SALARIES OF OTHER PERSONS

Consider, for a moment, the salaries paid to entertainers. The fastest way to become a millionaire is not to become a corporate executive, but to become a big rock 'n' roll star or a superstar in professional sports. In 1973, for example, there were an estimated fifty music performers earning between $1 million and

[11]*Forbes* (October 15, 1976), p. 78.
[12]W. Mark Crain, "Can Corporate Executives Set Their Own Wages?" in M. Bruce Johnson, ed., *The Attack on Corporate America: The Corporate Issues Sourcebook* (New York: McGraw-Hill, 1978), pp. 272–275.

$6 million a year.[13] These thirty-five persons and fifteen groups made, annually, between three and seven times the salary paid to America's highest-paid executive. While the musicians performed, that highest-paid executive directed, and was responsible for, a company that employed 376,000 persons, had sales of over $11 billion and assets of over $10 billion, and earned almost $400 million in profits. Rock stars, moreover, earn their fortunes sooner than business executives; most start their careers as teenage idols; few have their best earning years after thirty. The average chief executive in each of the 500 largest industrial corporations does not attain that degree of success until the age of fifty-five.

Or, examine the compensation paid to the superstars in professional sports. 14 The most interesting stories on sports pages now are not reports of games but stories about the fabulous salaries received by star athletes: $3 million to Julius Erving, $1.5 million each to O.J. Simpson and Pele, $500,000 to Kareem Abdul-Jabbar, $450,000 each to Tiny Archibald and Joe Namath, $400,000 to Catfish Hunter, $360,000 to Bob Lanier, $325,000 to Bill Bradley, $302,000 to Spencer Haywood, $250,000 to John Havlicek, $237,500 to Rick Barry, $230,000 to Tom Seaver, and $225,000 to Dick Allen.[14] More names from golf, hockey, and tennis could easily be added to the list. The reported incomes of these superstars are probably understated, since they exclude payments for endorsements and the like. These people, furthermore, work only part of the year, while the average chief executive has a forty-nine-week season.

When considered in the light of the compensation paid to extremely talented 15 persons in other areas, the rewards earned by corporate executives do not appear excessive. A competitive economy ensures that highly productive persons command high rewards.

QUESTIONS

1. After reading the first paragraph of this article, how inclined are you to agree with Ralph Nader? Why does Thomas open with such a paragraph?
2. How effectively does Thomas begin to turn the tables on Nader's position in paragraphs 2 and 3?
3. In paragraph 4, Thomas returns to Nader and his coauthors and extracts from their work a second position, more subtle and demanding than the one introduced in paragraph 2. Just what is this second position, and how does it differ from the other?
4. From paragraph 6 on, Thomas begins to answer this second objection. How well has he answered it by the end of paragraph 12? Are you convinced at that point? Why or why not?
5. Why do you suppose Thomas adds his last three paragraphs? Are they relevant to his argument? Do they contain reasons more or less convincing than the reasons already given?

---

[13]*Forbes* (April 15, 1973), p. 28.
[14]*Fortune* (May, 1976), p. 170.

6. Probably very few workers think they are being paid enough. You, on the other hand, might not always agree with what other persons think they ought to be paid. Choose one kind of work that you know something about or have an interest in, and write an argument for its compensation being either markedly more or less than it now is.

7. Write a rebuttal to Thomas's argument. You might begin with some of Nader's criticisms. Perhaps there is more that can be said about them. Perhaps Thomas didn't answer them effectively enough. Or begin with the information in his last three paragraphs. Perhaps you can use that information to different advantage. Or begin with something else if you see a better point of departure.

THE SEXUAL
ENLIGHTENMENT
OF CHILDREN
Sigmund Freud

Sigmund Freud (1856–1939) spent most of his life in Vienna and would have died there if he had not, like many other Jews, had to leave Austria when Nazi Germany invaded in 1938. As a young man he studied medicine in Vienna, became a doctor, and specialized in mental illness. His researches in this area led him to the study of unconscious mental processes and to the development of psychoanalysis as a way of understanding and treating certain emotional problems. The following essay first appeared in 1907 as a letter to the editor of a medical journal, Soziale Medizin und Hygiene.

DEAR SIR—When you ask me for an expression of opinion on the matter of   1
sexual enlightenment for children, I assume that what you want is the independent opinion of an individual physician whose professional work offers him special opportunities for studying the subject, and not a regular conventional treatise dealing with all the mass of literature that has grown up around it. I am aware that you have followed my scientific efforts with interest, and that, unlike many other colleagues, you do not dismiss my ideas without a hearing because I regard the psychosexual constitution and certain noxiae in the sexual life as the most important causes of the neurotic disorders that are so common.[1] My *Drei Abhandlungen zur Sexualtheorie*,[2] in which I describe the components of which the sexual instinct is made up, and the disturbances which may occur in its development into the function of sexuality, has recently received favorable mention in your Journal.

I am therefore to answer the questions whether children may be given any   2
information at all in regard to the facts of sexual life, and at what age and in what way this should be done. Now let me confess at the outset that discussion with regard to the second and third points seems to me perfectly reasonable, but that to my mind it is quite inconceivable how the first of these questions could ever be the subject of debate. What can be the aim of withholding from

---

[1] noxiae: faults. [Eds.]
[2] *Drei Abhandlungen zur Sexualtheorie: Three Essays on Sexual Theory.* [Eds.]

children, or let us say from young people, this information about the sexual life of human beings? Is it a fear of arousing interest in such matters prematurely, before it spontaneously stirs in them? Is it a hope of retarding by concealment of this kind the development of the sexual instinct in general, until such time as it can find its way into the only channels open to it in the civilized social order? Is it supposed that children would show no interest or understanding for the facts and riddles of sexual life if they were not prompted to do so by outside influence? Is it regarded as possible that the knowledge withheld from them will not reach them in other ways? Or is it genuinely and seriously intended that later on they should consider everything connected with sex as something despicable and abhorrent, from which their parents and teachers wish to keep them apart as long as possible?

I am really at a loss to say which of these can be the motive for the customary   3 concealment from children of everything connected with sex. I only know that these arguments are one and all equally foolish, and that I find it difficult to pay them the compliment of serious refutation. I remember, however, that in the letters of that great thinker and friend of humanity, Multatuli,[3] I once found a few lines which are more than adequate as an answer.

> To my mind it seems that certain things are altogether too much wrapped in mystery. It is well to keep the fantasies of children pure, but their purity will not be preserved by ignorance. On the contrary, I believe that concealment leads a girl or boy to suspect the truth more than ever. Curiosity leads to prying into things which would have roused little or no interest if they were talked of openly without any fuss. If this ignorance could be maintained I might be more reconciled to it, but that is impossible; the child comes into contact with other children, books fall into his hands, which lead him to reflect, and the mystery with which things he has already surmised are treated by his parents actually increases his desire to know more. Then this desire that is only incompletely and secretly satisfied gives rise to excitement and corrupts his imagination, so that the child is already a sinner while his parents still believe he does not know what sin is.[4]

I do not know how the case could be better stated, though perhaps one might   4 amplify it. It is surely nothing else but habitual prudery and a guilty conscience in themselves about sexual matters which causes adults to adopt this attitude of mystery towards children; possibly, however, a piece of theoretical ignorance on their part, to be counteracted only by fresh information, is also responsible. It is commonly believed that the sexual instinct is lacking in children, and only begins to arise in them when the sexual organs mature. This is a grave error, equally serious from the point of view both of theory and of actual practice. It is so easy to correct it by observation that one can only wonder how it can ever

---

[3]Multatuli: the pseudonym of Edward Douwes Dekker (1820–1887), a Dutch writer who became famous through his attacks on the Dutch colonial system.[Eds.]

[4]Multatuli, *Briefe*, 1906, Bd. I. S. 26.

have arisen. As a matter of fact, the new-born infant brings sexuality with it into the world; certain sexual sensations attend its development while at the breast and during early childhood, and only very few children would seem to escape some kind of sexual activity and sexual experiences before puberty. A more complete exposition of this statement can be found in my *Drei Abhandlungen zur Sexualtheorie*, to which reference has been made above. The reader will learn that the specific organs of reproduction are not the only portions of the body which are a source of pleasurable sensation, and that Nature has stringently ordained that even stimulation of the genitals cannot be avoided during infancy. This period of life, during which a certain degree of directly sexual pleasure is produced by the stimulation of various cutaneous areas (erotogenic zones),[5] by the activity of certain biological impulses and as an accompanying excitation during many affective states, is designated by an expression introduced by Havelock Ellis as the period of auto-erotism.[6] Puberty merely brings about attainment of the stage at which the genitals acquire supremacy among all the zones and sources of pleasure, and in this way presses erotism into the service of reproduction, a process which naturally can undergo certain inhibitions; in the case of those persons who later on become perverts and neurotics this process is only incompletely accomplished. On the other hand, the child is capable long before puberty of most of the mental manifestations of love, for example, tenderness, devotion, and jealousy. Often enough the connection between these mental manifestations and the physical sensation of sexual excitation is so close that the child cannot be in doubt about the relation between the two. To put it briefly, the child is long before puberty a being capable of mature love, lacking only the ability for reproduction; and it may be definitely asserted that the mystery which is set up withholds him only from intellectual comprehension of achievements for which he is psychically and physically prepared.

The intellectual interest of a child in the riddle of sexual life, his desire for knowledge, finds expression at an earlier period of life than is usually suspected. If they have not often come across such cases as I am about to mention, parents must either be afflicted with blindness in regard to this interest in their children, or, when they cannot overlook it, must make every effort to stifle it. I know a splendid boy, now four years old, whose intelligent parents abstain from forcibly suppressing one side of the child's development. Little Herbert, who has certainly not been exposed to any seducing influence from servants, has for some time shown the liveliest interest in that part of his body which he calls his weewee-maker. When only three years old he asked his mother, "Mamma, have you got a weewee-maker, too?" His mother answered, "Of course, what did you think?" He also asked his father the same question repeatedly. At about

---

[5]Cutaneous areas: parts of the skin. [Eds.]
[6]Havelock Ellis (1859–1939): British author of many works on human sexual development. [Eds.]

the same age he was taken to a barn and saw a cow milked for the first time. "Look, milk is coming out of the weewee-maker!" he called in surprise. At the age of three and three-quarters he was well on the way to establish correct categories by means of his own independent observation. He saw how water is run off from a locomotive and said, "See, the engine is making weewee, but where is its weewee-maker?" Later on he added thoughtfully, "Dogs and horses have weewee-makers, but tables and chairs don't have them." Recently he was watching his little sister of one week old being bathed, and remarked, "Her weewee-maker is still tiny; it will get bigger when she grows." (I have heard of this attitude towards the problem of sex difference in other boys of the same age.) I must expressly assert that Herbert is not a sensual child nor even morbidly disposed; in my opinion, since he has never been frightened or oppressed with a sense of guilt, he gives expression quite ingenuously to what he thinks.

The second great problem which exercises a child's mind—probably at a 6 rather later date—is that of the origin of children, and is usually aroused by the unwelcome arrival of a baby brother or sister. This is the oldest and most burning question that assails immature humanity; those who understand how to interpret myths and legends can detect it in the riddle which the Theban Sphinx set to Oedipus. The answers usually given to children in the nursery wound the child's frank and genuine spirit of investigation, and generally deal the first blow at his confidence in his parents; from this time onwards he commonly begins to mistrust grown-up people and keeps to himself what interests him most. The following letter may show how torturing this very curiosity may become in older children; it was written by a motherless girl of eleven and a half who had been puzzling over the problem with her younger sister.

DEAR AUNT MALI—Please will you be so kind as to write and tell me how you got Chris or Paul. You must know because you are married. We were arguing about it yesterday, and we want to know the truth. We have nobody else to ask. When are you coming to Salzburg? You know, Aunt Mali, we simply can't imagine how the stork brings babies. Trudel thought the stork brings them in a shirt. Then we want to know, too, how the stork gets them out of the pond, and why one never sees babies in ponds. And please will you tell me, too, how you know beforehand when you are going to have one. Please write and tell me *all* about it. Thousands of kisses from all of us.—Your inquiring niece,

LILY.

I do not think that this touching request brought the two sisters the infor- 7 mation they wanted. Later on the writer developed the neurosis that arises in unanswered unconscious questions—obsessive speculating.

I do not think that there is even one good reason for denying children the 8 information which their thirst for knowledge demands. To be sure, if it is the purpose of educators to stifle the child's power of independent thought as early as possible, in order to produce that "good behavior" which is so highly prized, they cannot do better than deceive children in sexual matters and intimidate them by religious means. The stronger characters will, it is true, withstand these influences; they will become rebels against the authority of their parents and later against every other form of authority. When children do not receive the explanations for which they turn to their elders, they go on tormenting themselves in secret with the problem, and produce attempts at solution in which the truth they have guessed is mixed up in the most extraordinary way with grotesque inventions; or else they whisper confidences to each other which, because of the sense of guilt in the youthful inquirers, stamp everything sexual as horrible and disgusting. These infantile sexual theories are well worth collecting and examining. After these experiences children usually lose the only proper attitude to sexual questions, many of them never to find it again.

It would seem that the overwhelming majority of writers, both men and women, who have dealt with the question of explaining sexual matters to children have expressed themselves in favor of enlightenment. The clumsiness, however, of most of their proposals how and when this enlightenment should be carried out leads one to conclude that they have not found it very easy to venture this admission. As far as my knowledge of the literature goes, the charming letter of explanation which a certain Frau Emma Eckstein gives as written to her ten-year-old boy stands out conspicuously.[7] The customary method is obviously not the right one. All sexual knowledge is kept from children as long as possible, and then on one single occasion an explanation, which is even then only half the truth and generally comes too late, is proffered them in mysterious and solemn language. Most of the answers to the question "How can I tell my children?" make such a pitiful impression, at least upon me, that I should prefer parents not to concern themselves with the explanation at all. It is much more important that children should never get the idea that one wants to make more of a secret of the facts of sexual life than of any other matter not suited to their understanding. To ensure this it is necessary that from the very beginning everything sexual should be treated like everything else that is worth knowing about. Above all, schools should not evade the task of mentioning sexual matters; lessons about the animal kingdom should include the great facts of reproduction, which should be given their due significance, and emphasis should be laid at the same time on the fact that man shares with the higher animals everything essential to his organization. Then, if the atmosphere of the home does not make for suppression of all reasoning, something similar to what I once overheard in a nursery would probably occur oftener. A small boy said to his little sister, "How can you think the stork brings babies! You know that man is a mammal, do you suppose that storks bring other mammals their young too?" In this way the curiosity of children will never become very intense, for at each stage in its inquiries it will find the satisfaction it needs. Explanations about the

---

[7]Emma Eckstein, *Die Sexualfrage in der Erziehung des Kindes*, 1904.

493

specific circumstances of human sexuality and some indication of its social significance should be provided before the child is eleven years old. The age of confirmation would be a more suitable time than any other at which to instruct the child, who already has full knowledge of the physical facts involved, in those social obligations which are bound up with the actual gratification of this instinct. A gradual and progressive course of instruction in sexual matters such as this, at no period interrupted, in which the school takes the initiative, seems to me to be the only method of giving the necessary information that takes into consideration the development of the child and thus successfully avoids ever-present dangers.

QUESTIONS

1. Summarize Freud's argument in your own words.

2. In his second paragraph, Freud mentions three questions. The second two he finds "perfectly reasonable" but the first hardly worth debate. Yet he doesn't leave that first question until paragraph 9, the last paragraph of his essay. What do you make of this imbalance? What does it indicate about Freud's argumentative purpose?

3. What counterpositions does Freud acknowledge? How does he present them and deal with them?

4. Freud quotes two long passages from other writers (Multatuli and Lily), and he gives us several quotations from little Herbert. What is the function of the material drawn from each of these three sources in Freud's argument?

5. Compare Freud's term *sexual enlightenment* with the contemporary term *sex education*. Do they have the same denotation? Do they have the same connotations?

6. What is the balance between appeal to reason and appeal to emotion in this essay? Can you point to specific places where Freud shifts from one to the other?

7. Paragraph 2 has a long string of rhetorical questions. What is the function of such questions? How do you respond to them?

8. Perhaps you have a younger brother or sister or know some young children. If not, you can certainly imagine having a child who might ask you questions about sex. What do you think your proper role would be in that situation? Write an essay in which you, first, specify the age and relationship to you of the person you imagine, and, second, outline the nature of the information you think proper to provide and the manner in which you might do that.

9. Write a critique of sex education as you have known it. This does not necessarily mean that you have to agree with all of Freud's ideas. Sex education as you have known it may have been well informed, well planned, and useful; or it may have been, for any number of reasons, a bungled job, an embarrassment, and a disaster. Most likely it held a place between those extremes. In any case, write an essay that describes sex education as you knew it, and make some suggestions for its improvement.

THE FIRST
TELEVISED WAR
Phillip Knightley

*Phillip Knightley was born in Australia in 1929. He began
his career as a copyboy on a newspaper in Sydney, later
becoming a reporter and an editor. For over twenty years he
has lived and worked in London as a journalist and historian of journalism, acting as a special correspondent for the*
Sunday Times *of London. He says that he has never heard
a shot fired in anger and hopes he never will. The following
selection is taken from chapter 16 of his book* The First
Casualty: From the Crimea to Vietnam: The War Correspondent as Hero, Propagandist, and Myth Maker *(1975).
The title of the book is based on a statement made by United
States Senator Hiram Johnson in 1917: "The first casualty
when war comes is truth."*

The most intrusive medium in Vietnam was television, and, as the war went   1
on, the hunger of editors for combat footage increased. "Before they were satisfied with a corpse," Richard Lindley, a British television reporter, said. "Then
they had to have people dying in action."[1] Michael Herr described a truck
carrying a dying ARVN soldier that stopped near a group of correspondents.
The soldier, who was only nineteen or twenty, had been shot in the chest. A
television cameraman leaned over the Vietnamese and began filming. The other
correspondents watched. "He opened his eyes briefly a few times and looked
back at us. The first time he tried to smile . . . then it left him. I'm sure he
didn't even see us the last time he looked, but we all knew what it was that he
had seen just before that."[2] The Vietnamese had seen the zoom lens of a sixteen-
millimeter converted Auricon sound camera capturing his last moments of life
on film that, if the flight connections worked and the editors back at the network
liked it, would be shown in American living rooms within forty-eight hours.

This little item would not be exceptional. During the Tet offensive,[3] a Vi-   2
etnamese in a checked shirt appeared on television being walked—that is, dragged—
between two soldiers. The soldiers took him over to a man holding a pistol,
who held it to the head of the man in the checked shirt and blew his brains

---

[1] *London Sunday Times*, November 26, 1967.
[2] *Christian Science Monitor*, May 29–June 30, 1970.
[3] Tet offensive: the campaign by the Vietcong begun during the Tet (lunar new year) festival in
January 1968. [Eds.]

Phillip Knightley

out. All of it was seen in full color on television (and later in a memorable series of photographs taken by Eddie Adams of the AP).

Any viewer in the United States who watched regularly the television re- 3 porting from Vietnam—and it was from television that 60 per cent of Americans got most of their war news—would agree that he saw scenes of real-life violence, death, and horror on his screen that would have been unthinkable before Vietnam. The risk and intrusion that such filming involved could, perhaps, be justified if it could be shown that television had been particularly effective in revealing the true nature of the war and thus had been able to change people's attitudes to it. Is there any evidence to this effect?

The director of CBS News in Washington, William Small, wrote: "When 4 television covered its 'first war' in Vietnam it showed a terrible truth of war in a manner new to mass audiences. A case can be made, and certainly should be examined, that this was cardinal to the disillusionment of Americans with this war, the cynicism of many young people towards America, and the destruction of Lyndon Johnson's tenure of office."[4] A *Washington Post* reporter, Don Oberdorfer, amply documents, in his book *Tet*, the number of commentators and editors (including those of Time Inc.) who had to re-examine their attitudes after extensive television—and press—coverage brought home to them the bewildering contradictions of a seemingly unending war.

Television's power seems to have impressed British observers even more than 5 American. The director-general of the Royal United Service Institution, Air Vice-Marshal S. W. B. Menaul, believes that television had "a lot to answer for [in] the collapse of American morale in relation to the Vietnam war." The then editor of the *Economist*, Alistair Burnet, wrote that the television reporting of Vietnam had made it very difficult for two American administrations to continue that war, "which was going on in American homes," irrespective of the merits or demerits of why the United States was actually involved in Vietnam. Robin Day, the BBC commentator, told a seminar of the Royal United Service Institution that the war on color-television screens in American living rooms had made Americans far more anti-militarist and anti-war than anything else: "One wonders if in future a democracy which has uninhibited television coverage in every home will ever be able to fight a war, however just. . . . The full brutality of the combat will be there in close up and color, and blood looks very red on the color television screen." And the Director of Defence Operations, Plans and Supplies at the Ministry of Defence, Brigadier F. G. Caldwell, said that the American experience in Vietnam meant that if Britain were to go to war again, "we would have to start saying to ourselves, are we going to let the television cameras loose on the battlefield?"[5]

All this seems very persuasive, and it would be difficult to believe that the 6

---

[4]*Sunday Times*, October 19 and October 10, 1971; *The Times*, July 12, 1971.
[5]J. Lucas, *Dateline Vietnam* (New York: Award Books, 1967), p. 15.

sight, day after day, of American soldiers and Vietnamese civilians dying in a war that seemed to make no progress could not have had *some* effect on the viewer. Yet a survey conducted for *Newsweek* in 1967 suggested a remarkably different conclusion: that television had encouraged a majority of viewers to *support* the war. When faced with deciding whether television coverage had made them feel more like "backing up the boys in Vietnam" or like opposing the war, 64 per cent of viewers replied that they were moved to support the soldiers and only 26 per cent to oppose the war. A prominent American psychiatrist, Fredric Wertham, said, in the same year, that television had the effect of conditioning its audience to accept war, and a further *Newsweek* enquiry, in 1972, suggested that the public was developing a tolerance of horror in the newscasts from Vietnam—"The only way we can possibly tolerate it is by turning off a part of ourselves instead of the television set."

Edward Jay Epstein's survey of television producers and news editors, for his book *News from Nowhere*, showed that more than two-thirds of those he interviewed felt that television had had little effect in changing public opinion on Vietnam. An opinion commonly expressed was that people saw exactly what they wanted to in a news report and that television only served to reinforce existing views. *The New Yorker's* television critic, Michael J. Arlen, reported, on several occasions, that viewers had a vague, unhappy feeling that they were not getting "the true picture" of Vietnam from the medium.[6] So if it was true that television did not radically change public opinion about the war, could it have been because of the quality of the coverage?

Television is a comparatively new medium. There were 10,000 sets in the United States in 1941; at the time of Korea there were 10 million, and at the peak of the Vietnam War 100 million. There was some television reporting in Korea, a lot of it daring—an American general had to order the BBC cameraman Cyril Page to get down off the front of a tank to which he had tied himself so as to get a grandstand view of the battle as the tank went into action. But, until Vietnam, no one knew what problems the prolonged day-by-day coverage of a war by television would produce. The first was surprising—a lack of reality. It had been believed that when battle scenes were brought into the living room the reality of war would at last be brought home to a civilian audience. But Arlen was quick to point out, in *The New Yorker*, that by the same process battle scenes are made less real, "diminished in part by the physical size of the television screen, which, for all the industry's advances, still shows one a picture of men three inches tall shooting at other men three inches tall."[7] Sandy Gall of ITN found shooting combat footage difficult and dangerous, and the end result very disappointing. "I think you lose one dimension on television's small screen and things look smaller than life; the sound of battle, for example, never

---

[6]F. Harvey, *Air War Vietnam* (New York: Bantam, 1967), p. 115.
[7]Harvey, p. 184.

coming across. I am always let down when I eventually see my footage and think, Is that all? The sense of danger never comes across on television and you, the correspondent, always look as though you had an easy time of it."[8]

For many Americans in Vietnam, there emerged a strange side to the war that became directly related to television—the fact that the war seemed so unreal that sometimes it became almost possible to believe that everything was taking place on some giant Hollywood set and all the participants were extras playing a remake of *Back to Bataan*.[9] GIs—and even correspondents—brought up on Second World War movies shown on television, used to seeing Errol Flynn sweeping to victory through the jungles of Burma or Brian Donlevy giving the Japanese hell in the Coral Sea,[10] tended to relate their experiences in Vietnam to the Hollywood version of America at war.[11] Michael Herr, making a dash, with David Greenway of *Time*, from one position at Hué to another, caught himself saying to a Marine a line from a hundred Hollywood war films: "We're going to cut out now. Will you cover us?" One should not be surprised, therefore, to find that GIs sometimes behaved, in the presence of television cameras, as if they were making *Dispatch from Da Nang*. Herr describes soldiers running about during a fight because they knew there was a television crew nearby. "They were actually making war movies in their heads, doing little guts and glory Leatherneck tap dances under fire, getting their pimples shot off for the networks."[12]

So it is not difficult to understand how, when seen on a small screen, in the enveloping and cosy atmosphere of the household, sometime between the afternoon soap-box drama and the late-night war movie, the television version of the war in Vietnam could appear as just another drama, in which the hero is the correspondent and everything will come out all right at the end. Jack Laurence of CBS, an experienced war correspondent, who spent a lot of time in Vietnam, had this possibility brought home to him in Israel during the 1973 conflict. He was in a hotel lobby, and a couple who had just arrived from the United States recognized him and said, "We saw you on television and we knew everything was going to be all right because you were there."[13] There is not much a television correspondent can do about such a situation as that; it seems inherent in the nature of the medium. However, correspondents, or, more fairly, their editors, do have something to answer for in their selection of news in Vietnam.

Years of television news of the war have left viewers with a blur of images consisting mainly of helicopters landing in jungle clearings, soldiers charging

9

10

11

---

[8]*Washington Post*, February 23, 1966.
[9]*Back to Bataan*: a 1945 John Wayne film about the retaking of Bataan in the Philippines during World War II. [Eds.]
[10]Errol Flynn (1909–1959) and Brian Donlevy (1899–1972): Hollywood filmstars. [Eds.]
[11]The arrival in 1965 of Flynn's son, Sean, as a correspondent tended to confirm this feeling.
[12]Interview with John Shaw.
[13]Harvey, p. 104.

into undergrowth, wounded being loaded onto helicopters, artillery and mortar fire, air strikes on distant targets, napalm canisters turning slowly in the sky, and a breathless correspondent poking a stick microphone under an army officer's nose and asking, "What's happening up there, Colonel?" (The only honest answer came, in 1972, from a captain on Highway 13. "I wish the hell I knew," he said.) The networks claimed that combat footage was what the public wanted; that concentrating on combat prevented the film's being out of date if it was delayed in transmission; that it was difficult to shoot anything other than combat film when only three or four minutes were available in the average news program for events in Vietnam; and that the illusion of American progress created by combat footage shot from only one side was balanced by what the correspondent had to say.

This is simply not true. To begin with, combat footage fails to convey all   12 aspects of combat. "A cameraman feels so inadequate, being able to record only a minute part of the misery, a minute part of the fighting," said Kurt Volkert, a CBS cameraman. "You have to decide what the most important action is. Is it the woman holding her crying baby? Is it the young girl cringing near her house because of the exploding grenades? Or is it the defiant looking Vietcong with blood on his face just after capture?"[14] When the cameraman's thirty minutes of combat footage are edited down to three minutes—not an unusual editing ratio—the result is a segment of action that bears about as much relation to the reality in Vietnam as a battle scene shot in Hollywood does. In fact, the Hollywood version would probably appear more realistic.

The American viewer who hoped to learn something serious about Vietnam   13 was subjected, instead, to a television course in the techniques of war, and he was not sufficiently exposed either to what the war meant to the people over whose land it was being fought, or to the political complexities of the situation, or even to the considered personal views of reporters who had spent years covering the situation. Yet, even by the networks' own standards, the limited aspects of the war that the viewer was permitted to see could produce excellent television. One of the most dramatic pieces of film on the war was shot by a CBS team on Highway 13 late in April 1972. A South Vietnamese mine, intended to stop advancing enemy tanks, had caught a truck loaded with refugees. The film showed deaf children, distressed babies, and a woman weeping over the body of her son. The reporter, Bob Simon, described what had happened and then, with perhaps the best sign-off line from Vietnam, said simply, "There's nothing left to say about this war, nothing at all." "Morley Safer's Vietnam," an hour-long report by the CBS correspondent in Saigon, was Safer's own explicit view, and was hailed by *The New Yorker*'s critic, Michael J. Arlen, as "one of the best pieces of journalism to come out of the Vietnam war in any medium." But film like this was rare.

---

[14]P. Jones Griffiths, *Vietnam Inc.* (New York: Macmillan, 1971), p. 60.

Phillip Knightley

Competition for combat footage was so intense that it not only forced American television teams to follow each other into what the BBC's correspondent Michael Clayton called "appallingly dangerous situations," but it also made editors reluctant to risk allowing a team the time and the freedom to make its own film of the war. Where were the television equivalents of Martha Gellhorn's series on Vietnamese orphanages and hospitals, or Philip Jones Griffiths' searing book on the nature of the war, *Vietnam Inc.?* True, television was handicapped by its mechanics—a three-man, or even a two-man, team loaded with camera, sound equipment, and film is less mobile and more dependent on military transport, and in a dangerous situation more vulnerable, than a journalist or a photographer. In its presentation, too, television is sometimes handicapped by its commercial associations. The Vietnamese cameraman Vo Suu filmed the brutal shooting of a Vietcong suspect by General Nguyen Ngoc Loan during the Tet offensive. NBC blacked out the screen for three seconds after the dead man hit the ground, so as to provide a buffer before the commercial that followed. (What television *really* wanted was action in which the men died cleanly and not too bloodily. "When they get a film which shows what a mortar does to a man, really shows the flesh torn and the blood flowing, they get squeamish," says Richard Lindley. "They want it to be just so. They want television to be cinema."[15]) 14

American television executives showed too little courage in their approach to Vietnam. They followed each other into paths the army had chosen for them. They saw the war as "an American war in Asia—and that's the only story the American audience is interested in," and they let other, equally important, aspects of Vietnam go uncovered. 15

QUESTIONS

1. What is the meaning of the incident Knightley describes in his first paragraph? How does that example relate to his essay?

2. What is Knightley's thesis? Where do you find the clearest statement of it? What position is Knightley arguing *against?*

3. Paragraphs 4 and 5 summarize a position frequently heard about the Vietnam War, yet it turns out to be a position Knightley attacks. What are his major points of disagreement with that position? How convincingly does Knightley develop them?

4. Trace the theme of Hollywood as it develops in this essay. What does it add to Knightley's argument? How does it relate to his thesis?

5. Knightley isn't the first person to observe that the movies and television have taught us how to behave in certain critical situations, not always having to do with war. Can you think of a time when your behavior was not just influenced but almost defined by how people in movies act? Write an essay about that event. What were you doing, or

---

[15]Jones Griffiths, p. 62.

what did you need to do? What models of behavior influenced your own? How well did that learning enable you to meet the demands of the moment?

6. For a week or more, study television coverage of an important political event. Write a report on the coverage as you find it. How realistic and thorough do you judge it to be? What hints of distortion and misunderstanding do you find? Try to develop a thesis about the success or failure of the coverage of this event.

7. Compare television and newspaper coverage of any significant event. To what extent do the different media focus on different features of the event? What are the values, as you see them, of the differences you find?

ANALYTIC IVORY TOWERS
Thomas J. Peters
and Robert H. Waterman, Jr.

Thomas Peters has degrees from Cornell and Stanford universities in civil engineering and business; Robert Waterman, Jr., is a mining engineer with a degree from Colorado School of Mines and an M.B.A. from Stanford. Waterman is a director of the business consulting firm McKinsey & Company. Peters heads his own consulting firm in Palo Alto. Both of these men are currently associated with the Stanford Business School. Their recent book, In Search of Excellence: Lessons from America's Best-Run Companies *(1982) has had both a popular and critical success. The following selection has been taken from chapter 2 of that book, a critique of excessive concern with rational efficiency in American business management.*

The reason behind the absence of focus on product or people in so many 1
American companies, it would seem, is the simple presence of a focus on
something else. That something else is overreliance on analysis from corporate
ivory towers and overreliance on financial sleight of hand,[1] the tools that would
appear to eliminate risk but also, unfortunately, eliminate action.

"A lot of companies overdo it," says Ed Wrapp. "They find planning more 2
interesting than getting out a salable product. . . . Planning is a welcome respite
from operating problems. It is intellectually more rewarding, and does not carry
the pressures that operations entail. . . . Formal long-range planning almost
always leads to overemphasis of technique." Fletcher Byrom of Koppers offers
a suggestion. "As a regimen," he says, "as a discipline for a group of people,
planning is very valuable. My position is, go ahead and plan, but once you've
done your planning, put it on the shelf. Don't be bound by it. Don't use it as
a major input to the decision-making process. Use it mainly to recognize change
as it takes place." In a similar vein, *Business Week* recently reported: "Significantly, neither Johnson & Johnson, nor TRW, nor 3M—all regarded as forward
thinking—has anyone on board called a corporate planner."

---

[1]ivory towers: places or situations remote or aloof from worldly or practical affairs. [Eds.]

David Ogilvy, founder of Ogilvy and Mather, states bluntly: "The majority 3
of businessmen are incapable of original thought because they are unable to
escape from the tyranny of reason." Harvard's renowned marketing professor
Theodore Levitt said recently: "Modelers build intricate decision trees whose
pretension to utility is exceeded only by the awe in which high-level line managers hold the technocrats who construct them." Finally, we have a recent
account of a Standard Brands' new product strategy that was an abject failure.
The reason, according to a *Business Week* cover story, was that Standard Brands
hired a bevy of GE planners and then gave them something akin to operating
responsibility. After letting most of them go, the chairman noted: "The guys
were bright, [but they] were not the kind of people who could implement the
programs."

Now, all of this is apparently bad news for many who have made a life's 4
work of number crunching. But the problem is not that companies ought not
to plan. They damn well should plan. The problem is that the planning becomes
an end in itself. It goes far beyond Byrom's sensible dictum to use it to enhance
mental preparedness. Instead, the plan becomes the truth, and data that don't
fit the preconceived plan (e.g., real customer response to a pre-test market
action) are denigrated or blithely ignored. Gamesmanship replaces pragmatic
action. ("Have you polled the corporate staffs yet about the estimate?" was a
common query in one corporate operating committee that we observed for
years.)

Business performance in the United States has deteriorated badly, at least 5
compared to that of Japan, and sometimes to other countries—and in many
cases absolutely, in terms of productivity and quality standards. We no longer
make the best or most reliable products and we seldom make them for less,
especially in internationally competitive industries (e.g., autos, chips).

The first wave of attack on the causes of this problem focused on government 6
regulators. That, however, seemed to be an incomplete answer. Then, in mid-
1980, the quest for root causes took thoughtful executives, business reporters,
and academics alike into the heartland of management practice, all trying to
figure out what had gone wrong. Not surprisingly, America's recent dependence
on overanalysis and a narrow form of rationality bore the brunt of the attack.
Both seemed especially at odds with the Japanese approach to the work force
and to quality—even allowing for cultural differences.

The inquiry ran into two formidable roadblocks. The first was inherent de- 7
fensiveness. The businessman's intellect and soul were finally under attack.
Until then he had been encouraged by the press simply to increase his finger
pointing at others, namely, the government. Second, the attack ran into a
language problem. It wasn't seen as an attack on "a narrow form of rationality,"
what we have termed the "rational model," thereby calling for a broader form.
It was seen as an attack on rationality and logical thought per se, thus implicitly

Thomas J. Peters and Robert H. Waterman, Jr.

encouraging escape into irrationality and mysticism. One was led to believe that the only solution was to move Ford board meetings to the local Zen center. And, obviously, that wasn't going to be the solution.

But let us stop for a moment and ask: What exactly do we mean by the fall of the rational model? We really are talking about what Thomas Kuhn,[2] in his landmark book *The Structure of Scientific Revolutions*, calls a paradigm shift. Kuhn argues that scientists in any field and in any time possess a set of shared beliefs about the world, and for that time the set constitutes the dominant paradigm. What he terms "normal science" proceeds nicely under this set of shared beliefs. Experiments are carried out strictly within the boundaries of those beliefs and small steps toward progress are made. An old but excellent example is the Ptolemaic view of the universe (which held until the sixteenth century) that the earth was at the center of the universe, and the moon, sun, planets, and stars were embedded in concentric spheres around it. Elaborate mathematical formulas and models were developed that would accurately predict astronomical events based on the Ptolemaic paradigm. Not until Copernicus and Kepler found that the formula worked more easily when the sun replaced the earth as the center of it all did an instance of paradigm shift begin.

After a paradigm shift begins, progress is fast though fraught with tension. People get angry. New discoveries pour in to support the new belief system (e.g., those of Kepler and Galileo), and scientific revolution occurs. Other familiar examples of paradigm shift and ensuing revolution in science include the shift to relativity in physics, and to plate techtonics in geology. The important point in each instance is that the old "rationality" is eventually replaced with a new, different, and more useful one.

We are urging something of this kind in business. The old rationality is, in our opinion, a direct descendant of Frederick Taylor's school of scientific management and has ceased to be a useful discipline. Judging from the actions of managers who seem to operate under this paradigm, some of the shared beliefs include:

- Big s better because you can always get economies of scale. When in doubt, consolidate things; eliminate overlap, duplication, and waste. Incidentally, as you get big, make sure everything is carefully and formally coordinated.
- Low-cost producers are the only sure-fire winners. Customer utility functions lead them to focus on cost in the final analysis. Survivors always make it cheaper.
- Analyze everything. We've learned that we can avoid big dumb decisions through good market research, discounted cash-flow analysis, and good budgeting. If a little is good, then more must be better, so apply things like discounted cash flow to risky investments like research and development. Use budgeting as a model for long-range planning. Make forecasts. Set hard nu-

---

[2]Thomas Kuhn (b. 1922): American historian of science. [Eds.]

merical targets on the basis of those forecasts. Produce fat planning volumes whose main content is numbers. (Incidentally, forget the fact that most long-range forecasts are bound to be wrong the day they are made. Forget that the course of invention is, by definition, unpredictable.)

· Get rid of the disturbers of the peace—i.e., fanatical champions. After all, we've got a plan. We want one new product development activity to produce the needed breakthrough, and we'll put 500 engineers on it if necessary, because we've got a better idea. 14

· The manager's job is decision making. Make the right calls. Make the tough calls. Balance the portfolio. Buy into the attractive industries. Implementation, or execution, is of secondary importance. Replace the whole management team if you have to to get implementation right. 15

· Control everything. A manager's job is to keep things tidy and under control. Specify the organization structure in great detail. Write long job descriptions. Develop complicated matrix organizations to ensure that every possible contingency is accounted for. Issue orders. Make black and white decisions. Treat people as factors of production. 16

· Get the incentives right and productivity will follow. If we give people big, straightforward monetary incentives to do right and work smart, the productivity problem will go away. Over-reward the top performers. Weed out the 30 to 40 percent dead wood who don't want to work. 17

· Inspect to control quality. Quality is like everything else; order it done. Triple the quality control department if necessary (forget that the QC force per unit of production in Japanese auto companies is just a third the size of ours). Have it report to the president. We'll show them (i.e., workers) that we mean business. 18

· A business is a business is a business. If you can read the financial statements, you can manage anything. The people, the products, and the services are simply those resources you have to align to get good financial results. 19

· Top executives are smarter than the market. Carefully manage the cosmetics of the income statement and balance sheet, and you will look good to outsiders. Above all, don't let quarterly earnings stop growing. 20

· It's all over if we stop growing. When we run out of opportunity in our industry, buy into industries we don't understand. At least we can then continue growing. 21

Much as the conventional business rationality seems to drive the engine of business today, it simply does not explain most of what makes the excellent companies work. Why not? What are its shortcomings? 22

For one, the numerative, analytical component has an in-built conservative bias. Cost reduction becomes priority number one and revenue enhancement takes a back seat. This leads to obsession with cost, not quality and value; to patching up old products rather than fooling with untidy new product or business devel- 23

505

opment; and to fixing productivity through investment rather than revitalization of the work force. A buried weakness in the analytic approach to business decision making is that people analyze what can be most readily analyzed, spend more time on it, and more or less ignore the rest.

As Harvard's John Steinbruner observes, "If quantitative precision is demanded, it is gained, in the current state of things, only by so reducing the scope of what is analyzed that most of the important problems remain external to the analysis." This leads to fixation on the cost side of the equation. The numbers are "hardest" there. The fix, moreover, is mechanical and easy to picture—buy a new machine to replace nineteen jobs, reduce paperwork by 25 percent, close down two lines and speed up the remaining one.

Numerative analysis leads simultaneously to another unintended devaluation of the revenue side. Analysis has no way of valuing the extra oomph, the overkill, added by an IBM or Frito-Lay sales force. In fact, according to a recent observer, every time the analysts got their hands on Frito's "99.5 percent service level" (an "unreasonable" level of service in a so-called commodity business) their eyes began to gleam and they proceeded to show how much could be saved if only Frito would reduce its commitment to service. The analysts are "right"; Frito would immediately save money. But the analysts cannot possibly demonstrate the impact of a tiny degree of service unreliability on the heroic 10,000-person sales force—to say nothing of the Frito's retailers—and, therefore, on eventual market share loss or margin decline. Viewed analytically, the overcommitment to reliability by Caterpillar ("Forty-eight-hour parts service anywhere in the world—or Cat pays") or Maytag ("Ten years' trouble-free operation") makes no sense. Analytically, purposeful duplication of effort by IBM and 3M on product development, or cannibalization of one P&G brand by another P&G brand is, well, just that, duplication. Delta's family feeling, IBM's respect for the individual, and McDonald's and Disney's fetish for cleanliness make no sense in quantitative terms.

The exclusively analytic approach run wild leads to an abstract, heartless philosophy. Our obsession with body counts in Viet Nam and our failure to understand the persistence and long-time horizon of the Eastern mind culminated in America's most catastrophic misallocation of resources—human, moral, and material. But McNamara's[3] fascination with numbers was just a sign of the times. One of his fellow whiz kids at Ford, Roy Ash, fell victim to the same affliction. Says *Fortune* of his Litton misadventures, "Utterly abstract in his view of business, [Ash] enjoyed to the hilt exercising his sharp mind in analyzing the most sophisticated accounting techniques. His brilliance led him to think in the most regal of ways: building new cities; creating a shipyard that would roll off the most technically advanced vessels the way Detroit builds automobiles."

24

25

26

---

[3]Robert McNamara (b. 1916): president of the Ford Motor Company, 1960–1961; Secretary of Defense, 1961–1968; president of the World Bank, 1968–1981. [Eds.]

Sadly, *Fortune's* analysis speaks not only of Ash's Litton failure but also of the similar disaster ten years later that undid AM International under his leadership.

The rationalist approach takes the living element out of situations that should, 27 above all, be alive. Lewis Lapham, the editor of *Harper's*, describes the fallacy of the numerative bias in an Easy Chair piece entitled "Gifts of the Magi": "The magi inevitably talk about number and weight—barrels of oil, the money supply—always about material and seldom about human resources; about things; not about people. The prevailing bias conforms to the national prejudice in favor of institutions rather than individuals." John Steinbeck made the same point about lifeless rationality:

> The Mexican Sierra has 17 plus 15 plus 9 spines in the dorsal fin. These can easily be counted. But if the sierra strikes hard on the line so that our hands are burned, if the fish sounds and nearly escapes and finally comes in over the rail, his colors pulsing and his tail beating the air, a whole new relational externality has come into being—an entity which is more than the sum of the fish plus the fisherman. The only way to count the spines of the sierra unaffected by this second relational reality is to sit in a laboratory, open an evil-smelling jar, remove a stiff colorless fish from the formalin solution, count the spines and write the truth.
> . . . There you have recorded a reality which cannot be assailed—probably the least important reality concerning either the fish or yourself. . . . It is good to know what you are doing. The man with this pickled fish has set down one truth and recorded in his experience many lies. The fish is not that color, that texture, that dead, nor does he smell that way.

To be narrowly rational is often to be negative. Peter Drucker gives a good 28 description of the baleful influence of management's analytic bias: " 'Professional' management today sees itself often in the role of a judge who says 'yes' or 'no' to ideas as they come up. . . . A top management that believes its job is to sit in judgment will inevitably veto the new idea. It is always 'impractical.' " John Steinbruner makes a similar point commenting on the role of staffs in general: "It is inherently easier to develop a negative argument than to advance a constructive one." In his analysis of the MLF (NATO's proposed shared nuclear multi-lateral force) decision, Steinbruner recounts an exchange between a conservative academic and a real-world statesman. Secretary of State Dean Acheson said to the Harvard-trained presidential adviser Richard Neustadt, "You think Presidents should be warned. You're wrong. Presidents should be given confidence." Steinbruner goes on to analyze the roles of "warners" versus "bolsterers." Notwithstanding his attempt to present a balanced case, it is clear that the weight of the neutrally applied analytic model falls on the side of the warning, not the bolstering.

Mobil's chief executive, Rawleigh Warner, Jr., echoed the theme in explain- 29 ing why his company decided not to bid on the 1960 offshore oil tracks in Prudhoe Bay: "The financial people in this company did a disservice to the exploration people. . . . The poor people in exploration were adversely impacted

Thomas J. Peters and Robert H. Waterman, Jr.

by people who knew nothing about oil and gas." Hayes and Abernathy, as usual, are eloquent on the subject: "We believe that during the past two decades American managers have increasingly relied on principles which prize analytical detachment and methodological elegance over insight . . . based on experience. Lacking hands-on experience, the analytic formulas of portfolio theory push managers even further toward an extreme of caution in allocating resources." Finally, George Gilder in *Wealth and Poverty* says, "Creative thought [the precursor to invention] requires an act of faith." He dissects example after example in support of his point, going back to the laying out of railroads, insisting that "when they were built they could hardly be justified in economic terms."

Today's version of rationality does not value experimentation and abhors mistakes. The conservatism that leads to inaction and years-long "study groups" frequently confronts businessmen with precisely what they were trying to avoid—having to make, eventually, one big bet. Giant product development groups analyze and analyze until years have gone by and they've designed themselves into one home-run product, with every bell and whistle attractive to every segment. Meanwhile, Digital, 3M, HP, and Wang, amid a hotbed of experimentation, have proceeded "irrationally" and chaotically, and introduced ten or more new products each during the same period. Advancement takes place only when we do something: try an early prototype on a customer or two, run a quick and dirty test market, stick a jury-rig device on an operating production line, test a new sales promotion on 50,000 subscribers.

The dominant culture in most big companies demands punishment for a mistake, no matter how useful, small, invisible. This is especially ironic because the most noble ancestor of today's business rationality was called *scientific* management. Experimentation is the fundamental tool of science: if we experiment successfully, by definition, we will make many mistakes. But overly rational businessmen are in pretty good company here, because even science doesn't own up to its messy road to progress. Robert Merton, a respected historian of science, describes the typical paper:

> [There is a] rockbound difference between scientific work as it appears in print and the actual course of inquiry. . . . The difference is a little like that between textbooks of scientific method and the ways in which scientists actually think, feel, and go about their work. The books on methods present ideal patterns, but these tidy, normative patterns . . . do not reproduce the typically untidy, opportunistic adaptations that scientists really make. The scientific paper presents an immaculate appearance which reproduces little or nothing of the intuitive leaps, false starts, mistakes, loose ends, and happy accidents that actually cluttered up the inquiry.

Sir Peter Medawar, Nobel laureate in immunology, flatly declares, "It is no use looking to scientific 'papers,' for they do not merely conceal but actively misrepresent the reasoning which goes into the work they describe."

Anti-experimentation leads us inevitably to overcomplexity and inflexibility.

508

The "home-run product" mentality is nowhere more evident than in the pursuit of the "superweapon" in defense. A *Village Voice* commentator notes:

> The quickest way to understand the dread evoked in the Pentagon by Spinney [senior analyst with the Program Analysis and Evaluation division of the Department of Defense] is to quote his bottom line: "Our strategy of pursuing ever-increasing technical complexity and sophistication has made high-technology solutions and combat readiness mutually exclusive." That is, the more money the U.S. presently spends on defense, the less able it is to fight. . . . More money has produced fewer but more complex planes which do not work much of the time. Deployment of fewer planes means a more elaborate and delicate communication system which is not likely to survive in war conditions.

Caution and paralysis-induced-by-analysis lead to an anti-experimentation bias. That, in turn, ironically leads to an ultimately risky "big bet" or the "superweapon" mentality. The screw turns once more. To produce such superproducts, hopelessly complicated and ultimately unworkable management structures are required. The tendency reaches its ultimate expression in the formal matrix organizational structure. Interestingly, some fifteen years before the mid-seventies matrix heyday, the researcher Chris Argyris identified the key matrix pathologies:

> Why are these new administrative structures and strategies having trouble? . . . The assumption behind this [matrix] theory was that if objectives and critical paths to these objectives were defined clearly, people would tend to cooperate to achieve these objectives according to the best schedule they could devise. However, in practice, the theory was difficult to apply. . . . It was not long before the completion of the paperwork became an end in itself. Seventy-one percent of the middle managers reported that the maintenance of the product planning and program review paper flow became as crucial as accomplishing the line responsibility assigned to each group. . . . Another mode of adaptation was to withdraw and let the upper levels become responsible for the successful administration of the program. "This is their baby—let them make it work.". . . Still another frequently reported problem was the immobilization of the group with countless small decisions.

One can beat the complexity syndrome, but it is not easy. The IBM 360 is one of the grand product success stories in American business history, yet its development was sloppy. Along the way, chairman Thomas Watson, Sr., asked vice-president Frank Cary to "design a system to ensure us against a repeat of this kind of problem." Cary did what he was told. Years later, when he became chairman himself, one of his first acts was to get rid of the laborious product development structure that he had created for Watson. "Mr. Watson was right," he conceded. "It [the product development structure] will prevent a repeat of the 360 development turmoil. Unfortunately, it will also ensure that we don't ever invent another product like the 360."

Thomas J. Peters and Robert H. Waterman, Jr.

The excellent company response to complexity is fluidity, the administrative   35
version of experimentation. Reorganizations take place all the time. "If you've
got a problem, put the resources on it and get it fixed," says one Digital executive. "It's that simple." Koppers's Fletcher Byrom adds support: "Of all the
things that I have observed in corporations, the most disturbing has been a
tendency toward over-organization, producing a rigidity that is intolerable in an
era of rapidly accelerating change." HP's David Packard notes, "You've got to
avoid having too rigid an organization. . . . If an organization is to work effectively, the communication should be through the most effective channel regardless of the organization chart. That is what happens a lot around here. I've
often thought that after you get organized, you ought to throw the chart away."
Speaking on the subject of American organizational rationality, our Japanese
colleague Ken Ohmae says: "Most Japanese companies don't even have a reasonable organization chart. Nobody knows how Honda is organized, except that
it uses lots of project teams and is quite flexible. . . . Innovation typically occurs
at the interface, requiring multiple disciplines. Thus, the flexible Japanese organization has now, especially, become an asset."

The rationalist approach does not celebrate informality. Analyze, plan, tell,   36
specify, and check up are the verbs of the rational process. Interact, test, try,
fail, stay in touch, learn, shift direction, adapt, modify, and see are some of
the verbs of the informal managing processes. We hear the latter much more
often in our interviews with top performers. Intel puts in extra conference rooms,
simply to increase the likelihood of informal problem solving among different
disciplines. 3M sponsors clubs of all sorts specifically to enhance interaction.
HP and Digital overspend on their own air and ground transportation systems
just so people will visit one another. Product after product flows from Patrick
Haggerty's bedrock principle of "tight coupling" at TI. It all means that people
talk, solve problems, and fix things rather than posture, debate, and delay.

Unfortunately, however, management by edict feels more comfortable to   37
most American managers. They shake their heads in disbelief at 3M, Digital,
HP, Bloomingdale's, or even IBM, companies whose core processes seem out
of control. After all, who in his right mind would establish Management By
Wandering Around as a pillar of philosophy, as HP does? It turns out that the
informal control through regular, casual communication is actually much tighter
than rule by numbers, which can be avoided or evaded. But you'd have a hard
time selling that idea outside the excellent companies.

The rational model causes us to denigrate the importance of values. We have   38
observed few, if any, bold new company directions that have come from goal
precision or rational analysis. While it is true that the good companies have
superb analytic skills, we believe that their major decisions are shaped more by
their values than by their dexterity with numbers. The top performers create a
broad, uplifting, shared culture, a coherent framework within which charged-
up people search for appropriate adaptations. Their ability to extract extraordi-

510

nary contributions from very large numbers of people turns on the ability to create a sense of highly valued purpose. Such purpose invariably emanates from love of product, providing top-quality services, and honoring innovation and contribution from all. Such high purpose is inherently at odds with 30 quarterly MBO objectives, 25 measures of cost containment, 100 demeaning rules for production-line workers, or an ever-changing, analytically derived strategy that stresses costs this year, innovation next, and heaven knows what the year after.

There is little place in the rationalist world for internal competition. A com-   39
pany is not supposed to compete with itself. But throughout the excellent companies research, we saw example after example of that phenomenon. Moreover, we saw peer pressure—rather than orders from the boss—as the main motivator. General Motors pioneered the idea of internal competition sixty years ago; 3M, P&G, IBM, HP, Bloomingdale's, and Tupperware are its masters today. Division overlap, product-line duplication, multiple new product development teams, and vast flows of information to spur productivity comparison—and improvements—are the watchwords. Why is it that so many have missed the message?

Again, the analyze-the-analyzable bias is ultimately fatal. It is true that costs   40
of product-line duplication and nonuniformity of manufacturing procedures can be measured precisely. But the incremental revenue benefits from a steady flow of new products developed by zealous champions and the increment of productivity gains that come from continuous innovation by competing shop floor teams are much harder, if not impossible, to get a handle on.

QUESTIONS

1. What is the thesis of this article? What is wrong with the rational model?
2. What examples of more sensible business practice do Peters and Waterman offer? Why, according to them, are those successful models not more copied?
3. The book from which this essay has been taken has had an exceptional run on the best-seller lists. Why do you suppose this is so? Does the book's commercial success say something good, bad, or neither about the book itself?
4. This essay uses a number of extended examples from outside the business world. Consider the uses of Kuhn (paragraphs 8–11) and Steinbeck (paragraph 27). What function does each example serve in the argument?
5. How is the argument of Spinney about defense spending (parragraph 32) related to Peters and Waterman's own argument?
6. A subtheme of this essay is the threat and example of Japanese businesses. If you locate all the references to Japan and things Japanese in this essay, what attitude toward Japan are Peters and Waterman adopting?
7. Select an organization or institution you know or can find out about (a school, a business, a team). Using the criteria developed by Peters and Waterman, write an essay in which you develop an argument about the relative success or failure of your chosen organization.

YOU HAVEN'T COME
A LONG WAY,
BABY: WOMEN
IN TELEVISION
COMMERCIALS
Carol Caldwell

*Carol Caldwell has worked as an advertising copywriter and
is now a free-lance writer, whose work has appeared in* Rolling Stone *and* Esquire *magazines. She covers the popular
culture scene, interviewing and writing on figures from the
entertainment world. The following essay appeared first in*
New Times *magazine in 1977. The essay's title is a play
on the advertising slogan of one product aimed at women:
"You've come a long way, baby."*

It's the beginning of the age of television, and all around it's black and white.   1
Millions of minuscule scan dots collide in electronic explosion to create Woman
in her Immaculate Kitchen. She is Alpha, Omega,[1] eternal and everlasting
Mother Video, toasting and frying, cleansing and purifying, perfectly formed of
fire and ice. Permanent-waved, magenta-lipped, demurely collared and cuffed,
cone-shaped from her tightly cinched waist down through yards and yards of
material that brush coquettishly mid-calf, she is Betty Furness for Westinghouse;
and you can be *sure* if it's Westinghouse.

The year is 1951. On the set of CBS-TV's *Studio One,* Furness has just   2
captured the part to become America's first full-time product spokeswoman on
television. Advertising execs at Westinghouse are taking a stab at having someone other than the host sell their product; they reason (and quite correctly) that
Furness, with her Brearley School cool and her Broadway glamor, is a figure
thousands of women will admire and listen to. During the audition Betty alters
the script supplied by the casting director. Later, she tells *Time* magazine that
she ad-libbed the refrigerator routine because "it was written like men think
women talk!"

1952. While John Daly, Bill Henry, and Walter Cronkite monitor Ike and   3

---

[1]Alpha, Omega: the first and last letters of the Greek alphabet; hence, the beginning and the
end. [Eds.]

Adlai at the conventions, Betty Furness opens and shuts forty-nine refrigerators, demonstrates the finer points of forty-two television sets, twenty-three dishwashers and twelve ovens for a total of four-and-a-half hours of air time. General Eisenhower is on the air approximately an hour and twenty minutes; Mr. Stevenson, fifty minutes.

1956. Bright and blondeened, twenty-eight-year-old Julia Meade is the commercial spokeswoman for Lincoln on the *Ed Sullivan Show*, for Richard Hudnut hair products on *Your Hit Parade*, for *Life* magazine on John Daly's news show. She is pulling down a hundred thousand dollars a year, which moves *Time* to comment, "Julia (34–20–34) is one of a dozen or so young women on TV who find self-effacement enormously profitable." Howard Wilson, a vice-president of Kenyon & Eckhardt, Lincoln's ad agency, hired Julia for the spots with trepidation: a woman just couldn't be convincing about such things as high torque, turbo drive, and ball-joint suspensions. His fears, it turns out, were unfounded, and Meade becomes the perky prototype for a whole slew of carefully coiffed women selling cars—selling *anything*—by means other than their technical knowledge. And so Julia Meade begat Bess Myerson, who begat Anita Bryant, who begat Carmelita Pope, who begat Florence Henderson, each wholesome, flawless, clear of eye and enunciation, in short, sixty-second reminders of everything the American woman ought to be.

Times change, however, and eventually infant TV's ideal, untouchable dozen spokeswomen were replaced by hundreds of nameless actresses who portray "the little woman" in scenarios believed, by the agencies who create them, to be honest-to-God, middle-American, slice-of-life situations. As early as 1955, this new wave of commercial realism got a pat on the back by the industry's weekly trade paper, *Advertising Age*. Procter & Gamble had just come out with a revolutionary new way to sell soap on TV: "It is very difficult for a soap commercial to emerge from the mass of suds, with every known variant on the familiar theme of the woman holding up a box of 'X' soap powder with a grisly smile pointing to a pile of clothes she has just washed. Cheer has come up with the unique approach of dramatizing an everyday washing problem from the poor woman's point of view with a sound-over technique of stream of consciousness."

That stream of consciousness flowed unchecked until Bill Free's famous National Airlines "Fly Me" faux pas in 1971. Women activists carried signs, stormed Free's and National's offices, read proclamations, and permeated the media with protest. Free talks of this trying and critical time with a humor and stoicism that comes from a six-year perspective, and from no longer handling the account. "The women's movement was identifying itself—and our 'Fly Me' campaign was an opportunity for a public platform. We were deluged with letters and calls. I even got an absurd letter from one of the leaders of the movement (who must go unnamed) demanding that I surely planned the sexual innuendo in the word 'fly'—she meant as in men's trouser pants." He paused.

513

"The ad community continues to demean women, far more subtly than in our campaign."

There are some easy hints at why this is so: Of the seventy-five thousand people currently employed in advertising, only 16.7 percent are women in other than clerical positions—not exactly an overwhelming voice. And, while advertising executives often live in the suburbs of large cities, they just as often tend to have a low regard for anyone who isn't an urbanite. As one New York agency executive quipped, "All I really know about the Middle America I sell to everyday is that it's the place I fly over to get to L.A."

But these notations still don't answer the question: Why have advertisers, who make their living keeping up with trends, been so slow to get on board with the women's revolution? Where was everybody the recent night David Brinkley closed the book on America's traditional homelife structure, citing the fact that a mere seven percent of our nation's homes still maintained the time-honored tradition of the everyday housewife. Mom has officially flown the coop just about everywhere, except on TV in the commercials.

At a roundtable on women's advertising sponsored by the agency trade publication *Madison Avenue*, Harriet Rex, a vice-president at J. Walter Thompson, had this comment to make: "There's always been a lag between what is and what the ad business has codified as what 'is.'" And Rena Bartos, a senior VP at the same agency, said, "Advertising may be a mirror of society but somehow the image in that mirror is a little out of focus. It plays back a 1950s reflection in a 1970s world."

Madison Avenue's "little woman" is hardly new, and only partially improved. When feminists cite advertising that is "acceptable," it's invariably print ads. This isn't surprising, since magazine ads are prepared for specific subscribers whose personal backgrounds and attitudes have been carefully documented by the publication and noted by the agency. Television, on the other hand, commands a much larger and subsequently less definable audience.

So it is left to the advertisers and their agencies to define who television's consuming woman might be and what type of commercial she might like. The reward is compelling: Americans heap a total $9.2 billion every year into the coffers of the nation's top three TV advertisers—Procter & Gamble, Bristol-Myers, and General Foods. Still, the women portrayed aren't always to the customer's liking, and last year agitated viewers marched en masse outside P&G headquarters in Cincinnati, suggesting in rather unladylike terms what to do with Mr. Whipple and his grocery store groupies. Inside, P&G stockholders took little heed, voting down a suggestion that their commercial portrayal of women be reconsidered.

Others in the business did listen. When the National Organization for Women sent all major advertising agencies a position paper on the role of women in commercials, no one was surprised that most of the commercials on the air didn't jibe with the NOW requirements. Several agencies, fearing intervention by the Federal Trade Commission, prodded their own regulatory outfit to consider the matter. The National Advertising Review Board formed a panel, including Patricia Carbine, publisher of *Ms.*; Joyce Snyder, coordinator of the task force on the image of women for NOW; the vice-presidents of broadcast standards for ABC and NBC; and a number of officers of sponsoring companies. A twenty-one page directive came out in 1975, in which the panel made a number of suggestions concerning ways in which advertisers could improve their portrayal of women. Here's what came out in the wash: "Advertising must be regarded as one of the forces molding society," the study asserted. "Those who protest that advertising merely reflects society must reckon with the criticism that much of the current reflection of women in advertising is out of date." Before airing a commercial, the panel urged advertisers to run down the NARB checklist, which included the following points:

· Are sexual stereotypes perpetuated in my ads? Do they portray women as weak, silly and over-emotional?
· Are the women portrayed in my ads stupid?
· Do my ads portray women as ecstatically happy over household cleanliness or deeply depressed because of their failure to achieve near-perfection in household tasks?
· Do my ads show women as fearful of not being attractive, of not being able to keep their husbands or lovers, fearful of in-law disapproval?
· Does my copy promise unrealistic psychological rewards for using the product?

Well now, does it? With these self-regulatory commandments in mind, I 13 spent four weeks in front of daytime TV, logging current household product commercials and trying to determine just where women stand in the advertising scheme of things. During that time, Iris dickered with Rachel and Mac's teetering marriage, Beth died, Stacy miscarried, and Jennifer killed John's wife so they could finally be together.

Now a word from our sponsors. 14

Ring around the collar lives. After eight long years, the little woman is still 15 exposing hubby and the kids to this awful embarrassment. It can strike virtually anywhere—in taxis, at ballgames, even on vacation doing the limbo. Our lady of the laundry is always guilty, always lucky to have a next-door neighbor who knows about Wisk, the washday miracle, and always back in hubby's good, but wary, graces by the happy ending. The Wisk woman faces the same unspoken commercial threat that the Geritol woman faces: "My wife, I think I'll keep her . . ." *if* she keeps in line.

Jim Jordan is president of Batten, Barton, Durstine and Osborn Advertising. 16 Eight years ago, in a fit of cosmic inspiration, he came up with "ring around the collar" for his agency's client, Lever Bros. Since then, Jordan has run checkout-counter surveys on his commercials, asking shoppers who were purchasing

515

Wisk, "You must be buying this product because you like the commercials." The reply he got was always the same: "Why no! I hate those commercials; but why should I hold that against the product?"

Jim Jordan echoes advertising's premier axiom: "The purpose of the com- 17 mercial is not the aesthetic pleasure of the viewer—it's to sell the product." And Wisk is selling like gangbusters. He doesn't believe "ring around the collar" commercials show women in an embarrassing light; and to assume that, he says, "would be giving commercials more credit than they deserve."

Perhaps. And perhaps his "ring around the collar" campaign is getting more 18 credit than it deserves for selling Wisk. Take any commercial with a simple message, repeat it again and again, and the product, if it's good, will sell, even if the spot is mindless and annoying. It's fixing the name of the product in the consumer's mind with a quick, catchy phrase that's important.

The household slice-of-life commercial is one of the classic offenders of the 19 NARB checklist. (Are sexual stereotypes perpetuated? You'd best believe it. Are the women portrayed stupid? And how.) Crisco's current campaign is a flawless example of this much-imitated genre, which has been developed and designed by Proctor & Gamble. In it various long-suffering husbands and condescending neighbors are put through the heartache of greasy, gobby chicken and fries, all because some unthinking corner cutter spent "a few pennies less" on that main-stay of American cookery, lard. These pound-foolish little women cause their loved ones to live through "disasters" and "catastrophes." At the cue word "ca-tastrophe," our video crumples into wavy electronic spasms and thrusts us back to the scene of the crime: to that excruciating point in the Bicentennial picnic or the backyard cookout when Dad has to wrinkle his upper lip and take Mom aside for a little set-to about her greasy chicken. The moral, delivered by some unseen pedantic male announcer, is plain: "Ladies who've learned—buy Crisco."

These examples are, sad to say, still very much the rule for women's portrayals 20 in thirty- and sixty-second spots. They occur with alarming regularity during the daytime hours, when stations may sell up to sixteen commercial minutes an hour. (The nighttime rate is a mere eight minutes, forty seconds per hour.) Now, you are probably not the average American who spends some six hours a day in front of the old boob tube (which, when the maximum number of commercials per hour is computed, means over an hour and a half of product propaganda). And you probably are quite sure that commercials have absolutely no effect on you. Maybe they don't. But a shaken agency copywriter told me the first word his child spoke was "McDonald's," and I've stood in a grocery line and watched while a mother, tired of her child's tears, lets him wander off and return—not with a candy bar, but with a roll of Charmin. Make no mistake about it: the cumulative effects of commercials are awesome. As the NARB study argues: "An endless procession of commercials on the same theme, all showing women using household products in the home, raises very strong im-plications that women have no other interests except laundry, dishes, waxing floors, and fighting dirt in any form. . . . Seeing a great many such advertisements in succession reinforces the traditional stereotype that a 'woman's place is *only* in the home.' "

There have, in the past few years, been commercials that break the homebody   21
mold. The Fantastik spray commercial, "I'm married to a man, not a house" (which, incidentally, was written and produced by men), has reaped much praise, as has L'Oreal's "I'm worth it" campaign. "Ten years ago, it would have been, 'John thinks I'm worth it,' " says Lenore Hershey, editor of *Ladies' Home Journal. Ms.*' Pat Carbine thinks United Airlines is flying right when they address women executives, "You're the boss." She also likes the Campbell's soup "working wife" commercial, in which a man scurries around the kitchen, preparing soup for his woman, but adds, "I'm afraid they took the easy route and resorted to total role reversal—making her look good at the expense of the man."

Indeed, Lois Wyse of Wyse Advertising fears that advertisers are not only   22
failing to talk to today's women, but they're missing men as well. The reason for this, as she sees it, is research—the extensive demographic studies done on who buys what product. Last winter Wyse told *Madison Avenue*, "About twenty years ago we were all little Ozzies and Harriets to all the people who do research, and now their idea of contemporizing is to make the Ozzies into Harriets and the Harriets into Ozzies."

Marketing research, with its charts and graphs and scientific jargon, has   23
increased in importance over the last ten years or so, while creativity, the keystone to the Alka-Seltzer, Volkswagen, and Benson & Hedges campaigns of the sixties, has taken the backseat. Ask anybody in advertising why commercials still show the little woman bumbling around in a fearful daze, and you'll find the answer is always the same: "Because our research tells us it is so." Agencies devote hundreds of thousands of dollars to find out who's buying their client's stuff and why. And it's not just Mom up there on the charts and graphs. Marketing researchers dissect and analyze the buying habits, educational and income levels of every member of the family. They even know what we do with our leisure time, and how much God we've got.

The subjective form of research is amorphously titled life-style research,   24
explained by the respected *Journal of Marketing* in the following brave-new-world lingo: "Life-style data—activities, interests, opinions—have proved their importance as a means of *duplicating* the consumer for the marketing researcher. . . ." And more: "Life-style attempts to answer questions like: What do women think about the job of housekeeping? Do they see themselves as homebodies or swingers? Life-style provides definitions like 'housewife role haters,' 'old fashioned homebodies' and 'active affluent urbanites.' "

But life-style research is still in its infancy and very, very expensive. The   25
trendiest and most attainable form of research going is called focus-group research, the grassroots movement of advertising research. From lairs of hidden cameras and tape-recording devices, agency and client-types, despite the experts'

517

warnings that focus-group samples are far too small to be projected on a national scale, eke out a vision of their consumer that almost invariably fits just the stereotype they had in mind in the first place, and proceed to advertise accordingly.

The theory, quite simply, is to get inside women's heads in order to get inside their pocketbooks. From Satellite Beach to Spokane, fact-finding specialists are retained at grand sums to commune with the natives and document their particular buying habits. For instance: 26

The canned-meat industry's advertising wasn't paying off in the Southeast. 27 Focus-group researchers were called in and groups of eight women were randomly selected from Memphis neighborhoods. The women fit the product's buyer profile—in this case, all came from families with middle to lower-middle incomes. Each woman was paid ten dollars. On an assigned day each focus group would meet for a two-hour session at the suburban home of the researcher's field representative—a woman who was a veteran of several similar exercises. As the women took their seats around the dining room table, loosening up with coffee and homemade cake, the client and agency folk sat, out of sight, in the rumpus room, carefully scanning the meeting on closed-circuit monitors. This is what they heard.

MODERATOR: Do any of you ever buy canned meats?

VOICES: Oh yes. Yeah. Uh, huh.

MODERATOR: When do you buy them?

ANN: Well, my husband went to New Orleans, so I bought a lot of canned goods. The children enjoy them.

LOU: Well, I bought Vienna sausage the other day 'cause the Giant had a special on it—seventy-nine cents a can—it's usually a dollar nine, a dollar nineteen. You could only get four at a time, so I went back twice that week.

MODERATOR: Do you buy these for particular members of the family?

NORMA: If they didn't like it, I wouldn't buy it.

DELORES: Melvin loves the hot dog chili. And the baby—you can just stick a Vienna sausage in her hand and she'll go 'round happy all day.

MODERATOR: Do you read the labels on canned meats?

VOICES: Oh sure. Yes.

NORMA: The children read the labels first and called my attention to it. When I saw it had things like intestines and things like that, I didn't want to buy potted meat any more.

LOU: Fats, tissues, organs. If you read the labels on this stuff—when they say hearts . . . I don't know. I don't like hearts.

VIRGINIA: Well, psychologically you're not geared to it.

ALMA: They could lie on the label a little bit. Just don't tell us so much. (Laugh.) It would taste pretty good, but . . . yeah. I'd rather not know.

MODERATOR: What do you think ought to be on the labels?

ANNE: I think you ought to know about the chemicals.

NORMA: I love to read calories on the side of a can.

DELORES: I wonder what all's in those preservatives?

IDA: The side of this Hormel can here says that this meat is made by the same company that makes Dial soap. Says Armour-Dial.

NORMA: At least you think it's clean.

DELORES: Some preservatives do taste like soap. . . .

IDA: I wouldn't be eating that stuff with them chemicals.

ANN: Well, if you worry about that, you're going to starve to death.

VIRGINIA: You'd never eat in a restaurant if you ever got back in the kitchen.

MODERATOR: Would you buy a product because of the advertising?

VOICES: No. No. Maybe.

IDA: My children love that Libby's—the one, "Libby's, Libby's, Libby's. . . ."

NORMA: Now, if there's young kids that go to the grocery store with you, everytime they'll pick up something . . . "Libby's, Libby's, Libby's."

DELORES: Every time I see Hormel chili . . . I think about them people out at a fireside by the beach eating that chili. One of them is playing a guitar and they start singing.

VIRGINIA: Armour has a cute hot dog commercial, that's where they're all marching around, weenies, ketchup and mustard. . . .

IDA: Yeah. That's cute.

MODERATOR: Do any of you ever buy Spam?

IDA: What's Spam?

ANNE: It's chopped something. Or pressed.

LOU: It's beaver board.

MODERATOR: Beaver what?

Most researchers claim that their studies are only as good as the people who [28] interpret them. The interpreters are usually the agency and clients who—many advertising executives will admit, but only off the record—read their own product concerns into the comments of the panelists. Quite often, complaints about daytime commercials ("They're awful!" "Ridiculous!" "Laughable!") are brushed aside. "You can formulate breakthrough approaches in order to reach this new woman," Joan Rothberg, a senior VP at Ted Bates, told *Madison Avenue*, "and yet the traditional 'Ring Around the Collar' approach wins out in terms of creating awareness and motivating people to buy the product."

One of the final research tests a commercial can go through after it's been [29] created and storyboarded is the Burke test. One day up at my old agency, the creative director, a writer, and an art director came blazing through the halls with hats and horns, announcing at 120 decibels, "We Burked twenty-nine! We Burked twenty-nine!" Now this may sound to you as it did to me that day, as if these people were talking in tongues. What having "Burked twenty-nine" actually means is the percentage the commercial scored in recall after one viewing by a large audience. The average number on the Burke scale for the particular product my friends were testing was twenty-five—so you can understand the celebration.

Because the agencies and their clients accept Burke scores as valid, the scores   30
become a powerful factor in what types of commercials will run. It's no accident that the Burke company is located in Cincinnati, since Cincinnati is the birthplace of Crest, Crisco, Comet, Charmin, Cheer, Bonus, Bounce, Bounty, Bold, Lava, Lilt, Pampers, Prell, Downy, Dash, and Duz—in other words, Cincinnati is the home of the King Kong of Household Cleanliness, Procter & Gamble. From high atop magnificent offices, P&G executives control daytime television and a goodly portion of prime time, too. They are the top-dollar spender on TV, having put out $260 million last year alone in commercial time bought. They produce and have editorial control over five of the biggest soap operas on TV: *As the World Turns, Another World, Edge of Night, Guiding Light,* and *Search for Tomorrow,* which reach some forty million women every day.

Procter & Gamble is the most blatant offender in perpetuating "the little   31
woman" commercial stereotype. Because of its monopoly on both media and marketplace (it pulls in $3.6 billion every year) and because its research is the most expensive and extensive, P&G is the recognized leader and arbiter of format and content in household product commercials—where P&G goes, others will follow.

This does not spur innovation. In one P&G agency, the creative people have   32
two formulae they use for "concepting" a commercial: regular slice-of-life (problem in the home, solution with the wonderful product) or what the agency guys call "two C's in a K." The "K" stands for kitchen; the "C" is a four-letter word.

Once a commercial is written, tested, and approved by the client, it's got to   33
be cast and shot. I asked Barbara Claman to talk about what agency people and their clients ask for when they're casting housewife roles. She should know: Barbara's built up one of the largest commercial casting agencies in the country. The day we talked all hell was breaking loose outside her office door. Scores of women and children had come to try out for a McDonald's commercial.

I wondered if agencies ever called for a P&G-type housewife for their com-   34
mercials.

"Absolutely. She should be blond—or, if brunette, not too brunette. Pretty,   35
but not too pretty. Midwestern in speech, middle-class looking, gentile. If they want to use blacks, they want *waspy* blacks."

"What about P&G-type husbands?"   36

"Same thing," Claman said. "But you'll find that the husband is getting to   37
play the asshole more and more in American commercials."

"But do you see a change occurring? A trend in women's portrayals away   38
from the traditional P&G type?"

"A little. I think they'd like to be a little more real. They're realizing, very   39
slowly, that the working woman has a lot of money."

"What if they want a Rosie, a Madge or a Cora—one of the Eric Hoffer   40
working-class philosopher-queens?"

Barbara laughed. "They'll say, 'Let's cast a ballsy one.' "   41

"Are you offended by the roles they want to put women in? Do you try to   42
change their thinking on this?"

"I'm totally offended. I'm tired of seeing women hysterical over dirt spots on   43
their glasses. I get lady producers in here all the time. We've tried to change
their minds about the roles. You see how successful we've been."

Jane Green is another casting director in New York. She tells of a friend   44
who was auditioning for a P&G spot in which the agency's creative people were
trying to break out of the housewife mold. They'd called interesting faces—real
people who wore real clothes. A couple of hours passed and the P&G client
was obviously agitated. He turned to the agency producer: "What are you people
trying to pull over on me? The woman in this commercial needs to be *my* wife,
in *my* bathroom in Cincinnati—not some hip little chickie. Whom do you
think we're selling to?"

One wonders. Recently an agency producer asked me and my cat Rayette to   45
be in a kitty litter commercial. I arrived wearing blue jeans and a shirt, my
usual at-home ensemble. The art director, who was wearing jeans himself,
wasn't pleased: "Where is your shirtwaist? I told the producer I wanted a *housewife* look in this commercial." I tried to explain that most women—housewives
and otherwise—had left those McMullans and Villagers back at the Tri Delt
house in '66. The shoot was postponed until we found something that looked
more housewifey.

Some commercial trends have passed: The damsel in distress has, for the   46
time being, retreated to her tower. (Remember the thundering White Knight?
The mystical, spotless Man from Glad? Virile, barrel-chested Mr. Clean?) But
others remain, the most blatantly offensive, perhaps, being those commercials
using women as sex objects to entice the consumer into buying the product.
Most agency people aren't allowed to comment on the scheme of things in such
commercials (one slip of the tongue and that multimillion-dollar account might
choose another, more circumspect agency). But Dwight Davis, VP and creative
director on the Ford dealers' account with J. Walter Thompson in Detroit, says
it's no secret Detroit is still the national stronghold of selling with sex. Why?
The male is still the decision maker in car buying ("Our research tells us it is
so"); and the auto is still an extension of the American male libido. So we've
got Catherine Deneuve hawking Lincoln-Mercurys. She circles the car in her
long, slinky gown and slips inside to fondle the plush interior. Catherine signs
off, sprawled across the hood of the car, with a seductive grrrrr. She is, as Davis
describes the phenomenon, the car advertisers' "garnish on the salad."

Commercials like this, and the little woman slice-of-life, are caricatures of   47
themselves. That's precisely why Carol Burnett and the people at *Saturday Night
Live* have so much fun with them. Even the new wave of women's commercials

521

isn't spared. In a spoof Anne Beatts wrote for *Saturday Night*, a middle-class Mom, dressed not in a shirtwaist but a polyester pantsuit, rushes into the kitchen, crashing through a café-curtained dutch door. She starts to have a heart-to-heart with the camera: "I'm a nuclear physicist and Commissioner of Consumer Affairs." She starts to put her groceries away.

"In my spare time, I do needlepoint, read, sculpt, take riding lessons, and   48
brush up on my knowledge of current events. Thursday's my day at the day-care center, and then there's my work with the deaf; but I still have time left over to do all my own baking and practice my backhand, even though I'm on call twenty-four hours a day as a legal aid lawyer in Family Court. . . ." Our New-Wave Mom is still running on, all the time very carefully folding the grocery bags and stuffing them into a cabinet where literally hundreds of other carefully folded bags are stacked incredibly neatly, when the omniscient announcer comes in:

"How does Ellen Sherman, Cleveland housewife, do it all? She's smart! She   49
takes Speed. Yes, Speed—the tiny blue diet pill you don't have to be overweight to need."

If the "average" woman is true to her portrayal in commercials, we've got a   50
pretty bitter pill to swallow. But you know, we all know, commercials don't portray real life. Nice Movies' Dick Clark, who's done spots for Coca-Cola, Toyota, and Glade, points out, most commercials are "formula answers to advertising questions—bad rip-offs of someone else's bad commercials." They are bad rip-offs of their viewers too. But, someday, some bright young advertising prodigy will begin a whole new trend of commercials that don't talk down, don't demean or debase, and still sell soap or toothpaste or cars like crazy. And then everyone will be doing it. Double your money back, guaranteed.

Why am I so sure? Because, as Brinkley so neatly points out, only seven   51
percent of our homes have the traditional resident Mom. Because there are more women doctors, engineers, copywriters, jockeys, linesmen, you name it, than ever before. Because women are becoming more selective in their buying habits. Because, quite simply, research tells me it is so.

QUESTIONS

1. What is the thesis of this essay? Does it concern the past, the future, or the present? Or does it concern them all? Is more than one main idea being argued?

2. What conclusions do you draw from the market research portrayed in paragraph 28? Do you think your conclusions differ much from those of the researchers and their sponsors?

3. How important to Caldwell's argument is her way of writing? Would you consider her style serious, frivolous, lively, dull, inspiring, solemn, or what? What would you call it? Why?

4. Caldwell often takes over phrases from advertising to use in her own prose, as in paragraphs 14 and 15. What is the purpose of this? What is its effect?

5. This article appeared in 1977. Have things changed since then? If you were updating this piece by adding a new section at the end, what would you say? Write a new conclusion for this essay, adding what you think should be said to bring it up to date.

6. If you disagree with the point of this argument, write your own counterargument, either reinterpreting Caldwell's evidence or adding new evidence of your own.

7. Classify the types of women characters you see in commercials, providing specific examples for each type. Then work with a small group of your classmates and critique the categories each of you has developed. Together, prepare a refined classification system of types of women characters with examples.

8. Do some research on the use of women in a particular category of advertising—in a single magazine, for a single product or kind of product, or during a particular stretch of television time—and use the evidence you gather for an argument of your own.

THE CAUSES OF ENVIRONMENTAL STRESS

Barry Commoner

Barry Commoner (b. 1917), biologist, ecologist, and educator, is widely recognized as one of America's most articulate authorities on energy policy. He has written over two hundred scientific articles and has received numerous awards for his writing. In his book The Closing Circle *(1971) he seeks to examine as a scientist—but in language intelligible to the general public—the causes of environmental stress. In the eighth chapter, reprinted here, he examines and argues against two causes frequently put forth as explanations for the problem: population increases and a rise in the wealth of individuals, calling the chapter "Population and 'Affluence.' " Because this title makes sense only in its original context (as one of several chapters examining different proposed explanations for environmental stress), we have substituted the title you find here.*

The environmental crisis tells us that there is something seriously wrong with the way in which human beings have occupied their habitat, the earth. The fault must lie not with nature, but with man. For no one has argued, to my knowledge, that the recent advent of pollutants on the earth is the result of some natural change independent of man. Indeed, the few remaining areas of the world that are relatively untouched by the powerful hand of man are, to that degree, free of smog, foul water, and deteriorating soil. Environmental deterioration must be due to some fault in the human activities on the earth. 1

One explanation that is sometimes offered is that man is a "dirty" animal— that unlike other animals man is likely to "foul his own nest." Somehow, according to this view, people lack other animals' tidy nature and increasingly foul the world as their numbers increase. This explanation is basically faulty, for the "neatness" of animals in nature is not the result of their own sanitary activities. What removes these wastes is the activity of *other* living things, which use them as nutrients. In an ecological cycle no waste can accumulate because nothing is wasted. Thus, a living thing that is a natural part of an ecosystem cannot, by its own biological activities, degrade that ecosystem; an ecosystem is always stressed from without. Human beings, as animals, are no less tidy than 2 other living organisms. They pollute the environment only because they have broken out of the closed, cyclical network in which all other living things are held.

So long as human beings held their place in the terrestrial ecosystem— 3 consuming food produced by the soil and oxygen released by plants, returning organic wastes to the soil and carbon dioxide to the plants—they could do no serious ecological harm. However, once removed from this cycle, for example to a city, so that bodily wastes are not returned to the soil but to surface water, the human population is separated from the ecosystem of which it was originally a part. Now the wastes become external to the aquatic system on which they intrude, overwhelm the system's self-adjustment, and pollute it.

Certain human activities—agriculture, forestry, and fishing—directly exploit 4 the productivity of a particular ecosystem. In these cases, a constituent of the ecosystem that has economic value—an agricultural crop, timber, or fish—is withdrawn from the ecosystem. This represents an external drain on the system that must be carefully adjusted to natural and man-made inputs to the ecosystem if collapse is to be avoided. A heavy drain may drive the system out of balance toward collapse. Examples include destructive erosion of agricultural or forest lands following overly intense exploitation or the incipient destruction of the whaling industry due to the extinction of whales.

Environmental stress may also arise if the amount of a particular ecosystem 5 component is deliberately augmented from without, either to dispose of human waste or in an effort to accelerate the system's rate of turnover and thereby increase the yield of an extractable good. An example of the first sort is the dumping of sewage into surface waters. An example of the second sort is the use of nitrogen fertilizer in agriculture.

Finally, since human beings are uniquely capable of producing materials not 6 found in nature, environmental degradation may be due to the resultant intrusion into an ecosystem of a substance wholly foreign to it. Perhaps the simplest example is a synthetic plastic, which unlike natural materials, is not degraded by biological decay. It therefore persists as rubbish or is burned—in both cases causing pollution. In the same way, a toxic substance such as DDT or lead, which plays no role in the chemistry of life and interferes with the actions of substances that do, is bound to cause ecological damage if sufficiently concentrated. In general, any productive activity which introduces substances foreign to the natural environment runs a considerable risk of polluting it.

Our task, then, is to discover how human activities generate *environmental* 7 *impacts*—that is, external intrusions into the ecosystem which tend to degrade its natural capacity for self-adjustment.

As a first step we might look at the history of the pollution problem in a 8 highly industrialized country such as the United States. Unfortunately, despite the national proclivity to collect and store in the memories of the ubiquitous computer all sorts of statistics—from an individual's tax records to his attendance at political rallies—historical data on pollution levels are very spotty. However, a rather striking picture does emerge from the data that are available: *most pollution problems made their first appearance, or became very much worse, in the years following World War II.*

A good example of this trend is provided by phosphate, an important pollutant   9
of surface waters. In the thirty-year period from 1910 to 1940 annual phosphate output from municipal sewage somewhat more than doubled, from about 17 million pounds (calculated as phosphorus) to about 40 million pounds. Thereafter the rate of phosphate output rose rapidly, so that in the next thirty-year period, 1940 to 1970, it increased more than sevenfold to about 300 million pounds per year. Some other examples of increases in annual pollutant output since 1946: nitrogen oxides from automobiles (which trigger the formation of smog), 630 per cent; tetraethyl lead from gasoline, 415 per cent; mercury from chloralkali plants, 2,100 per cent; synthetic pesticides (between 1950 and 1967 only), 270 per cent; inorganic nitrogen fertilizer (some of which leaches into surface water and pollutes it), 789 per cent; nonreturnable beer bottles, 595 per cent. Many pollutants were totally absent before World War II, having made their environmental debut in the war years: smog (first noticed in Los Angeles in 1943), man-made radioactive elements (first produced in the wartime atomic bomb project), DDT (widely used for the first time in 1944), detergents (which began to displace soap in 1946), synthetic plastics (which became a contributor to the rubbish problem only after the war).

These striking changes in the postwar pace of environmental deterioration   10
provide an important clue to the origin of the pollution problem. The last fifty years have seen a sweeping revolution in science, which has generated powerful changes in technology and in its application to industry, agriculture, transportation, and communication. World War II is a decisive turning point in this historical transition. The twenty-five years preceding the war is the main period of the sweeping modern revolution in basic science, especially in physics and chemistry, upon which so much of the new productive technology is based. In the approximate period of the war itself, under the pressure of military demands, much of the new scientific knowledge was rapidly converted into new technologies and productive enterprises. Since the war, the technologies have rapidly transformed the nature of industrial and agricultural production. The period of World War II is, therefore, a great divide between the scientific evolution that preceded it and the technological revolution that followed it.

We can find important clues to the development of postwar technology in   11
the nature of the prewar scientific revolution. Beginning in the 1920's, physics broke away from the ideas that had dominated the field since Newton's time. Spurred by discoveries about the properties of atoms, a wholly new conception of the nature of matter was developed. Experiment and theory advanced until physicists gained a remarkably effective understanding of the properties of subatomic particles and of the ways in which they interact to generate the properties

of the atom as a whole. This new knowledge produced new, more powerful techniques for smashing the hitherto indestructible atom, driving out of its nucleus extremely energetic particles. Natural and artificial radioactivity was discovered. By the late 1930's it became clear, on theoretical grounds, that vast quantities of energy could be released from the atomic nucleus. During World War II, this theory was converted into practice, giving rise to nuclear weapons and reactors—and to the hazards of artificial radioactivity and the potential for catastrophic war.

The new physical theories also helped to explain the behavior of electrons, 12 especially in solids—knowledge that in the postwar years led to the invention of the transistor and to the proliferating solid-state electronic components. This provided the technological base for the modern computer, not to speak of the transistor radio.

Chemistry, too, made remarkable progress in the prewar period. Particularly 13 significant for later environmental effects were advances in the chemistry of organic compounds. These substances were first discovered by eighteenth-century chemists in the juices of living things. Gradually chemists learned the molecular composition of some of the simpler varieties of natural organic substances. Chemists developed a powerful desire to imitate nature—to synthesize in the laboratory the organic substances uniquely produced by life.

The first man-made organic substance, urea, was synthesized in 1828. From 14 this simple beginning (urea contains only one carbon atom), chemists learned how to make laboratory replicas of increasingly complex natural products. Once techniques for putting together organic molecules were worked out, an enormous variety of different products could be made. This is the natural consequence of the escalating mathematics of the possible atomic combinations in organic compounds. For example, although molecules that are classed as sugars contain only three types of atoms—carbon, oxygen, and hydrogen—which can be related to each other in only a few different ways, there are sixteen different molecular arrangements for sugars that contain six carbons (one of these is the familiar glucose, or grape sugar). The number of different kinds of organic molecules that can, in theory, exist is so large as to have no meaningful limit.

Around the turn of the century chemists learned a number of practical ways 15 of creating many of the theoretically possible molecular arrangements. This knowledge—that the variety of possible organic compounds is essentially limitless and that ways of achieving at least some of the possible combinations were at hand—proved irresistible. It was as though language had suddenly been invented, followed inevitably by a vast outburst of creative writing. Instead of new poems, the chemists created new molecules. Like some poems, some of the new molecules were simply the concrete end-product of the joyful process of creation—testimony to what the chemist had learned. Other molecules, again like certain poems, were created for the sake of what they taught the creator— newly defined steps toward more difficult creations. Finally, there were new

527

molecules created with a particular purpose in mind—let us say to color a fabric—the analogy, perhaps, of an advertising jingle.

The net result represents, in terms of the number of new man-made objects, 16 probably the most rapid burst of creativity in human history. Acceleration was built into the process, for each newly created molecule became, itself, the starting point for building many new ones.

As a result, there accumulated on the chemists' shelves a huge array of new 17 substances, similar to the natural materials of life in that they were based on the chemistry of carbon, but most of them absent from the realm of living things. As new useful materials were sought, some of the chemicals were taken off the shelf—either because of a resemblance to some natural substance or at random—and tried out in practice. This is how sulfanilamide—which a dyestuff chemist had synthesized in 1908—was found in 1935 to kill bacteria, and DDT—which had sat on a Swiss chemical laboratory shelf since 1874—was found in 1939 to kill insects.

Meanwhile a good deal was learned about the chemical basis of important 18 molecular properties—the kind of molecular structure that governed a substance's color, elasticity, fibrous strength, or its ability to kill bacteria, insects, or weeds. It then became possible to *design* new molecules for a particular purpose, rather than search the chemical storeroom for likely candidates. Although many such advances had occurred by the time of World War II, very few had as yet been converted to industrial practice on a significant scale. That came later.

Thus, the prewar scientific revolution produced, in modern physics and 19 chemistry, sciences capable of manipulating nature—of creating, for the first time on earth, wholly new forms of matter. But until World War II the practical consequences were slight compared to the size and richness of the accumulated store of knowledge. What the physicists had learned about atomic structure appeared outside the laboratory only in a few kinds of electrical equipment, such as certain lamps and x-ray apparatus. In industry, physical phenomena still appeared largely in the form of mechanical motion, electricity, heat, and light. In the same way the chemical industry was largely based on the older substances—minerals and other inorganic chemicals. But the new tools, unprecedented in their power and sweeping in their novelty, were there, waiting only on the urgency of the war and the stimulus of postwar reconstruction to be set to work. Only later was the potentially fatal flaw in the scientific foundation of the new technology discovered. It was like a two-legged stool: well founded in physics and chemistry, but flawed by a missing third leg—the biology of the environment.

All this is a useful guide in our search for the causes of the environmental 20 crises. Is it only a coincidence that in the years following World War II there was not only a great outburst of technological innovation, but also an equally large upsurge in environmental pollution? Is it possible that the new technology is the major cause of the environmental crisis?

This is part of the background of the sharp rise in pollution levels in the   21
United States since 1946. But there have been other changes as well, and these
too might be related to the pollution problem. Pollution is often blamed, for
example, on a rising population and level of affluence. It is easy to demonstrate
that the changes in pollution level in the United States since World War II
cannot be accounted for simply by the increased population, which in that
period rose by only 42 per cent. Of course, this is but a simplistic response to
a simplistic proposal. It is conceivable that even a 40 to 50 per cent increase in
population size *might* be the real cause of a much larger increase in pollution
intensity. For example, in order to provide the food, clothing, and shelter necessary for that many more people, it might be necessary to intensify production—
and therefore the resulting pollution—by a much greater proportion because
the increased production of goods might require the use of inefficient activities
(for example, obsolete factories might need to be pressed into use). In this case,
production activities would need to expand much more than 40 to 50 per cent
to meet the needs of so large an increase in population. In effect, this would
imply a reduction in productivity (that is, the value produced per unit labor
used in the process). In actual fact, matters are just the other way around; there
have been sharp *increases* in productivity since 1946. Moreover, the chemical
industries, which are particularly heavy polluters, have shown especially large
increases in productivity; between 1958 and 1968 productivity in chemical industries increased by 73 per cent as compared with a 39 per cent increase for
all manufacturing. So changes in productive efficiency can hardly account for
the discrepancy between recent increases in pollution levels and the growth of
the population.

Another popular idea is that increased population has led to the rapid growth   22
of cities, where internal crowding and deteriorated social conditions lead to a
worsening of the pollution problem. This notion, too, fails to account for the
actual intensity of the environmental crisis. For one thing, a number of serious
pollution problems, such as those due to radioactive fallout, fertilizer, pesticides,
mercury, and many other industrial pollutants are not of urban origin. It is
true, however, that the size and population density of a city will have a dispro-
portionately large effect on the amount of pollution produced per person, because of the "edge" effect. (That is, as a city becomes larger, the ratio between
its circumference and its area declines; since wastes must be removed at the
city's boundaries, one might expect waste levels to rise for the same effort to
remove them per unit area.) This effect may explain differences in the incidence
of diseases related to air pollution among cities of different sizes. Thus the per
capita incidence of lung cancer in the largest cities (1 million or more population) is about 37 per cent higher than it is in cities from 250,000 to 1 million
population. However, here too, the effect is too small to explain the observed
increases in the intensity of pollution.

The distribution of population does have a serious effect on environmental   23
pollution due to automotive transport. Consider, for example, the consequences

of the population shifts that are so typical of United States cities: rising populations of blacks and other minority groups in urban ghettos; migration of more affluent social groups to the suburbs. These processes separate the homes and places of work of both ghetto dwellers and suburbanites. Those suburbanites who work in the city, but are unwilling to live there, need to commute; ghetto dwellers who seek work in outlying industries, but are unable to live in the suburbs, must also commute, in reverse. This helps to explain why automobile vehicle-miles traveled within metropolitan areas, per capita, have increased from 1,050 in 1946 to 1,790 in 1966. Thus, the intensification of environmental problems associated with urbanization is not so much due to the increasing size of the population as it is to the maldistribution of the living and working places in metropolitan areas.

In sum, there appears to be no way to account for the rapid growth in   24
pollution levels in the United States since 1946 by the concurrent growth in the overall size of the population. Neither simple increase in numbers, the multiplicative effects of urban crowding, nor a supposed decrease in productive efficiency can explain the sharp increases in pollution which are the mark of the environmental crisis. The explanation must lie elsewhere.

The upshot of these considerations is that the ratio between the amount of   25
pollution generated in the United States and the size of the population has increased sharply since 1946. The country produces more pollution, for the size of its population, than it used to. This relationship can be converted to a mathematically equivalent but—as we shall see—highly misleading statement: that there has been a sharp increase in the amount of pollution produced *per person*. For example, if pollution has increased tenfold while population has increased by 43 per cent, then pollution per person has increased about sevenfold ($1.43 \times 7 = 10$ approximately). Since biological wastes produced per person have certainly not increased by this much, this observation usually leads to the further conclusion that each of us has become more affluent, responsible for the use of more goods and therefore for the production of more wastes. A favorite statistic introduced at this point is that the United States contains about 6 per cent of the world's population, but uses from 40 to 50 per cent of the world's goods and that this kind of affluent society is, in the nature of things, also an "effluent society."

Again, it is useful to look at the facts about "affluence" in the United States.   26
We can think of affluence in terms of the average amount of goods devoted, per person, to individual welfare. As a very rough measure—which, as we shall see, is vastly inflated—we might use the Gross National Product available per person. In 1946 GNP per capita was $2,222; in 1966 it was $3,354 (expressed in 1958 dollars to correct for inflation). This represents an increase of about 50 per cent, which by itself is clearly insufficient to account for the observed increases in pollution per capita.

Since the GNP is a crude over-all average of the goods and services produced   27
in the country, it is more informative to break it down into specific items,

especially as between those essential to life, such as food, clothing, and shelter, and amenities, such as personal automobiles, television sets, and electric corn-poppers.

With respect to food, the over-all picture for the 1946–68 period is quite   28 clear: no significant changes have taken place in per capita availability of the major food categories, such as total calories and protein, in the United States. Total calories actually declined somewhat, from about 3,380 per person per day in 1946 to about 3,250 per person per day in 1968. Protein available dropped slightly in the first few years after World War II, remained constant at about 95 grams per person per day until 1963, when it began to rise slightly, reaching the value of 99 grams per person per day in 1968; this represents a slight decrease from 1946 to 1968.

These figures are reflected in over-all agricultural production data for the   29 United States. In the postwar period, total grain production per capita has not varied from year to year by more than a few per cent. In the same period, per capita consumption of certain important diet accessories—calcium, vitamins A and C, and thiamin—actually declined about 11 to 20 per cent. This situation may reflect the temporary improvement in nutritional balance due to wartime food programs, and the unfortunate decline in the quality of the United States diet when these programs were abandoned.

In general, then, in total quantity per capita, food consumption in the United   30 States during the 1946–68 period has remained essentially unchanged, although there has been some decline in certain aspects of diet quality. Clearly, there is no sign of increasing affluence with respect to food consumption.

The situation with respect to clothing is quite similar: essentially no change   31 in per capita production. For example, annual production of shoes per capita in the United States remained constant at about three pairs between 1946 and 1966. In that period, per capita domestic production of all types of hosiery was more variable, but there was no significant over-all change between 1946 and 1966. While rapidly changing styles in that period caused large variations in the relative proportion of different types of outer clothing used per capita (for example, men's and women's suits declined considerably, while the production of separate skirts, blouses, trousers, and sport shirts increased), the overall per capita production of clothing remained essentially unchanged. Total use of fiber was forty-five pounds per capita in 1950 and forty-nine pounds per capita in 1968—an increase of only 9 per cent. Again, we must conclude that, at least in the crude terms of the amounts of clothing produced per capita, there is no sign of increasing affluence in the United States in the period following 1946.

With respect to shelter, the following figures are relevant: housing units   32 occupied in 1946 were 0.272 per capita, in 1966 they were 0.295 per capita. These figures do not take into account the quality of housing. In any case, they do not indicate any marked increase in affluence with respect to housing. This situation is also reflected in the production figures for housing materials, which show little change per capita in the period following 1946.

We can sum up the possible contribution of increased affluence to the United   33
States pollution problem as follows: per capita production of goods to meet major human needs—food, clothing, and shelter—have not increased significantly between 1946 and 1968 and have even declined in some respects. There has been an increase in the per capita utilization of electric power, fuels, and paper products, but these changes cannot fully account for the striking rise in pollution levels. If affluence is measured in terms of certain household amenities, such as television sets, radios, and electric can-openers and corn-poppers, and in leisure items such as snowmobiles and boats, then there have been certain striking increases. But again, these items are simply too small a part of the nation's over-all production to account for the observed increase in pollution level.

What these figures tell us is that, in the most general terms—apart from   34
certain items mentioned above—United States production has about kept pace with the growth of the United States population in the period from 1946 to 1968. This means that over-all production of basic items, such as food, steel, and fabrics has increased in proportion to the rise in population, let us say from 40 to 50 per cent. This over-all increase in total United States production falls far short of the concurrent rise in pollution levels, which is in the range of 200 to 2,000 per cent, to suffice as an explanation of the latter. It seems clear, then, that despite the frequent assertions that blame the environmental crisis on "overpopulation," "affluence," or both, we must seek elsewhere for an explanation.

QUESTIONS

1. This is a peculiar argument in that Commoner argues more for what is not the case than for what is. What is his conclusion? Summarize the main point of his essay.

2. What is meant by an ecosystem or an ecological cycle? What two abuses of particular ecological cycles does Commoner categorize in his opening paragraphs?

3. One of the more explicitly argumentative sections is from paragraph 21 to paragraph 24. What particular arguments are taken up in those paragraphs, and how are they answered?

4. Paragraphs 25 through 33 make up another explicitly argumentative section. In what ways does this section parallel paragraphs 21 through 24? How similar are Commoner's methods here in taking up and answering specific arguments?

5. What is the overall structure of this argument? What are its main sections? Pay particular attention to paragraphs 7 and 20. What is their function?

6. What overall purpose do paragraphs 8 through 19 serve? In what ways are they preparatory for the paragraphs that follow?

7. Because the essay concludes without answering the question raised, can you anticipate where an investigator might look next? Where should we look, do you suppose, for an answer to this vexing question?

8. Monitor your own habits of use and consumption for a week. Write a report on your personal contribution to environmental pollution. Commoner's essay should indicate enough categories of activity to give you plenty of ideas as to what to look for.

WHAT IS THE BUSINESS OF ORGANIZED CRIME?
Thomas C. Schelling

Thomas C. Schelling (b. 1921) is a professor of economics at Harvard. He has written books on international economics, global strategy, and arms control. He also served as a consultant to President Lyndon Johnson's Commission on Crime. The essay reprinted here is a slightly abridged version of a paper presented at a symposium on organized crime, first published in a legal journal in 1971.

It is becoming widely accepted that the business of organized crime is to provide the public with illicit goods and services like bets, narcotics, sex out of wedlock, and unregulated loans. . . . Federal law even *defines* organized crime as those unlawful activities in which a highly organized, disciplined association supplies illegal goods and services. The appendix on organized crime in the Staff Report to the Commission on Violence states, "It is well known that organized crime exists and thrives because it provides services the public demands," and "Organized crime depends not on victims, but on customers." The Task Force on Organized Crime of the 1967 President's Commission opened its report with the assertion, "The core of organized crime activity is the supplying of illegal goods and services—gambling, loan-sharking, narcotics, and other forms of vice—to countless numbers of citizen customers." 1

And indeed this conception of organized crime corresponds to part of the image, though only a part, of the gangs that thrived when liquor was nationally prohibited in the 1920's and early 1930's. (Supplying liquor was the quieter part; suppressing rival supply was the part that made Chicago famous.) 2

At first glance, this is in some contrast to a quite different line of business that, at different times and particularly in the later 1930's, appeared to characterize the organized racketeers. This business was extortion, based on the threat of damage, together with occasional efforts to monopolize "legitimate" lines of business by physically destroying or intimidating competition. 3

The Task Force in 1967 gave lesser emphasis—nevertheless some emphasis—to the use by organized crime of "illegitimate methods" in connection with legitimate business and labor unions. These illegitimate methods were identified as "monopolization, terrorism, extortion, tax evasion." The contrast seems to be that in the "core" activities the racketeers are busy providing illicit goods and 4

534

services whereas, when they turn to legitimate business, they terrorize, blackmail, and monopolize.

In his appendix to that Task Force Report, Donald Cressey, one of the outstanding academic investigators of this subject, draws a "basic distinction" between ordinary criminals and "organized criminals," the former being wholly predatory while the latter "offers a return to the respectable members of society." Hardly anybody will miss the burglars if they suddenly disappear. "But if the confederation of men employed in illicit businesses were suddenly abolished, it would be sorely missed because it performs services for which there is a great public demand."

And all are agreed that, as the Task Force stated, "To carry on its many activities secure from governmental interference, organized crime corrupts public officials. Indeed some, like the Kefauver committee, found that corruption procured not only immunity from the law but employment of the police as enforcers of the mob's authority."[1]

The purpose of my paper is to dissent from this widespread interpretation of what it is that *organized crime* is engaged in. Mine will not be a disagreement with the facts, fragmentary as they are, from which most of the authors and commissions and lawmakers and law enforcers start. The difference will be one of analysis, of interpretation of what it is that is going on. But before dissenting let me try to state in a purely descriptive, not analytical, way, what it is we all seem to be talking about when we speak of *organized crime*.

Evidently we do not merely mean "crime that is organized." The term, *organized crime*, is not composed merely of two words in the English language that keep their ordinary meanings when joined. Donald Cressey does not mean, I am sure, that burglars are never organized. If it should suit their purpose to work in small gangs; to share the take as a partnership; to vote new members into the club; to insure each other against accident or arrest and to maintain a common retirement fund; to have exclusive contracts with merchants who dispose of their goods, and to regularize their relations with the police; to have a research staff, a retained lawyer, and a technological consultant; and to divide the labor among scouts, lookouts, breakers and enterers, and disposers of merchandise, they indeed deserve to be called "organized" in the ordinary English-language sense of the word. But they are a different kind of "organized crime" from what this symposium is discussing, which is *organized crime*.

Still, while it may be easy to say what we do not mean by *organized crime*, it is not easy to tell from the professional literature exactly what we should mean. There is no problem, of course, if we can simply point to a unique organization. There is no problem in defining what we mean by a "religious organization" if there is only one church, or by a "political party" if there is

---

[1] Kefauver Committee, 3rd Interim Report, S. Rep. No. 307, 82nd Cong. 1st Sess. 182, 184 (1951).

only one party. If there is a single "Mafia" that either governs and operates everywhere or has no counterpart in those places where it has no operations, we can give *organized crime* a proper name and call it "Mafia" with a capital M, "La Cosa Nostra" with capital letters, or "The Organization," just as some people refer to "The Establishment" in relation to overworld society, and need not define the species because it has but a single member. But if we take that route we are committed to a particular hypothesis, one that is limited to a particular time and place, and one that precludes comparative analysis because the definition precludes comparison.

There is, I believe, a characteristic of *organized crime* that is consistent with all of these definitions and characterizations (even the one that treats *organized crime* as a proper noun), and that is consistent with most of the prevailing images of racketeers, whether based on stories of Chicago in the 1920's, New York in the 1930's, Miami in the 1940's, or any of these places in the 1960's. This key characteristic is suggested by the term "society." But "society" is too broad and too loose for my purpose. "Government" would come closer to what I have in mind. The characteristic is *exclusivity*, or, to use a more focused term, *monopoly*. From all accounts, organized crime does not merely extend itself broadly, but brooks no competition. It seeks not merely influence, but exclusive influence. In the overworld its counterpart would be not just organized business, but monopoly. And we can apply to it some of the adjectives that are often associated with monopoly—ruthless, unscrupulous, greedy, exploitative, unprincipled.

Now, it is clear that governments have to have an element of monopoly. We cannot all be obeying two conflicting sets of laws, two competing sets of traffic lights, or two contradictory building codes, and paying taxes to maintain duplicate street systems or armies. If there are several governments they must work out jurisdictional or territorial arrangements, the way towns and counties and states and port authorities and the federal government do. So if an organization seeks governing authority in the underworld we should expect it to seek exclusive authority, or at least to seek stable jurisdictional sharing with other authorities and, all together, to constitute a hierarchy without competition. That is what we should expect them to seek. We should not be surprised when civil war breaks out.

We now have a hint of what to look for when we ask about the business that organized crime is in. Part of my argument will be that organized crime is usually monopolized crime. What distinguishes the burglars from the loan sharks or the gamblers is not only that one steals what we have and the other sells what we want. It is also that burglars are never reported to be fighting each other in gangs for exclusive control over their hunting grounds. Burglars are busy about their burglary, not staking claims and fighting off other burglars. It is when a gang of burglars begins to police their territory against the invasion of other gangs of burglars, and makes interloping burglars join up and share their loot or get out of town, and collectively negotiates with the police not only for their

536

own security but to enlist the police in the war against rival burglar gangs or nonjoining mavericks, that we should, I believe, begin to identify the burglary gangs as *organized crime*. Until then we should use a different term, like "organized burglary."

We can ask, at this point, the question why burglars are not *organized* in the   13
more ambitious way I just described. More generally, why are some kinds of crime apparently *organized* in exclusivist monopoly fashion, and characterized by occasional gang wars and truces and market-sharing arrangements, while other kinds of crime are more like competitive business, the individual criminal or the criminal organization going about its business without a major effort to destroy or intimidate competition and obtain exclusive control?

There is probably no simple answer. The same question can be asked about   14
business enterprise in the overworld. And there we find that some businesses lend themselves more than others to monopolization. And if we examine the businesses that seem rarely to be monopolized, or rarely to stay monopolized, and those that show a universal tendency to become monopolized, we may discover characteristics of the technology, the market, the consumer demand, the personnel requirements, or the financial and legal requirements that determine whether a business is ineluctably monopolized, sometimes monopolized, or hardly susceptible to monopolization. We can then turn to the underworld and see whether some corresponding principles apply.

In a purely descriptive sense this tendency toward monopolization surely   15
seems to characterize *organized crime*. We have to keep in mind that rival claimants to monopoly position sometimes find it cheaper to merge than to make war, or cheaper to stabilize their boundaries than to fight over them, and that even war may lead to surrender and empire rather than to total destruction or massive retaliation. Where there is no governmental authority that can exert itself, or where a government is sympathetic or subservient to business, broad cartel arrangements may provide a framework for comparatively nonviolent resolution of competitive conflict.

It is worthwhile remembering that the Chicago gangster deaths of the 1920's,   16
like the alleged Boston gangster deaths of the 1960's, were usually characterized, if not identified, as arising out of gang rivalry. Pickpockets, burglars, car thieves, embezzlers, people who cheat on their income taxes, shoplifters, muggers and bank robbers usually don't go around killing each other. There's nothing in it for them. Two bank robbers who pick the same day for the same bank may have to fight for the privilege if they arrive at the same time, and two purse snatchers who grab the same purse may fight for possession; but these are rare instances, and the man who embezzles the bank he works for has neither the knowledge nor the interest that would motivate him to make war on other embezzlers at other banks. But evidently the people in what the Crime Commission Task Force called "the core of organized crime"—the people in illegal gambling and loan-sharking—like the people who delivered illegal beer and gin

in the days of the Untouchables, fought like the devil for the market, and patched up truces, and imposed hierarchical empires that were continually susceptible to breakdown, defection, and challenge.

One could of course give a particularist explanation of this. The big gangs have power and are greedy for more; the urge to exclusivity is natural, and when they get around to taking over burglary as they may have taken over the protection rackets and loan-sharking, we'll find burglary displaying these monopolistic tendencies. But I think that would be wrong. An alternative hypothesis is that we find *organized crime* in the lines of business that lend themselves to monopoly. The reason they are not in burglary may be that burglary is hard to monopolize.

It may be useful to remind ourselves of how many illegal goods and services are provided competitively, rather than by monopoly organizations of the underworld. An ideal example for my purpose is the sale of cigarettes below the legal age. Why is this market not monopolized? If it could be, there might be a few hundred million dollars in it of monopoly profits. But obviously it can't be. Nobody can keep a nineteen-year-old from buying a pack of cigarettes for a seventeen-year-old; the competition is everywhere. There is just no room for a black market differential, because the law itself is virtually impossible to enforce. If you can't control the market and police it against competition, excluding competitors or making them pay for the franchise, you cannot do any more than sell cigarettes to minors, and that's not an occupation in which a criminal, organized or not, could make a living.

Monopolize shoplifting? Try it: if you succeed, department stores may hire you as security guards, because you can presumably spot your competition better than the store detectives, and you may have a competitive advantage on the side of law and order.

At this point it might appear that we've reached the question, why does illegal gambling so readily lend itself to monopolization? Why is it that it not only occurs, as burglary and shoplifting occur, but is the object of monopolistic enterprise as those other criminal trades are not? But I'm going to ask a different question instead, a question that may help to answer the first question. What is the relation of organized crime to illegal gambling, at least as it shows up in such investigations as those of Senator Kefauver's committee?

The interpretation that I want to suggest is that *organized crime* does indeed have a victim. The victim is the bookmaker—the man who sells illicit services to the public. And the crime of which he is the victim is the crime of extortion. He pays to stay in business. Nominally he may seem to procure a "wire service" or occasionally to borrow money or to use the clearing-house facilities of the extortionate monopoly organization. But basically he is in a very simple business, one that needs no such organization; and he could do without The Organization. He might find organization useful, as many small businessmen find trade associations and lobbies and even public relations offices useful. But he does not need The Organization. It needs him. It lives off him. It lives off him the way it lives off anyone else, who, either in the underworld or the overworld, buys "protection."

And it is easier to see why extortion has to be monopolized than why gam-   22
bling itself would have to be monopolized. Large-scale systematic extortion cannot really stand competition any more than a local taxing authority; I cannot take half the bookie's earnings if you took it before I got there. We can divide the bookies between us, territorially or otherwise, but if nine other mobs are demanding half his earnings, all ten are in trouble. "Protection" is primarily against the one who offers it, but it has to include protection against rival taxing authorities.

And if the nominal basis for the extortion is the sale of a wire service or   23
something of the sort, then evidently there will be an apparent monopoly of wire service in the underworld, but as a by-product of the monopolization of the protection racket.

We come now to the central question in this whole line of investigation. If   24
the business of organized crime is extortion, in the underworld as well as in the overworld, why is the "core" of organized crime activity in the underworld itself? That is, why is the biggest victim of organized crime an illegal business rather than some legal business? (It may not be, but the traditional estimates as published, say, by the President's Commission in 1967, use figures between 5 and 10 billion dollars as the gross earnings of the illegal gambling business, and impute the larger part of it to the profits of "organized crime.")

It is worthwhile to pause a moment and notice a certain anomaly. Making   25
book is indeed a "crime without a victim," to use the name that Edwin Schur gave these activities[2] but is itself victimized by organized crime. The victims of most crimes are not in the underworld. A department store may violate some laws and regulations, cheat its customers, or the taxing authorities, or otherwise commit occasional crimes, but basically a department store is a "legitimate activity," and is the target of shoplifters. Shoplifters and pickpockets and burglars and embezzlers do not typically pick their victims in the underworld. Even if their victims are not altogether pure, they nevertheless do not usually have underworld careers. But what is generally referred to as the primary target of organized crime is itself an underworld activity. It is criminals who are victimized, if we accept my interpretation of the business of organized crime as that of extortion.

Should we be surprised? Can we identify characteristics of illegal bookmaking   26
that make it a prime target for organized extortion? Can we possibly then look at other activities, legitimate activities and underworld activities, and infer which among them may be easy targets for organized extortion?

---

[2]Schur used the term in relation to the consumer as well as to the purveyor, and did not limit it to marketplace activities but let it include private deviance, like homosexuality, as well. See E. Schur, *Crimes Without Victims* (1965).

Thomas C. Schelling

My first candidate, as a criterion for target selection by organized extortionists, is that the victims should be poor at protecting themselves. In particular, one would like victims who have no ready access to the law. Criminals would therefore usually be ideal victims. The attractiveness of underworld victims is even greater if the police can actually be used as an instrument; if harassment can take the form of vigorous law enforcement by the police, the extortionists may not even need to engage in illegal violence to keep their victims in line.

Second, the extortionist wants a victim who cannot hide from him. Burglary is a very private affair, and the burglar has no need to advertise himself and his business and his location. A bookmaker or prostitute who was as hard to locate and to identify as a burglar might well escape the racketeer, but he would lose his customers. If a customer can find a bookie when he wants to place a bet, the racketeer can find him. Those who sell illicit services to the public are therefore more visible, more easily located and identified, than embezzlers, pickpockets, shoplifters, car thieves, and people who cheat on their income tax. All criminals may be susceptible to blackmail, but those who cannot hide without losing their business are especially vulnerable.

Third, it is probably important to be able to monitor the victim's activity and his earnings. Those who operate in the open, dealing with a standard commodity, one that has a face value in money and few complicated costs, are probably those with whom an extortionist can reach an enforceable contract. Even if one can find and recognize an embezzler or jewel thief, one would have a hard time going shares with him, because the embezzler can fool the extortionist if he can fool the firm he embezzles from, and the jewel thief needn't put his best prizes on display. A bookmaker may get away with some business on the side, and avoid taxation by the extortionist organization, but his business is basically simpler and more public than most criminal activities.

Fourth, it helps if the victim has a regular business that he cannot carry away in an attempt to escape extortion. A bookmaker or prostitute or loan shark has to have a place of business; much of his business assets consist of goodwill, personal acquaintance, knowledge of the customers and their credit ratings, trust, access to a grapevine communication system, and perhaps personal relations with the police. A bookmaker or prostitute can probably always escape, but not and still do business within the jurisdiction of The Organization.

Fifth, all of this may work best if it works smoothly and regularly. The victim has to be treated "fairly." He has to know that he is treated like other victims. The business has to be depersonalized. Rules of the game are needed so that the victim knows where he stands. He has to compare his situation with that of others in the same business. There probably has to be a set of simple and fairly uniform arrangements. The bookmaker has the choice of paying or not paying; it might burden the system too much if each had to negotiate his own unique arrangement with The Organization, and renegotiate it month by month.

Consider for example the sharing arrangement that Senator Kefauver's com- $\quad$ 32
mittee turned up in Miami. The "syndicate" took 50 percent of the bookmaker's
proceeds. This was a standardized percentage. Furthermore, it was not 40 percent or 55 percent or 29 percent or 83 percent. It was a nice round number,
the nicest and roundest there is, an even 50-50. Oil-producing countries in the
Middle East tend to converge on standard royalty arrangements with the Western
companies they deal with. A king or a shah or a sultan or a sheik cannot explain
to himself or to his constituents a lesser percentage share than the country next
door receives, and he cannot persuasively hold out for a much more favorable
share. So it may be that the very standardized nature and visibility of bookmaking
lends itself to standardized, visible, and institutionalized arrangements, known
to all and applied without much discrimination. Bookmakers probably can compare notes and tell whether they are receiving equal treatment far more readily
than my neighbor and I can compare assessed valuations on our houses.

Perhaps another characteristic is that bookmaking, like prostitution, is a fairly $\quad$ 33
petty activity, especially when it is illegal. That is, it can be a one-man or one-
person job, or at least the retail organizations can be pretty small and decentralized. The bookmaker is probably his own bookkeeper, and he cannot readily
plead inability when asked to pay. An officer of a bank would have to be a first-
rate embezzler to pay large and regular amounts of blackmail out of the bank's
resources without its becoming known to anybody else in the bank. In large
organizations, too many people have to sign the checks, initial the vouchers,
audit the books, scrutinize budgets, take inventory, and otherwise tangle things
up in red tape. The small independent entrepreneur, whether in the underworld
or the overworld, may be more able to meet the demands than a complex
organization would be.

These are only suggestions. There may be other characteristics of illegal $\quad$ 34
bookmaking that I have missed, that are even more important in determining
why it is such an attractive target for extortion. If we knew more about these
activities in cities of different sizes, on the insides of large organizations as well
as on the streets, and in different parts of the country, and particularly if we
compared them with comparable activities in other countries, we could learn
more. My conjectures may at least help to alert investigators to what they should
be looking for: unless one raises the right questions, no amount of hearings and
inquiries and investigations will turn up the pertinent answers.

It may be equally useful to look at many black markets that are immune to $\quad$ 35
organized crime. There have been elaborate black markets in foreign currency
and gold, but while those engaged may occasionally have been subject to blackmail, there is no sign that it has been at the hands of large extortionate organizations. There is apparently an enormous black market in drugs, if one is willing
to construe all the abuses of prescriptioning procedures as part of the black
market, and apparently Organized Crime gets its hands on at most a small

portion of it. If firearms should ever be banned in the United States, there will probably be an extensive black market, but the chances are overwhelmingly against its ever being monopolized by a criminal organization. . . .

When we turn to the overworld we can similarly ask, what characteristics of 36 a business would tend to make it an attractive target for organized extortion? An equally interesting and important question may be, what forms should we expect the tribute to take? It is of some interest that even in dealing with the petty bookmaker, The Organization sometimes goes through the motion of providing a wire service, or otherwise pretending that it offers something more than sheer brutal "protection." That may explain why *organized crime* is so widely alleged to have been engaged in businesses like the provision of laundry service. The reason for selecting laundry may not lie so much with the laundry business as with the nature of the customer. Restaurants may be comparatively easy targets for racketeers. They are so easily harassed, because their business is really rather fragile. Noises and bad odors and startling events can spoil the clientele, and even physical damage cannot be guarded against. Furthermore, restaurants do a great deal of business in cash, are often small proprietorships or partnerships, and are therefore financially capable of meeting the demands for tribute. But why not demand cash, then, rather than take it as a monopoly profit on a high-priced laundry service?

Or, to take another familiar example, why is it so often alleged that vending 37 machines as well as pinball machines and slot machines are often "organized" by *organized crime*? Maybe *organized crime* likes gambling, and pinball machines are a little like slot machines, and then once you're in the machine business you may as well deal in cigarettes, too. Or maybe the machines are attractive for some other reason.

My conjecture is that the machines, like the laundry service, meet certain 38 criteria that make them attractive means both of exacting tribute and of paying it. Again, if we were attempting organized extortion against restaurateurs in a city, planning to hit them all and to protect them all from rival extortionists, in what medium would we want them to pay us?

One criterion is that it should be tax-deductible. There is no sense imposing 39 a cost that is greater than what we get, when we could find a form in which we get everything that the victim loses. The high-priced laundry service is a deductible expense: profits from the cigarette machine are excludable income, as long as the concessionaire receives them, not the restaurateur.

Second, the victim wants to be able to keep books without showing that he 40 pays tribute. He does not want creditors, revenue agents, or grand juries to be able to identify the tribute he pays, especially if it is illegal.

Third, the victim may want a manner of payment that minimizes embar- 41 rassment and the loss of self-respect. He may prefer to feel himself the victim of a monopoly linen service, and to complain to his wife and his employees about how the linen industry has been victimized and he is indirectly suffering, rather than to remind himself periodically that he is simply paying cash for protection. He may even be able to feel that the vending machines are monopolized, not that he is providing rent-free space for somebody else's vending machine in return for "protection."

Indeed, from most accounts, gambling machines were used for this purpose in the 1930's and perhaps were still so used in the 1960's. A gambling machine in a neighborhood store may represent two kinds of criminal activity. One is illicit gambling; the other is extortion. It tends to get listed under the heading of gambling; but the more brutal crime is that some poor store owner is being shaken down by a protection racketeer. And his tribute takes the form of having machines put in his store. He may despise the machines and make nothing off them: but that's the price he pays. If the laws against gambling were properly enforced, the "crime without a victim" might disappear, but the extortion might continue with payment taking another guise. It may hurt the extortionist somewhat to be denied his favorite medium of tribute; but we miss the point if we suppose that the only crime we're dealing with is gambling. 42

The machines and the laundry services and the other ostensible businesses that are used by the racketeers may also meet another need. That's the need for institutionalized practices, uniform arrangements, nondiscrimination, etc. If each victim privately pays cash he has no way of knowing how his treatment compares with that of other victims; but if they all get their linen or beer or meat from the same monopolistic provider, or all provide their vestibules for similar kinds of machinery concessions, they know they're getting standard treatment. 43

Incidentally, if news vendors, neighborhood store owners, or barbershops became universal victims of organized extortion, perhaps sharing their earnings and nominally receiving some service in return, perhaps paying extortionate prices for supplies or rent on the building, we would probably not describe haircuts and magazines and chewing gum as the businesses that organized crime were engaged in. We'd describe them as the victimized trades. We would distinguish the barbers and the news vendors from the personnel of *organized crime*. Even if The Organization helped to enforce union membership, uniform prices and uniform closing days; lobbied for legislation favorable to barbers; occasionally intervened on their behalf with their landlords, lent them money, and occasionally got them barbershop space in new hotels, we still wouldn't consider the barber a criminal nor consider organized crime to be in the business of providing haircuts. We would not be afraid that a successful crackdown on organized crime would close up the barbershops and leave us no place to get our hair trimmed. We'd expect instead that prices might fall, just as if a heavy tax on haircuts had just been repealed. 44

This thought may put illegal gambling back into better perspective. It is undoubtedly true that, as Donald Cressey said in the passage quoted earlier, "if the confederation of men employed in illicit businesses were suddenly abolished, 45 it would be sorely missed because it performs services for which there is a great public demand." But it is only true if we take the "confederation" to include the bookmakers as well as the racketeers who prey on them. Even then it is true only if we permit no newcomers to enter the business in replacement of the abolished "confederation." Even if the customer wants his bookie, he has no use for the organization that restricts competition in the betting industry.

I must at this point offer two qualifications, one substantive and the other a matter of point of view. The substantive one is this. Maybe bookmakers, prostitutes, loan sharks, and drug peddlers would, if left alone by the racketeers, be unable to come to proper terms with the police and unable to engage in their business. Maybe corruption is best handled collectively, and an illicit trade consisting only of individualistic competitors could not buy off the public officials. Perhaps they would be unable to form their own organization: nobody likes to pay dues, people may drift in and out of the business, some may have satisfactory arrangements and no need for the union. In that case it might be worth a fairly high price to have discipline and organization imposed from outside. The Organization may levy a high tax once it imposes its own governance on the gambling business; but a high tax may be better than no governance at all.

Conceivably, then, bookmakers gain by being victims of a predatory organization; without it they would have no organization. Furthermore, much of the tax, perhaps most of it, may be passed along to the customer. Gasoline stations do not suffer enormously when gasoline taxes go up a nickel; they suffer only to the extent that motorists reduce their driving because of the higher price of gasoline, and on the whole the tax gets passed along to the buyer. Thus the direct victim of extortion is the bookmaker, or the prostitute, or the barber, or the restaurateur; but if the tax is uniformly levied on all bookmakers or restaurateurs, and if it is a tax on transactions and not on residual profits, it probably is passed along so that the one who "pays" the tribute is the customer, not the nominal taxpayer. Just as the tenants in apartment houses "pay" the property tax, though the landlord forwards the check to the tax collector, the person who places the bet receives less favorable odds than if bookmaking were a purely competitive and "untaxed" consumer service.

The second qualification is that any organization can be viewed in different ways. It is possible to say with some truth that General Motors does not produce automobiles; the Chevrolet and Pontiac divisions do. Many businesses, small and large, are decentralized; General Motors may deliberately allow the Chevrolet division a good deal of autonomy, just as Chevrolet grants its sales agents so much autonomy that they are considered to be "authorized dealers," dealing in their own names, rather than branches of Chevrolet. Many firms let their salesmen work on commission; farm owners often prefer going shares with a tenant rather than hiring him for a wage. Many hotel and restaurant chains lay down architectural and other standards, but do not directly manage the individual establishments that bear their name.

By analogy, one could say that *organized crime* is indeed in the gambling 49
business but finds it expedient to run that business by licensing individual bookmakers rather than hiring them as employees. It may even do it on an "open
shop" basis, according to which anybody can get into the business as long as
he pays the franchise tax. A specific test might be whether The Organization
could move into a locale where there was no off-track betting and establish a
bookmaking business, and if so whether it would own and operate the business
or instead set it up in the familiar pattern, inviting independent operators to
operate under the "protection" of the racketeering organization, which would
protect them from molestation either by police or rival organizations. If it did
the latter, we'd have to admit that though the arrangement has all the characteristics of extortion, and may often arise directly out of extortion, it can be
construed as well as a monopolized business in which independent operators
are allowed on condition that they pay standardized tribute to the licensing
organization.

All of this has some bearing on the question, if gambling were made legal 50
would it continue to attract racketeers? It is often alleged that organized crime
is so skilled and experienced in the gambling business that it would have an
edge over "legitimate" entrepreneurs, and would not only entrench itself in
legitimized gambling but would enjoy the greater profits that would go with
enlarged business. One suggestion of this paper is that The Organization is not
really skilled and experienced in the provision of gambling services. It is skilled
and experienced in the *suppression* of rival gambling services, especially in
suppressing rival *illegal* gambling by collusion with the police. Its success, with
or without the police, is appreciably due to the inability of the bookmaker to
seek the protection of the law. It is also due to the inability of the bookmaker
to protect himself through corporate organization, trade association, and all the
other ways that modern business protects itself from crude and petty interlopers,
chiselers, and even racketeers.

Thus the important question is not whether the *bookmakers* would show up 51
as the sellers of legal bets if off-track betting were made legal. The question is
whether The Organization could get a monopolized extortionist grip on the
industry. That may not be an easy question to answer, but it is at least clear
that some of the characteristics of off-track betting that presently make it an
ideal target for monopolized extortion would not be present if it were made as
legal to bet in front of a television screen as it is to bet in the presence of the
horses themselves. The history of prohibition and its aftermath in the liquor
business strongly suggests that *organized crime* may not thrive or survive in the
face of legal competition.

In any event, those among us who are so hypocritical as to want off-track 52
betting illegal, prostitution abolished, and the credit laws enforced, but still
want to place their bets, visit the bawdy houses, and borrow on the side to
preserve their credit ratings, needn't be afraid of a crackdown on organized
crime. They may suffer, as Donald Cressey suggests they will, from a crackdown

Thomas C. Schelling

on gambling, prostitution and loan-sharking; they can benefit, though, from a crackdown on *organized crime*, just as the consumer always hopes to benefit from trustbusting.

The purpose of monopoly has always been to suppress, not to enlarge, supply. 53 People who like monopoly prices and punitive taxes on the naughty activities may be pleased that the long arm of organized crime reaches out and levies a tax on the retailer that is passed along to the consumer. The consumers will prefer to see the activities become more freely competitive, whether by being released from illegality, or released from the grip of *organized crime*: so will those who dislike corruption, especially when it is centralized and regularized by large monopoly organizations that can build corruption directly into our institutions, rather than leave it to gnaw away at the edges.

QUESTIONS

1. In paragraph 7, Schelling explains the purpose of this essay as "dissent," thus making the essay an argument as well as an interpretation. What is he dissenting from, and why?

2. In paragraph 9, Schelling begins to define *organized crime*. He also begins to discuss what is at stake in the process of definition itself. For how many paragraphs does this particular definition extend? How does Schelling define *organized crime*? That is, what is his definition, and how does he go about the process of defining?

3. In paragraph 17, Schelling offers us two hypotheses, calling one an "alternative." What are they? Why does he offer two?

4. In paragraph 20, Schelling presents one question and then offers a substitute. Why? What does this paragraph suggest about the use of questions in developing an argument?

5. In paragraph 35, Schelling uses the term "large extortionate organizations." What is that equivalent to? What does it indicate about the progress of this argument that Schelling can suddenly insert that term?

6. Paragraph 44 is crucial to this argument. Can you restate what it says in your own words?

7. How is Schelling using the word *tax* in paragraph 47?

8. Consider the last paragraph. How do such expressions as "the long arm of organized crime," "levies a tax," "retailer," and "consumer" strike you in this context? What is their function and their effect?

9. Paragraphs 50 and 51 make a small argument in themselves about the possible results of legalizing gambling. What position does Schelling take in those two paragraphs? Develop that position in a longer argument of your own, or, if you prefer, dissent from it and develop a position opposed to Schelling's.

10. Throughout this essay Schelling uses the term *victimless crime*. Write an essay in which you first define that term as it is generally used outside this essay—that definition will require some research—and then reconsider the term in the light of Schelling's argument. You might want to argue for decriminalizing some victimless crimes or, conversely, argue that some so-called victimless crime is not actually victimless.

A MODEST PROPOSAL
Jonathan Swift

Jonathan Swift (1667–1745) was born in Dublin, Ireland, of English parents and educated in Irish schools. A graduate of Trinity College, Dublin, he received an M.A. from Oxford and was ordained a priest in the Church of England in 1695. He was active in politics as well as religion, becoming an editor and pamphlet writer for the Tory party in 1710. After becoming Dean of St. Patrick's Cathedral, Dublin, in 1713, he settled in Ireland and began to take an interest in the English economic exploitation of Ireland, gradually becoming a fierce Irish patriot. By 1724 the English were offering a reward for the discovery of the writer of the Drapier's Letters, *a series of pamphlets secretly written by Swift, attacking the British for their treatment of Ireland. In 1726 Swift produced the first volume of a more universal satire, known to modern readers as* Gulliver's Travels, *which has kept his name alive for two hundred and fifty years. A* Modest Proposal, *his best-known essay on Irish affairs, appeared in 1729. In 1742 he was found to be of unsound mind and three years later he died, leaving most of his estate for the founding of a hospital for the insane.*

A *Modest Proposal*
*for Preventing the Children of Poor People in Ireland
from Being a Burden to Their Parents or Country,
and for Making Them Beneficial to the Public*

It is a melancholy object to those who walk through this great town,[1] or travel in the country, when they see the streets, the roads and cabin-doors crowded with beggars of the female sex, followed by three, four, or six children, all in rags, and importuning every passenger for an alms. These mothers, instead of being able to work for their honest livelihood, are forced to employ all their time in strolling, to beg sustenance for their helpless infants, who, as they grow up, either turn thieves for want of work, or leave their dear native country to fight for the Pretender in Spain,[2] or sell themselves to the Barbadoes.[3]

---

[1]this great town: Dublin. [Eds.]

[2]Pretender in Spain: the Catholic descendant of the British royal family (James I, Charles I, and Charles II) of Stuart. Exiled so that England could be governed by Protestant rulers, the Stuarts lurked in France and Spain, preparing various disastrous schemes for regaining the throne. [Eds.]

[3]sell themselves to the Barbadoes: sell themselves as indentured servants, a sort of temporary slavery, to the sugar merchants of the British Carribean islands. [Eds.]

Jonathan Swift

I think it is agreed by all parties that this prodigious number of children, in the arms, or on the backs, or at the heels of their mothers, and frequently of their fathers, is in the present deplorable state of the kingdom a very great additional grievance; and therefore whoever could find out a fair, cheap, and easy method of making these children sound and useful members of the commonwealth would deserve so well of the public as to have his statue set up for a preserver of the nation.

But my intention is very far from being confined to provide only for the children of professed beggars; it is of a much greater extent, and shall take in the whole number of infants at a certain age who are born of parents in effect as little able to support them as those who demand our charity in the streets.

As to my own part, having turned my thoughts for many years upon this important subject, and maturely weighed the several schemes of other projectors, I have always found them grossly mistaken in their computation. It is true a child just dropped from its dam may be supported by her milk for a solar year with little other nourishment, at most not above the value of two shillings,[4] which the mother may certainly get, or the value in scraps, by her lawful occupation of begging, and it is exactly at one year old that I propose to provide for them, in such a manner as, instead of being a charge upon their parents, or the parish, or wanting food and raiment for the rest of their lives, they shall, on the contrary, contribute to the feeding and partly to the clothing of many thousands.

There is likewise another great advantage in my scheme, that it will prevent those voluntary abortions, and that horrid practice of women murdering their bastard children, alas, too frequent among us, sacrificing the poor innocent babes, I doubt, more to avoid the expense than the shame, which would move tears and pity in the most savage and inhuman breast.

The number of souls in Ireland being usually reckoned one million and a half, of these I calculate there may be about two hundred thousand couples whose wives are breeders, from which number I subtract thirty thousand couples who are able to maintain their own children, although I apprehend there cannot be so many under the present distresses of the kingdom, but this being granted, there will remain an hundred and seventy thousand breeders. I again subtract fifty thousand for those women who miscarry, or whose children die by accident or disease within the year. There only remain an hundred and twenty thousand children of poor parents annually born: the question therefore is, how this number shall be reared, and provided for, which as I have already said, under the present situation of affairs is utterly impossible by all the methods hitherto proposed, for we can neither employ them in handicraft or agriculture; we neither build houses (I mean in the country), nor cultivate land: they can very seldom pick up a livelihood by stealing until they arrive at six years old, except

---

[4]shillings: a shilling used to be worth about one day's labor. [Eds.]

where they are of towardly parts, although I confess they learn the rudiments much earlier, during which time they can however be properly looked upon only as probationers, as I have been informed by a principal gentleman in the County of Cavan, who protested to me that he never knew above one or two instances under the age of six, even in a part of the kingdom so renowned for the quickest proficiency in that art.

I am assured by our merchants that a boy or girl before twelve years old, is   7
no saleable commodity, and even when they come to this age, they will not yield above three pounds, or three pounds and half-a-crown at most on the Exchange, which cannot turn to account either to the parents or the kingdom, the charge of nutriment and rags having been at least four times that value.

I shall now therefore humbly propose my own thoughts, which I hope will   8
not be liable to the least objection.

I have been assured by a very knowing American of my acquaintance in   9
London, that a young healthy child well nursed is at a year old a most delicious, nourishing and wholesome food, whether stewed, roasted, baked, or boiled, and I make no doubt that it will equally serve in a fricassee, or a ragout.

I do therefore humbly offer it to public consideration, that of the hundred   10
and twenty thousand children already computed, twenty thousand may be re-served for breed, whereof only one fourth part to be males, which is more than we allow to sheep, black-cattle, or swine, and my reason is that these children are seldom the fruits of marriage, a circumstance not much regarded by our savages, therefore one male will be sufficient to serve four females. That the remaining hundred thousand may at a year old be offered in sale to the persons of quality, and fortune, through the kingdom, always advising the mother to let them suck plentifully in the last month, so as to render them plump, and fat for a good table. A child will make two dishes at an entertainment for friends, and when the family dines alone, the fore or hind quarter will make a reasonable dish, and seasoned with a little pepper or salt will be very good boiled on the fourth day, especially in winter.

I have reckoned upon a medium, that a child just born will weigh twelve   11
pounds, and in a solar year if tolerably nursed increaseth to twenty-eight pounds.

I grant this food will be somewhat dear, and therefore very proper for land-   12
lords, who, as they have already devoured most of the parents, seem to have the best title to the children.

Infant's flesh will be in season throughout the year, but more plentiful in   13
March, and a little before and after, for we are told by a grave author, an eminent French physician,[5] that fish being a prolific diet, there are more chil-dren born in Roman Catholic countries about nine months after Lent than at any other season; therefore reckoning a year after Lent, the markets will be more

---

[5]French physician: François Rabelais (1494?–1553), physician and satirist known for his *Gargantua* and *Pantagruel*. [Eds.]

glutted than usual, because the number of Popish infants is at least three to one in this kingdom, and therefore it will have one other collateral advantage by lessening the number of Papists among us.

I have already computed the charge of nursing a beggar's child (in which list 14 I reckon all cottagers, labourers, and four-fifths of the farmers) to be about two shillings *per annum*, rags included, and I believe no gentleman would repine to give ten shillings for the carcass of a good fat child, which, as I have said, will make four dishes of excellent nutritive meat, when he hath only some particular friend of his own family to dine with him. Thus the Squire will learn to be a good landlord and grow popular among his tenants, the mother will have eight shillings net profit, and be fit for work until she produces another child.

Those who are more thrifty (as I must confess the times require) may flay 15 the carcass; the skin of which artifically dressed, will make admirable gloves for ladies, and summer boots for fine gentlemen.

As to our city of Dublin, shambles[6] may be appointed for this purpose, in 16 the most convenient parts of it, and butchers we may be assured will not be wanting, although I rather recommend buying the children alive, and dressing them hot from the knife, as we do roasting pigs.

A very worthy person, a true lover of his country, and whose virtues I highly 17 esteem was lately pleased, in discoursing on this matter to offer a refinement upon my scheme. He said that many gentlemen of this kingdom, having of late destroyed their deer, he conceived that the want of venison might be well supplied by the bodies of young lads and maidens, not exceeding fourteen years of age, nor under twelve, so great a number of both sexes in every county being now ready to starve, for want of work and service: and these to be disposed of by their parents if alive, or otherwise by their nearest relations. But with due deference to so excellent a friend, and so deserving a patriot, I cannot be altogether in his sentiments. For as to the males, my American acquaintance assured me from frequent experience that their flesh was generally tough and lean, like that of our schoolboys, by continual exercise, and their taste disagreeable, and to fatten them would not answer the charge. Then as to the females, it would, I think with humble submission, be a loss to the public, because they soon would become breeders themselves: and besides, it is not improbable that some scrupulous people might be apt to censure such a practice (although indeed very unjustly) as a little bordering upon cruelty, which I confess, hath always been with me the strongest objection against any project, howsoever well intended.

But in order to justify my friend, he confessed that this expedient was put 18 into his head by the famous Psalmanazar, a native of the island Formosa, who came from thence to London, above twenty years ago, and in conversation told my friend that in his country when any young person happened to be put to

---

[6]shambles: slaughterhouses. [Eds.]

death, the executioner sold the carcass to persons of quality, as a prime dainty, and that, in his time, the body of a plump girl of fifteen, who was crucified for an attempt to poison the emperor, was sold to his Imperial Majesty's Prime Minister of State, and other great Mandarins of the Court, in joints from the gibbet, at four hundred crowns. Neither indeed can I deny that if the same use were made of several plump young girls in this town who, without one single groat to their fortunes, cannot stir abroad without a chair, and appear at the playhouse and assemblies in foreign fineries, which they never will pay for, the kingdom would not be the worse.

Some persons of a desponding spirit are in great concern about that vast   19 number of poor people, who are aged, diseased, or maimed, and I have been desired to employ my thoughts what course may be taken to ease the nation of so grievous an encumbrance. But I am not in the least pain upon that matter, because it is very well known that they are every day dying, and rotting, by cold, and famine, and filth, and vermin, as fast as can be reasonably expected. And as to the younger labourers they are now in almost as hopeful a condition. They cannot get work, and consequently pine away from want of nourishment, to a degree that if at any time they are accidentally hired to common labour, they have not strength to perform it; and thus the country and themselves are in a fair way of being soon delivered from the evils to come.

I have too long digressed, and therefore shall return to my subject. I think   20 the advantages by the proposal which I have made are obvious and many, as well as of the highest importance.

For first, as I have already observed, it would greatly lessen the number of   21 Papists, with whom we are yearly over-run, being the principal breeders of the nation, as well as our most dangerous enemies, and who stay at home on purpose with a design to deliver the kingdom to the Pretender, hoping to take their advantage by the absence of so many good Protestants, who have chosen rather to leave their country than stay at home and pay tithes against their conscience to an idolatrous Episcopal curate.

Secondly, the poorer tenants will have something valuable of their own,   22 which by law may be made liable to distress, and help to pay their landlord's rent, their corn and cattle being already seized, and money a thing unknown.

Thirdly, whereas the maintenance of an hundred thousand children, from   23 two years old, and upwards, cannot be computed at less than ten shillings a piece *per annum*, the nation's stock will be thereby increased fifty thousand pounds *per annum*, besides the profit of a new dish, introduced to the tables of all gentlemen of fortune in the kingdom, who have any refinement in taste, and the money will circulate among ourselves, the goods being entirely of our own growth and manufacture.

Fourthly, the constant breeders, besides the gain of eight shillings sterling   24 *per annum*, by the sale of their children, will be rid of the charge of maintaining them after the first year.

Fifthly, this food would likewise bring great custom to taverns, where the   25
vintners will certainly be so prudent as to procure the best receipts for dressing
it to perfection, and consequently have their houses frequented by all the fine
gentlemen, who justly value themselves upon their knowledge in good eating;
and a skilful cook, who understands how to oblige his guests, will contrive to
make it as expensive as they please.

Sixthly, this would be a great inducement to marriage, which all wise nations   26
have either encouraged by rewards, or enforced by laws and penalties. It would
increase the care and tenderness of mothers towards their children, when they
were sure of a settlement for life, to the poor babes, provided in some sort by
the public to their annual profit instead of expense. We should soon see an
honest emulation among the married women, which of them could bring the
fattest child to the market. Men would become as fond of their wives, during
the time of their pregnancy, as they are now of their mares in foal, their cows
in calf, or sows when they are ready to farrow, nor offer to beat or kick them
(as it is too frequent a practice) for fear of a miscarriage.

Many other advantages might be enumerated. For instance, the addition of   27
some thousand carcasses in our exportation of barrelled beef; the propagation of
swine's flesh, and improvement in the art of making good bacon, so much
wanted among us by the great destruction of pigs, too frequent at our tables,
are no way comparable in taste or magnificence to a well-grown, fat yearling
child, which roasted whole will make a considerable figure at a Lord Mayor's
feast, or any other public entertainment. But this and many others I omit, being
studious of brevity.

Supposing that one thousand families in this city would be constant cus-   28
tomers for infants' flesh, besides others who might have it at merry meetings,
particularly weddings and christenings; I compute that Dublin would take off
annually about twenty thousand carcasses, and the rest of the kingdom (where
probably they will be sold somewhat cheaper) the remaining eighty thousand.

I can think of no one objection that will possibly be raised against this   29
proposal, unless it should be urged that the number of people will be thereby
much lessened in the kingdom. This I freely own, and it was indeed one principal design in offering it to the world. I desire the reader will observe, that I
calculate my remedy *for this one individual Kingdom of* Ireland, *and for no
other that ever was, is, or, I think, ever can be upon earth.* Therefore let no
man talk to me of other expedients: *Of taxing our absentees at five shillings a
pound: Of using neither clothes, nor household furniture, except what is of our
own growth and manufacture: Of utterly rejecting the materials and instruments
that promote foreign luxury: Of curing the expensiveness of pride, vanity, idleness, and gaming in our women: Of introducing a vein of parsimony, prudence,
and temperance: Of learning to love our country, wherein we differ even from*
Laplanders, *and the inhabitants of* Topinamboo: *Of quitting our animosities*

and factions, nor act any longer like the Jews, *who were murdering one another at the very moment their city was taken: Of being a little cautious not to sell our country and consciences for nothing: Of teaching landlords to have at least one degree of mercy towards their tenants.* Lastly, *of putting a spirit of honesty, industry, and skill into our shopkeepers, who, if a resolution could now be taken to buy only our native goods, would immediately unite to cheat and exact upon us in the price, the measure and the goodness, nor could ever yet be brought to make one fair proposal of just dealing, though often and earnestly invited to it.*

Therefore I repeat, let no man talk to me of these and the like expedients, till he hath at least a glimpse of hope that there will ever be some hearty and sincere attempt to put them in practice.   30

But as to myself, having been wearied out for many years with offering vain, idle, visionary thoughts, and at length utterly despairing of success, I fortunately fell upon this proposal, which as it is wholly new, so it hath something solid and real, of no expense and little trouble, full in our own power, and whereby we can incur no danger in disobliging England. For this kind of commodity will not bear exportation, the flesh being of too tender a consistence to admit a long continuance in salt, *although perhaps I could name a country which would be glad to eat up our whole nation without it.*   31

After all I am not so violently bent upon my own opinion as to reject any offer, proposed by wise men, which shall be found equally innocent, cheap, easy and effectual. But before some thing of that kind shall be advanced in contradiction to my scheme, and offering a better, I desire the author, or authors, will be pleased maturely to consider two points. First, as things now stand, how they will be able to find food and raiment for a hundred thousand useless mouths and backs? And secondly, there being a round million of creatures in human figure, throughout this kingdom, whose whole subsistence put into a common stock would leave them in debt two millions of pounds sterling; adding those who are beggars by profession, to the bulk of farmers, cottagers, and laborers with their wives and children, who are beggars in effect; I desire those politicians who dislike my overture, and may perhaps be so bold to attempt an answer, that they will first ask the parents of these mortals whether they would not at this day think it a great happiness to have been sold for food at a year old, in the manner I prescribe, and thereby have avoided such a perpetual scene of misfortunes as they have since gone through, by the oppression of landlords, the impossibility of paying rent without money or trade, the want of common sustenance, with neither house nor clothes to cover them from the inclemencies of weather, and the most inevitable prospect of entailing the like, or greater miseries upon their breed for ever.   32

I profess in the sincerity of my heart that I have not the least personal interest in endeavoring to promote this necessary work, having no other motive than the *public good of my country, by advancing our trade, providing for infants,*   33

Jonathan Swift

relieving the poor, and giving some pleasure to the rich. I have no children by which I can propose to get a single penny; the youngest being nine years old, and my wife past child-bearing.

QUESTIONS

1. A proposal always involves a proposer. What is the character of the proposer here? Do we perceive his character to be the same throughout the essay? Compare, for example, paragraphs 21, 26, and 33.

2. When does the proposer actually offer his proposal? What does he do before making his proposal? What does he do after making his proposal? How does the order in which he does things affect our impression of him and of his proposal?

3. What kind of counterarguments to his own proposal does this proposer anticipate? How does he answer and refute proposals that might be considered alternatives to his?

4. In reading this essay, most persons are quite certain that the author, Swift, does not himself endorse the proposer's proposal. How do we distinguish the two of them? What details of style help us make this distinction?

5. Consider the proposer, the counterarguments the proposer acknowledges and refutes, and Swift himself, who presumably does not endorse the proposer's proposal. To what extent is Swift's position essentially that which his proposer refutes? To what extent is it a somewhat different position still?

6. To what extent does an ironic essay like this depend upon the author and reader sharing certain values without question or reservation? Can you discover any such values explicitly or implicitly present in Swift's essay?

7. Use Swift's technique to write a "modest proposal" of your own about some contemporary situation. That is, use some outlandish proposal as a way of drawing attention to a situation that needs correcting. Consider carefully the character you intend to project for your proposer and the way you intend to make your own view distinguishable from hers or his.

THE DECLARATION OF INDEPENDENCE
Thomas Jefferson

Thomas Jefferson (1743–1826) was born in Shadwell, Virginia, attended William and Mary College, and became a lawyer. He was elected to the Virginia House of Burgesses in 1789 and was a delegate to the Continental Congress in 1776. When the Congress voted in favor of Richard Henry Lee's resolution that the colonies "ought to be free and independent states," a committee of five members, including John Adams, Benjamin Franklin, and Jefferson, was appointed to draw up a declaration. Jefferson, because of his eloquence as a writer, was asked by this committee to draw up a first draft. Jefferson's text, with a few changes suggested by Franklin and Adams, was presented to the Congress. After a debate in which further changes were made, including striking out a passage condemning the slave trade, the Declaration was approved on the fourth of July, 1776. Jefferson said of it that, "Neither aiming at originality of principles or sentiments, nor yet copied from any particular and previous writing, it was intended to be an expression of the American mind."

In Congress, July 4, 1776
*The unanimous Declaration of the
thirteen united States of America*

When in the Course of human events it becomes necessary for one people   1
to dissolve the political bands which have connected them with another, and to assume among the powers of the earth, the separate and equal station to which the Laws of Nature and of Nature's God entitle them, a decent respect to the opinions of mankind requires that they should declare the causes which impel them to the separation.

We hold these truths to be self-evident, that all men are created equal, that   2
they are endowed by their Creator with certain unalienable Rights, that among these are Life, Liberty and the pursuit of Happiness. That to secure these rights, Governments are instituted among Men, deriving their just powers from the consent of the governed, That whenever any Form of Government becomes destructive of these ends, it is the Right of the People to alter or to abolish it,

and to institute new Government, laying its foundation on such principles and organizing its powers in such form, as to them shall seem most likely to affect their Safety and Happiness. Prudence, indeed, will dictate that Governments long established should not be changed for light and transient causes; and accordingly all experience hath shewn that mankind are more disposed to suffer, while evils are sufferable, than to right themselves by abolishing the forms to which they are accustomed. But when a long train of abuses and usurpations, pursuing invariably the same Object evinces a design to reduce them under absolute Depotism, it is their right, it is their duty, to throw off such Government, and to provide new Guards for their future security. Such has been the patient sufferance of these Colonies; and such is now the necessity which constrains them to alter their former Systems of Government. The history of the present King of Great Britain is a history of repeated injuries and usurpations, all having in direct object the establishment of an absolute Tyranny over these States. To prove this, let Facts be submitted to a candid world.

He has refused his Assent to Laws, the most wholesome and necessary for the public good. 3

He has forbidden his Governors to pass laws of immediate and pressing importance, unless suspended in their operation till his Assent should be obtained; and when so suspended, he has utterly neglected to attend to them. 4

He has refused to pass other Laws for the accommodation of large districts of people, unless those people would relinquish the right of Representation in the Legislature, a right inestimable to them and formidable to tyrants only. 5

He has called together legislative bodies at places unusual, uncomfortable, and distant from the depository of their Public Records, for the sole purpose of fatiguing them into compliance with his measures. 6

He has dissolved Representative Houses repeatedly, for opposing with manly firmness his invasions on the rights of the people. 7

He has refused for a long time, after such dissolutions, to cause others to be elected; whereby the Legislative Powers, incapable of Annihilation, have returned to the People at large for their exercise; the State remaining in the mean time exposed to all the dangers of invasion from without, and convulsions within. 8

He has endeavored to prevent the population of these States; for that purpose obstructing the Laws for Naturalization of Foreigners; refusing to pass others to encourage their migration hither, and raising the conditions of new Appropriations of Lands. 9

He has obstructed the Administration of Justice, by refusing his Assent to Laws for Establishing Judiciary Powers. 10

He has made Judges dependent on his Will alone, for the tenure of their offices, and the amount and payment of their salaries. 11

He has erected a multitude of New Offices, and sent hither swarms of Officers to harass our people, and eat out their substance. 12

He has kept among us, in times of peace, Standing Armies without the 13
Consent of our legislatures.

He has affected to render the Military independent of and superior to the 14
Civil Power.

He has combined with others to subject us to a jurisdiction foreign to our 15
constitution, and unacknowledged by our laws; giving his Assent to the Acts of
pretended Legislation: For quartering large bodies of armed troops among us:
For protecting them, by a mock Trial, from punishment for any Murders which
they should commit on the Inhabitants of these States: For cutting off our Trade
with all parts of the world: For imposing Taxes on us without our Consent: For
depriving us in many cases, of the benefits of Trial by Jury; For Transporting
us beyond Seas to be tried for pretended offenses: for abolishing the free System
of English Laws in a neighboring Province, establishing therein an Arbitrary
government, and enlarging its Boundaries so as to render it at once an example
and fit instrument for introducing the same absolute rule into these Colonies:
For taking away our Charters, abolishing our most valuable Laws and altering
fundamentally the Forms of our Governments: For suspending our own Legislatures, and declaring themselves invested with power to legislate for us in all
cases whatsoever.

He has abdicated Government here, by declaring us out of his Protection 16
and waging War against us.

He has plundered our seas, ravaged our Coasts, burnt our towns, and de- 17
stroyed the lives of our people.

He is at this time transporting large Armies of foreign Mercenaries to com- 18
plete the works of death, desolation and tyranny, already begun with circumstances of Cruelty & Perfidy scarcely paralleled in the most barbarous ages, and
totally unworthy the Head of a civilized nation.

He has constrained our fellow Citizens taken Captive on the high Seas to 19
bear Arms against their Country, to become the executioners of their friends
and Brethren, or to fall themselves by their Hands.

He has excited domestic insurrections amongst us, and has endeavored to 20
bring on the inhabitants of our frontiers, the merciless Indian Savages, whose
known rule of warfare, is an undistingushed destruction of all ages, sexes, and
conditions.

In every stage of these Oppressions We have Petitioned for Redress in the 21
most humble terms: Our repeated petitions have been answered only by repeated
injury. A Prince, whose character is thus marked by every act which may define
a Tyrant, is unfit to be the ruler of a free people.

Nor have We been wanting in attention to our British brethren. We have 22
warned them from time to time of attempts by their legislature to extend an
unwarrantable jurisdiction over us. We have reminded them of the circumstances of our emigration and settlement here. We have appealed to their native
justice and magnanimity, and we have conjured them by the ties of our common

Thomas Jefferson

kindred to disavow these usurpations, which would inevitably interrupt our connections and correspondence. They too have been deaf to the voice of justice and of consanguinity. We must, therefore, acquiesce in the necessity, which denounces our Separation, and hold them, as we hold the rest of mankind, Enemies in War, in Peace Friends.

We, THEREFORE, the Representatives of the UNITED STATES OF AMERICA,   23
in General Congress, Assembled, appealing to the Supreme Judge of the world for the rectitude of our intentions, do, in the Name, and by Authority of the good People of these Colonies, solemnly publish and declare, That these United Colonies are, and of Right ought to be FREE AND INDEPENDENT STATES; that they are Absolved from all Allegiance to the British Crown, and that all political connection between them and the State of Great Britain, is and ought to be totally dissolved; and that as Free and Independent States, they have full Power to levy War, conclude Peace, contract Alliances, establish Commerce, and to do all other Acts and Things which Independent States may of right do. And for the support of this Declaration, with a firm reliance on the protection of Divine Providence, we mutually pledge to each other our Lives, our Fortunes, and our sacred Honor.

QUESTIONS

1. The Declaration of Independence is frequently cited as a classic deductive argument. A deductive argument is based on a general statement, or premise, that is assumed to be true. What does this document assume that the American colonists are entitled to and on what basis? Look at the reasoning in paragraph 2. What are these truths that are considered self-evident? What does *self-evident* mean?

2. What accusations against the king of Great Britain are the facts presented meant to substantiate? If you were the British king presented with this document, how might you reply to it? Would you first attack its premise or reply to its accusations? Or would you do both? (How did George III respond anyway?)

3. To what extent is the audience of the Declaration intended to be the king and people of Great Britain?

4. What other audiences were intended for this document? Define at least two other audiences, and describe how each might be expected to respond.

5. Although this declaration could have been expected to lead to war and all the horrors thereof, it is a most civilized document, showing great respect throughout for certain standards of civility among people and among nations. Try to define the civilized standards the declaration assumes. Write an essay that tries to identify and characterize the nature and variety of those expectations.

6. Write a declaration of your own, announcing your separation from some injurious situation (an uncompatible roommate, a noisy sorority or fraternity house, an awful job, or whatever). Start with a premise, give reasons to substantiate it, provide facts that illustrate the injurious conditions, and conclude with a statement of what your new condition will mean to you and to other oppressed people.

Sciences and
Technologies

THE ART OF
TEACHING SCIENCE
Lewis Thomas

*Lewis Thomas (b. 1913), a graduate of the Harvard Medical
School, is chancellor of Memorial Sloan-Kettering Cancer
Center in New York City and chairman of the board of the
Scientists' Institute for Public Information. He has won both
the National Book Award and the American Book Award
for his collections of essays,* The Lives of a Cell *(1974) and*
The Medusa and the Snail *(1979). This piece, which was
given as a talk at a conference sponsored by the Alfred P.
Sloan Foundation, appeared in the* New York Times Mag-
azine *in 1982.*

Everyone seems to agree that there is something wrong with the way science   1
is being taught these days. But no one is at all clear about when it went wrong
or what is to be done about it. The term "scientific illiteracy" has become
almost a cliché in educational circles. Graduate schools blame the colleges;
colleges blame the secondary schools; the high schools blame the elementary
schools, which, in turn, blame the family.

I suggest that the scientific community itself is partly, perhaps largely, to   2
blame. Moreover, if there are disagreements between the world of the humanities and the scientific enterprise as to the place and importance of science in a
liberal-arts education and the role of science in 20th-century culture, I believe

that the scientists are themselves responsible for a general misunderstanding of what they are really up to.

During the last half-century, we have been teaching the sciences as though they were the same collection of academic subjects as always, and—here is what has really gone wrong—as though they would always be the same. Students learn today's biology, for example, the same way we learned Latin when I was in high school long ago: first, the fundamentals; then, the underlying laws; next, the essential grammar and, finally, the reading of texts. Once mastered, that was that: Latin was Latin and forever after would always be Latin. History, once learned, was history. And biology was precisely biology, a vast array of hard facts to be learned as fundamentals, followed by a reading of the texts.

Furthermore, we have been teaching science as if its facts were somehow superior to the facts in all other scholarly disciplines—more fundamental, more solid, less subject to subjectivism, immutable. English literature is not just one way of thinking; it is all sorts of ways; poetry is a moving target; the facts that underlie art, architecture and music are not really hard facts, and you can change them any way you like by arguing about them. But science, it appears, is an altogether different kind of learning: an unambiguous, unalterable and endlessly useful display of data that only needs to be packaged and installed somewhere in one's temporal lobe in order to achieve a full understanding of the natural world.

And, of course, it is not like this at all. In real life, every field of science is incomplete, and most of them—whatever the record of accomplishment during the last 200 years—are still in their very earliest stages. In the fields I know best, among the life sciences, it is required that the most expert and sophisticated minds be capable of changing course—often with a great lurch—every few years. In some branches of biology the mind-changing is occurring with accelerating velocity. Next week's issue of any scientific journal can turn a whole field upside down, shaking out any number of immutable ideas and installing new bodies of dogma. This is an almost everyday event in physics, in chemistry, in materials research, in neurobiology, in genetics, in immunology.

On any Tuesday morning, if asked, a good working scientist will tell you with some self-satisfaction that the affairs of his field are nicely in order, that things are finally looking clear and making sense, and all is well. But come back again on another Tuesday, and the roof may have just fallen in on his life's work. All the old ideas—last week's ideas in some cases—are no longer good ideas. The hard facts have softened, melted away and vanished under the pressure of new hard facts. Something strange has happened. And it is this very strangeness of nature that makes science engrossing, that keeps bright people at it, and that ought to be at the center of science teaching.

The conclusions reached in science are always, when looked at closely, far more provisional and tentative than are most of the assumptions arrived at by our colleagues in the humanities. But we do not talk much in public about this, nor do we teach this side of science. We tend to say instead: These are the facts of the matter, and this is what the facts signify. Go and learn them, for they will be the same forever.

By doing this, we miss opportunity after opportunity to recruit young people 8 into science, and we turn off a good many others who would never dream of scientific careers but who emerge from their education with the impression that science is fundamentally boring.

Sooner or later, we will have to change this way of presenting science. We 9 might begin by looking more closely at the common ground that science shares with all disciplines, particularly with the humanities and with social and be-havioral science. For there is indeed such a common ground. It is called be-wilderment. There are more than seven times seven types of ambiguity in sci-ence, all awaiting analysis. The poetry of Wallace Stevens is crystal clear alongside the genetic code.

One of the complaints about science is that it tends to flatten everything. In 10 its deeply reductionist way, it is said, science removes one mystery after another, leaving nothing in the place of mystery but data. I have even heard this claim as explanation for the drift of things in modern art and modern music: Nothing is left to contemplate except randomness and senselessness; God is nothing but a pair of dice, loaded at that. Science is linked somehow to the despair of the 20th-century mind. There is almost nothing unknown and surely nothing un-knowable. Blame science.

I prefer to turn things around in order to make precisely the opposite case. 11 Science, especially 20th-century science, has provided us with a glimpse of something we never really knew before, the revelation of human ignorance. We have been accustomed to the belief, from one century to another, that except for one or two mysteries we more or less comprehend everything on earth. Every age, not just the 18th century, regarded itself as the Age of Reason, and we have never lacked for explanations of the world and its ways. Now, we are being brought up short. We do not understand much of anything, from the episode we rather dismissively (and, I think, defensively) choose to call the "big bang," all the way down to the particles in the atoms of a bacterial cell. We have a wilderness of mystery to make our way through in the centuries ahead. We will need science for this but not science alone. In its own time, science will produce the data and some of the meaning in the data, but never the full meaning. For perceiving real significance when significance is at hand, we will need all sorts of brains outside the fields of science.

It is primarily because of this need that I would press for changes in the way 12 science is taught. Although there is a perennial need to teach the young people who will be doing the science themselves, this will always be a small minority. Even more important, we must teach science to those who will be needed for thinking about it, and that means pretty nearly everyone else—most of all, the poets, but also artists, musicians, philosophers, historians and writers. A few of these people, at least, will be able to imagine new levels of meaning which may be lost on the rest of us.

In addition, it is time to develop a new group of professional thinkers, perhaps 13 a somewhat larger group than the working scientists and the working poets, who can create a discipline of scientific criticism. We have had good luck so far in the emergence of a few people ranking as philosophers of science and historians and journalists of science, and I hope more of these will be coming along. But we have not yet seen specialists in the fields of scientific criticism who are of the caliber of the English literary and social critics F. R. Leavis and John Ruskin or the American literary critic Edmund Wilson. Science needs critics of this sort, but the public at large needs them more urgently.

I suggest that the introductory courses in science, at all levels from grade 14 school through college, be radically revised. Leave the fundamentals, the so-called basics, aside for a while, and concentrate the attention of all students on the things that are not known. You cannot possibly teach quantum mechanics without mathematics, to be sure, but you can describe the strangeness of the world opened up by quantum theory. Let it be known, early on, that there are deep mysteries and profound paradoxes revealed in distant outline by modern physics. Explain that these can be approached more closely and puzzled over, once the language of mathematics has been sufficiently mastered.

At the outset, before any of the fundamentals, teach the still imponderable 15 puzzles of cosmology. Describe as clearly as possible, for the youngest minds, that there are some things going on in the universe that lie still beyond comprehension, and make it plain how little is known.

Do not teach that biology is a useful and perhaps profitable science; that can 16 come later. Teach instead that there are structures squirming inside each of our cells that provide all the energy for living. Essentially foreign creatures, these lineal descendants of bacteria were brought in for symbiotic living a billion or so years ago. Teach that we do not have the ghost of an idea how they got there, where they came from, or how they evolved to their present structure and function. The details of oxidative phosphorylation and photosynthesis can come later.

Teach ecology early on. Let it be understood that the earth's life is a system 17 of interdependent creatures, and that we do not understand at all how it works. The earth's environment, from the range of atmospheric gases to the chemical constituents of the sea, has been held in an almost unbelievably improbable state of regulated balance since life began, and the regulation of stability and balance is somehow accomplished by the life itself, like the autonomic nervous system of an immense organism. We do not know how such a system works, much less what it means, but there are some nice reductionist details at hand, such as the bizarre proportions of atmospheric constituents, ideal for our sort of planetary life, and the surprising stability of the ocean's salinity, and the fact that the average temperature of the earth has remained quite steady in the face of at least a 25 percent increase in heat coming in from the sun since the earth began. That kind of thing: something to think about.

Go easy, I suggest, on the promises sometimes freely offered by science. 18 Technology relies and depends on science these days, more than ever before, but technology is far from the first justification for doing research, nor is it necessarily an essential product to be expected from science. Public decisions about the future of technology are totally different from decisions about science, and the two enterprises should not be tangled together. The central task of science is to arrive, stage by stage, at a clearer comprehension of nature, but this does not at all mean, as it is sometimes claimed to mean, a search for mastery over nature.

Science may someday provide us with a better understanding of ourselves, 19 but never, I hope, with a set of technologies for doing something or other to improve ourselves. I am made nervous by assertions that human consciousness will someday be unraveled by research, laid out for close scrutiny like the workings of a computer, and then—and *then* . . . ! I hope with some fervor that we can learn a lot more than we now know about the human mind, and I see no reason why this strange puzzle should remain forever and entirely beyond us. But I would be deeply disturbed by any prospect that we might use the new knowledge in order to begin doing something about it—to improve it, say. This is a different matter from searching for information to use against schizophrenia or dementia, where we are badly in need of technologies, indeed likely one day to be sunk without them. But the ordinary, everyday, more or less normal human mind is too marvelous an instrument ever to be tampered with by anyone, science or no science.

The education of humanists cannot be regarded as complete, or even ade- 20 quate, without exposure in some depth to where things stand in the various branches of science, particularly, as I have said, in the areas of our ignorance. Physics professors, most of them, look with revulsion on assignments to teach their subject to poets. Biologists, caught up by the enchantment of their new power, armed with flawless instruments to tell the nucleotide sequences of the entire human genome, nearly matching the physicists in the precision of their measurements of living processes, will resist the prospect of broad survey courses; each biology professor will demand that any student in his path master every fine detail within that professor's research program.

The liberal-arts faculties, for their part, will continue to view the scientists 21 with suspicion and apprehension. "What do the scientists want?" asked a Cambridge professor in Francis Cornford's wonderful "Microcosmographia Academica." "Everything that's going," was the quick answer. That was back in 1912, and scientists haven't much changed.

But maybe, just maybe, a new set of courses dealing systematically with 22 ignorance in science will take hold. The scientists might discover in it a new and subversive technique for catching the attention of students driven by curiosity, delighted and surprised to learn that science is exactly as the American scientist and educator Vannevar Bush described it: an "endless frontier." The humanists, for their part, might take considerable satisfaction in watching their scientific colleagues confess openly to not knowing everything about everything. And the poets, on whose shoulders the future rests, might, late nights, thinking things over, begin to see some meanings that elude the rest of us. It is worth a try.

I believe that the worst thing that has happened to science education is that 23 the fun has gone out of it. A great many good students look at it as slogging work to be got through on the way to medical school. Others are turned off by the premedical students themselves, embattled and bleeding for grades and class standing. Very few recognize science as the high adventure it really is, the wildest of all explorations ever taken by human beings, the chance to glimpse things never seen before, the shrewdest maneuver for discovering how the world works. Instead, baffled early on, they are misled into thinking that bafflement is simply the result of not having learned all the facts. They should be told that everyone else is baffled as well—from the professor in his endowed chair down to the platoons of postdoctoral students in the laboratories all night. Every important scientific advance that has come in looking like an answer has turned, sooner or later—usually sooner—into a question. And the game is just beginning.

If more students were aware of this, I think many of them would decide to 24 look more closely and to try and learn more about what *is* known. That is the time when mathematics will become clearly and unavoidably recognizable as an essential, indispensable instrument for engaging in the game, and that is the time for teaching it. The calamitous loss of applied mathematics from what we might otherwise be calling higher education is a loss caused, at least in part, by insufficient incentives for learning the subject. Left by itself, standing there among curriculum offerings, it is not at all clear to the student what it is to be applied to. And there is all of science, next door, looking like an almost-finished field reserved only for chaps who want to invent or apply new technologies. We have had it wrong, and presented it wrong to class after class for several generations.

An appreciation of what is happening in science today, and how great a 25 distance lies ahead for exploring, ought to be one of the rewards of a liberal-arts education. It ought to be good in itself, not something to be acquired on the way to a professional career but part of the cast of thought needed for getting into the kind of century that is now just down the road. Part of the intellectual equipment of an educated person, however his or her time is to be spent, ought to be a feel for the queernesses of nature, the inexplicable thing, the side of life for which informed bewilderment will be the best way of getting through the day.

QUESTIONS

1. What is the thesis of Thomas's argument? What parts of the essay present evidence to support it? What parts of the essay offer alternatives to present methods of teaching science? Do you think Thomas presents valid reasons for adopting these alternatives?

2. In Thomas's view, what is wrong with the way science is taught now? What suggestions does he offer for the improvement of science teaching?

3. What does Thomas mean by giving poets responsibility for the future (paragraph 22)? Can he be serious? Or is this a rhetorical trick of some kind?

4. What would it take to be the kind of critic of science that Thomas mentions in paragraph 13?

5. Who is Thomas's audience? What is his attitude toward his audience?

6. Thomas concludes by saying, "Part of the intellectual equipment of an educated person . . . ought to be a feel for the queernesses of nature, the inexplicable thing, the side of life for which informed bewilderment will be the best way of getting through the day." What does he mean by "informed bewilderment"? How does one develop that?

7. What points made by Thomas apply to your experience in science courses you elected or were required to take? Drawing on your own experience and those points in the essay which are relevant to it, or those points you wish to take issue with, write a letter to a friend who is to attend your college, and present an agrument either for or against taking a particular science course.

8. If Lewis Thomas were teaching a biology course at your school next semester, would you take it? Give reasons.

MISLEADING MYTHS ABOUT COMPUTERS
Bertram Raphael

Born in New York in 1936, Bertram Raphael has degrees from Rensselaer Polytechnic Institute, Brown University, and MIT. He has published over twenty scientific articles and reviews, has been editor of Artificial Intelligence *and a patrol leader of the Sierra Club Ski Patrol. He is currently Director of the Artificial Intelligence Center of the Stanford Research Institute. The selection that follows here is from the opening chapter of his book,* The Thinking Computer.

Many people share the belief that computers are inherently stupid, and that [1] even a suggestion that computers might be made smarter is ridiculous. This belief is so widespread that most people—scientists as well as laymen—never even consider the many ways in which smarter computers might help them. Misconceptions about a computer's limitations seem to be based upon two widely accepted but basically untrue premises. Let us examine these myths in turn. By pointing out some of their fallacies, perhaps I can open your mind to the fascinating prospects for smarter computers.

THE ARITHMETIC MYTH. *A computer is nothing but a big fast arithmetic machine.*

This myth seems to be based upon the following erroneous reasoning. [2]

1. Computers were originally needed to do the kinds of large arithmetic calculations that arose in the tasks of aiming ballistic weapons and of producing approximate solutions to equations of nuclear physics. [True.]
2. Therefore, the designers of computers intended them to be only big, fast arithmetic calculating machines. [Doubtful. The basic design and operations of computers are much more general, as we shall see below.]
3. Therefore, computers are nothing but big fast arithmetic machines. [False! Although the intentions of the original designers of computers are subject to wide interpretation,[1] when we study the capabilities of today's machines objectively we find much more powerful, more flexible systems.]

---

[1] I am reminded of the story of the little old lady who walked up to Wernher von Braun, the rocket expert, at the end of his lecture and asked, "Dr. von Braun, why do people want to fly to the moon? Why don't they sit home and watch television, like the good Lord intended?"

Computers are arithmetic machines, certainly; virtually every computer has   3
wired into it the ability to add and subtract. But are they "nothing but" arithmetic machines? Certainly not. Take the reference manual for any computer,
and scan through its "instruction set": the collection of basic operations it has
been designed and wired to perform. You will see a few, perhaps as many as
ten or twenty, operations that bear some close resemblance to arithmetic—e.g.,
ADD, DIVIDE, FLOATING SUBTRACT, MULTIPLY STEP, and so on—
but you will also see many, perhaps one or two hundred, operations that have
relatively little to do with arithmetic—e.g., STORE, LOAD, TEST, SHIFT,
READ, WRITE, REWIND TAPE, SKIP, MOVE, MASK, MATCH,
TRANSFER, and so on.

To see why computers must be able to perform so many nonarithmetic   4
operations, consider as an example the simple task of preparing the pay checks
for a business firm. This is a common job for a computer. But is it a job for a
"big fast arithmetic machine"? If a human accountant did the job, he might sit
down with the record books, time cards, check forms, and a small calculating
machine. In a simple case, he would use the machine to multiply each employee's hourly salary by the number of hours the employee had worked and
write the answer on a check.

Now suppose we want a computer to do a similar job. What *program*—   5
sequence of elementary operations—must we give it? The program will have to
do everything that both the accountant and his calculating machine did when
the job was done by hand. True, the computer will have to do an occasional
MULTIPLY operation, just as the calculator did; but it will also be very busy
doing all the things the accountant did: looking up an employee's name, looking
up his hourly salary, noting the salary in a convenient place, checking whether
the employee was listed as away on vacation or sick leave and if he was not
then looking for the record of his time card, finding where the total hours worked
was noted, copying that total in a convenient place, supervising the MULTIPLY
calculation, finding and positioning the next blank check (if the book of blank
checks is empty then starting another book), copying the employee's name onto
the check, dating the check, copying the calculated pay onto the check, im-
printing a facsimile of a signature on the check, and moving the check to the
"done" pile. Even in this trivial job a computer would have to spend almost all
its effort doing what a man would do, and very little doing what a calculator
would do.

Almost all the time that a computer works on the problem just described,   6
and in fact much of the time that any computer works on any problem, the
computer is positioning, comparing, moving, choosing, copying . . . , but it is
not doing arithmetic. Rather than calling a computer "nothing but a big fast
arithmetic machine," it is much more accurate to say that a computer is *a big,
fast, general-purpose symbol-manipulating machine*. With this definition as a

Bertram Raphael

foundation, we can progress in later chapters to an appreciation of how it is possible to develop flexible, decision-making, problem-solving, perceiving computers—in short, smart computers.

THE STUPID COMPUTER MYTH. *A computer is an obedient intellectual slave that can do only what it is told to do.*

This second myth is even more persistent than the first one, and even more [7] damaging in the way it tends to constrain our thinking. Suppose I gave you the pieces of a jigsaw puzzle and told you, "by the way, these pieces cannot be fit together." Would you try very hard to fit the pieces together? Why should anyone try to build a smart computer, if he is told over and over again that computers are inherently stupid?

The stupid-computer myth has been repeated and generally accepted for [8] more than a hundred years. In 1842, after Professor Babbage of Cambridge designed his Analytical Engine, a large-scale mechanical digital computer (which unfortunately was never completed), his friend Lady Lovelace wrote,[2] "The Analytical Engine has no pretensions to *originate* anything. It can do *whatever we know how to order* it to perform." There is no question that Lady Lovelace's argument, and all the subsequent versions of the stupid-computer myth, are true, in a certain literal sense: a computer must be given its program of instructions, and it will always do exactly what those instructions tell it to do (unless, of course, one of its circuits fails). And yet this basic truth is not a real restriction on the intelligence of computers at all.

A couple of examples will resolve this paradox. One of the first scientists to [9] challenge the stupid-computer myth was A. L. Samuel of IBM. In 1961, he developed a program to make a computer play checkers. After practicing by playing against itself for a while on the new computers in the basement of an IBM manufacturing plant, the program could consistently beat Samuel, its creator. How was this possible? Samuel had figured out how to order the computer to learn to play a better game. . . .

In 1969, "Shakey," a computer-controlled robot at Stanford Research Insti- [10] tute, could find its way from room to room, avoiding or rearranging obstacles according to general instructions such as "Block Door 3 with Box 5," even though its program had never before considered that particular task or that particular arrangement of obstacles. How? Shakey's designers had figured out how to program a robot to find its own way around and to solve, for itself, a wide class of problems. . . .

The claim that a computer "can only do what it is told to do" does not mean [11] that computers must be stupid; rather, it clarifies the challenge of how to make computers smarter; we must figure out how to tell (i.e., program) a computer

---

[2]Lady Lovelace (1814–1852): the daughter of Lord Byron; keenly interested in mathematics, she tried to promote interest in the Analytical Engine among members of the scientific establishment. [Eds.]

to be smarter. Can we tell a computer how to learn? To create? To invent? Why not? I'd bet even Lady Lovelace would have agreed that the task of figuring out "how to order" a computer "to originate" something would be a fascinating and meaningful research challenge.

QUESTIONS

1. What is the general position against which Raphael argues?

2. What is the arithmetic myth? How does Raphael answer it? Are you satisfied with the answer? Does his answer lead convincingly to his revised definition of a computer in paragraph 6?

3. What is the stupid-computer myth? How does Raphael answer it?

4. Devise a sequence of questions or instructions that would lead a computer to learn something, to get smarter. What kind of instructions would those have to be?

5. Describe whatever experience you have had with a computer. What is your sense of that computer's intelligence and of yours in relation to it? Did you see any evidence that it was getting smarter? Were you, as you worked with it, getting smarter in relation to it?

6. Could a computer be called a person, ever, under any circumstances? Take one side or the other of this question and present the strongest argument you can to prove your case. Obviously you will have to define "person" to do this, and you will have to consider what being a person involves. Whichever side you take, try to anticipate the main points on the opposite side of the argument and deal with them.

EVOLUTION AS FACT AND THEORY
Stephen Jay Gould

Born in 1941 in New York City, Stephen Jay Gould has degrees from Antioch College and Columbia University. For the past fifteen years he has been teaching geology at Harvard University, but he is best known for his monthly column in Natural History *magazine, which has a wide readership. The author of over a hundred scientific articles, he has recently collected some of his more popular writings in* The Panda's Thumb *(1980). The essay reprinted here appeared first in* Discover *magazine, a journal of popular science, in 1981.*

Kirtley Mather, who died last year at age 89, was a pillar of both science and 1 the Christian religion in America and one of my dearest friends. The difference of half a century in our ages evaporated before our common interests. The most curious thing we shared was a battle we each fought at the same age. For Kirtley had gone to Tennessee with Clarence Darrow to testify for evolution at the Scopes trial of 1925. When I think that we are enmeshed again in the same struggle for one of the best documented, most compelling and exciting concepts in all of science, I don't know whether to laugh or cry.

According to idealized principles of scientific discourse, the arousal of dor- 2 mant issues should reflect fresh data that give renewed life to abandoned notions. Those outside the current debate may therefore be excused for suspecting that creationists have come up with something new, or that evolutionists have generated some serious internal trouble. But nothing has changed; the creationists have not a single new fact or argument. Darrow and Bryan were at least more entertaining than we lesser antagonists today.[1] The rise of creationism is politics, pure and simple; it represents one issue (and by no means the major concern) of the resurgent evangelical right. Arguments that seemed kooky just a decade ago have re-entered the mainstream.

CREATIONISM IS NOT SCIENCE

The basic attack of the creationists falls apart on two general counts before 3

---

[1]Darrow and Bryan: Clarence Darrow (1857–1938) was the defense attorney in the 1925 trial of John Thomas Scopes for teaching evolution; William Jennings Bryan (1860–1925), was an orator and politician who aided the prosecution in the Scopes trial. (See "The End of the Scopes Trial" in Reporting.) [Eds.]

we even reach the supposed factual details of their complaints against evolution. First, they play upon a vernacular misunderstanding of the word "theory" to convey the false impression that we evolutionists are covering up the rotten core of our edifice. Second, they misuse a popular philosophy of science to argue that they are behaving scientifically in attacking evolution. Yet the same philosophy demonstrates that their own belief is not science, and that "scientific creationism" is therefore meaningless and self-contradictory, a superb example of what Orwell[2] called "newspeak."[3]

In the American vernacular, "theory" often means "imperfect fact"—part of   4 a hierarchy of confidence running downhill from fact to theory to hypothesis to guess. Thus the power of the creationist argument: evolution is "only" a theory, and intense debate now rages about many aspects of the theory. If evolution is less than a fact, and scientists can't even make up their minds about the theory, then what confidence can we have in it? Indeed, President Reagan echoed this argument before an evangelical group in Dallas when he said (in what I devoutly hope was campaign rhetoric): "Well, it is a theory. It is a scientific theory only, and it has in recent years been challenged in the world of science—that is, not believed in the scientific community to be as infallible as it once was."

Well, evolution *is* a theory. It is also a fact. And facts and theories are   5 different things, not rungs in a hierarchy of increasing certainty. Facts are the world's data. Theories are structures of ideas that explain and interpret facts. Facts do not go away when scientists debate rival theories to explain them. Einstein's theory of gravitation replaced Newton's, but apples did not suspend themselves in mid-air pending the outcome. And human beings evolved from apelike ancestors whether they did so by Darwin's proposed mechanism or by some other, yet to be discovered.

Moreover, "fact" does not mean "absolute certainty." The final proofs of   6 logic and mathematics flow deductively from stated premises and achieve certainty only because they are *not* about the empirical world. Evolutionists make no claim for perpetual truth, though creationists often do (and then attack us for a style of argument that they themselves favor). In science, "fact" can only mean "confirmed to such a degree that it would be perverse to withhold provisional assent." I suppose that apples might start to rise tomorrow, but the possibility does not merit equal time in physics classrooms.

Evolutionists have been clear about this distinction between fact and theory   7 from the very beginning, if only because we have always acknowledged how far we are from completely understanding the mechanisms (theory) by which evolution (fact) occurred. Darwin continually emphasized the difference between

---

[2]George Orwell (1903–1950): English journalist and novelist, author of *Animal Farm* and *1984*. [Eds.]

[3]"Newspeak": the official language in Orwell's *1984*, devised to meet the ideological needs of the ruling party and to make all other modes of thought impossible. [Eds.]

his two great and separate accomplishments: establishing the fact of evolution, and proposing a theory—natural selection—to explain the mechanism of evolution. He wrote in *The Descent of Man:* "I had two distinct objects in view; firstly, to show that species had not been separately created, and secondly, that natural selection had been the chief agent of change . . . Hence if I have erred in . . . having exaggerated its [natural selection's] power . . . I have at least, as I hope, done good service in aiding to overthrow the dogma of separate creations."

Thus Darwin acknowledged the provisional nature of natural selection while affirming the fact of evolution. The fruitful theoretical debate that Darwin initiated has never ceased. From the 1940s through the 1960s, Darwin's own theory of natural selection did achieve a temporary hegemony that it never enjoyed in his lifetime. But renewed debate characterizes our decade, and, while no biologist questions the importance of natural selection, many now doubt its ubiquity. In particular, many evolutionists argue that substantial amounts of genetic change may not be subject to natural selection and may spread through populations at random. Others are challenging Darwin's linking of natural selection with gradual, imperceptible change through all intermediary degrees; they are arguing that most evolutionary events may occur far more rapidly than Darwin envisioned. 8

Scientists regard debates on fundamental issues of theory as a sign of intellectual health and a source of excitement. Science is—and how else can I say it?—most fun when it plays with interesting ideas, examines their implications, and recognizes that old information may be explained in surprisingly new ways. Evolutionary theory is now enjoying this uncommon vigor. Yet amidst all this turmoil no biologist has been led to doubt the fact that evolution occurred; we are debating *how* it happened. We are all trying to explain the same thing: the tree of evolutionary descent linking all organisms by ties of genealogy. Creationists pervert and caricature this debate by conveniently neglecting the common conviction that underlies it, and by falsely suggesting that we now doubt the very phenomenon we are struggling to understand. 9

Using another invalid argument, creationists claim that "the dogma of separate creations," as Darwin characterized it a century ago, is a scientific theory meriting equal time with evolution in high school biology curricula. But a prevailing viewpoint among philosophers of science belies this creationist argument. Philosopher Karl Popper has argued for decades that the primary criterion of science is the falsifiability of its theories. We can never prove absolutely, but we can falsify. A set of ideas that cannot, in principle, be falsified is not science. 10

The entire creationist argument involves little more than a rhetorical attempt to falsify evolution by presenting supposed contradictions among its supporters. Their brand of creationism, they claim, is "scientific" because it follows the Popperian model in trying to demolish evolution. Yet Popper's argument must apply in both directions. One does not become a scientist by the simple act of 11 trying to falsify another scientific system; one has to present an alternative system that also meets Popper's criterion—it too must be falsifiable in principle.

"Scientific creationism" is a self-contradictory, nonsense phrase precisely be-   12
cause it cannot be falsified. I can envision observations and experiments that would disprove any evolutionary theory I know, but I cannot imagine what potential data could lead creationists to abandon their beliefs. Unbeatable systems are dogma, not science. Lest I seem harsh or rhetorical, I quote creationism's leading intellectual, Duane Gish, Ph.D., from his recent (1978) book *Evolution? The Fossils Say No!* "By creation we mean the bringing into being by a supernatural Creator of the basic kinds of plants and animals by the process of sudden, or fiat, creation. We do not know how the Creator created, what processes He used, *for He used processes which are not now operating anywhere in the natural universe* [Gish's italics]. This is why we refer to creation as special creation. We cannot discover by scientific investigations anything about the creative processes used by the Creator." Pray tell, Dr. Gish, in the light of your last sentence, what then is "scientific" creationism?

THE FACT OF EVOLUTION

Our confidence that evolution occurred centers upon three general argu-   13
ments. First, we have abundant, direct, observational evidence of evolution in action, from both the field and the laboratory. It ranges from countless experiments on change in nearly everything about fruit flies subjected to artificial selection in the laboratory to the famous British moths that turned black when industrial soot darkened the trees upon which they rest. (The moths gain protection from sharp-sighted bird predators by blending into the background.) Creationists do not deny these observations; how could they? Creationists have tightened their act. They now argue that God only created "basic kinds," and allowed for limited evolutionary meandering within them. Thus toy poodles and Great Danes come from the dog kind and moths can change color, but nature cannot convert a dog to a cat or a monkey to a man.

The second and third arguments for evolution—the case for major changes—   14
do not involve direct observation of evolution in action. They rest upon inference, but are no less secure for that reason. Major evolutionary change requires too much time for direct observation on the scale of recorded human history. All historical sciences rest upon inference, and evolution is no different from geology, cosmology, or human history in this respect. In principle, we cannot observe processes that operated in the past. We must infer them from results that still survive: living and fossil organisms for evolution, documents and artifacts for human history, strata and topography for geology.

The second argument—that the imperfection of nature reveals evolution—   15
strikes many people as ironic, for they feel that evolution should be most elegantly displayed in the nearly perfect adaptation expressed by some organisms—

573

the chamber of a gull's wing, or butterflies that cannot be seen in ground litter because they mimic leaves so precisely. But perfection could be imposed by a wise creator or evolved by natural selection. Perfection covers the tracks of past history. And past history—the evidence of descent—is our mark of evolution.

Evolution lies exposed in the *imperfections* that record a history of descent. 16 Why should a rat run, a bat fly, a porpoise swim, and I type this essay with structures built of the same bones unless we all inherited them from a common ancestor? An engineer, starting from scratch, could design better limbs in each case. Why should all the large native mammals of Australia be marsupials, unless they descended from a common ancestor isolated on this island continent? Marsupials are not "better," or ideally suited for Australia; many have been wiped out by placental mammals imported by man from other continents. This principle of imperfection extends to all historical sciences. When we recognize the etymology of September, October, November, and December (seventh, eighth, ninth, and tenth, from the Latin), we know that two additional items (January and February) must have been added to an original calendar of ten months.

The third argument is more direct: transitions are often found in the fossil 17 record. Preserved transitions are not common—and should not be, according to our understanding of evolution (see next section)—but they are not entirely wanting, as creationists often claim. The lower jaw of reptiles contains several bones, that of mammals only one. The non-mammalian jawbones are reduced, step by step, in mammalian ancestors until they become tiny nubbins located at the back of the jaw. The "hammer" and "anvil" bones of the mammalian ear are descendants of these nubbins. How could such a transition be accomplished? the creationists ask. Surely a bone is either entirely in the jaw or in the ear. Yet paleontologists have discovered two transitional lineages or therapsids (the so-called mammal-like reptiles) with a double jaw joint—one composed of the old quadrate and articular bones (soon to become the hammer and anvil), the other of the squamosal and dentary bones (as in modern mammals). For that matter, what better transitional form could we desire than the oldest human, *Australopithecus afarensis*, with its apelike palate, its human upright stance, and a cranial capacity larger than any ape's of the same body size but a full 1,000 cubic centimeters below ours? If God made each of the half dozen human species discovered in ancient rocks, why did he create in an unbroken temporal sequence of progressively more modern features—increasing cranial capacity, reduced face and teeth, larger body size? Did he create to mimic evolution and test our faith thereby?

AN EXAMPLE OF CREATIONIST ARGUMENT

Faced with these facts of evolution and the philosophical bankruptcy of their 18 own position, creationists rely upon distortion and innuendo to buttress their rhetorical claim. If I sound sharp or bitter, indeed I am—for I have become a major target of these practices.

I count myself among the evolutionists who argue for a jerky, or episodic, rather than a smoothly gradual, pace of change. In 1972 my colleague Niles Eldredge and I developed the theory of punctuated equilibrium [*Discover*, October]. We argued that two outstanding facts of the fossil record—geologically "sudden" origin of new species and failure to change thereafter (stasis)—reflect the predictions of evolutionary theory, not the imperfections of the fossil record. In most theories, small isolated populations are the source of new species, and the process of speciation takes thousands or tens of thousands of years. This amount of time, so long when measured against our lives, is a geological microsecond. It represents much less than 1 per cent of the average life span for a fossil invertebrate species—more than 10 million years. Large, widespread, and well-established species, on the other hand, are not expected to change very much. We believe that the inertia of large populations explains the stasis of most fossil species over millions of years.

We proposed the theory of punctuated equilibrium largely to provide a different explanation for pervasive trends in the fossil record. Trends, we argued, cannot be attributed to gradual transformation within lineages, but must arise from the differential success of certain kinds of species. A trend, we argued, is more like climbing a flight of stairs (punctuations and stasis) than rolling up an inclined plane.

Since we proposed punctuated equilibria to explain trends, it is infuriating to be quoted again and again by creationists—whether through design or stupidity, I do not know—as admitting that the fossil record includes no transitional forms. Transitional forms are generally lacking at the species level, but are abundant between larger groups. The evolution from reptiles to mammals, as mentioned earlier, is well documented. Yet a pamphlet entitled "Harvard Scientists Agree Evolution Is a Hoax" states: "The facts of punctuated equilibrium which Gould and Eldredge . . . are forcing Darwinists to swallow fit the picture that Bryan insisted on, and which God has revealed to us in the Bible."

Continuing the distortion, several creationists have equated the theory of punctuated equilibrium with a caricature of the beliefs of Richard Goldschmidt, a great early geneticist. Goldschmidt argued, in a famous book published in 1940, that new groups can arise all at once through major mutations. He referred to these suddenly transformed creatures as "hopeful monsters." (I am attracted to some aspects of the non-caricatured version, but Goldschmidt's theory still has nothing to do with punctuated equilibrium.) Creationist Luther Sunderland talks of the "punctuated equilibrium hopeful monster theory" and tells his hopeful readers that "it amounts to tacit admission that anti-evolutionists are correct in asserting there is no fossil evidence supporting the theory that all life is connected to a common ancestor." Duane Gish writes, "According to Goldschmidt, and now apparently according to Gould, a reptile laid an egg from which the first bird, feathers and all, was produced." Any evolutionist who

19

20

21

22

believed such nonsense would rightly be laughed off the intellectual stage; yet the only theory that could ever envision such a scenario for the evolution of birds is creationism—God acts in the egg.

CONCLUSION

I am both angry at and amused by the creationists; but mostly I am deeply sad. Sad for many reasons. Sad because so many people who respond to creationist appeals are troubled for the right reason, but venting their anger at the wrong target. It is true that scientists have often been dogmatic and elitist. It is true that we have often allowed the white-coated, advertising image to represent us—"Scientists say that Brand X cures bunions ten times faster than . . ." We have not fought it adequately because we derive benefits from appearing as a new priesthood. It is also true that faceless bureaucratic state power intrudes more and more into our lives and removes choices that should belong to individuals and communities. I can understand that requiring that evolution be taught in the schools might be seen as one more insult on all these grounds. But the culprit is not, and cannot be, evolution or any other fact of the natural world. Identify and fight your legitimate enemies by all means, but we are not among them. 23

I am sad because the practical result of this brouhaha will not be expanded coverage to include creationism (that would also make me sad), but the reduction or excision of evolution from high school curricula. Evolution is one of the half dozen "great ideas" developed by science. It speaks to the profound issues of genealogy that fascinate all of us—the "roots" phenomenon writ large. Where did we come from? Where did life arise? How did it develop? How are organisms related? It forces us to think, ponder, and wonder. Shall we deprive millions of this knowledge and once again teach biology as a set of dull and unconnected facts, without the thread that weaves diverse material into a supple unity? 24

But most of all I am saddened by a trend I am just beginning to discern among my colleagues. I sense that some now wish to mute the healthy debate about theory that has brought new life to evolutionary biology. It provides grist for creationist mills, they say, even if only by distortion. Perhaps we should lie low and rally round the flag of strict Darwinism, at least for the moment—a kind of old-time religion on our part. 25

But we should borrow another metaphor and recognize that we too have to tread a straight and narrow path, surrounded by roads to perdition. For if we ever begin to suppress our search to understand nature, to quench our own intellectual excitement in a misguided effort to present a united front where it does not and should not exist, then we are truly lost. 26

QUESTIONS

1. Summarize the difference between *fact* and *theory* as Gould uses those terms in paragraphs 3 through 12.

2. Why, in paragraph 13, does Gould return to the "fact of evolution"? What turn does his argument take there?

3. In paragraphs 18 through 22 Gould claims that the creationists have distorted his work. How well do you think Gould has substantiated this claim? Are all his examples and arguments convincing? If there are problems, what are they?

4. Consider the proposition that "a set of ideas that cannot, in principle, be falsified is not science" (paragraph 10). How does that proposition set evolution theory apart from creationism? What underlying notion does it point to in the history and nature of science?

5. Insofar as you can tell, does the teaching of evolution continue in schools in your area? Have the fears Gould voices at the end of his essay come to pass? Perhaps you can draw upon your own memory of high school, and write a report on this subject. Or perhaps you can interview one or more high school biology teachers.

6. Gould opens his essay with a reference to the Scopes trial in 1925. Do some library research about that trial and about the current debate. (See also the *New York Times* report on the trial in this book, pp. 135) Write an essay arguing that the same battle continues or that significant differences exist between the two situations.

7. In paragraph 12 Gould criticizes Gish for assuming that God created the world, using "processes which are not now operating anywhere in the natural universe." Does this mean that to be a scientist, one must accept the opposite assumption, namely, that *natural processes are always the same throughout the universe?* Write an essay in which you consider a science that you have studied, exploring the extent to which it depends upon this assumption. What are the main theories and facts established by this science? Do they require this assumption? Is the assumption itself scientific? Or is it an article of faith?

THE EVOLUTION
OF LANGUAGE
Julian Jaynes

*A research psychologist at Princeton University, Julian Jaynes
was born in Massachusetts in 1923 and has degrees from
McGill and Yale universities. The author of numerous articles on psychology and neurology, he is widely known for
his original and controversial book,* The Origin of Consciousness in the Breakdown of the Bicameral Mind *(1976).
The material reprinted here, from the section of that book
called "The Origin of Civilization," is typical of Jaynes's
writing in its reasoned opposition to a widely accepted view
of the matter it discusses.*

WHEN DID LANGUAGE EVOLVE?

It is commonly thought that language is such an inherent part of the human   1
constitution that it must go back somehow through the tribal ancestry of man
to the very origin of the genus *Homo*, that is, for almost two million years.
Most contemporary linguists of my acquaintance would like to persuade me
that this is true. But with this view, I wish to totally and emphatically disagree.
If early man, through these two million years, had even a primordial speech,
why is there so little evidence of even simple culture or technology? For there
is precious little archaeologically up to 40,000 B.C., other than the crudest of
stone tools.

Sometimes the reaction to a denial that early man had speech is, how then   2
did man function or communicate? The answer is very simple: just like all other
primates, with an abundance of visual and vocal signals which were very far
removed from the syntactical language that we practice today. And when I even
carry this speechlessness down through the Pleistocene Age, when man developed various kinds of primitive pebble choppers and hand axes, again my linguist
friends lament my arrogant ignorance and swear oaths that in order to transmit
even such rudimentary skills from one generation to another, there had to be
language. But consider that it is almost impossible to describe chipping flints
into choppers in language. This art was transmitted solely by imitation, exactly
the same way in which chimpanzees transmit the trick of inserting straws into
ant hills to get ants. It is the same problem as the transmission of bicycle riding;
does language assist at all?

578

Because language *must* make dramatic changes in man's attention to things 3 and persons, because it allows a transfer of information of enormous scope, it must have developed over a period that shows archaeologically that such changes occurred. Such a one is the late Pleistocene, roughly from 70,000 B.C. to 8000 B.C. This period was characterized climatically by wide variations in temperature, corresponding to the advance and retreat of glacial conditions, and biologically by huge migrations of animals and man caused by these changes in weather. The hominid population exploded out of the African heartland into the Eurasian subarctic and then into the Americas and Australia. The population around the Mediterranean reached a new high and took the lead in cultural innovation, transferring man's cultural and biological focus from the tropics to the middle latitudes.[1] His fires, caves, and furs created for man a kind of transportable microclimate that allowed these migrations to take place.

We are used to referring to these people as late Neanderthalers. At one time 4 they were thought to be a separate species of man supplanted by Cro-Magnon man around 35,000 B.C. But the more recent view is that they were part of the general human line, which had great variation, a variation that allowed for an increasing pace of evolution, as man, taking his artificial climate with him, spread into these new ecological niches. More work needs to be done to establish the true patterns of settlement, but the most recent emphasis seems to be on its variation, some groups continually moving, others making seasonal migrations, and others staying at a site all the year round.[2]

I am emphasizing the climate changes during this last glacial age because I 5 believe these changes were the basis of the selective pressures behind the development of language through several stages.

CALLS, MODIFIERS, AND COMMANDS

The first stage and the *sine qua non* of language is the development out of 6 incidental calls of *intentional calls*,[3] or those which tend to be repeated unless turned off by a change in behavior of the recipient. Previously in the evolution of primates, it was only postural or visual signals such as threat postures which were intentional. Their evolution into auditory signals was made necessary by the migration of man into northern climates, where there was less light both in the environment and in the dark caves where man made his abode, and where visual signals could not be seen as readily as on the bright African savannahs.

---

[1] See J. D. Clark, "Human ecology during the Pleistocene and later times in Africa south of the Sahara," *Current Anthropology*, 1960, I:307–324.

[2] See Karl W. Butzer, *Environment and Archaeology: An Introduction to Pleistocene Geography* (Chicago: Aldine Press, 1964), p. 378.

[3] *sine qua non*: a Latin phrase meaning "without which not," that is, something essential. [Eds.]

This evolution may have begun as early as the Third Glaciation Period or possibly even before. But it is only as we are approaching the increasing cold and darkness of the Fourth Glaciation in northern climates that the presence of such vocal intentional signals gave a pronounced selective advantage to those who possessed them.

I am here summarizing a theory of language evolution which I have developed more fully and with more caution elsewhere.[4] It is not intended as a definitive statement of what occurred in evolution so much as a rough working hypothesis to approach it. Moreover, the stages of language development that I shall describe are not meant to be necessarily discrete. Nor are they always in the same order in different localities. The central assertion of this view, I repeat, is that *each new stage of words literally created new perceptions and attentions, and such new perceptions and attentions resulted in important cultural changes which are reflected in the archaeological record.*

The first real elements of speech were the final sounds of intentional calls differentiating on the basis of intensity. For example, a danger call for immediately present danger would be exclaimed with more intensity, changing the ending phoneme.[5] An imminent tiger might result in "wahee!" while a distant tiger might result in a cry of less intensity and so develop a different ending such as "wahoo." It is these endings, then, that become the first modifiers meaning "near" and "far." And the next step was when these endings, "hee" and "hoo," could be separated from the particular call that generated them and attached to some other call with the same indication.

The crucial thing here is that the differentiation of vocal qualifiers had to precede the invention of the nouns which they modified, rather than the reverse. And what is more, this stage of speech had to remain for a long period until such modifiers became stable. This slow development was also necessary so that the basic repertoire of the call system was kept intact to perform its intentional functions. This age of modifiers perhaps lasted up to 40,000 B.C., where we find archaeologically retouched hand axes and points.

The next stage might have been an age of commands, when modifiers, separated from the calls they modify, now can modify men's actions themselves. Particularly as men relied more and more on hunting in the chilled climate, the selective pressure for such a group of hunters controlled by vocal commands must have been immense. And we may imagine that the invention of a modifier meaning "sharper" as an instructed command could markedly advance the making of tools from flint and bone, resulting in an explosion of new types of tools from 40,000 B.C. up to 25,000 B.C.

7

8

9

10

---

[4]Julian Jaynes, "The evolution of language in the Late Pleistocene," *Annals of the New York Academy of Sciences*, Vol. 280, 1976.

[5]phoneme: one of the smallest units of speech that distinguish one word or utterance from another. [Eds.]

NOUNS

Once a tribe has a repertoire of modifiers and commands, the necessity of   11
keeping the integrity of the old primitive call system can be relaxed for the first
time, so as to indicate the referents of the modifiers or commands. If "wahee!"
once meant an imminent danger, with more intensity differentiation, we might
have "wak ee!" for an approaching tiger, or "wab ee!" for an approaching bear.
These would be the first sentences with a noun subject and a predicative modifier, and they may have occurred somewhere between 25,000 and 15,000 B.C.

These are not arbitrary speculations. The succession from modifiers to com-   12
mands and, only when these become stable, to nouns is no arbitrary succession.
Nor is the dating entirely arbitrary. Just as the age of modifiers coincides with the
making of much superior tools, so the age of nouns for animals coincides with the
beginning of drawing animals on the walls of caves or on horn implements.

The next stage is the development of thing nouns, really a carry-over from   13
the preceeding. And just as life nouns began animal drawings, so nouns for
things beget new things. This period corresponds, I suggest, to the invention of
pottery, pendants, ornaments, and barbed harpoons and spearheads, the last two
tremendously important in spreading the human species into more difficult
climates. From fossil evidence we know factually that the brain, particularly the
frontal lobe in front of the central sulcus, was increasing with a rapidity that
still astonishes the modern evolutionist. And by this time, perhaps what corresponds to the Magdalenian culture,[6] the language areas of the brain as we know
them had developed.

QUESTIONS

1. What is the position against which Jaynes argues? State it as clearly as you can.
What are the main reasons that "linguists" believe in this position?

2. What is Jaynes's position? What are the main reasons he gives for his belief in it?

3. After reviewing paragraph 6, explain in your own words what incidental calls are
and how intentional calls develop from them. Why do you suppose that Jaynes maintains
that language grew from calls? What other possibilities can you think of?

4. What is the essential difference between paragraphs 1 through 6 and paragraphs
7 through 13?

5. What does Jaynes mean by "perceptions and attentions" (paragraph 7)? Why are
those nouns in plural form?

---

[6]Magdalenian culture: the Stone Age period during which Cro-Magnon man reached his highest
level of industry and art. [Eds.]

Julian Jaynes

6. Make up a small vocabulary for an invented language (something like Jaynes's "wahee," "wahoo," and so on) that could serve in a few basic situations in your everyday life. Provide a word list and a description of how those words or parts of words could combine to form calls, commands, statements, or whatever. That is, provide a grammar as well as a lexicon for your invented language. What will prevent your language from having much of a future?

7. Do linguists disagree with Jaynes as he says? Locate some reviews of his book in linguistic journals. Summarize the reactions to his book, identifying any consensus that seems to exist.

IT'S ONLY HUMAN NATURE: THE SOCIOBIOLOGIST'S FAIRYLAND

Steven Rose

Steven Rose (b. 1938) teaches biology at the Open University in England and has written extensively on the politics of science. He edited, with Hilary Rose, The Political Economy of Science (1976) and has coauthored a pamphlet, Race, Education and Intelligence (1978), for the National Union of Teachers in Great Britain. The following article first appeared in the British professional journal Race and Class in 1979. It represents Rose's response to the fashionable interdisciplinary movement called "sociobiology."

Football crowds shout for rival teams and, at the end of the match, fights 1
break out between supporters of the two sides. Advanced industrial nations spend
up to 10 per cent of their gross national product on armaments of greater and
greater sophistication when their stock-piles are already sufficient to obliterate
all life on earth many times over. Why? "It's only human nature. Man is by
nature aggressive, and these are two ways of showing it."

Schoolchildren compete in exams for top place; adults compete for jobs 2
against a background of unemployment; businesses compete with each other for
contracts and profits. Why? "It's only human nature. Man is by nature greedy
and competitive and seeks power over others; some people are naturally superior
in the competition, others inferior, and the struggle sorts out natural winners
from natural losers."

Entry into Britain by foreigners, especially those with black, brown or yellow 3
skins, is restricted by law. Once inside, groups with different religions or skin
colors are discriminated against in housing or jobs and their families physically
and mentally assaulted. Why? "It's only human nature. Men are by nature
territorial, group-living animals, asserting of their rights of ownership over land,
and xenophobic."[1]

Throughout society, men occupy the highest positions, in government, in- 4
dustry, science, medicine; women, the inferior ones as secretaries, technicians,

---

[1]xenophobic: fearing strangers. [Eds.]

schoolteachers, nurses. Why? "It's only human nature. Men have naturally higher skills than women for these demanding tasks—women are essentially nurturative, concerned with child-rearing, and at work only incidentally—and only in the jobs which mimic their roles as home-makers; office wives, tenders of the sick, teachers of the young. In all societies patriarchy is inevitable."

How often, when oppressed people in struggle query some aspect of the social order, does the answer come back like that, full of the heavy certainty of the "naturalness" of any piece of human conduct, that "things are so and rightly and inevitably so." "You can't change human nature," we are told, with an air of either smug satisfaction or pious resignation, when we are moved to protest about any seeming injustice. Yet what is this mysterious, looming abstraction which seemingly lies at the core of any piece of human conduct, any type of social relation?

Up until the middle of the last century, the inevitabilities of human nature were seen as part of god's ordering of the universe, a god which had created humanity in a given mold, provided rules for the proper conduct of human affairs and established an unquestionable hierarchy: "the rich man in his castle, the poor man at his gate." With the final death of god—already wounded fearfully by the rise of Newtonian science in the seventeenth century—at the hands of the triumphant Darwinism of the nineteenth, then science, in the form of biology, replaced him as the arbiter of human nature and destiny. Biology, rather than god, was responsible for setting the limits to human conduct and potential: class, race and sexual struggles were to be seen as the workings out of the inevitable consequences of the iron laws of evolution: the struggle for existence, the survival of the fittest, were the Darwinian categories that lay beneath Victorian laissez-faire capitalism,[2] and Britain's imperial expansion. Social Darwinism,[3] given its full ideological form by Herbert Spencer,[4] was seductive as a mode of describing and rationalizing "the way the world was" not merely to philosophers and politicians, but to many biologists as well, and did not Darwin's own "solution" to the mechanism of evolution derive from Malthus's view of the inevitability of competition for scarce resources in human populations?[5]

Over recent years, after a period of disrepute, this tendency towards biological law-giving has once again become high fashion, dignified now by names which lay claim to new scientific legitimacy. Ethology, which has a long and in many ways distinguished intellectual history, has become aggrandized into "socio-

---

[2]laissez-faire capitalism: the doctrine that an economic system functions best without any interference from government. [Eds.]

[3]Social Darwinism: the theory of evolution and natural selection applied to the social-political world; in other words, the belief that wealth and power reflect biological superiority. [Eds.].

[4]Herbert Spencer (1820–1903): English philosopher who coined the phrase "Survival of the fittest." [Eds.]

[5]Thomas Malthus (1766–1834): an English economist who first argued that world population would outstrip our food supply. [Eds.]

biology," whose prophets claim it as the science of the future into which will
be merged as well not merely the brain sciences such as neurobiology and
psychology, but also the sciences of human society, sociology, economics, politics. The mainsprings of human conduct will be discovered deep in all of our
biological histories and as a result not only will human nature be understood
and quantified, it will become predictable as well; from the position you and
your partner adopt while copulating and your neighbor's quarrel with his mother-
in-law, through the protests over nuclear power to the date and form of the
coming revolution in South Africa—sociobiology's claim to the ownership of
the inscribed tablets of the iron laws of history are universalistic to the point of
megalomania.

It is easy to imagine a better world than the present—one for example, where,   8
across large areas of the globe people do *not* die routinely of famine and famine-
induced disease; where the perinatal mortality of Liverpool or the Rhondda is
no higher than in Hampstead or Bournemouth;[6] where unemployment and
routine alienated labor is eliminated and our children educated to develop their
human and creative possibilities to the full; where we live without the imminent
threat of destruction from nuclear war begun by accident or design; and where
humanity's relationships with nature are harmonious rather than exploitative.
Yet at the same time our imagination of, our striving for, the new world runs
full tilt into the claims of "hard-nosed realism." What is, is what must be. It is
only human nature. Offered a vision of Utopia, the realist defenders of the status
quo substitute sociobiology. For them, in the kingdom of the blind, the one-
eyed prophets are to be defined as mad, and have their eyes removed.

So it is important to look at the method and reasoning employed by this law-   9
giving subject which claims to tell us who we are and how we must live. In this
article, I want to discuss some of the general claims made by sociobiology to be
able to provide explanatory or predictive knowledge of the behavior of humans,
individually or in groups.

Now it is relatively easy to respond simply by saying that sociobiology tells   10
us what *is*, but not what *ought* to be: that one cannot derive moral precepts
from biological observations; that biology is neutral about human morality whatever it says about human animality—indeed, many sociobiologists, though not
all by any means, would offer such a disclaimer. The substance of my disagreement with sociobiology's claims, however, is far deeper than this truism. I would
argue that the entire structure of the method and reasoning employed by sociobiology contains a series of fundamental flaws. Hence the general claims that
it makes to provide explanatory or predictive knowledge of the behavior of humans, individually or in groups, are *scientifically* invalid, and not merely mor-
ally neutral or otiose. Note that this critique of sociobiology is written from a

---

[6]Liverpool . . . Bournemouth: Rhondda is an urban district in a coal mining region of Wales.
Rose contrasts industrial (Rhondda and Liverpool) with suburban (Hampstead and Bournemouth)
England. [Eds.]

standpoint which accepts that there is a field of *science* for discussion here—a field which may become, and in the case of sociobiology *has* become a battle-ground between science and ideology, but one in which, nonetheless, it *is* possible to distinguish truth from falsity, science from ideology or social relations. I am specifically *not* discussing here the social determinants of the renewed interest in biological determinism, nor its manifestly ideological functions.

I am setting this discussion against two backgrounds. The first is the surge of popular and semi-popular books which have appeared over the last few years, by people like Desmond Morris, Konrad Lorenz, Robert Ardrey, Tiger and Fox, and more recently Richard Dawkins (*The Selfish Gene*, London, 1976). All of these claim to provide accounts of some of the terrain which E. O. Wilson, in a more academic but no less controversial book, has called *Sociobiology—the New Synthesis* (Harvard University Press, 1975), a pared down and popular version of which is *On Human Nature*. The second background point to be made is that these sociobiologists do not all speak with one voice; indeed there are quite bitter disputes over theory and methodology between them, as between, for example, the school which claims that the "unit of selection" in the evolution of societies is the group, and that which believes it is the individual or the genes packaged inside that individual and his or her near relatives. These disputes do not concern me here. For the purpose of my present discussion, whether one is a group- or kin-selectionist is irrelevant. I want to try to demonstrate that all types of contemporary sociobiological thinking embody within them a set of interlocking fallacies, which render their claim to scientificity spurious. And in order to do this—and this is the final caveat I wish to make—I propose to use examples wider, perhaps, than some advocates of sociobiology would want to accept as falling within their framework. Having exposed these fallacies, I am then able to ask: what ideological function—whose interests—do they serve? Who benefits from sociobiological thinking?

First, what the sociobiologists do is to take aspects of human behavior and attempt to abstract certain common features from them. A mother protecting her baby from attack, a doctor risking his or her life in a cholera epidemic, a soldier leading a doomed assault on a machine-gun post, all express "altruism." A child's logical and numerical skills, its reading ability and conformity to its teacher's expectations are all measures of an underlying, unitary "intelligence." Note how this trick works, by taking a process with a dynamic and a history of its own involving individuals and their relations, that is a social interaction, and isolating out an abstract, underlying, fixed thing, or "quality." This process, of *reification,* is not dissimilar to the phrenology of the early nineteenth century, in which a human was seen as a mosaic of different pieces of behavior—a person's brain had a "bump of philoprogenitiveness," another for "love of music" and so forth.

Now sociobiologists would dispute this claim, arguing that far from lumping together disparate activities and reifying them in a phrenological manner, they

586

were doing no more and no less than Newton when he saw the fall of an apple and the motion of the moon as different cases of the same law of gravity. The difference between the sociobiologists and Newton is, however, profound. It is as if Newton had defined gravity as a "property" of the apple, rather than as law describing an aspect of the relationship between the apple and the earth. It was precisely because he transcended the reified property and understood the relationship between objects that Newtonian mechanics advanced, and it is because they do not do this that the sociobiologists' attempt to reduce disparate phenomena to a common denominator must fail. In the sociobiological universe, characteristics such as altruism or aggression, locked inside individuals' heads as reified properties, also become abstract forces which move the individuals who possess them like clockwork mechanisms. One can see this at work when sociobiologists attempt to measure the quality that they have reified, as for example when they attempt to quantify aggression by reducing it to a measure of how fast rats kill mice placed in cages along with them—an experimental approach dignified with the name of the study of "muricidal" behavior.

What happens in this approach is that the fixed and reified property becomes attached to an individual rather than emerging from a situation. It is individuals who then become aggressive, altruistic, intelligent and so forth, and the *same property* becomes manifest in different circumstances. The aggressive male is essentially playing the same role whether on a picket line, in a football crowd or beating his wife; he is expressing, in different forms, aspects of the same underlying biological property (contrast this, for example, with a definition of "intelligence" not as a property of the individual but of a relationship—of that individual with others and with the social and natural worlds which confront her or him).

Once you've performed this labelling trick, the way is open to seek for the location of the quality inside the individual—for if a person is aggressive, it is clear that there must be, for instance, a region of the brain which is *responsible* for the aggression—from which it follows that one can eliminate "undesirable" aggression, whether of strikers or football fans, by removing or modifying the bit of the brain which is responsible for it.

Examples of this first fallacy, of reification, are numerous. One is the Russian practice of labelling political dissidents as mad and treating them for schizophrenia. A second is a book by a couple of American psychosurgeons, *Violence and the Brain*,[7] which, in the face of the inner city riots which raged through the U.S., argued that whatever the social reasons which might be involved, the riots might be best explained by there being something wrong with the "aggression centres" in the brains of a number of ghetto leaders, and that urban violence could be cured by removing a small region of the brain—the amygdala—from some 5 to 10 per cent of ghetto dwellers. A couple of years ago, I came across

---

[7]V. Mark and L. Ervin, London, 1970.

587

a copy of a letter from an American prison governor which made the same case—it asked for neurosurgical examination and intervention for a black prisoner whose signs of "illness" were "organizing a prison work strike, learning karate, hatred for white society and reading revolutionary literature." In similar vein, it is common practice in American inner cities now to define children who are disrespectful of their teachers and poor learners (with a high proportion of blacks and Chicanos) as suffering from "minimal brain dysfunction" and to drug them with an amphetamine-like substance called Ritalin. It is estimated that some 600,000 pre-puberty inner city school children are currently being dosed with daily Ritalin pills on the basis of school reports—not because there are any physical or neurological "signs of disorder," but because their teachers and psychiatrists have reified, out of the complex interaction of these school kids with their schools, homes and the wider society, a "disease" of too little amphetamine in the brain! What this reification does is to reverse the old slogan "do not adjust your mind, the fault is in reality."[8] Instead, the "fault" is located within the individual, a phrenological bump of aggression, or social dissatisfaction.

Having abstracted—reified—aspects of a social interaction into uniform qualities of an individual participant in that interaction, the next fallacy of sociobiological thinking is to quantify the quality. That's easy: you simply ask "how much" aggression, intelligence, altruism or whatever an individual possesses. We are accustomed to thinking in linear, ordinal terms. If someone is intelligent, we ask "how intelligent?" "more or less intelligent than some other person?"—and so on, till we end up with a ranking scale against which the entire citizenry can be categorized and their "quality," intelligence, given a number, like the infamous IQ. The spurious numerology which masquerades as science has such a grip on day-to-day thinking that it is often not hard to accept the apparent scientificity of this type of sociobiological argumentation. 17

Asking the question "how much" in an ordinal, linear way, is only very seldom a sensible scientific question and is often quite meaningless—to reply to the question "how many bananas make six" by saying "two apples" may be grammatically correct, but is empty of scientific content. 18

So there are the first two fallacies of sociobiology—the reification, then the quantification. Now for the third. This is the appeal to biological "evidence" from the study of non-human animals. As humans are a particular animal species, with a continuity of evolutionary links with the rest of the biological world, it is not unreasonable to expect to find analogies for human behavior amongst other animals. The strength of ethology has lain in its study of animals in their natural environments and in social interaction. However, the problem that such studies run into is just the same as that of the study of human behavior, 19

---

[8]For more details see the discussion in Hilary Rose and Steven Rose, *The Political Economy of Science*, London, 1976.

but more so, for it is now necessary to look in non-humans for "qualities" abstracted out of human experience. If it is hard enough to study an aspect of human relations without reifying, what happens when we take terms for human behavior—intelligence, curiosity, altruism, aggression—and look for their analogies in animals? So we find species of ants which introduce others into their nest, where they perform certain of the tasks of the ant economy, classified as "slave-making" ants. Some strains of rats, in appropriate conditions, tend to kill mice placed in their cages, and these become labelled as "aggressive" rats. The use of an identical label, which may be no more than a sort of pun, or observer's shorthand, becomes an explanation. Unitary labels must imply unitary mechanisms, and "aggression" in other animals must imply the "innate aggression" of humans too. Thus a sort of conjuring trick takes place in which the sociobiologist looks at the natural world in terms of human categories, and then turns back to the social world once more and claims that because such phenomena occur in other animals as well as humans, they must be biologically based in humans, and hence they represent inevitable and immutable categories of human behavior. It is a world of looking-glass logic, to which E. O. Wilson is particularly prone.

The final trick—the fourth of the sociobiological fallacies—is to play a sort 20 of fairy-tale game. In it, one says "just suppose" that any particular human or social character was biologically—genetically—determined, then what would the consequences be? A good example of this comes in Dawkins's book, in which he uses the "just suppose" game for sexual constancy. "Just suppose," he argues, that all females were sexually genetically constant, whilst a proportion of males had a gene for constancy and the rest a gene for "philandering"—then what would the consequences be? He concludes that a population with a given proportion of male "philanderers" would form an "evolutionary stable strategy," and presumably, therefore, that a male's propensity to be faithful or unfaithful to his spouse is just another of those biologically determined variables of human behavior which is immune to social explanation. Whether you are (as a male) a Casanova or an Abelard is genetically laid down before you start (so, according to one of Wilson's most favored acolytes, R. Trivers, may be the alleged like of adults and dislike of children for spinach!).[9] The point is not that one shouldn't make models of behavior, it is that we are in constant danger of being seduced by our models, of being so enchanted by the fact that they "fit" the data that we ignore that an infinity of *other* models could equally well fit one's observations. The point about models is that they must be testable and refutable. The trouble with the sociobiologist's models is that they become a closed world—there is no sort of situation to which one cannot get a fit granted enough

---

[9]Casanova . . . Abelard: Giovanni Giacomo Casanova (1725–1798) was a legendary seducer of women. His memoirs became world famous. Peter Abelard (1079–1142) was a French philosopher, a teacher, and, after his famous romance with Heloise, a monk. Abelard is a legendary example of romantic constancy and devotion. [Eds.]

Steven Rose

suppositions about genes for this or that piece of behavior and some other genetic properties like dominance or partial expressivity. Some of the wilder reaches of this sort of fairyland model-building come when we discover that according to some psychometricians of the Eysenck school,[10] not only are differences in intelligence largely inherited but so are children's capacity to learn French at school, neuroticism, radicalism versus conservatism in political thought and even twins' tendencies to answer consistently or inconsistently on questionnaires (thereby "saving the phenomenon" with a vengeance!).

The charge that the sociobiological world is "closed" to possible experimental refutation, whilst serious, does not make sociobiology unique. Many fields of science operate within paradigms—general overarching theories—which are so comprehensive and adaptable to "new" facts that they are not capable of refutation in the classical sense of philosophy of science—evolutionary theory itself is an example. So is astronomy, whether in its Ptolemaic or Galilean form.   21

Yet evolutionary theory, despite the unresolved paradoxes within it—and they are many and powerful—is *the* great unifying hypothesis within which so much of biology can be encompassed that its strengths are unchallengeable. My charge against the tautologies and self-fulfilling prophecies of sociobiology is that, because of the set of fallacies embedded within them, which result in the reduction of living organisms in all their richness to jerky caricatured puppets pulled by strings of "selfish genes," its tautologies are scientifically sterile[11]—the tautologies of pre-Copernican astronomy, not those of evolutionary theory. Far from being much abused "new Galileos," as their advocates have claimed for them, the sociobiologists are mere Ptolemaic medieval schoolmen. Finally, sociobiology's claim to biologize away the study of human societies by the methods of sociology, economics, political science, and history fails the very simple test that there is no way that sociobiology can possibly account for either differences between particular existing human societies—for instance between South Africa and Tanzania—nor rapid changes of social form within a given society—for instance between China pre-1948 and after 1968. If it can't do these things, at best the exercise becomes a piece of fashionable Harvard or Oxford intellectual games-playing; at worst a way of ideologically justifying the status quo. These reflections on the methodology of sociobiology in general can be seen as applying to Wilson's *On Human Nature* in particular, as the book represents a pared-down version of his earlier *Sociobiology*, emphasizing how the "new" thinking of sociobiology affects our understanding of human societies, though a substantial proportion of the book has appeared earlier in magazine and journal articles and a part of it merely reprints a section of the final chapter of *Sociobiology*. The latter book was heavily criticized both for its ideology and its biological and   22

---

[10]Hans Jurgen Eysenck (b. 1916): a British psychologist associated with the measurement of human intelligence. [Eds.]

[11]Note that, as I emphasized earlier, I am saying nothing here about the ideological function of these sociobiological propositions, but rather viewing them from the "inside" of a science-versus-pseudoscience battleground.

anthropological claims.[12] Nowhere in the present book does Wilson acknowledge these criticisms explicitly and nowhere in his quite extensive bibliography does he refer to a single one of the many articles and books published by his critics. Despite this surprising lack—of academic courtesy if nothing else—Wilson's claims in the present book are moderated from some of the more incautious phrases of *Sociobiology*. Gone, for example, are "genes" for "spite" or "indoctrinability" or whatever, in the crudely phrenological style of his earlier book; now caveats surround each assertion to the point where it often virtually disappears into a cloud of "tendencies."

The book takes us through a series of topics which are the now familiar   23
hunting ground for sociobiological theorizing and which have been discussed above; the evolution of human society, aggression, sexual behavior and differentiation, "altruism," and religion. It concludes with a call for hope, based upon what he describes as the "seemingly fatal deterioration of the myths of traditional religion and of its secular equivalents," chief amongst which he places Marxism, and their replacement by an ethic of the search for "scientific truth," previously called for in *Chance and Necessity* (London, 1971) by the molecular biologist Jacques Monod—the sort of philosophical naïveté that the French immediately dubbed Monodtheism. In Wilson's case this call is the less credible in that whilst he has clearly read his Bible, he shows little evidence of even having read *Marx for Beginners*.

What Wilson wants to claim is that the organism and its behavior represent   24
no more than the gene's way of making another gene; that is, the richness of our biological, mental and social life may be reinterpreted simply in terms of strategies for the survival of selfish genes. This is what we may call hard sociobiology. The fallacy inherent in this neat formulation (deriving, I believe, from Samuel Butler, who argued a century or so ago that a chicken was merely the egg's way of making another egg) is seen if the paradox is inverted; after all it is equally plausible, paradoxical, and fallacious to argue that the gene is merely human behavior's way of creating another piece of human behavior.

In the book, Wilson slips uneasily between defense of this hard sociobiology   25
and a much softer version. Sometimes he does this explicitly, as when he claims there are two forms of altruism, hardcore and softcore, and sometimes implicitly, when he lowers his sights to something little more contentious than the claim that one cannot understand human society in the absence of an understanding of human biology. Now while it is easy to understand the relevance of such a soft claim in reaction to the sort of sociological or psychological reductionism (for instance Skinnerian behaviorism)[13] which has been an important intellec-

---

[12]For instance, the various publications of the U.S. Science for the People Study Group on Sociobiology, including their review in the *New York Review of Books* and, most recently their book, *Biology as a Social Weapon*. Cambridge, Mass., 1978, or the very useful anthropological demolition by Marshall Sahlins, *The Use and Abuse of Biology*. London, 1977.

[13]Skinnerian behaviorism: school of psychology that, following B. F. Skinner (b. 1904), inventor of the Skinner box for conditioning experiments with animals, restricts its interest to observable behavior in response to stimuli. [Eds.]

tual strand in the U.S., or even in response to some of those ideologues who wish to debiologize the human condition entirely, it is scarcely a serious theoretical challenge to any sort of Marxist thinking.

The real failure of the sociobiologists lies in their seeming inability to avoid the either/or trap. Behavior must be *either* socially *or* biologically determined, or must represent the arithmetic sum of a biological (genetic) and an environmental component. On the contrary, a proper understanding of the interaction of the biological and the social in the production of humans and their society will only be possible following the simple recognition that *both* genes *and* environment are perfectly necessary to the expression of any behavior. That humans have two legs and speak depends upon their genotype; if they were, say four-legged and incapable of spoken communication, human society would be very different. Hence human society is genetically determined. This proposition, which is all soft sociobiology boils down to, is trivial. But intermingled with the soft sociobiology are the harder Wilsonian claims.   26

Perhaps most of human sex differences in cognition are environmentally determined, but an itsy-bitsy is genetic and in favor of the men, and if "we" "choose" a society which minimizes these differences "we" may, but in doing so "we" will be going against nature (note Wilson's deliberate avoidance of the question of who "we" are in this context). In the same way, although he does not go as far as Dawkins in proposing sex-linked genes for "philandering," for Wilson human males have a genetic tendency towards polygyny, females towards constancy; having a bit on the side is a male characteristic, while females who are sexually attractive have a genetic tendency to rise upward through the social classes. Genetic determinism constantly creeps in at the back door.   27

The aim of a truly human science of sociobiology would not be to debiologize or to desocialize our understanding of the human condition. It is vital that an integrated dialectical account of human nature be achieved and the traps of either biological or sociological reductionism avoided. Wilsonian sociobiology is, however, a travesty of this goal, marred by grandiloquent claims, falsely dichotomous thinking, and an incapacity to distance itself from the particularist assumptions of the dominant racist, sexist, and class bound ideology of late twentieth-century western society.   28

It is against this that we must pose a real science and vision of humanity—one which says that it is the biological and social nature of humanity to transform itself, reach beyond itself constantly: that what seems fixed or constant is so only in the historical moment which itself is always in flux, that the human nature of feudal, preindustrial society was not the human nature of the industrial revolution, is not the human nature of today's advanced capitalism—and will not be the human nature of the transformed societies of tomorrow—those that will at length have truly achieved that old goal, the freedom of necessity.   29

QUESTIONS

1. Insofar as you can infer it from this essay, what is sociobiology? What is the theory against which Rose takes his stand?

2. In paragraph 12, Rose mentions a "trick" of analysis that sociobiologists allegedly perform: it involves abstracting a quality from its context; *reification* is his word for it. Look that word up, and *phrenology*, which he also mentions. Do you sympathize with those assertions, with Rose's choice of words?

3. Think of gravity first as a property of an apple and then as "an aspect of the relationship between the apple and the earth" (paragraph 13). What is the difference between those ways of thinking? Draw up a list of similar "properties": the hardness of your chair, the sharpness of your pencil, or the acuity of your mind. Then try to think about them less as properties than as symptoms or aspects of relationships between things. How does that shift in perspective alter your understanding of the "property" in question?

4. What fallacies does Rose find in the sociobiologists' method of argument? Explain each in your own words.

5. In paragraph 22, Rose claims that Wilson, especially in *Sociobiology*, employed a "phrenological style." What kind of "trick" is Rose playing with that term?

6. Taking hints from paragraphs 6, 23, 25, 28, and 29, define the perspective from which Rose writes. What is the nature of his quarrel with Wilson?

7. Identify an admirable quality in a person you know—intelligence, attractiveness, kindness, or whatever—and write a paper of two parts. In the first part, write of that quality as if it were a property of the person. In the second, describe it as an aspect of the relationship of that person with other people and with the environment. Add a note in which you indicate which of the two definitions seems the more convincing to you.

8. Describe an incident in which you see evidence of a serious social problem, racial prejudice, joblessness, deficiencies in the educational system, or something of that sort. Try to see the problem, again, less as a property of one person or group than as an aspect of the relationship of two or more elements within a system. Thus you might be led not simply to say that a person is prejudiced, or is the victim of prejudice, but that the person participates in a prejudicial system.

9. Do some library research about the sociobiologists mentioned by Rose (especially in paragraph 11) and about their reception by other critics. Write an argumentative paper that supports or supplements Rose's position or that disagrees with his views, using the information you have found as evidence for your case.

THE TREE OF KNOWLEDGE

J. Robert Oppenheimer

J. Robert Oppenheimer (1904–1967) was the director of the Los Alamos Scientific Laboratory, which exploded the first atomic bomb in 1945. After the war, as head of the general advisory committee of the Atomic Energy Commission, he opposed the manufacture of the H-bomb. In 1963 the AEC awarded Oppenheimer its prestigious Enrico Fermi award "in recognition of his outstanding contributions to theoretical physics and his scientific and administrative leadership not only in development of the atomic bomb, but also in establishing the groundwork for the many peaceful uses of atomic energy." In 1947 he was appointed director and professor of physics at the Institute for Advanced Study at Princeton. In 1958 he spoke from notes to a group of journalists in Washington, D.C., and the following article is an edited version of the recorded text of his talk, as it appeared in Harper's Magazine *in October 1958.*

When I speak to the press I am aware that I am talking to a group of men who have a singularly critical destiny in these rather peculiar times. Those of us whose work it is to preserve old learning, and to find new, look to the press to keep the channels of truth and communication open and to keep men in some sense united in common knowledge and common humanity. 1

I want to talk about the nature and structure of our knowledge today and how it has altered and complicated the problems of the press. There are enormous differences between our world of learning today—our Tree of Knowledge—and those of Athens,[1] or the Enlightenment,[2] or the dawn of science in fifteenth- and sixteenth-century Europe. You can get some suggestion of how shattering these changes have been if you remember that Plato, when he tried to think about human salvation and government, recommended mathematics as one of the ways to learn to know the truth, to discriminate good from evil 2

---

[1] Athens: Oppenheimer probably refers to the Athens of the fifth and fourth centuries B.C., the age of Athenian democracy under Pericles and the age of Socrates, Plato, and Aristotle during and after the Peloponnesian War. [Eds.]

[2] the Enlightenment: a period of European intellectual history in the eighteenth century, associated with names such as Newton, Locke, Descartes, Voltaire, Hume, Kant, Jefferson, Franklin, and Diderot. [Eds.]

and the wise from the foolish. Plato was not a creative mathematician, but students confirm that he knew the mathematics of his day, and understood it, and derived much from it.

Today, it is not only that our kings do not know mathematics, but our philosophers do not know mathematics and—to go a step further—our mathematicians do not know mathematics. Each of them knows a branch of the subject and they listen to each other with a fraternal and honest respect; and here and there you find a knitting together of the different fields of mathematical specialization. In fact, a great deal of progress in mathematics is a kind of overarching generalization which brings things that had been separate into some kind of relation. Nevertheless, it is not likely today that our most learned advisers—the men who write in the press and tell us what we may think—would suggest that the next President of the United States be able to understand the mathematics of the day.

YIELDING BOUNDARIES

The first characteristic of scientific knowledge today—a trivial and pedestrian characteristic—is that its growth can be measured. When I talk of "science" here I would like to use the word in the broadest sense to include all man's knowledge of his history and behavior, his knowledge, in fact, of anything that can be talked of in an objective way so that people all over the world can understand it, know what the scientist has done, reproduce it, and find out if it is true or not. It is hard to measure the growth of science defined in these terms in a sensible way but it can be measured in fairly foolish ways.

One way of measuring science, for example, is to find out how many people are engaged in it. I know a young historian of science who has amused himself by counting the scientists of the last two centuries and he has found that their number has, quite accurately, doubled about every ten years. Professor Purcell of Harvard put the same conclusion another way the other day when he said, "Ninety per cent of all scientists are alive." This gives some notion of the changes involved.

I must, however, qualify this trend in two ways. First, it cannot continue, because if it went on for another century, then everyone would be a scientist—there would be nobody else left. So a kind of saturation is setting in and the rate of science's growth is slowing down. The second qualification is that what might be called the "stature" of science is not proportional to its volume; it may be proportional to the cube root of its volume or something like that. In short, every scientist is not a Newton and the proportion of Newtons among all scientists tends to decline as the number of people involved gets bigger.

Despite all qualification, though, the fact remains that the growth in the number of people in science and the growth in firm knowledge—important,

J. Robert Oppenheimer

non-trivial knowledge of the kind that appears in learned journals and books—have been more or less parallel; and this growth will continue, although the increase in it is bound to taper off. The result is that nearly everything that is now known was not in any book when most of us went to school; we cannot know it unless we have picked it up since. This in itself presents a problem of communication that is nightmarishly formidable.

On the other hand, there is a more encouraging aspect of this scientific   8
knowledge. As it grows, things, in some ways, get much simpler. They do not get simpler because one discovers a few fundamental principles which the man in the street can understand and from which he can derive everything else. But we do find an enormous amount of order. The world is not random and whatever order it has seems in large part "fit," as Thomas Jefferson said, for the human intelligence. The enormous variety of facts yields to some kind of arrangement, simplicity, generalization.

One great change in this direction—and it has not yet, I think, fully come   9
to public understanding—is that we are beginning to see that the hard boundaries which once seemed to separate the parts of the natural world from each other are now yielding to some kind of inquiry. We are beginning to see ways across the gaps between the living and the dead, the physical and the mental.

Let me give just a few illustrations: 10

· It is probably not an accident, although it is not really understood, that the age of the earth—some six or seven billion years according to calculation by radioactive techniques—is very close to the period required for the most distant nebulae to recede into the furthest reaches of space. We can picturesquely define that time by saying that during it things were a lot closer together than they are now and the state of the material universe was very different. Some years ago the brilliant Russian biochemist Oparin suggested that when the atmosphere had no oxygen in it,[3] certain conditions could have prevailed on earth under which life could have originated from inorganic matter. There has since been confirmation in Urey's laboratory and this hypothesis turns out to be true.[4] Although mermaids and heroes do not walk out of the test tube, we do see that quite reasonable accounts of the origin of life are not too far from our grasp.

· The recent research on how the genetic mechanisms of all living material operate shows how certain proteins have special information-bearing properties—how they can store information and transmit it from one generation to another.[5]

---

[3](Alexander Ivanovich) Oparin (1894–1980): Soviet biochemist who first advanced the idea that the origin of life was chemical. [Eds.]

[4](Harold Clayton) Urey (1893–1981): American scientist and Nobel Prize winner for chemistry in 1934. [Eds.]

[5]An account of this development, by F. H. C. Crick, appeared in *Scientific American*, September 1957. (See also *The Double Helix* (1968) by James D. Watson; "The Molecular Structure of Nucleic Acids," by Watson and Crick, in *Nature* (25 April 1953), 737. Watson and Crick were also awarded Nobel Prizes.) [Eds.]

· The study of how the nerve impulses from our sense organs to the brain can be modulated and altered by the perceptive apparatus of the animal—often it is an animal rather than a man—give us some notion both of the unreliability of our sense impressions and of the subtlety of the relations between thought and the object of thought.

All these problems, which even in the nineteenth century seemed to obstruct 11 the possibility of a unified view of the great arch of nature, are yielding to discovery; and in all science there is a pervasive, haunting sense that no part of nature is really irrelevant to any other.

GAY AND WONDERFUL MYSTERY

But the model of science which results from all this investigation is entirely 12 different from a model which would have seemed natural and understandable to the Greeks or the Newtonians. Although we do start from common human experience, as they did, we so refine what we think, we so change the meaning of words, we build up so distinctive a tradition, that scientific knowledge today is not an enrichment of the general culture. It is, on the contrary, the possession of countless, highly specialized communities who love it, would like to share it, would very much like to explain it, and who make some efforts to communicate it; but it is not part of the common human understanding. This is the very strange predicament to which the press addresses itself today and to which it can give, I believe, only a partial solution.

It would of course be splendid—and one often hears this—if we could say 13 that while we cannot know the little details about the workings of atoms and proteins and the human psyche, we *can* know the fundamental principles of science. But I am afraid that this is only marginally true. The fundamentals of physics are defined in terms of words that refer to an experience that lay people have not had and that very few people have run across in their education.

For example, in my opinion, it is almost impossible to explain what the 14 fundamental principle of relativity is about, and this is even more true of the quantum theory. It is only possible to use analogies, to evoke some sense of understanding. And as for the recent discovery—the very gay and wonderful discovery for which Dr. Yang and Dr. Lee were awarded the Nobel Prize[6]— that nature has a preference for right-handed or left-handed screws in certain situations and is not indifferent to the handedness of the screw—to explain this is, I believe, quite beyond my capacity. And I have never heard anyone do it in a way that could be called an enrichment of culture.

---

[6]Dr. Yang and Dr. Lee: the Nobel Prize in physics in 1957 was shared by Chen Ning Yang (b. 1922), Einstein Professor of Physics at the State University of New York at Stony Brook, and Tsung Dao Lee (b. 1925), Enrico Fermi Professor of Physics at Columbia. [Eds.]

To sum up the characteristics of scientific knowledge today, then, I would say 15
that it is mostly new; it has not been digested; it is not part of man's common
knowledge; it has become the property of specialized communities who may on
occasion help one another but who, by and large, pursue their own way with
growing intensity further and further from their roots in ordinary life.

We must always remember that, like most human accomplishments, the 16
sciences have grown out of a long, accumulating experience of error, astonishment, invention, and understanding. Taken as a whole, they constitute a series
of traditions; and these traditions—once largely common, now largely separate—
are as essential to understanding a part of biology or astronomy or physics as
the general human tradition is to the existence of civilized life. I know that a
complete immersion in these many different, related, yet specific traditions is
beyond the reach of any one person—that as things stand today, most of us are
without any experience, really, in any. We have much in common from the
simple ways in which we have learned to live and talk and work together. Out
of this have grown the specialized disciplines like the fingers of the hand, united
in origin but no longer in contact.

PRACTICAL BOOBY TRAPS

Now I am going to make a distinction which may seem arbitrarily sharp but 17
which is I think important both to the learned community and the press. I have
been talking until now about science as the things we have discovered about
nature—incredible things and beautiful and astonishing, but defined, usually
not by any use to which they are put, but simply in terms of the ways in which
they were found out. Pure science is thus inherently circumscribed but immensely revealing, showing as it does that left to itself, man's imagination was
not a patch on reality.[7]

Seeking out this knowledge is one problem and I am not through with it. 18
But the other problem is that, of course, this knowledge has practical consequences. On it is built the world we live in and the face of that world has been
changed, probably more than in any other period of history, by the scientific
revolution. Now these practical consequences, because they are intended in
some way to be responsive to man's needs, can be talked about in an intelligible
way. It is not necessary to know how a nucleus is put together, or what are the
laws which determine its behavior, in order to explain what nuclear energy is
all about. It may be very hard to explain it well because it involves human
choices, options, decisions, prejudices. But I believe that it is no more difficult
to write about nuclear energy than about where people go for a holiday. It is

---

[7]man's . . . reality: to paraphrase, man's imagination cannot begin to compete with reality.
[Eds.]

not much harder to write about nuclear weapons, except that, to the problems of human variety, there is added the problem of a very great deal of secrecy.

To take another example, it has not been hard to write about the use of vaccines in the prevention of disease and these can be described without elaborate theory. As a matter of fact the vaccines were discovered without much theoretical background and the atomic bomb was made before we had much idea what held nuclei together; we do not have very much idea today. 19

The press has done an admirable job in explaining these and other practical applications of science—I think it is aware that it has to do a much, much greater one. But there are, I think, some booby traps which stand in its way. I would like to list three of them. 20

One of the simplest traps is that when technical people talk they always emphasize the fact that they are not sure. Sometimes, as in the case of knowing all the effects of radiation on life, we are not, in fact, sure, because experience takes so long to acquire. But usually the statement that we are not sure is more like the polite comment, "I don't want to bore you but . . ." Statements about scientific matters are not entirely sure—nothing is—but compared to politics they are so extremely sure as to be of a different order of certainty. If a scientist says he is not sure, pay attention to the limits within which he says this—the margin for error he insists on allowing. This margin will not be so wide. Within what limits we are uncertain about the genetic damages of radiation, for example, is not something to worry or wonder about. We know something of the effects on the genes. The differences of opinion over this question lie in quite a different field. They lie in conflicting assessments of the relative gravity of these damages and of other vaster dangers of total nuclear war. 21

A second trap to beware of is the strange fact that the words scientists use have taken on special meaning so that there is a confusing quality of punning when they discuss technical things and describe their aims. "Relativity" sounds like something that occurs in daily life; it is not. Scientists talk about the "adventure" of science and they are right; but of course in the public mind this is very likely to be identified with looking to see if the other side of the moon is really there. Here the public is wrong. The adventures of science are intellectual adventures, involving discoveries of the inadequacy of our means of describing nature, because it is so unfamiliar and strange. Space travel has, no doubt, its value and virtue, but it is in no way related to the great adventures of science. It would be, of course, if we could go out two or three billion light-years and see what is going on there, because it is hard to see that far with telescopes. But this is not the same thing as the progress of human learning and understanding. 22

A third trap and a serious one—it has infested the discussion of radioactive fallout—is that in most technical explanations, very large numbers occur, and it is often hard to convey their implications sensitively. It may be equally true to say, for instance, that something will cause 10,000 casualties and that these 23 casualties will affect a hundred-thousandth of the population of the world; but one statement can make the effect seem rather small and the other can make it very big. We cannot get over the habit of talking in numbers but it takes some exposition if we are to avoid creating the wrong impression.

I have one example of this. It has to do with radioactive fallout. I know   24
nothing about the main efforts being made to eliminate fallout at present but it is obvious that they have to do with the elimination of fissionable material from bombs. The first step is to take the casing away from big bombs and the next step, presumably, is to take away much—or even all—of the rest.

I have some understanding of this as a technical problem and some idea of   25
the benefits which will accrue from it. But in an old day, when we had the first primitive, tiny, atomic weapons, there was also a contrast. The story is in the public domain and I am surprised that no reporter has dug it out. We were thinking then in terms of casualties of hundreds of thousands and not hundreds of millions. It was a much more innocent age but it was warfare and in that sense it was not innocent. All the bombs then had fissionable material and the first one we set off at Trinity near Los Alamos was dirty. It was set off practically at ground level, the fireball touched the ground and in fact a great deal of radioactive contamination was spread, by the standard of those days. The government had a lot of trouble with a herd of cattle whose hair turned white as a result. It was a very dirty bomb.

The bombs at Hiroshima and Nagasaki on the other hand were clean. They   26
were exploded high in the air and few if any casualties were produced by fallout. Possibly there were a handful on a global scale, but practically all the hundreds of thousands who died, and the others who were maimed from radiation and blast, did not have the benefit of fallout. Nevertheless, I vastly prefer our first dirty bomb to those two clean ones.

When all is said and done about these problems—essentially soluble prob-   27
lems—of describing the practical consequences of scientific progress, there remains the central, perplexing question, to which I keep returning, of bringing an appreciation of the new scientific knowledge to the world. It is a question of high importance; it deserves study.

I do not see, for example, how the scientist can evoke the same understanding   28
and grateful warmth from his fellows as the actor who gives them pleasure and insight, and reveals their own predicament to them, or the musician or dancer or writer or athlete, in whom they see their talents in greater perfection, and often their own limitations and error in larger perspective. The power of the new knowledge itself to excite the intelligent public's mind is very different from the days of Newton when the problems under discussion—the course of the heavenly bodies, the laws of dynamics—were not far from ordinary human experience. People could go to demonstrations to see the new principles in action; they could discuss them in salons and cafés. The ideas were revolutionary but not very hard to understand. It is no wonder that the excitement and change

and enrichment of culture in Europe that came about as a result of these discoveries were without parallel.

Today there are sciences like that, which are just starting. During the nineteenth century the theory of evolution certainly played this role. And today, in the psychological sciences there are many fundamental points that anyone can understand if he is willing to take the trouble—science here is just beginning to leave the common experience, and the accumulated tradition has not yet grown very far.

Yet as a whole, the problem is formidable. It is not hopeless—much can and should be done. But I do not believe it can be done by the press alone. Part of the solution lies in education, and, I think, part of it lies with just learning to live with it. Our tradition and culture and community of learning have become reticulated,[8] complicated, and non-hierarchal. They have their own nobility if one brings to them the right attitudes of affection, interest, and indefatigability. The new knowledge is not the kind of thing one can ever finally master; there is no place a man can go to get it all straight. But it has its beauty if one knows how to live with it. And the main thing is to recognize this and not to talk in terms of cultures which are unattainable for us, but to welcome those that are at hand.

Because beyond the need for explanation of the practical, beyond the need for information, there will always be the need for a community of meaning and understanding. To my mind this is a basic and central need. It is a very grave circumstance of our time that the overwhelming part of new knowledge is available only to a few people and does not enrich common understanding. I think, nevertheless, that learned folk do have some sense of this community; and I think this furnishes a clue for others, because it comes in part from the similarities of experience in our professional lives—from recognizing points in common and differences in our separate traditions. We have lived in parallel ways through experience and wonder and have some glimmering of a kind of new-found harmony.

This suggests to me that all of us in our years of learning, and many if not most of us throughout our lives, need some true apprenticeship, some hard and concentrated work, in the specialized traditions. This will make us better able to understand one another but, most important of all, it will clarify for us the extent to which we do not understand one another. It will not be easy. It means a major change in the way we look at the world and in our educational practices. It means that an understanding of the scope, depth, and nature of our ignorance should be among the primary purposes of education. But to me, it seems necessary for the coherence of our culture, and for the very future of any free civilization. A faithful image of this in the public press could do a great deal to help us all get on with it.

---

[8]Reticulated: netlike, intricate, entangled. [Eds.]

J. Robert Oppenheimer

QUESTIONS

1. Oppenheimer develops his central metaphor, "the tree of knowledge," with words and phrases like "branch," "over-arching generalization," and "growth that can be measured." How do these terms, and others like them, clarify his main idea?

2. Oppenheimer spoke to an audience of editors and journalists who had their own role to play in relation to that "tree of knowledge." What do you suppose Oppenheimer took their role to be?

3. In paragraph 16, Oppenheimer alters his language to speak of "traditions" rather than "branches" of study. What does he gain by that change?

4. Discuss the relation of "pure" to "practical" science, both as Oppenheimer mentions it in paragraphs 17 and 18 and as you may have encountered those terms before.

5. Oppenheimer finally argues that our best way of understanding "the tree of knowledge" is to advance, each one of us, well along one of its branches. Understanding the whole, that is, derives from close study of a part. What do you make of that argument?

6. Write a report on a branch of knowledge in which you specialize as a student, a worker, a hobbyist, or whatever. Try to let your reader know what that area of learning is like and what it takes to become proficient in it.

7. Write a report on someone else who is a specialist at something that interests you. Define the specialty, and explain its relation to larger systems of knowledge that surround it.

8. Oppenheimer's idea of a "tree of knowledge" and his advocacy for proficiency along one of its branches raises the old question of the relative merits of being a generalist or a specialist. Write an argument in which you advocate either a general or a highly specialized education as the best course for you during your undergraduate years.

WRITING SUGGESTIONS
FOR ARGUING

1. How does Ursula Le Guin's argument about fantasy in "Why Are Americans Afraid of Dragons?" relate to Stanley Kauffmann's and Judith Crist's very different reactions to *Star Wars*? How do Le Guin's arguments relate to your own reactions to *Star Wars* or its sequels, to Disneyland, or to other popular versions of fantasy? Develop your own argument on this topic that takes account of positions represented by Le Guin, Crist, and Kauffmann.

2. Both Robert Oppenheimer in "The Tree of Knowledge" and Lewis Thomas in "The Art of Teaching Science" suggest that the general public misperceives the nature and methodology of scientific thought. In an essay compare their two arguments. Which in your view goes further toward correcting this misperception? Why?

3. Ursula Le Guin ("Why Are Americans Afraid of Dragons?"), Thomas J. Peters and Robert H. Waterman ("Analytic Ivory Towers"), and Carol Caldwell ("You Haven't Come a Long Way, Baby") all react against the inherent conservatism of corporate America. How does each go about exploring the fallacies of such conservatism? In an essay compare their criticisms and the importance of these criticisms to the overall argument being presented.

4. Arthur Miller in "Tragedy and the Common Man," Barry Commoner in "The Causes of Environmental Stress," and Steven Rose in "It's Only Human Nature" are all concerned with current explanations of the forces that determine human behavior. Where do they seem to be in agreement or disagreement with one another? In an essay discuss the role the writer's evaluation of deterministic theories plays in each argument.

5. Richard Robinson and Richard Taylor represent two sides of a debate concerning "reason" and "faith." Compare their positions with Stephen Jay Gould's argument in "Evolution as Fact and Theory." In an essay consider how effectively one may "reasonably" argue against (or in favor of) "faith."

6. Thomas Jefferson opens his Declaration of Independence by stating directly the "self-evident truths" upon which his argument will be based. In fact, every argument depends on an appeal to such unquestioned values, to a body of "truths" that the writer assumes his audience must accept (although not every writer states these "truths" as explicitly as Jefferson). Consider three essays, perhaps one from each sub-section of "Arguing" (such as John Berger's "The Question of Zoos," Sigmund Freud's "The Sexual Enlightenment of Children," and Steven Rose's "It's Only Human Nature"). Try to determine in each case the values the writer *assumes*—not the views being argued but the accepted "truths" on which the argument depends. Write an essay in which you develop a thesis about the relationship between the values a writer assumes in constructing an argument and the audience to whom the argument is directed. For example, are some values likely to have a greater influence (on particular audiences) than others?

7. How much does the audience—or the writer's assumptions about the audience—affect argumentative writing? Select three essays from "Arguing" (perhaps Ursula Le

603

Guin's "Why Are Americans Afraid of Dragons?," Thomas J. Peters's and Robert H. Waterman's "Analytic Ivory Towers," and J. Robert Oppenheimer's "The Tree of Knowledge"), and describe the ways in which these authors' presumed audiences seem to have shaped the essays. Consider such matters as the presumed relationship between author and audience in each case: friendly, hostile, or neutral; familiar or unfamiliar; writing for specialists or the general public; and so on. Consider also yourself as audience and the way your situation compares with that of the original audience. In an essay develop a thesis about the way that the author-audience relationship influences arguments or their effectiveness.

8. Has any one of the arguments in this section persuaded you to hold a view that you did not hold before you read the essay? Select the essay that you feel had the greatest effect on your own values or your own view of a particular situation. Do not pick the one you were most in agreement with before you read it. Pick the one that changed your mind the most. Try to explain exactly what caused the change. Was it reasoning? Examples? Emotional language? Or what? Use your personal experience as a persuaded reader to develop a thesis about what sorts of things are actually convincing in argumentative writing. You may wish to bring in examples, including negative examples, from other essays in this section.

9. Select the essay from "Arguing" that you found the least convincing. Assuming that you are addressing the same audience, write a reply to that essay in which you attack its weak points and bring in any additional evidence that will help you argue your case.

10. Of the essays in this section that you have read, which do you consider the best argued? Which is the worst? Write an essay in which you try to substantiate both of these judgments (that is, make an effective argument for your position), and from this, develop a thesis about what makes for good and bad argumentative writing.

11. Of the essays you have read in this section, which one do you think faced the most difficult problems in terms of the position being argued and the beliefs of the audience addressed? Discuss these problems and evaluate the author's attempts to solve them. Taking examples from other essays as well, develop a thesis about what makes an argument difficult to develop and what are the best solutions for such difficulties. You may also wish to consider the relationship between difficulty and the interest generated by any given essay.

REFLECTING

REFLECTING

Here in "Reflecting," as in other parts of this collection, you will encounter writing that touches upon a wide range of topics—from the secrets of warts to the significances of the Eiffel Tower, from the courage of turtles to the profession of engineering. But you will also find that, in their discussions of these and other topics, the authors in this section often turn out to be as much concerned with their own perceptions, thoughts, and feelings as with the matter at hand. This subjective, self-conscious, or personal quality results in part from the solitary nature of reflection. When we are reflecting, after all, we are alone with ourselves and thus are naturally inclined to become very conscious of our own immediate situation—of ourselves and our thoughts. At one moment we may be reflecting upon the flight of a hawk and the next be contemplating the drift of our own minds. So you should not be surprised to find that some of the authors here are primarily, even exclusively, concerned with themselves—with their own thoughts, thought processes, or, as in autobiography, with some aspect of their past experience. Ultimately, the subjective element is a hallmark of reflection because it involves writers in exploring some aspect of their knowledge or experience as a means of discovering and defining its personal significance—its bearing upon themselves, their ideas, and their beliefs.

This essential quality of reflective writing can be seen in the following passage from Loren Eiseley's "The Bird and the Machine":

> I suppose their little bones have years ago been lost among the stones and winds of those high glacial pastures. I suppose their feathers blew eventually into the piles of tumbleweed beneath the straggling cattle fences and rotted there in the mountain snows, along with dead steers and all the other things that drift to an end in the corners of the wire. I do not quite know why I should be thinking of birds over the *New York Times* at breakfast, particularly the birds of my youth half a continent away. It is a funny thing what the brain will do with memories and how it will treasure them and finally bring them into odd juxtapositions with other things, as though it wanted to make a design, or get some meaning out of them, whether you want it or not, or even see it.
>
> It used to seem marvelous to me, but I read now that there are machines that can do these things in a small way, machines that can crawl about like animals,

and that it may not be long now until they do more things—maybe even make themselves—I saw that piece in the *Times* just now.

This passage, from the beginning of Eiseley's essay, clearly presents him as being in a contemplative frame of mind. Indeed, the opening sentence portrays him as being so absorbed in his thoughts that he does not even bother to identify exactly what he is thinking about in his reference to "their little bones." It is as if we overhear Eiseley talking to himself rather than to us. The subject of his thoughts becomes somewhat clearer in the second sentence, but only by implication, by his reference to "their feathers." Not until the third sentence, when he mentions "the birds of my youth half a continent away," does it become clear that he has been speculating about the fate of some birds that he had evidently seen in the western mountains when he was a young man. But by this point he is no longer wondering about the fate of the birds, so much as about the focus of his thoughts, about why he "should be thinking of birds over the *New York Times* at breakfast." Eiseley's self-absorption, his curiosity about the movement of his own mind, then provokes him to reflect on the workings of the human brain, especially on "what the brain will do with memories." His thoughts about the brain together with a "piece in the *Times*" then lead him in the next paragraph to move rapidly from thinking about mechanical brains and robots to imagining the possibility of self-reproducing machines. So, over the course of a few sentences, Eiseley's mind ranges widely from thinking about the birds of his youth to contemplating machines of the future. As is typical of reflection, he seeks to make sense of things through the process of contemplating various experiences, images, ideas, or memories.

Though he ranges widely in his thoughts, each image or idea that comes to his mind is evidently occasioned either by a preceding reflection or by some aspect of his immediate situation, such as his reading of the *Times*. His thoughts develop, then, by a process of association and suggestion. This process of association is reflected by the way that a word or phrase in one sentence—"I suppose their little bones . . ."—is echoed by a word or phrase in the next—"I suppose their feathers . . ." Or by the way that one phrase seems to give rise to another, much as the "winds" of the first sentence seem to have occasioned the "feathers" that "blew" in the second. Words and phrases reverberate here, much as they do when we are actually in the process of reflecting upon something ourselves. Not only does one reflection lead into the next, but the sequence as a whole suggests that his thoughts are guided by a fascination with exploring the tension between nature and technology, between the bird and the machine. This associatively and thoughtfully linked sequence of memories, images, and ideas is typical of reflection. Reflective writing thus echoes the process that Eiseley attributes to the brain—calling upon memories, bringing them into "odd juxtapositions with other things," in order "to make a design, or get some meaning out of them."

THE RANGE OF REFLECTIVE WRITING

When writers are involved in reflecting, they are not constrained by the demands of a particular field, profession, or specialized public purpose. Though they aim to "get some meaning out of" their writing and convey it to others, the solitary and personal nature of reflection allows authors considerable freedom in their choice and development of material. Given this freedom, they can let their thoughts develop associatively, and if they wish they can also draw on the techniques of reporting, explaining, and arguing. So it is not surprising to find a broad range in the form and content of reflective writing.

You can get an initial sense of that range just by turning from the reflections of Eiseley to those of Roland Barthes on the Eiffel Tower. Whereas Eiseley ranges broadly between the images from his past and his reading of the moment, between the workings of his mind and the mentality of machines, Barthes focuses relentlessly, as in a meditation, on a single object directly within his line of vision:

> . . . at the moment I begin writing these lines about it, the Tower is there, in front of me, framed by my window; and at the very moment the January night blurs it, apparently trying to make it invisible, to deny its presence, two little lights come on, winking gently as they revolve at its very tip; all this night, too, it will be there, connecting me above Paris to each of my friends that I know are seeing it: with it we all comprise a shifting figure of which it is the steady center: the Tower is friendly.
>
> The Tower is also present to the entire world. First of all as a universal symbol of Paris, it is everywhere on the globe where Paris is to be stated as an image; from the Midwest to Australia, there is no journey to France which isn't made, somehow, in the Tower's name. . . .

The Tower is so clearly at the center of Barthes's attention that it figures as the subject or object of every sentence in the piece. Looking out at the Tower, Barthes moves back and forth in this passage between reporting more or less literal observations about it to generating metaphoric conceptions about it that grow out of his observations. In this way, he moves from noting that it is at the center of his attention to recognizing that it is also central in the lives of his Parisian friends, and this perception stimulates him, in turn, to conceive of the Tower as a living symbol of the social community that binds people to each other in friendship—"the Tower is friendly." One perspective on it suggests another, and so having meditated on its centrality in the life of Paris, Barthes is moved to consider and explain the sense in which it "is also present to the entire world."

By contrast with Barthes's concentration on a visible object, a piece of architecture, which he comes to see as a universally significant symbol, other authors turn their attention inward to reflect upon aspects of their lives as writers. Some, like James Baldwin in "Autobiographical Notes," range widely in the experiences and images that they call to mind, as they seek to make sense of how their careers and their works have been shaped by their personal and cultural experiences. Others, such as William Stafford in "A Way of Writing," focus very closely on their writing process, trying to shed light on how they "bring about new things." Still others, like George Orwell in "Why I Write," attempt to account for the complex motives that have driven them to write at various times in their lives.

The range of reflective writing is open even to imaginary experience, as you can see in the following passage from Walter Lippmann's thoughts "On Political Writing":

> The other night I sat up late reading one of those books on politics which are regarded as essential to any sort of intellectual respectability. It was a book that might be referred to in the Constitutional Convention at Albany. As I read along I was possessed with two convictions about the author. The first was that he had worn a high hat when he wrote the book; the second, that he had no teeth, which made him a little difficult to understand.

With a playful image such as Lippmann generates here at the opening of his reflections, even the drabbest subject can be brought to life—both for a writer and a reader. In fact, Lippmann manages to use his imaginary portrait as a stimulating focus for his entire reflection on political writing, continually adding details so as to build up a ludicrous picture of the unidentified author and, by extension, of political writing.

Lippman's calculated bit of satiric portraiture also reminds us that for all its freedom and variety, reflective writing does, at last, involve more than simply letting our minds wander idly, as if in reverie or daydreaming. When writers are reflecting, after all, they are using language to explore themselves and their world in a form that will make sense both to themselves and to others. So like other kinds of writing, reflecting is the outcome of various methods for achieving a particular purpose.

METHODS OF REFLECTING

Given the personal and subjective nature of reflecting, there are no hard-and-fast rules for carrying it on in writing. Still, it can be helpful to see how a few academic and professional writers conduct their reflections, if only to get some hints from them that you can try out on your own. So in the following paragraphs we have put together several observations about the methods that appear to be at work in the pieces we have collected in this section. Some of these methods may work for you, others may not. Only you can know what is best for you, and you can only know by trying some out for yourself—remembering that in exploratory writing such as this, whatever works is right.

To begin with, we have noticed that most of the writers here seem to use some method of getting started, of initially stimulating their reflections. Some writers do so by managing to have the object of their thoughts directly within their field of observation, much as Barthes is able to see the Eiffel Tower through his window while he meditates on its significance. For other writers, of course, the subject of their thoughts is out of reach, in which case they usually call up a distinctive image of the subject in their mind's eye, or their mind's ear, as does Geoffrey Wolff here at the beginning of his piece about his dead father:

> I listen for my father and I hear a stammer. This was explosive and unashamed, not a choking on words but a spray of words. His speech was headlong, edgy, breathless: there was neither room in his mouth nor time in the day to contain what he burned to utter. I have a remnant of that stammer, and I wish I did not; I stammer and blush, my father would stammer and grim. He depended on a listener's good will. My father depended excessively upon people's good will.

Though Wolff's father is dead, his father's stammer is vividly present here in this passage, partly because Wolff calls it back in the opening sentence by a conscious act of willing to hear it in his mind's ear, partly because Wolff admits to hearing it in his own echoing stammer. In some cases, however, a writer's image of the past depends not on an act of will or an echo, but on imaginative conjecture, as in Eiseley's opening suppositions about the decayed bones and rotted feathers of the birds. Whatever its source, a vivid image of the subject evidently helps many writers to begin the process of meditating or reflecting.

Some subjects, of course, initially appear to be colorless or intangible, if not downright abstract, and thus they do not seem to offer the possibility of getting started by means of contemplating a lively and suggestive image. For example, you might reasonably wonder how an author could possibly find a stimulating image with which to begin meditating on the subject of keeping a notebook. But as Joan Didion shows in the opening of her piece, "On Keeping a Notebook," one need only find a provocative, suggestive, or perplexing entry in a personal notebook to get some thoughts flowing:

> " 'That woman Estelle,' " the note reads, " 'is partly the reason why George Sharp and I are separated today' *Dirty crepe-de-Chine wrapper, hotel bar, Wilmington RR, 9:45 a.m. August Monday morning.*"
>
> Since the note is in my notebook, it presumably has some meaning to me. I study it for a long while. At first I have only the most general notion of what I was doing on an August Monday morning in the bar of the hotel across from the Pennsylvania Railroad station in Wilmington, Delaware (waiting for a train? missing one? 1960? 1961? why Wilmington?), but I do remember being there.

The lively details in her note together with the probing questions that she puts to herself about her own situation help Didion recall several paragraphs of vivid memories, which in turn raise further questions in her mind, and thus she is able to spin out a lively and thoughtful set of reflections on the value of keeping a notebook.

In some cases, however, what is lacking in fact can only be supplied by a lively fiction, as in Walter Lippmann's reflections on political writing. Lippmann, of course, is able to build an entire piece around the image of the toothless, high-hatted author, not only because the image is vivid and suggestive but also because Lippmann is alive to its suggestiveness. The initial image of a high-hatted writer immediately suggests a highly inflated and pretentious prose style, which Lippmann illustrates with a few sample phrases, such as "social con-sciousness . . . sovereign will . . . electoral duties . . . national obligations." These phrases, in turn, evidently provoke Lippmann to conjure up further details about the imaginary author, which then suggest additional qualities about his prose style. So Lippmann plays back and forth between imaginary portraiture and thoughts about the style of political writing.

Like other writers in this section, Lippmann sustains the flow of his thoughts by repeatedly playing upon the suggestive possibilities of an image or idea, a phrase or simply a word. In fact, if you look back through the several passages that we have referred to in this introduction, examining them closely with an eye to noting how authors develop their reflections, you will probably be able to discover numerous points at which they work with the implications of an image or idea by repeating or echoing a key word or phrase in a sequence of statements, as we observed Eiseley doing in "The Bird and the Machine," or as Wolff does here in his reflections on his father's stammer:

> I have a remnant of that stammer, and I wish I did not; I stammer and blush, my father would stammer and grin. He depended on a listener's good will. My father depended excessively upon people's good will.

With each echo or repetition, of course, Wolff introduces some element of variation, and as you can see from those last two sentences, just a few variations can produce very startling shifts in the thought and feeling of a reflection. "It is," as Eiseley reminds us, "a funny thing what the brain will do with memories and how it will treasure them and finally bring them into odd juxtapositions with other things."

But as Eiseley also reminds us, the brain does such funny things as if "to make a design, or get some meaning out of them." So, too, we have noticed that the authors in this section seem compelled "to get some meaning out of" the process of reflecting. They do not seem content simply to keep their thoughts flowing suggestively from one phrase to the next. So you will find that they persistently press their thoughts beyond the limits of their immediate perceptions or recollections. For some authors, this process leads to more or less clear and satisfying conclusions, as in the case of Didion, whose questioning not only helps her to call back all of the missing details from her notebook, but also enables her to see the value for herself of keeping a notebook:

It all comes back. Perhaps it is difficult to see the value in having one's self back in that kind of mood, but I do see it; I think we are well advised to keep on nodding terms with the people we used to be, whether we find them attractive company or not.

For other authors, such as Barthes, the process will seem to yield not only irresolution, but frustrating contradictions. At one point in his piece on the Tower, for example, Barthes goes so far as to say that *"it means everything,"* only to reverse himself later by asserting that "the Tower is *nothing.*" But though his piece may thus seem tantalizingly inconclusive, you will also see that in the process he has clearly pushed his reflections to the point of enabling himself— and us—to recognize that the Tower is at last a far more complex symbol than anyone may ever be able to fathom. So his reflections do enable him to get at least "some" meaning out of the Tower.

In the collection of pieces that follow, you will have the opportunity to see how nineteen writers use language to get some meaning for themselves out of reflecting on various memories, images, and ideas. And we hope that the pleasure of following their reflective movements will lead you to try some contemplative writing of your own.

Arts and Humanities

A WAY OF WRITING
William Stafford

William Stafford (b. 1914) is a writer and teacher (now at Lewis and Clark College in Oregon) who achieved recognition as a poet in the 1960s when his Traveling Through the Dark *(1963) won the National Book Award. Since then he has published several other volumes, including his collected poems,* Stories That Could Be True *(1977). The selection from his work that follows is an essay on his way of writing. It first appeared in the Oberlin College literary magazine,* Field, *in 1970.*

A writer is not so much someone who has something to say as he is someone who has found a process that will bring about new things he would not have thought of if he had not started to say them. That is, he does not draw on a reservoir; instead, he engages in an activity that brings to him a whole succession of unforeseen stories, poems, essays, plays, laws, philosophies, religions, or—but wait! 1

Back in school, from the first when I began to try to write things, I felt this richness. One thing would lead to another; the world would give and give. Now, after twenty years or so of trying, I live by that certain richness, an idea hard to pin, difficult to say, and perhaps offensive to some. For there are strange implications in it. 2

One implication is the importance of just plain receptivity. When I write, I like to have an interval before me when I am not likely to be interrupted. For me, this means usually the early morning, before others are awake. I get pen and paper, take a glance out the window (often it is dark out there), and wait. It is like fishing. But I do not wait very long, for there is always a nibble—and this is where receptivity comes in. To get started I will accept anything that 3 occurs to me. Something always occurs, of course, to any of us. We can't keep from thinking. Maybe I have to settle for an immediate impression: it's cold, or hot, or dark, or bright, or in between! Or—well, the possibilities are endless. If I put down something, that thing will help the next thing come, and I'm off. If I let the process go on, things will occur to me that were not at all in my mind when I started. These things, odd or trivial as they may be, are somehow connected. And if I let them string out, surprising things will happen.

If I let them string out. . . . Along with initial receptivity, then, there is 4
another readiness: I must be willing to fail. If I am to keep on writing, I cannot bother to insist on high standards. I must get into action and not let anything stop me, or even slow me much. By "standards" I do not mean "correctness"— spelling, punctuation, and so on. These details become mechanical for anyone who writes for a while. I am thinking about what many people would consider "important" standards, such matters as social significance, positive values, con- sistency, etc. I resolutely disregard these. Something better, greater, is happen- ing! I am following a process that leads so wildly and originally into new territory that no judgment can at the moment be made about values, significance, and so on. I am making something new, something that has not been judged before. Later others—and maybe I myself—will make judgments. Now, I am headlong to discover. Any distraction may harm the creating.

So, receptive, careless of failure, I spin out things on the page. And a won- 5
derful freedom comes. If something occurs to me, it is all right to accept it. It has one justification: it occurs to me. No one else can guide me. I must follow my own weak, wandering, diffident impulses.

A strange bonus happens. At times, without my insisting on it, my writings 6
become coherent; the successive elements that occur to me are clearly related. They lead by themselves to new connections. Sometimes the language, even the syllables that happen along, may start a trend. Sometimes the materials alert me to something waiting in my mind, ready for sustained attention. At such times, I allow myself to be eloquent, or intentional, or for great swoops (treach- erous! not to be trusted!) reasonable. But I do not insist on any of that; for I know that back of my activity there will be the coherence of my self, and that indulgence of my impulses will bring recurrent patterns and meanings again.

This attitude toward the process of writing creatively suggests a problem for 7
me, in terms of what others say. They talk about "skills" in writing. Without denying that I do have experience, wide reading, automatic orthodoxies and maneuvers of various kinds, I still must insist that I am often baffled about what "skill" has to do with the precious little area of confusion when I do not know what I am going to say and then I find out what I am going to say. That precious interval I am unable to bridge by skill. What can I witness about it? It remains mysterious, just as all of us must feel puzzled about how we are so inventive as to be able to talk along through complexities with our friends, not needing to plan what we are going to say, but never stalled for long in our confident forward

progress. Skill? If so, it is the skill we all have, something we must have learned before the age of three or four.

A writer is one who has become accustomed to trusting that grace, or luck, or—skill.   8

Yet another attitude I find necessary: most of what I write, like most of what   9
I say in casual conversation, will not amount to much. Even I will realize, and even at the time, that it is not negotiable. It will be like practice. In conversation I allow myself random remarks—in fact, as I recall, that is the way I learned to talk—, so in writing I launch many expendable efforts. A result of this free way of writing is that I am not writing for others, mostly; they will not see the product at all unless the activity eventuates in something that later appears to be worthy. My guide is the self, and its adventuring in the language brings about communication.

This process-rather-than-substance view of writing invites a final, dual re-   10
flection:

1) Writers may not be special—sensitive or talented in any usual sense. They are simply engaged in sustained use of a language skill we all have. Their "creations" come about through confident reliance on stray impulses that will, with trust, find occasional patterns that are satisfying.

2) But writing itself is one of the great, free human activities. There is scope for individuality, and elation, and discovery, in writing. For the person who follows with trust and forgiveness what occurs to him, the world remains always ready and deep, an inexhaustible environment, with the combined vividness of an actuality and flexibility of a dream. Working back and forth between experience and thought, writers have more than space and time can offer. They have the whole unexplored realm of human vision.

William Stafford

A sample daily-writing sheet and the poem as revised.

15 December 1969

[handwritten draft, largely illegible]

Shadows

I

Out in places like Wyoming some of the shadows

are cut out and pasted on fossils.

There are mountains that erode when
clouds drag across them. You can hear *the tick*

~~the tick~~ of the light breaking edges off white stones.

618

At a fountain on Main Street I saw
our shadow. It did not drink but
waited on cement and water while I drank.
There were two people and but one shadow.
I looked up so hard outward that a bird
flying past made a shadow on the sky.

There is a place in the air where our house
used to be.

Once I crawled through grassblades to hear
the sounds of their shadows. One of the shadows
moved, and it was the earth where a mole
was passing. I could hear little
paws in the dirt, and fur brush along
the tunnel, and even, somehow, the mole shadow.
In churches their hearts pump sermons
from wells full of shadows.
In my prayers I let yesterday begin
and then go behind this hour now.

SHADOWS

Out in places like Wyoming some of the shadows
are cut out and pasted on fossils.
There are mountains that erode when
clouds drag across them. You hear the tick
of sunlight breaking edges off white stones.

At a fountain on Main Street I saw
our shadow. It did not drink but
waited on cement and water while I drank.
There were two people and but one shadow.

619

William Stafford

I looked up so hard outward that a bird
flying past made a shadow on the sky.
There is a place in the air where
our old house used to be.

Once I crawled through grassblades to hear
the sounds of their shadows. One shadow
moved, and it was the earth where a mole
was passing. I could hear little
paws in the dirt, and fur brush along
the tunnel, and even, somehow, the mole shadow.

In my prayers I let yesterday begin
and then go behind this hour now,
in churches where hearts pump sermons
from wells full of shadows.

QUESTIONS

1. What was your definition of a creative writer before you read this essay? In what
ways did this essay agree with your definition? In what ways did it challenge your definition?

2. To what "others" do you think Stafford is referring in paragraph 7 when he says,
"They talk about 'skills' in writing"? How does he define skill?

3. In what ways does this essay itself reflect the way of writing that Stafford is reflecting
on? What, for example, does he mean in the second point of the last paragraph when
he writes: ". . .Writing itself is one of the great, free human activities"?

4. First, describe your own process of writing. Then summarize Stafford's process of
writing as he describes it. In what ways is his similar to or different from your own
process? Compare your process with the processes of your classmates. Can you say there
is one process of writing, or are there several or many? What similarities and differences
are most outstanding in the processes described by you and your classmates?

5. Look at the sample daily-writing sheet, the typescript, and the final version of the
poem "Shadows." Consider the changes made from one version to the next. What
material has been cut out, rearranged, or added? Write an analysis of the changes made,
considering whether they strengthen or weaken the final version of the poem.

6. Try Stafford's method by making daily-writing sheets for a week. Use your sheets
to develop a poem, a story, or an essay. Then revise your draft.

7. Use the different versions you wrote for question 6 to analyze your own revision
process. Or work with a classmate, exchanging versions and analyzing each other's changes.
Consider, as in question 5, what has been cut out, rearranged, or added and how the
changes strengthen or weaken the final version.

MEMORIES OF
MY FATHER
Geoffrey Wolff

*Geoffrey Wolff (b. 1937) went to the Choate School and
Princeton University, after which he became a journalist,
an editor, a free-lance writer, a novelist, a professor, and
his father's biographer. The following essay is chapter 1 of
his life of his father,* The Duke of Deception, *published in
1979.*

I listen for my father and I hear a stammer. This was explosive and un-   1
ashamed, not a choking on words but a spray of words. His speech was headlong,
edgy, breathless: there was neither room in his mouth nor time in the day to
contain what he burned to utter. I have a remnant of that stammer, and I wish
I did not; I stammer and blush, my father would stammer and grin. He depended
on a listener's good will. My father depended excessively upon people's good
will.

As he spoke straight at you, so did he look at you. He could stare down   2
anyone, though this was a gift he rarely practiced. To me, everything about
him seemed outsized. Doing a school report on the Easter Islanders I found in
an encyclopedia pictures of their huge sculptures, and there he was, massive
head and nose, nothing subtle or delicate. He was in fact (and how diminishing
those words, *in fact*, look to me now) an inch or two above six feet, full bodied,
a man who lumbered from here to there with deliberation. When I was a child
I noticed that people were respectful of the cubic feet my father occupied; later
I understood that I had confused respect with resentment.

I recollect things, a gentleman's accessories, deceptively simple fabrications   3
of silver and burnished nickel, of brushed Swedish stainless, of silk and soft
wool and brown leather. I remember his shoes, so meticulously selected and
cared for and used, thin-soled, with cracked uppers, older than I was or could
ever be, shining dully and from the depths. Just a pair of shoes? No: I knew
before I knew any other complicated thing that for my father there was nothing
he possessed that was "just" something. His pocket watch was not "just" a
timepiece, it was a miraculous instrument with a hinged front and a representation on its back of porcelain ducks rising from a birch-girt porcelain pond. It
struck the hour unassertively, musically, like a silver tine touched to a crystal
glass, no hurry, you might like to know it's noon.

He despised black leather, said black shoes reminded him of black attaché   4
cases, of bankers, lawyers, look-before-you-leapers anxious not to offend their

621

clients. He owned nothing black except his dinner jacket and his umbrella. His umbrella doubled as a shooting-stick, and one afternoon at a polo match at Brandywine he was sitting on it when a man asked him what he would do if it rained, sit wet or stand dry? I laughed. My father laughed also, but tightly, and he did not reply; nor did he ever again use this quixotic contraption. He took things, *things*, seriously.

My father, called Duke, taught me skills and manners; he taught me to shoot 5 and to drive fast and to read respectfully and to box and to handle a boat and to distinguish between good jazz music and bad jazz music. He was patient with me, led me to understand for myself why Billie Holiday's understatements were more interesting than Ella Fitzgerald's complications. His codes were not novel, but they were rigid, the rules of decorum that Hemingway prescribed. A gentleman kept his word, and favored simplicity of sentiment; a gentleman chose his words with care, as he chose his friends. A gentleman accepted responsibility for his acts, and welcomed the liberty to act unambiguously. A gentleman was a stickler for precision and punctilio; life was no more than an inventory of small choices that together formed a man's character, entire. A gentleman was this, and not that; a *man* did, did not, said, would not say.

My father could, however, be coaxed to reveal his bona fides. He had been 6 schooled at Groton and passed along to Yale. He was just barely prepared to intimate that he had been tapped for "Bones," and I remember his pleasure when Levi Jackson, the black captain of Yale's 1949 football team, was similarly honored by that secret society. He was proud of Skull and Bones for its hospitality toward the exotic. He did sometimes wince, however, when he pronounced Jackson's Semitic Christian name, and I sensed that his tolerance for Jews was not inclusive; but I never heard him indulge express bigotry, and the first of half a dozen times he hit me was for having called a neighbor's kid a guinea.

There was much luxury in my father's affections, and he hated what was 7 narrow, pinched, or mean. He understood exclusion, mind you, and lived his life believing the world to be divided between a few *us's* and many *them's*, but I was to understand that aristocracy was a function of taste, courage, and generosity. About two other virtues—candor and reticence—I was confused, for my father would sometimes proselytize the one, sometimes the other.

If Duke's preoccupation with bloodlines was finite, this did not cause him 8 to be unmindful of his ancestors. He knew whence he had come, and whither he meant me to go. I saw visible evidence of this, a gold signet ring which I wear today, a heavy bit of business inscribed arsy-turvy with lions and flora and a motto, *nulla vestigium retrorsit.* "Don't look back" I was told it meant.

After Yale—class of late nineteen-twenty something, or early nineteen-thirty 9 something—my father batted around the country, living a high life in New York among school and college chums, flying as a test pilot, marrying my mother, the daughter of a rear admiral. I was born a year after the marriage, in 1937, and three years after that my father went to England as a fighter pilot with Eagle Squadron, a group of American volunteers in the Royal Air Force. Later he transferred to the OSS, and was in Yugoslavia with the partisans; just before the Invasion he was parachuted into Normandy, where he served as a sapper with the Resistance, which my father pronounced *ray-zee-staunce.*

His career following the war was for me mysterious in its particulars; in the service of his nation, it was understood, candor was not always possible. This much was clear: my father mattered in the world, and was satisfied that he mattered, whether or not the world understood precisely why he mattered. 10

A pretty history for an American clubman. Its fault is that it was not true. My father was a bullshit artist. True, there were many boarding schools, each less pleased with the little Duke than the last, but none of them was Groton. There was no Yale, and by the time he walked from a room at a mention of Skull and Bones I knew this, and he knew that I knew it. No military service would have him; his teeth were bad. So he had his teeth pulled and replaced, but the Air Corps and Navy and Army and Coast Guard still thought he was a bad idea. The ring I wear was made according to his instructions by a jeweler two blocks from Schwab's drugstore in Hollywood, and was never paid for. The motto, engraved backwards so that it would come right on a red wax seal, is dog Latin and means in fact "leave no trace behind," but my father did not believe me when I told him this. 11

My father was a Jew. This did not seem to him a good idea, and so it was his notion to disassemble his history, begin at zero, and re-create himself. His sustaining line of work till shortly before he died was as a confidence man. If I now find his authentic history more surprising, more interesting, than his counterfeit history, he did not. He would not make peace with his actualities, and so he was the author of his own circumstances, and indifferent to the consequences of this nervy program. 12

There were some awful consequences, for other people as well as for him. He was lavish with money, with others' money. He preferred to stiff institutions: jewelers, car dealers, banks, fancy hotels. He was, that is, a thoughtful buccaneer, when thoughtfulness was convenient. But people were hurt by him. Much of his mischief was casual enough: I lost a tooth when I was six, and the Tooth Fairy, "financially inconvenienced" or "temporarily out of pocket," whichever was then his locution, left under my pillow an IOU, a sight draft for two bits, or two million. 13

I wish he hadn't selected from among the world's possible disguises the costume and credentials of a yacht club commodore. Beginning at scratch he might have reached further, tried something a bit more bold and odd, a bit less inexorably conventional, a bit less calculated to please. But it is true, of course, that a confidence man who cannot inspire confidence in his marks is nothing at all, so perhaps his tuneup of his bloodline, educational *vita*, and war record was merely the price of doing business in a culture preoccupied with appearances. 14

623

Geoffrey Wolff

I'm not even now certain what I wish he had made of himself: I once believed   15
that he was most naturally a fictioneer. But for all his preoccupation with make-
believe, he never tried seriously to write it. A confidence man learns early in
his career that to commit himself to paper is to court trouble. The successful
bunco artist does his game, and disappears himself: Who *was* that masked man?
No one, no one at all, *nulla vestigium* [*sic*] *retrorsit* [*sic*],[1] not a trace left behind.

Well, I'm left behind. One day, writing about my father with no want of   16
astonishment and love, it came to me that I am his creature as well as his get.
I cannot now shake this conviction, that I was trained as his instrument of
perpetuation, put here to put him into the record. And that my father knew
this, calculated it to a degree. How else explain his eruption of rage when I
once gave up what he and I called "writing" for journalism? I had taken a job
as the book critic of *The Washington Post*, was proud of myself; it seemed then
like a wonderful job, honorable and enriching. My father saw it otherwise: "You
have failed me," he wrote, "you have sold yourself at discount" he wrote to me,
his prison number stamped below his name.

He was wrong then, but he was usually right about me. He would listen to   17
anything I wished to tell him, but would not tell me only what I wished to
hear. He retained such solicitude for his clients. With me he was strict and
straight, except about himself. And so I want to be strict and straight with him,
and with myself. Writing to a friend about this book, I said that I would not
now for anything have had my father be other than what he was, except happier,
and that most of the time he was happy enough, cheered on by imaginary
successes. He gave me a great deal, and not merely life, and I didn't want to
bellyache; I wanted, I told my friend, to thumb my nose on his behalf at
everyone who had limited him. My friend was shrewd, though, and said that
he didn't believe me, that I couldn't mean such a thing, that if I followed out
its implications I would be led to a kind of ripe sentimentality, and to mere
piety. Perhaps, he wrote me, you would not have wished him to lie to himself,
to lie about being a Jew. Perhaps you would have him fool others but not so
deeply trick himself. "In writing about a father," my friend wrote me about our
fathers, "one clambers up a slippery mountain, carrying the balls of another in
a bloody sack, and whether to eat them or worship them or bury them decently
is never cleanly decided."

So I will try here to be exact. I wish my father had done more headlong,   18
more elegant inventing. I believe he would respect my wish, be willing to speak
with me seriously about it, find some nobility in it. But now he is dead, and
he had been dead two weeks when they found him. And in his tiny flat at the
edge of the Pacific they found no address book, no batch of letters held with a
rubber band, no photograph. Not a thing to suggest that he had ever known
another human being.

---

[1] *nulla vestigium* [*sic*] *retrorsit* [*sic*]: the correct Latin would be *nulla vestigia retrorsum*. [Eds.]

QUESTIONS

1. Summarize in your own words Wolff's attitude toward his father.

2. Wolff's translation of his father's motto is "leave no trace behind." How does this motto relate to Duke's life? Consider especially paragraphs 15 through 18.

3. In paragraph 12, Wolff calls his father an "author." What does he mean by this? What else does he call him?

4. This essay does not have the structure of an argument, a report, or even an explanation. It moves with the mind, as a reflection, a meditation, or a memoir. Do you find any structure in it—any principles of organization? If so, what are these principles?

5. Consider the structure of the first two paragraphs. How does the last sentence of each relate to the preceding material in the paragraph? How does the last sentence change your interpretation of what you have read in the rest of the paragraph?

6. Paragraphs 6 through 10 give an account of Duke's life. How does reading paragraph 11 change your interpretation of this account? What has the supposed motto "Don't look back" to do with the way these paragraphs are organized? Why does Wolff allow the reader to believe Duke's lies for several paragraphs before the deception is revealed?

7. Wolff's vocabulary and his sentence construction range widely from the elegant to the vulgar, the delicate to the blunt. Locate some instances of rapid shifting from one to the other. What is the effect of these switches?

8. Reflect on an incident in your childhood involving a parent or older relative or friend. Describe the incident as you saw it then and as you now see it. What did you learn about this person—and perhaps about yourself? Try to avoid (as Wolff's friend warns) "ripe sentimentality" and "mere piety" (paragraph 17).

THE DEATH
OF THE MOTH
Virginia Woolf

Born in 1882, Virginia Woolf became one of England's major modern novelists before her death in 1941. She is also known as the author of important critical essays and such personal documents as letters, journals, and familiar essays. The selection from her work reprinted here stands somewhere between the observations of a naturalist and the familiar essay, as the observations become an occasion for reflection. Ironically, this selection was first published for a wide audience in the posthumous collection The Death of the Moth and Other Essays *(1942), seen into print by her husband, Leonard Woolf.*

Moths that fly by day are not properly to be called moths; they do not excite that pleasant sense of dark autumn nights and ivy-blossom which the commonest yellow-underwing asleep in the shadow of the curtain never fails to rouse in us. They are hybrid creatures, neither gay like butterflies nor sombre like their own species. Nevertheless the present specimen, with his narrow hay-colored wings, fringed with a tassel of the same color, seemed to be content with life. It was a pleasant morning, mid-September, mild, benignant, yet with a keener breath than that of the summer months. The plough was already scoring the field opposite the window, and where the share had been, the earth was pressed flat and gleamed with moisture. Such vigor came rolling in from the fields and the down beyond that it was difficult to keep the eyes strictly turned upon the book. The rooks too were keeping one of their annual festivities;[1] soaring round the tree tops until it looked as if a vast net with thousands of black knots in it had been cast up into the air; which, after a few moments sank slowly down upon the trees until every twig seemed to have a knot at the end of it. Then, suddenly, the net would be thrown into the air again in a wider circle this time, with the utmost clamor and vociferation, as though to be thrown into the air and settle slowly down upon the tree tops were a tremendously exciting experience.

The same energy which inspired the rooks, the ploughmen, the horses, and even, it seemed, the lean bare-backed downs, sent the moth fluttering from side to side of his square of the window-pane. One could not help watching him. One was, indeed, conscious of a queer feeling of pity for him. The possibilities

---

[1]rooks: European birds, similar to American crows. [Eds.]

of pleasure seemed that morning so enormous and so various that to have only a moth's part in life, and a day moth's at that, appeared a hard fate, and his zest in enjoying his meagre opportunities to the full, pathetic. He flew vigorously to one corner of his compartment, and, after waiting there a second, flew across to the other. What remained for him but to fly to a third corner and then to a fourth? That was all he could do, in spite of the size of the downs, the width of the sky, the far-off smoke of houses, and the romantic voice, now and then, of a steamer out at sea. What he could do he did. Watching him, it seemed as if a fibre, very thin but pure, of the enormous energy of the world had been thrust into his frail and diminutive body. As often as he crossed the pane, I could fancy that a thread of vital light became visible. He was little or nothing but life.

Yet, because he was so small, and so simple a form of the energy that was   3
rolling in at the open window and driving its way through so many narrow and intricate corridors in my own brain and in those of other human beings, there was something marvelous as well as pathetic about him. It was as if someone had taken a tiny bead of pure life and decking it as lightly as possible with down and feathers, had set it dancing and zigzagging to show us the true nature of life. Thus displayed one could not get over the strangeness of it. One is apt to forget all about life, seeing it humped and bossed and garnished and cumbered so that it has to move with the greatest circumspection and dignity. Again, the thought of all that life might have been had he been born in any other shape caused one to view his simple activities with a kind of pity.

After a time, tired by his dancing apparently, he settled on the window ledge   4
in the sun, and, the queer spectacle being at an end, I forgot about him. Then, looking up, my eye was caught by him. He was trying to resume his dancing, but seemed either so stiff or so awkward that he could only flutter to the bottom of the window-pane; and when he tried to fly across it he failed. Being intent on other matters I watched these futile attempts for a time without thinking, unconsciously waiting for him to resume his flight, as one waits for a machine, that has stopped momentarily, to start again without considering the reason of its failure. After perhaps a seventh attempt he slipped from the wooden ledge and fell, fluttering his wings, onto his back on the window sill. The helplessness of his attitude roused me. It flashed upon me he was in difficulties; he could no longer raise himself; his legs struggled vainly. But, as I stretched out a pencil, meaning to help him to right himself, it came over me that the failure and awkwardness were the approach of death. I laid the pencil down again.

The legs agitated themselves once more. I looked as if for the enemy against   5
which he struggled. I looked out of doors. What had happened there? Presumably it was midday, and work in the fields had stopped. Stillness and quiet had replaced the previous animation. The birds had taken themselves off to feed in the brooks. The horses stood still. Yet the power was there all the same, massed outside indifferent, impersonal, not attending to anything in particular. Some-

how it was opposed to the little hay-colored moth. It was useless to try to do anything. One could only watch the extraordinary efforts made by those tiny legs against an oncoming doom which could, had it chosen, have submerged an entire city, not merely a city, but masses of human beings; nothing, I knew, had any chance against death. Nevertheless after a pause of exhaustion the legs fluttered again. It was superb this last protest, and so frantic that he succeeded at last in righting himself. One's sympathies, of course, were all on the side of life. Also, when there was nobody to care or to know, this gigantic effort on the part of an insignificant little moth, against a power of such magnitude, to retain what no one else valued or desired to keep, moved one strangely. Again, some-how, one saw life, a pure bead. I lifted the pencil again, useless though I knew it to be. But even as I did so, the unmistakable tokens of death showed them-selves. The body relaxed, and instantly grew stiff. The struggle was over. The insignificant little creature now knew death. As I looked at the dead moth, this minute wayside triumph of so great a force over so mean an antagonist filled me with wonder. Just as life had been strange a few minutes before, so death was now as strange. The moth having righted himself now lay most decently and uncomplainingly composed. O yes, he seemed to say, death is stronger than I am.

QUESTIONS

1. A moth is a creature so small and insignificant that most of us would not pay attention to its dying. Why does Woolf pay attention? How does she engage our attention?

2. What most impresses Woolf as she watches the moth? What are the symbolic overtones of what she sees?

3. Why does Woolf describe in paragraph 1 the scene beyond the window? How does this description connect with her purpose in writing this essay?

4. In this essay, we are presented with the flow of events concerning the death of the moth and Woolf's thoughts concerning the dying of the moth. Analyze how these different strands are woven together to create the symbolic effect of the essay.

5. If you have had an experience similar to Woolf's involving an insect or small animal, write a description of that experience, in which you include what you saw and what you thought.

6. For many of us, our first experience with death involves the death of an animal— a pet or some creature we've seen die as the victim of a car or of another animal. Write an essay in which you consider such an event and whether it helped you understand and accept the reality of death.

THE IGUANA
Isak Dinesen

Karen Dinesen (1885–1962) was a Danish woman who married a Swedish baron and went to Kenya in East Africa with him in 1914 to manage their coffee plantation. After their divorce she stayed in Kenya, managing the plantation until its failure in 1931. During this time she began to write in English (the language of whites in Kenya), taking the male first name of Isak. Her best-known books are Seven Gothic Tales *(1934), a volume of stories, and* Out of Africa *(1937), her reminiscences of Kenya. The following brief selection from the latter volume appeared in the section called "From an Immigrant's Notebook."*

In the Reserve I have sometimes come upon the Iguana, the big lizards,[1] as they were sunning themselves upon a flat stone in a river-bed. They are not pretty in shape, but nothing can be imagined more beautiful than their coloring. They shine like a heap of precious stones or like a pane cut out of an old church window. When, as you approach, they swish away, there is a flash of azure, green and purple over the stones, the color seems to be standing behind them in the air, like a comet's luminous tail. 1

Once I shot an Iguana. I thought that I should be able to make some pretty things from his skin. A strange thing happened then, that I have never afterwards forgotten. As I went up to him, where he was laying dead upon his stone, and actually while I was walking the few steps, he faded and grew pale, all color died out of him as in one long sigh, and by the time that I touched him he was grey and dull like a lump of concrete. It was the live impetuous blood pulsating within the animal, which had radiated out all that glow and splendor. Now that the flame was put out, and the soul had flown, the Iguana was as dead as a sandbag. 2

Often since I have, in some sort, shot an Iguana, and I have remembered the one of the Reserve. Up at Meru I saw a young Native girl with a bracelet on, a leather strap two inches wide, and embroidered all over with very small turquoise-colored beads which varied a little in color and played in green, light blue and ultramarine. It was an extraordinarily live thing; it seemed to draw breath on her arm, so that I wanted it for myself, and made Farah buy it from her.[2] No sooner had it come upon my own arm than it gave up the ghost. It 3

---

[1] the Reserve: the game reserve in the Ngong Hills of Kenya, Africa. [Eds.]
[2] Farah Aden: Dinesen's Somali servant. [Eds.]

was nothing now, a small, cheap, purchased article of finery. It had been the play of colors, the duet between the turquoise and the "nègre",—that quick, sweet, brownish black, like peat and black pottery, of the Native's skin,—that had created the life of the bracelet.

In the Zoological Museum of Pietermaritzburg, I have seen, in a stuffed deep-water fish in a showcase, the same combination of coloring, which there had survived death; it made me wonder what life can well be like, on the bottom of the sea, to send up something so live and airy. I stood in Meru and looked at my pale hand and at the dead bracelet, it was as if an injustice had been done to a noble thing, as if truth had been suppressed. So sad did it seem that I remembered the saying of the hero in a book that I had read as a child: "I have conquered them all, but I am standing amongst graves."

In a foreign country and with foreign species of life one should take measures to find out whether things will be keeping their value when dead. To the settlers of East Africa I give the advice: "For the sake of your own eyes and heart, shoot not the Iguana."

QUESTIONS

1. In this essay the act of shooting an iguana comes to stand as a type or model of other actions; it becomes a symbolic event. This is expressed explicitly at the beginning of paragraph 3: "Often since I have, *in some sort*, shot an Iguana" (italics added). How do the incidents described in paragraphs 3 and 4 help us to understand the full meaning of the symbolic action of shooting an iguana? Restate this meaning in your own words.

2. An argument that lurks beneath the surface of this meditative essay is made explicit in its last sentence. How do you understand that sentence and that argument?

3. The power of this essay grows from its effective representation—its ability to put us in the picture, to make us see and feel the events represented. Find a phrase of description or comparison that seems to you especially vivid, and explain why it is effective.

4. Dinesen uses three concrete examples here. How are the three related? Why do you suppose she arranged them in the order in which she did?

5. In her meditation, Dinesen moves from lizard, to bracelet, to fish, and then uses these three specific, concrete instances to make the jump to generalizations about foreign species and foreign countries. Try this technique yourself. Find some incident in your own life that reminds you of other similar events, so that they can be brought together as being symbolic of a certain *kind* of event. To what broader point can you leap from these few recollected events?

AUTOBIOGRAPHICAL NOTES

James Baldwin

James Baldwin was born in Harlem in 1924 and followed his father's vocation, becoming a preacher at age fourteen. At seventeen, he left the ministry and devoted himself to writing. Baldwin's most frequent subject has been the relationship between blacks and whites, about which he writes, "The color of my skin makes me, automatically, an expert." He has written five novels, a book of stories, one play, and several collections of essays. This essay, "Autobiographical Notes," introduces his collection, Notes of a Native Son *(1955).*

I was born in Harlem thirty-one years ago. I began plotting novels at about the time I learned to read. The story of my childhood is the usual bleak fantasy, and we can dismiss it with the restrained observation that I certainly would not consider living it again. In those days my mother was given to the exasperating and mysterious habit of having babies. As they were born, I took them over with one hand and held a book with the other. The children probably suffered, though they have since been kind enough to deny it, and in this way I read *Uncle Tom's Cabin* and *A Tale of Two Cities* over and over and over again; in this way, in fact, I read just about everything I could get my hands on—except the Bible, probably because it was the only book I was discouraged to read. I must also confess that I wrote—a great deal—and my first professional triumph, in any case, the first effort of mine to be seen in print, occurred at the age of twelve or thereabouts, when a short story I had written about the Spanish revolution won some sort of prize in an extremely short-lived church newspaper. I remember the story was censored by the lady editor, though I don't remember why, and I was outraged.

Also wrote plays, and songs, for one of which I received a letter of congratulations from Mayor La Guardia, and poetry, about which the less said, the better. My mother was delighted by all these goings-on, but my father wasn't; he wanted me to be a preacher. When I was fourteen I became a preacher, and when I was seventeen I stopped. Very shortly thereafter I left home. For God knows how long I struggled with the world of commerce and industry—I guess they would say they struggled with *me*—and when I was about twenty-one I had enough done of a novel to get a Saxton Fellowship. When I was twenty-two the fellowship was over, the novel turned out to be unsalable, and I started

1

2

James Baldwin

waiting on tables in a Village restaurant and writing book reviews—mostly, as it turned out, about the Negro problem, concerning which the color of my skin made me automatically an expert. Did another book, in company with photographer Theodore Pelatowski, about the store-front churches in Harlem. This book met exactly the same fate as my first—fellowship, but no sale. (It was a Rosenwald Fellowship.) By the time I was twenty-four I had decided to stop reviewing books about the Negro problem—which, by this time, was only slightly less horrible in print than it was in life—and I packed my bags and went to France, where I finished, God knows how, *Go Tell It on the Mountain*.

Any writer, I suppose, feels that the world into which he was born is nothing   3
less than a conspiracy against the cultivation of his talent—which attitude certainly has a great deal to support it. On the other hand, it is only because the world looks on his talent with such a frightening indifference that the artist is compelled to make his talent important. So that any writer, looking back over even so short a span of time as I am here forced to assess, finds that the things which hurt him and the things which helped him cannot be divorced from each other; he could be helped in a certain way only because he was hurt in a certain way; and his help is simply to be enabled to move from one conundrum to the next—one is tempted to say that he moves from one disaster to the next. When one begins looking for influences one finds them by the score. I haven't thought much about my own, not enough anyway; I hazard that the King James Bible, the rhetoric of the store-front church, something ironic and violent and perpetually understated in Negro speech—and something of Dickens' love for bravura—have something to do with me today; but I wouldn't stake my life on it. Likewise, innumerable people have helped me in many ways; but finally, I suppose, the most difficult (and most rewarding) thing in my life has been the fact that I was born a Negro and was forced, therefore, to effect some kind of truce with this reality. (Truce, by the way, is the best one can hope for.)

One of the difficulties about being a Negro writer (and this is not special   4
pleading, since I don't mean to suggest that he has it worse than anybody else) is that the Negro problem is written about so widely. The bookshelves groan under the weight of information, and everyone therefore considers himself informed. And this information, furthermore, operates usually (generally, popularly) to reinforce traditional attitudes. Of traditional attitudes there are only two—For or Against—and I, personally, find it difficult to say which attitude has caused me the most pain. I am speaking as a writer; from a social point of view I am perfectly aware that the change from ill-will to good-will, however motivated, however imperfect, however expressed, is better than no change at all.

But it is part of the business of the writer—as I see it—to examine attitudes,   5
to go beneath the surface, to tap the source. From this point of view the Negro problem is nearly inaccessible. It is not only written about so widely; it is written about so badly. It is quite possible to say that the price a Negro pays for becoming articulate is to find himself, at length, with nothing to be articulate about. ("You

taught me language," says Caliban to Prospero,[1] "and my profit on't is I know how to curse.") Consider: the tremendous social activity that this problem generates imposes on whites and Negroes alike the necessity of looking forward, of working to bring about a better day. This is fine, it keeps the waters troubled; it is all, indeed, that has made possible the Negro's progress. Nevertheless, social affairs are not generally speaking the writer's prime concern, whether they ought to be or not; it is absolutely necessary that he establish between himself and these affairs a distance which will allow, at least, for clarity, so that before he can look forward in any meaningful sense, he must first be allowed to take a long look back. In the context of the Negro problem neither whites nor blacks, for excellent reasons of their own, have the faintest desire to look back; but I think that the past is all that makes the present coherent, and further, that the past will remain horrible for exactly as long as we refuse to assess it honestly.

I know, in any case, that the most crucial time in my own development came 6 when I was forced to recognize that I was a kind of bastard of the West; when I followed the line of my past I did not find myself in Europe but in Africa. And this meant that in some subtle way, in a really profound way, I brought to Shakespeare, Bach, Rembrandt, to the stones of Paris, to the cathedral at Chartres, and to the Empire State Building, a special attitude. These were not really my creations, they did not contain my history; I might search in them in vain forever for any reflection of myself. I was an interloper; this was not my heritage. At the same time I had no other heritage which I could possibly hope to use—I had certainly been unfitted for the jungle or the tribe. I would have to appropriate these white centuries, I would have to make them mine—I would have to accept my special attitude, my special place in this scheme—otherwise I would have no place in *any* scheme. What was the most difficult was the fact that I was forced to admit something I had always hidden from myself, which the American Negro has had to hide from himself as the price of his public progress; that I hated and feared white people. This did not mean that I loved black people; on the contrary, I despised them, possibly because they failed to produce Rembrandt. In effect, I hated and feared the world. And this meant, not only that I thus gave the world an altogether murderous power over me, but also that in such a self-destroying limbo I could never hope to write.

One writes out of one thing only—one's own experience. Everything depends 7 on how relentlessly one forces from this experience the last drop, sweet or bitter, it can possibly give. This is the only real concern of the artist, to recreate out of the disorder of life that order which is art. The difficulty then, for me, of being a Negro writer was the fact that I was, in effect, prohibited from examining my own experience too closely by the tremendous demands and the very real dangers of my social situation.

I don't think the dilemma outlined above is uncommon. I do think, since 8

---

[1]Caliban to Prospero: characters in Shakespeare's *The Tempest*. Caliban, a savage and deformed creature, is the slave of Prospero, the rightful Duke of Milan. [Eds.]

writers work in the disastrously explicit medium of language, that it goes a little way towards explaining why, out of the enormous resources of Negro speech and life, and despite the example of Negro music, prose written by Negroes has been generally speaking so pallid and so harsh. I have not written about being a Negro at such length because I expect that to be my only subject, but only because it was the gate I had to unlock before I could hope to write about anything else. I don't think that the Negro problem in America can be even discussed coherently without bearing in mind its context; its context being the history, traditions, customs, the moral assumptions and preoccupations of the country; in short, the general social fabric. Appearances to the contrary, no one in America escapes its effects and everyone in America bears some responsibility for it. I believe this the more firmly because it is the overwhelming tendency to speak of this problem as though it were a thing apart. But in the work of Faulkner, in the general attitude and certain specific passages in Robert Penn Warren, and, most significantly, in the advent of Ralph Ellison, one sees the beginnings—at least—of a more genuinely penetrating search. Mr. Ellison, by the way, is the first Negro novelist I have ever read to utilize in language, and brilliantly, some of the ambiguity and irony of Negro life.

About my interests: I don't know if I have any, unless the morbid desire to   9 own a sixteen-millimeter camera and make experimental movies can be so classified. Otherwise, I love to eat and drink—it's my melancholy conviction that I've scarcely ever had enough to eat (this is because it's *impossible* to eat enough if you're worried about the next meal)—and I love to argue with people who do not disagree with me too profoundly, and I love to laugh. I do *not* like bohemia, or bohemians, I do not like people whose principal aim is pleasure, and I do not like people who are *earnest* about anything. I don't like people who like me because I'm a Negro; neither do I like people who find in the same accident grounds for contempt. I love America more than any other country in the world, and, exactly for this reason, I insist on the right to criticize her perpetually. I think all theories are suspect, that the finest principles may have to be modified, or may even be pulverized by the demands of life, and that one must find, therefore, one's own moral center and move through the world hoping that this center will guide one aright. I consider that I have many responsibilities, but none greater than this: to last, as Hemingway says, and get my work done.

I want to be an honest man and a good writer.   10

QUESTIONS

1. What does Baldwin believe is the business of the writer? With what should a writer be concerned?

2. What circumstances have influenced Baldwin as a writer? What does he consider the most important point in his development as a writer?

3. Explain what you think Baldwin means when he writes in paragraph 8: "I have not written about being a Negro at such length because I expect that to be my only subject, but only because it was the gate I had to unlock before I could hope to write about anything else."

4. What is Baldwin's point of view toward himself and his life as a writer? That is, what sense of himself does he project? Find specific passages in the essay to support your answer.

5. What is Baldwin's tone? What is the effect of this tone with an autobiographical topic?

6. Baldwin finds it hard to separate the things that helped him as a writer from those that hurt him. Consider your own experiences with writing, and write an essay in which you reflect on what has been most helpful and most harmful in your development as a writer.

7. What central fact of your life—race, religion, parents, birthplace, special abilities, and so on—has influenced you the most? Write your own "Autobiographical Notes" in which you focus on the influence of this central fact on the shaping of your life.

ON KEEPING A NOTEBOOK

Joan Didion

*Joan Didion was born in Sacramento, California, in 1934
and graduated with a B.A. in English from the University
of California at Berkeley in 1956. Until the publication of
her first novel,* Run River, *in 1963, she worked as an associate feature editor for* Vogue *magazine. Since then she
has written two more novels,* Play It as It Lays *(1971) and*
A Book of Common Prayer *(1977), as well as three books
of essays,* Slouching Towards Bethlehem *(1969),* The White
Album *(1982), and* Salvador *(1983). As an essayist, she has
shown herself to be a trenchant observer and interpreter of
American society. The selection reprinted here is from*
Slouching Towards Bethlehem.

" 'That woman Estelle,' " the note reads, " 'is partly the reason why George   1
Sharp and I are separated today' *Dirty crepe-de-Chine wrapper, hotel bar, Wilmington RR, 9:45 a.m. August Monday morning.*"

Since the note is in my notebook, it presumably has some meaning to me.   2
I study it for a long while. At first I have only the most general notion of what
I was doing on an August Monday morning in the bar of the hotel across from
the Pennsylvania Railroad station in Wilmington, Delaware (waiting for a train?
missing one? 1960? 1961? why Wilmington?), but I do remember being there.
The woman in the dirty crepe-de-Chine wrapper had come down from her
room for a beer, and the bartender had heard before the reason why George
Sharp and she were separated today. "Sure," he said, and went on mopping the
floor, "You told me." At the other end of the bar is a girl. She is talking,
pointedly, not to the man beside her but to a cat lying in the triangle of sunlight
cast through the open door. She is wearing a plaid silk dress from Peck & Peck,
and the hem is coming down.

Here is what it is: the girl has been on the Eastern Shore, and now she is   3
going back to the city, leaving the man beside her, and all she can see ahead
are the viscous summer sidewalks and the 3 A.M. long-distance calls that will
make her lie awake and then sleep drugged through all the steaming mornings
left in August (1960? 1961?). Because she must go directly from the train to
lunch in New York, she wishes that she had a safety pin for the hem of the
plaid silk dress, and she also wishes that she could forget about the hem and
the lunch and stay in the cool bar that smells of disinfectant and malt and make

friends with the woman in the crepe-de-Chine wrapper. She is afflicted by a little self-pity, and she wants to compare Estelles. That is what that was all about.

Why did I write it down? In order to remember, of course, but exactly what 4
was it I wanted to remember? How much of it actually happened? Did any of it? Why do I keep a notebook at all? It is easy to deceive oneself on all those scores. The impulse to write things down is a peculiarly compulsive one, inexplicable to those who do not share it, useful only accidentally, only secondarily, in the way that any compulsion tries to justify itself. I suppose that it begins or does not begin in the cradle. Although I have felt compelled to write things down since I was five years old, I doubt that my daughter ever will, for she is a singularly blessed and accepting child, delighted with life exactly as life presents itself to her, unafraid to go to sleep and unafraid to wake up. Keepers of private notebooks are a different breed altogether, lonely and resistant rearrangers of things, anxious malcontents, children afflicted apparently at birth with some presentiment of loss.

My first notebook was a Big Five tablet, given to me by my mother with the 5
sensible suggestion that I stop whining and learn to amuse myself by writing down my thoughts. She returned the tablet to me a few years ago; the first entry is an account of a woman who believed herself to be freezing to death in the Arctic night, only to find, when day broke, that she had stumbled onto the Sahara Desert, where she would die of the heat before lunch. I have no idea what turn of a five-year-old's mind could have prompted so insistently "ironic" and exotic a story, but it does reveal a certain predilection for the extreme which has dogged me into adult life; perhaps if I were analytically inclined I would find it a truer story than any I might have told about Donald Johnson's birthday party or the day my cousin Brenda put Kitty Litter in the Aquarium.

So the point of my keeping a notebook has never been, nor is it now, to 6
have an accurate factual record of what I have been doing or thinking. That would be a different impulse entirely, an instinct for reality which I sometimes envy but do not possess. At no point have I ever been able successfully to keep a diary; my approach to daily life ranges from the grossly negligent to the merely absent, and on those few occasions when I have tried dutifully to record a day's events, boredom has so overcome me that the results are mysterious at best. What is this business about "shopping, typing piece, dinner with E, depressed"? Shopping for what? Typing what piece? Who is E? Was this "E" depressed, or was I depressed? Who cares?

In fact I have abandoned altogether that kind of pointless entry; instead I tell 7
what some would call lies. "That's simply not true," the members of my family frequently tell me when they come up against my memory of a shared event. "The party was *not* for you, the spider was *not* a black widow, *it wasn't that way at all.*" Very likely they are right, for not only have I always had trouble

distinguishing between what happened and what merely might have happened, but I remain unconvinced that the distinction, for my purposes, matters. The cracked crab that I recall having for lunch the day my father came home from Detroit in 1945 must certainly be embroidery, worked into the day's pattern to lend verisimilitude; I was ten years old and would not now remember the cracked crab. The day's events did not turn on cracked crab. And yet it is precisely that fictitious crab that makes me see the afternoon all over again, a home movie run all too often, the father bearing gifts, the child weeping, an exercise in family love and guilt. Or that is what it was to me. Similarly, perhaps it never did snow that August in Vermont; perhaps there never were flurries in the night wind, and maybe no one else felt the ground hardening and summer already dead even as we pretended to bask in it, but that was how it felt to me, and it might as well have snowed, could have snowed, did snow.

How it felt to me: that is getting closer to the truth about a notebook. I 8
sometimes delude myself about why I keep a notebook, imagine that some thrifty virtue derives from preserving everything observed. See enough and write it down, I tell myself, and them some morning when the world seems drained of wonder, some day when I am only going through the motions of doing what I am supposed to do, which is write—on that bankrupt morning I will simply open my notebook and there it will all be, a forgotten account with accumulated interest, paid passage back to the world out there: dialogue overheard in hotels and elevators and at the hat-check counter in Pavillon (one middle-aged man shows his hat check to another and says, "That's my old football number"); impressions of Bettina Aptheker and Benjamin Sonnenberg and Teddy ("Mr. Acapulco") Stauffer; careful *aperçus* about tennis bums and failed fashion models and Greek shipping heiresses, one of whom taught me a significant lesson (a lesson I could have learned from F. Scott Fitzgerald, but perhaps we all must meet the very rich for ourselves) by asking, when I arrived to interview her in her orchid-filled sitting room on the second day of a paralyzing New York blizzard, whether it was snowing outside.

I imagine, in other words, that the notebook is about other people. But of 9
course it is not. I have no real business with what one stranger said to another at the hat-check counter in Pavillon; in fact I suspect that the line "That's my old football number" touched not my own imagination at all, but merely some memory of something once read, probably "The Eighty-Yard Run." Nor is my concern with a woman in a dirty crepe-de-Chine wrapper in a Wilmington bar. My stake is always, of course, in the unmentioned girl in the plaid silk dress. *Remember what it was to be me:* that is always the point.

It is a difficult point to admit. We are brought up in the ethic that others, 10
any others, all others, are by definition more interesting than ourselves; taught to be diffident, just this side of self-effacing. ("You're the least important person in the room and don't forget it," Jessica Mitford's governess would hiss in her

ear on the advent of any social occasion; I copied that into my notebook because it is only recently that I have been able to enter a room without hearing some such phrase in my inner ear.) Only the very young and the very old may recount their dreams at breakfast, dwell upon self, interrupt with memories of beach picnics and favorite Liberty lawn dresses and the rainbow trout in a creek near Colorado Springs. The rest of us are expected, rightly, to affect absorption in other people's favorite dresses, other people's trout.

And so we do. But our notebooks give us away, for however dutifully we   11 record what we see around us, the common denominator of all we see is always, transparently, shamelessly, the implacable "I." We are not talking here about the kind of notebook that is patently for public consumption, a structural conceit for binding together a series of graceful *pensées*; we are talking about something private, about bits of the mind's string too short to use, an indiscriminate and erratic assemblage with meaning only for its maker.

And sometimes even the maker has difficulty with the meaning. There does   12 not seem to be, for example, any point in my knowing for the rest of my life that, during 1964, 720 tons of soot fell on every square mile of New York City, yet there it is in my notebook, labeled "FACT." Nor do I really need to remember that Ambrose Bierce liked to spell Leland Stanford's name "£eland $tanford" or that "smart women almost always wear black in Cuba," a fashion hint without much potential for practical application. And does not the relevance of these notes seem marginal at best?:

> In the basement museum of the Inyo County Courthouse in Independence, California, sign pinned to a mandarin coat: "This MANDARIN COAT was often worn by Mrs. Minnie S. Brooks when giving lectures on her TEAPOT COLLECTION."
> Redhead getting out of car in front of Beverly Wilshire Hotel, chinchilla stole, Vuitton bags with tags reading:

> MRS LOU FOX
> HOTEL SAHARA
> VEGAS

Well, perhaps not entirely marginal. As a matter of fact, Mrs. Minnie S.   13 Brooks and her MANDARIN COAT pull me back into my own childhood, for although I never knew Mrs. Brooks and did not visit Inyo County until I was thirty, I grew up in just such a world, in houses cluttered with Indian relics and bits of gold ore and ambergris and the souvenirs my Aunt Mercy Farnsworth brought back from the Orient. It is a long way from that world to Mrs. Lou Fox's world, where we all live now, and is it not just as well to remember that? Might not Mrs. Minnie S. Brooks help me to remember what I am? Might not Mrs. Lou Fox help me to remember what I am not?

But sometimes the point is harder to discern. What exactly did I have in   14 mind when I noted down that it cost the father of someone I know $650 a month to light the place on the Hudson in which he lived before the Crash?

What use was I planning to make of this line by Jimmy Hoffa: "I may have my faults, but being wrong ain't one of them"? And although I think it interesting to know where the girls who travel with the Syndicate have their hair done when they find themselves on the West Coast, will I ever make suitable use of it? Might I not be better off just passing it on to John O'Hara? What is a recipe for sauerkraut doing in my notebook? What kind of magpie keeps this notebook? "*He was born the night the Titanic went down.*" That seems a nice enough line, and I even recall who said it, but is it not really a better line in life than it could ever be in fiction?

But of course that is exactly it: not that I should ever use the line, but that I should remember the woman who said it and the afternoon I heard it. We were on her terrace by the sea, and we were finishing the wine left from lunch, trying to get what sun there was, a California winter sun. The woman whose husband was born the night the *Titanic* went down wanted to rent her house, wanted to go back to her children in Paris. I remember wishing that I could afford the house, which cost $1,000 a month. "Someday you will," she said lazily. "Someday it all comes." There in the sun on her terrace it seemed easy to believe in someday, but later I had a low-grade afternoon hangover and ran over a black snake on the way to the supermarket and was flooded with inexplicable fear when I heard the checkout clerk explaining to the man ahead of me why she was finally divorcing her husband. "He left me no choice," she said over and over as she punched the register. "He has a little seven-month-old baby by her, he left me no choice." I would like to believe that my dread then was for the human condition, but of course it was for me, because I wanted a baby and did not then have one and because I wanted to own the house that cost $1,000 a month to rent and because I had a hangover.

It all comes back. Perhaps it is difficult to see the value in having one's self back in that kind of mood, but I do see it; I think we are well advised to keep on nodding terms with the people we used to be, whether we find them attractive company or not. Otherwise they turn up unannounced and surprise us, come hammering on the mind's door at 4 A.M. of a bad night and demand to know who deserted them, who betrayed them, who is going to make amends. We forget all too soon the things we thought we could never forget. We forget the loves and the betrayals alike, forget what we whispered and what we screamed, forget who we were. I have already lost touch with a couple of people I used to be; one of them, a seventeen-year-old, presents little threat, although it would be of some interest to me to know again what it feels like to sit on a river levee drinking vodka-and-orange-juice and listening to Les Paul and Mary Ford and their echoes sing "How High the Moon" on the car radio. (You see I still have the scenes, but I no longer perceive myself among those present, no longer could even improvise the dialogue.) The other one, a twenty-three-year-old, bothers me more. She was always a good deal of trouble, and I suspect she will reappear when I least want to see her, skirts too long, shy to the point of aggravation,

15

16

always the injured party, full of recriminations and little hurts and stories I do not want to hear again, at once saddening me and angering me with her vulnerability and ignorance, an apparition all the more insistent for being so long banished.

It is a good idea, then, to keep in touch, and I suppose that keeping in touch 17 is what notebooks are all about. And we are all on our own when it comes to keeping those lines open to ourselves: your notebook will never help me, nor mine you. "So *what's new in the whiskey business?*" What could that possibly mean to you? To me it means a blonde in a Pucci bathing suit sitting with a couple of fat men by the pool at the Beverly Hills Hotel. Another man approaches, and they all regard one another in silence for a while. "So what's new in the whiskey business?" one of the fat men finally says by way of welcome, and the blonde stands up, arches one foot and dips it in the pool, looking all the while at the cabaña where Baby Pignatari is talking on the telephone. That is all there is to that, except that several years later I saw the blonde coming out of Saks Fifth Avenue in New York with her California complexion and a voluminous mink coat. In the harsh wind that day she looked old and irrevocably tired to me, and even the skins in the mink coat were not worked the way they were doing them that year, not the way she would have wanted them done, and there is the point of the story. For a while after that I did not like to look in the mirror, and my eyes would skim the newspapers and pick out only the deaths, the cancer victims, the premature coronaries, the suicides, and I stopped riding the Lexington Avenue IRT because I noticed for the first time that all the strangers I had seen for years—the man with the seeing-eye dog, the spinster who read the classified pages every day, the fat girl who always got off with me at Grand Central—looked older than they once had.

It all comes back. Even that recipe for sauerkraut: even that brings it back. I 18 was on Fire Island when I first made that sauerkraut, and it was raining, and we drank a lot of bourbon and ate the sauerkraut and went to bed at ten, and I listened to the rain and the Atlantic and felt safe. I made the sauerkraut again last night and it did not make me feel any safer, but that is, as they say, another story.

QUESTIONS

1. As described here, what is the difference between a diary and a notebook? Why does Didion reject the use of a diary? What does she mean by "instead I tell what some would call lies" (paragraph 7)?

2. Why is it important to the writer to "*Remember what it was to be me*" (paragraph 9)? What purpose do other people serve in the writer's remembrance of her past selves?

3. Trace the pattern of reflection and meditation in the essay. How much of the text is made up of notebook entries? How much is reflection on that material, and how much is meditation on what is reflected?

4. Find a picture of yourself, alone or with family or friends, that was taken at least

five years ago. Write an essay in which you both describe yourself at that time and reflect on that former self as you see it now.

5. Recall some experience from your past, and write about it. Embroider the truth with details to suggest how you felt about the experience rather than what actually occurred.

6. In the library, find a copy of *Time* or *Life* or another magazine that might have been in your home in the month and year of your seventh birthday. Carefully study the pictures, the text, and the advertisements. Choose some material that will help you; then write about the world you remember at that time and about your place in it.

THE SILENCES OF
WOMEN AS WRITERS
Tillie Olsen

*Tillie Olsen was born in Omaha, Nebraska, in 1913. She
tells some of the circumstances of her life in the following
selection. What she does not say is that her collection of four
stories,* Tell Me a Riddle *(1951), has been widely hailed as
a major work of American fiction. "The Silences of Women
as Writers," which is the conclusion of the first chapter of
her book* Silences *(1978), originated as a talk delivered from
notes at a weekly meeting of the Radcliffe Institute in 1962.
The lecture was taped, transcribed, and then edited by the
author before publication in* Harper's *magazine in 1965.*

In the last century, of the women whose achievements endure for us in one   1
way or another,[1] nearly all never married (Jane Austen, Emily Brontë, Christina
Rossetti, Emily Dickinson, Louisa May Alcott, Sarah Orne Jewett) or married
late in their thirties (George Eliot, Elizabeth Barrett Browning, Charlotte Brontë,
Olive Schreiner). I can think of only four (George Sand, Harriet Beecher Stowe,
Helen Hunt Jackson, and Elizabeth Gaskell) who married and had children as
young women.[2] All had servants.

In our century, until very recently, it has not been so different. Most did not   2
marry (Selma Lagerlof, Willa Cather, Ellen Glasgow, Gertrude Stein, Gabriela
Mistral, Elizabeth Madox Roberts, Charlotte Mew, Eudora Welty, Marianne
Moore) or, if married, have been childless (Edith Wharton, Virginia Woolf,
Katherine Mansfield, Dorothy Richardson, H. H. Richardson, Elizabeth Bowen,
Isak Dinesen, Katherine Anne Porter, Lillian Hellman, Dorothy Parker). Col-
ette had one child (when she was forty). If I include Sigrid Undset, Kay Boyle,
Pearl Buck, Dorothy Canfield Fisher, that will make a small group who had
more than one child. All had household help or other special circumstances.

Am I resaying the moldy theory that women have no need, some say no   3
capacity, to create art, because they can "create" babies? And the additional
proof is precisely that the few women who have created it are nearly all childless?
No.

The power and the need to create, over and beyond reproduction, is native   4
in both women and men. Where the gifted among women (*and men*) have

---

[1]"One Out of Twelve" has a more extensive roll of women writers of achievement.
[2]I would now add a fifth—Kate Chopin—also a foreground silence.

remained mute, or have never attained full capacity, it is because of circumstances, inner or outer, which oppose the needs of creation.

Wholly surrendered and dedicated lives; time as needed for the work; totality   5
of self. But women are traditionally trained to place others' needs first, to feel these needs as their own (the "infinite capacity"); their sphere, their satisfaction to be in making it possible for others to use their abilities. This is what Virginia Woolf meant when, already a writer of achievement, she wrote in her diary:

> Father's birthday. He would have been 96, 96, yes, today; and could have been 96, like other people one has known; but mercifully was not. His life would have entirely ended mine. What would have happened? No writing, no books;—inconceivable.

It took family deaths to free more than one woman writer into her own   6
development.[3] Emily Dickinson freed herself, denying all the duties expected of a woman of her social position except the closest family ones, and she was fortunate to have a sister, and servants, to share those. How much is revealed of the differing circumstances and fate of their own as-great capacities, in the diaries (and lives) of those female bloodkin of great writers: Dorothy Wordsworth, Alice James, Aunt Mary Moody Emerson.

And where there is no servant or relation to assume the responsibilities of   7
daily living? Listen to Katherine Mansfield in the early days of her relationship with John Middleton Murry, when they both dreamed of becoming great writers:[4]

> The house seems to take up so much time. . . . I mean when I have to clean up twice over or wash up extra unnecessary things, I get frightfully impatient and want to be working [writing]. So often this week you and Gordon have been talking while I washed dishes. Well someone's got to wash dishes and get food. Otherwise "there's nothing in the house but eggs to eat." And after you have gone I walk about with a mind full of ghosts of saucepans and primus stoves and "will there be enough to go around?" And you calling, whatever I am doing, writing, "Tig, isn't there going to be tea? It's five o'clock."
>
> I loathe myself today. This woman who superintends you and rushes about slamming doors and slopping water and shouts "You might at least empty the pail and wash out the tea leaves." . . . O Jack, I wish that you would take me in your arms and kiss my hands and my face and every bit of me and say, "It's all right, you darling thing, I understand."

A long way from Conrad's favorable circumstances for creation: the flow of daily life made easy and noiseless.[5]

---

[3]Among them: George Eliot, Helen Hunt Jackson, Mrs. Gaskell, Kate Chopin, Lady Gregory, Isak Dinesen. Ivy Compton-Burnett finds this the grim reason for the emergence of British women novelists after World War I: ". . . The men were dead, you see, and the women didn't marry so much because there was no one for them to marry, and so they had leisure, and, I think, in a good many cases they had money because their brothers were dead, and all that would tend to writing, wouldn't it, being single, and having some money, and having the time—having no men, you see."

[4]Already in that changed time when servants were not necessarily a part of the furnishings of almost anyone well educated enough to be making literature.

[5]Joseph Conrad (1857–1924): Polish-born English novelist, author of *Lord Jim*. [Eds.]

And, if in addition to the infinite capacity, to the daily responsibilities, there 8
are children?

Balzac, you remember, described creation in terms of motherhood.[6] Yes, in 9
intelligent passionate motherhood there are similarities, and in more than the
toil and patience. The calling upon total capacities; the reliving and new using
of the past; the comprehensions; the fascination, absorption, intensity. All almost
certain death to creation—(so far).

Not because the capacities to create no longer exist, or the need (though for 10
a while, as in any fullness of life, the need may be obscured), but because the
circumstances for sustained creation have been almost impossible. The need
cannot be first. It can have at best, only part self, part time. (Unless someone
else does the nurturing. Read Dorothy Fisher's "Babushka Farnham" in *Fables
for Parents*.) More than in any other human relationship, overwhelmingly more,
motherhood means being instantly interruptable, responsive, responsible. Children need one *now* (and remember, in our society, the family must often try
to be the center for love and health the outside world is not). The very fact that
these are real needs, that one feels them as one's own (love, not duty); *that
there is no one else responsible for these needs*, gives them primacy. It is distraction, not meditation, that becomes habitual; interruption, not continuity; spas-
modic, not constant toil. The rest has been said here. Work interrupted, deferred, relinquished, makes blockage—at best, lesser accomplishment. Unused
capacities atrophy, cease to be.

When H. H. Richardson, who wrote the Australian classic *Ultima Thule*, 11
was asked why she—whose children, like all her people, were so profoundly
written—did not herself have children, she answered: "There are enough women
to do the childbearing and childrearing. I know of none who can write my
books." I remember thinking rebelliously, yes, and I know of none who can
bear and rear my children either. But literary history is on her side. Almost no
mothers—as almost no part-time, part-self persons—have created enduring literature . . . so far.

If I talk now quickly of my own silences—almost presumptuous after what 12
has been told here—it is that the individual experience may add.

In the twenty years I bore and reared my children, usually had to work on 13
a paid job as well, the simplest circumstances for creation did not exist. Nevertheless writing, the hope of it, was "the air I breathed, so long as I shall breathe
at all." In that hope, there was conscious storing, snatched reading, beginnings
of writing, and always "the secret rootlets of reconnaissance."

When the youngest of our four was in school, the beginnings struggled toward 14
endings. This was a time, in Kafka's words, "like a squirrel in a cage: bliss of
movement, desperation about constriction, craziness of endurance."

Bliss of movement. A full extended family life; the world of my job (tran- 15

---

[6]Honoré de Balzac (1799–1850): prolific French novelist and short-story writer; he is best known
for a series of novels with the comprehensive title, *The Human Comedy*. [Eds.]

scriber in a dairy-equipment company); and the writing, which I was somehow able to carry around within me through work, through home. Time on the bus, even when I had to stand, was enough; the stolen moments at work, enough; the deep night hours for as long as I could stay awake, after the kids were in bed, after the household tasks were done, sometimes during. It is no accident that the first work I considered publishable began: "I stand here ironing, and what you asked me moves tormented back and forth with the iron."

In such snatches of time I wrote what I did in those years, but there came a 16 time when this triple life was no longer possible. The fifteen hours of daily realities became too much distraction for the writing. I lost craziness of endurance. What might have been, I don't know; but I applied for, and was given, eight months' writing time. There was still full family life, all the household responsibilities, but I did not have to hold an eight-hour job. I had continuity, three full days, sometimes more—and it was in those months I made the mysterious turn and became a writing writer.

Then had to return to the world of work, someone else's work, nine hours, 17 five days a week.

This was the time of festering and congestion. For a few months I was able 18 to shield the writing with which I was so full, against the demands of jobs on which I had to be competent, through the joys and responsibilities and trials of family. For a few months. Always roused by the writing, always denied. "I could not go to write it down. It convulsed and died in me. I will pay."

My work died. What demanded to be written, did not. It seethed, bubbled, 19 clamored, peopled me. At last moved into the hours meant for sleeping. I worked now full time on temporary jobs, a Kelly, a Western Agency girl (girl!), wandering from office to office, always hoping to manage two, three writing months ahead. Eventually there was time.

I had said: always roused by the writing, always denied. Now, like a woman 20 made frigid, I had to learn response, to trust this possibility for fruition that had not been before. Any interruption dazed and silenced me. It took a long while of surrendering to what I was trying to write, of invoking Henry James's "passion, piety, patience," before I was able to re-establish work.

When again I had to leave the writing, I lost consciousness. A time of 21 anesthesia. There was still an automatic noting that did not stop, but it was as if writing had never been. No fever, no congestion, no festering. I ceased being peopled, slept well and dreamlessly, took a "permanent" job. The few pieces that had been published seemed to have vanished like the not-yet-written. I wrote someone, unsent: "So long they fed each other—my life, the writing—; —the writing or hope of it, my life—; but now they begin to destroy." I knew, but did not feel, the destruction.

A Ford grant in literature, awarded me on nomination by others, came almost 22 too late. Time granted does not necessarily coincide with time that can be most fully used, as the congested time of fullness would have been. Still, it was two years.

Drowning is not so pitiful as the attempt to rise, says Emily Dickinson. I do 23 not agree, but I know whereof she speaks. For a long time I was that emaciated survivor trembling on the beach, unable to rise and walk. Said differently, I could manage only the feeblest, shallowest growth on that devastated soil. Weeds, to be burned like weeds, or used as compost. When the habits of creation were at last rewon, one book went to the publisher, and I dared to begin my present work. It became my center, engraved on it: "Evil is whatever distracts." (By now had begun a cost to our family life, to my own participation in life as a human being.) I shall not tell the "rest, residue, and remainder" of what I was "leased, demised, and let unto" when once again I had to leave work at the flood to return to the Time-Master, to business-ese and legalese. This most harmful of all my silences has ended, but I am not yet recovered; may still be a one-book silence.

However that will be, we are in a time of more and more hidden and 24 foreground silences, women *and* men. Denied full writing life, more may try to "nurse through night" (that part-time, part-self night) "the ethereal spark," but it seems to me there would almost have had to be "flame on flame" first; and time as needed, afterwards; and enough of the self, the capacities, undamaged for the rebeginnings on the frightful task. I would like to believe this for what has not yet been written into literature. But it cannot reconcile for what is lost by unnatural silences.

QUESTIONS

1. Olsen's subject is silences. What does she mean by "silence"? To what causes does she attribute silences?

2. According to Olsen, what special circumstances account for the silences of women writers—as opposed to men? What is the significance of the two lists of writers in paragraphs 1 and 2?

3. Compare the excerpt from Virginia Woolf's diary with the passage written by Katherine Mansfield. What do these two excerpts have in common? How do they differ? To whom are they addressed? Do you think the Mansfield selection also comes from a diary? How do both excerpts function in relation to Olsen's thesis?

4. Like many essays, this one blends reflection and argument. Locate those parts of the essay that seem to belong most directly to each mode. How are they related to each other? Which would you say dominates the essay, or are they equally balanced?

5. Consider paragraphs 18 to 21. How does Olsen describe the process of literary creation or writing? What metaphors dominate this description? What is their effect?

6. How would you describe Olsen's writing style? Is it literary? Conversational? Hard or easy to follow? What might be the reason for her many sentence fragments? How are they related to her theme?

7. Olsen shows how her difficulties are similar to those of others who have tried to do what she does. Taken together, her personal reflections and her research powerfully explain the situation of a woman trying to be a writer. Have you ever run into obstacles and problems when you tried to do something? Can you find evidence that others have

had the same experience? Write an essay that combines personal experience with evidence from accounts of other people's experience—an essay in which you think about your own difficulties in a truly reflective way, going beyond the merely personal to larger themes and issues.

THE EIFFEL TOWER
Roland Barthes

Roland Barthes (1915–1980) has been a major force in the intellectual life of France for the past two decades, and his influence is still spreading around the world. He wrote frequently on literary subjects and on popular culture from the special perspective we have learned to call semiology or semiotics: the study of signs. In the portion of his essay on the Eiffel Tower reprinted here, we find him considering the tower as a sign, asking not so much what it means as how it means. This work first appeared in English as the opening essay in a collection translated by Richard Howard, called The Eiffel Tower and Other Mythologies *(1979).*

Maupassant often lunched at the restaurant in the tower,[1] though he didn't care much for the food: *It's the only place in Paris,* he used to say, *where I don't have to see it.* And it's true that you must take endless precautions, in Paris, not to see the Eiffel Tower; whatever the season, through mist and cloud, on overcast days or in sunshine, in rain—wherever you are, whatever the landscape of roofs, domes, or branches separating you from it, *the Tower is there*; incorporated into daily life until you can no longer grant it any specific attribute, determined merely to persist, like a rock or the river, it is as literal as a phenomenon of nature whose meaning can be questioned to infinity but whose existence is incontestable. There is virtually no Parisian glance it fails to *touch* at some time of day; at the moment I begin writing these lines about it, the Tower is there, in front of me, framed by my window; and at the very moment the January night blurs it, apparently trying to make it invisible, to deny its presence, two little lights come on, winking gently as they revolve at its very tip: all this night, too, it will be there, connecting me above Paris to each of my friends that I know are seeing it: with it we all comprise a shifting figure of which it is the steady center: the Tower is friendly.

The Tower is also present to the entire world. First of all as a universal symbol of Paris, it is everywhere on the globe where Paris is to be stated as an image; from the Midwest to Australia, there is no journey to France which isn't made, somehow, in the Tower's name, no schoolbook, poster, or film about France which fails to propose it as the major sign of a people and of a place: it belongs to the universal language of travel. Further: beyond its strictly Parisian statement, it touches the most general human image-repertoire: its simple, primary shape confers upon it the vocation of an infinite cipher: in turn and

[1]Guy de Maupassant (1850–1893): French novelist and short-story writer. [Eds.]

649

Roland Barthes

according to the appeals of our imagination, the symbol of Paris, of modernity, of communication, of science or of the nineteenth century, rocket, stem, derrick, phallus, lightning rod or insect, confronting the great itineraries of our dreams, it is the inevitable sign; just as there is no Parisian glance which is not compelled to encounter it, there is no fantasy which fails, sooner or later, to acknowledge its form and to be nourished by it; pick up a pencil and let your hand, in other words your thoughts, wander, and it is often the Tower which will appear, reduced to that simple line whose sole mythic function is to join, as the poet says, *base and summit*, or again, *earth and heaven*.

This pure—virtually empty—sign—is ineluctible, *because it means everything*. In order to negate the Eiffel Tower (though the temptation to do so is rare, for this symbol offends nothing in us), you must, like Maupassant, get up on it and, so to speak, identify yourself with it. Like man himself, who is the only one not to know his own glance, the Tower is the only blind point of the total optical system of which it is the center and Paris the circumference. But in this movement which seems to limit it, the Tower acquires a new power: an object when we look at it, it becomes a lookout in its turn when we visit it, and now constitutes as an object, simultaneously extended and collected beneath it, that Paris which just now was looking at it. The Tower is an object which sees, a glance which is seen; it is a complete verb, both active and passive, in which no function, no *voice* (as we say in grammar, with a piquant ambiguity) is defective. This dialectic is not in the least banal, it makes the Tower a singular monument; for the world ordinarily produces either purely functional organisms (camera or eye) intended to see things but which then afford nothing to sight, what *sees* being mythically linked to what remains *hidden* (this is the theme of the voyeur), or else spectacles which themselves are blind and are left in the pure passivity of the visible. The Tower (and this is one of its mythic powers) transgresses this separation, this habitual divorce of *seeing* and *being seen*; it achieves a sovereign circulation between the two functions; it is a complete object which has, if one may say so, both sexes of sight. This radiant position in the order of perception gives it a prodigious propensity to meaning: the Tower attracts meaning, the way a lightning rod attracts thunderbolts; for all lovers of signification, it plays a glamorous part, that of a pure signifier, i.e., of a form in which men unceasingly put *meaning* (which they extract at will from their knowledge, their dreams, their history), without this meaning thereby ever being finite and fixed: who can say what the Tower will be for humanity tomorrow? But there can be no doubt it will always be something, and something of humanity itself. Glance, object, symbol, such is the infinite circuit of functions which permits it always to be something other and something much more than the Eiffel Tower.

In order to satisfy this great oneiric function,[2] which makes it into a kind of total monument, the Tower must escape reason. The first condition of this

---

[2]oneiric function: function as the basis for dreaming, for the imaginary. [Eds.]

victorious flight is that the Tower be an utterly *useless* monument. The Tower's inutility has always been obscurely felt to be a scandal, i.e., a truth, one that is precious and inadmissible. Even before it was built, it was blamed for being useless, which, it was believed at the time, was sufficient to condemn it; it was not in the spirit of a period commonly dedicated to rationality and to the empiricism of great bourgeois enterprises to endure the notion of a useless object (unless it was declaratively an *objet d'art*, which was also unthinkable in relation to the Tower); hence Gustave Eiffel, in his own defense of his project in reply to the Artists' Petition, scrupulously lists all the future uses of the Tower: they are all, as we might expect of an engineer, scientific uses: aerodynamic measurements, studies of the resistance of substances, physiology of the climber, radioelectric research, problems of telecommunication, meteorological observations, etc. These uses are doubtless incontestable, but they seem quite ridiculous alongside the overwhelming myth of the Tower, of the human meaning which it has assumed throughout the world. This is because here the utilitarian excuses, however ennobled they may be by the myth of Science, are nothing in comparison to the great imaginary function which enables men to be strictly human. Yet, as always, the gratuitous meaning of the work is never avowed directly: it is rationalized under the rubric of *use*: Eiffel saw his Tower in the form of a serious object, rational, useful; men return it to him in the form of a great baroque dream which quite naturally touches on the borders of the irrational.

This double movement is a profound one: architecture is always dream and 5 function, expression of a utopia and instrument of a convenience. Even before the Tower's birth, the nineteenth century (especially in America and in England) had often dreamed of structures whose height would be astonishing, for the century was given to technological feats, and the conquest of the sky once again preyed upon humanity. In 1881, shortly before the Tower, a French architect had elaborated the project of a sun tower; now this project, quite mad technologically, since it relied on masonry and not on steel, also put itself under the warrant of a thoroughly empirical utility; on the one hand, a bonfire placed on top of the structure was to illuminate the darkness of every nook and cranny in Paris by a system of mirrors (a system that was undoubtedly a complex one!), and on the other, the last story of this sun tower (about 1,000 feet, like the Eiffel Tower) was to be reserved for a kind of sunroom, in which invalids would benefit from an air "as pure as in the mountains." And yet, here as in the case of the Tower, the naïve utilitarianism of the enterprise is not separate from the oneiric, infinitely powerful function which, actually, inspires its creation: use never does anything but shelter meaning. Hence we might speak, among men, of a true Babel complex: Babel was supposed to *serve* to communicate with God, and yet Babel is a dream which touches much greater depths than that of the theological project; and just as this great ascensional dream, released from its utilitarian prop, is finally what remains in the countless Babels represented by the painters, as if the function of art were to reveal the profound uselessness of

651

objects, just so the Tower, almost immediately disengaged from the scientific considerations which had authorized its birth (it matters very little here that the Tower should be in fact useful), has arisen from a great human dream in which movable and infinite meanings are mingled: it has reconquered the basic use-lessness which makes it live in men's imagination. At first, it was sought—so paradoxical is the notion of an empty monument—to make it into a "temple of Science"; but this is only a metaphor; as a matter of fact, the Tower is *nothing*, it achieves a kind of zero degree of the monument; it participates in no rite, in no cult, not even in Art; you cannot visit the Tower as a museum: there is nothing to see *inside* the Tower. This empty monument nevertheless receives each year twice as many visitors as the Louvre and considerably more than the largest movie house in Paris.

QUESTIONS

1. This is in some ways a difficult piece of writing. If you had difficulties in following it, try to locate them specifically, and discuss any problems in reading or interpretation. Are the difficulties mainly in the vocabulary, the sentence structure, or the ideas being presented?

2. A meditative essay will not move with the logic of a piece of argumentation or explanation, but it should have an order or structure of its own. Analyze this essay's structure by isolating a central subject for each of the five paragraphs and tracing the movements of mind that lead from one paragraph to the next.

3. Consider the structure of the first paragraph, which concludes with "the Tower is friendly." What does that statement mean in its context? What elements of the paragraph prepare for it or support it as a conclusion? Choose another paragraph for a similar analysis.

4. Reconstruct the information Barthes required in order to produce this meditation on the Eiffel Tower. How much did he rely on facts obtainable by research? How much on direct observation? How much on a consistent way of thinking about his subject? Examine each paragraph for traces of research. What would *you* need to know to write in a similar way on some public building or monument in Washington, D.C., New York City, or some other city or town in your experience?

5. Write an essay in which you compare some other public monument to Barthes's Eiffel Tower or in which you meditate on a monument of your choice.

THE WAY TO RAINY MOUNTAIN
N. Scott Momaday

N. Scott Momaday was born in Lawton, Oklahoma, in 1934. His father is a full-blooded Kiowa and his mother is part Cherokee. After attending schools on Navaho, Apache, and Pueblo Indian reservations, Momaday graduated from the University of New Mexico and took his Ph.D. at Stanford University. He has published two collections of poetry, Angle of Geese and Other Poems *(1974) and* The Gourd Dancer *(1976), and a memoir,* The Names *(1976). In 1969, his novel* House Made of Dawn *won the Pulitzer Prize. The following essay appeared first in the* Reporter *magazine in 1967 and later as the introduction to* The Way to Rainy Mountain *(1969), a collection of Kiowa legends.*

A single knoll rises out of the plain in Oklahoma, north and west of the 1
Wichita range. For my people, the Kiowas, it is an old landmark, and they gave it the name Rainy Mountain. The hardest weather in the world is there. Winter brings blizzards, hot tornadic winds arise in the spring, and in summer the prairie is an anvil's edge. The grass turns brittle and brown, and it cracks beneath your feet. There are green belts along the rivers and creeks, linear groves of hickory and pecan, willow and witch hazel. At a distance in July or August the steaming foliage seems almost to writhe in fire. Great green and yellow grasshoppers are everywhere in the tall grass, popping up like corn to sting the flesh, and tortoises crawl about on the red earth, going nowhere in the plenty of time. Loneliness is an aspect of the land. All things in the plain are isolate; there is no confusion of objects in the eye, but *one* hill or *one* tree or *one* man. To look upon that landscape in the early morning, with the sun at your back, is to lose the sense of proportion. Your imagination comes to life, and this, you think, is where Creation was begun.

I returned to Rainy Mountain in July. My grandmother had died in the 2
spring, and I wanted to be at her grave. She had lived to be very old and at last infirm. Her only living daughter was with her when she died, and I was told that in death her face was that of a child.

I like to think of her as a child. When she was born, the Kiowas were living 3
the last great moment of their history. For more than a hundred years they had controlled the open range from the Smoky Hill River to the Red, from the

headwaters of the Canadian to the fork of the Arkansas and Cimarron. In alliance with the Comanches, they had ruled the whole of the Southern Plains. War was their sacred business, and they were the finest horsemen the world has ever known. But warfare for the Kiowas was pre-eminently a matter of disposition rather than of survival, and they never understood the grim, unrelenting advance of the U.S. Cavalry. When at last, divided and ill provisioned, they were driven onto the Staked Plains in the cold of autumn, they fell into panic. In Palo Duro Canyon they abandoned their crucial stores to pillage and had nothing then but their lives. In order to save themselves, they surrendered to the soldiers at Fort Sill and were imprisoned in the old stone corral that now stands as a military museum. My grandmother was spared the humiliation of those high gray walls by eight or ten years, but she must have known from birth the affliction of defeat, the dark brooding of old warriors.

Her name was Aho, and she belonged to the last culture to evolve in North   4
America. Her forebears came down from the high country in western Montana nearly three centuries ago. They were a mountain people, a mysterious tribe of hunters whose language has never been classified in any major group. In the late seventeenth century they began a long migration to the south and east. It was a journey toward the dawn, and it led to a golden age. Along the way the Kiowas were befriended by the Crows, who gave them the culture and religion of the Plains. They acquired horses, and their ancient nomadic spirit was suddenly free of the ground. They acquired Tai-me, the sacred sun-dance doll, from that moment the object and symbol of their worship, and so shared in the divinity of the sun. Not least, they acquired the sense of destiny, therefore courage and pride. When they entered upon the Southern Plains they had been transformed. No longer were they slaves to the simple necessity of survival; they were a lordly and dangerous society of fighters and thieves, hunters and priests of the sun. According to their origin myth, they entered the world through a hollow log. From one point of view, their migration was the fruit of an old prophecy, for indeed they emerged from a sunless world.

Though my grandmother lived out her long life in the shadow of Rainy   5
Mountain, the immense landscape of the continental interior lay like memory in her blood. She could tell of the Crows, whom she had never seen, and of the Black Hills, where she had never been. I wanted to see in reality what she had seen more perfectly in the mind's eye, and drove fifteen hundred miles to begin my pilgrimage.

A dark mist lay over the Black Hills, and the land was like iron. At the top   6
of a ridge I caught sight of Devil's Tower upthrust against the gray sky as if in the birth of time the core of the earth had broken through its crust and the motion of the world was begun. There are things in nature that engender an awful quiet in the heart of man; Devil's Tower is one of them. Two centuries

ago, because of their need to explain it, the Kiowas made a legend at the base of the rock. My grandmother said:

"Eight children were there at play, seven sisters and their brother. Suddenly   7
the boy was struck dumb; he trembled and began to run upon his hands and feet. His fingers became claws, and his body was covered with fur. There was a bear where the boy had been. The sisters were terrified; they ran, and the bear after them. They came to the stump of a great tree, and the tree spoke to them. It bade them climb upon it, and as they did so, it began to rise into the air. The bear came to kill them, but they were just beyond its reach. It reared against the tree and scored the bark all around with its claws. The seven sisters were borne into the sky, and they became the stars of the Big Dipper." From that moment, and so long as the legend lives, the Kiowas have kinsmen in the night sky. Whatever they were in the mountains, they could be no more. However tenuous their well-being, however much they had suffered and would suffer again, they had found a way out of the wilderness.

My grandmother had a reverence for the sun, a holy regard that now is all   8
but gone out of mankind. There was a wariness in her, and an ancient awe. She was a Christian in her later years, but she had come a long way about, and she never forgot her birthright. As a child she had been to the sun dances; she had taken part in that annual rite, and by it she had learned the restoration of her people in the presence of Tai-me. She was about seven when the last Kiowa sun dance was held in 1887 on the Washita River above Rainy Mountain Creek. The buffalo were gone. In order to consummate the ancient sacrifice—to impale the head of a buffalo bull upon the Tai-me tree—a delegation of old men journeyed into Texas, there to beg and barter for an animal from the Goodnight herd. She was ten when the Kiowas came together for the last time as a living sun-dance culture. They could find no buffalo; they had to hang an old hide from the sacred tree. Before the dance could begin, a company of soldiers rode out from Fort Sill under orders to disperse the tribe. Forbidden without cause the essential act of their faith, having seen the wild herds slaughtered and left to rot upon the ground, the Kiowas backed away forever from the tree. That was July 20, 1890, at the great bend of the Washita. My grandmother was there. Without bitterness, and for as long as she lived, she bore a vision of deicide.[1]

Now that I can have her only in memory, I see my grandmother in the   9
several postures that were peculiar to her: standing at the wood stove on a winter morning and turning meat in a great iron skillet; sitting at the south window, bent above her beadwork, and afterwards, when her vision failed, looking down for a long time into the fold of her hands; going out upon a cane, very slowly as she did when the weight of age came upon her; praying. I remember her

---

[1]deicide: the killing of a deity or god. [Eds.]

most often at prayer. She made long, rambling prayers out of suffering and hope, having seen many things. I was never sure that I had the right to hear, so exclusive were they of all mere custom and company. The last time I saw her she prayed standing by the side of her bed at night, naked to the waist, the light of a kerosene lamp moving upon her dark skin. Her long black hair, always drawn and brained in the day, lay upon her shoulders and against her breasts like a shawl. I do not speak Kiowa, and I never understood her prayers, but there was something inherently sad in the sound, some merest hesitation upon the syllables of sorrow. She began in a high and descending pitch, exhausting her breath to silence; then again and again—and always the same intensity of effort, of something that is, and is not, like urgency in the human voice. Transported so in the dancing light among the shadows of her room, she seemed beyond the reach of time. But that was illusion; I think I knew then that I should not see her again.

Houses are like sentinels in the plain, old keepers of the weather watch. 10
There, in a very little while, wood takes on the appearance of great age. All colors wear soon away in the wind and rain, and then the wood is burned gray and the grain appears and the nails turn red with rust. The window panes are black and opaque; you imagine there is nothing within, and indeed there are many ghosts, bones given up to the land. They stand here and there against the sky, and you approach them for a longer time than you expect. They belong in the distance; it is their domain.

Once there was a lot of sound in my grandmother's house, a lot of coming 11
and going, feasting and talk. The summers there were full of excitement and reunion. The Kiowas are a summer people; they abide the cold and keep to themselves, but when the season turns and the land becomes warm and vital they cannot hold still; an old love of going returns upon them. The aged visitors who came to my grandmother's house when I was a child were made of lean and leather, and they bore themselves upright. They wore great black hats and bright ample shirts that shook in the wind. They rubbed fat upon their hair and wound their braids with strips of colored cloth. Some of them painted their faces and carried the scars of old and cherished enmities. They were an old council of warlords, come to remind and be reminded of who they were. Their wives and daughters served them well. The women might indulge themselves; gossip was at once the mark and compensation of their servitude. They made loud and elaborate talk among themselves, full of jest and gesture, fright and false alarm. They went abroad in fringed and flowered shawls, bright beadwork and German silver. They were at home in the kitchen, and they prepared meals that were banquets.

There were frequent prayer meetings, and nocturnal feasts. When I was a 12
child I played with my cousins outside, where the lamplight fell upon the ground and the singing of the old people rose up around us and carried away into the

darkness. There were a lot of good things to eat, a lot of laughter and surprise. And afterwards, when the quiet returned, I lay down with my grandmother and could hear the frogs away by the river and feel the motion of the air.

Now there is a funereal silence in the rooms, the endless wake of some final 13 word. The walls have closed in upon my grandmother's house. When I returned to it in mourning, I saw for the first time in my life how small it was. It was late at night, and there was a white moon, nearly full. I sat for a long time on the stone steps by the kitchen door. From there I could see out across the land; I could see the long row of trees by the creek, the low light upon the rolling plains, and the stars of the Big Dipper. Once I looked at the moon and caught sight of a strange thing. A cricket had perched upon the handrail, only a few inches away. My line of vision was such that the creature filled the moon like a fossil. It had gone there, I thought, to live and die, for there, of all places, was its small definition made whole and eternal. A warm wind rose up and purled like the longing within me.

The next morning, I awoke at dawn and went out on the dirt road to Rainy 14 Mountain. It was already hot, and the grasshoppers began to fill the air. Still, it was early in the morning, and birds sang out of the shadows. The long yellow grass on the mountain shone in the bright light, and a scissortail hied above the land. There, where it ought to be, at the end of a long and legendary way, was my grandmother's grave. She had at last succeeded to that holy ground. Here and there on the dark stones were ancestral names. Looking back once, I saw the mountain and came away.

QUESTIONS

1. What is this essay about? Explain whether it is a history of the Kiowas, or a biography of the writer's grandmother, or a narrative of the writer's journey.

2. Trace the movement in time in this essay. How much takes place in the present, the recent past, the distant past, or legendary time? What effect does such movement create?

3. How much of the essay reports events, and how much of the essay represents a sense of place or of persons through description of what the writer sees and feels? Trace the pattern of reporting and representing, and consider the writer's purpose in such an approach to his subject.

4. The first paragraph ends by drawing the reader into the writer's point of view: "Your imagination comes to life, and this, you think, is where Creation was begun." Given the description of the Oklahoma landscape that precedes this in the paragraph, how do you react to Momaday's summarizing statement? Why? What other passages in the essay evoke a sense of place?

5. Visit a place that has historical significance. It may be a place where you or

members of your family lived in the past, or it may be a place of local or national historical significance. Describe the place as it appears now, and report on events that took place there in the past. What, if any, evidence do you find in the present of those events that took place in the past?

6. If you have a grandparent or an older friend living nearby, ask this person about his or her history. What does this person remember about the past that is no longer in the present? Are there also objects—pictures, clothing, medals, and so on—that can speak to you of your subject's past life? Reflect on the person's present life as well as on those events from the past that seem most memorable. Write an essay in which you represent your subject's life by concentrating on the place where he or she lives and the surrounding objects that help you to understand the past and present life.

Social Sciences and
Public Affairs

COLLEGE: DePAUW
Margaret Mead

As the headnote on page 66 indicates, Margaret Mead was a cultural anthropologist whose work continues to be important and influential. The present selection is from her memoir of her early life, Blackberry Winter *(1972), where it appears as chapter 8. In her memoir Mead wrote: "I speak out of the experience of my own lifetime of seeing past and future as aspects of the present."*

American families differ greatly in their expectations about what going to 1
college will mean in their children's lives. In the intellectual community to which my parents belonged, college was as necessary as learning to read. It was an intellectual experience and the gateway to the rest of life. All my life I expected to go to college, and I was prepared to enjoy it.

My mother had included drawing lessons in the advantages she had wrested 2
for me out of the various strange environments in which we lived, and I had enough talent to be encouraged to become a painter. However, when I was told by my artist cousins that in order to become a painter I should go to art school and skip college, I gave up the idea. For me, not to go to college was, in a sense, not to become a full human being.

This did not mean, of course, that all the children in the family felt as I did. 3
My brother very dutifully went to college and took a Ph.D. But he never cared much for reading books. Instead, he fastened on the applied aspects of my father's essentially very intellectual but very concrete interests. What interested Richard primarily were the business aspects of the ongoing world—such matters

as the relationship of highway legislation to bus lines and trucking, or working out the best locations for chain stores, or the uses of coal. Had he come from a different kind of family, he might have gone very contentedly straight into business. As it was, he became for most of his life a college professor in schools of business concerned with the kinds of projects in which he himself did consulting. He exemplified in his own person one of the things that has happened in America as higher education has become instrumental in business, industry, and agriculture, as well as in professions like law and medicine which once had their own exclusive forms of preparation.

For my sister Elizabeth, college never was more than a background—and   4
not a very relevant background at that—for the development of her gifts. She willingly left college to go to Italy with my mother and spent a happy year in Rome studying architecture. Afterward she continued to study architecture at the University of Pennsylvania and Columbia University and, still later, took courses both in fine arts and in education at New York University. When it was necessary to write papers, she wrote them. When it was necessary to read books, she read them and knew how to get a great deal out of them. Although her delight in painting and music and dancing made her seem to be a changeling in our midst, she too received the family intellectual imprint and she became a teacher and only secondarily—and sometimes and still with delight—a painter. And she married William Steig, an artist from a family of artists, who left college after one semester and made a name for himself as a cartoonist, one of the most ironic and compassionate of our time.

And there was my youngest sister, Priscilla, who was so responsive to the   5
standards of the wider society. Having begun to read at five, she read what she chose, reached out for science fiction and formulas of dissent and assent, and used her reading as a weapon against the rest of the family. By the time she was ready for college, she was entrancingly beautiful: she was also competent and had a mind that could do anything asked of it. I decided, then, that if she were to resist the temptation to become a well-bred, well-dressed young woman who could talk intelligently about any subject but who cared really deeply about none, she would have to have an overdose of the kind of social life that at Vassar or Smith College would have been tempered by her relationships with fine women teachers who were using their own minds and hoped that some students would become intellectually active. So I helped her choose the University of Wisconsin, saw to it that she had the right introductions and the right clothes, made the right sorority, and was showered with the attentions to which her looks entitled her. She herself decided that she would make Phi Beta Kappa in three years. When she succeeded in this, she left the fraternity-sorority life of the Wisconsin campus behind, took what she had gained from the good teaching of professors who cared about their subject, and, in her own phrasing, went to the University of Chicago to learn something. In the same spirit, she resisted the attractions of young men with impeccable Ivy League backgrounds. Instead, she married Leo Rosten, a brilliant young political scientist who had worked

his way through college by giving lectures on Great Literature to women's clubs and by teaching English to immigrants, an experience that he later utilized in *The Education of Hyman Kaplan*. Throughout her married life she restrained the exuberant imagination of her gifted husband by periodically advocating the kind of economies my mother had insisted on when she had made my father return the lapis lazuli necklace because the money should be given to a fellowship fund. In the last years of her life, she was studying to become a social worker.

So the overriding academic ethos shaped all our lives. This was tempered by 6 my mother's sense of responsibility for society, by my father's greater interest in real processes than in theoretical abstractions, and by my grandmother's interest in real children, in chickens, and in how to season stewed tomatoes with toasted bread. But at the heart of their lives, the enjoyment of the intellect as mediated by words in books was central, and I was the child who could make the most of this—the child who was not asked to constrain or distort some other gift.

And so, even though it was decided that I was to go to DePauw rather than 7 Bryn Mawr or Wellesley, I approached the idea of college with the expectation of taking part in an intellectual feast. I looked forward to studying fascinating subjects taught by people who understood what they were talking about. I imagined meeting brilliant students, students who would challenge me to stretch my mind and work instead of going skating with my lessons done well enough so that I led my classmates who hated what they were studying. In college, in some way that I devoutly believed in but could not explain, I expected to become a person.

At DePauw in 1919 I found students who were, for the most part, the first 8 generation to go to college and whose parents appeared at Class Day poorly dressed while their daughters wore the raccoon or the muskrat coats that were appropriate to the sorority they had made. It was a college to which students had come for fraternity life, for football games, and for establishing the kind of rapport with other people that would make them good Rotarians in later life and their wives good members of the garden club.

I arrived with books of poetry, portraits of great personalities to hang on the 9 wall, and the snobberies of the East, such as the expectation that one dressed in the evening for the members of one's own family. And I was confronted by the snobbery and cruelty of the sorority system at its worst, with rules against rushing that prevented the women who had gone to college with my father and who had married my father's fraternity brothers from ever speaking to me or inviting me to their homes—rules made by the Panhellenic Association in order to control competition that was so harsh and so unashamed that the very rules designed to control it made it even worse. This was my first and only real experience of discrimination—mild enough in all conscience.

It is very difficult to know how to evaluate how essential it is to have one's 10 soul seared by the great injustices of one's own time—being born a serf or slave, a woman believed to have no mind or no soul, a black man or woman in a white man's world, a Jew among Christians who make a virtue of anti-Semitism, a miner among those who thought it good sport to hire Pinkertons to shoot down miners on strike.[1] Such experiences sear the soul. They make their victims ache with bitterness and rage, with compassion for fellow sufferers or with blind determination to escape even on the backs of fellow sufferers. Such experiences can breed the desire to fight unrelentingly against the injustice that has let one's mother die because no doctor would attend her or let one's brother work in a mine because there was no school to recognize his talents—an injustice that substitutes arbitrary social categories for the recognition of humanity. Injustice experienced in the flesh, in deeply wounded flesh, is the stuff out of which change explodes. But the passionate fight for humanity—the fight to free slaves, free colonies, free women and children—also has been carried by those who have never experienced, and in the case of whites fighting for blacks or men for women, never could experience in their own persons the depths of injustice against which they have fought.

There is a great deal of talk today about the inexperience of the suburban children of affluent middle-class families, who have never seen an open wound, or a baby born, or anyone die, whose conceptions of humiliation, deprivation, and suffering are drawn wholly from films and television. But such discussions do not take into account the different kinds of fighters, all of whom are needed in any cause—both those who know at first hand the searing effects of discrimination and those who are shocked to the core by their encounters with the tragedies that are part of others' everyday experience.

The point of John Howard Griffin's book, *Black Like Me*, was precisely that he was not black. For a brief period he experienced the humiliation and hostility that a black man can expect to experience daily—and throughout his life in the United States. But Griffin experienced this *not* as a black man but as a white man with temporarily blackened skin, a white man who had been reared to expect something else and who suddenly drew back from his own image when he called his own wife—white and far away at the other end of a telephone line—by an endearing term. Out of his experience, Griffin was able to tell men and women in the white world things that no black individual had ever thought to tell them. And I think it is no accident that some of the most impassioned statements about woman's rights have been made by men, or that anti-imperialist movements in colonial countries have been inspired and even led by Europeans who were outraged by the consequences of social arrangements through which they, as members of a privileged group, had never suffered.

Yet it is very difficult to draw a line. Certainly, positions of privilege can breed a kind of hardened insensitivity, an utter inability to imagine what it is to be an outsider, an individual who is treated with contempt or repulsion for

---

[1]Pinkertons: employees of the Pinkerton National Detective Agency, often used as guards in industrial disputes. [Eds.]

reasons of skin color, or sex, or religion, or nationality, or the occupation of his parents and grandparents. Some kind of experience is necessary to open one's eyes and so to loosen the ties of unimaginative conformity. It can come from a terrible shock—through the brutal experience of having a close companion ejected from a restaurant or even shot down in the street. But there is another kind of initiation into humiliation—through the experience of hardship in some petty caricature of the real world which, by its very pettiness, engages one's emotions and enlarges one's consciousness of the destructive effects of every kind of social injustice.

All my life I had been a leader in children's groups that were democratically constituted. In our family, my mother's idealistic altruism and egalitarian principles meant that the children of farm laborers were treated with no less—and perhaps even more—gentleness and consideration than were the children of educated, professional parents. From this position of security, I believed that I could dictate egalitarian behavior. I had been brought up to the American standard of good breeding, based on the assumption that a well-bred person never intentionally hurt anyone—an assumption that reverses the English conception of a well-bred person as someone who is never rude unintentionally. My father sometimes paraphrased Chesterfield's admonition to be considerate of one's inferiors, courteous to one's equals, and stiff with one's superiors. But no one suggested that we had any superiors, only people who had more money or who were more interested in validating their social position. My father refused to make social efforts and my mother's position was, therefore, related to her own associations with other women who were equally concerned with good works. My mother used to complain because my father would not make the effort, but no one suggested that he would not have succeeded had he wanted to.

In some ways I was in the position of a child who is brought up in a leading family in a sequestered minority group, in the position, for example, of the daughter of the rabbi in a Jewish community or of the pastor in a segregated black community, a girl who has never questioned her privileged status but who has absorbed an ethic that is deeply critical of injustice in the world. In *Ex-Prodigy*, Norbert Wiener describes how he was reared, in a setting of anti-Semitism, with an attributed superiority as a Russian. When he discovered that he himself was Jewish, he could not identify only with Jews but had to identify with all oppressed peoples. The stigmata of privilege remained.

When I arrived at DePauw, I found that I had two roommates. One was a girl who had come to college to join a sorority, and this had been arranged in advance; the other expected to be rushed by a sorority that had little prestige. I soon learned that no one belonging to a sorority could speak to an unpledged freshman. This, of course, explained why I heard nothing from the effusive girl who had written me so many letters during the summer. When the invitations came out, I was invited to the Kappa rushing party. But when I arrived wearing

663

Margaret Mead

my unusual and unfashionable dress that was designed to look like a wheat field with poppies blooming in it, my correspondent turned her back on me and never spoke to me again. I found the whole evening strangely confusing. I could not know, of course, that everyone had been given the signal that inviting me had been a mistake. Afterward, my two roommates got the bids they expected, but I did not get a bid.

It still took a little time for me to realize the full implications of what it meant to be an unpledged freshman in a college where everything was organized around the fraternities and sororities. For one thing, I had no dates; these were all arranged through commands to the freshman pledges of certain fraternities to date the freshman pledges of certain sororities. Although all freshmen had to live in dormitories, it meant also that there was a widening gulf between the pledges, who spent a lot of time at their sorority houses being disciplined and shaped up, and the unpledged freshmen and the few upperclassmen in the dormitories.

With a very few exceptions, these upperclassmen were pretty dismal. But there was Katharine Rothenberger, who became my lifelong friend; she had transferred from a college where she had turned down a sorority bid because it was too expensive. And there was an English girl, very tall and very serious, also a transfer, who in later life became a very well-known missionary. By and large, however, the girls who were, by sorority standards, ineligible were less attractive and less sparkling than their classmates who were among the chosen. Moreover, all those who still hoped had one characteristic in common—their fear of making friends with others of their own kind. Although I was experiencing the bitter injustice of being excluded, on grounds that I did not respect, I experienced also what I have come to regard as a principal reason for abolishing such exclusive institutions, that is, the damage done to the arbitrarily excluded who continue to believe that one day they still may enter the ranks of the chosen.

It also took some little time for me to discover that previously rejected students might nevertheless be accepted later if they displayed some special ability that would help a chapter keep up the kind of competitive records that were cherished by rival chapters on the campus or within the intrafraternity and -sorority rivalries that were fostered by the national Greek-letter societies. So a student could continue to hope that the members of a chapter would eventually recognize in him—or her—some sign of high scholarship or an outstanding ability in some extracurricular field or a strong political potential and then, overlooking the initial disability, they would invite the girl or boy to join the chapter and perhaps even make some effort to like the person who once had been so harshly excluded.

It was many years before liberal white Americans came to realize that what they offered Negro Americans was not so very different from this. In the period between the two wars, Negro physicians, lawyers, scientists, and men with other recognized talents and outstanding abilities were admitted to the fraternal rela-

664

tionships of occupations that hitherto had been closed to them and they were treated almost as though they had been accepted by the group they had joined.

During the next forty years, before fraternities and clubs lost almost all their 21 power on campuses in the general rejection of elitism that developed in the 1960's, various efforts were made to democratize an institution that was essentially incapable of democratization—for the only point of exclusiveness is that someone is excluded. But the main result of such efforts was that they strengthened the conviction of members of Greek-letter societies that students who were left out had not wanted to join or could not afford to do so. And the unchosen seldom talked.

The blandness with which the privileged accept their status was illustrated 22 when the Panhellenic Association of Syracuse University, during World War II, invited me to be a dinner speaker on "Democracy," a topic that was particularly fashionable at that time. The organizers had not bothered to find out whether I had ever attended a college where there were Greek-letter societies. So they heard a lot of stories they had previously been protected from hearing.

During the year I studied at DePauw, I did not deny that I was hurt, nor did 23 I pretend to myself that I would have refused the chance to be accepted by a sorority. The truth is, I would not have known enough to refuse. And once inside, it is quite possible that I would have been as unseeing as the rest. As it was, what particularly offended me as the year wore on was the contrast between the vaunted democracy of the Middle West and the blatant, strident artificiality of the Greek-letter societies on that midwestern campus, the harshness of the rules that prevented my father's classmates from ever addressing a hospitable word to me, and, more than anything else, the lack of loyalty that rejection engendered among the unchosen.

I discovered, too, that simple rejection was not enough. It had to be rubbed 24 in. At that time it was fashionable for girls to wear what were called Peter Thompson suits—tailored middy suits in dark-colored wool or pastel-colored linen. In the spring, when I too acquired a Peter Thompson suit, a prominent Theta, meeting me on the campus, roughly turned down my collar to look at the label, certainly expecting to find that my new dress was not authentic—as it was.

My unusual clothing was not all that was held against me. There was my 25 room with its carefully planned color scheme, my books and pictures, and, above all, my tea set. And I did not chew gum. Then, as if these things were not enough, there was my accent. The big Freshman English Literature course was taught by a New Englander who conceived it to be his principal task to educate provincial Americans. The very first day he glared around the room and asked, "Does anyone in this class know how to pronounce c-a-l-f?" I volunteered, and when I used the broad *a* he commented, "Oh, you come from the East, don't you? Out here they say 'calf,' " and mockingly drew out the flat *a* sound. A third of the freshman class heard that doubtful compliment. There were two other students from the East. One was the daughter of a Methodist bishop who had formerly been the president of DePauw; the other was her close friend. That saved them. But I was branded. After a while some of my friends thought it was fun to get me to say, "I have been there," using the Bryn Mawr pronunciation, "bean," instead of the Middle Western "bin." This usually happened when mothers came to visit and the girls wanted to show off the local curiosities.

And, although the sorority rejection was the sharper blow, there was another. I found out that I was also ineligible to belong to the Y.W.C.A. because, as an Episcopalian, I did not belong to an Evangelical religion. There were five of us at DePauw who were religious rejects—myself, one Roman Catholic, one Greek Orthodox, one Lutheran, and one Jew. The Jew was David Lilienthal. On one occasion he was asked to give a talk to the Methodist Sunday School on the Jewish conception of Jesus. The rest of us were simply beyond the pale. 26

So I was confronted, for the first time in my life, with being thoroughly unacceptable to almost everyone and on grounds in which I had previously been taught to take pride. I responded by setting out to see what I could do within this system, which I found sufficiently uncongenial so that I spent no time lamenting my exclusion. 27

I wrote a stunt that was performed by the freshman dormitory, Mansfield Hall, as part of a competition in which we challenged the senior dormitory and the sororities—the first time this was done. I set to work to make the English honors society, Tusitala, which was the Samoan name that had been given Robert Louis Stevenson. I wrote and directed the pageant that the entire feminine student body, under the direction of the Department of Physical Education, gave each year. I also designed the freshman float for this occasion. And, finally, I went into the political arena and succeeded in getting Katharine Rothenberger elected vice-president of the class by setting the sororities against one another. I was satisfied that by the end of the year I would have received a bid to join a sorority—probably at least two. For although no sorority might want to have me, each one would be afraid that I might become the property of a rival. 28

The teaching at DePauw was far less disappointing than the college social organization. In my catalogue I had marked courses totaling over 200 hours, even though 120 hours was all that a student could take in four years. I thoroughly enjoyed the magnificent teaching given by men who were first and foremost teachers, interested in their students and unharassed by the demand that they "publish or perish," an attitude that later came to haunt even small colleges like DePauw. The training in writing given me by Professor Pence was never equaled by anyone else. At DePauw I was introduced to discussions of the Old Testament prophets and the Social Gospel, and this firmly established association between the Old and the New Testament and the demands of social justice provided me with an ethical background up to the time of the develop- 29 ment of ecumenicism and Vatican II. These courses were taught by deeply religious men who regarded it a privilege to be teaching where they were.

At DePauw, too, I took a course in History as Past Ethics, to which I still 30 refer. However, there were only two girls and a couple of dozen boys in that class, and the two girls received the highest marks. As long as I was in high school, the greater maturity of adolescent girls had not struck me. But in the setting of this coeducational college it became perfectly clear both that bright girls could do better than bright boys and that they would suffer for it.

This made me feel that coeducation was thoroughly unattractive. I neither 31 wanted to do bad work in order to make myself attractive to boys nor did I want them to dislike me for doing good work. It seemed to me that it would be much simpler to go to a girl's college where one could work as hard as one pleased.

This preference foreshadowed, I suppose, my anthropological field choices— 32 not to compete with men in male fields, but instead to concentrate on the kinds of work that are better done by women. Actually, there are two kinds of field work that women can do better than men. One is working with women and children in situations in which male investigators are likely to be suspected and resented by the men of a society. The other is working with both men and women as an older woman, using a woman's postmenopausal high status to achieve an understanding of the different parts of a culture, particularly in those cultures in which women past the reproductive period are freed from the constraints and taboos that constrict the lives of younger women. The first choice can be effectively exercised only in a situation in which the culture is being studied by a male-female pair or a team. For when a woman explicitly classifies herself with excluded women and uninitiated children, she does not have access to the rest of the culture. The second role is very practical for an older woman who is working alone in a culture that has already been explored by a male and female pair.

Nevertheless, as long as I remained at DePauw, I felt I was an exile. I used 33 to sit in the library and read the drama reviews in *The New York Times*. Like so many other aspiring American intellectuals and artists, I developed the feeling that American small towns were essentially unfriendly to the life of the mind and the senses. I believed that the center of life was in New York City, where Mencken and George Jean Nathan were publishing *Smart Set*, where *The Freeman*, *The New Republic*, and *The Nation* flourished, where F. P. A. and Heywood Broun were writing their diatribes,[2] and where the theater was a living world of contending ideas.

And Luther Cressman was in New York. I had had enough of the consolation 34 of knowing that I was engaged, so that all the nonsense about having dates—or not having dates—was irrelevant. I wanted a life that demonstrated in a more

---

[2]F. P. A.: pseudonym of Franklin Pierce Adams (1881–1960), newspaper columnist and writer. [Eds.]

real and dramatic form that I was not among the rejected and unchosen. And so, at the end of the year, I persuaded my father to let me leave DePauw and enter Barnard College.

What did I learn from this essentially very mild experience of being treated   35
as an outsider and a reject from my own society? Just enough to know more clearly than ever that this is not the way to organize society—that those who reject or those who are rejected, and usually both, suffer irreversible character damage. It is true that sometimes one or the other may show magnificent character traits. I believe that the ideal of the English gentleman, embodied in the belief that he alone—and no one else—can destroy his position, is valuable. Equally, the position of the Jews, steadily persecuted but sustained by their conception of themselves as a chosen people, has produced an enormous number of highly intelligent, humanly sensitized, valuable men and women. But the reciprocal, the belief of the Nazis that they were the proper heirs of European civilization, from which all whom they regarded as lesser men should be excluded, was an evil that the world cannot face again. Whatever advantages may have arisen, in the past, out of the existence of a specially favored and highly privileged aristocracy, it is clear to me that today no argument can stand that supports unequal opportunity or any intrinsic disqualification for sharing in the whole of life.

By the very contrast that it provided, DePauw clarified my picture of the kind   36
of college at which I wanted to be a student—a place where people were intellectually stirred and excited by ideas, where people stayed up all night talking about things that mattered, where one would meet one's peers and, still more important, people with different and superior minds, and, not least, where one would find out what one could do in life.

I left DePauw, sorry only to leave Katharine Rothenberger. At the time, I   37
hardly realized how lasting some of my impressions would be. I never again went to a football game as a partisan, but more than twenty-five years later, when I was asked to lecture at Wabash College, the college that was DePauw's football rival, I felt a little like a traitor.

Even now, when I lecture in the Middle West, if I want my voice to be free   38
of a carping note, I have to think myself back into the world of my grandmother and my mother—the Middle West as they presented it to me—and will myself to omit my own experience of DePauw in 1920. The dream glowed; the reality had been more than disappointing.

QUESTIONS

1. What were Mead's expectations of college? What did she hope to learn and become?

2. On what grounds was Mead judged unacceptable by the sororities? How did this judgment square with her sense of herself?

3. What impressions do you have of Mead from this essay? What is Mead's point of view toward herself? Find passages in this essay to support your answer.

4. This is a chapter from Mead's autobiography in which she is looking back at her first college experiences and trying to make sense of those experiences in light of what she knew later. Trace the movement of Mead's mind. How does one thought or experience suggest another? At what points does she move back and forth between the past and the present?

5. In what ways does Mead show her anthropological bent in telling her own story? How does she attempt to make it of public significance?

6. What does going to college mean to you? What were your expectations of college, and what were your parents' expectations for you? Write an essay in which you consider these questions, and discuss what the reality of your college experience has been so far.

7. Have you ever experienced discrimination such as being excluded or rejected by a club or organization? How has this experience affected you? Use this experience, as Mead has, to reflect upon the meaning of this experience for your life.

WHY I WRITE
George Orwell

George Orwell (1903–1950) was the pen name of Eric Blair, the son of a British customs officer serving in Bengal, India. As a boy he was sent home to prestigious schools, where he learned to dislike the rich and powerful. After finishing his schooling at Eton, he served as an officer of the British police in Burma, where he became disillusioned with imperialism. Then he studied conditions among the urban poor and the coal miners of Wigan, a city in northwestern England, which confirmed him as a socialist. He was wounded in the Spanish civil war, defending the lost cause of the left against the fascists. Under the name of Orwell, he wrote accounts of all these experiences, as well as the anti-Stalinist fable Animal Farm *(1945) and the dystopian novel* 1984 *(1949). The following essay was first published in a little magazine called* Gangrel *in 1946. It has since been reprinted in several collections of Orwell's essays.*

From a very early age, perhaps the age of five or six, I knew that when I grew up I should be a writer. Between the ages of about seventeen and twenty-four I tried to abandon this idea, but I did so with the consciousness that I was outraging my true nature and that sooner or later I should have to settle down and write books.

I was the middle child of three, but there was a gap of five years on either side, and I barely saw my father before I was eight. For this and other reasons I was somewhat lonely, and I soon developed disagreeable mannerisms which made me unpopular throughout my schooldays. I had the lonely child's habit of making up stories and holding conversations with imaginary persons, and I think from the very start my literary ambitions were mixed up with the feeling of being isolated and undervalued. I knew that I had a facility with words and a power of facing unpleasant facts, and I felt that this created a sort of private world in which I could get my own back for my failure in everyday life. Nevertheless the volume of serious—i.e. seriously intended—writing which I produced all through my childhood and boyhood would not amount to half a dozen pages. I wrote my first poem at the age of four or five, my mother taking it down to dictation. I cannot remember anything about it except that it was about a tiger and the tiger had "chair-like teeth"—a good enough phrase, but I fancy the poem was a plagiarism of Blake's "Tiger, Tiger." At eleven, when the war of 1914–18 broke out, I wrote a patriotic poem which was printed in the local newspaper, as was another, two years later, on the death of Kitchener.[1] From time to time, when I was a bit older, I wrote bad and usually unfinished "nature poems" in the Georgian style.[2] I also, about twice, attempted a short story which was a ghastly failure. That was the total of the would-be serious work that I actually set down on paper during all those years.

However, throughout this time I did in a sense engage in literary activities. 3 To begin with there was the made-to-order stuff which I produced quickly, easily and without much pleasure to myself. Apart from school work, I wrote *vers d'occasion*,[3] semicomic poems which I could turn out at what now seems to me astonishing speed—at fourteen I wrote a whole rhyming play, in imitation of Aristophanes,[4] in about a week—and helped to edit school magazines, both printed and in manuscript. These magazines were the most pitiful burlesque stuff that you could imagine, and I took far less trouble with them than I now would with the cheapest journalism. But side by side with all this, for fifteen years or more, I was carrying out a literary exercise of a quite different kind: this was the making up of a continuous "story" about myself, a sort of diary existing only in the mind. I believe this is a common habit of children and adolescents. As a very small child I used to imagine that I was, say, Robin Hood, and picture myself as the hero of thrilling adventures, but quite soon my "story" ceased to be narcissistic in a crude way and became more and more a mere description of what I was doing and the things I saw. For minutes at a time this kind of thing would be running through my head: "He pushed the door open and entered the room. A yellow beam of sunlight, filtering through the muslin curtains, slanted on to the table, where a matchbox, half open, lay beside the inkpot. With his right hand in his pocket he moved across to the window. Down in the street a tortoiseshell cat was chasing a dead leaf," etc. etc. This habit continued till I was about twenty-five, right through my non-literary years. Although I had to search, and did search, for the right words, I seemed to be making this descriptive effort almost against my will, under a kind of compulsion from outside. The "story" must, I suppose, have reflected the styles of the various writers I admired at different ages, but so far as I remember it always had the same meticulous descriptive quality.

When I was about sixteen I suddenly discovered the joy of mere words, i.e. 4 the sounds and associations of words. The lines from *Paradise Lost*,[5]

> So hee with difficulty and labour hard
> Moved on: with difficulty and labour hee,

---

[1]Horatio Kitchener (1850–1916): British general who extended the empire from Egypt into the Sudan in 1898. [Eds.]

[2]Georgian style: from *Georgian Poetry*, an anthology of contemporary verse; five volumes were published between 1912 and 1922. [Eds.]

[3]*vers d'occasion*: verse prepared for a particular event. [Eds.]

[4]Aristophanes (448?–380? B.C.): Greek dramatist. [Eds.]

[5]*Paradise Lost*: English epic poem written by John Milton (1608–1674). [Eds.]

which do not now seem to me so very wonderful, sent shivers down my back-bone; and the spelling "hee" for "he" was an added pleasure. As for the need to describe things, I knew all about it already. So it is clear what kind of books I wanted to write, in so far as I could be said to want to write books at that time. I wanted to write enormous naturalistic novels with unhappy endings, full of detailed descriptions and arresting similes, and also full of purple passages in which words were used partly for the sake of their sound. And in fact my first completed novel, *Burmese Days*, which I wrote when I was thirty but projected much earlier, is rather that kind of book.

I give all this background information because I do not think one can assess   5
a writer's motives without knowing something of his early development. His subject matter will be determined by the age he lives in—at least this is true in tumultuous, revolutionary ages like our own—but before he ever begins to write he will have acquired an emotional attitude from which he will never completely escape. It is his job, no doubt, to discipline his temperament and avoid getting stuck at some immature stage, or in some perverse mood: but if he escapes from his early influences altogether, he will have killed his impulse to write. Putting aside the need to earn a living, I think there are four great motives for writing, at any rate for writing prose. They exist in different degrees in every writer, and in any one writer the proportions will vary from time to time, according to the atmosphere in which he is living. They are:

1. Sheer egoism. Desire to seem clever, to be talked about, to be remem-   6
bered after death, to get your own back on grown-ups who snubbed you in childhood, etc. etc. It is humbug to pretend that this is not a motive, and a strong one. Writers share this characteristic with scientists, artists, politicians, lawyers, soldiers, successful businessmen—in short, with the whole top crust of humanity. The great mass of human beings are not acutely selfish. After the age of about thirty they abandon individual ambition—in many cases, indeed, they almost abandon the sense of being individuals at all—and live chiefly for others, or are simply smothered under drudgery. But there is also the minority of gifted, wilful people who are determined to live their own lives to the end, and writers belong in this class. Serious writers, I should say, are on the whole more vain and self-centered than journalists, though less interested in money.

2. Aesthetic enthusiasm. Perception of beauty in the external world, or, on   7
the other hand, in words and their right arrangement. Pleasure in the impact of one sound on another, in the firmness of good prose or the rhythm of a good story. Desire to share an experience which one feels is valuable and ought not to be missed. The aesthetic motive is very feeble in a lot of writers, but even a pamphleteer or a writer of textbooks will have pet words and phrases which appeal to him for non-utilitarian reasons; or he may feel strongly about typog-raphy, width of margins, etc. Above the level of a railway guide, no book is quite free from aesthetic considerations.

3. Historical impulse. Desire to see things as they are, to find out true facts   8
and store them up for the use of posterity.

4. Political purpose—using the word "political" in the widest possible sense. 9
Desire to push the world in a certain direction, to alter other people's idea of
the kind of society that they should strive after. Once again, no book is genuinely
free from political bias. The opinion that art should have nothing to do with
politics is itself a political attitude.

It can be seen how these various impulses must war against one another, and 10
how they must fluctuate from person to person and from time to time. By
nature—taking your "nature" to be the state you have attained when you are
first adult—I am a person in whom the first three motives would outweigh the
fourth. In a peaceful age I might have written ornate or merely descriptive books,
and might have remained almost unaware of my political loyalties. As it is I
have been forced into becoming a sort of pamphleteer. First I spent five years
in an unsuitable profession (the Indian Imperial Police, in Burma), and then I
underwent poverty and the sense of failure. This increased my natural hatred
of authority and made me for the first time fully aware of the existence of the
working classes, and the job in Burma had given me some understanding of the
nature of imperialism: but these experiences were not enough to give me an
accurate political orientation. Then came Hitler, the Spanish civil war, etc. By
the end of 1935 I had still failed to reach a firm decision. I remember a little
poem that I wrote at that date, expressing my dilemma:

> A happy vicar I might have been
> Two hundred years ago,
> To preach upon eternal doom
> And watch my walnuts grow;
>
> But born, alas, in an evil time,
> I missed that pleasant haven,
> For the hair has grown on my upper lip
> And the clergy are all clean-shaven.
>
> And later still the times were good,
> We were so easy to please,
> We rocked our troubled thoughts to sleep
> On the bosoms of the trees.
>
> All ignorant we dared to own
> The joys we now dissemble;
> The greenfinch on the apple bough
> Could make my enemies tremble.
>
> But girls' bellies and apricots,
> Roach in a shaded stream,
> Horses, ducks in flight at dawn,

George Orwell

All these are a dream.

It is forbidden to dream again;
We maim our joys or hide them;
Horses are made of chromium steel
And little fat men shall ride them.

I am the worm who never turned,
The eunuch without a harem;
Between the priest and the commissar
I walk like Eugene Aram;

And the commissar is telling my fortune
While the radio plays,
But the priest has promised an Austin Seven,
For Duggie always pays.

I dreamed I dwelt in marble halls,
And woke to find it true;
I wasn't born for an age like this;
Was Smith? Was Jones? Were you?

The Spanish war and other events in 1936–37 turned the scale and thereafter I knew where I stood. Every line of serious work that I have written since 1936 has been written, directly or indirectly, *against* totalitarianism and *for* democratic Socialism, as I understand it. It seems to me nonsense, in a period like our own, to think that one can avoid writing of such subjects. Everyone writes of them in one guise or another. It is simply a question of which side one takes and what approach one follows. And the more one is conscious of one's political bias, the more chance one has of acting politically without sacrificing one's aesthetic and intellectual integrity.

What I have most wanted to do throughout the past ten years is to make political writing into an art. My starting point is always a feeling of partisanship, a sense of injustice. When I sit down to write a book, I do not say to myself, "I am going to produce a work of art." I write it because there is some lie that I want to expose, some fact to which I want to draw attention, and my initial concern is to get a hearing. But I could not do the work of writing a book, or even a long magazine article, if it were not also an aesthetic experience. Anyone who cares to examine my work will see that even when it is downright propaganda it contains much that a full-time politician would consider irrelevant. I am not able, and I do not want, completely to abandon the world-view that I acquired in childhood. So long as I remain alive and well I shall continue to feel strongly about prose style, to love the surface of the earth, and to take

674

pleasure in solid objects and scraps of useless information. It is no use trying to suppress that side of myself. The job is to reconcile my ingrained likes and dislikes with the essentially public, non-individual activities that this age forces on all of us.

It is not easy. It raises problems of construction and of language, and it raises   12
in a new way the problem of truthfulness. Let me give just one example of the cruder kind of difficulty that arises. My book about the Spanish civil war, *Homage to Catalonia*, is, of course, a frankly political book, but in the main it is written with a certain detachment and regard for form. I did try very hard in it to tell the whole truth without violating my literary instincts. But among other things it contains a long chapter, full of newspaper quotations and the like, defending the Trotskyists who were accused of plotting with Franco. Clearly such a chapter, which after a year or two would lose its interest for any ordinary reader, must ruin the book. A critic whom I respect read me a lecture about it. "Why did you put in all that stuff?" he said. "You've turned what might have been a good book into journalism." What he said was true, but I could not have done otherwise. I happened to know, what very few people in England had been allowed to know, that innocent men were being falsely accused. If I had not been angry about that I should never have written the book.

In one form or another this problem comes up again. The problem of lan-   13
guage is subtler and would take too long to discuss. I will only say that of late years I have tried to write less picturesquely and more exactly. In any case I find that by the time you have perfected any style of writing, you have always outgrown it. *Animal Farm* was the first book in which I tried, with full consciousness of what I was doing, to fuse political purpose and artistic purpose into one whole. I have not written a novel for seven years, but I hope to write another fairly soon. It is bound to be a failure, every book is a failure, but I know with some clarity what kind of book I want to write.

Looking back through the last page or two, I see that I have made it appear   14
as though my motives in writing were wholly public-spirited. I don't want to leave that as the final impression. All writers are vain, selfish and lazy, and at the very bottom of their motives there lies a mystery. Writing a book is a horrible, exhausting struggle, like a long bout of some painful illness. One would never undertake such a thing if one were not driven on by some demon whom one can neither resist nor understand. For all one knows that demon is simply the same instinct that makes a baby squall for attention. And yet it is also true that one can write nothing readable unless one constantly struggles to efface one's own personality. Good prose is like a window pane. I cannot say with certainty which of my motives are the strongest, but I know which of them deserve to be followed. And looking back through my work, I see that it is invariably where I lacked a *political* purpose that I wrote lifeless books and was betrayed into purple passages, sentences without meaning, decorative adjectives and humbug generally.

George Orwell

QUESTIONS

1. What relation between politics and art does Orwell advocate in this essay? What are other possible views of this matter? If you disagree with Orwell, write a counterstatement.

2. Do you understand Orwell's poem? What is its point as a poem? What purpose does it serve in the context of the essay?

3. In this essay we find a writer reflecting on his own motives, looking over his past, and seeking the pattern of his own development. This reflective movement involves both explanation and argumentation as well as reflection. Try to sort out these different strands of writing in this essay.

4. Where is the line between why writers *do* write and why they *should* write? How does Orwell evaluate his own writing, discriminating between better and worse work?

5. What sense of himself does Orwell convey to his readers? How would you describe his personality, his character? What in his writing leads you to see him as you do? Is it what he says, or how he says it? Be as specific as you can.

6. How would you describe Orwell's prose? Is he accurate about himself when he discusses his own style? Does his writing have the qualities he would like it to have? Consider specific phrases and sentences.

7. After thinking about Orwell's reasons for writing, consider your own. Are Orwell's reasons applicable to your writing? Write a short essay that considers the question, Why do I write?

ON POLITICAL WRITING
Walter Lippmann

Walter Lippmann (1889–1974) received his A.B. degree from Harvard at the age of twenty and went on to graduate study in philosophy. He is best known as a political commentator and journalist. He served as an editor and columnist on the New Republic, *the* New York World, *and the* Herald Tribune, *and he held office as an assistant to the Secretary of War in 1917. Between 1913 and 1955 he wrote more than ten books on political and philosophical subjects. The following essay (which we have supplied with a title) appeared as Lippmann's "Books and Things" column in the* New Republic *in 1915.*

The other night I sat up late reading one of those books on politics which are regarded as essential to any sort of intellectual respectability. It was a book that might be referred to in the Constitutional Convention at Albany. As I read along I was possessed with two convictions about the author. The first was that he had worn a high hat when he wrote the book; the second, that he had no teeth, which made him a little difficult to understand. And all through that hot and mosquito-ridden night the disintegration of his vocabulary went churning through my head . . . "social consciousness . . . sovereign will . . . electoral duties . . . national obligations . . . on moral, economic, political, and social grounds . . . social consciousness . . . sovereignty . . . electoral . . . social . . . sovereign . . . national . . . sovereign . . . ." Each word was as smooth and hard and round as a billiard ball, and in the malice of my sleeplessness I saw the toothless but perfectly groomed man in a high hat making patterns of the balls which were handed to him by his butler.

As the night dragged along, the callowest prejudices came to the surface and all fairer and reputable judgment deserted me. I heard myself say that this ass who plagued me couldn't possibly have any ideas because he didn't have any vocabulary. How is it possible, I asked, to write or think about the modern world with a set of words which were inchoate lumps when Edmund Burke used them? Political writing is asphyxiated by the staleness of its language. We are living in a strange world, and we have to talk about it in a kind of algebra. And of course if we deal only with colorless and vacant symbols, the world we see and the world we describe soon becomes a colorless and vacant place. Nobody can write criticism of American politics if the only instruments at his command are a few polysyllables of Greek and Latin origin. You can't put Bryan and Hearst and Billy Sunday into the vocabulary of Aristotle, Bentham, or Burke. Yet if you are going to write about American politics, can you leave out Bryan and Hearst and Billy Sunday, or even Champ Clark? The author I had been reading did leave them out completely. He talked about the national will of America as if it were a single stream of pure water which ran its course through silver pipes laid down by the Constitutional Fathers.

I tried to recall any new words which had been added to the vocabulary of   3
social science. Boss, heeler, machine, logrolling, pork-barrel—those were the words which meant something at Washington or in Tammany Hall,[1] but my author would no more have used them than he would have eaten green peas with a knife. Anyone who did use them he would have regarded as a mere journalist, and probably a cocksure young man at that. Then I remembered that the diplomats had made current a few fresh words within the last genera-tions—hinterland, pacific penetration, sphere of influence, sphere of legitimate aspiration; they had meaning, because nations went to war about them. But the real contributions, curiously enough, have come not from the political theorist, but from novelists, and from philosophers who might have been novelists.

H. G. Wells and William James,[2] I said to myself, come nearer to having a   4
vocabulary fit for political uses than any other writers of English. They write in terms which convey some of the curiosity and formlessness of modern life. Speech with them is pragmatic, and accurate in the true sense. They are exact when exactness is possible, blurred when the thought itself is blurred. They have almost completely abandoned the apparatus of polysyllables through which no direct impression can ever penetrate. They do not arrange concepts, they gather precepts, and never do you lose the sense that the author is just a man trying to find out what he thinks. But the political writer who gave me the nightmare never admitted that he was just a man. He aimed at that impersonal truth which is like the inscription on monuments.

He regarded himself as a careful person. His method was to retrieve in   5
qualifying clause whatever he had risked in assertion. So he achieved a com-pendium of things-that-can't-be-done, a kind of anthology of the impossible. His notion of getting at the truth was to peel it, like Peer Gynt's onion,[3] though Peer Gynt had the sense to be surprised that there was nothing to an onion but the layers.

My temper grew worse as I reflected on the hypnotic effect of books done in   6
this manner, on the number of men whose original vision is muffled by verbal

---

[1]Tammany Hall: the Democratic political organization in New York City that was famous for its corruption. [Eds.]

[2]H. G. Wells (1866–1946): English novelist and writer on politics and education. William James (1842–1910): American psychologist and philosopher. [Eds.]

[3]Peer Gynt: a character in the 1869 play of the same name by Henrik Ibsen. In Act V Peer Gynt peels a wild onion, each layer of which represents a chapter of his life, and finds nothing at its core. [Eds.]

red tape and officialism of the spirit. The true speech of man is idiomatic, if not of the earth and sky, then at least of the saloon and the bleachers. But no smelly or vivid impression can win its way through these opaque incantations with which political science is afflicted. They forbid fresh seeing. An innocence of the eye is impossible, for there are no words to report a vision with; and visions which cannot be expressed are not cultivated. No wonder, I thought, political philosophizing means so little in human life. Its woodenness is the counterpart of a wooden politics, its inhumanity is the inhumanity of a state machine. The language is callous, unmoved, and unmoving, because it aims to reflect rather than to lead the life upon which it comments. Dead speech is good enough for thoughts that bring no news, and it is to the timidity of political thought that we must ascribe its preference for a dead language. In these tomes over which we yawn at night, there are occasionally ideas which might shake the world. But they do not shake it, for they are written for people who do not like to shake it. They are hedged with reservations, fortified with polysyllables, and covered over with the appalling conceit that here is truth—objective, impersonal, cold.

I generalized rashly: That is what kills political writing, this absurd pretense 7 that you are delivering a great utterance. You never do. You are just a puzzled man making notes about what you think. You are not building the Pantheon,[4] then why act like a graven image? You are drawing sketches in the sand which the sea will wash away. What more is your book but your infinitesimal scratching, and who the devil are you to be grandiloquent and impersonal? The truth is you're afraid to be wrong. And so you put on these airs and use these established phrases, knowing that they will sound familiar and will be respected. But this fear of being wrong is a disease. You cover and qualify and elucidate, you speak vaguely, you mumble because you are afraid of the sound of your own voice. And then you apologize for your timidity by frowning learnedly on anyone who honestly regards thoughts as an adventure, who strikes ahead and takes his chances. You are like a man trying to be happy, like a man trying too hard to make a good mashie shot in golf. It can't be done by trying so hard to do it. Whatever truth you contribute to the world will be one lucky shot in a thousand misses. You cannot be right by holding your breath and taking precautions.

QUESTIONS

1. Like many meditations, this one contains an argument. What is Lippmann's point or thesis in his argument? What do H. G. Wells and William James (paragraph 4) represent in his argument?

2. Consider the people named in paragraph 2: Edmund Burke, William Jennings

---

[4]the Pantheon: famous Roman temple dedicated to all the gods. [Eds.]

Bryan, William Randolph Hearst, Billy Sunday, Aristotle, Jeremy Bentham, and Champ Clark. Can you understand what they represent without knowing exactly who each was? If you look them up, how does this affect your reading of the paragraph? As Lippmann groups them, what do the groups represent?

3. This piece first appeared in a magazine column in which Lippmann frequently reviewed books, so it might have been a book review. Instead, it turned into a meditation. What would have been different if this had been a book review? That is, what would have been present in the text that now isn't, and what *is* present that would have been absent or different if this had been a review?

4. Look at the first sentence of each paragraph in this essay. In how many of them does Lippmann mention himself? Why does he do this? What has this to do with the method or form of his essay?

5. In the last paragraph, Lippmann changes to the second person (*you*). Why does he do this—and why in this paragraph? What has this change to do with the structure of his essay?

6. Lippmann seems to be against using long words: "polysyllables of Greek and Latin origin" (paragraph 2). Does he use many such words himself? Try making a list of those he uses. Is *polysyllable* a long word of Greek or Latin origin? Is Lippmann ignoring his own practice in making his criticism, or does he mean to include himself? Provide evidence for your answer to this last question.

7. Write an essay in which you consider a book not in itself but as a representative of a type of writing that you either admire or deplore. Instead of criticizing the single work, reflect upon the whole kind of writing represented in that work. Remember to push your thought to a conclusion. (Or instead of a book, you might consider a particular film as representative of a certain type of filmmaking.)

CONFESSIONS OF
A NEWS ADDICT
Stanley Milgram

In addition to his work on obedience to authority (see pages 329–352), Stanley Milgram is known for his studies of the relationship between television watching and antisocial behavior. The present essay, which appeared first in the Antioch Review *in 1977, was reprinted that same year in the* New York Times. *It is more a personal reflection than a psychological study, but, as Milgram has observed, "Social psychologists are part of the very social matrix they have chosen to analyze, and thus they can use their experience as a source of insight."*

Let me begin with a confession. I am a news addict. Upon awakening I flip 1
on the *Today* show to learn what events transpired during the night. On the
commuter train which takes me to work, I scour *The New York Times*, and find
myself absorbed in tales of earthquakes, diplomacy and economics. I read the
newspaper as religiously as my grandparents read their prayerbooks. The sacra-
mental character of the news extends into the evening. The length of my work-
day is determined precisely by my need to get home in time for Walter Cronkite.
My children understand that my communion with Cronkite is something serious
and cannot be interrupted for light and transient causes.

But what is it, precisely, that is happening when I and millions of others 2
scour our newspapers, stare at the tube, and pore over the news magazines that
surround us? Does it make sense? What is news, and why does it occupy a place
of special significance for so many people?

Let us proceed from a simple definition: News is information about events 3
that are going on outside immediate experience. In this sense, news has always
been a part of the human situation. In its earliest form, it took the shape of an
account brought by a traveler, or a member of the group who wandered farther
than the rest and found water, game or signs of a nearby enemy. The utility of
such information is self-evident. News is a social mechanism that extends our
own eyes and ears to embrace an ever-wider domain of events. A knowledge of
remote events allows us to prepare for them and take whatever steps are needed
to deal with them. This is the classic function of news.

News is the consciousness of society. It is the means whereby events in the 4
body politic are brought into awareness. And it is curious that regimes which
we call *repressive* tend to exhibit the same characteristic of repressed personalities;

they are unable, or unwilling, to allow conflictive material into awareness. The disability stems from deep insecurities. The censoring of the repressed material does not eliminate it, but forces it to fester without anyone's rationally coming to grips with it.

Inevitably news comes to be controlled by the dominant political forces of a 5 society. In a totalitarian regime the government attempts to create the image of a world, and of events, that reflects most favorably on those in power. The democratization of news, which goes hand in hand with the diffusion of political power among those governed, is a relatively recent development whose permanence cannot be assured.

Democracies are far better able to cope with the reality of events than are 6 totalitarian regimes. Such regimes promulgate a myth of their omnipotence, and are threatened even by events outside the control of the political process. Thus, typically, the Soviet press does not report air crashes, and even natural disasters such as earthquakes are suppressed, out of the notion—rooted in political insecurity—that the event in some manner reflects badly on the regime.

The question for any society is not whether there shall be news, but rather 7 who shall have access to it. Every political system may be characterized by the proportion of information it has which is shared with the people and the proportion withheld. That is why the growth of secret news-gathering agencies, such as the C.I.A., is a troubling one for a democracy. It appears our Government wants to keep some news to itself.

At a deeper historical level we can see that news in its present form is closely 8 tied to the rise of economy, and specifically to the exploitative and risk elements of capitalism. For the 19th-century merchant, news meant reports of his ship, of resources to exploit, and the means of minimizing the risk element inherent in entrepreneurship by gaining as much information as possible before his competitors. News services, such as Reuters, developed to serve business and investment interests, who discovered that getting the news quickly was the first step to financial gain.

In a civilization in which all activities tend toward commercial expression— 9 for example, our own—news becomes a product to manufacture and dispense to the consumer. Thus a large-scale industry for the production and consumption of news has evolved. We ingest it with the same insatiable appetite that moves us to purchase the manifold products of our commercial civilization.

News under such circumstances tends toward decadent use. It no longer 10 serves first the classic function of giving us information on which to act, or even to help us construct a mental model of the larger world. It serves mainly as entertainment. The tales of earthquakes, political assassinations and bitterly fought elections are the heady stuff of which drama or melodrama is made. Happily, we are able to indulge our taste for thriller, romance or murder mystery under the guise of a patently respectable pursuit. All enlightened people are supposed to know what is going on in the world. If what is going on also happens to be thrilling and exciting, so much the better.

Another feature of the decadent use of news is its increasing ritualization.   11
The information becomes subservient to the form in which it is delivered. News is broadcast every evening, whether or not there is vital information to be conveyed. Indeed, the problem for the news networks is to generate sufficient news to fill a given time period. The time period becomes the fundamental fact, the framework into which events must be fitted. As in any ritual, the form persists even when a meaningful content is missing.

Those groups whose survival and well-being are most affected by remote   12
events will be most persistently attuned to them. For example, Israelis, who view the survival of their state as a day-to-day contingency, are among the most news-oriented people in the world. During periods of crisis, portable radios blare in buses and in the marketplace. Jews, in general, have felt the need to develop antennae for remote events because of a communal insecurity. Any event, no matter how remote—even a farcical *putsch* in Munich led by a paperhanger— may grow into a formidable threat. Thus, constant monitoring of events is strongly reinforced.

Although I am a news addict, my addiction is strongest for news that in many   13
respects seems most remote from my own life and experience. International news receives top priority, followed by national domestic news, and finally— and of least interest—local news. I feel more concerned reading about a student strike in Paris than a murder in my own neighborhood. I am especially uninterested in those news programs that provide a constant litany of fires and local crimes as their standard fare.

Yet there is a paradox in this. Surely a criminal loose in my city is of greater   14
personal consequence than an election outcome in Uruguay. Indeed, I sometimes ask what difference it makes to the actual conduct of my life to know about a fracas in Zaire, or a train wreck in Sweden.

The total inconsequence of the news for my life is most strikingly brought   15
home when we return from a vacation of several weeks where we have been without any news. I normally scan the accumulated pile of newspapers, but cannot help noticing how little difference it all made to me. And least consequential of all were those remote international events that so rivet my attention in the normal course of the week.

Why this interest in things far away, with a lesser interest in events close at   16
home? Perhaps it is essentially a romantic impulse in the projection of meaning into remote countries, places and people. Such a romantic impulse stems from a dissatisfaction with the mundane reality of everyday life. The events and places described in the news are remote, and thus we can more readily fix our imaginative sentiments to them.

Moreover, an interest in news reinforces the "cosmopolitan" attitude which   17
characterizes modern life, a desire to focus not only on the immediate com-

munity, but on the larger world. It is thus the opposite of the "provincialism" which characterized an earlier rural existence.

Living in the modern world, I cannot help but be shaped by it, suckered by   18
the influence and impact of our great institutions. *The New York Times*, CBS and *Newsweek* have made me into a news addict. In daily life I have come to accept the supposition that if *The New York Times* places a story on the front page, it deserves my attention. I feel obligated to know what is going on. But sometimes, in quieter moments, another voice asks: If the news went away, would the world be any worse for it?

QUESTIONS

1. Most of this essay is devoted to what Milgram calls his news addiction. What does Milgram mean when he calls himself a "news addict"?

2. Summarize in your own words Milgram's attitude about what news is and why it holds special significance for so many people.

3. What does Milgram mean when he writes that "News is the consciousness of society" (paragraph 4)? Analyze and critique this statement.

4. In this essay, the writer is reflecting, but he is also explaining and interpreting. What are his different aims in this essay?

5. For Milgram, "International news receives top priority" (paragraph 13). What kind of news interests you the most? What are your primary sources of news? Write an essay in which you reflect on your own interest (or lack of interest) in news.

6. Milgram begins this essay with a confession that he is a news addict. Write an essay in which you confess to a reader about one of your addictions or obsessions, and consider what effects this addiction or obsession has had on your life.

OBSESSED WITH SPORT
Joseph Epstein

*Born in Chicago in 1937, Joseph Epstein graduated from
the University of Chicago in 1959 and began a career as a
writer and editor. Since 1975 he has been the editor of
American Scholar, the quarterly review of Phi Beta Kappa,
writing occasional essays for that magazine under the pseudonym of Aristides. He is the author of several books on
American life and culture. Since 1974 he has regularly been
a Visiting Lecturer in English at Northwestern University.
The essay reprinted here appeared in Harper's magazine in
1976.*

I cannot remember when I was not surrounded by sports, when talk of sports
was not in the air, when I did not care passionately about sports. As a boy in
Chicago in the late Forties, I lived in the same building as the sister and brother-
in-law of Barney Ross, the welterweight champion. Half a block away, down
near the lake, the Sullivan High School football team worked out in the spring
and autumn. Summers the same field was given over to baseball and men's
softball on Sundays. A few blocks to the north was the Touhy Avenue Field-
house, where basketball was played, and lifeguards trained, and behind which,
in a softball field frozen over in winter, crack-the-whip, hockey, and speed
skating took over. To the west, a block or so up Morse Avenue, was the Morse
Avenue "L" Recreations, a combined pool hall and bowling alley. Life, in short,
was games.

My father had no interest in sports. He had grown up, one of the ten children 2
of Russian Jewish immigrant parents, on tough Notre Dame Street in Montreal,
where the major sports were craps, poker, and petty larceny. He left Montreal
at seventeen to come to Chicago, where he worked hard and successfully so
that his sons might play. Two of his boyhood friends from Notre Dame Street,
who had the comic-book names of Sammy and Danny Spunt, had also come
to Chicago, where they bought the Ringside Gym on Dearborn Street in the
Loop. All the big names worked out at Ringside for their Chicago fights: Willie
Pep, Tony Zale, Joe Louis. At eight or nine I would take the El downtown to
the Ringside, be introduced around by Danny Spunt ("Tony Zale, I'd like you
to meet the son of an old friend of mine. Kid, I'd like you to meet the mid-
dleweight champion of the world"), and return home with an envelope filled
with autographed 8-by-10 glossies of Gus Lesnevich, Tammy Maurielo, Kid
Gavilan, and the wondrous Sugar Ray.

Joseph Epstein

I lived on, off, and in sports. *Sport* magazine had recently begun publication, [3] and I gobbled up its issues cover to cover, soon becoming knowledgeable not only about the major sports—baseball, football, and basketball—but about golf, hockey, tennis, and horse racing, so that I scored reputably on the Sport Quiz, a regular department at the front of the magazine. Another regular department was the Sport Classic, which featured longish profiles of the legendary figures in the history of sports: Ty Cobb, Jim Thorpe, Bobby Jones, Big Bill Tilden, Red Grange, Man o' War. I next moved on to the sports novels of John R. Tunis—*All-American, The Iron Duke, The Kid from Tomkinsville, The Kid Comes Back, World Series,* the lot—which I read with as much excitement as any books I have read since.

The time was, as is now apparent, a splendid era in sports. Ted Williams, [4] Joe DiMaggio, and Stan Musial were afield; first Jack Kramer, then Pancho Gonzales, dominated tennis; George Mikan led the Minneapolis Lakers, and the Harlem Globetrotters could still be taken seriously; Doc Blanchard and Glen Davis, Mr. Inside and Mr. Outside, were playing for Army, Johnny Lujack was at Notre Dame; in the pros Sammy Baugh, Bob Waterfield, and Sid Luckman were the major T-formation quarterbacks; Joe Louis and Sugar Ray Robinson fought frequently; the two Willies, Mosconi and Hoppe, put in regular appearances at Bensinger's in the Loop; Eddie Arcaro seemed to ride three, four winners a day. Giants, it truly seemed, walked the earth.

All learning of craft—which sport, like writing, most assuredly is—involves [5] imitation, especially in the early stages; and I was an excellent mimic. By the time I was ten years old I had mastery over all the big-time moves: the spit in the mitt, the fluid infield chatter, the knocking of dirt from the spikes; the rhythmic barking out of signals, hands high under the center's crotch to take the ball; the three bounces and deep breath before shooting the free throw (on this last, I regretted not being a Catholic, so that I might be able to make the sign of the cross before shooting, as was then the fashion among Catholic high-school and college players). I went in for athletic haberdashery in a big way, often going beyond mimicry to the point of flat-out phoniness—wearing, for example, a knee pad while playing basketball, though my knees were always, exasperatingly, intact.

I always looked good, which was important, because form is intrinsic to sports; [6] but in my case it was doubly important, because the truth is that I wasn't really very good. Or at any rate not good enough. Two factors accounted for this. The first was that, without being shy about body contact, I lacked a certain indispensable aggressiveness; the second connected closely to the first, was that, when it came right down to it, I did not care enough about winning. I would rather lose a point attempting a slashing cross-court backhand than play for an easier winner down the side; the long jump shot always had more allure for me than the safer drive to the basket. Given a choice between the two vanities of winning and looking good, I almost always preferred looking good.

I shall never forget the afternoon, sometime along about my thirteenth year, when, shooting baskets alone, I came upon the technique for shooting the hook. Although today it has nowhere near the consequence of the jump shot—an innovation that has been to basketball what the jet has been to air travel—the hook is still the single most beautiful shot in the game. The rhythm and grace of it, the sway of the body off the pivot, the release of the ball behind the head and off the fingertips, the touch and instinct involved in its execution, make the hook altogether a balletic thing, and to achieve it is to feel one of the most delectable sensations in sports. That afternoon, on a deserted side street, shooting on a rickety wooden backboard and a black rim without a net, I felt it and grew nearly drunk on the feeling. Rain came down, dirt washed in the gutters, flecks of it spattering my clothes and arms and face, but, soaked and cold though I was, I do not think I would have left that basket on that afternoon for anything. I threw up hook after hook, from every angle, from farther and farther out, off the board, without the board, and hook after hook went in. Only pitch darkness drove me home. 7

I do not say that not to have shot the hook is never to have lived, but only that, once having done so, the pleasure it gives is not so easily forgotten. Every sport offers similar pleasures, the pleasures taken differing by temperament: the canter into the end zone to meet a floating touchdown pass, or the clean, crisp feel of a perfect block or tackle; the long straight drive or the precisely played approach shot to the green; the solid overhead; the pickup on the tricky short hop or the long ball down one of the power alleys. Different sports, different pleasures. But so keen are these pleasures—pleasures of execution, of craft completed—that, along with being unforgettable, they are also worth recapturing in any available way, and the most available way, when reflexes have slowed, when muscle no longer responds so readily to brain, is from the grandstand or, perhaps more often nowadays, from the chair before the television. 8

PLEASURES OF THE SPECTATOR

I have put in days on the bench, but years in my chair before the television set. Recently it has occurred to me that over the years I have heard more hours of talk from the announcer Curt Gowdy than from my own father, who is not a reticent man. I have been thoroughly Schenkeled, Mussbergered, Summeralled, Cosselled, DeRogotissed, and Garagiolaed. How many hundreds—thousands?—of hours have I spent watching sports of all sorts, either at parks or stadiums or over television? I am glad I shall never have a precise answer. Yet neither apparently can I get enough. What is the fascination? Why is it that, with the prospect of a game to watch in the evening or on the weekend, the day seems lighter and brighter? What do I get out of it? 9

What I get out of it, according to one fairly prominent view, is an outlet for my violent emotions. Knee-wrenching, rib-cracking, headbusting, this view has 10 it, is what sports are really about, with sports fans being essentially sadists, and cowardly sadists at that, for they take their violence not at firsthand but at second remove. Enthusiasm for sports among Americans is little more than a reflection of the national penchant for violence. Military men talk about game plans; the long touchdown pass is called the bomb. The average pro-football fan, seeing a quarterback writhing on the ground at midfield as a result of the ministrations of Joe Green, Carl Eller, or Lyle Alzado, twitters with glee, finds his ultimate reward, and declares a little holiday in the blackest corner of his heart.

But this is a criticism that comes at sports by way of politics. To believe it 11 one has to believe that the history of the United States is chiefly one of rape, expropriation, and aggressive imperialism. To dismiss it, however, one need only know something about sports. Violence is indubitably a part of some sports; in some—hockey is an example—it sometimes comes close to being featured. But in no sport—not even boxing, that most rudimentary of sports—is it the main item, and in many other sports it plays no part at all. A distinction worth insisting on is that between violence and roughness. Roughness, a willingness to mix it up, to take if need be an elbow in the jaw, is part of rebounding in basketball, yet violence is not. Even in pro football, most maligned of modern American sports, more of roughness than of violence is involved. Roughness raises the stakes, provides the pressure, behind execution. A splendid because true phrase has come about in pro football to cover the situation in which a pass receiver, certain that he will be tackled upon the instant he makes his reception, drops a ball he should otherwise have caught easily—the phrase, best delivered in a Southern accent such as Don Meredith's, is "He heard footsteps on that one, Howard." Although a part of the attraction, it is not so much those footsteps that fill the stands and the den chairs on Sunday afternoons as it is those men who elude them: the Lynn Swanns, the Fran Tarkentons, the O. J. Simpsons. The American love of violence theory really will not wash. Dick Butkus did not get us into Vietnam.

Many who would not argue that sports reflect American violence nevertheless 12 claim that they imbue one with the competitive spirit. In some who are already amply endowed with it, sports doubtless do tend to refine (or possibly brutalize) the desire to win. Yet sports also teach a serious respect for craft. Competition, though it flourishes as always, is in bad odor nowadays; but craft, officially respected, does not flourish greatly outside the boutique.

If the love of violence or the competitive urge does not put me in my chair 13 for the countless games I watch, is it, then, nostalgia, a yearning to regain the more glowing moments of adolescence? Many argue that this is precisely so, that American men exist in a state of perpetual immaturity, suspended between boy- and manhood. "The difference between men and boys," says Liberace, "is the price of their toys." (I have paid more than $300 for two half-season tickets to the Chicago Bulls games, parking fees not included.) Such unending enthusiasm for games may have something to do with adolescence, but little, I suspect, with regaining anything whatever. Instead, it has more to do with watching men do regularly and surpassingly what, as an adolescent, one did often bumblingly though with an occasional flash of genius. To have played these games oneself as a boy or a young man helps immeasurably the appreciation that in watching a sport played at professional caliber one is witnessing the extraordinary made to look ordinary. That a game may have no consequence outside itself—no effect on history, on one's own life, on anything really—does not make it trivial but only makes the enjoyment of it all the purer.

The notion that men watch sports to regain their adolescence pictures them   14
sitting in the stands or at home watching a game and, within their psyches, muttering, "There, but for the lack of grace of God, go I." And it is true that a number of contemporary authors who are taken seriously have indeed written about sports with a strong overlay of yearning. In the men's softball games described in the fiction of Philip Roth, center field is a place akin to Arcady. Arcadian, too, is the outfield in Willie Morris's memoir of growing up in the South, *North Toward Home*. In the first half of *Rabbit Run* John Updike takes up the life of a man whose days are downhill all the way after hitting his peak as a high-school basketball star—and in the writing Updike himself evinces a nice soft touch of undisguised longing. In *A Fan's Notes*, a book combining yearning and self-disgust in roughly equal measure, Frederick Exley makes plain that he would much prefer to have been born into the skin of Frank Gifford rather than into his own.

But most men who are enraptured by sports do not think any such thing. I   15
should like to have Kareem Abdul-Jabbar's sky hook, but not, especially for civilian life, the excessive height that is necessary to its execution. I should like to have Jimmy Connors's ground strokes, but no part of his mind. These are men born with certain gifts, gifts honed by practice and determination, that I, and millions along with me, enjoy seeing on display. But the reality principle is too deeply ingrained, at least in a man of my years, for me to even imagine exchanging places with them. One might as well imagine oneself in the winner's circle at Churchill Downs as the horse.

Fantasy is an element in sports when they are played in adolescence—an   16
alley basket becomes the glass backboard at Madison Square Garden, a concrete park district tennis court with grass creeping out of the service line becomes center court at Wimbledon—but fantasy of this kind is hard to come by. Part of this has to do with age; but as large a part has to do with the age in which we live. Sport has always been a business but never more so than currently, and nothing lends itself less to fantasy than business. Reading the sports section has become rather like reading the business section—mergers, trades, salary negotiations, contract disputes, options, and strikes fill the columns. Along with the details of business, those of the psychological and social problems of athletes have come to the fore. The old *Sport* magazine concentrated on play on the

field, with only an occasional digressive reference to personal life. ("Yogi likes plenty of pizza in the off-season and spends a lot of his time at his teammate Phil Rizzuto's bowling alley," is a rough facsimile of a sentence from its pages that I recall.) But the magazine in its current version, as well as the now more popular *Sports Illustrated*, expends much space on the private lives of athletes— their divorces, hang-ups, race relations, need for approval, concern for security, potted philosophies—with the result that the grand is made to seem small.

On the other side of the ledger, there is a view that finds a shimmering significance in everything having to do with sports. Literary men in general are notoriously to be distrusted on the subject. They dig around everywhere, and can be depended upon to find much treasure where none is buried. Norman Mailer mining metaphysical ore in every jab of Muhammad Ali's, an existential nugget in each of his various and profuse utterances, is a particularly horrendous example. Even the sensible William Carlos Williams was not above this sort of temptation. In a poem entitled "At the Ball Game," we find the lines "It is the Inquisition, the/Revolution." Dr. Williams could not have been much fun at the ball park. — 17

THE REAL THING

If enthusiasm for sports has little to do with providing an outlet for violent emotions, regaining adolescence, discovering metaphysical truths, the Inquisition or the Revolution, then what, I ask myself, am I doing past midnight, when I have to be up at 5:30 the next morning, watching on television what will turn out to be a seventeen-inning game between the New York Mets and the St. Louis Cardinals? The conversation coming out of my television set is of a very low grade, even for sports announcing. But even the dreary talk cannot put me off—the rehash of statistics, the advise to youngsters to keep their gloves low when in the field, the thin jokes. Neither the Mets nor the Cards figure to be contenders this year. The only possible effect that this game can have on my life is to make me dog-tired the next day. Yet I cannot pull myself away. I want to know how it is going to end. True, the score will be available in the morning paper. But that is not the same thing. What is going on here? — 18

One thing that is going on is the practice of craft of a very high order, which is intrinsically interesting. But something as important is involved, something rarer in contemporary life, the spectacle of which gives enormous satisfaction. To define this satisfaction negatively, it is the absence of fraudulence and fakery. No small item, this, when one stops to think that in nearly every realm of contemporary life fraud and fakery have an established—some would say a preponderant—place. Advertising, politics, business, and journalism are only the most obvious examples. Fraud seems similarly pervasive in modern art: in painters whose reputations rest on press agentry; in writers who write one way — 19 and live quite another; in composers who are taken seriously but whose work cannot be seriously listened to. At a time when *image* is one of the most frequently used words in American speech and writing, one does not too often come upon the real thing.

Sport may be the toy department of life, but one of its abiding compensations is that, at least on the field, it is the real thing. Much has been done in recent years in the attempt to ruin sport—the ruthlessness of owners, the greed of players, the general exploitation of fans. But even all this cannot destroy it. On the court, down on the field, sport is fraud-free and fakeproof. With a full count, two men on, his team down by one run in the last of the eighth, a batter (as well as a pitcher) is beyond the aid of public relations. At match point at Forest Hills a player's press clippings are of no help. Last year's earnings will not sink a twelve-foot putt on the eighteenth at Augusta. Alan Page, galloping up along a quarterback's blind side, figures to be neglectful of that quarterback's image as a swinger. In all these situations, and hundreds of others, a man either comes through or he doesn't. He is alone out there, naked but for his ability, which counts for everything. Something there is that is elemental about this, and something greatly satisfying.

Another part of the satisfaction to be got from sports—from playing them, but also from watching them being played—derives from their special clarity. Sports offer clarity of a kind sufficient to engage the most serious minds. That the Cambridge mathematician G. H. Hardy closely followed cricket and avidly read cricket scores is not altogether surprising. Numbers in sports are ubiquitous. Scores, standings, averages, times, records—comfort is found in such numbers. ERA, RBI, FGP, pass completions, turnovers, category upon category of statistics are kept for nearly every aspect of athletic activity. (Why, I recently heard someone ask, are records not kept for catchers throwing out runners attempting to steal? Because, the answer is, often runners steal on pitchers, and so it would be unfair to charge these stolen bases against catchers.) As perhaps in no other sphere, numbers in sports tell one where things stand. No loopholes here, where figures, for once, do not lie. Nowhere else is such specificity of result available.

Clarity about character is also available in sports. "You Americans hold to the proposition that it is self-evident that all men are created equal," I not long ago heard an Englishman say, adding, "it had better be self-evident, for no other evidence for it exists." Sport coldly demonstrates physical inequalities—there are the larger, the faster, the stronger, the more graceful athletes—but it also throws up human types who have devised ways to redress these inequalities. One such type is the hustler. In every realm but that of sports the word *hustle* is pejorative, whereas in sports it is approbative. Two of the hustler breed, Pete Rose of the Cincinnati Reds and Jerry Sloan of the Chicago Bulls, are men who supplement reasonably high levels of ability with unreasonably high levels of courage and desire. Other athletes—Joe Morgan and Oscar Robertson come

20

21

22

691

to mind—bring superior athletic intelligence to bear upon their play. And Bill Russell, late of the Boston Celtics, who if the truth be known was not an inherently superior athlete, blended hustle and intelligence with what abilities he did have and through force of character established supremacy.

Whence do hustle, intelligence, and character in sports derive, especially since they apparently do not necessarily carry over into life? Joe DiMaggio and Sugar Ray Robinson, two of the most instinctively intelligent and physically elegant athletes, brought little of either of these qualities over into their business or personal activities. Some athletes can do all but one important thing well: Wilt Chamberlain at the free-throw line, for those who recall his misery there, leaves a permanent picture of a mental block in action. Other athletes—Connie Hawkins, Ilie Nastase, Dick Allen—have all the physical gifts in superabundance, yet, because of some insufficiency of character, some searing flaw, never come near to fulfilling their promise. Coaches supply yet another gallery of human types, from the fanatical Vince Lombardi to the comical Casey Stengel to the measured and aptly named John Wooden. The cast of characters in sport, the variety of situations, the complexity of behavior it puts on display, the overall human exhibit it offers—together these supply an enjoyment akin to that once provided by reading interminably long but inexhaustibly rich nineteenth-century novels. 23

In a wider sense, sport is culture. For many American men it represents a common background, a shared interest. It has a binding power that transcends social class and education. Some years ago I found myself working in the South among men with whom I shared nothing in the way of region, religion, education, politics, or general views; we shared nothing, in fact, but sports, which was enough for us to get along and grow to become friends, in the process showing how superficial all the things that might have kept us apart in fact were. More recently, in Chicago, at a time when race relations were in a particularly jagged state, I recall emerging from an NBA game, in which the Chicago Bulls in overtime beat the Milwaukee Bucks, into a snowy night and an aura of common good feeling that, for a time, submerged the enmity between races; laughing, throwing snowballs, exuberant generally, the crowd leaving the Chicago Stadium that night was not divided by being black and white but unified by being Bull fans. Last year's Boston-Cincinnati World Series, one of the most gratifying in memory, coming hard upon a year of extreme political divisiveness, performed, however briefly, something of the same function. How much better it felt to agree about the mastery of Luis Tiant than to argue about the wretchedness of Richard Nixon. 24

In sports as in life, character does not much change. I have recently begun to play a game called raquet ball, and I find I would still rather look good than win, which is what I usually do: look good and lose. I beat the rum-dums but go down before quality players. I get compliments in defeat. Men who beat me 25 admire the whip of my strokes, my wrist action, my anticipation, the power I get behind the ball. When this occurs I feel like a woman who is complimented for the shape of her bottom when it is her mind she craves admiration for, though of course she will take what praise she can get.

R. H. Tawney, the great historian of religion and capitalism, once remarked that the only progress he could note during the course of his lifetime was in the deportment of dogs. For myself, I would say that the chief progress in the course of my lifetime has been in the quality and variety of athletic gear. Racquets made of metal, aluminum, wood, and fiberglass, balls of different colors, sneakers of all materials and designs, posh warm-up suits, tube socks, sweatbands for the head and wrist in various colors and pipings; only the athletic supporter, the old jockstrap, remains unornamented, but perhaps even now Vera or Peter Max is at the drawing board. In any event, with all this elegant plumage available, it is a nice time to be playing ball again.

Sports can be impervious to age. My father-in-law, a man of style, seriousness, and great good humor who died a year ago in his late sixties, was born in South Bend, Indiana, and in his early manhood left the Catholic Church—two facts that conjoined to give him an intense interest in the fortunes of the teams from Notre Dame. He loved to see them lose. The torch has been passed on. I now love to see Notre Dame lose, and when it does I think of him and remember his smile.

When I was a boy I had a neighbor, a man who, after retirement, had a number of strokes. An old man and a young boy, we had in common a love of sports, which, when we met on the street, was our only topic of conversation. He once inspected a new glove of mine, and instructed me to rub it down with neat's-foot-oil, place a ball firmly in the pocket, wrap string tightly around the glove, and leave it like that for the winter. I did, and it worked. After his last stroke but one, he seldom left his house. Afternoons he spent in a chair in his bedroom, a blanket over his lap, listening to Cub games over the radio. It was while listening to a ball game that he quietly died. I cannot imagine a better way.

QUESTIONS

1. What distinction does Epstein make between violence and roughness? Is the distinction valid?

2. Outline the reasons given for being "obsessed with sport," and consider their order of presentation. Is there any hierarchy in this order, or is one reason as important as any other?

3. If you removed the first eight paragraphs from this essay, would the rest of the essay be just as effective? Explain.

4. Locate passages in which Epstein's own experience is used to introduce larger issues and questions. What purpose do these passages serve within the essay?

5. Examine your own obsession, whether it be with sports, music, movies, cooking, reading, or whatever. Write a history of your obsession, including, as Epstein does, the most important places, people, and things connected with it.

6. Write an essay in which you reflect on something you tried to do well as a child. Your conclusion should describe your feelings about your youthful efforts from your present point of view.

Sciences and
Technologies

THE BIRD AND
THE MACHINE
Loren Eiseley

Loren Eiseley (1907–1977) rode the rails as a young hobo before he finished college, went to graduate school at the University of Pennsylvania, and began a distinguished career as an anthropologist, archaeologist, essayist, and poet. Through his writing, Eiseley made the ideas and findings of anthropology comprehensible to the public. He found significance in small incidents—the flights of birds, the web of a spider, and the chance encounter with a young fox. Eiseley once wrote that animals understand their roles, but that man, "bereft of instinct, must search continually for meanings." This essay is taken from his collection The Immense Journey *(1957).*

I suppose their little bones have years ago been lost among the stones and winds of those high glacial pastures. I suppose their feathers blew eventually into the piles of tumbleweed beneath the straggling cattle fences and rotted there in the mountain snows, along with dead steers and all the other things that drift to an end in the corners of the wire. I do not quite know why I should be thinking of birds over the *New York Times* at breakfast, particularly the birds of my youth half a continent away. It is a funny thing what the brain will do with memories and how it will treasure them and finally bring them into odd juxtapositions with other things, as though it wanted to make a design, or get some meaning out of them, whether you want it or not, or even see it.

It used to seem marvelous to me, but I read now that there are machines 2 that can do these things in a small way, machines that can crawl about like animals, and that it may not be long now until they do more things—maybe even make themselves—I saw that piece in the *Times* just now. And then they will, maybe—well, who knows—but you read about it more and more with no one making any protest, and already they can add better than we and reach up and hear things through the dark and finger the guns over the night sky.

This is the new world that I read about at breakfast. This is the world that 3 confronts me in my biological books and journals, until there are times when I sit quietly in my chair and try to hear the little purr of the cogs in my head and the tubes flaring and dying as the messages go through them and the circuits snap shut or open. This is the great age, make no mistake about it; the robot has been born somewhat appropriately along with the atom bomb, and the brain they say now is just another type of more complicated feedback system. The engineers have its basic principles worked out; it's mechanical, you know; nothing to get superstitious about; and man can always improve on nature once he gets the idea. Well, he's got it all right and that's why, I guess, that I sit here in my chair, with the article crunched in my hand, remembering those two birds and that blue mountain sunlight. There is another magazine article on my desk that reads "Machines Are Getting Smarter Every Day." I don't deny it, but I'll still stick with the birds. It's life I believe in, not machines.

Maybe you don't believe there is any difference. A skeleton is all joints and 4 pulleys, I'll admit. And when man was in his simpler stages of machine building in the eighteenth century, he quickly saw the resemblances. "What," wrote Hobbes, "is the heart but a spring, and the nerves but so many strings, and the joints but so many wheels, giving motion to the whole body?" Tinkering about in their shops it was inevitable in the end that men would see the world as a huge machine "subdivided into an infinite number of lesser machines."

The idea took on with a vengeance. Little automatons toured the country— 5 dolls controlled by clockwork. Clocks described as little worlds were taken on tours by their designers. They were made up of moving figures, shifting scenes and other remarkable devices. The life of the cell was unknown. Man, whether he was conceived as possessing a soul or not, moved and jerked about like these tiny puppets. A human being thought of himself in terms of his own tools and implements. He had been fashioned like the puppets he produced and was only a more clever model made by a greater designer.

Then in the nineteenth century, the cell was discovered, and the single 6 machine in its turn was found to be the product of millions of infinitesimal machines—the cells. Now, finally, the cell itself dissolves away into an abstract chemical machine—and that into some intangible, inexpressible flow of energy. The secret seems to lurk all about, the wheels get smaller and smaller, and they turn more rapidly, but when you try to seize it the life is gone—and so, by popular definition, some would say that life was never there in the first place. The wheels and the cogs are the secret and we can make them better in time— machines that will run faster and more accurately than real mice to real cheese.

I have no doubt it can be done, though a mouse harvesting seeds on an   7 autumn thistle is to me a fine sight and more complicated, I think, in his multiform activity, than a machine "mouse" running a maze. Also, I like to think of the possible shape of the future brooding in mice, just as it brooded once in a rather ordinary mousy insectivore who became a man. It leaves a nice fine indeterminate sense of wonder that even an electronic brain hasn't got, because you know perfectly well that if the electronic brain changes, it will be because of something man has done to it. But what man will do to himself he doesn't really know. A certain scale of time and a ghostly intangible thing called change are ticking in him. Powers and potentialities like the oak in the seed, or a red and awful ruin. Either way, it's impressive; and the mouse has it, too. Or those birds, I'll never forget those birds—yet before I measured their signif- icance, I learned the lesson of time first of all. I was young then and left alone in a great desert—part of an expedition that had scattered its men over several hundred miles in order to carry on research more effectively. I learned there that time is a series of planes existing superficially in the same universe. The tempo is a human illusion, a subjective clock ticking in our own kind of pro- toplasm.

As the long months passed, I began to live on the slower planes and to   8 observe more readily what passed for life there. I sauntered, I passed more and more slowly up and down the canyons in the dry baking heat of midsummer. I slumbered for long hours in the shade of huge brown boulders that had gathered in tilted companies out on the flats. I had forgotten the world of men and the world had forgotten me. Now and then I found a skull in the canyons, and these justified my remaining there. I took a serene cold interest in these discoveries. I had come, like many a naturalist before me, to view life with a wary and subdued attention. I had grown to take pleasure in the divested bone.

I sat once on a high ridge that fell away before me into a waste of sand   9 dunes. I sat through hours of a long afternoon. Finally, as I glanced beside my boot an indistinct configuration caught my eye. It was a coiled rattlesnake, a big one. How long he had sat with me I do not know. I had not frightened him. We were both locked in the sleep-walking tempo of the earlier world, baking in the same high air and sunshine. Perhaps he had been there when I came. He slept on as I left, his coils, so ill discerned by me, dissolving once more among the stones and gravel from which I had barely made him out.

Another time I got on a higher ridge, among some tough little wind-warped   10 pines half covered over with sand in a basin-like depression that caught every- thing carried by the air up to those heights. There were a few thin bones of birds, some cracked shells of indeterminable age, and the knotty fingers of pine roots bulged out of shape from their long and agonizing grasp upon the crevices of the rock. I lay under the pines in the sparse shade and went to sleep once more.

It grew cold finally, for autumn was in the air by then, and the few things that lived thereabouts were sinking down into an even chillier scale of time. In the moments between sleeping and waking I saw the roots about me and slowly, slowly, a foot in what seemed many centuries, I moved my sleep-stiffened hands over the scaling bark and lifted my numbed face after the vanishing sun. I was a great awkward thing of knots and aching limbs, trapped up there in some long, patient endurance that involved the necessity of putting living fingers into rock and by slow, aching expansion bursting those rocks asunder. I suppose, so thin and slow was the time of my pulse by then, that I might have stayed on to drift still deeper into the lower cadences of the frost, or the crystalline life that glisters in pebbles, or shines in a snowflake, or dreams in the meteoric iron between the worlds.

It was a dim descent, but time was present in it. Somewhere far down in that scale the notion struck me that one might come the other way. Not many months thereafter I joined some colleagues heading higher into a remote windy tableland where huge bones were reputed to protrude like boulders from the turf. I had drowsed with reptiles and moved with the century-long pulse of trees; now, lethargically, I was climbing back up some invisible ladder of quickening hours. There had been talk of birds in connection with my duties. Birds are intense, fast-living creatures—reptiles, I suppose one might say, that have escaped out of the heavy sleep of time, transformed fairy creatures dancing over sunlit meadows. It is a youthful fancy, no doubt, but because of something that happened up there among the escarpments of that range, it remains with me a lifelong impression. I can never bear to see a bird imprisoned.

We came into that valley through the trailing mists of a spring night. It was a place that looked as though it might never have known the foot of man, but our scouts had been ahead of us and we knew all about the abandoned cabin of stone that lay far up on one hillside. It had been built in the land rush of the last century and then lost to the cattlemen again as the marginal soils failed to take to the plow.

There were spots like this all over that country. Lost graves marked by un-lettered stones and old corroding rim-fire cartridge cases lying where somebody had made a stand among the boulders that rimmed the valley. They are all that remain of the range wars; the men are under the stones now. I could see our cavalcade winding in and out through the mist below us: torches, the reflection of the truck lights on our collecting tins, and the far-off bumping of a loose dinosaur thigh bone in the bottom of a trailer. I stood on a rock a moment looking down and thinking what it cost in money and equipment to capture the past.

698

We had, in addition, instructions to lay hands on the present. The word had   15
come through to get them alive—birds, reptiles, anything. A zoo somewhere
abroad needed restocking. It was one of those reciprocal matters in which science
involves itself. Maybe our museum needed a stray ostrich egg and this was the
payoff. Anyhow, my job was to help capture some birds and that was why I was
there before the trucks.

The cabin had not been occupied for years. We intended to clean it out and   16
live in it, but there were holes in the roof and the birds had come in and were
roosting in the rafters. You could depend on it in a place like this where everything blew away, and even a bird needed some place out of the weather and
away from coyotes. A cabin going back to nature in a wild place draws them
till they come in, listening at the eaves, I imagine, pecking softly among the
shingles till they find a hole and then suddenly the place is theirs and man is
forgotten.

Sometimes of late years I find myself thinking the most beautiful sight in the   17
world might be the birds taking over New York after the last man has run away
to the hills. I will never live to see it, of course, but I know just how it will
sound because I've lived up high and I know the sort of watch birds keep on
us. I've listened to sparrows tapping tentatively on the outside of air conditioners
when they thought no one was listening, and I know how other birds test the
vibrations that come up to them through the television aerials.

"Is he gone?" they ask, and the vibrations come up from below, "Not yet,   18
not yet."

Well, to come back, I got the door open softly and I had the spotlight all   19
ready to turn on and blind whatever birds there were so they couldn't see to get
out through the roof. I had a short piece of ladder to put against the far wall
where there was a shelf on which I expected to make the biggest haul. I had all
the information I needed just like any skilled assassin. I pushed the door open,
the hinges squeaking only a little. A bird or two stirred—I could hear them—
but nothing flew and there was a faint starlight through the holes in the roof.

I padded across the floor, got the ladder up and the light ready, and slithered   20
up the ladder till my head and arms were over the shelf. Everything was dark
as pitch except for the starlight at the little place back of the shelf near the eaves.
With the light to blind them, they'd never make it. I had them. I reached my
arm carefully over in order to be ready to seize whatever was there and I put
the flash on the edge of the shelf where it would stand by itself when I turned
it on. That way I'd be able to use both hands.

Everything worked perfectly except for one detail—I didn't know what kind   21
of birds were there. I never thought about it at all, and it wouldn't have mattered
if I had. My orders were to get something interesting. I snapped on the flash
and sure enough there was a great beating and feathers flying, but instead of
my having them, they, or rather he, had me. He had my hand, that is, and for
a small hawk not much bigger than my fist he was doing all right. I heard him

699

give one short metallic cry when the light went on and my hand descended on the bird beside him; after that he was busy with his claws and his beak was sunk in my thumb. In the struggle I knocked the lamp over on the shelf, and his mate got her sight back and whisked neatly through the hole in the roof and off among the stars outside. It all happened in fifteen seconds and you might think I would have fallen down the ladder, but no, I had a professional assassin's reputation to keep up, and the bird, of course, made the mistake of thinking the hand was the enemy and not the eyes behind it. He chewed my thumb up pretty effectively and lacerated my hand with his claws, but in the end I got him, having two hands to work with.

He was a sparrow hawk and a fine young male in the prime of life. I was 22 sorry not to catch the pair of them, but as I dripped blood and folded his wings carefully, holding him by the back so that he couldn't strike again, I had to admit the two of them might have been more than I could have handled under the circumstances. The little fellow had saved his mate by diverting me, and that was that. He was born to it, and made no outcry now, resting in my hand hopelessly, but peering toward me in the shadows behind the lamp with a fierce, almost indifferent glance. He neither gave nor expected mercy and something out of the high air passed from him to me, stirring a faint embarrassment.

I quit looking into that eye and managed to get my huge carcass with its fist 23 full of prey back down the ladder. I put the bird in a box too small to allow him to injure himself by struggle and walked out to welcome the arriving trucks. It had been a long day, and camp still to make in the darkness. In the morning that bird would be just another episode. He would go back with the bones in the truck to a small cage in a city where he would spend the rest of his life. And a good thing, too. I sucked my aching thumb and spat out some blood. An assassin has to get used to these things. I had a professional reputation to keep up.

In the morning, with the change that comes on suddenly in that high coun- 24 try, the mist that had hovered below us in the valley was gone. The sky was a deep blue, and one could see for miles over the high outcroppings of stone. I was up early and brought the box in which the little hawk was imprisoned out onto the grass where I was building a cage. A wind as cool as a mountain spring ran over the grass and stirred my hair. It was a fine day to be alive. I looked up and all around and at the hole in the cabin roof out of which the other little hawk had fled. There was no sign of her anywhere that I could see.

"Probably in the next county by now," I thought cynically, but before be- 25 ginning work I decided I'd have a look at my last night's capture.

Secretively, I looked again all around the camp and up and down and opened 26 the box. I got him right out in my hand with his wings folded properly and I was careful not to startle him. He lay limp in my grasp and I could feel his heart pound under the feathers but he only looked beyond me and up.

The Bird and the Machine

I saw him look that last look away beyond me into a sky so full of light that 27
I could not follow his gaze. The little breeze flowed over me again, and nearby
a mountain aspen shook all its tiny leaves. I suppose I must have had an idea
then of what I was going to do, but I never let it come up into consciousness.
I just reached over and laid the hawk on the grass.

He lay there a long minute without hope, unmoving, his eyes still fixed on 28
that blue vault above him. It must have been that he was already so far away
in heart that he never felt the release from my hand. He never even stood. He
just lay with his breast against the grass.

In the next second after that long minute he was gone. Like a flicker of light, 29
he had vanished with my eyes full on him, but without actually seeing even a
premonitory wing beat. He was gone straight into that towering emptiness of
light and crystal that my eyes could scarcely bear to penetrate. For another long
moment there was silence. I could not see him. The light was too intense.
Then from far up somewhere a cry came ringing down.

I was young then and had seen little of the world, but when I heard that 30
cry my heart turned over. It was not the cry of the hawk I had captured; for,
by shifting my position against the sun, I was now seeing further up. Straight
out of the sun's eye, where she must have been soaring restlessly above us for
untold hours, hurtled his mate. And from far up, ringing from peak to peak of
the summits over us, came a cry of such unutterable and ecstatic joy that it
sounds down across the years and tingles among the cups on my quiet breakfast
table.

I saw them both now. He was rising fast to meet her. They met in a great 31
soaring gyre that turned to a whirling circle and a dance of wings. Once more,
just once, their two voices, joined in a harsh wild medley of question and
response, struck and echoed against the pinnacles of the valley. Then they were
gone forever somewhere into those upper regions beyond the eyes of men.

I am older now, and sleep less, and have seen most of what there is to see 32
and am not very much impressed any more, I suppose, by anything. "What
Next in the Attributes of Machines?" my morning headline runs. "It Might Be
the Power to Reproduce Themselves."

I lay the paper down and across my mind a phrase floats insinuatingly: "It 33
does not seem that there is anything in the construction, constituents, or behavior of the human being which it is essentially impossible for science to
duplicate and synthesize. On the other hand . . ."

All over the city the cogs in the hard, bright mechanisms have begun to 34
turn. Figures move through computers, names are spelled out, a thoughtful
machine selects the fingerprints of a wanted criminal from an array of thousands.
In the laboratory an electronic mouse runs swiftly through a maze toward the
cheese it can neither taste nor enjoy. On the second run it does better than a
living mouse.

"On the other hand . . ." Ah, my mind takes up, on the other hand the machine does not bleed, ache, hang for hours in the empty sky in a torment of hope to learn the fate of another machine, nor does it cry out with joy nor dance in the air with the fierce passion of a bird. Far off, over a distance greater than space, that remote cry from the heart of heaven makes a faint buzzing among my breakfast dishes and passes on and away.

QUESTIONS

1. According to Eiseley, what is the difference between birds and machines?
2. Why does Eiseley tell the story about his experience as a young anthropologist exploring life in the American desert? How does this story relate to the rest of the essay?
3. Trace the associative movement of the writer's mind. How does one thought suggest another? How does this movement help illustrate his point?
4. Eiseley projects himself from the beginning as someone remembering and reflecting upon his experience. How did the meditative process of this essay, with its various twists and turns of thought, affect you as a reader?
5. Eiseley writes: "It is a funny thing what the brain will do with memories and how it will treasure them and finally bring them into odd juxtapositions with other things, as though it wanted to make a design, or get some meaning out of them, whether you want it or not, or even see it." (paragraph 1) Begin reflecting on some important memories from your childhood, and see where these reflections take you. As your mind wanders between past and present, see if any kind of design or meaning emerges for you. You may want to start with the first memory that comes to you by freewriting, writing down anything that goes through your mind for fifteen minutes without stopping. Then go back, and read what you've written. See what associations can be shaped into your own essay.

THE COURAGE
OF TURTLES
Edward Hoagland

Edward Hoagland's first published book was a novel about circus life called Cat Man *(1955). (See earlier biographical note, page 151, for additional details.) His interest in animals and the wilderness has continued all his life, leading to his best-known books of travel and observation of nature, including* The Courage of Turtles *(1971), a collection to which the following essay gave its title.*

Turtles are a kind of bird with the governor turned low. With the same attitude of removal, they cock a glance at what is going on, as if they need only to fly away. Until recently they were also a case of virtue rewarded, at least in the town where I grew up, because, being humble creatures, there were plenty of them. Even when we still had a few bobcats in the woods the local snapping turtles, growing up to forty pounds, were the largest carnivores. You would see them through the amber water, as big as greeny wash basins at the bottom of the pond, until they faded into the inscrutable mud as if they hadn't existed at all.

When I was ten I went to Dr. Green's Pond, a two-acre pond across the road. When I was twelve I walked a mile or so to Taggart's Pond, which was lusher, had big water snakes and a waterfall; and shortly after that I was bicycling way up to the adventuresome vastness of Mud Pond, a lake-sized body of water in the reservoir system of a Connecticut city, possessed of cat-backed little islands and empty shacks and a forest of pines and hardwoods along the shore. Otters, foxes and mink left their prints on the bank; there were pike and perch. As I got older, the estates and forgotten back lots in town were parceled out and sold for nice prices, yet, though the woods had shrunk, it seemed that fewer people walked in the woods. The new residents didn't know how to find them. Eventually, exploring, they did find them, and it required some ingenuity and doubling around on my part to go for eight miles without meeting someone. I was grown by now, I lived in New York, and that's what I wanted on the occasional weekends when I came out.

Since Mud Pond contained drinking water I had felt confident nothing untoward would happen there. For a long while the developers stayed away, until the drought of the mid-1960s. This event, squeezing the edges in, convinced the local water company that the pond really wasn't a necessity as a catch basin, however; so they bulldozed a hole in the earthen dam, bulldozed the banks to

Edward Hoagland

fill in the bottom, and landscaped the flow of water that remained to wind like an English brook and provide a domestic view for the houses which were planned. Most of the painted turtles of Mud Pond, who had been inaccessible as they sunned on their rocks, wound up in boxes in boys' closets within a matter of days. Their footsteps in the dry leaves gave them away as they wandered forlornly. The snappers and the little musk turtles, neither of whom leave the water except once a year to lay their eggs, dug into the drying mud for another siege of hot weather, which they were accustomed to doing whenever the pond got low. But this time it was low for good; the mud baked over them and slowly entombed them. As for the ducks, I couldn't stroll in the woods and not feel guilty, because they were crouched beside every stagnant pothole, or were slinking between the bushes with their heads tucked into their shoulders so that I wouldn't see them. If they decided I had, they beat their way up through the screen of trees, striking their wings dangerously, and wheeled about with that headlong, magnificent velocity to locate another poor puddle.

I used to catch possums and black snakes as well as turtles, and I kept dogs 4 and goats. Some summers I worked in a menagerie with the big personalities of the animal kingdom, like elephants and rhinoceroses. I was twenty before these enthusiasms began to wane, and it was then that I picked turtles as the particular animal I wanted to keep in touch with. I was allergic to fur, for one thing, and turtles need minimal care and not much in the way of quarters. They're personable beasts. They see the same colors we do and they seem to see just as well, as one discovers in trying to sneak up on them. In the laboratory they unravel the twists of a maze with the hot-blooded rapidity of a mammal. Though they can't run as fast as a rat, they improve on their errors just as quickly, pausing at each crossroads to look left and right. And they rock rhythmically in place, as we often do, although they are hatched from eggs, not the womb. (A common explanation psychologists give for our pleasure in rocking quietly is that it recapitulates our mother's heartbeat *in utero*.)

Snakes, by contrast, are dryly silent and priapic.[1] They are smooth movers, 5 legalistic, unblinking, and they afford the humor which the humorless do. But they make challenging captives; sometimes they don't eat for months on a point of order—if the light isn't right, for instance. Alligators are sticklers too. They're like war-horses, or German shepherds, and with their bar-shaped, vertical pupils adding emphasis, they have the *idée fixe* of eating,[2] eating, even when they choose to refuse all food and stubbornly die. They delight in tossing a salamander up towards the sky and grabbing him in their long mouths as he comes down. They're so eager that they get the jitters, and they're too much of a proposition for a casual aquarium like mine. Frogs are depressingly defenseless: that moist, extensive back, with the bones almost sticking through. Hold a frog

---

[1]priapic: phallic; derived from Priapus, a god of male procreative power in Greek and Roman mythology. [Eds.]

[2]*idée fixe*: fixed idea, obsession. [Eds.]

and you're holding its skeleton. Frogs' tasty legs are the staff of life to many animals—herons, raccoons, ribbon snakes—though they themselves are hard to feed. It's not an enviable role to be the staff of life, and after frogs you descend down the evolutionary ladder a big step to fish.

Turtles cough, burp, whistle, grunt and hiss, and produce social judgments. They put their heads together amicably enough, but then one drives the other back with the suddenness of two dogs who have been conversing in tones too low for an onlooker to hear. They pee in fear when they're first caught, but exercise both pluck and optimism in trying to escape, walking for hundreds of yards within the confines of their pen, carrying the weight of that cumbersome box on legs which are cruelly positioned for walking. They don't feel that the contest is unfair; they keep plugging, rolling like sailorly souls—a bobbing, infirm gait, a brave, sea-legged momentum—stopping occasionally to study the lay of the land. For me, anyway, they manage to contain the rest of the animal world. They can stretch out their necks like a giraffe, or loom underwater like an apocryphal hippo.[3] They browse on lettuce thrown on the water like a cow moose which is partly submerged. They have a penguin's alertness, combined with a build like a Brontosaurus when they rise up on tiptoe. Then they hunch and ponderously lunge like a grizzly going forward. 6

Baby turtles in a turtle bowl are a puzzle in geometrics. They're as decorative as pansy petals, but they are also self-directed building blocks, propping themselves on one another in different arrangements, before upending the tower. The timid individuals turn fearless, or vice versa. If one gets a bit arrogant he will push the others off the rock and afterwards climb down into the water and cling to the back of one of those he has bullied, tickling him with his hind feet until he bucks like a bronco. On the other hand, when this same milder-mannered fellow isn't exerting himself, he will stare right into the face of the sun for hours. What could be more lionlike? And he's at home in or out of the water and does lots of metaphysical tilting. He sinks and rises, with an infinity of levels to choose from; or, elongating himself, he climbs out on the land again to perambulate, sits boxed in his box, and finally slides back in the water, submerging into dreams. 7

I have five of these babies in a kidney-shaped bowl. The hatchling, who is a painted turtle, is not as large as the top joint of my thumb. He eats chicken gladly. Other foods he will attempt to eat but not with sufficient perseverance to succeed because he's so little. The yellow-bellied terrapin is probably a year-ling, and he eats salad voraciously, but no meat, fish or fowl. The Cumberland terrapin won't touch salad or chicken but eats fish and all of the meats except for bacon. The little snapper, with a black crenelated shell,[4] feasts on any kind 8

---

[3]apocryphal: of doubtful authority, false. [Eds.]
[4]crenelated shell: a shell that looks as if it has battlements in which elevated walls alternate with spaces. [Eds.]

of meat, but rejects greens and fish. The fifth of the turtles is African. I acquired him only recently and don't know him well. A mottled brown, he unnerves the green turtles, dragging their food off to his lairs. He doesn't seem to want to be green—he bites the algae off his shell, hanging meanwhile at daring, steep, head-first angles.

The snapper was a Ferdinand until I provided him with deeper water. Now 9
he snaps at my pencil with his downturned and fearsome mouth, his swollen face like a napalm victim's. The Cumberland has an elliptical red mark on the side of his green-and-yellow head. He is benign by nature and ought to be as elegant as his scientific name (*Pseudemys scripta elegans*), except he has contracted a disease of the air bladder which has permanently inflated it; he floats high in the water at an undignified slant and can't go under. There may have been internal bleeding, too, because his carapace is stained along its ridge.[5] Unfortunately, like flowers, baby turtles often die. Their mouths fill up with a white fungus and their lungs with pneumonia. Their organs clog up from the rust in the water, or diet troubles, and, like a dying man's, their eyes and heads become too prominent. Toward the end, the edge of the shell becomes flabby as felt and folds around them like a shroud.

While they live they're like puppies. Although they're vivacious, they would 10
be a bore to be with all the time, so I also have an adult wood turtle about six inches long. Her shell is the equal of any seashell for sculpturing, even a Cellini shell;[6] it's like an old, dusty, richly engraved medallion dug out of a hillside. Her legs are salmon-orange bordered with black and protected by canted,[7] heroic scales. Her plastron—the bottom shell—is splotched like a margay cat's coat, with black ocelli on a yellow background.[8] It is convex to make room for the female organs inside, whereas a male's would be concave to help him fit tightly on top of her. Altogether, she exhibits every camouflage color on her limbs and shells. She has a turtleneck neck, a tail like an elephant's, wise old pachydermous hind legs and the face of a turkey—except that when I carry her she gazes at the passing ground with a hawk's eyes and mouth. Her feet fit to the fingers of my hand, one to each one, and she rides looking down. She can walk on the floor in perfect silence, but usually she lets her shell knock portentously, like a footstep, so that she resembles some grand, concise, slow-moving id.[9] But if an earthworm is presented, she jerks swiftly ahead, poises above it and strikes like a mongoose, consuming it with wild vigor. Yet she will climb on my lap to eat bread or boiled eggs.

If put into a creek, she swims like a cutter, nosing forward to intercept a 11

---

[5]carapace: a shell, especially one that covers the back. [Eds.]
[6]Benevenuto Cellini (1500–1571): Italian sculptor and metalsmith known for extremely ornate work and for having written an exciting and readable autobiography. [Eds.]
[7]canted: sloped or beveled. [Eds.]
[8]ocelli: eyelike spots. [Eds.]
[9]id: a psychological term for the instinctual part of the self. [Eds.]

strange turtle and smell him. She drifts with the current to go downstream, maneuvering behind a rock when she wants to take stock, or sinking to the nether levels, while bubbles float up. Getting out, choosing her path, she will proceed a distance and dig into a pile of humus, thrusting herself to the coolest layer at the bottom. The hole closes over her until it's as small as a mouse's hole. She's not as aquatic as a musk turtle, not quite as terrestrial as the box turtles in the same woods, but because of her versatility she's marvelous, she's everywhere. And though she breathes the way we breathe, with scarcely perceptible movements of her chest, sometimes instead she pumps her throat ruminatively, like a pipe smoker sucking and puffing. She waits and blinks, pumping her throat, turning her head, then sets off like a loping tiger in slow motion, hurdling the jungly lumber, the pea vine and twigs. She estimates angles so well that when she rides over the rocks, sliding down a drop-off with her rugged front legs extended, she has the grace of a rodeo mare.

But she's well off to be with me rather than at Mud Pond. The other turtles 12 have fled—those that aren't baked into the bottom. Creeping up the brooks to sad, constricted marshes, burdened as they are with that box on their backs, they're walking into a setup where all their enemies move thirty times faster than they. It's like the nightmare most of us have whimpered through, where we are weighted down disastrously while trying to flee; fleeing our home ground, we try to run.

I've seen turtles in still worse straits. On Broadway, in New York, there is a 13 penny arcade which used to sell baby terrapins that were scrawled with bon mots in enamel paint,[10] such as KISS MY BABY. The manager turned out to be a wholesaler as well, and once I asked him whether he had any larger turtles to sell. He took me upstairs to a loft room devoted to the turtle business. There were desks for the paper work and a series of racks that held shallow tin bins atop one another, each with several hundred babies crawling around in it. He was a smudgy-complexioned, serious fellow and he did have a few adult terrapins, but I was going to school and wasn't actually planning to buy; I'd only wanted to see them. They were aquatic turtles, but here they went without water, presumably for weeks, lurching about in those dry bins like handicapped citizens, living on gumption. An easel where the artist worked stood in the middle of the floor. She had a palette and a clip attachment for fastening the babies in place. She wore a smock and a beret, and was homely, short and eccentric-looking, with funny black hair, like some of the ladies who show their paintings in Washington Square in May. She had a cold, she was smoking, and her hand wasn't very steady, although she worked quickly enough. The smile that she produced for me would have looked giddy if she had been happier, or drunk. Of course the turtles' doom was sealed when she painted them, because their bodies inside would continue to grow but their shells would not. Gradually,

---

[10]bon mots: choice expressions; clever, witty sayings. [Eds]

invisibly, they would be crushed. Around us their bellies—two thousand belly shells—rubbed on the bins with a mournful, momentous hiss.

Somehow there were so many of them I didn't rescue one. Years later, however, I was walking on First Avenue when I noticed a basket of living turtles in front of a fish store. They were as dry as a heap of old bones in the sun; nevertheless, they were creeping over one another gimpily, doing their best to escape, I looked and was touched to discover that they appeared to be wood turtles, my favorites, so I bought one. In my apartment I looked closer and realized that in fact this was a diamondback terrapin, which was bad news. Diamondbacks are tidewater turtles from brackish estuaries, and I had no sea water to keep him in. He spent his days thumping interminably against the baseboards, pushing for an opening through the wall. He drank thirstily but would not eat and had none of the hearty, accepting qualities of wood turtles. He was morose, paler in color, sleeker and more Oriental in the carved ridges and rings that formed his shell. Though I felt sorry for him, finally I found his unrelenting presence exasperating. I carried him, struggling in a paper bag, across town to the Morton Street Pier on the Hudson. It was August but gray and windy. He was very surprised when I tossed him in; for the first time in our association, I think, he was afraid. He looked afraid as he bobbed about on top of the water, looking up at me from ten feet below. Though we were both accustomed to his resistance and rigidity, seeing him still pitiful, I recognized that I must have done the wrong thing. At least the river was salty, but it was also bottomless; the waves were too rough for him, and the tide was coming in, bumping him against the pilings underneath the pier. Too late, I realized that he wouldn't be able to swim to a peaceful inlet in New Jersey, even if he could figure out which way to swim. But since, short of diving in after him, there was nothing I could do, I walked away.

14

QUESTIONS

1. Hoagland claims in paragraph 4 that turtles became "the particular animal I wanted to keep in touch with." Describe what he sees in turtles. Do you sympathize with his choice?

2. Describe the means by which Hoagland tries to get you to sympathize with his partiality for turtles.

3. Hoagland's vocabulary is literary and sophisticated. We have glossed some of his less common words and phrases. How does his diction—that is, his choice of words—help convey a sense of himself in this essay?

4. We have classified this essay as an example of reflective writing, but it also contains a good deal of reporting and explaining. Which passages are most given to those other modes of writing, and how do they relate to the reflective element in this essay.

5. Mud Pond plays a prominent role in this essay, notably in paragraph 3; then it seems forgotten until it is mentioned suddenly again in paragraph 12. What is the significance of Mud Pond for this essay?

6. Turtles seem to remind Hoagland of everything else in the animal kingdom. Select another animal—whatever one, no matter how strange or how ordinary, that you know fairly well—and write of that creature so as to suggest how it reminds you of the rest of the animal world.

7. Consider the end of Hoagland's essay. Can you think of a similar moment in your life when you have been incapable or unwilling—understandably, perhaps, but sadly nevertheless—to do or to risk doing the right thing? Write an account of that experience. Try to write matter-of-factly as Hoagland does, letting the experience speak for itself. Resist any urge to preach or moralize about it. Just try to make your account clear enough and detailed enough that your reader won't be able to miss its significance.

ON WARTS
Lewis Thomas

Born in 1913, Thomas is a medical doctor, biologist, re-
searcher, and professor as well as a writer. (See earlier bio-
graphical note, page 559.) He is most widely known, how-
ever, for essays that he published first in the New England
Journal of Medicine *and that have been gathered since in*
collections entitled The Lives of a Cell *(winner of the Na-*
tional Book Award in 1975) and The Medusa and the Snail
(1979). The following selection is taken from The Medusa
and the Snail.

Warts are wonderful structures. They can appear overnight on any part of   1
the skin, like mushrooms on a damp lawn, full grown and splendid in the
complexity of their architecture. Viewed in stained sections under a microscope,
they are the most specialized of cellular arrangements, constructed as though
for a purpose. They sit there like turreted mounds of dense, impenetrable horn,
impregnable, designed for defense against the world outside.

In a certain sense, warts are both useful and essential, but not for us. As it   2
turns out, the exuberant cells of a wart are the elaborate reproductive apparatus
of a virus.

You might have thought from the looks of it that the cells infected by the   3
wart virus were using this response as a ponderous way of defending themselves
against the virus, maybe even a way of becoming more distasteful, but it is not
so. The wart is what the virus truly wants; it can flourish only in cells undergoing
precisely this kind of overgrowth. It is not a defense at all; it is an overwhelming
welcome, an enthusiastic accommodation meeting the needs of more and more
virus.

The strangest thing about warts is that they tend to go away. Fully grown,   4
nothing in the body has so much the look of toughness and permanence as a
wart, and yet, inexplicably and often very abruptly, they come to the end of
their lives and vanish without a trace.

And they can be made to go away by something that can only be called   5
thinking, or something like thinking. This is a special property of warts which
is absolutely astonishing, more of a surprise than cloning or recombinant DNA
or endorphin or acupuncture or anything else currently attracting attention in
the press. It is one of the great mystifications of science: warts can be ordered
off the skin by hypnotic suggestion.

Not everyone believes this, but the evidence goes back a long way and is   6
persuasive. Generations of internists and dermatologists, and their grandmothers

for that matter, have been convinced of the phenomenon. I was once told by a distinguished old professor of medicine, one of Sir William Osler's original bright young men,[1] that it was his practice to paint gentian violet over a wart and then assure the patient firmly that it would be gone in a week,[2] and he never saw it fail. There have been several meticulous studies by good clinical investigators, with proper controls. In one of these, fourteen patients with seemingly intractable generalized warts on both sides of the body were hypnotized, and the suggestion was made that all the warts on one side of the body would begin to go away. Within several weeks the results were indisputably positive; in nine patients, all or nearly all of the warts on the suggested side had vanished, while the control side had just as many as ever.

It is interesting that most of the warts vanished precisely as they were instructed, but it is even more fascinating that mistakes were made. Just as you might expect in other affairs requiring a clear understanding of which is the right and which the left side, one of the subjects got mixed up and destroyed the warts on the wrong side. In a later study by a group at the Massachusetts General Hospital, the warts on both sides were rejected even though the instructions were to pay attention to just one side.   7

I have been trying to figure out the nature of the instructions issued by the unconscious mind, whatever that is, under hypnosis. It seems to me hardly enough for the mind to say, simply, get off, eliminate yourselves, without providing something in the way of specifications as to how to go about it.   8

I used to believe, thinking about this experiment when it was just published, that the instructions might be quite simple. Perhaps nothing more detailed than a command to shut down the flow through all the precapillary arterioles in and around the warts to the point of strangulation.[3] Exactly how the mind would accomplish this with precision, cutting off the blood supply to one wart while leaving others intact, I couldn't figure out, but I was satisfied to leave it there anyhow. And I was glad to think that my unconscious mind would have to take the responsibility for this, for if I had been one of the subjects I would never have been able to do it myself.   9

But now the problem seems much more complicated by the information concerning the viral etiology of warts,[4] and even more so by the currently plausible notion that immunologic mechanisms are very likely implicated in the rejection of warts.   10

If my unconscious can figure out how to manipulate the mechanisms needed for getting around that virus, and for deploying all the various cells in the correct order for tissue rejection, then all I have to say is that my unconscious is a lot   11

---

[1]Sir William Osler (1849–1919): Canadian physician and renowned professor at McGill, the University of Pennsylvania, Johns Hopkins, and Oxford. [Eds.]
[2]gentian violet: a purple dye. [Eds.]
[3]precapillary arterioles: small, terminal branches of arteries, connecting to capillaries. [Eds.]
[4]etiology: a study of causes. [Eds.]

further along than I am. I wish I had a wart right now, just to see if I am that talented.

There ought to be a better word than "Unconscious," even capitalized, for 12 what I have, so to speak, in mind. I was brought up to regard this aspect of thinking as a sort of private sanitarium, walled off somewhere in a suburb of my brain, capable only of producing such garbled information as to keep my mind, my proper Mind, always a little off balance.

But any mental apparatus that can reject a wart is something else again. This 13 is not the sort of confused, disordered process you'd expect at the hands of the kind of Unconscious you read about in books, out at the edge of things making up dreams or getting mixed up on words or having hysterics. Whatever, or whoever, is responsible for this has the accuracy and precision of a surgeon. There almost has to be a Person in charge, running matters of meticulous detail beyond anyone's comprehension, a skilled engineer and manager, a chief executive officer, the head of the whole place. I never thought before that I possessed such a tenant. Or perhaps more accurately, such a landlord, since I would be, if this is in fact the situation, nothing more than a lodger.

Among other accomplishments, he must be a cell biologist of world class, 14 capable of sorting through the various classes of one's lymphocytes,[5] all with quite different functions which I do not understand, in order to mobilize the right ones and exclude the wrong ones for the task of tissue rejection. If it were left to me, and I were somehow empowered to call up lymphocytes and direct them to the vicinity of my wart (assuming that I could learn to do such a thing), mine would come tumbling in all unsorted, B cells and T cells, suppressor cells and killer cells, and no doubt other cells whose names I have not learned, incapable of getting anything useful done.

Even if immunology is not involved, and all that needs doing is to shut off 15 the blood supply locally, I haven't the faintest notion how to set that up. I assume that the selective turning off of arterioles can be done by one or another chemical mediator, and I know the names of some of them, but I wouldn't dare let things like these loose even if I knew how to do it.

Well, then, who does supervise this kind of operation? Someone's got to, 16 you know. You can't sit there under hypnosis, taking suggestions in and having them acted on with such accuracy and precision, without assuming the existence of something very like a controller. It wouldn't do to fob off the whole intricate business on lower centers without sending along a quite detailed set of specifications, way over my head.

Some intelligence or other knows how to get rid of warts, and this is a 17 disquieting thought.

It is also a wonderful problem, in need of solving. Just think what we would 18 know, if we had anything like a clear understanding of what goes on when a

[5]lymphocytes: white blood cells formed in lymphoid tissue. [Eds.]

wart is hypnotized away. We would know the identity of the cellular and chemical participants in tissue rejection, conceivably with some added information about the ways that viruses create foreignness in cells. We would know how the traffic of these reactants is directed, and perhaps then be able to understand the nature of certain diseases in which the traffic is being conducted in wrong directions, aimed at the wrong cells. Best of all, we would be finding out about a kind of superintelligence that exists in each of us, infinitely smarter and possessed of technical know-how far beyond our present understanding. It would be worth a War on Warts, a Conquest of Warts, a National Institute of Warts and All.

QUESTIONS

1. Though we have presented this piece as a reflective essay, it begins with the writer reporting on the nature of warts. Summarize what Thomas reports.

2. Where in this essay would you say the movement from reporting to reflecting begins? What signals that move? What guides it?

3. A second stage of reflection begins somewhere in paragraphs 11, 12, or possibly 13. What is the nature of this second stage, and where do *you* think it begins?

4. Consider this "Person in charge" of whom Thomas begins to speak in paragraph 13. Write a page or so in which you reflect on the nature of that person. How do you understand him or her, especially in relation to yourself?

5. We've all heard of powers of mind quite beyond our understanding. How do you know just when to shuffle a step in order to jump cleanly over a puddle in the walk? Or how do you know to wake up, sometimes just minutes before your alarm? Pick some such happening that allows you to suspect that someone other than the self you know best may be "in charge," and write a short essay reflecting on that fact or on that suspicion.

WHY A SURGEON
WOULD WRITE
Richard Selzer

*Richard Selzer is a surgeon who has written widely, pub-
lishing articles in popular magazines as well as occasional
short fiction. (See earlier biographical note, page 147, for
additional details.) The following essay is from Selzer's collection of autobiographical pieces,* Mortal Lessons.

Someone asked me why a surgeon would write. Why, when the shelves are   1
already too full? They sag under the deadweight of books. To add a single adverb
is to risk exceeding the strength of the boards. A surgeon should abstain. A
surgeon, whose fingers are more at home in the steamy gullies of the body than
they are tapping the dry keys of a typewriter. A surgeon, who feels the slow slide
of intestines against the back of his hand and is no more alarmed than were a
family of snakes taking their comfort from such an indolent rubbing. A surgeon,
who palms the human heart as though it were some captured bird.

Why should he write? Is it vanity that urges him? There is glory enough in   2
the knife. Is it for money? One can make too much money. No. It is to search
for some meaning in the ritual of surgery, which is at once murderous, painful,
healing, and full of love. It is a devilish hard thing to transmit—to find, even.
Perhaps if one were to cut out a heart, a lobe of the liver, a single convolution
of the brain, and paste it to a page, it would speak with more eloquence than
all the words of Balzac.[1] Such a piece would need no literary style, no mass of
erudition or history, but in its very shape and feel would tell all the frailty and
strength, the despair and nobility of man. What? Publish a heart? A little piece
of bone? Preposterous. Still I fear that is what it may require to reveal the truth
that lies hidden in the body. Not all the undressings of Rabelais, Chekhov, or
even William Carlos Williams have wrested it free,[2] although God knows each
one of those doctors made a heroic assault upon it.

I have come to believe that it is the flesh alone that counts. The rest is that   3
with which we distract ourselves when we are not hungry or cold, in pain or
ecstasy. In the recesses of the body I search for the philosophers' stone.[3] I know
it is there, hidden in the deepest, dampest cul-de-sac. It awaits discovery. To

---

[1]Honoré de Balzac (1799–1850): French novelist. [Eds.]

[2]François Rabelais (1494?–1553): French writer and satirist; Anton Pavlovich Chekhov (1860–1904):
Russian dramatist and short-story writer; William Carlos Williams (1883–1963): American poet; all
three writers also were physicians. [Eds.]

[3]philosophers' stone: an imaginary substance supposed to turn other metals to gold. [Eds.]

find it would be like the harnessing of fire. It would illuminate the world. Such a quest is not without pain. Who can gaze on so much misery and feel no hurt? Emerson has written that the poet is the only true doctor.[4] I believe him, for the poet, lacking the impediment of speech with which the rest of us are afflicted, gazes, records, diagnoses, and prophesies.

I invited a young diabetic woman to the operating room to amputate her leg.   4 She could not see the great shaggy black ulcer upon her foot and ankle that threatened to encroach upon the rest of her body, for she was blind as well. There upon her foot was a Mississippi Delta brimming with corruption, sending its raw tributaries down between her toes. Gone were all the little web spaces that when fresh and whole are such a delight to loving men. She could not see her wound, but she could feel it. There is no pain like that of the bloodless limb turned rotten and festering. There is neither unguent or anodyne to kill such a pain yet leave intact the body.[5]

For over a year I trimmed away the putrid flesh, cleansed, anointed, and   5 dressed the foot, staving off, delaying. Three times each week, in her darkness, she sat upon my table, rocking back and forth, holding her extended leg by the thigh, gripping it as though it were a rocket that must be steadied lest it explode and scatter her toes about the room. And I would cut away a bit here, a bit there, of the swollen blue leather that was her tissue.

At last we gave up, she and I. We could not longer run ahead of the gangrene.   6 We had not the legs for it. There must be an amputation in order that she might live—and I as well. It was to heal us both that I must take up knife and saw, and cut the leg off. And when I could feel it drop from her body to the table, see the blessed *space* appear between her and that leg, I too would be well.

Now it is the day of the operation. I stand by while the anesthetist administers   7 the drugs, watch as the tense familiar body relaxes into narcosis. I turn then to uncover the leg. There, upon her kneecap, she has drawn, blindly, upside down for me to see, a face; just a circle with two ears, two eyes, a nose, and a smiling upturned mouth. Under it she has printed SMILE, DOCTOR. Minutes later I listen to the sound of the saw, until a little crack at the end tells me it is done.

So, I have learned that man is not ugly, but that he is Beauty itself. There   8 is no other his equal. Are we not all dying, none faster or more slowly than any other? I have become receptive to the possibilities of love (for it is love, this thing that happens in the operating room), and each day I wait, trembling in the busy air. Perhaps today it will come. Perhaps today I will find it, take part in it, this love that blooms in the stoniest desert.

All through literature, the doctor is portrayed as a figure of fun. Shaw was   9 splenetic about him;[6] Molière delighted in pricking his pompous medicine

---

[4]Ralph Waldo Emerson (1803–1882): American essayist and poet. [Eds.]
[5]unguent: salve or ointment; anodyne: soothing medicine that relieves pain. [Eds.]
[6]George Bernard Shaw (1856–1950): British playwright and critic. [Eds.]

men,[7] and well they deserved it. The doctor is ripe for caricature. But I believe that the truly great writing about doctors has not yet been done. I think it must be done *by* a doctor, one who is through with the love affair with his technique, who recognizes that he has played Narcissus,[8] raining kisses on a mirror, and who now, out of the impacted masses of his guilt, has expanded into self-doubt, and finally into the high state of wonderment. Perhaps he will be a nonbeliever who, after a lifetime of grand gestures and mighty deeds, comes upon the knowledge that he has done no more than meddle in the lives of his fellows, and that he has done at least as much harm as good. Yet he may continue to pretend, at least, that there is nothing to fear, that death will not come, so long as people depend on his authority. Later, after his patients have left, he may closet himself in his darkened office, sweating and afraid.

There is a story by Unamuno in which a priest,[9] living in a small Spanish   10
village, is adored by all the people for his piety, kindness, and the majesty with which he celebrates the Mass each Sunday. To them he is already a saint. It is a foregone conclusion, and they speak of him as Saint Immanuel. He helps them with their plowing and planting, tends them when they are sick, confesses them, comforts them in death, and every Sunday, in his rich, thrilling voice, transports them to paradise with his chanting. The fact is that Don Immanuel is not so much a saint as a martyr. Long ago his own faith left him. He is an atheist, a good man doomed to suffer the life of a hypocrite, pretending to a faith he does not have. As he raises the chalice of wine, his hands tremble, and a cold sweat pours from him. He cannot stop for he knows that the people need this of him, that their need is greater than his sacrifice. Still . . . still . . . could it be that Don Immanuel's whole life is a kind of prayer, a paean to God?

A writing doctor would treat men and women with equal reverence, for what   11
is the "liberation" of either sex to him who knows the diagrams, the inner geographies of each? I love the solid heft of men as much as I adore the heated capaciousness of women—women in whose penetralia is found the repository of existence. I would have them glory in that. Women are physics and chemistry. They are matter. It is their bodies that tell of the frailty of men. Men have not their cellular, enzymatic wisdom. Man is albuminoid, proteinaceous, laked pearl; woman is yolky, ovoid, rich. Both are exuberant bloody growths. I would use the defects and deformities of each for my sacred purpose of writing, for I know that it is the marred and scarred and faulty that are subject to grace. I would seek the soul in the facts of animal economy and profligacy. Yes, it is the exact location of the soul that I am after. The smell of it is in my nostrils. I have caught glimpses of it in the body diseased. If only I could tell it. Is there

---

[7]Jean-Baptiste Poquelin Molière (1622–1673): French playwright and actor. [Eds.]

[8]Narcissus: After rejecting the love of Echo, this character in Greek mythology pined away for his own beautiful reflection in a pool, and then was turned into the flower that bears his name. [Eds.]

[9]Miguel de Unamuno (1864–1936): Spanish writer and philosopher. [Eds.]

no mathematical equation that can guide me? So much pain and pus equals so much truth? It is elusive as the whippoorwill that one hears calling incessantly from out the night window, but which, nesting as it does low in the brush, no one sees. No one but the poet, for he sees what no one else can. He was born with the eye for it.

Once I thought I had it: Ten o'clock one night, the end room off a long corridor in a college infirmary, my last patient of the day, degree of exhaustion suitable for the appearance of a vision, some manifestation. The patient is a young man recently returned from Guatemala, from the excavation of Mayan ruins. His left upper arm wears a gauze dressing which, when removed, reveals a clean punched-out hole the size of a dime. The tissues about the opening are swollen and tense. A thin brownish fluid lips the edge, and now and then a lazy drop of the overflow spills down the arm. An abscess, inadequately drained. I will enlarge the opening to allow better egress of the pus. Nurse, will you get me a scalpel and some . . . ?

What happens next is enough to lay Francis Drake avomit in his cabin.[10] No explorer ever stared in wilder surmise than I into that crater from which there now emerges a narrow gray head whose sole distinguishing feature is a pair of black pincers. The head sits atop a longish flexible neck arching now this way, now that, testing the air. Alternately it folds back upon itself, then advances in new boldness. And all the while, with dreadful rhythmicity, the unspeakable pincers open and close. Abscess? Pus? Never. Here is the lair of a beast at whose malignant purpose I could but guess. A Mayan devil, I think, that would soon burst free to fly about the room, with horrid blanket-wings and iridescent scales, raking, pinching, injecting God knows what acid juice. And even now the irony does not escape me, the irony of my patient as excavator excavated.

With all the ritual deliberation of a high priest I advance a surgical clamp toward the hole. The surgeon's heart is become a bat hanging upside down from his rib cage. The rim achieved—now thrust—and the ratchets of the clamp close upon the empty air. The devil has retracted. Evil mocking laughter bangs back and forth in the brain. More stealth. Lying in wait. One must skulk. Minutes pass, perhaps an hour. . . . A faint disturbance in the lake, and once again the thing upraises, farther and farther, hovering. Acrouch, strung, the surgeon is one with his instrument; there is no longer any boundary between its metal and his flesh. They are joined in a single perfect tool of extirpation. It is just for this that he was born. Now—thrust—and clamp—and *yes*. Got him!

Transmitted to the fingers comes the wild thrashing of the creature. Pinned and wriggling, he is mine. I hear the dry brittle scream of the dragon, and a

---

[10]Francis Drake (1540?–1596): English admiral who raided the Spanish treasures from the New World and circumnavigated the world. [Eds.]

hatred seizes me, but such a detestation as would make of Iago a drooling sucktit.[11] It is the demented hatred of the victor for the vanquished, the warden for his prisoner. It is the hatred of fear. Within the jaws of my hemostat is the whole of the evil of the world, the dark concentrate itself, and I shall kill it. For mankind. And, in so doing, will open the way into a thousand years of perfect peace. Here is Surgeon as Savior indeed.

Tight grip now . . . steady, relentless pull. How it scrabbles to keep its tentacle-hold. With an abrupt moist plop the extraction is complete. There, writhing in the teeth of the clamp, is a dirty gray body, the size and shape of an English walnut. He is hung everywhere with tiny black hooklets. Quickly . . . into the specimen jar of saline . . . the lid screwed tight. Crazily he swims round and round, wiping his slimy head against the glass, then slowly sinks to the bottom, the mass of hooks in frantic agonal wave. 16

"You are going to be all right," I say to my patient. "We are *all* going to be all right from now on." 17

The next day I take the jar to the medical school. "That's the larva of the botfly," says a pathologist. "The fly usually bites a cow and deposits its eggs beneath the skin. There, the egg develops into the larval form which, when ready, burrows its way to the outside through the hide and falls to the ground. In time it matures into a fullgrown botfly. This one happened to bite a man. It was about to come out on its own, and, of course, it would have died." 18

The words *imposter, sorehead, servant of Satan* sprang to my lips. But now he has been joined by other scientists. They nod in agreement. I gaze from one gray eminence to another, and know the mallet-blow of glory pulverized. I tried to save the world, but it didn't work out. 19

No, it is not the surgeon who is God's darling. He is the victim of vanity. It is the poet who heals with his words, stanches the flow of blood, stills the rattling breath, applies poultice to the scalded flesh. 20

Did you ask me why a surgeon writes? I think it is because I wish to be a doctor. 21

QUESTIONS

1. What are Selzer's reasons for writing? In what ways do his reasons surprise you?
2. Throughout this essay, Selzer compares the doctor with the poet. Why does he believe that the poet "sees what no one else can" (paragraph 11)? What is his reason for comparing the doctor with the poet?
3. Why does Selzer introduce the examples of his patients, the diabetic amputee (paragraphs 4 through 7) or the excavator (paragraphs 12 through 19)? How do these examples enhance the meaning of Selzer's reflections?
4. Trace the movement of the writer's thoughts from any one paragraph to the next.

[11]Iago: the villain in Shakespeare's *Othello*. [Eds.]

5. Ask one or two people in the field you plan to enter about the kind of writing that is required in that profession. Find out if the writing they do is helpful in understanding the profession and their place in it. Ask them what they would write if they were asked to write about what they do and why they do it. Use this information in an essay considering the importance of writing in your chosen field.

6. Write a reflective essay that considers why writing is important to you. If writing is not important to you, consider why this is so.

THE PROFESSION
OF ENGINEERING
Herbert Hoover

*Born in West Branch, Iowa, Herbert Hoover (1874–1964)
is often remembered only as the president of the United
States who lost to Franklin D. Roosevelt in the election of
1932 during the depression. Actually, he was a man whose
great achievements should overshadow that particular event.
Hoover graduated from Stanford University in 1895 as an
engineer and rapidly became one of the world's top mining
engineers. In 1909 he and his wife published a translation
of Georgius Agricola's* De Re Metallica *(1556), the most
important engineering work written in the Renaissance. He
organized relief operations for devastated Europe after two
world wars. When the Mississippi flooded in 1927, six state
governors asked that Hoover be in charge of federal aid. As
president he supported such projects as the San Francisco
Bay Bridge and the Colorado River Dam. In the following
selection from his* Memoirs *(1951), he reflects on the profession
that had given shape to his life.*

I cannot leave my profession without some general comment upon it. Within 1
my lifetime it had been transformed from a trade into a profession. It was the
American universities that took engineering away from rule-of-thumb surveyors,
mechanics, and Cornish foremen and lifted it into the realm of application of
science, wider learning in the humanities with the higher ethics of a profession
ranking with law, medicine and the clergy. And our American profession had
brought a transformation in another direction through the inclusion of administrative
work as part of the engineer's job.

The European universities did not acknowledge engineering as a profession 2
until long after America had done so. I took part in one of the debates at Oxford
as to whether engineering should be included in its instruction. The major
argument put forward by our side was the need of University setting and its
cultural influences on the profession. We ventured to assert that not until Oxford
and Cambridge recognized engineering as a profession equal to others would
engineering secure its due quota of the best English brains, because able young
men would always seek the professions held in the highest public esteem. I cited
the fact that while various special technical colleges had been existent in Eng-

land for a long time, yet there were more than a thousand American engineers of all breeds in the British Empire, occupying top positions.

Soon after the Oxford discussions, I returned to America. At my ship's table 3 sat an English lady of great cultivation and a happy mind, who contributed much to the evanescent conversation on government, national customs, literature, art, industry, and whatnot. We were coming up New York harbor at the final farewell breakfast, when she turned to me and said:

"I hope you will forgive my dreadful curiosity, but I should like awfully to 4 know—what is your profession?"

I replied that I was an engineer. She emitted an involuntary exclamation, 5 and "Why, I thought you were a gentleman!"

Hundreds of times students and parents have consulted me upon engineering 6 compared with the other professions. My comment usually is: "Its training deals with the exact sciences. That sort of exactness makes for truth and conscience. It might be good for the world if more men had that sort of mental start in life even if they did not pursue the profession. But he who would enter these precincts as a life work must have a test taken of his imaginative faculties, for engineering without imagination sinks to a trade. And those who would enter here must for years abandon their white collars except for Sunday."

In the mining branch of the profession, those who follow the gods of engi- 7 neering to that success marked by an office of one's own in a large city must be prepared to live for years on the outside borders of civilization; where beds are hard, where cold bites and heat burns, where dress-up clothes are a new pair of overalls, where there is little home life—not for weeks but for years—where often they must perform the menial labor necessary to keep soul and body together. Other branches of the profession mean years on the lower rungs of the ladder—shops, works, and powerhouses—where again white collars are not a part of the engineer uniform. But the engineer learns through work with his own hands not only the mind of the worker but the multitude of true gentlemen among them. On the other hand, men who love a fight with nature, who like to build and see their building grow, men who do not hold themselves above manual labor, men who have the moral courage to do these things soundly, some day will be able to move to town, wear white collars every day, and send out the youngsters to the lower rungs and frontiers of industry.

It is a great profession. There is the fascination of watching a figment of the 8 imagination emerge through the aid of science to a plan on paper. Then it moves to realization in stone or metal or energy. Then it brings jobs and homes to men. Then it elevates the standards of living and adds to the comforts of life. That is the engineer's high privilege.

The great liability of the engineer compared to men of other professions is 9 that his works are out in the open where all can see them. His acts, step by step, are in hard substance. He cannot bury his mistakes in the grave like the doctors. He cannot argue them into thin air or blame the judge like the lawyers.

He cannot, like the architects, cover his failures with trees and vines. He cannot, like the politicians, screen his shortcomings by blaming his opponents and hope that the people will forget. The engineer simply cannot deny that he did it. If his works do not work, he is damned. That is the phantasmagoria that haunts his nights and dogs his days. He comes from the job at the end of the day resolved to calculate it again. He wakes in the night in a cold sweat and puts something on paper that looks silly in the morning. All day he shivers at the thought of the bugs which will inevitably appear to jolt its smooth consummation.

On the other hand, unlike the doctor his is not a life among the weak. Unlike the soldier, destruction is not his purpose. Unlike the lawyer, quarrels are not his daily bread. To the engineer falls the job of clothing the bare bones of science with life, comfort, and hope. No doubt as years go by people forget which engineer did it, even if they ever knew. Or some politician puts his name on it. Or they credit it to some promoter who used other people's money with which to finance it. But the engineer himself looks back at the unending stream of goodness which flows from his successes with satisfactions that few professions may know. And the verdict of his fellow professionals is all the accolade he wants.

With the industrial revolution and the advancement of engineers to the administration of industry as well as its technical direction, the governmental, economic and social impacts upon the engineers have steadily increased. Once, lawyers were the only professional men whose contacts with the problems of government led them on to positions of public responsibility. From the point of view of accuracy and intellectual honesty the more men of engineering background who become public officials, the better for representative government.

The engineer performs many public functions from which he gets only philosophical satisfactions. Most people do not know it, but he is an economic and social force. Every time he discovers a new application of science, thereby creating a new industry, providing new jobs, adding to the standards of living, he also disturbs everything that is. New laws and regulations have to be made and new sorts of wickedness curbed. He is also the person who really corrects monopolies and redistributes national wealth.

Four hundred years ago Georgius Agricola wrote of my branch of the profession words as true today as they were then:

> Inasmuch as the chief callings are those of the moneylender, the soldier, the merchant, the farmer, and miner, I say, inasmuch as usury is odious, while the spoil cruelly captured from the possessions of the people innocent of wrong is wicked in the sight of God and man, and inasmuch as the calling of the miner excels in honor and dignity that of the merchant trading for lucre, while it is not less noble though far more profitable than agriculture, who can fail to realize that mining is a calling of peculiar dignity?

722

QUESTIONS

1. What do you think Hoover means when he says "engineering without imagination sinks to a trade" (paragraph 6)? Does he illustrate the importance of imagination at any point in his essay? What other qualities must an engineer possess?

2. What purpose does Hoover's anecdote about the English lady serve?

3. Consider Hoover's style. Find examples of his use of parallel structure within sentences and of his grouping of sentences of the same structure. What effect does such parallelism create?

4. Given what you know of Hoover from his diction, syntax, and comments on his profession, how would you describe him?

5. Consider a profession you are in or a job you have had, and write a short essay about it. Reflect on its challenges, its problems and pleasures, and its requirements for success. Consider how it compares with other jobs or professions and how it prepares people for public office. You can be perfectly serious in your essay, but if you once held what you consider to be the world's worst job, you can be perfectly serious with satirical intent.

WRITING SUGGESTIONS
FOR REFLECTING

1. Contrast Joan Didion's meaning for *notes* ("On Keeping a Notebook") with that of James Baldwin in his "Autobiographical Notes." How are the differences in these definitions related to each writer's methods? How are these methods determined by each writer's sense of self?

2. Consider how living creatures are used as symbols in the reflections by two or three of the following writers: Virginia Woolf, Isak Dinesen, Edward Hoagland, and Loren Eiseley. How do the ways the writers use their symbols differ? How do these differences relate to each writer's larger purpose?

3. A number of writers in this section write about personal obsessions (Geoffrey Wolff, Joseph Epstein, and Stanley Milgram, for example). Why is such a subject suitable for reflective writing? Drawing on these essays or others you think are appropriate, write an essay defining *obsession* or defining and classifying different types of obsessions.

4. James Baldwin, Margaret Mead, and Herbert Hoover all consider prejudice in the course of reflecting on their past experiences. How is the development of this topic in each case determined by the writer's particular concerns? Based on these three readings, what conclusions can you draw about how people respond to and overcome the prejudice of others?

5. Certain writers in "Reflecting" consider professions (for example, James Baldwin, Tillie Olsen, and George Orwell on the profession of writing; Lewis Thomas and Richard Selzer on medicine; Herbert Hoover on engineering). Select two or three of these essays, either about the same profession or about different professions. Compare and contrast what the writers say about the profession and how they say it. In what ways do they challenge or support your assumptions about the profession?

6. Select two or three of the essays that present extended portraits of particular people. You might choose from those by Geoffrey Wolff, Scott Momaday, Margaret Mead, Joseph Epstein, and Richard Selzer. How do these writers differ in their techniques for presenting their subjects? In what ways do these differences relate to the purposes of each essay?

7. Examine the tones of two or three autobiographical pieces. How are they similar and different? How does the tone of each relate to the purposes of the writer?

8. A number of writers in this section offer their reflections in order to justify a belief or an opinion or a strong feeling about a subject. In other words, their reflections constitute a kind of argument. Consider one or more of these (for example, the essays by Isak Dinesen, Tillie Olsen, Walter Lippmann, Joseph Epstein, Loren Eiseley). How convincing is the argument in each case? How has the writer used purely personal responses to make a persuasive case? How would you go about developing a more objective argument for the same position? What would be the difference in effect?

9. Choose one essay from each of the three disciplinary areas in this section. (The

724

essays by Scott Momaday, Margaret Mead, and Richard Selzer would be one possibility; or Roland Barthes, Stanley Milgram, and Lewis Thomas.) In each case, trace the writer's movement of mind. How does each writer seem to be led from one thought to the next? Explore any particular similarities or differences among the three. Can you draw any conclusion about the relationship between a writer's field of interest and his or her process of thought?

Reading and Rereading

READING AND RESPONDING

Readers of the *New York Times* editorial page on September 23, 1967, would have encountered, along with several other editorials, the following featured article:

Dear Mr. ⑈O 2 ⑈⑊⑈ ⑈O6 3⑈⑈ ⑈⑊O 2⑈⑈ ⑈O 7 3O⑈⑈8⑈⑈

By E. B. WHITE

My bank, which I have forgotten the name of in the excitement of the moment, sent me a warning the other day. It was headed: "An important notice to all our checking account customers." The burden of this communication was that I would no longer be allowed to write checks that did not bear the special series of magnetic ink numbers along the base. 1

My bank said the Federal Reserve System had notified them that it will not accept for processing any checks that don't show these knobby little digits. For example, I would no longer be free to write a check on a blank form, because it would lack a certain magnetism that computers insist on. 2

Slightly Rheumatoid

I first encountered these spooky numbers a few years back and took a dislike to them. They looked like numbers that had been run over by a dump truck or that had developed rheumatoid arthritis and their joints had swollen. But I kept my mouth shut, as they seemed to be doing me no harm. 3

Now, however, it appears that we are all going to knuckle under to the machines that admire these numbers. We must all forgo the pleasure and convenience of writing a check on an ordinary nonmagnetic piece of paper. My signature used to be enough to prod my bank into dispatching some of my money to some deserving individual or firm. Not any more. 4

This, I think, is a defeat for all—a surrender. In order to accommodate the Federal Reserve System, we are asked to put ourselves out. 5

Reading and Rereading

I Embarrass Easily

The notice I received says that if I try to palm off a check that lacks the magnetic ink numbers, the check cannot be processed without "delay, extra handling charges, and possible embarrassment." I embarrass easily—it doesn't take much, really—and naturally I am eager to learn what form this embarrassment will take if I should decide to write a check using the old blank form that has proved so convenient, for I don't know how many decades, on those occasions when one is stuck without his checkbook or enough lettuce to carry the day.

"The tremendous increase in the use of checks," writes my bank, warming to its subject, "made it necessary for the Federal Reserve to establish a completely computerized operation for processing all checks from all banks. Their computer can function only when proper magnetic numbers are used."

Well, I can believe that last part, about the computer requiring a special diet of malformed numbers; but I am suspicious of that first statement, about how the Federal Reserve would have been unable to carry on unless it went completely over to machines. I suspect that the Federal Reserve simply found machines handy and adventurous. But suppose we had had, in this country, a tremendous increase in the use of checks before anybody had got round to inventing the computer—what would have happened then? Am I expected to believe that the Federal Reserve and all its members would have thrown in the sponge?

I know banks better than that. Banks love money and are not easily deflected from the delicious act of accumulating it. Love would have found a way. Checks would have cleared.

I'm not against machines, as are some people who feel that the computer is leading us back into the jungle. I rather like machines, particularly the egg beater, which is the highest point the machine has yet reached. I'm against machines only when the convenience they afford to some people is regarded as more important than the inconvenience they cause to all.

In short, I don't think computers should wear the pants, or make the decisions. They are deficient in humor, they are not intuitive, and they are not aware of the imponderables. The men who feed them seem to believe that everything is made out of ponderables, which isn't the case. I read a poem once that a computer had written, but didn't care much for it. It seemed to me I could write a better one myself, if I were to put my mind to it.

Time to Find Out

And now I must look around for a blank check. It's time I found out what form my new embarrassment is going to take. First, though, I'll have to remember the name of my bank. It'll come to me, if I sit here long enough. Oddly enough, the warning notice I received contained no signature. Imagine a bank forgetting to sign its name!

Obviously, reading this essay in a textbook for a course in English composition, as you have just done, is not quite the same as reading it in a daily newspaper purchased at the corner newsstand. Not only does the format—the layout, the page size, the typeface—of a newspaper differ from that of a textbook,

728

but the reasons we have for reading each and, consequently, the *way* we read will differ, as well.

Think for a moment, though, about the similarities between your reading of this essay here and now and someone's reading of it in the fall of 1967. First of all, both readings are based on recognizing and interpreting an arrangement of printed symbols, symbols most of us were familiar with long before we began to learn them systematically in the first grade. This aspect of reading is so elemental that you probably never stop to consider what a feat it really is. Second, both readings begin with the title and work their way sequentially through the final line of the text (though seeing the process as purely sequential is somewhat misleading; in fact, our minds may very well flash back to an earlier paragraph or sentence, comparing what was read there to what is being read at the moment, as we work to grasp the text as a whole). Third, neither reading can be simply passive, a reader mentally "absorbing" words on a page. As that *Times* buyer read and as you read, a constant flow of responses—questions, judgments, appreciations, rejections—accompanied and arose from the reading.

Of course, all of these elements of reading take place simultaneously. Consider, for example, the title, "Dear Mr. 021 1063 02 10730 8." How can it be "read"? The first two words are easy enough: we recognize them immediately as the conventional salutation of a business letter. We could even speak them aloud (taking into account that the unpronounceable *Mr.* is an abbreviated form of *Mister*). But the following series of "knobby little digits" presents a more complicated problem. "What are they?" we might ask. "What do they mean?" Even if we recognize them as the sort of figures that are printed at the bottom of a check, we cannot, in fact, *read* them, particularly as the markings between the numbers represent nothing in our language or our grammar; they are not even meant to be read by human beings, but by machines. Trying to read such a title, however, will set off any number of responses: perhaps an inkling of what the writer may be getting at ("Ah, a send-up of banks"), perhaps confusion ("I can't imagine what to make of this"), perhaps the desire to read on, and probably a less than fully articulated combination of several of these.

Next, the name of the author will create another round of responses. Perhaps you (and our imaginary reader of the *Times*) will be familiar with the name E. B. White and will associate it with *Charlotte's Web* or *Elements of Style* or a piece in *The New Yorker* magazine or something else you've read by White or know he wrote. You (and our imaginary *Times* reader) might respond positively ("I loved *Charlotte's Web*") or negatively ("I hate that *New Yorker* stuff") or less familiarly ("Is E. B. a man or a woman?"), but you will certainly have some response. This complicated sequence of responses, of course, occurs in just the second or two it takes you to comprehend the symbols on the page.

As you continue to read, you will continue to respond. Thoughts and impressions, no matter how tentative and ill-formed, will play through your consciousness, and the closer your attention, the more these impressions will rise directly from the words you are reading. (You may even feel compelled to jot down some of these responses in the margin of the page.) Our minds can only make sense of the information we receive by testing this information against what we already know and feel. Such testing is a peculiarly human activity—at least we regard it as "human" when we observe it in other species—and only by allowing, even encouraging, ourselves to make these mental connections can we participate fully in the collaboration necessary to create meaning. Reading, as you probably realize, is a *transaction* that spans at least two human minds; reader and writer both must work actively for a meaningful transaction to take place.

If either participant fails to regard the human responsibilities of communication, the collaboration must necessarily break down, the transaction will be ultimately unsatisfying. White provides a particularly unpleasant example of this: an impersonal letter, written not by a human being but by "a bank," has had an unsettling effect because it indicates to White the abrupt dehumanization of what was previously a human transaction. In his essay "On Political Writing" (p. 677), Walter Lippmann raises the problem more explicitly. He describes how, as he read through "one of those books on politics which are regarded as essential to any sort of intellectual respectability," his responses become increasingly exasperated because, as he says, the author "never admitted that he was just a man. He aimed at that impersonal truth which is like the inscription on monuments." In both these cases, the collaboration between reader and writer has failed because the writer has hidden behind a mask of impersonality.

Readers can fail, as well, when they approach the transaction impersonally, when they neglect to pay attention to their reactions and responses, when they don't participate actively in making meaning of what they read. Such passivity is, of course, what impersonal writers expect of their readers; the mask is meant to be impenetrable, intimidating, so objections won't be raised and questions won't be asked. Perhaps you have found yourself, on occasion, intimidated by such all-knowing texts or bureaucratic pronouncements. But keep in mind that it is active readers like White and like Lippmann, who approach whatever they read inquisitively, ready to respond and to examine their responses, who help us see more clearly and understand more fully. As an intelligent human being, it is your responsibility to read with all your mind.

As we have said, your reading will always involve responses of some kind. The important step for thoughtful readers is to move from the responses themselves to a serious examination of them. To read White's reflections on his bank's warning and respond simply with "It's dumb" or "It's funny" or "I agree" or "I disagree" or the implacable "I can't relate to this" is not enough. Examining such responses will reveal a complex interaction between the structures of the text, the intentions and abilities of the writer, and what you as a reader bring to the text from your own experience. You may find White's essay "funny" because his treatment of his bank as a letter-writing entity that forgets to sign its name sets off a particularly exact set of images in your mind. You may "disagree" with White because you find his comment that the egg beater "is the highest point the machine has yet reached" to be overly flippant and because you think the computer's greater accuracy does in fact afford convenience to all. You may feel you "can't relate to" White's experience because you've never known checks *without* the magnetic code and because you've never received a similarly impersonal letter from a bureaucratic institution. Whatever the case, your responses will remain superficial and ill-formed until you examine them closely enough to explain them in detail.

Clearly, our own experiences will deeply affect our reading. Whatever we have seen or done or felt or heard, even the room we are in and our last meal, will contribute to a data bank from which our responses arise. Consider the following excerpt from the memoirs of Frederick Douglass (the complete chapter from which this was taken appears on p. 21). Born into slavery, Douglass managed to learn to read and at the age of twelve saved enough money—fifty cents— to buy his first book, *The Columbian Orator*. This was a popular school book containing speeches by famous orators and dialogues for students of rhetoric to practice and memorize. Here are Douglass's reactions to one of his readings:

> I was now about twelve years old, and the thought of being *a slave for life* began to bear heavily upon my heart. Just about this time, I got hold of a book entitled "The Columbian Orator." Every opportunity I got, I used to read this book. Among much of other interesting matter, I found in it a dialogue between a master and his slave. The slave was represented as having run away from his master three times. The dialogue represented the conversation which took place between them, when the slave was retaken the third time. In this dialogue, the whole argument in behalf of slavery was brought forward by the master, all of which was disposed of by the slave. The slave was made to say some very smart as well as impressive things in reply to his master—things which had the desired though unexpected effect; for the conversation resulted in the voluntary emancipation of the slave on the part of the master.
>
> In the same book, I met with one of Sheridan's mighty speeches on and in behalf of Catholic emancipation. These were choice documents to me. I read them over and over again with unabated interest. They gave tongue to interesting thoughts of my own soul, which had frequently flashed through my mind, and died away for want of utterance. The moral which I gained from the dialogue was the power of truth over the conscience of even a slaveholder. What I got from Sheridan was a bold denunciation of slavery, and a powerful vindication of human rights. The reading of these documents enabled me to utter my thoughts, and to meet the arguments brought forward to sustain slavery; but while they relieved me of one difficulty, they brought on another even more painful than the one of which I was relieved. The more I read, the more I was led to abhor and detest my enslavers.

Obviously, Douglass's experience as a slave determined his strong response to his reading. The words he read spoke directly to his condition, shaping his previously inexpressible desires and emotions into language. He was of course the perfect audience for Richard Brinsley Sheridan's "bold denunciation of slavery and powerful vindication of human rights." But had Douglass's master and mistress read the same speech, they might well have reacted in a strongly negative way, finding Sheridan subversive of their position as slave owners. They might have characterized his denunciation as "too bold" and his vindication of human rights as "wrongheaded" rather than "powerful." We might read Sheridan today and respond to his speech as an effective piece of eighteenth-century rhetoric or as an interesting historical document. On the other hand, if we have lived in places where human rights are greatly restricted, we might find Sheridan's speech as powerful and bold as Douglass did.

This does not mean, of course, that one's responses are limited to a strictly personal point of view. As we determine the basis for our most personal responses, we can begin to read with greater discipline and to think more systematically about what we read. First of all, we are able to realize that not everyone will have the same responses that we do. This, in turn, can help us recognize what may be limitations in our original responses, limitations imposed perhaps by our *lack* of experience ("Well, sure, I guess if I had been using blank checks all my life and got a letter like that out of the blue, threatening me with 'possible embarrassment' if I didn't start using the magnetically coded ones, I wouldn't have liked it very much either. But what's his point in making a joke of it?"). Opening up a text for ourselves will almost always mean moving beyond those important initial responses to asking ourselves implicit questions about what is being said, how it is being said, and why it is being said in this particular way.

Obviously, we can't fully comprehend what we are reading until we have read it once completely through. Not until we reach White's final line ("Imagine a bank forgetting to sign its name!") do all the various strands of thought that he has been pursuing begin to fall clearly into place. At this point a second reading (and maybe even a third or a fourth) will allow us to pay more attention to how a writer has presented the material, because our curiosity has been satisfied as to what the text is about and we have a sense of it as a whole. In rereading it, we may discover points we have missed or misinterpreted; other of our experiences may begin to come to bear ("This is like that letter I got from the registrar's office informing me that from now on I'd have to have financial aid forms notarized and submit them with my term bill"). Consequently, our responses will be different and we may significantly revise our initial reading. We can also begin in this second reading to question the text more closely to discover its intentions and its structure. This questioning may take a number of forms (which we'll be considering later in this discussion), but in all cases it's a good idea to write down your responses, beginning with those that arise during the initial reading. Writing helps us to think more clearly and deeply about what we read and to preserve our thoughts for further development.

732

ELEMENTS OF READING

Earlier we pointed out some basic similarities between reading E. B. White's "Dear Mr. . . ." on the editorial page of the *New York Times* and reading the same essay in a textbook as an assignment for an English composition course. However, as you already know from experience, many elements of your reading can vary, depending on the situation. What you read and why you read will always influence the way you read.

For example, a *Times* buyer in the fall of 1968 would have read White's essay primarily for what we can call "pleasure." "Pleasure," of course, can take many forms: we may read for amusement, for escape, for intellectual discovery and stimulation, even to get angry or to make ourselves more depressed. But it's clear that we *choose* to do such reading because of a definite personal interest. No one is asking us to look for anything or remember anything. Ironically, though, we will often remember what we read for pleasure more clearly and more fully than what we read under pressure, because our minds are more relaxed. On such occasions, we have time to pause over a word or a phrase just because we like the sound of it or the feeling it expresses. So, while the pleasure that arises from personal interest may be our primary purpose for reading, we may also be assimilating new information, analyzing a particularly striking passage to understand how it works, even evaluating how successfully a writer has achieved certain effects, all because we enjoy what we are doing.

Douglas L. Wilson's account of his wide-ranging research into the intellectual sources of Robert Frost's famous poem "Mending Wall" ("The Other Side of the Wall," p. 261) provides a good example of this sort of reading. Personal experience has led Wilson to question prevailing interpretations of Frost's meaning. Intrigued, he begins to read biographies of the poet, letters Frost wrote during the poem's composition, even treatises on wall-building; he returns again and again to the poem itself. Bit by bit, Wilson arms himself with evidence that he hopes will substantiate his unorthodox analysis, his re-evaluation, of the work. His purposes in doing such reading are obviously varied. Yet what links them together and, in fact, underlies them all is Wilson's intense personal interest, his *pleasure* in the task. Thoughtful, responsible, and truly responsive reading will always involve an element of personal interest.

Taking account of how you read for pleasure, then, can help you read more effectively in other situations; you can even use your personal reading to help you develop habits that will make you a better reader generally.

One way is to take the time to make note of your immediate responses. For example, you may want to remember a particular piece of information or to hold on to a word or phrase that made an impression; to respond evaluatively, agreeing or disagreeing with what the writer has to say; or to explore responses that the writer has triggered. Begin to record such responses in writing. Keep a notebook handy to use as a journal of observations, information, and impressions. You can then refer to this journal for ideas to use in your own writing. Taking pleasure in working with new concepts and new information is an important step in becoming a better reader.

Reading in its broadest sense (as White's bank's computer *reads* his magnetic "code-name") always implies taking in information. We do so whenever and whatever we read: symbols on a page become meaningful data. But grasping the information a text presents will require an awareness of the author's purpose for writing. For example, in the essay you are now reading, our main purpose is to *explain*, to help a reader understand more about the process of reading. Most textbook material is primarily explanatory, and your task as a student will often be clear-cut: to memorize a body of information and give it back pretty much in its original form on an "objective" test. Therefore, as you read a chapter or assigned article, you will want to sort out the most pertinent information. If, as is the case here, this information is fairly limited, underlining short passages (in a book that belongs to you) or jotting study notes for yourself may be sufficient. Usually, though, you'll be faced with a considerable amount of information to assimilate, in which case underlining won't help much in your process of sorting and memorizing. Actually transcribing data in your own handwriting is a far better aid to memory, and a transcription that provides a complete accounting of what you read is the most useful way to clarify pertinent information for yourself.

Making a formal outline can be an invaluable aid as you read complicated explanatory material. Outlining requires that you read more closely in order to sort out a writer's major points from the supporting data. When the information from a chapter or article is abstracted and arranged according to the author's plan of organization, you can see the important information and the supporting details much more quickly and easily than mere underlining of the text will allow. Obviously, this kind of detailed outlining is an arduous, time-consuming activity, but then so is any enforced study for information. You'll find that for much of the material you'll be reading in college, the benefits of such an outline can be enormous. (A sample of outlining technique and some suggestions for practice appear in the questions that follow this section on pp. 738–739.)

Summarizing is another way to incorporate writing when you read explanatory material. A summary requires you to tell in your own words the gist of what the writer has said. You must understand the material at a deeper level than that required for memorization because you must "rethink" the writer's words and make them your own. Consequently, summaries are most useful for studying articles and books of fairly limited scope where the author's point of view is important. (For studying chapters of large textbooks that require memorizing a wide range of information, an outline is generally more helpful.) The process of summarizing is an indispensable tool for comprehension, and the ability to summarize is a necessary skill for writing research papers in which you must smoothly integrate source material with your own interpretation.

There are times when you may need to summarize an entire article or a complete chapter of a book. This sort of summary is called an *abstract*, and it is conventional for many academic writers, particularly in the sciences or social sciences, to provide their own very brief summary of this sort at the beginning of a longer article. (See Barbara Landau *et al.*, "Spatial Knowledge and Geometric Representation in a Child Blind from Birth," p. 379, or Peter Marler and Susan Peters, "Sparrows Learn Adult Song and More from Memory," p. 415.) For purposes of study, however, you may want your abstract to be more detailed, including important supporting data as well as the article's main ideas. On the other hand, for purposes of research and preparing to integrate another writer's ideas into an essay of your own, you will probably need to summarize only a pertinent passage rather than the article as a whole. (Examples of a detailed abstract along with some suggestions for practice, appear in the questions that follow this section on p. 739.)

Because they allow a reader to see how a writer has arranged his or her points and what evidence is supplied to back them up, outlines and summaries can also be useful for analyzing texts where the purpose is not simply explaining. However, other modes of analysis may be even more helpful. (The introductions to the sections "Reporting," "Explaining," "Arguing," and "Reflecting" offer some specific suggestions.) In general, though, after your initial reading, you should return to the piece of writing and pose questions that will help reveal how and why the text works as it does. We will use White's "Dear Mr. . . ." as an example of how to go about questioning a text.

What is the writer's purpose? White's immediate purpose is to describe his responses to the letter from his bank, ranging from personal annoyance to ironic evaluations of why a change should be required to a note of wry defiance. These personal reflections revolve around a more general and serious point, which he states fairly directly in paragraph 5 and again in paragraph 10: he thinks it is a "defeat," a "surrender" to allow machines to inconvenience "all" (and himself, in particular) for the sake of making life easier for a powerful few. Allied with this idea is White's belief that computers are "deficient" in the qualities which make us human and that, consequently, they should not be allowed to usurp human transactions (paragraph 11). His conclusion is a refusal to "knuckle under" to the dictates of such machines.

How does the writer organize his or her material? White's reflections are organized around the information contained in the letter he received from his bank. His title is an ironic version of the letter's salutation, and his concluding sentence refers to the lack of a closing signature. In paragraphs 1, 2, 6, and 7, he quotes from the letter, directly or indirectly, and goes on to offer his specific responses. Paragraphs 10 and 11 represent a new, more general direction of thought that grows out of his specific responses to the letter. Paragraph 12 returns to the letter and reinforces White's reactionary position on encroaching impersonality.

Does the writer provide evidence to back up the points he or she is trying to make? White is not offering a formal argument but a more personal consideration of his subject, so we would not expect "evidence" in the traditional sense. But, as his reflective structure would suggest, he does offer imaginative evidence and evidence based on personal experience, particularly in paragraphs 4–5, 8–9, and 11.

What are the writer's assumptions about his or her audience? White's essay was written for the *New York Times*, so he could assume that his readers would be a reasonably well-informed group, many of whom would have themselves received similar letters from their banks. Even so, he is careful to explain the change the bank is demanding as well as its practical effects. (A further question you might consider is whether the writer assumes his readers will be generally sympathetic with, antagonistic toward, or neutral about the ideas being raised. What would you say about White's assumptions?)

What kind of language and imagery does the writer use? White is responding to what he regards as a ridiculous letter with very serious implications. His language is resolutely informal and conversational; phrases like "spooky numbers," "kept my mouth shut," "palm off," "enough lettuce," and "wear the pants" can be contrasted to the kind of communication he is criticizing. Yet when he has a serious point to make (for example, that computers "are deficient in humor, they are not intuitive, and they are not aware of the imponderables"), his language becomes more formal. His images—particularly his personification of the bank as a letter-writing entity—are comic or wryly sarcastic, but, as with his language, they don't overwhelm his underlying seriousness.

In responding to questions such as these, a reader is able to take a piece of writing apart and examine its components to see how it works. In many situations, so careful an analysis won't be necessary: you would have little reason, for example, to analyze a comprehensive textbook in this way. However, analytical skill can be applied to a wide variety of activities and, in particular, can help a reader move beyond simply personal responses to a more systematic evaluation of a piece of writing.

Suppose that your initial response to the White essay was something like, "I enjoyed this; it was funny." A second analytical reading then helped you to understand the workings of the essay and how the tone and imagery contributed to your interest and appreciation. Further analysis of your own initial responses perhaps led you to realize that you share White's suspicion of computers and his subversive reaction to impersonal, bureaucratic pronouncements. This, in turn, has given you a sense of how others, who do not particularly share your views, might respond. Now you may develop a more systematic evaluation of the essay.

Purpose. White has succeeded well in presenting his own reactions with wit and grace. His conversational tone and his wry imagery allow a reader to sympathize with his very human rebellion against being inconvenienced because of the requirements of a machine.

Organization. Organizing his essay around the letter he received from his bank is an effective way for White to move from his specific responses to his more general considerations about the relationship between technology and human life. This organization also leads him to his important central image of a bank that forgets "to sign its name."

Evidence. Because White is relating his responses rather than arguing a position, the personal evidence he presents (the inconvenience the new rules will cause him, the computer-composed poem, etc.) is sufficient to communicate aptly and forcefully his reason for feeling the way he does. What White's evidence does not do, however, is to convince us that carrying checks with the magnetic code is a terrible inconvenience. White simply assumes that his reader will agree. Consequently, his general comments on computer technology—particularly from the perspective of almost twenty years—don't carry the weight they might.

Summary. White's essay is an entertaining and thought-provoking reflection on what it's like to be told to modify old habits in order to conform to the dictates of new technology. The personality of the writer, the grace and cleverness of his expression, and the clarity of his design engage the reader's attention and sympathy. Although we may not immediately agree with the specific basis for his objections or with his underlying argument, we can't help but be persuaded by his sincerity, skill, and good sense that his position is admirably and sanely humane.

This, of course, is only the beginning of only one evaluation. These notations—or another set that might be entirely contradictory—could be expanded and developed into an evaluative essay that presented reasons and evidence based on further research, perhaps into other essays by White or studies of computerized banking. Such an essay might be highly supportive (as our sample summary would indicate) or highly critical ("Though White's essay is very clever, the subversive point of view he expresses here is just a few steps from anarchy"), or it might take an intermediate position. It might concentrate on the consequences of the writer's ideas or the success of the writer's methods or some combination of the two.

As you may already have begun to realize, becoming a more astute reader can lay the groundwork for becoming a more effective writer. The more reading we do—the more we understand our role as a reader—the more we learn about what it means to be an audience. By paying attention to our responses, by examining them in order to analyze and evaluate what we read, we can begin to see more clearly *why* we feel well or poorly treated by a writer. Transferring such knowledge from our own experience as an audience to the audience for whom we are writing, we become more aware of what that intended audience will require. We become more concerned about the appropriate tone to take, about what does and doesn't need to be said about a topic, given our purpose, and we have a better idea of the organization necessary to gain and hold our audience's interest and bring our work to a satisfactory conclusion. We realize more fully the transaction that must take place, and how we as writers can encourage a reader to collaborate in the making of meaning. In "Writing and Rewriting" we will consider this subject in more detail.

SUGGESTIONS FOR DISCUSSION AND WRITING

1. Choose something you habitually read for pleasure (a particular magazine, for example, or the sports pages or even a comic book or the liner notes of a new record album). As you read, take the time to record your responses in writing. It may be interesting to share the responses with the rest of the class.

2. Prepare a formal summarizing outline of all or part of one of the readings in this text. Some suggestions are Barbara Tuchman's " 'This is the End of the World': The Black Death," Annemarie de Waal Malefijt's "*Homo Monstrosus*," E. H. Gombrich's "Art for Eternity," Edward Hall's "The Anthropology of Manners," Charles Darwin's "Worms and the Soil," Barbara Landau's "Spatial Knowledge . . .," O. H. Ammann's "Report on the Hudson River Bridge," and Barry Commoner's "The Causes of Environmental Stress." (Your instructor may have other suggestions.) As an example of this method, we've started you on the first eight paragraphs of the Malefijt essay below.

I. Introduction
    A. Linnaeus included *homo monstrosus*, "a species related to *Homo sapiens* but markedly different in physical appearance," in his eighteenth-century classification of living things.
    B. Belief in monstrous races had endured 2,000 years, stimulated by the following sources:
        1. Accounts from explorers and travelers, probably based on malformed individuals.
        2. Explorers' desire to enhance their own fame at home.

      3. Ignorance of distant lands and limits of human variation stimulated imaginative production of and belief in such races.

    C. Credulity of those who believed in monstrous races comparable to "unfounded prejudices" held today.

II. Early Greece

    A. Herodotus (5th c. B.C.) was an objective historian about the known world, but the further away the land the more unusual its customs and inhabitants appeared to him.

      1. Herodotus believed that if strange habits existed, then strange physical differences could also.

      2. Herodotus's sources were his own travels and earlier writers such as Hesiod and Homer.

      3. Herodotus didn't invent monsters, but was "first to locate them in actual geographical areas."

      4. Possible reasons for Greek acceptance of reality of monstrous races.

3. Choose one of the essays mentioned above (or another that your instructor suggests), and write a detailed summary of the information it contains. Again, we have provided an example based on the first eight paragraphs of the Malefijt essay.

Malefijt's intention is to describe and account for the belief in monstrous races that existed for at least 2,000 years before Linnaeus's inclusion of them in his eighteenth-century classification of natural things. Accounts of monstrous races by early Greek travelers and explorers arose from their ignorance of birth defects, desire for fame at home, and accounts of monstrous races in previous literature, all of which stimulated imagination. *The Greek historian Herodotus, whose reports of the world known to him may be considered objective, nonetheless included reports in his works of monstrous races in such places as Libya, Ethiopia, and India. The "first to locate monsters in actual geographical areas," Herodotus did not invent monsters. His sources were stories heard in his travels, and previous literature such as the work of Hesiod, who spoke of one-eyed, dog-headed, and breast-eyed tribes, and Homer, who wrote of one-eyed Cyclops as well as of giants and pygmies.* Possible reasons for the Greeks' acceptance of such accounts were their awareness that differences existed in the cultures surrounding them, and Empedocles' theory of evolution, which postulated that men and animals evolved from the random combination of separate parts, thus leaving open the possibility of the survival of peculiar combinations.

(Note that if you were doing research for a paper on the Greek historian Herodotus, you might have included in your summary only the sentences presented here in italics.)

4. Suppose you were doing research on the subject of how college English textbooks treat the subject of reading. Summarize portions of this appendix that might be pertinent.

5. Return to E. B. White's "Dear Mr. . . ." and attempt first to outline and then to summarize his essay. Note any particular difficulties you may have. How does the form of White's reflective essay contribute to these difficulties?

6. Choose one of the readings in this text for a careful written analysis. Begin by jotting down your responses to your initial reading. Then consider the questions for analysis that follow. You may, as well, want to prepare an outline or summary as a means of analyzing the writer's methods.

Reading and Rereading

a. What was the writer's purpose for writing? That is, what did the writer set out to show, to explain, to prove, to reflect on?

b. How did the writer organize the material? Does the organization reflect the purpose for writing? Was the arrangement of material easy for the reader to follow?

c. Does the writer provide evidence to back up the points he or she is making? Here you should look for any sweeping general statements with no evidence to back them up, or reasons why we should accept them.

d. What kind of diction is used? Here you would look for overly formal or too informal language, or for imagery and metaphor that help to convey meaning.

e. What are the writer's assumptions about his or her audience? Such assumptions would include a sense of the level of intelligence of the audience and an awareness of what general knowledge about the topic the audience might have.

After this preparation, write an essay of your own in which you analyze the essay you have read.

7. Based on the suggestions outlined on page 737 prepare an evaluation of the reading you analyzed in question 5 above or another reading in this text. After this preparation, write an essay in which you evaluate this reading.

Writing and Rewriting

As we discussed in "Reading and Rereading," expressing your ideas will often begin with recording your most immediate responses, jotting them down on a pad, in a journal, or in the margin of a book. Clearly such jottings are not intended for a reader. You may be surprised to realize, however, that with thought and care and concern for an eventual audience, even the sketchiest notes can evolve into a significant, controlled piece of writing. This process of development and revision is rarely apparent when we read: all we see is the finished product, the piece of writing in its final form. But the polished work that is presented to an audience may, in fact, barely resemble what the writer started out with.

E. B. White didn't simply sit down the afternoon he received the warning from his bank and allow "Dear Mr. . . . ." to flow out onto a page (if you haven't yet read White's essay, you'll find it at the beginning of "Reading and Rereading," p. 727). The letter sparked a response, however—a sense of injustice, of annoyance at the threat of "embarrassment" and concern about the effects of technology—and White realized that here was at least the germ of an essay that might eventually find its way into print, earning him a bit of money and the satisfaction of reaching an audience with his concerns. His first thought, though, was merely to provide himself with a rough rendering of his immediate response. Consequently, his original notes (which we include below) do little more than sketch out his basic intentions and establish a point of view.

I seldom carry a checkbook,
because I like to travel light
But I always have money
in the bank (it is an
old habit of mine that
I can't seem to break)
and I feel that I should
be free to dispense this
money without any
embarrassment to myself.
Nw, because of the Federal
Reserve's knuckly ander,
I will not be privileged to
write a blank check.

The ~~only that~~ danger ^in^ ~~of~~ a
machine ~~culture~~ is that ~~it~~
in the enjoyment of
the convenience of machines,
~~will to ^we^ ever~~, will ~~outweigh~~ ^overshadow^
their disadvantages to others

The danger in a machine
culture is not that ~~machines~~
~~will take over our thinking~~
~~and dominate us as lives~~, but
~~that even, who~~ the convenience
of machines may come ~~to~~
overshadow the losses we suffer
~~from them~~ by reason of their
peculiar requirements.

Computers free the Federal Reserve from arduous and voluminous ~~operations~~ operations in clearing checks. But in so doing they deprive the ^{narrow} consumer's of ~~but the privilege~~ ^{right} of instructing his bank in a casual, agreeable manner

The man who foresaw all
this was a man named
Orwell. and he foresaw
pretty good. If we're
not careful. we may
wake up some morning
and find that what he
predicted has come to
pass.

Writing and Rewriting

White's notes bear almost no resemblance to his polished final draft as it appeared in the *New York Times*. We see White beginning with his immediate personal response—his desire to dispense his money without any embarrassment or inconvenience to himself—and then moving on to generalize, to expand his annoyance over the particular letter to the larger issue of "the danger in a machine culture." Thus, he establishes the meaning and purpose that will govern his final essay. But there is little attempt to formulate a coherent design at this point. In fact, it is almost comforting to see how messy these initial notes are, when we realize what they will provide the foundation for.

Even as White is scribbling notes to himself, however, with little concern for coherence and the needs of his eventual reader, he is his own critic. He is listening to himself as he writes, thinking about how his words go together, and revising when he's not quite satisfied. He has, for example, reworked the sentence about "the danger in a machine culture" several times, trying to get it right (although, as we'll see in his subsequent drafts, this central idea would continue to give him trouble). But he is not particularly concerned with correctness; for instance, he lets stand a sentence like "The man who forsaw all of this was a man named Orwell and he foresaw pretty good." No sentence like this will, in fact, appear in the final draft, but what White seems to be after here is a kind of aptness. Orwell is a touchstone for the writer's ideas, a way of getting at what he wants to say and finding the words to generalize about his particular situation.

Based on these very rough notes, White typed a first draft, onto which he wrote in further revisions:

which I don't often do but which I
consider a great convenience in
certain circumstances.

My bank, which I have forgotten the name of
in the excitement of the moment, sent me a ~~notice~~ warning the other
day. It ~~read~~ was headed: "An important notice to all our checking account
customers." The burden of this communication was ~~this~~ that
~~the Federal Reserve System~~ I would no longer be allowed to write
~~submit~~ checks that did not bear the special series of
"magnetic ink numbers" along the base. ~~They~~ My bank said ~~that~~
the Federal Reserve System had notified them that it will not
accept for processing any checks that don't bear these curious form
numbers. For example, I would not be allowed to write a check on a blank
~~(I~~ (I've never been very fond of these numbers, since
I first laid eyes on them---they look to me like numbers that
have been ~~run over~~ backed into by a dump truck, or have deve,oped rheumatoid
joints
arthritis, and their knuckles have swollen. But, I have kept my
mouth shut, until now.) Now it appears that we are going
to knuckle under to machines, and that I am no longer privelegd
to write a check on a blank form, because it lacks these spooky
litttle numbers. This, I thinkm is a defeat, a surrender.
I plan to go on ~~writ~~ instructing my bank, and I can't think of its
name, to dispense my money in the way I want it dispensed, witjout
any reference to magnetic ink numbers. I will be ~~~~ interested t
to see what gappens.

The notice I received says that if I try to
~~put over~~ a check that lacks the magnetic ink numbers, it cannot
be processed without "delay, extra handling charges, and possible
embarrassment."

rather easily embarrassed---it doesn't take much----and I ~~would like~~ am ~~keen~~ eager

to ~~know~~ learn what form this embarrassment is going to take if I should

decide to write a check using the old blank form that has proved

so convenient for I don't know how many decades, when one is stuck
without one's checkbook or enough lettuce to carry the day.
The reason given by my bank for this tightening

of its service is ~~that~~ this: "The tremendous increase in the use of

checks made it necessary for the Federal Reserve to establish a

completely computerized operation for processing all checks from all

banks. Their computer can function only when proper magnetic numbers
Well, I can believe that last
are used." ~~I~~ part, about the computer requiring

a special diet of funny numbers, ---this I can believe. But I am

suspicious of that first statement, about how the Federal Reserve
would have been unable   had gone over
cou dn't carry on unless it went over to machines. I think the truth
and adventurous
is ~~it~~ the Federal Reserve found machines handy, and that's
But   we had had, in this country
why it went over to them. Suppose there had been a tremendous increase
and nobody had got round to inventing the computer
in the use of checks but the computer hadn't been invented---what would

h ve happened then? Would ~~banks~~ banks have ~~given up~~
Would the Federal Reserve system have collapsed from exhaustion
thrown in the sponge? I know banks better than that---they would
and educ
have cleared those checks ~~if they had to employ retarded children~~ to
and they are not easily deflected from accumulating it.
~~don't~~ Banks love money. ~~So~~

Come to think it, I love money, too. I am a lifelong checking account

patron and have had to be ~~tremend~~ extremely thrifty because of my

refusal to balance my checkbook in the space on the left where you

are supposd to keep track of what you've been spending and depositing.

I've never done that, on the theory that it is a waste of time--also
I subtract quick
I don't add good, and my figures would be ~~deceptive~~ misleading because inaccurate.

Instead, I practice thrift and never know my balance until I receive my
in the days before machines
statement. Speaking of bank statements, mine used to arrive the first

3

of the month and was legible and decipherable and coherent. Now,
since machines have taken over, it arrives anywhere from the
largely
first of the month to the eighth of the month, and is indecipherable,
except to a man hell bent on deciphering something.

The notice

To get back to the warning from my bank, it ended:
"So remember...be sure to use only your own personal checks with
pre-encoded magnetic ink numbering. It takes both your account
number and your signature for your check to clear properly. Thank you
very much."

Writing and Rewriting

This step from notes to first draft is significant: the essay is actually beginning to take shape here. White has used the letter from his bank to provide an opening and conclusion, but you'll note that he hasn't yet discovered the precise design that will allow his finished work to revolve around this letter. In fact, he has to wrench his attention back to the letter in the final paragraph, after a digression about his bank statement and balancing his checkbook. Nor has he quite developed the important image of the bank as a letter writer (although, he *has* begun to personify the bank in his opening sentence and later on when he writes, "Banks love money . . ."; and he has also—perhaps for very practical reasons—assumed the pose of not being able to remember his bank's name). The idea about "the danger of a machine culture," which he struggled with in his original notes, appears here in a quite different form—a specific reference to the bank accommodating the Federal Reserve rather than customers—and, consequently, the incident has not yet been fully generalized.

Again, though, White is his own critic. The draft is messy and chewed over, with typed emendations as well as handwritten ones. Some of these changes seem to show White trying to capture fleeting thoughts, slapping them down on paper, as he did in his notes, to save and cull from later on. Others are based on his concern for how an audience will respond (the deletion of the line about banks employing "retarded children" is a good example), while still others are "improvements," revisions of vocabulary and syntax to clarify meaning or create more graceful, forceful expression.

In his second draft, White continues to revise, to tighten his structure and refine his language.

My bank, which I have forgotten the name of
in the excitement of the moment, sent me a warning the other
day. It was headed: "An important notice to all our checking
account customers." The burden of this communication was that
I would no longer be allowed to write checks that did not bear
the special series of magnetic ink numbers along the base. My
bank said the Federal Reserve System had notified them that it
will not accept for processing any checks that don't show these
knobby little digits. For example, I would no longer be free
to write a check on a blank form, because it would lack ~~the~~ a
~~magnetic numbers~~ certain magnetism that computers insist on.

I first encountered these spooky numbers a few
years back and took a dislike to them. ~~They~~ They looked like numbers
that had been run over by a dump truck, or that had developed
rheumatoid arthritis and their joints had swollen. But I kept
my mouth shut [about them] as they seemed to be doing me no harm.
Now, however, it appears that we are all going to knuckle under
to machines ~~and will have to forego~~ the pleasure and convenience
of writing a check on an ordinary, non-magnetic piece of paper.
My signature used to be enough to prod my bank into dispatching
some of my money to some needy individual or firm, ~~but~~ not any
more. This, I think, is a defeat for all---a surrender. In
order to accommodate the Federal Reserve system, we are ~~going~~ asked
to put ourselves out.

The notice I received says that if I try to

270

2

palm off a check that lacks the magnetic ink numbers, the check
cannot be processed without "delay, extra handling charges, and
possible embarrassment."   I embarrass easy---it doesn't take
much, really---and naturally I am eager to learn what form this
embarrassment will take if I should decide to write a check using
the old blank form that has proved so convenient for I don't know
how many decades on those occasions when one is stuck without
his checkbook or enough lettuce to carry the day.

          "The tremendous increase in the use of checks,"
writes my bank , warming to its subject, "made it necessary for
the Federal Reserve to establish a completely computerized operation for processing all checks from all banks. Their computer
can function only when proper magnetic numbers are used." Well,
I can believe that last part, about the computer requiring a
special diet of ~~darangedxnumbers~~ malformed numbers; but I am
suspicious of that first statement, about how the Federal Reserve
would have been unable to carry on unless it went _completely_ over to machines.
I suspect that the Federal Reserve simply found machines ~~useful,~~
handly, and ~~sustaining to its age.~~ _adventurous_ But suppose ~~there~~ we had had,
in this country, a tremendous increase in the use of checks and
nobody had _yet_ got round to inventing the computer---what would have
happened then? Am I ~~supposed~~ _expected_ to believe that the Federal Reserve
and all ~~their~~ _its_ member banks would have thrown in the sponge? I
know banks better than that. Banks love money and are not easily
deflected from the ~~anaknexxing~~ delicious business of accumulating
it. ~~Samehowxtheyxwouldxhavexfoundx~~ Love would have found a way.
Checks would have cleared.

          I'm not against machines, as are some people

3

who feel that the computer is leading us down the primrose

trail. I ~~laxaxmmxkixx~~ like machines---particularly the egg

the highest point   has yet reached)

beater, which is the machine at its finest and most mysterious.

~~Rmt~~ I8m only against machines when the convenience they afford

some   is considered) more important than

to ~~xemexix xextxixvpempix~~ overshadwos the ~~im~~inconvience they

all

cause to ~~mix many~~. In short, I don't think computers should

wear the pants, or even make the decisions---~~sixxxxixx~~. They

lack humor, and they are not intuitive--or even aware ofthe

mponderables. I read a poem once written by a computer but

didn't care much for it. It seemed to me I could write a better

100

one myself, if I put my mind to it, and my heart in it.

     And now I must look around for a blank check.

It's time I found out what form ~~thxxxxxkxxxx~~ my new embarrssment

is going to take. First, thoulg, I'll have o remember the

150

name of my bank. It'll come to me, if I sit here long enough.

Oddly enough the warning notice I received

contained no signature. Imagine a bank

forgetting to sign its name!

174

278

270

722

Writing and Rewriting

The pieces have begun to fall more gracefully into place here. Most important, perhaps, White gets rid of the digression about bank statements at the end of his first draft and replaces it with the more general reflections he has been aiming toward all along. Note how the troublesome sentence from his notes about "the danger of a machine culture" has found its place in the penultimate paragraph of this second draft. (Note, as well, how White has continued to rework and refine it.)

In the handwritten emendations of this draft, we also see White sharpening the wit of his reflections, particularly as he develops his wry personification of his bank and computers in general ("a certain magnetism that computers insist on" and "machines that admire these numbers"). And it is not until now, in his attempt to bring the essay to a satisfactory close, that White adds the final, memorable image of "a bank forgetting to sign its name," an image that eventually grows very naturally out of his process of revising, of focusing and clarifying his ideas in order to make his point most vividly for his audience. Names are no longer important; all that matters now is a magnetic code for computers to read.

Reading White's finished essay as it appeared in the *New York Times*, we have a hard time realizing that the writer didn't know exactly what he had in mind when he sat down to write. When a piece of writing is successful, we do not see the seams; the words carry us along so that we are not aware of the writer's process. But it is clear from White's notes and his drafts that this graceful, carefully conceived essay required a great deal of work: jotting, scratching out, drafting, rewriting, private questions and decisions, moments of inspiration when the connections began to seem clear, when the work seemed to pay off. What we learn from White's manuscripts is that ideas don't spring full blown from a writer's mind into a clear, coherent form. Rather, ideas may tumble out in unformed, fragmented ways that can be developed, modified, and sharpened draft after draft.

Composition is, then, a process, and the practical implications for student writers are readily apparent. It takes time to put what you have to say, your most personal and immediate responses, into a form that an audience can understand and appreciate, into words that will best express your intentions. Waiting to begin a writing assignment until the night before it is due will not allow this sort of time. Fully developed ideas are the result of revising, of working step by step, and will require a series of working sessions over the course of several days or several weeks. Only then can you take full advantage of your reading and writing skills in order to produce a final draft that seems to be ready for an audience. What you end with will very likely come a long way from how you begin.

You've just seen, of course, how E. B. White began. You'll find what he ended with at the beginning of "Reading and Rereading," p. 727.

SUGGESTIONS FOR DISCUSSION AND WRITING

1. We have suggested several changes that White made in the course of drafting his essay in order to take into account his readers' attitudes and interests. What other changes like these do you find? What do these changes tell you about the audience White had in mind? How does he encourage the responses he wants from his readers?

2. Compare White's final pattern of organization to the initial notes he made for himself. Do the notes provide any sense of his final pattern? (You may also want to look at the first and final drafts of a poem that William Stafford includes in his "A Way of Writing," p. 615. How does Stafford's final pattern for the poem correspond to his original worksheet? What similarities and differences can you discover between White's process of composing an essay and Stafford's process of composing poetry?)

3. What does White achieve in the course of revising? How has he determined what to keep from earlier drafts and what to delete?

4. Consider some of the words and expressions White chooses that may seem a bit out of the ordinary, either in themselves or in the way they are used. Looking at the words and expressions you have selected, what can you say about White's style, about what gives his essay its particular tone of voice? Look also through the drafts to see the words and expressions which were deleted. In what way do the selected words and expressions best serve White's purpose.

5. Have you ever felt oppressed or victimized by a machine or an institution? Write an essay in which you express your feelings and seek to gain sympathy for your cause or redress for your grievance.

Suggestions for Writing
Across the Disciplines

The following writing suggestions are based on the topical groupings of essays in the Topical Guide to the Contents, p. xv.

WRITING

1. Select one of the essays in the "Writing" section that you find interesting. Analyze it using Orwell's four reasons for writing as your primary means of analysis. That is, try to determine the relative strength of each of the four motives in the essay you have selected to study. Make sure you understand Orwell thoroughly before you begin your analysis, and reread his definitions as you need to. Write an essay in which you set forth your findings. Obviously, unexpected findings are likely to be the most interesting. You shouldn't neglect the obvious, but you should try to go beyond it.

2. First, proceed as directed in question 1 above, but this time extend your analysis to a second essay. Then, write a paper in which you compare and contrast the two essays with respect to Orwell's motives for writing.

HISTORY

3. Consider the question of the historian's distance from or closeness to the subject matter of his or her inquiry. Select four or five essays from the "History" group that will serve to illustrate the advantages and disadvantages of being close to or distant from one's subject. You might seek to answer some of the following questions:

    a. Can your chosen historians be ranked in order of distance from their subject? (If they can't, better reconsider your choices.)

    b. How does a "distant" historian seek to compensate for the disadvantages of distance—and how does a "close" historian compensate for those of closeness?

    c. How many kinds of distance and closeness are important for you to consider?

    d. What conclusion can you draw about the historian and the question of distance?

4. Among the essays in the "History" section are two reports on the stock market. Examine these reports in the light of Carr's views about the historian and historical fact.

Is there a difference between "historical" facts and "journalistic" facts? Do you agree or disagree with Carr? Try to take a stand on this matter. You may bring in other essays from this section as evidence if your wish.

MYTH AND FANTASY

5. What is a monster? What is a hero? Can a monster ever become a hero? Consider these problems in the light of the essays by Malefijt, Kennedy, Auden (including the fairy tale), and any other material you think appropriate. (That is, you may bring in other things, but you should not ignore Malefijt, Kennedy, and Auden.) You should produce an essay *in* definition and *on* definition, not simply defining "monster" and "hero" but considering how such notions as monstrosity and heroism come to be defined. (You may find the two essays on sports helpful here.)

6. What is the relationship between myth or fantasy and real life? Present an answer to this question based on a reading of the essays in the "Myth and Fantasy" section. Consider such matters as why we turn to myth or fantasy and what these works do to us or for us.

SYMBOLS AND SYMBOLISM

7. How does a moth or a lizard or a tower or a wart become a symbol of something other than itself? You will find the trick done right before your eyes in most of the essays in the "Symbols and Symbolism" group, and you will find it discussed in the others. Giving an object symbolic meaning is, of course, much more than a trick. It is a major element in human thought. Choose three essays from this section that turn objects into symbols, and try to explain exactly how their central objects are given that extra dimension of meaning. Write an essay in which you develop a thesis about how symbolism is accomplished, presenting examples from your chosen essays in support of your thesis.

8. If you have read a number of the essays in the "Symbols and Symbolism" section, you have seen writers raising objects to a symbolic level of meaning. Can you do it yourself? Take these essays as your models, and write an essay in which some object or creature known to you is the center of attention. See if you can give your chosen object symbolic power by your treatment of it. Don't choose something like a flag, which has an established symbolic value, but something that will be made a symbol by the way you present it. Remember, you are not making an argument in a direct way, proving that something is a symbol; you are doing something more subtle and delicate.

ART

9. Anyone who writes about the visual and performing arts has to do a lot of describing. Take the pieces by Agee, Bryden, White, and the *New York Times* on King Tut,

757

and look especially at the descriptive passages in them. Can you rank them in order from most to least successful? Try to find at least one example of really good description, and explain what makes it good. Try to find at least one example of poor description, and explain what is wrong with it. Use all of this material to support a thesis about written description.

10. Here are three generalizations about art:

    a. Art is a representation of life.

    b. Art is an expression of the artist's personality.

    c. Art is for the satisfaction of its consumers.

Consider the essays by Miller, Bentley, Gombrich, and Barthes. Can you say for each of them which of the three views is closest to their own? Select two essays that express quite different views on the nature of art. Discuss these views, and indicate which you find most congenial and why.

MEDIA

11. The "Media" section contains essays on TV news, TV advertising, zoos, newspapers, and movies and three samples of reporting from the *New York Times*. We all know that TV is a medium of mass communication, that newspapers and films are media as well. Are zoos media too? Does it make sense to think of news and advertising as somewhat different media even when they are carried by the same medium? What are media, anyway? Present a definition of the term that will enable you to answer the above questions. Use the various essays as sources of information to support, illustrate, and qualify your definition.

12. What's news? Using the essays by Milgram, Oppenheimer, and Knightley and the three *New York Times* pieces, discuss the question of what the news is and what it ought to be. Are the problems built into the nature of the media, or are they difficulties that might be overcome—or both? Develop your own view of what the news ought to be and what it can be, using the essays in the "Media" section as resource material.

EDUCATION

13. Education can be divided into three subtopics: learning, schooling, and teaching. Using the essays in the "Education" section as resource material, write an essay in which you express your own views about the proper relationship of these three elements in education. That is, present your own thesis about the way that individual learning, schools as institutions, and teachers as individuals should function so as to produce the best results. Use the essays to support your ideas and to provide good or bad examples.

14. Using the essays by Douglass, Angelou, and Mead as models, write a personal reminiscence about some important experience in your own history of learning and schooling. Remember, do not simply tell a story, but use the story to make a point about education.

CULTURE

15. Moments of contact between different cultures are especially revealing for the ethnographer. Most of the essays in the "Culture" section are based upon observation of cross-cultural interaction. Write an essay in which you consider the various ways in which these different writers use cross-cultural interaction for their own purposes in these essays. Include the Geertz essay and at least three other essays on culture in your discussion.

16. What do we mean by the word "primitive"? What range of values—positive or negative—do we attribute to such notions as wild, uncivilized, barbaric, savage? Discuss the different values attached to the "primitive" in the essays by Mead, Momaday, Dinesen, Berger, Malefijt, and any other essays in the "Culture" section that seem useful to you.

ANIMAL BEHAVIOR

17. Using the essays by Berger, Goodall, and Mowat, write an essay in which you discuss the observations of animals by humans. Consider such questions as why we look at animals, how we look at them, and whether they look back. Try to develop a thesis about what we can and cannot learn from animals by observing them. You may wish to consider the questions of how the manner of observing influences the creatures under observation and what our attempts to observe animals teach us about ourselves.

18. The essays by Hoagland, Woolf, Marler and Peters, and Darwin all concern animals operating under the pressure of drives and instincts, behaving in ways that are more or less programmed for them genetically. How do the different writers respond to these patterns of behavior? How do they relate or compare them to human needs and actions? Write an essay in which you develop a thesis about "instinctive" or "programmed" behavior and its meaning for humans. Draw your examples from these essays.

HUMAN BEHAVIOR

19. What does it mean to be human? Is there such a thing as human nature? What qualities or characteristics can we say belong to all human beings? Consider especially the essays by Rose, Kübler-Ross, Milgram, Raphael, Jaynes, Piaget, Freud, and Bettelheim in answering this question.

20. What is human personality? What makes a human being distinctive, individual, unique? In formulating your answer to this question, consider especially the essays by Bettelheim, Wolff, Selzer, and Epstein.

21. How free are human beings? Consider the essays by Rose, Milgram, and Bettelheim and any other essays from the "Human Behavior" section that you find appropriate in formulating your response to this question.

759

Suggestions for Writing Across the Disciplines

PUBLIC AFFAIRS

22. Two of the most famous pieces of political writing ever composed in English are included in the "Public Affairs" section: the work of Swift and of Jefferson. Both pieces are over two hundred years old now but have lasted well, though perhaps for different reasons. We ask you to compare the two of them from the viewpoints provided by Lippmann and Orwell. What reasons for writing are visible in these two old texts? Would they satisfy Lippmann, do you think? Should they? What do you think are the strongest and weakest points of each text *as writing?*

23. If the proverbial Martian were browsing in an intergalactic library and found only the essays by Jefferson, the U.S. Government, Schelling, Commoner, and Brown, what would he think of the United States? Basing your views upon these essays only, and not drawing upon your personal knowledge, write an essay in which you describe the country revealed in this group of essays. Be as balanced as you can. Look for signs of hope as well as danger and difficulty.

BUSINESS AND ECONOMICS

24. What makes for success in business? Using the essays by Peters and Waterman, Thomas, MacLeod, Kaye, and Schelling, develop your own view of the secrets of success in the world of business. You may wish to recognize more than one kind of success, and you will certainly have to define the word "success" itself, but you will find plenty of ideas and information on the subject in these essays.

25. Thurow presents a theory of economics in his essay "A Zero-Sum Game." Do you agree with this theory? Using the material in the essays by Allen and Smith and the *New York Times* report, and any other information you consider appropriate, write an essay in which you take a stand on Thurow's thesis, agreeing or disagreeing with it. Support your position with material from the other essays as well as from whatever other sources you use.

TECHNOLOGY

26. Using Miller and Saidla's commentary at the end of the Ammann essay as a guide, consider the writing in Ammann's essay and the other essays in the "Technology" section from the point of view of organization and style. Try to describe how each essay is put together. How many different types of organization do you find in these essays? What are the relationships between the subject matter and the style and organization of each one? Can you develop a thesis about the proper "fit" between subject and writing in essays on technological subjects aimed at general audiences?

27. Consider the camera, the telephone, the bridge, and the computer as devices. What features, if any, do they have in common? Which has the longest history and which the shortest? What sorts of effort have gone into their development? Write an

essay in which you use the material in the "Technology" section as the basis for developing a thesis about the human dimension of technology—how it affects us, what it costs us, and why it concerns us.

LIFE SCIENCE

28. Write an essay in which you describe the relationship between biology and medicine. Using the essays in the "Life Science" section as your source material, you might consider Gould and Scopes as biologists, Selzer and Selby as physicians. What qualities do they share? What differences do you see in their concerns and procedures? The essays by Gold and Thomas should provide additional evidence about what biologists do, what they are most concerned about, and how they work. You might consider whether the goals of biology and medicine are the same or different. Try to develop a thesis about the relationship between the two fields.

29. Selby and Selzer are surgeons who write about their experience. Why do they do this? Many people find their essays powerful. Some are offended by them. What are the sources of the power in these essays? How much is in the subject matter and how much is in the presentation? Can you distinguish between Selby and Selzer as writers? Write an essay in which you develop a thesis about these surgeons as writers.

TIME, SPACE, NUMBER

30. Knowledge about the universe is the result of a transaction between human mechanisms for perceiving the world and whatever those mechanisms allow us to perceive and understand. Using the essays in the "Time, Space, Number" section as your source material, discuss the relationship between human beings as perceiving, thinking creatures and the universe as we perceive it. How are the mathematical and physical sciences related to our ordinary ways of perceiving and understanding the world? What difficulties do scientists experience in communicating their information to others? How do they attempt to solve these difficulties?

31. Every essay in the "Time, Space, Number" section was written by a scientist, and most of them by very eminent scientists indeed. However, we ask you to consider them not as scientists but as writers. Specifically, we ask you to write an essay on the relationship between the occasion or situation for writing and the kind of writing that results. Consider each of these essays in relation to its occasion and audience, commenting on the organization and style of each as a response to its situation. Then, use these discussions as the basis for some generalization about the relationship between an essay and its original situation.

KNOWLEDGE AND BELIEF

32. When is it right to believe in someone or something? When is it right to doubt? What are proper and improper grounds for belief? Discuss these questions in the light

761

of the essays by Taylor and Robinson on faith, Asimov on doubt, Oppenheimer on knowledge, and Milgram on obedience. Develop your own position, but attend to the views presented in these five essays.

33. Many people find values that sustain them through their commitment to a profession or discipline. Considering the essays in the "Knowledge and Belief" section by Hoover, Selzer, Eiseley, Gould, and Oppenheimer, discuss the relationship between career commitment and belief. Consider such questions as whether there is a common pattern to the values of all these writers or whether different professions seem to make for different beliefs; how the beliefs or values are related to each professional commitment; whether the values are strictly tied to professional ethics or seem to extend beyond the career to a whole way of life—or any other aspects of the relationship between profession and belief that emerges from your reading of these essays.

ACKNOWLEDGMENTS

ACKNOWLEDGMENTS (continued from page iv)

Edward Hallett Carr, "The Historian and His Facts", from *What Is History?* by Edward Hallett Carr. Copyright © 1961 by Edward Hallett Carr. Reprinted by permission of Alfred A. Knopf, Inc. Edward Hallett Carr, "The Historian and His Facts," from *What Is History?* Reprinted by permission of Macmillan, London and Basingstroke.

Barry Commoner, "The Causes of Environmental Stress," from *The Closing Circle: Nature, Man and Technology*, by Barry Commoner. Copyright © 1971 by Barry Commoner. Reprinted by permission of Alfred A. Knopf, Inc. Portions of this book originally appeared in *The New Yorker*.

Francis Crick, "Times and Distances, Large and Small," from *Life Itself*. Copyright © 1981 by Francis Crick. Reprinted by permission of Simon & Schuster, Inc.

Judith Crist, "Review of *Star Wars*." Copyright © 1977, *Saturday Review* Magazine. Reprinted by permission.

Joan Didion, "On Keeping a Notebook," from *Slouching Towards Bethlehem* by Joan Didion. Copyright © 1966, 1968 by Joan Didion. Reprinted by permission of Farrar, Straus and Giroux, Inc.

Isak Dinesen, "The Iguana," by permission of Random House, Inc., and the Rungstedlund Foundation. From *Out of Africa* by Isak Dinesen, copyright by Random House, Inc., 1937 and renewed 1965 by the Rungstedlund Foundation.

Albert Einstein, "What Is the Theory of Relativity?" from *Ideas and Opinions* by Albert Einstein. Copyright © 1954, renewed 1982 by Crown Publishers, Inc. Used by permission of Crown Publishers, Inc.

Loren Eiseley, "The Bird and the Machine." Copyright © 1955 by Loren Eiseley. Reprinted from *The Immense Journey*, by Loren Eiseley, by permission of Random House, Inc.

Joseph Epstein, "Obsessed with Sport." Reprinted by permission of Joseph Epstein. Copyright © 1976 by Joseph Epstein.

Frances FitzGerald, "America Revised," from *America Revised* by Frances FitzGerald. Copyright © 1979 by Frances FitzGerald. By permission of Little, Brown and Company in association with the Atlantic Monthly Press.

Robert Frost, "Mending Wall," from *The Poetry of Robert Frost* edited by Edward Connery Lathem. Copyright 1930, 1939, © 1960 by Holt, Rinehart and Winston. Copyright © 1958 by Robert Frost. Copyright © 1967 by Leslie Frost Ballantine. Reprinted by permission of Holt, Rinehart and Winston, Publishers.

Clifford Geertz, "Anthropology as Thick Description." Reprinted by permission of the Author.

Michael Gold, "The Cells That Would Not Die." Reprinted by the permission of *Science '83* Magazine. Copyright, The American Association for the Advancement of Science.

E. H. Gombrich, "Art for Eternity," from E. H. Gombrich, *The Story of Art*, © 1972, pp. 32–42. Reprinted by permission of Prentice-Hall, Inc., Englewood Cliffs, New Jersey.

Jane Van Lawick-Goodall, "First Observations," from *In the Shadow of Man* by Jane Van Lawick-Goodall. Copyright © 1971 by Hugo and Jane Van Lawick-Goodall. Reprinted by permission of Houghton Mifflin Company. From *In the Shadow of Man* by Jane Van Lawick-Goodall. Reprinted by permission of Collins Publishers, London.

Stephen Jay Gould, "Evolution As Fact and Theory." Stephen Jay Gould, © 1981 *Discover* Magazine, Time, Inc.

Edward T. Hall, Jr., "The Anthropology of Manners." Reprinted by permission. Copyright © 1958 by Scientific American, Inc. All rights reserved.

Edward Hoagland, "River-Gray, River-Green." Copyright © 1976 by Edward Hoagland.

Edward Hoagland, "The Courage of Turtles." Copyright © 1970 by Edward Hoagland. Reprinted from *The Edward Hoagland Reader* by permission of Random House, Inc.

Herbert Hoover, "The Profession of Engineering." Reprinted by permission of the Hoover Foundation.

David Hounshell, "Two Paths to the Telephone." Reprinted by permission. Copyright © 1981 by Scientific American, Inc. All rights reserved.

Bill Jay, "Death in the Darkroom." © 1982 by Bill Jay.

Julian Jaynes, "The Evolution of Language," from *The Origins of Consciousness in the Breakdown of the Bicameral Mind* by Julian Jaynes. Reprinted by permission of Houghton Mifflin Co.

Acknowledgments

James Jeans, "Why the Sky Is Blue," from *The Stars in Their Courses* by James Jeans. Reprinted by permission of Cambridge University Press.

Stanley Kauffmann, "Review of *Star Wars*" (pp. 289–291) in *Before My Eyes: Film Criticism and Comment* by Stanley Kauffmann. Copyright © 1980 by Stanley Kauffmann. By permission of Harper & Row, Publishers, Inc.

Marvin Kaye, "The Toy with One Moving Part." Copyright © 1973 by Marvin Kaye. From the book *The Story of Monopoly, Silly Putty, Bingo, Twister, Frisbee, Scrabble Etc.* Reprinted with permission of Stein and Day Publishers.

X. J. Kennedy, "Who Killed King Kong?" From *Dissent*, Spring 1960. Reprinted by permission of *Dissent*.

Phillip Knightley, "The First Televised War." From *The First Casualty*, copyright © 1975 by Phillip Knightley. Reprinted by permission of Harcourt Brace Jovanovich, Inc.

Elizabeth Kübler-Ross, "On the Fear of Death." Reprinted with permission of Macmillan Publishing Company from *On Death and Dying*, by Elizabeth Kübler-Ross. Copyright © 1969 by Elizabeth Kübler-Ross.

Barbara Landau, et al., "Spatial Knowledge and Geometric Representation in a Child Blind from Birth," by Barbara Landau, Henry Gleitman and Elizabeth Spelke. From *Science*, vol. 213, 11 September 1981, pp. 1275–8. Copyright © 1981 by the American Association for the Advancement of Science.

Ursula Le Guin, "Why Are Americans Afraid of Dragons?" Reprinted by permission of the Berkley Publishing Group from *Language of the Night* edited by Susan Wood. "Why Are Americans Afraid of Dragons?" Copyright © 1982 by Ursula Le Guin.

Walter Lippmann, "On Political Writing," from *The New Republic*, vol. IV, 7 August 1915. Used with the permission of the President and Fellows of Harvard College.

Celeste MacLeod, "Some People Always Make It: The Optionaires." Reprinted by permission of the Putnam Publishing Group from *Horatio Alger, Farewell: The End of the American Dream* by Celeste MacLeod. Copyright © 1980 by Celeste MacLeod.

Annemarie de Waal Malefijt, "Homo Monstrosus." Reprinted by permission. Copyright © 1968 by Scientific American, Inc. All rights reserved.

Peter Marler and Susan Peters, "Sparrows Learn Adult Song and More from Memory." From *Science*, vol. 213, pp. 780–782, 14 August 1981. Copyright 1981 by the American Association for the Advancement of Science.

Margaret Mead, "A Day in Samoa," from *Coming of Age in Samoa* by Margaret Mead. Copyright © 1938, 1955 by Margaret Mead. By permission of William Morrow & Company.

Margaret Mead, "College: DePauw," from *Blackberry Winter* by Margaret Mead. By permission of William Morrow & Company.

Stanley Milgram, "Obedience and Disobedience to Authority." Reprinted by permission of the author.

Stanley Milgram, "Confessions of a News Addict." Copyright © 1977 by *The Antioch Review*, Inc. First appeared in *The Antioch Review*, vol. 35, no. 2–3 (Spring–Summer 1977). Reprinted by permission of the Editors.

Arthur Miller, "Tragedy and the Common Man." Reprinted by permission of International Creative Management. Copyright © 1949 by the New York Times for Arthur Miller.

Walter J. Miller and Lee E. A. Saidla, " 'Comment' in Ammann's Reports." From *Engineers as Writers* by Walter J. Miller and Lee E. A. Saidla. Copyright © 1969 by Van Nostrand Reinhold Company. Reprinted by permission of the publisher.

Horace Miner, "Body Ritual Among the Nacirema." Reproduced by permission of the American Anthropological Association from *American Anthropologist* 58 (3): 503–507, 1956. Not for further reproduction.

N. Scott Momaday, "The Way to Rainy Mountain." Reprinted from *The Way to Rainy Mountain*. Copyright © 1969, The University of New Mexico Press.

Farley Mowat, "Observing Wolves." From *Never Cry Wolf* by Farley Mowat. Copyright © 1963 by Farley Mowat. By permission of Little, Brown and Company in association with the Atlantic Monthly Press.

New York Times, "Tutankhamen's Tomb Is Opened." © 1923 by The New York Times Company. Reprinted by permission.

Acknowledgments

New York Times, "Weird Roar Surges from Exchange Floor." © 1929 by The New York Times Company. Reprinted by permission.

New York Times, "The End of the Scopes Trial." © 1925 by The New York Times Company. Reprinted by permission.

Tillie Olsen, "The Silences of Women as Writers." Excerpted from the book *Silences* by Tillie Olsen. Copyright © 1965, 1972, 1978 by Tillie Olsen. Reprinted by permission of Delacorte Press/Seymour Lawrence.

J. Robert Oppenheimer, "The Tree of Knowledge." Copyright © 1958, by *Harper's* Magazine. All rights reserved. Reprinted from the October 1958 issue by special permission.

George Orwell, "Why I Write," from *Such, Such Were the Joys* by George Orwell. Copyright © 1953 by Sonia Brownell Orwell; renewed 1981 by Mrs. George K. Perutz, Mrs. Miriam Gross, and Dr. Michael Dickson. Reprinted by permission of Harcourt Brace Jovanovich, Inc. Reprinted by permission of the estate of the late Sonia Brownell Orwell and Martin Secker & Warburg Ltd.

Winthrop Palmer, "Isadora Duncan," reprinted by permission of the author.

Thomas H. Peters and Robert H. Waterman, Jr., "Analytic Ivory Towers," from *In Search of Excellence* by Thomas J. Peters and Robert H. Waterman. Copyright © 1982 by Thomas J. Peters and Robert H. Waterman. By permission of Harper & Row, Publishers, Inc.

Jean Piaget, "How Children Form Mathematical Concepts," reprinted by permission. Copyright © 1953 by Scientific American, Inc. All rights reserved.

Bertram Raphael, "Syntax and Semantics," from *The Thinking Computer: Mind Inside Matter* by Bertram Raphael, W. H. Freeman and Company. Copyright © 1978.

Bertram Raphael, "Misleading Myths About Computers," from *The Thinking Computer: Mind Inside Matter* by Bertram Raphael. W. H. Freeman and Company. Copyright © 1978.

Richard Robinson, "Faith," from *An Atheist's Values* by Richard Robinson. By permission of Basil Blackwell, Publisher.

Steven Rose, "It's Only Human Nature: The Sociobiologist's Fairyland," from *Race and Class*, vol. 20, No. 3, 1979; published by The Institute of Race Relations, London.

Murray Ross, "Football Red and Baseball Green," reprinted by permission of the author.

Bertrand Russell, "Touch and Sight: The Earth and the Heavens," from *The ABC of Relativity* by Bertrand Russell. Reprinted by permission of George Allen & Unwin (Publishers) Ltd.

Thomas C. Schelling, "What Is the Business of Organized Crime?" Originally appeared in 20 *Journal of Public Law*, 1 (1971). Reprinted by permission of the *Emory Law Journal*, Emory University School of Law, Atlanta, Georgia 30322.

Roy C. Selby, Jr., "A Delicate Operation." Copyright © 1975 by *Harper's* Magazine. All rights reserved. Reprinted from the December 1975 issue by special permission.

Richard Selzer, "Why a Surgeon Would Write," from *Mortal Lessons: Notes on the Art of Surgery.* Copyright © 1974, 1975, 1976, by Richard Selzer. Reprinted by permission of Simon & Schuster, Inc.

"Adam Smith," "The Great Inflation," copyright © 1981 by George J. W. Goodman. Reprinted by permission of Summit Books, a division of Simon & Schuster, Inc.

William Stafford, "A Way of Writing," reprinted by permission.

Richard Taylor, "Faith," reprinted by permission of New York University Press from *Religious Experience and Truth: A Symposium*, edited by Sidney Hook. Copyright © 1961 by New York University.

Lewis Thomas, "On Warts," from *The Medusa and the Snail* by Lewis Thomas. Copyright © 1979 by Lewis Thomas. Reprinted by permission of Viking Penguin, Inc.

Lewis Thomas, "The Art of Teaching Science," Copyright © 1982 by The New York Times Company. Reprinted by permission.

Robert Thomas, "Is Corporate Executive Compensation Excessive?" From Bruce M. Johnson, ed., *The Attack on Corporate America: The Corporate Issues Sourcebook*, © 1978. Reprinted by permission of McGraw-Hill Book Company.

Lester Thurow, "A Zero-Sum Game," from *The Zero-Sum Society*, by Lester C. Thurow. Copyright © 1980 by Basic Books, Inc. Publishers. Reprinted by permission of the publisher.

Barbara Tuchman, " 'This Is the End of the World': The Black Death," from *A Distant Mirror*, by Barbara Tuchman. Copyright © 1979 by Barbara Tuchman. Reprinted by permission of Alfred A. Knopf, Inc.

765

Acknowledgments

E. B. White, "The Ring of Time," from *Essays of E. B. White*. Copyright © 1956 by E. B. White. Reprinted by permission of Harper & Row, Publishers, Inc.

E. B. White, "Dear Mr. 0214 1063 02 10730 8." Copyright © 1967 by The New York Times Company. Reprinted by permission.

E. B. White, "Drafts," reprinted by permission of Cornell University Library. Copyright © 1967 by The New York Times Company, reprinted by permission.

Douglas L. Wilson, "The Other Side of the Wall," reprinted by permission of *The Iowa Review*.

Geoffrey Wolff, "Memories of My Father," from *The Duke of Deception*, by Geoffrey Wolff. Copyright © 1979 by Geoffrey Wolff. Reprinted by permission of Random House, Inc.

Virginia Woolf, "The Death of the Moth," from *The Death of the Moth and Other Essays* by Virginia Woolf, copyright © 1942 by Harcourt Brace Jovanovich, Inc.; renewed 1970 by Marjorie T. Parsons. Reprinted by permission of the publisher. From *The Death of the Moth and Other Essays* by Virginia Woolf. By permission of the author's Literary Estate and the Hogarth Press.

ART ACKNOWLEDGMENTS

Annemarie de Waal Malefijt, "Homo Monstrosus," p. 90; "Representatives of Monstrous Tribes," p. 93; "Animal-Headed People," p. 95; "Latter-Day Monster," p. 97; "Apelike Men," p. 97; "Hirsute Aborigine." Reproduced by courtesy of the Picture Collection, The Branch Libraries, The New York Public Library. E. H. Gombrich, "Art for Eternity," p. 214; "Portrait Head of Limestone," courtesy of the Kunstlisches Museum von Vienna, p. 216; "Painting of a Pond," reproduced by courtesy of the Trustees of the British Museum. "Portrait of Hesire," p. 217, reproduced by courtesy of the Egyptian Museum. "King Amenophis IV," p. 222, reproduced by courtesy of the Staatsmuseum von Berlin. "The Pharaoh Tutankhamen and his Wife," p. 223, reproduced by courtesy of the Egyptian Museum. "A Dagger from Mycenae," p. 224, reproduced by courtesy of the National Archeological Museum, Athens, Greece. E. B. White, "Drafts," reprinted by permission of Cornell University Library, Copyright © 1967 by the New York Times Company. Reprinted by permission.

Rhetorical Index

Rhetorical Index

COMPARISON AND CONTRAST

Discussed in "Explaining," pp. 204–205

Exemplified by "America Revised," pp. 237–243; "To Impersonate, To Watch, and To Be Watched," pp. 245–250; "Football Red and Baseball Green," 251–259; "The Great Inflation," pp. 306–311; "On the Fear of Death," pp. 322–328; "Touch and Sight: The Earth and the Heavens," pp. 397–398

DEFINITION

Discussed in "Explaining," p. 204

Exemplified by "The Historian and His Facts," pp. 226–235; "To Impersonate, To Watch, and To Be Watched," pp. 245–250; "The Water of Life," pp. 274–276; "Some People Always Make It: The Optionaires," pp. 312–321; "Obedience and Disobedience to Authority," pp. 329–333; "Anthropology as Thick Description," pp. 368–372; "Syntax and Semantics," pp. 376–378; "Faith," pp. 473–474; "What Is the Business of Organized Crime?" pp. 534–536

DESCRIPTION

Discussed in "Reporting," pp. 8–9

Exemplified by "The Ring of Time" pp. 11–14; "Tutankhamen's Tomb Is Opened," pp. 18–19; "Graduation," pp. 27–30; "Buster Keaton," pp. 38–40; "Olivier's Moor," pp. 44–46; " 'This Is the End of the World': The Black Death," pp. 48–56; "Weird Roar Surges from Exchange Floor," pp. 59–64; "A Day in Samoa," pp. 66–68; "First Observations," pp. 74–80; "Body Ritual Among the Nacirema," pp. 82–86; "The Discus Thrower," pp. 147–150," "River-Gray, River-Green," pp. 151–154; "Anthropology as Thick Description," pp. 368–372; "Memories of My Father," pp. 621–624; "The Death of the Moth," pp. 626–628; "The Iguana," pp. 629–630; "The Way to Rainy Mountain," pp. 653–657; "The Bird and the Machine," pp. 697–701; "The Courage of Turtles," pp. 703–708

EXPLAINING

Discussed in "Explaining," pp. 199–206

Exemplified by all selections in "Explaining," pp. 207–437

RHETORICAL INDEX

769

Rhetorical Index

NARRATION

Discussed in "Reporting," pp. 8–9

Exemplified by "Tutankhamen's Tomb Is Opened," pp. 16–19; "Learning to Read and Write," pp. 21–25; "Graduation," pp. 30–36; "Isadora Duncan," pp. 41–43; "Olivier's Moor," pp. 44–46; "A Day in Samoa," pp. 66–68; "Observing Wolves," pp. 70–73; "First Observations," pp. 78–80; "Crash!" pp. 99–110; "The Toy with One Moving Part," pp. 112–118; "Love Canal and the Poisoning of America," pp. 119–132; "The End of the Scopes Trial," pp. 135–137; "A Delicate Operation," pp. 143–145; "The Discus Thrower," pp. 147–149; " The Cells That Would Not Die," pp. 156–162; "Two Paths to the Telephone," pp. 164–176," "Joey: A 'Mechanical Boy,' " pp. 294–304; "The Great Inflation," pp. 306–311; "The Anthropology of Manners," pp. 353–359; "The Death of the Moth," pp. 626–628; "College," pp. 659–668; "The Bird and the Machine," pp. 697–701

POINT OF VIEW

Discussed in "Reporting," pp. 3–5

Exemplified by all selections in the book

PROCESS ANALYSIS

Discussed in "Explaining," p. 205

Exemplified by "A Delicate Operation," pp. 143–145; "How Children Form Mathematical Concepts," pp. 286–292; "Obedience and Disobedience to Authority," pp. 332–336; "Anthropology as Thick Description," pp. 368–372; "Why the Sky Is Blue," pp. 373–374; "Sparrows Learn Adult Song and More from Memory," pp. 415–420

PROCESS OF ASSOCIATION

Discussed in "Reflecting," pp. 608–609

Exemplified by "A Way of Writing," pp. 615–617; "Memories of My Father," pp. 621–624; "The Death of the Moth," pp. 626–628; "On Keeping a Notebook," pp. 636–641; "The Eiffel Tower," pp. 649–652; "The Way to Rainy Mountain," pp. 653–658; "The Bird and the Machine," pp. 695–702